*Altering Ready-To-Wear Fashions*

# Altering Ready-To-Wear Fashions

**Mrs. Jeanne Brinkley**
Formerly Home Economics Supervisor
Occupational Consultant, and Teacher Educator in Florida

**Mrs. Ann Aletti**
Vocational Teacher and Consultant,
Ft. Lauderdale, Florida.

Consultant
**James Mosley**
Vocational Department Chairman,
Jones High School, Orlando, Florida.

**Chas. A. Bennett Co., Inc.**
Peoria, Illinois 61614

Copyright © 1976

**By Jeanne Brinkley
and Ann Aletti**

*All rights reserved*

80 81 82 83 84 KP 5 4 3 2

ISBN 87002-083-8

*Library of Congress Catalog No. 75-13742*

Printed in the United States of America

Drawings by Ann A. Russo

**Cover Illustration:**
Edmond Eldarzi's Clothing, Peoria, Ill.

## Preface

This book has been designed with a threefold purpose in mind. It is primarily planned to be used as a textbook in courses for training people for the career of clothing alterationist. Second, efforts have been made to make the units comprehensive enough so interested persons can practice at home on their own and teach themselves this trade. Third, it is set-up so that individuals who have problems finding ready-to-wear clothing to fit themselves, can use the book as a reference. Thus they can solve their own special problems in fitting and altering their own clothing.

Three areas are included. The first seven chapters cover the clothing industry, equipment, fabrics, pressing techniques, and clothing selection. This background material can help you make the greatest use of the actual skills involved. Chapters 8 through 12 consist solely of the most common fitting and altering problems encountered in working with ready-to-wear clothing. The last four chapters give helpful suggestions for actually using the skills acquired in a successful career. These deal with getting a job, working with people, and going into business for yourself.

To go into this trade, you do not need long years of experience in making clothing from scratch. In fact, this type of experience can sometimes be a disadvantage since so many of the techniques used are not the same as those used in home sewing methods. You *do* need to know how to operate a sewing machine well. You should also be familiar with handling various fabrics and with the general construction of a garment.

## Acknowledgments

With deep gratitude, the authors wish to acknowledge the following for their aid in giving information, locating resources, and reacting to the material in the text as work progressed.

- Mr. Jay Anderson and Mr. Fred Ackerman of POSH, INC., Miami, Fl.
- Mr. Len Coleman of Flair of Miami, and Mr. Jerry Berkowitz of Mr. B of Hallandale, Fl. and New York City—manufacturers.
- Mrs. Vivian Dempsey, Ft. Lauderdale, Fl. and New York—designer.
- Mrs. Leilani Peck, Communications Specialist, and other members of the staff of the Monroe County Cooperative Extension Service, Rochester, N.Y.
- Miss Margaret McGraw, The Blum Store, Phila., Pa.—Buyer.
- Mrs. Naomi Coyle, Sink 'r Swim, Beach Haven, N.J.—Owner-Buyer.
- Mrs. Gladys Hutchinson, Home Economics Adult Supervisor, Broward County, Fl.
- Mrs. Emiko Kudo, Director of Vocational Education, Hawaii.
- Mrs. Marian Hills, principal, Grand Rapids, Mich.
- Mrs. Edith Atcheson, high school teacher, Orlando, Fl.
- Mrs. Helen Jacobsen, teacher, Ft. Lauderdale, Fl.
- Mr. Napoleon Heck, student, Orlando, Fl.
- Mr. Austin Patrick Sullivan, tax consultant, Washington, D.C.
- Mrs. Ann DiNardo, Librarian, Ft. Lauderdale, Fl.
- Mr. and Mrs. Harold Heller, consultants, Appleton, Wisc.
- Mrs. Karen Nawrocki, artist, Grand Rapids, Mich.
- Commercial sources who supplied pictures.

Our special thanks to Mrs. Ann Aletti Russo, art teacher, Clearwater, Fl., for her drawings.

# Table of Contents

**PREFACE** .................................................. 5
**ACKNOWLEDGMENTS** ........................................ 5
**Chapter 1. OPPORTUNITIES IN THE NEEDLE TRADES** .......... 10
    Shop Opportunities ................................... 10
    Self-Employment Opportunities ........................ 14
    This Could Be You .................................... 15
    What You Will Need to Know ........................... 17
    The Metric System .................................... 17
**Chapter 2. THE GARMENT INDUSTRY** ........................ 18
    Garment Manufacturing ................................ 18
    Labels ............................................... 23
    Retail Stores ........................................ 25
    Designers ............................................ 28
    Sources of Trade Information ......................... 31
**Chapter 3. EQUIPMENT, TOOLS, AND SUPPLIES** .............. 33
    Equipment ............................................ 33
    Sewing Supplies ...................................... 48
**Chapter 4. LEARNING ABOUT FABRICS** ...................... 52
    Fibers ............................................... 53
    Yarns ................................................ 56
    Construction of Fabric ............................... 57
    Finishes ............................................. 62
    Compatible Trimming Fabrics .......................... 64
    Fabric Legislation ................................... 64
**Chapter 5. PRESSING** .................................... 72
    Pressing Equipment and Accessories ................... 72
    Using a Press Cloth .................................. 78
    General Pressing Information ......................... 78
    Short Cuts with an Iron .............................. 82
    Special Precautions in Pressing ...................... 83
    Instructions for Making Pressing Equipment ........... 83
**Chapter 6. COMMERCIAL SEWING METHODS** ................... 88
    Techniques ........................................... 88
    Supplies You Will Need for Samples ................... 89
    Construction Methods ................................. 91
    Variations ........................................... 114

## Contents

**Chapter 7. FLATTERING THE FEMALE FIGURE** .................................. 121
    Body Proportions ........................................... 121
    Selecting Clothes .......................................... 121

**Chapter 8. FITTING WOMEN'S CLOTHES** ............................................ 134
    Ready-To-Wear Sizes ....................................... 135
    Preparing for the Fitting .................................. 139
    Ready, Set, Go ............................................. 139
    Pin Fitting ................................................ 144
    Fittings to Avoid .......................................... 145
    Neckline Fittings .......................................... 145
    Shoulder Fittings .......................................... 150
    Bodice Fittings ............................................ 156
    Waistline Fittings ......................................... 166
    Skirt Fittings ............................................. 168
    Sleeve Fittings ............................................ 174
    Fitting the Princess Style Garment ......................... 178
    Fitting the Basic Shift .................................... 185
    Fitting Pants .............................................. 188
    Fitting Coats .............................................. 195
    Fitting Jackets and Suits .................................. 196

**Chapter 9. STANDARD ALTERATIONS FOR WOMEN** .................................. 197
    Helpful Hints .............................................. 197
    Transferring Pin Markings to Usable Markings ............... 198
    Doing the Alteration ....................................... 199
    Basic Dress Alterations .................................... 200
    Altering the Princess Style Garment ........................ 231
    Altering the Basic Shift ................................... 234
    Altering Pants ............................................. 236
    Coat Alterations ........................................... 243
    Jacket Alterations ......................................... 244
    Preparing for a Second Fitting ............................. 244

**Chapter 10. FITTING AND ALTERING HEMLINES** .................................. 245
    Preparing to Do Hem Fittings ............................... 245
    Fitting Street-Length Hems ................................. 247
    Fitting Floor Length Hems .................................. 250
    Hemming Techniques ......................................... 253
    Hem Alterations ............................................ 261

**Chapter 11. FINISHING TOUCHES** ............................................... 279
    Hand Stitches .............................................. 279
    Machine Stitches ........................................... 291

## Contents

    Fasteners and Other Controls................ 292
    Weights................................... 302
    Shoulder Pads............................. 303
    Labels.................................... 304

### Chapter 12. FITTING AND ALTERING MENSWEAR... 305
    Judging the Fit of Men's Jackets............ 309
    Judging the Fit of Men's Trousers........... 310
    Fitting Men's Clothes...................... 312
    Fitting Jackets............................ 314
    Fitting Trousers........................... 315
    Special Pointers for Alterations.............. 316
    Altering Trousers.......................... 316
    Jacket Alterations......................... 323
    Altering Vests............................. 330
    Shirt Alterations........................... 331

### Chapter 13. DEVELOPING SPEED AND EFFICIENCY... 334
    Time-Study Methods....................... 334
    Time-and-Energy Savers.................... 335
    Value Your Time........................... 339
    Learn to Say "No"......................... 339
    Take Care of Your Health................... 339
    Organize Your Day's Activities............... 341

### Chapter 14. WORKING WITH PEOPLE... 345
    Confidence................................ 345
    Competence............................... 347
    Courtesy.................................. 348
    Cooperation............................... 348
    Costs..................................... 350

### Chapter 15. GETTING A JOB... 351
    Where to Look............................. 351
    Appointment for an Interview................ 352
    Getting Ready for the Interview.............. 353
    Appearance............................... 355
    The Interview............................. 356
    Application Forms......................... 356
    Show What You Can Do.................... 357
    Accepting the Job.......................... 357
    Keeping the Job........................... 357

### Chapter 16. ESTABLISHING YOUR OWN BUSINESS... 360
    Advantages................................ 360

Contents

    Procedure . . . . . . . . . . . . . . . . . . . . . . . . . . . . . . . . . . . . . . 361
    Planning Your Work Area . . . . . . . . . . . . . . . . . . . . . . . . . . . 363
    Customer Contacts . . . . . . . . . . . . . . . . . . . . . . . . . . . . . . . 365
    Conducting Business. . . . . . . . . . . . . . . . . . . . . . . . . . . . . . 368
    Enlarging Your Business . . . . . . . . . . . . . . . . . . . . . . . . . . . 379
**APPENDIX A** . . . . . . . . . . . . . . . . . . . . . . . . . . . . . . . . . . . . . . . 384
**GLOSSARY** . . . . . . . . . . . . . . . . . . . . . . . . . . . . . . . . . . . . . . . 385
**REFERENCES** . . . . . . . . . . . . . . . . . . . . . . . . . . . . . . . . . . . . 393
**INDEX** . . . . . . . . . . . . . . . . . . . . . . . . . . . . . . . . . . . . . . . . . . 395

# Chapter 1
# Opportunities in the Needle Trades

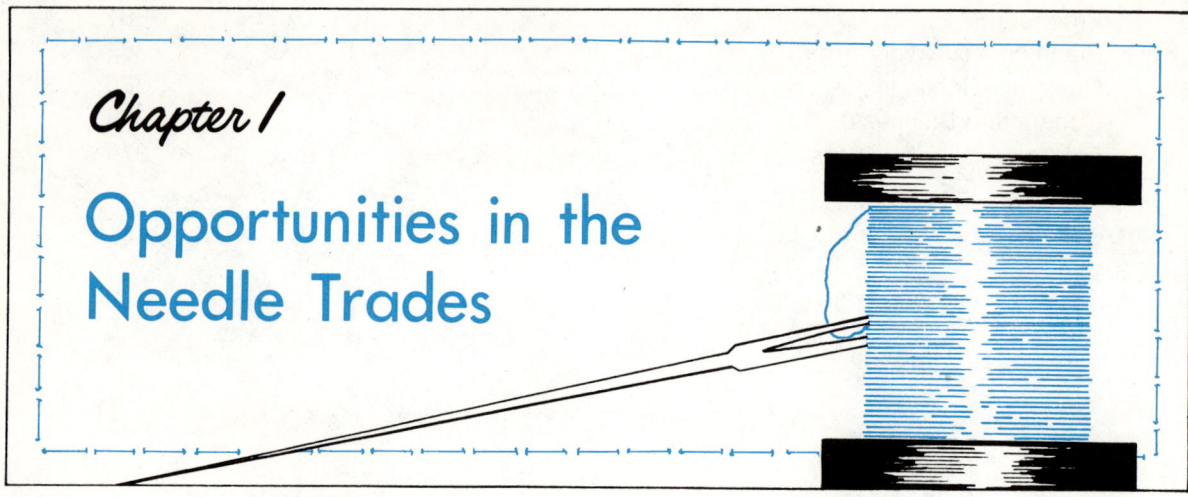

Everyone today needs a skill with which to earn a living. The more career opportunities that skill opens, the better it is. When it can be used as a hobby as well as a vocation, it doubles in value. Even more important is a skill that continues to be usable today, tomorrow, and ten or twenty years from now. Add the advantage of being able to use your talent either at home—part or full time—or in the business world, and you have an insurance policy in your pocket.

Where can you find such a skill to develop? You are holding one answer in your hands.

Too many people think of sewing skills as usable for making their own clothes, doing custom dressmaking for other people, or working in a clothing factory running a sewing machine. These are all possibilities, of course, but they are only part of the story.

One of the most profitable areas in sewing is alterations. Even here, there are more variations than you may have imagined. With the help of this book, a whole new world could open to you.

Perhaps you have dreamed of becoming a fashion designer. Both men and women have found satisfying outlets for their creative abilities in this field. If that is your goal, it is a worthy one. However, there is more to being a successful designer than being able to draw sketches of pretty clothes. You must understand fabrics, design, fitting, costs, and how clothes are put together.

Learning to alter ready-to-wear fashions can give you an important foundation for understanding many of these things. You will be able to support yourself while working toward your larger goal.

## SHOP OPPORTUNITIES

Many stores have an alteration department for the convenience of their customers. Such alterations usually are not free. They are a service for which the customer who does not sew is glad to pay. In a large store, a fitter suggests exactly what alterations need to be made in the garment the customer is buying. The fitter then marks the changes needed. In a workroom behind the scenes, alterationists do the sewing, making the changes marked by the fitter. When you have acquired skills, speed, a working knowledge of commercial equipment, and the ability to meet the pressure of shop production, you can find job opportunities which include many areas.

• Alterationist—carries out the fitter's directions for the changes to be made on the garments.

- Fitter—does the fitting on the garment while worn by the customer.
- Fitter - alterationist — does fittings as well as alterations and gives instructions to helpers.
- Fitter - alterationist - salesperson—functions in all these capacities in small specialty shops.
- Manager of specialty shop—combines sewing skill with knowledge of the retail trade to lead to promotion to a managerial position.
- Supervisor in alterations department—distributes the work to helpers, sees that the work is completed on time, checks the quality of work done, and gives a final inspection to the garments altered in the shop.
- Sewing specialist—uses special skills in such operations as putting in hems, pressing, and handwork in large alterations shops.

POSH, INC.
Fred Ackerman, designer

*Would you know how to put this gown together just by looking at the design?*

*Designer sketching new couture line. The fabric in the background is the inspiration for the design.*

POSH, INC., Fred Ackerman, designer

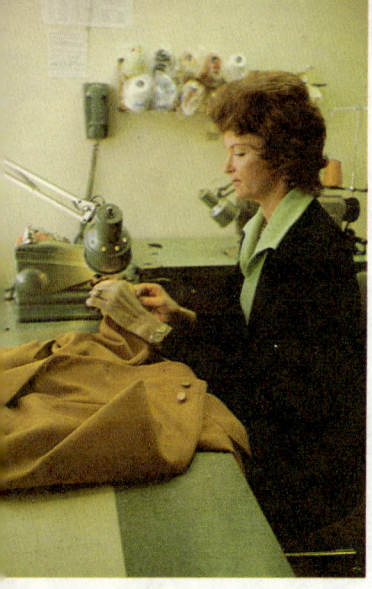

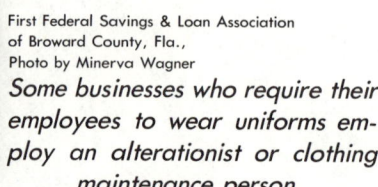

POSH, INC.

Manufacturers make up sample garments for display to potential buyers.

First Federal Savings & Loan Association of Broward County, Fla.,
Photo by Minerva Wagner

Some businesses who require their employees to wear uniforms employ an alterationist or clothing maintenance person.

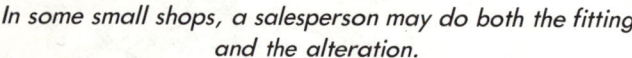

In some small shops, a salesperson may do both the fitting and the alteration.

Ft. Lauderdale News

- Monogram machine operator—puts individual initials or monograms on clothes and household linens for customers in some specialty shops.
- Mending and repair specialist—repairs pockets, replaces zippers, sews on buttons, and mends holes for drycleaners and some alterations shops.
- Salesperson and sample dressmaker in fabric shop—makes garments featuring certain fabrics or patterns offered for sale in the store.
- Sample hand (dressmaker) for garment manufacturer—makes complete garments of

Fur shops need people with special skills to line or alter fur garments.

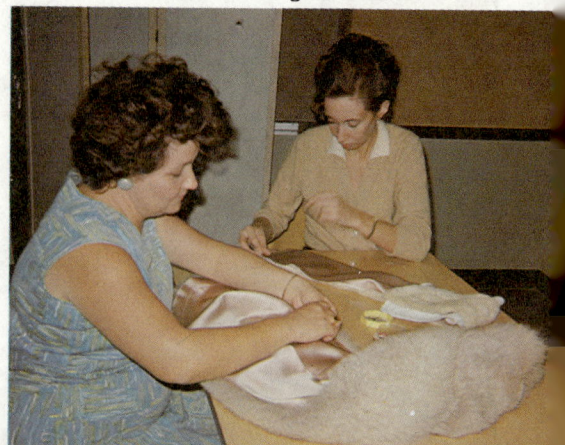

12

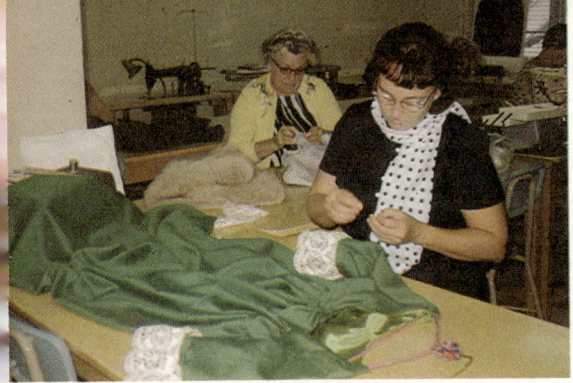

### Ch. 1: Opportunities in the Needle Trades

*Sewing specialists may do only one type of work such as special hand finishing.*

proposed styles before production is started. These may be used to determine the cost of manufacture and to show as sales samples to possible buyers.

- Finisher-alterationist in fur shop—does the handwork required for fur garments such as putting in linings or attaching hooks and eyes.
- Finisher—does all the handwork—hems, hooks, eyes, snaps, buttons, labels.
- Clothing maintenance specialist—fits, alters, and maintains costumes or uniforms for businesses who require their employees to wear them.

Photo by Deanna Laughlin
*Fitter adjusting the hem of a bridal gown worn by the customer.*

*A supervisor in a large alterations department is responsible for assigning work and checking it after it is completed.*

Lorenz Fashions in Monograming, Inc.,
Photo by Minerva Wagner
*Personal monograms on household linens and clothes are a special service offered by some shops.*

13

### Altering Ready-To-Wear Fashions

## SELF-EMPLOYMENT OPPORTUNITIES

All of the jobs listed in the preceding section involve working for someone else in a business. Besides these opportunities, you can do many kinds of sewing work for pay in your own home or shop.

Besides building your own business fitting and altering clothes for private customers, self-employment needle trade jobs could include:

- Making clothes for customers who cannot find what they desire in ready-made garments.
- Making wedding or "special event" clothes for people who cannot find what they want in a store.
- Making sample dresses for fabric shops and manufacturers.
- Making uniforms and costumes for special needs such as waitresses, waiters, cheerleaders, bands, theatrical performers, and employees in tourist attractions.
- Mending and reweaving damaged clothing.
- Pressing and restoring special garments such as bridal dresses, veils, and formals.
- Make unusual "boutique" items such as stoles, shawls, caftans, scarves, sashes, and handbags.
- Producing quantities of special items such as tennis dresses and bathing suits for specialty shops or private customers.
- Altering men's, women's, and children's clothing for shops with no alteration departments of their own.
- Developing into a small-scale private designer and producer of chic fashions.

Ft. Lauderdale News
*Alterationists carry out the fitter's instructions to make the necessary changes.*

*Make special-event clothes such as these bridesmaids' dresses.*

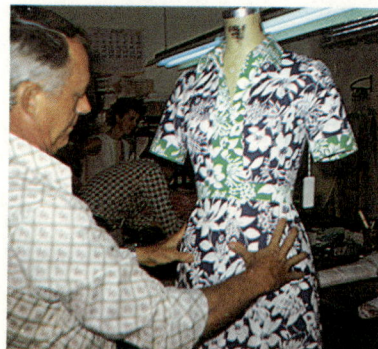

POSH, INC.
*Fabric stores need sample display garments to feature special patterns and fabrics.*

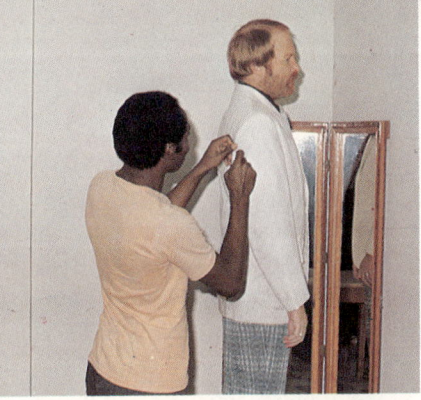

*Many people with fitting problems or special likes and dislikes prefer to have their clothes custom made.*

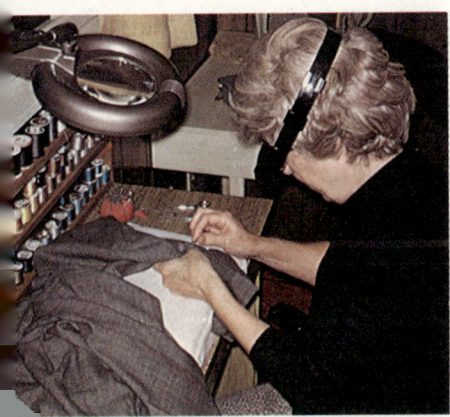

Photo by Bryan Hills

*Mending and reweaving damaged clothing is a highly developed skill for which people are willing to pay well.*

*Costumes for many special events are usually custom-made.*

Photo by Robert Howley

## THIS COULD BE YOU

Work in the needle trades is open to all people, regardless of race, age, or sex. Job possibilities are available at many different levels of ability. Even some physical disabilities need not stand in anyone's way.

The following stories are examples of real people who have found interesting careers using their skills in clothing alterations.

### She Has Designs on Life

Suzy Martin had always loved to design clothes. She spent many happy hours as a young girl drawing dress designs for herself, her dolls, and her friends. Sometimes her mother was able to copy her plans and make them into dresses for Suzy. Other times the designs were not practical and could not be made up into garments. So Suzy took clothing construction and alteration courses to learn how clothes are constructed, and also took courses in creative design. One summer she got a job in a dress manufacturing company working with the designers. Now she is well on her way to becoming a successful designer.

### New Land Brings New Life

Rose Fernandez and her family came to the United States as refugees from Cuba. Rose's husband had been a respected attorney in his homeland and she had never worked outside of

*Boutique items such as caftans are often easy to make and easy to sell.*

the home. Having to leave his professional standing, friends, and cherished life style in Cuba broke Mr. Fernandez' spirit. He did not speak English well enough to become an attorney in the United States and found it difficult to get any kind of work. Rose knew she had to learn to do something to help her family get established again.

Rose had a well-developed sense of style and enjoyed working with clothes, so she took a course in fitting and altering clothing. There she found she had a natural flair for fitting and a strong feeling for knowing what looked right.

15

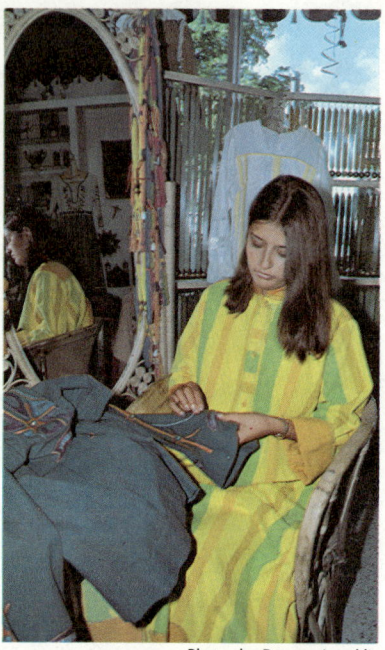

Stud Service, Inc.
Photos by Deanna Laughlin
Jane Drake Imports

*Adding unusual trimmings to standard ready-to-wear items can be exciting, creative, and profitable.*

She was soon able to get a job as a fitter in an exclusive dress shop where she became a valued employee. Her earnings enabled her to help her family regain their independence and pride.

### Doors Are Opened

Bessie Johnson was the divorced mother of six young children. She had very little education and had to rely on welfare to help her buy food and the other necessities of life. However, Bessie was not afraid of work. Her main goal was to be able to support herself and her family. Because she had so many handicaps, reaching her goal seemed almost impossible, but that didn't stop Bessie.

By taking basic education courses offered in her community, she improved her English, reading, and math. She took courses in self-improvement and in clothing construction. Then she enrolled in a fitting and alterations course.

Before long Bessie found a job in the alterations department of a dress shop. She worked there for a period of time, increasing her skill, speed, and understanding of clothing. Eventually she moved to a new and better position as head fitter in another shop.

Today Bessie is not only self supporting and off welfare, but she is also putting her children through college.

### Future Unlimited

Sven Sundberg enjoyed wearing clothes that were special and fit well. He especially liked to have his shirts fit smoothly around his body. However, since he was very slender, many of the shirts he bought were too big. What was his solution? Sewing machines fascinated Sven, and he enjoyed working with his hands. He learned how to stitch a straight seam and altered his shirts.

Sven's skill with the sewing machine impressed his brother, who asked him to shorten a pair of trousers. This was such an easy task that Sven decided to learn more about sewing. He signed up for a fitting and alterations course in his school. As he learned new skills, he decided to investigate career possibilities in the field. His first stop, a men's wear shop in his neighborhood, yielded results. The manager hired him for after-school hours to do pants cuffing and other alterations.

Not only does Sven earn all his spending money on his part-time job but he also has been guaranteed a full-time job by his employers when he graduates. Because there are so few

## Ch. 1: Opportunities in the Needle Trades

young men going into the trade today, his chances for advancement are excellent.

Can you see the possibilities of a career for yourself in a needle trade? Would you like to put your sewing skills to work for you?

### WHAT YOU WILL NEED TO KNOW

Skill itself is important in any work situation. However, sewing skill alone is not the total answer to a career in alterations. To be successful in this trade, you will need to understand:

- The garment industry and the clothing construction methods it uses.
- Fashion changes and the influences they have on the ready-to-wear market.
- The vocabulary of the fashion world.
- The equipment and supplies you will need and use.
- How fabrics are made and how they should be handled.
- The importance and techniques of pressing correctly.
- The principles of design and how to create a flattering effect.
- Where and how to make fitting corrections.
- Speed methods for making alterations.
- How to work with people.

All of these areas are discussed in this book to help you gain the broad background of knowledge you will need and use.

### THE METRIC SYSTEM

The metric system is a decimal system of weights and measures, based on the number ten and its multiples and divisibles.

Common units are used to specify a weight or measure. These are *metre* for length and distance, *gram* for weight or mass, and *litre* for volume or capacity. In this book, you need only be concerned with metres, used to measure clothing.

Prefixes are used to describe the size of the unit. The most common prefixes are *kilo* (1,000), *centi* (0.01 or 1/100), and *milli* (0.001 or 1/1,000).

The metre is approximately a yard long (39.4 inches). To specify fractions of a metre or inch equivalents, centi is used. A centimetre is 0.01 (1/100) metre.

It may be easier for you to understand the metric system if you compare it to the dollar monetary system used in the United States, which is also based on the number ten. In this monetary system, one hundred cents equal a dollar. In the metric system, 100 centimetres equal a metre. One centimetre is 1/100 of a metre, just as one cent is 1/100 of a dollar.

Instead of using the word centimetre, the symbol cm may be used, *c* for *centi* and *m* for *metre*. Since cm are symbols and not abbreviations, they are not followed by a period.

Following are common equivalents:

1 cm = .39 inch
1 inch = 2.54 cm

Throughout this book, measurements are given in inches, followed by the metric equivalent enclosed in parenthesis. Drawings, however, give metric measurements. Each drawing is accompanied by a conversion chart showing the customary inch equivalents for all the measurements.

# Chapter 2
# The Garment Industry

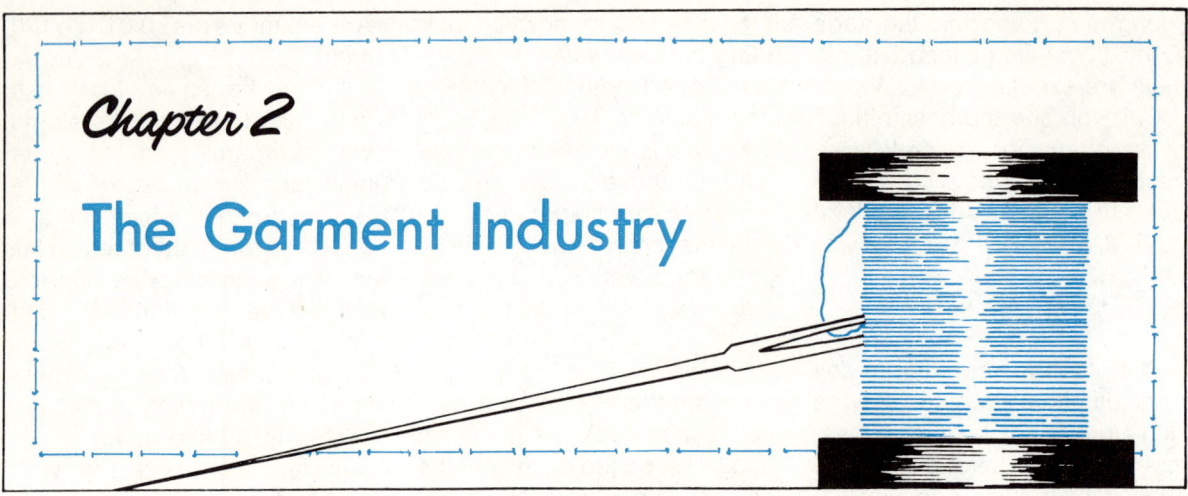

The garment industry is often called the "rag" business. It includes manufacturers, stores, and designers. It even involves the models, fashion magazines, and trade papers.

All of the skills used in producing the clothes people wear are included in the term, "needle trades."

## GARMENT MANUFACTURING

At one time most of the clothing manufacturers in the United States were located on or near 7th Avenue in New York City. In fact, the term "7th Avenue" came to mean the garment manufacturing industry. Today almost any city or community may have its own clothing factory and so have a "7th Avenue" of its own. The industry is now flourishing in many areas such as Greenville, North Carolina, Dallas, Texas, and Honolulu, Hawaii. However, no matter where manufacturers decide to set up their operations, their production sewing methods are basically the same.

Manufacturers determine the sewing methods they use by the prices they expect to receive for the garments. Production operations vary greatly, from the special, exclusive *designer* dresses to the mass-produced *budget* garments. You may find these sewing methods are very different from those you use at home. Understanding the different processes used in factories to construct garments will help you in altering them.

Expensive *designer* garments are cut a few at a time from several layers of fabric. One operator is responsible for stitching the whole garment. Another worker does all the handwork. Fine fabrics are used, with quality stressed throughout. More intricate lines appear in the designs. Seam and hem allowances are generous. These clothes are often altered to fit an individual customer at the time of purchase.

Less expensive clothes or *moderate*-priced garments are made with somewhat different methods. Many garments of the same size and style are cut at one time from many layers of material. These garments have adequate seams and hems and are made of the better fabrics. During the actual sewing, the mass-production speed methods described in Chapter 6 are used. Most of the clothes you might be asked to work on would probably fall in the medium-priced range.

"Justice—ILGWU"
*Row after row of operators, each specializing in one operation, work in an assembly line to produce ready-to-wear clothes.*

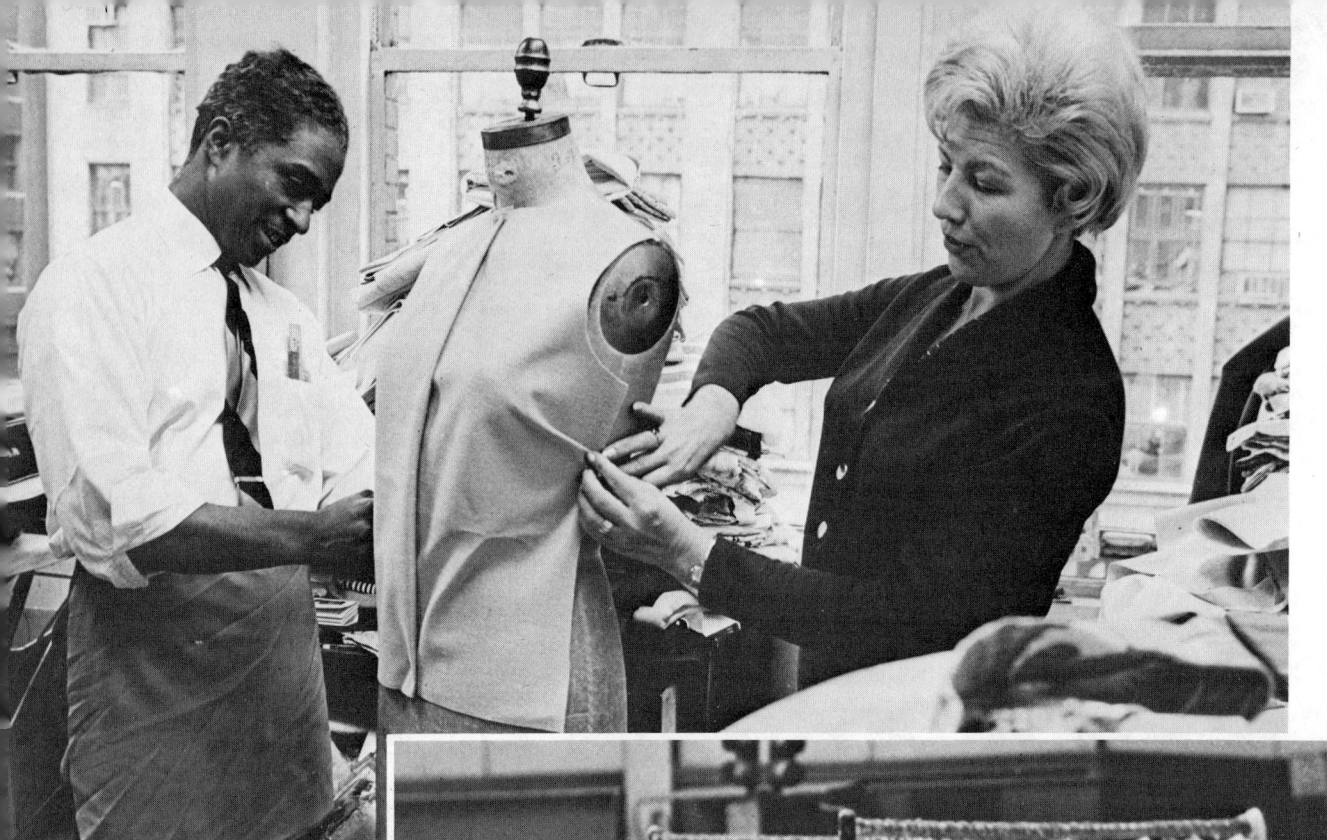

"Justice—ILGWU"
Designers for the garment industry draping a new style.

"Justice—ILGWU"
Racks of completed garments being hurried down the street are a common sight on 7th Avenue in New York City.

As the price of a garment goes down, the number of garments cut at one time goes up. In *budget*-priced clothes, sometimes as many as 350 garments are cut at one time from layers and layers of cloth piled on top of one another. Darts and pocket placements are marked by making small holes through all the layers at once with an electric needle. Seam allowances are narrowed to save cloth. Sometimes even the material under the darts is cut away. Hems are narrow and skirts short. Detail work for style lines is eliminated where possible. The sewing operations are all broken into units so speed can be developed on any one job. For example, one person may put in all the zippers and do *only* zippers. This worker can develop a rhythm that enables her to complete one zipper every three minutes.

Many budget-priced clothes are nearly impossible to alter because they have construction features that prevent changes. The more expensive garments are made with the allowances for basic changes necessary for individual customers.

Often the price you charge for alterations can depend on the original price of the garment. (You will find more information on what to charge for your alterations work in Chapter 16.) When you do not know the original price, estimate it by analyzing the label in the garment.

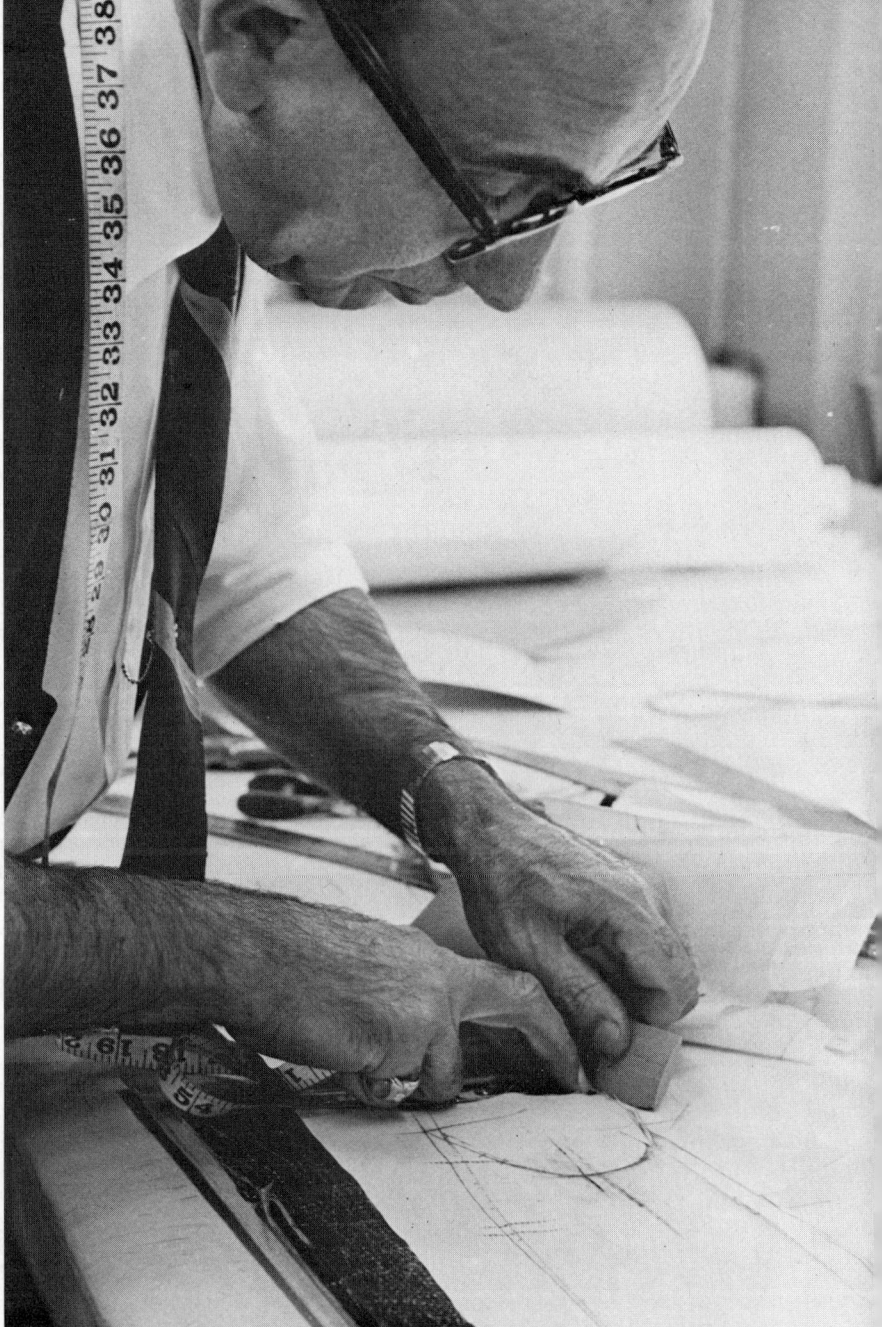

"Justice—ILGWU"
*Pattern maker drafts the pattern to create a "marker." Serving as a pattern, it will be placed on the many layers of cloth to be cut at one time.*

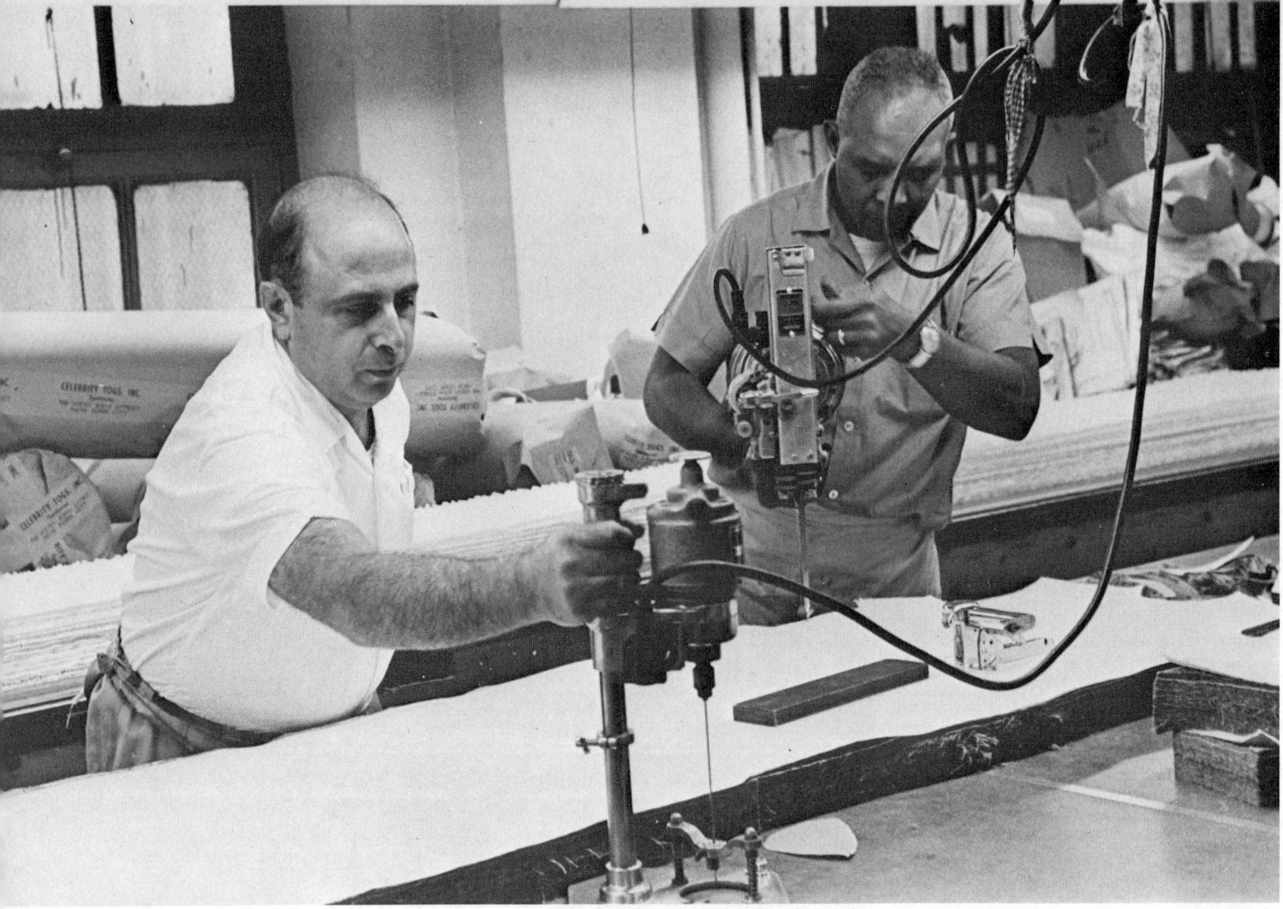

"Justice—ILGWU"
A garment cutter works on a thick pile of fabric for a budget line. Notice the pieces already cut and stacked at the lower right. The worker in the foreground is preparing to mark the layers with the electric needle marker.

"Justice—ILGWU"
Garment cutter in the process of cutting several garments at one time for a medium-priced line.

## Ch. 2: The Garment Industry

### LABELS

Labels in the clothing industry have as much meaning as they do in the food business. Certain food brands represent higher quality and are more expensive. Some brands identify the food processor while others identify the store selling them. Some represent an exclusive source, such as a famous restaurant. If you have done much food buying, you have probably learned to understand what these labels are telling you about the food they identify. However, you had to learn what they were saying.

Clothing labels give you the same kinds of information. You may find one of several types of labels in the garments you alter. Be familiar with the information these labels give.

Machine operators work at one operation on special machines for greater speed and efficiency.

"Justice—ILGWU"

*Altering Ready-To-Wear Fashions*

Mister B

Manufacturers usually limit their production to a relatively narrow price range. If you learn what market the manufacturer caters to, you will know the approximate cost of the garment carrying that label.

J. P. Stevens & Co.

Manufacturers of high quality cloth often have a label of their own to be sewn into the garments made from their fabrics.

Wool Council

The fibers used in the fabric must be identified on a label or hang-tag attached to the garment. Many manufacturers put this information on a permanent label sewn into the garments.

ILGWU

Garments made in shops employing union labor have a union label sewn into one of the seams.

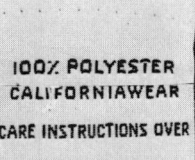

Californiawear

Care labels must give instructions for care of garment.

*POSH, INC.

Some manufacturers employ designers whose name adds prestige to their clothes and is included on the label.

Jurgens & Holtvluwer Dagmar

Many stores selling high quality merchandise prefer to remove the manufacturer's label and replace it with one giving the name of their own shop.

*Registered trademark, sole property of Posh, Inc.

## Ch. 2: The Garment Industry

- *Manufacturer's* label gives you the name of the company that made the garment. You will need to learn which manufacturer makes medium priced clothes, and which makes more expensive ones.
- *Designer's* label tells you who designed the garment. You, in turn, must know what price range they design for.
- *Store* label gives the name of the store where the garment was purchased. Some exclusive shops prefer to remove the manufacturer's or designer's label and replace it with one of their own. Recognizing some of the better-known retail shops in your town or city will help you to understand what this label means.
- *Signature* label (name or initials) tells you what designer was responsible for the design of the garment, print, or accessory item. These labels are worked into the design itself in some way. They are meant to be a part of the design and are not removable.
- *Combination manufacturer and designer label* indicates the manufacturer employs his own designers.
- *Fiber content and clothing care labels* are required by law in all garments. They can help you to select proper iron temperatures and care needs as you work on the garment.
- *Cloth manufacturer's label* tells you what mill produced the fabric from which the garment was made. Mills with their own labels have usually advertised and have built a reputation for a certain quality in their fabrics.
- *Labor union* label indicates that the garment was made in a factory employing only union labor.
- *Patch label* is a small symbol, perhaps in the shape of an animal or bird, adapted by a manufacturer as an identifying mark for a specific line of clothes. This patch is permanently attached to the outside of the garment, perhaps on the pocket or collar. It indicates a specific manufacturer and price range.

Learning to interpret information on labels can tell you what the garment may have cost and how it was made. Therefore how can you learn what they are saying?

- Start by examining the labels in your own closets. Compare the quality of those clothes with the price you paid.
- Make a habit of looking at labels and prices of clothes in clothing shops or department stores in your area. Do not hesitate to go into the more expensive shops to look.
- Read newspaper and magazine advertisements for clothes and for the stores that sell them. The ads will give you a great deal of information about prices. Make a scrapbook of these advertisements to help you study and remember what you have observed.
- Make a collection of labels or ads. Paste them on cards to test yourself as to how well you remember this information.

### RETAIL STORES

Once you learn alterations skills, you may be seeking a job in a store. Begin now to get well acquainted with the different kinds of retail stores in your area.

Clothes are sold in several different kinds of retail stores:

- *Quality department stores* usually arrange garments into little shops within the store. These groupings are based on the price or the kind of garment sold. You might find a Teen Shop, a Sportswear Department, a Bridal Department, or a Designer's Department along with many others.
- *Bargain department stores* arrange merchandise more by counters or areas rather than

*Bargain department stores may be large chains with outlets all over the country such as this one in Des Moines, Iowa. Their sales volume enables them to offer lower prices for quality goods.*

J. C. Penney Co. (Des Moines, Iowa)

25

into a special shop atmosphere. In these you will find sportswear, daytime, formal, children's, and men's wear in special areas.

• *Specialty shops* cater to specific needs of the buying public. These needs might be:

• *Price*—from the very expensive high-fashion, label-conscious shop to the bargain shop.

• *Sex*—clothes for men only or women only.

• *Sportswear*—specialize in clothes for all kinds of sports or just one kind—tennis clothes or ski clothes.

• *Bridal or formal wear*— usually cater to only one sex

Lynn Photo Service (Ship Bottom, N.J.)

*Quality department stores often arrange merchandise into little shops within a store.*

Lynn Photo Service

*Specialty shops may feature clothing for one sex only, such as this menswear store.*

*Resort shops are often designed to blend with the architecture of the area. They feature the clothes popular for the activities of the resort.*

Sink 'r Swim (Beach Haven, N.J.)

and carry only special affairs' clothing.

- *Size*—for specific body-build problems, such as tall, junior, half-size, or extra-large.
- *Resort shops*—clothes for area sports such as beachwear, or riding, ski, tennis, golf, or boating clothes.
- *Boutique*—for unusual or "trendy" clothes in many price ranges. These shops feature accessories, scarves, jewelry, belts, handbags, stoles, and vests.
- *Lingerie and Loungewear*—for undergarments, sleepwear, hostess gowns, and lounging clothes.

Lynn Photo Service

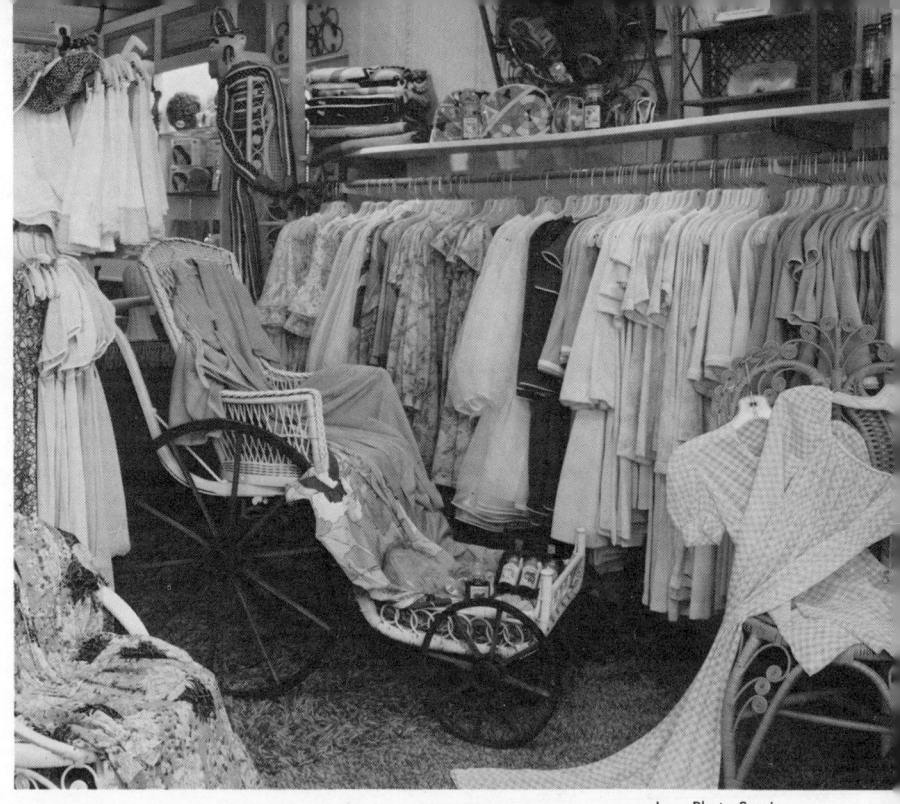

*Some shops specialize in one type of clothing exclusively, such as loungewear.*



*Boutique shops feature accessory items and special "up-to-the-minute" styles.*

Lynn Photo Service

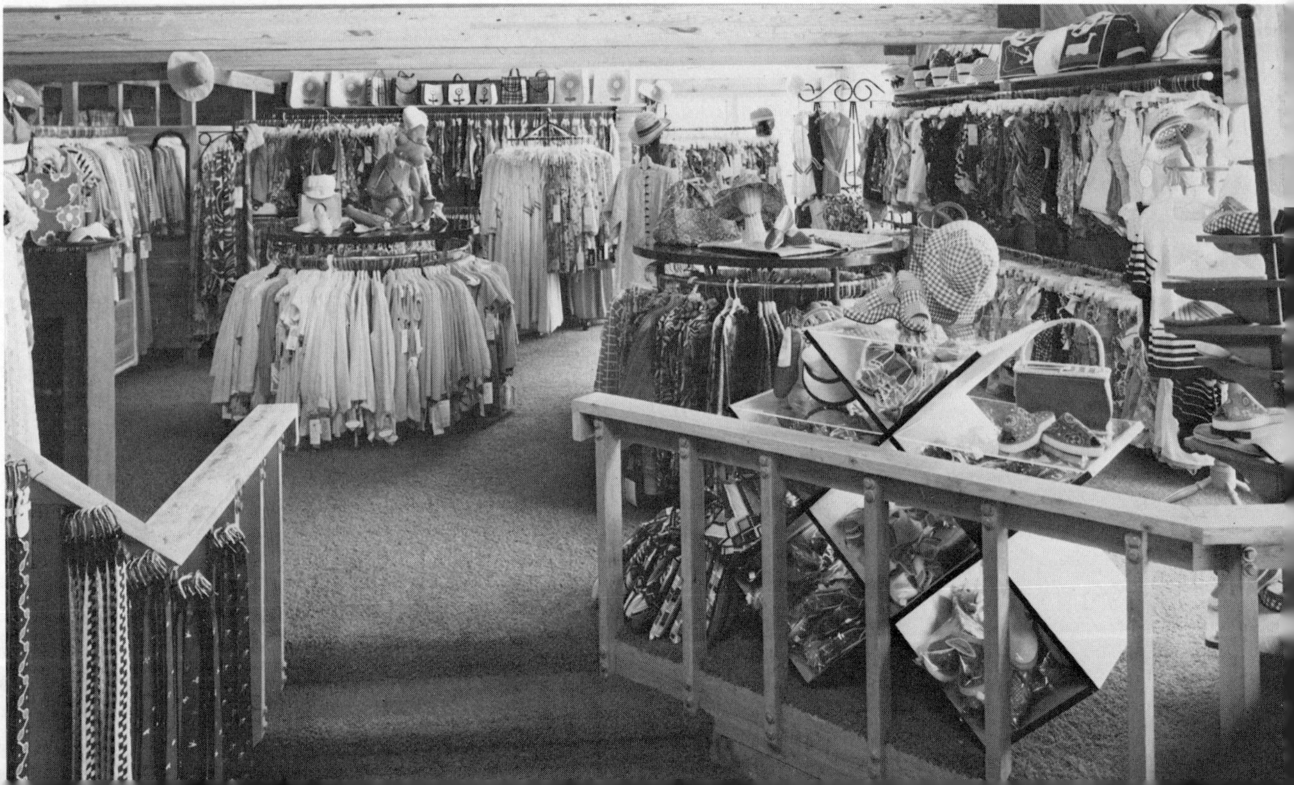

Coco Chanel

Adrian

Drawings by Karen Nawrocki
Dior

## DESIGNERS

You may never own a designer's original but the style of every garment you will work on has been influenced by a famous designer. Even large-volume catalogue sales companies recognize fashion awareness in their customers. Some identify their newest line each season with a particular designer.

As a worker in the trade, you should be familiar with current designers and how they are influencing fashion. Since fashions tend to repeat, become aware of designers who have contributed the most to fashion trends in the last fifty years.

### From Paris to Street Designers in Fifty Years

For many years, the fashion picture for women was controlled by the great designers and dressmakers of Paris. Their ideas were copied all over the world. Except for traditional native costumes, all clothes followed the influence of the Paris fashion salons.

At the same time, men's fashions were set primarily in England and Italy. They changed relatively little from year to year. However, in recent years, men's fashion styles have again come to world-wide attention. Many of today's designer's excel in both men's and women's fashions.

Fashion designs for both men and women have always been influenced by world events and trends in living patterns. Students of clothing history can usually describe the economic conditions of a given period by studying the fashions worn during the time. You might find it interesting to read one of the many good books available on the history of costume.

The purpose of this discussion is merely to call your attention to some of the main designers of the last fifty years who have made a definite impact on fashion.

*Coco Chanel* (French) influenced fashion in many areas

Ann Fogarty  Norman Norell  Pucci

Drawings by Karen Nawrocki

since the "flapper" era of the 20's. She started a trend toward casual comfort in clothes. She designed loose, simple, easy-to-wear clothes that did not require corsets. Chanel jackets with straight lines and braid trims have become fashion classics that keep reappearing. She also introduced and designed "costume" jewelry. Her inexpensive long chains and beads worn together over suits and shirts have enjoyed popularity for years.

*Edith Head and Adrian* (American) were prominent Hollywood designers for the motion picture studios and popular movie stars of the 1930's and 1940's. They became the pacesetters of the period and influenced fashion toward peplums, padded shoulders, and knee-length hemlines.

*Dior* (French) threw a bombshell on the fashion stage in the late 1940's with the mid-calf hemline, tight waist, and full skirt. Known as the "new look," it influenced women all over the world to throw out their old wardrobes and start totally new ones.

*Ann Fogarty* (American) concentrated on good-quality, moderately priced clothes styled with classic lines. She made it possible for the young clothes-conscious woman to own designer-original clothes on a limited income.

*Norman Norell* designs clothes in the best traditions of the high-fashion salons. He uses subtle lines, superior workmanship, and fine fabrics. His clothes are sold only in better shops or salons but are so popular they are quickly copied by manufacturers of lower-priced garments.

*Emilio Pucci* (Italian) is known for his vivid geometrical prints and wild color combinations, which he introduced in the early 1960's. The very name Pucci has become a word that means a certain style of casual elegance. His influence is felt most

*Givenchy*

*Courreges*

Drawings by Karen Nawrocki
*Mary Quant*

in the coordinated pants and shirts and the "little" nylon knit dresses.

*Givenchy* (French) concentrates on fine clothes with classic lines. He popularized the sleeveless daytime or evening dress with matching jacket or coat. This style almost eliminated the popular mink stole from the fashion scene. His name is closely linked with the two most prominent fashion pace-setters of the early 1960's—Jackie Kennedy and Audrey Hepburn.

*Courreges* (French) designed styles which were the beginning of the "youth cult." He inspired the first hemline explosion since Dior introduced the new look. He introduced tailored, above-the-knee dresses worn with calf-high boots. These mini-skirts were copied by manufacturers of pre-teen and children's clothes.

*Mary Quant* (England) created the craze for "Mod" look clothes, including the extremely short "micro-mini" skirt lengths. She also made the old-fashioned granny prints with crocheted collars popular. She was primarily responsible for London becoming the focal point of fashions for youths of many countries.

*St. Laurent* (French) was trained under Dior. He set up his own salon in the 1960's and decided to drop the hemline again in 1970. This attempt to influence fashion was called the midi-length. However, the target it sought to hit had changed—consumers refused to be led. Many manufacturers and retail stores learned the bitter, costly truth that fashion could no longer be dictated by one particular voice. This healthy turn of events made room for the many budding, imaginative designers in the industry today.

*Cardin* (French, now working in the United States) was one of the first well-known designers to start designing equally smart clothes for both men and women. He avoided the youth

St. Laurent    Cardin    Drawing by Karen Nawrocki / Halston

emphasis of the 1960's and is known for fine detail and precision tailoring.

*Halston* (American) is known for comfortable clothes with simple lines. He makes use of elastic, knits, or drawstrings instead of zippers and buttons. Natural, soft-finish fabrics are his trademark. Because of it's simplicity, the Halston look is easily copied at all price levels and is wearable by all ages.

*Betsy Johnson* (American) took advantage of the emphasis on the youthful look in the 1960's and made the layered look the signature of the early 1970's. The body suit, crocheted or knitted vests, shirt jackets, and pants all became part of this look. Along with many versions of Levi jeans, work shirts, and jackets, this became the uniform of the young people. Her baby-doll dress revived puffed sleeves.

*Willi Smith* (American) became a leader of the "store front" or street designers. They design and sell their clothes from their own small stores. His street happens to be Manhattan. However, this type of designer can flourish wherever young men and women want comfortable, colorful layers of coordinated clothes.

*Stephen Burrows* (American) is the first black designer to win the coveted Coty award for fashion leadership. He uses color with exuberance and spirit. The "lettuce" edge ruffle hems were his invention along with bright "pop art" accents.

## SOURCES OF TRADE INFORMATION

Since you are serious about learning this trade, keep abreast of current trends in fashions. This means you will want to know about new developments in fabrics, styles, garment manufacturers, retail stores, and national laws involving fabrics and clothing. You will also want to know what is new in accessories.

Betsy Johnson

Willi Smith

Drawing by Karen Nawrocki
Stephen Burrows

The easiest way to keep yourself informed is by reading the women's section of the daily newspaper. There are also many magazines, books, and trade papers you will find interesting and helpful.

You can either subscribe to these publications or look them up in a school or public library.

### Magazines (the advertisements are especially helpful)

Family Circle
Woman's Day
McCall's
Ladies' Home Journal
Good Housekeeping
Mademoiselle
Glamour
Seventeen
Ebony
Essence
Vogue
Harper's Bazaar
GQ—Gentlemen's Quarterly
Esquire

### Quarterly fashion catalogs of pattern companies

Vogue
Simplicity
Elegance (French)
McCall's
Butterick

### Books

Kieth, Judith. *I Haven't a Thing to Wear!* Tannersville, Pa.: Tandem Press, 1968 (paper back).

Dariaux, Genevieve Antoine. *Elegance*. New York: Doubleday, 1964.

Daves, Jessica. *Ready-Made Miracle*. New York: G.P. Putnam & Sons, 1967.

Hansen, Henny H., *Costumes and Styles*. New York: Dutton, 1972.

Levin, Phyllis Lee. *The Wheels of Fashion*. New York: Doubleday, 1965.

### Pamphlets

Pattern and textile company give-aways.

United States Extension Service bulletins.

# Chapter 3

# Equipment, Tools, and Supplies

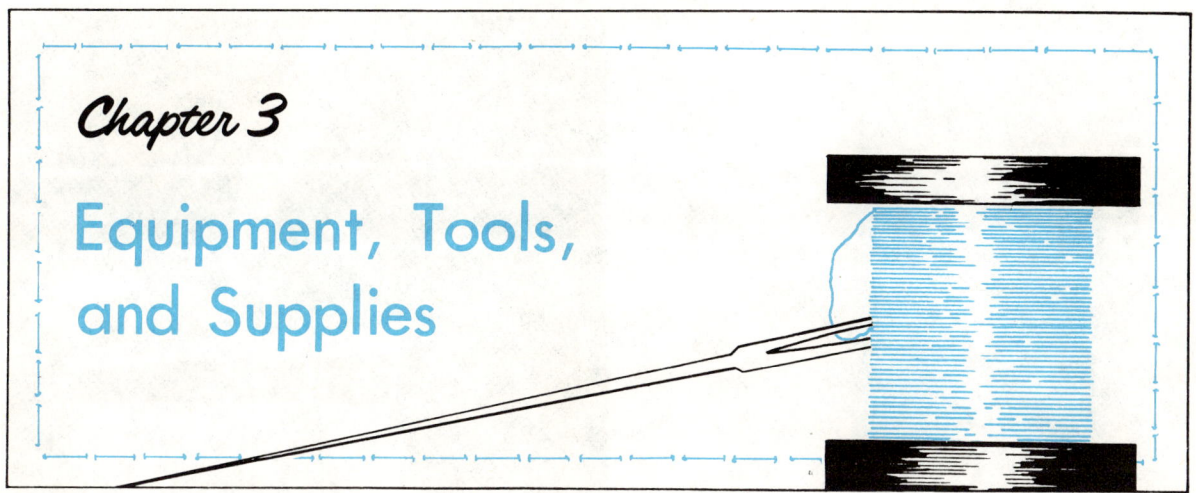

A well-planned alteration shop or department will have the right equipment, tools, lighting, and work space. It will also have on hand most of the small sewing supplies listed in this chapter. Proper tools and a good layout of equipment help to increase speed and save energy. A well-organized work area can help produce better quality alterations work and increase the skill of the worker.

To get off on the right foot and get used to a "shop" atmosphere, start by rearranging your own work area at home. Make it as efficient and well-organized as possible. This will help you form better work habits and develop a more professional attitude toward your own work. Start by bringing all your sewing tools, supplies, and large equipment into one space or corner of the work area.

Make a list of the equipment you already have on hand. Check your list with the information in this chapter. Then decide what equipment, tools, and supplies are worth keeping, what to get rid of, and what additional items you will need.

Only the very large alteration shops have industrial equipment requiring special installation and care. All the equipment listed in this chapter can be bought for home use. Even the industrial sewing machines described are easily installed in the home if your business should increase to that extent.

None of the tools or equipment suggested is very expensive. With proper care and handling, your major pieces should give good service for years.

In other words, this is a business you can start with a small initial investment of money. You can probably start out with the supplies and equipment you have on hand. Little by little, you can add other items you need as your business grows.

## EQUIPMENT

A few basic pieces of equipment will get you started.

### Sewing Machines

A properly operating sewing machine is the most important piece of equipment in the shop.

### DOMESTIC SEWING MACHINE

Any model of home sewing machine in any size can be used successfully. It can be a portable or a cabinet model but should be the regular lockstitch (straight stitch) type.

Chain stitch models are not practical for general alterations work. The chain stitch is not as versatile. It is also more difficult

### Altering Ready-To-Wear Fashions

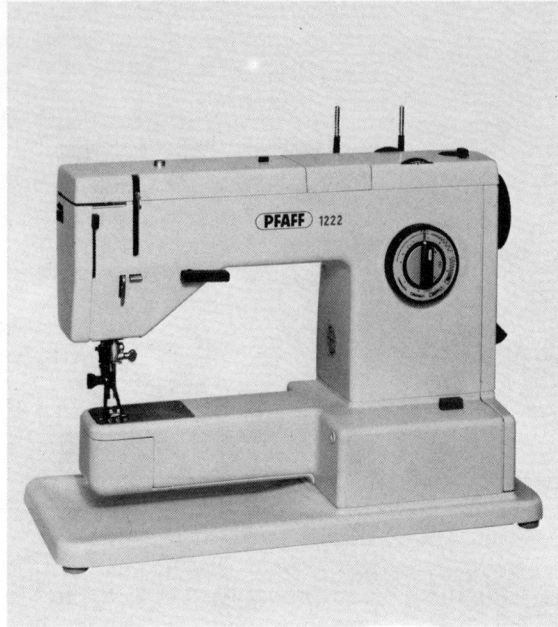
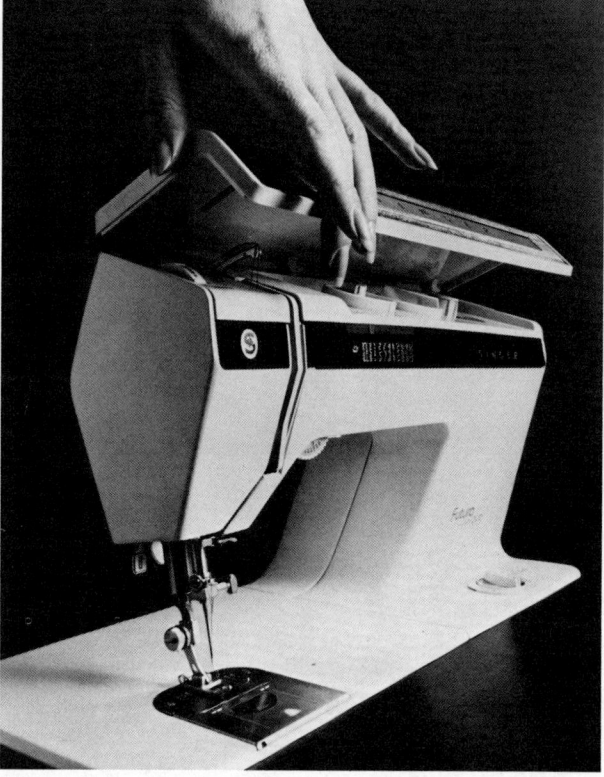

A.C. Webber & Co., Inc.
Singer Company

*Any model of home sewing machine in any size can be used successfully for alterations. The machine can be portable or a cabinet model but should be a lockstitch machine.*

to rip in small areas because once the thread is broken, the entire length of stitching comes out.

The zigzag stitch or a swing needle attachment is very useful and almost necessary for the best work.

### INDUSTRIAL SEWING MACHINE

Most of the well-known sewing machine companies make industrial models also. These machines may be for either general or highly specialized work. They have heavy power motors and much greater speed than home sewing models. If your business increases to the extent that you need to increase your speed, you may find you will wish to purchase an industrial straight stitch machine. Chain stitch or highly specialized machines would probably not be practical for the small shop since you would need to do a large volume of work to make them pay for themselves.

These machines have strong, sturdy table-type bases that cut down on vibration caused by the high speed of the machine. The bed of the machine sits flush with the table top to give a smooth work surface. Under the table is a large floor treadle for operating the machine by foot control. A knee press lever is used to raise and lower the presser foot. These two controls free the hands for smoother handling of your work. Some of the newer models have zigzag or swing needle and backstitch controls, which are worth the extra cost.

Since these machines must be grounded, they have a three-prong electrical plug with a ground wire. You will need

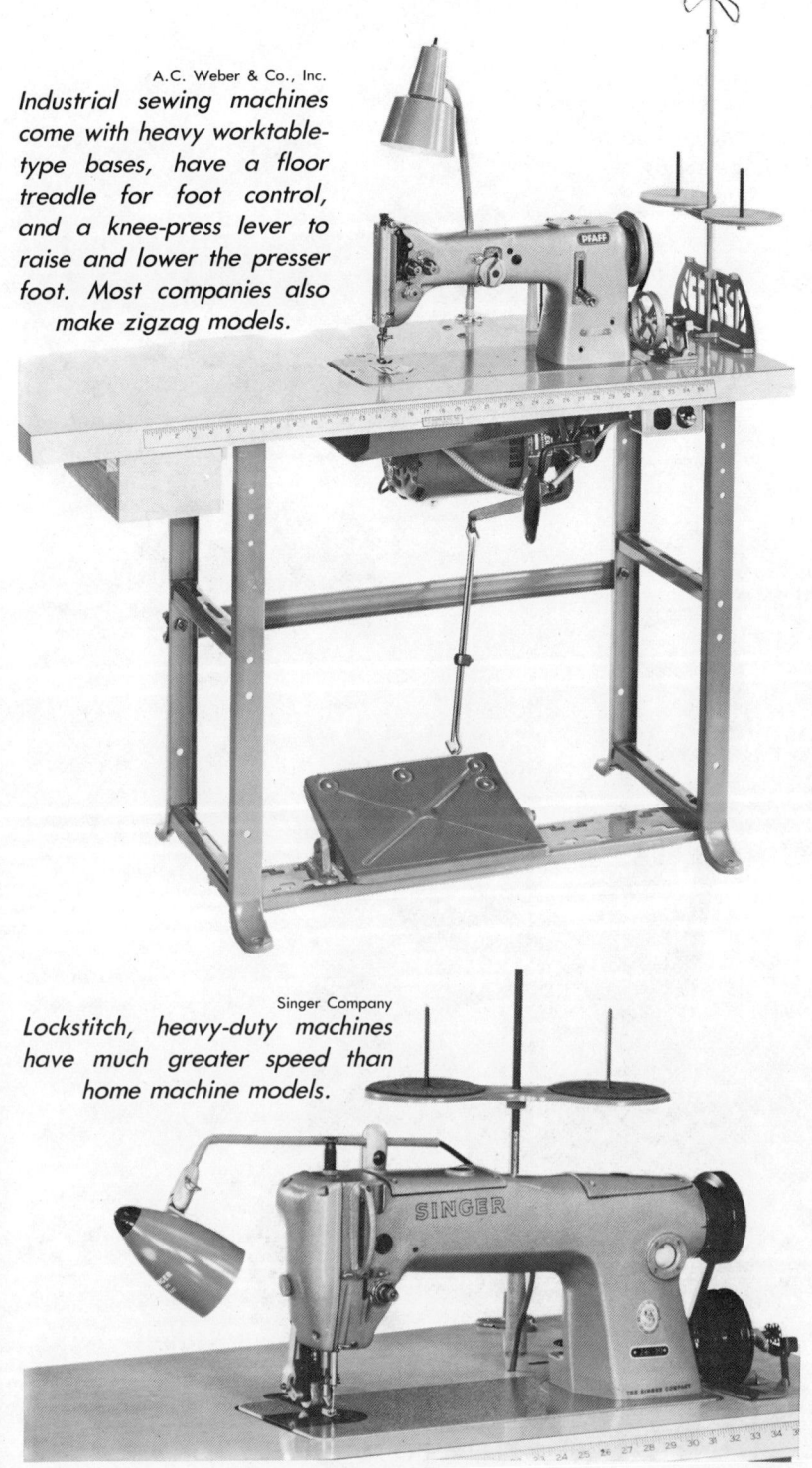

A.C. Weber & Co., Inc.
*Industrial sewing machines come with heavy worktable-type bases, have a floor treadle for foot control, and a knee-press lever to raise and lower the presser foot. Most companies also make zigzag models.*

Singer Company
*Lockstitch, heavy-duty machines have much greater speed than home machine models.*

either a three-hole wall socket or an adapter for a two-hole socket.

The cost of an industrial sewing machine is usually no greater than the deluxe model home sewing machines.

### BLINDSTITCH INDUSTRIAL MACHINE

Large alteration shops find it to their advantage to own a blindstitch machine. This highly specialized machine does only hemming. However, since seventy-five percent of all alterations work is rehemming garments, this machine can be very useful.

The blindstitch machine makes the loose-looped stitch used in hemming most ready-to-wear garments. It comes with controls for different weight materials and stitch sizes. It has the same type of worktable, foot treadle, knee press, and switch button controls found on the regular industrial machine.

These machines are priced about the same as any deluxe machine. You will find it will pay for itself in a short time if you have a large volume of hemming business.

NOTE: Often good buys can be had on secondhand industrial machines through a reputable dealer or classified ads.

### MACHINE ACCESSORIES

To get the maximum efficiency from your machine, you will need a supply of common accessories.

### Altering Ready-To-Wear Fashions

*The blindstitch machine is used for hemming. More garments require hemming than any other alteration, making this a helpful piece of equipment for large shops.*

Chandler Machine Company

*Many machines are available for specialized sewing. This Fowler Taping Attachment is used to apply tape to the edges of skirt hems.*

Singer Company

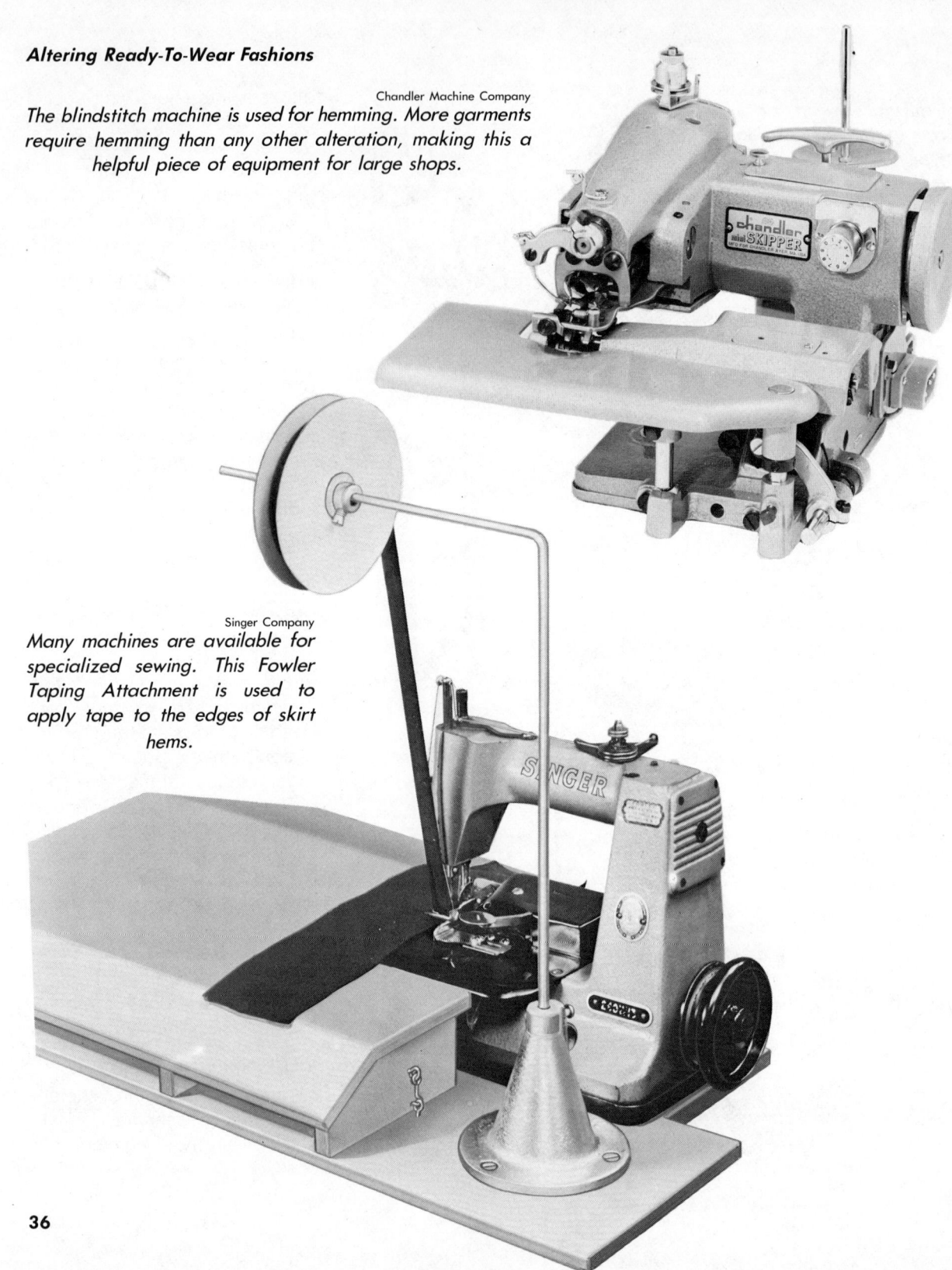

### Ch. 3: Equipment, Tools, and Supplies

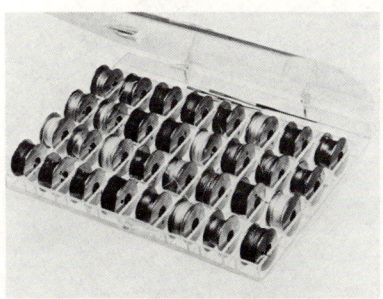

Scovill Mfg. Company

*Have at least a dozen extra bobbins for each machine in the shop. These bobbins should be kept in an organized manner so they are easy to find and use.*

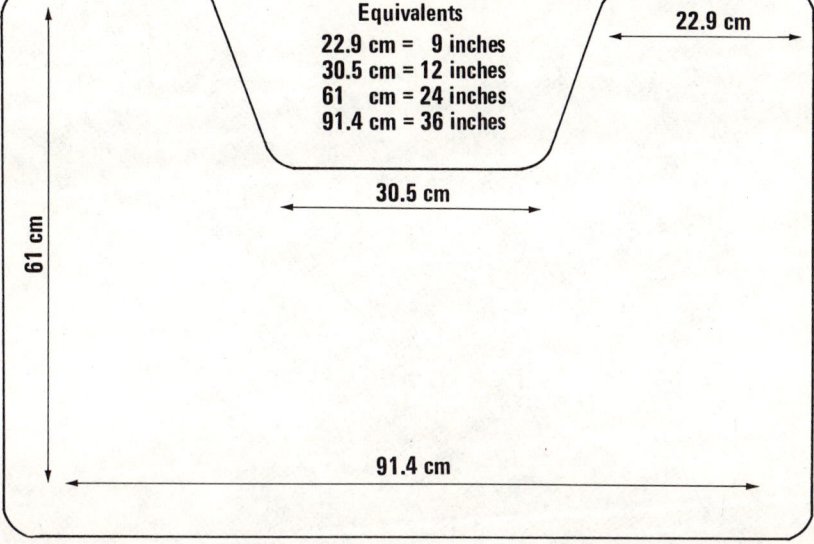

*A light plywood or masonite board shaped to fit around the body when held on the lap can make an effective work area if space is limited.*

### Special Presser Feet

You should have the following extra presser feet for your machines:
- Zipper foot to apply regular zippers.
- Right- and left-hand zipper feet (for industrial sewing machines only).
- Special zipper foot for invisible zippers.
- Walking foot or rolling foot for leather or many layers of cloth.
- Plastic foot to use with looped fabrics such as terry cloth.

### Extra Bobbins

You should have at least a dozen extra bobbins for each machine in the shop. If you keep these bobbins filled with the most commonly used colors of thread, you will save yourself a great deal of time. Some people wind a second color thread over the first. This wastes time. Keep extra empty bobbins for special colors.

### Sewing Machine Needles

Keep a supply of needles in all sizes for different weights of fabric and thread size. Be sure to have regular needles for woven fabrics and ball point needles for synthetic knits. Throw away all blunted and rough needles—they can snag fabric.

### Maintenance Supplies

For proper maintenance of your sewing machines, you should have the special oil, cleaning brushes, and screw drivers that are made for the machines. Do not allow these screw drivers to be used with other household tools. They may not be available when you need them, or they may become bent or damaged from heavy use.

### Worktable or Counter

You will need a table or work surface for laying out garments for marking, pinning, and cutting. If possible, this worktable should be the standard 30 inches (76 cm) high and should measure about 27 inches (69 cm) by 40 inches (102 cm) in size.

You can also use a card table, the leaf of a sewing machine, or a counter hinged to a wall. The work area should be as close to the sewing machine as possible.

"Justice—ILGWU"

A large, flat work surface area allows the worker to maintain good posture. Garments will not wrinkle as easily if they can be spread out as they are being worked on.

### Lap Board or Large Tray

If your space is limited, you can use a lightweight plywood or masonite board on your lap for hand work. This board should be shaped to fit around the waist when you are seated. Suggested dimensions for such a board are given on page 37.

### Storage Drawers

You will have many small items, such as buttons and trims, to store in a close-by, convenient location. Chests of drawers, boxes, or shelves, can be used for this purpose.

### Peg Board

A piece of peg board, hung in a convenient location, makes a handy place to store spools of thread, tape, and small tools and supplies.

### Chair or Stool

Being comfortable while you work can increase your efficiency. Thus it will pay you to invest in a good posture chair.

This chair should be the proper height so you can sit with your feet flat on the floor.

The seat should not slope backward or forward. You will want to sit erect with your head up and your back straight. A straight seat allows you to bend from the hips when operating the sewing machine. This position is less tiring than bending from a sloping seat.

Adding casters to the legs of your work chair will help you move from one work space to another with less effort.

CAUTION: Many posture chairs are designed with a central pedestal support and a broad base of four legs that extend the width of the chair or farther. These give the chair stability but they are easy to trip over when you walk away from the chair.

### Lighting

In doing any kind of close work, good lighting is essential. You will find a fluorescent light the most desirable. This type of light is called cool light because it does not give off the heat that a 100- or 150-watt incandescent light bulb does. It also gives less glare and fewer reflections.

The light should be placed about two or three feet (61 or 91.4 cm) above the sewing and pressing areas. You can buy the fluorescent light tubes in several different lengths so you can find one that fits the space you have available. They can be hung from a peg board or under a storage shelf. They can be plugged into any regular electrical outlet.

### Garment Storage

You will need some arrangement for hanging garments when you are not working on them. You can invest in a commercial rack, which is made of strong metal pipes in a frame shape supporting a hanging rod. The rod should be at least six feet (183 cm) from the floor. These frames have casters on the base so you can move the racks around easily.

If your space and volume of business are small, you may find several other ways to provide the hanging space you need. You might even use an over-the-door clothes bar. This attachment requires no installation, is inexpensive, and will hold about 12 garments. It just slips over the top of any door.

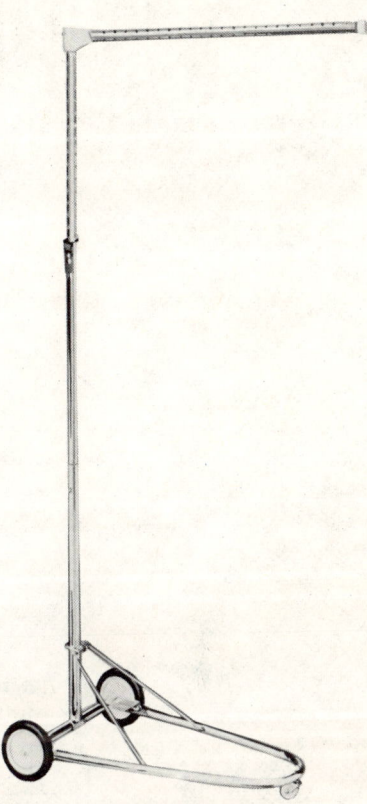

Seymour Housewares Lear Siegler, Inc.
*Commercial garment racks will hold several garments, can be moved around easily, and folded up for compact storage.*

In addition to a rack or closet, you will find metal clothes hooks attached to the wall over the sewing machine helpful. Attach one hook 2 feet (61 cm) above the machine for average-length garments and another one about 4 feet (1.2 m) above the machine for long garments. When you are working on the hem of a skirt, hang the garment on a hanger on the hook. This keeps the top of the garment from wrinkling or slipping off the machine table.

## Press Table or Counter

A pressing area is a necessity. However, a conventional ironing board takes up unnecessary space. You will find that a buckboard (see Chapter 5) is more satisfactory and takes less space. These small pressing boards can rest on top of your sewing supply cabinet, worktable, or chest of drawers. The area to be used for this purpose should be 30 inches (76 cm) from the floor and should measure no less than 18 by 40 inches (46 by 102 cm). The surface should be smooth and easy to keep clean.

Family Circle Magazine
Photo by Vincent Lisanti

*A well-planned work area with an efficient arrangement of peg board, shelves, and storage drawers as well as good lighting and a posture chair.*

Family Circle Magazine
Photo by Vincent Lisanti

*A storage closet where garments, extra supplies, and infrequently used equipment may be stored can help keep the clutter out of your work space. Notice the added advantage of putting the full-length mirrors on the inside of the closet doors. The doors can be adjusted to give your customer front, back, and side views of your work.*

*Altering Ready-To-Wear Fashions*

### Full Length Mirrors

A mirror enables the customer to view the garment while wearing it, and to see what alterations you are making.

#### ONE-PANEL MIRROR

Any area that will be used for fittings must have at least one full-length mirror. This mirror should be about 2 feet (61 cm) by 6 feet (183 cm) in size. Although inexpensive mirrors are available, they usually have some irregularities that can give a poor image. A good mirror with no distortion in the image is worth the higher price.

#### THREE-WAY MIRRORS

A three-way mirror is not absolutely necessary but can be a valuable tool if you have the space for it. Each mirror should be about the same size as the one-panel mirror described above. The three mirrors should be hinged together so the two side mirrors can be moved forward and adjusted. This gives customers a front, side, and back view of the garment. It will help clients keep track of what you are doing. The customers will be more apt to stand straight and hold still if they can watch you in the mirrors. Also, they may have some suggestions they can offer as to what they would like to have done.

### Fitting Platform

Shops that specialize in long, formal, or bridal wear find a fitting platform a useful piece of equipment. These platforms are usually 3 feet (1 m) square and made of hardwood. They are raised above the ground about 1 foot (30.5 cm) with the base 3 inches (7.6 cm) smaller on all sides than the platform. This equipment is optional and may take up too much room for a small shop.

### Adjustable Body Forms

These forms can be purchased for both men and women. They will adjust to several different sizes. They may be used for checking an alteration while working on a garment, for checking the drape of a difficult hemline, and for adjusting linings.

The work can be pinned right on the form so you will not have to call your customer in for many fittings. However, these forms need storage space.

If your space is very limited, they can be more of a burden than a help.

### TOOLS

As with any kind of skilled work, having the right tools for the job increases your speed and proficiency.

### Shears and Scissors

Scissors and shears are used for cutting but they differ in types of handles. Each of the two handles on shears is a different size. One handle is small, only large enough to insert the thumb. The other handle is larger and is meant to have at least two fingers inserted in it. Both handles on scissors are the same size.

Always keep scissors and shears sharp and ready for use. Make it a practice to use your sewing scissors and shears for cutting fabrics and threads only. Cutting other materials, such as paper, dulls the edges. Keep a pair of household shears handy for any other cutting jobs around the house.

The shears and scissors suggested here are listed in the order of their importance to your work.

#### SMALL SEWING SCISSORS

Your most important pair of scissors will be those about 5 or 6 inches (12.7 or 15 cm) long. Since these are used for clipping and trimming seams and threads, they must be sharp to the points. Be sure one blade is pointed and one rounded. The rounded blade keeps the scissors from digging into rough, bulky, or looped materials as you cut.

#### LARGE SHEARS

You will need one pair of dressmaking shears about 7 to 9 inches (17.8 to 22.9 cm) long. These are used for cutting seams or large areas of cloth.

#### EMBROIDERY SCISSORS

These small, two-pointed scissors are used for very fine

**Ch. 3: Equipment, Tools, and Supplies**

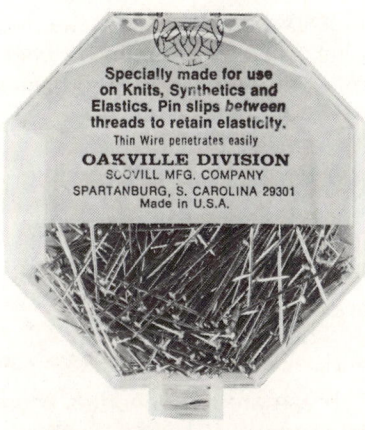

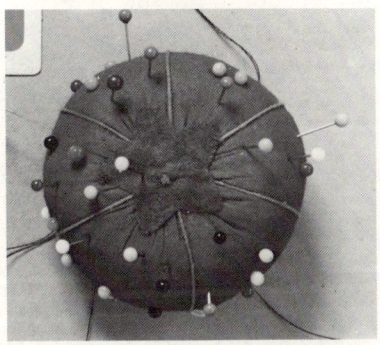

Scovill Mfg. Co.
Belding Heminway Co., Inc.

*Stainless steel or brass pins—ball point and sharp—should both be on hand. If you buy one kind with plastic ball ends, you can easily keep them separated.*

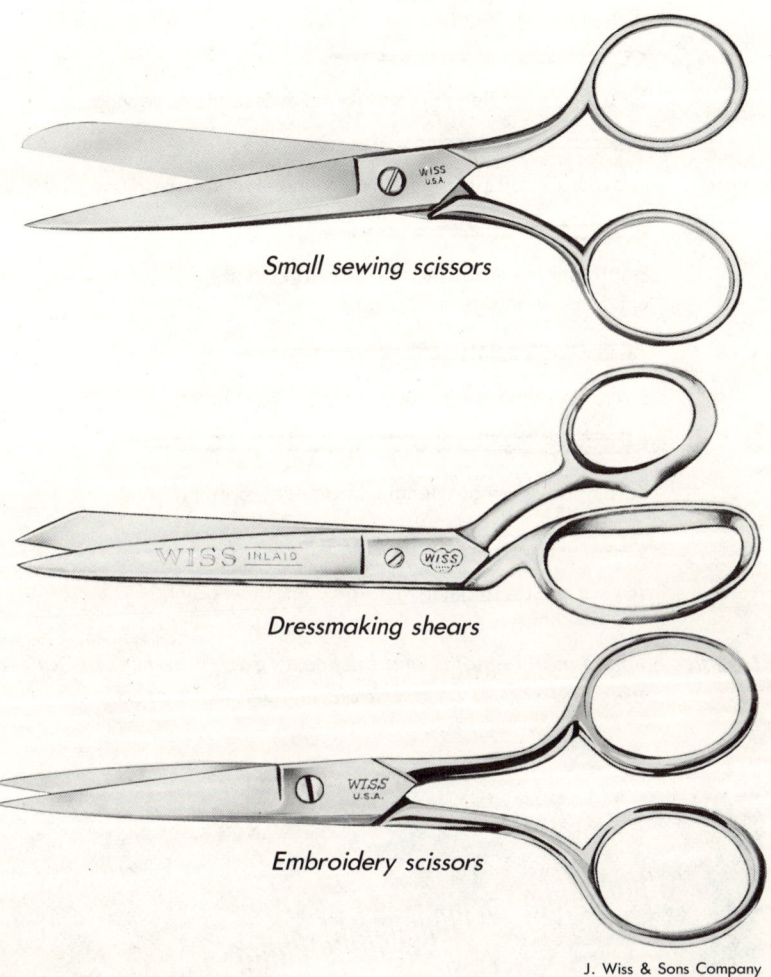

*Small sewing scissors*

*Dressmaking shears*

*Embroidery scissors*

J. Wiss & Sons Company

detail cutting or trimming such as in applique or lace work.

## ELECTRIC SCISSORS

If you plan to make boutique items or do custom sewing along with alterations, a pair of electric scissors can be time-savers. They require no muscular pressure and are easier and less tiring for long cutting jobs. They are especially convenient for people with arthritis in their fingers.

### Pins

Always buy brass or stainless steel dressmaker pins since steel pins have a tendency to corrode easily. They can rust and leave marks in light-colored fabrics.

You will need fine pins for sheer or delicate fabrics and longer and heavier pins for thicker cloth. You will also need ball point pins for working with synthetic knits. Keep the sharp pins separated from ball point pins. Some people find it helpful to buy one kind of pin with small colored plastic balls on the heads for identification. The

## Altering Ready-To-Wear Fashions

Actual size illustrations

Sharps: medium length, small round eyes; general sewing

Betweens: shortest length, small round eyes; fine work

Embroidery: medium length, large long eyes; embroidery and general sewing

Cotton darners: long length, large eyes; darning

Yarn darners: longest length, large eyes; darning

Tapestry: short and heavy, large eyes, blunt point; needlepoint

Belding Heminway Co., Inc.

*Needles come in many lengths and thickness. Each type has specialized uses and should be available in your work area.*

plastic heads also make the pins easier to find when dropped on the floor and easier to use.

### Needles for Hand Sewing

Needles are available in several types. Each type varies in length and thickness and has special uses.

### MILLINERS AND DARNERS

These are long needles used for speed in thread marking, basting, and handwork such as hemming. You will need all sizes.

### EMBROIDERY AND SHARPS

Keep all sizes for close stitching and applique work.

### TAPESTRY OR CREWEL

These needles have larger eyes and are used for special work with yarn or heavy thread.

### BALL POINT

These needles have rounded points which push fine yarns aside rather than piercing them. They are used for handwork on smooth-finish nylon and polyester knit fabrics.

### BEADING WIRE NEEDLES

If you are called upon to apply bead trimming by hand, you will find these long, fine needles a must.

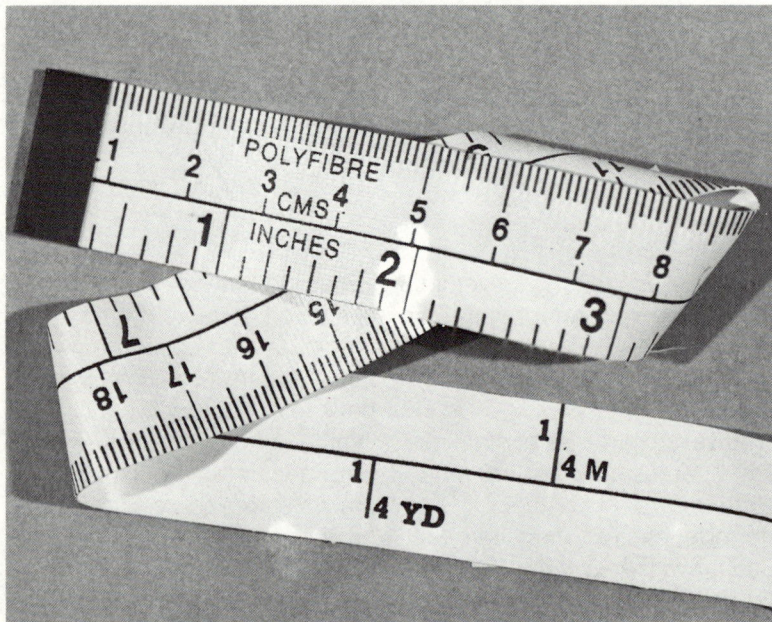

White Sewing Machine Company
*Tapes with both centimetre and inch markings are now available.*

*Ch. 3: Equipment, Tools, and Supplies*

### GLOVER NEEDLE

These needles, with wedge-shaped points, are used for stitching and repairing leather.

### Measuring Tools

Many alterations require careful measurements and having a variety of measuring tools will increase your efficiency.

### TAPES

You will need a good, soft, sixty-inch (152 cm) plastic measuring tape for taking body measurements. Be sure your tape is accurate and is not stretched or frayed at the end. Tapes are now available in both customary and metric measures, with inches marked on one side and centimetres on the other side.

If you expect to do any work on men's clothes, you will want the special tape made for this purpose. These tapes have a two-inch-long (5 cm) fiberboard piece attached at one end, called a crotch piece. See Chapter 12.

### MEASURING STICK

A plastic or wooden measuring stick is useful for measuring flat surfaces and marking hemlines.

### SIX-INCH GAUGE

These small rulers are used for marking hem, cuff, and seam widths and other small areas. They are also easier to use for

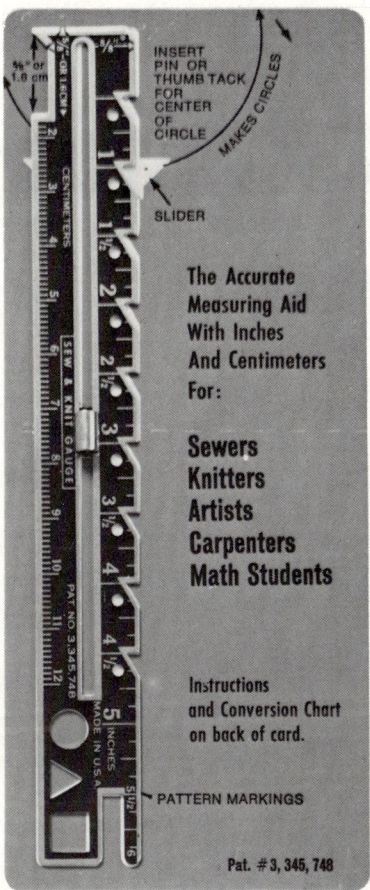

Belding Heminway Company, Inc.

*A six-inch gauge, showing both centimetre and inch measurements, has many uses.*

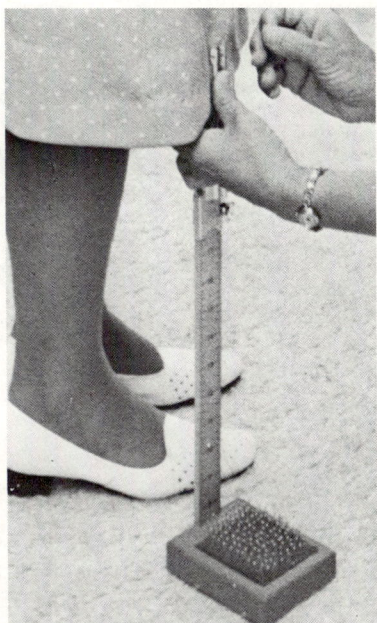

*Hem markers that stand alone and adjust to different heights increase accuracy and save time.*

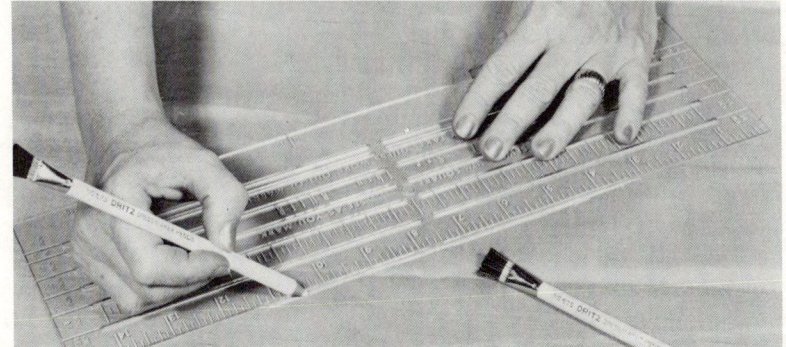

*Clear plastic measuring tools allow complete visibility as well as firm, straight edges for marking.*

Scovill Mfg. Company

### Altering Ready-To-Wear Fashions

marking hem lengths on long garments.

### PLASTIC SEE-THROUGH RULER

You will never know how useful this tool can be until you try one. It is made of clear plastic and is 4 inches (10 cm) wide by 15 inches (38 cm) long. It may be used as a T-square in checking grain lines and for measuring seam widths.

### HEM OR SKIRT MARKER

This is a specialized tool for marking hem lengths only. It consists of a ruler with braces and weights on the bottom so it will stand firmly in place alone. It has a clamp arrangement at the top that holds the hem of the garment firmly while the fitter marks the length with a pin. The clamp adjusts to the height of hem desired.

### Thimble

Thimbles protect your finger while doing handwork. People who have never been able to get accustomed to a thimble probably have not been using the correct size. To get the right size for comfort, try a thimble on before buying. Place on the middle finger of your sewing hand and shake your hand. If the thimble falls off, it is too large. If it pinches, it is too tight. A good-fitting thimble can be worn for hours without discomfort.

Thimbles come in two styles. The open-ended style consists of a band of metal to protect the sides of the finger tip. Men tailors usually prefer this type. The closed-ended thimble completely covers the fingertip and is usually preferred by women.

Any thimble should be made of hard metal. There have been cases where needles have gone through a soft material such as plastic or aluminum. Plastic thimbles can dissolve on contact with cleaning fluids.

### Marking Tools

Several methods of transferring markings from patterns to fabric or from the outside to the inside of a garment are described in Chapter 9. Only a few tools are needed to do the necessary marking.

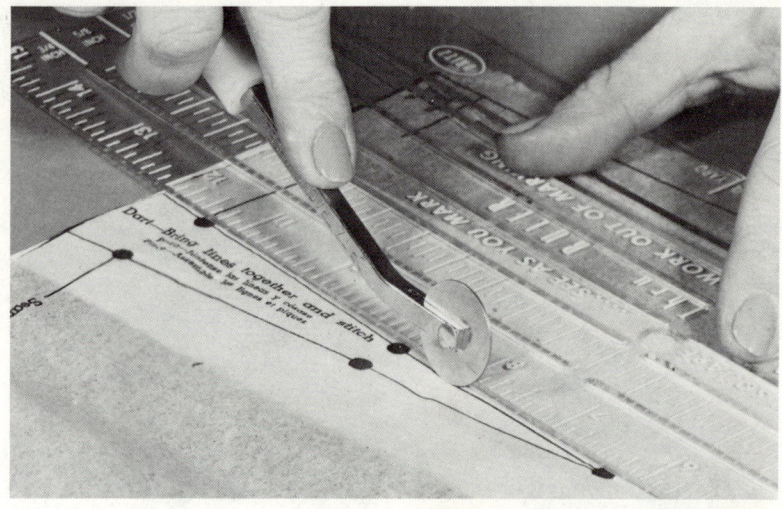

*Scovill Mfg. Company*

*Dressmaker's carbon paper and tracing wheels may be needed for transferring pattern markings to fabric for new linings or accessory items you might want to make.*

### TRACING WHEEL

This is a handy tool to be used with carbon paper to make markings on fabric. Three kinds of wheel edges are made—a needle edge, a dull saw-tooth edge, and a smooth edge. The smooth or saw-tooth wheels are the safest to use for they are not as apt to leave permanent marks on the fabric.

### DRESSMAKER'S CARBON PAPER

Dressmaker's carbon paper comes in basic colors and is used for speed in tracing patterns onto fabric. In alterations, it is used only for tracing lining and interlining patterns when new linings are needed for ready-made clothes.

## Ch. 3: Equipment, Tools, and Supplies

*Tailor's chalk is used for making temporary markings on the wrong side of the fabric to guide your sewing.*

### TAILOR'S CHALK

Tailor's chalk marks fabric easily and brushes off after it has served its purpose. It comes in squares of black, white, pink, and blue. It is also available in pencil form. Chalk is used to mark fitter's pin lines in clothes to be altered.

Wax markers are also available, but they are only safe to use on dark-colored double knits and wools. When heat is applied to the wax, it melts and may leave permanent marks on thin and light-colored fabrics.

### Pin Cushions

Commercial pin cushions are made of felt or cotton on the outside and filled with cotton batting. They can be purchased in 2-inch (5 cm) or 4-inch (10 cm) sizes. Many have a small strawberry-shaped emery bag attached to them.

The 4-inch (10 cm) size is best, as it holds many more pins and does not need constant refilling. The 2-inch (5 cm) size is useful for needles, which are handier to use if kept in their own cushion.

The emery bag should only be used to slide needles in and out to smooth or sharpen them. It should not be used to store needles or pins as they will rust rapidly.

Some fitters and alterationists prefer a wrist pin cushion. These cushions are made of the same materials as the round ones but are smaller and oblong in shape. They are attached to an elastic or a plastic bracelet to fit the wrist. If you get in the habit of wearing a wrist cushion, you will always have your pins handy as you move from one area to another.

Avoid pin cushions made from foam rubber—needles or pins do not slide in or out of this material easily.

### Other Small Tools

- Small pointed *pliers* are useful for straightening or mending metal items such as trims or buckles.
- *Tweezers* can be used to remove threads and knots stuck in the fabric or your sewing machine.
- *Emery boards* are handy for smoothing rough edges on metal or wood trims on garments. Use them to file fingernails or rough skin on fingertips before handling fine fabrics that snag easily.
- *Seam ripper* removes machine stitching easily. This is a double-pointed instrument with one point covered by a tiny plastic ball and the other point sharp. Between the two points is a tiny blade. CAUTION: All ripping must be done very carefully. A slight slip of a ripper and you could cut the fabric enough to ruin a whole garment.
- *Steel awl* makes small holes in fabric, leather, or plastic materials. For this work, the sharp-pointed awl is safer and easier to use than the points of your scissors.

### Trade Language as a Tool

Many specialized terms are used in the needle trades. Some of these terms, such as baste, findings, dart, facing, and pile, have several different meanings. Become familiar with the terms accepted as part of your trade so you will always know what you are expected to do.

Since so many terms are used, it would be impractical to list them all in this chapter. Wherever possible, the individual terms are explained as they

## Altering Ready-To-Wear Fashions

are used in the book. You will also find a glossary in the back of the book.

The different kinds of words to watch for will be:
- Fashion or style words.
- Sewing words.
- Names of tools and equipment.
- Fabric terms.
- Foreign words used in the trade.

### SEWING SUPPLIES

As you build up your business or department, you will find you can save valuable time if you keep several basic supplies on hand.

Most of the following supplies can be purchased through commercial dressmaker or tailor supply catalogues or a local business that caters to the needle trades.

If you specialize in menswear, you may have to contact a special supply house for "tailor's findings." If your specialty is formal or bridal clothes, special supply houses also stock items needed for that type of garment.

The area or climate in which you operate will determine the most common colors to order in your supplies. In summer resort areas, you will need most sewing supplies in white and pastel colors. In the north or non-resort areas of the south, dark colors are more common, so you will want to buy more dark-colored supplies.

As you work, build your supplies until you have a good selection.

### Thread

You should have the following on hand:
- A supply of No. 50 or 60 cotton basting thread in basic colors. These are used for thread markings and basting.
- A supply of No. 50 or 60 mercerized cotton thread in basic colors for hand- or machine-stitching.
- A supply of No. 50 or 60 cotton-polyester combination thread for knits and all stretch fabrics.
- A spool of clear nylon monofilament thread for invisible hand and machine stitching. It can be used on any color. These threads are available in large industrial-size spools.
- Buttonhole twist or heavy-duty thread in basic colors for attaching buttons or making thread loops and tacks on heavy garments. Buttonhole twist is used for hand work on sports clothes and menswear.
- A container of elastic sewing thread. Many garments are smocked or shirred by using elastic thread on the bobbin. If such a garment needs alterations, some of the elastic thread may have to be replaced.

### Fasteners

You will often need to replace a lost or broken fastener and should have a supply on hand.

### HOOKS AND EYES

Keep a supply of black and white metal hooks and eyes in all sizes. Be sure they are made of rustproof brass.

### SNAPS

All sizes of black and white snaps of good-quality, rustproof metal are essential. Nylon snaps are available in clear and black for use on sheer and fine single-knit fabrics.

### BUTTONS

Have cards of standard-size shirt buttons on hand for replacing any missing on tailored shirts. Also keep an assortment of buttons (single or in sets) on hand for replacement on garments.

Separate the buttons into sets, sizes, or colors. Keep them in plastic boxes, glass jars, or clear plastic pill containers. The buttons stay clean and are easy to identify.

### Hem and Seam Finishes

Many alterations will require some type of finish for hem or seam to protect the garment. Save time by keeping a supply of these on hand.

### SEAM BINDING

You are probably familiar with the one-half inch (1.3 cm) wide woven seam binding used by most manufacturers to finish hem and facing edges. It is available in 100-yard (90 m) rolls as well as the small 3-yard

## Ch. 3: Equipment, Tools, and Supplies

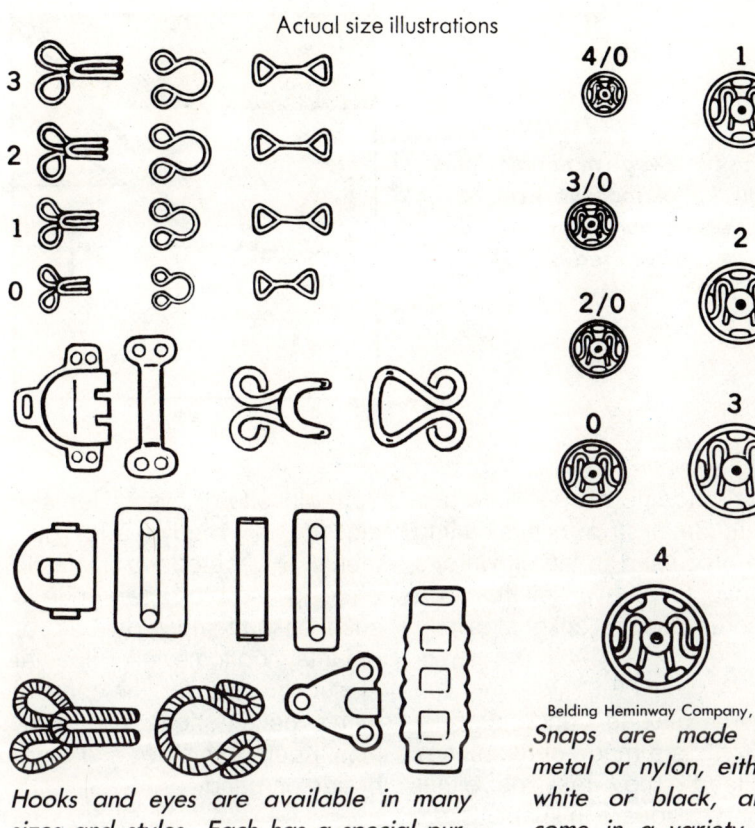

Hooks and eyes are available in many sizes and styles. Each has a special purpose.

Snaps are made of metal or nylon, either white or black, and come in a variety of sizes.

(3 m) lengths sold in fabric stores.

Since you will need to use binding frequently, you will find it wise to buy a supply of the large roles in white, beige, black, and navy. You may also want supplies of commonly used colors such as blue, pink, aqua, green, and red.

### LACE

Lace may be used in place of seam binding to give a special touch or when the garment color cannot be matched with the same binding color. Keep a supply of 1/2-inch (1.3 cm) and 2-inch (5 cm) wide nylon lace in all basic colors. White lace can be used anytime on light-colored garments. Black lace is acceptable on dark-colored garments.

The pliability and stretch of the lace make it especially useful for knits. The finished edges save time in application as there are no cut edges to be finished or seamed. Wide lace makes an easily applied hem facing when garment hems must be lowered.

### Lining Materials

Alterations often require the addition of small pieces of lining fabric. For instance, you may have to add to the original lining when the garment must be released to make it larger. Keep all the odds and ends of lining pieces left from other alterations. Sort them by fiber content and store in separate plastic bags—all polyester, polyester-cotton, nylon, acetate, and cotton. Solid-color single-knit fabrics are also handy to have on hand.

When necessary, these fabrics can be used with a compatible garment fabric for hem, sleeve, armhole, or neck facings and even zipper seam facings.

### Interfacings

Interfacings come in many weights and textures. Both woven and non-woven interfacings give added body and shaping to garments. Either kind may be purchased in varying weights from lightweight to heavy. Many have a special adhesive on one side, making it possible to iron them in place rather than sewing them. Each kind serves special purposes.

The non-woven interfacings are crisp in texture and usually

### Altering Ready-To-Wear Fashions

do not shape easily around curved areas. They are used mainly for areas that should remain fairly flat. The all-bias, non-woven interfacing is softer and will shape better than the other forms.

Lightweight woven interfacings are used to give slight extra body to lightweight fabrics in areas such as collars and buttonholes. The heaviest weights are used mainly for coats and suits of heavy woven fabrics.

The adhesive types of interfacings usually make the outer fabric stiffer than the rest of the garment. They can show on the outside and should be used carefully.

Study the type of interfacing originally used in the garment by the manufacturer before selecting one as an addition or replacement. Match the type already in use as much as possible. Sometimes a garment will have no interfacing but you may have a good reason to add one. In that case, use a weight of interfacing as near the weight of the outside fabric as possible.

A one-yard supply of each type of weight interfacing available is a wise purchase. You will always have the correct weight of interfacing on hand when you need it.

### Padding Materials

Keep a small supply of polyester or cotton batting for making shoulder pads or any other extra padding needed for a better fit. Small strips of this batting are also used in the crown of a sleeve to give a soft roll to a tailored coat or jacket sleeve.

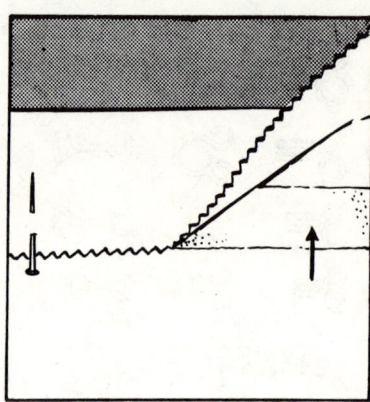

Educational Bureau Coats & Clark Inc.
*Fusible web materials offer a quick, permanent way to hold layers of fabric together. They are often used on hems.*

### Weights

Dressmaking and drapery weights are made of flat pieces of lead. They may be either round or square in shape. Sizes vary from 5/8 inch (1.6 cm) to 1 1/8 inch (2.8 cm) across. The size determines how much the weight weighs—the shape is not important.

These weights are used in hems of loose-fitting jackets to improve the way the jacket hangs and stays in place. They are also used to control the drape of a cowl neckline or a panel. (See Chapter 11 under Finishing Touches.)

### Elastic Braid

A supply of different widths of elastic braids, from 1/8 inch (.3 cm) to 1 inch (2.5 cm) is useful. You will often have to replace elastic in ready-made garments. Lace-edged elastic braid is used to repair lingerie such as half-slips, panties, or pajama bottoms. A special elastic is sold for the tops of men's boxer shorts and pajamas. Keep both black and white braids on hand.

### Belt Backing

A supply of 1-yard (1 m) lengths in the different widths of belt stiffening is a help in piecing out belts that have to be lengthened. Keep a supply of black and white in widths from 1/2 inch (1.3 cm) to 2 inches (5 cm.).

If a new belt has to be made for a garment, it is best to purchase the proper backing to match as needed.

### Adhesives

Some alterations can be done best by gluing the fabrics together rather than sewing.

## Ch. 3: Equipment, Tools, and Supplies

### RUBBER CEMENT

Use rubber cement for hem alterations on leather garments.

### WHITE GLUE

White glue can be used for gluing fabric, metal, wood, or leather trims in place. It is also used for gluing fabric in place when covering a buckle.

### FUSIBLE WEB MATERIAL

Fusible web material is made of matted synthetic fibers with an adhesive substance holding them together. It is sold by the yard in 18-inch (46 cm) widths or packaged as a 3-yard (1 m) by 1-inch (2.5 cm) strip.

Fusible web material holds two pieces of fabric together when pressed in place with an ordinary steam iron. It is useful for mending or gluing down seams that tend to curl. In addition, it can be used for holding hems in place or tacking down facings.

### Silicone Spray

Silicone spray helps make stubborn zippers slide more easily.

It can also be sprayed on the surface of the sewing machine bed before sewing materials such as vinyl, polyurethane coated fabrics, or any type of leather. These materials tend to stick to the sewing machine bed. Silicone spray on the bed makes the garment slide more easily while you stitch.

# Chapter 4
# Learning About Fabrics

When you alter ready-to-wear garments, you will have better results if you understand something about the fabrics you are working with. Fabrics vary greatly depending upon the fibers, yarns, constructions, and finishes used in making them. It can all be very confusing.

Have you ever had any of these problems with your sewing?

• The garment did not hang right. There were wrinkles or ripples you could not explain or correct. The skirt was supposed to drape softly in front but kept pulling to the sides. Or, the side seams wouldn't hang straight.

• The cut edges frayed and raveled so badly you could hardly sew the garment together. Seam finishing was difficult or almost impossible.

• The zipper seams, or hem puckered after the garment was washed.

• You started to press and the fabric melted under the iron, causing a hard, shiny surface or even a hole.

• The cut edges rolled up as you worked on them and were difficult to make lie flat.

• The fabric kept stretching and getting larger and larger as you worked on it. Perhaps one piece stretched more than another.

These and other problems could be due to the way the fabric was made. They could also result from improper handling because you did not understand what was needed for that particular piece of material.

You are probably familiar with cotton, linen, wool, silk, nylon, rayon, polyester, spandex, and many other fibers. You may already know that some of these are used together in blends. Many of these names are listed on the hangtags and labels of garments you purchase or alter. However, do you understand the differences in these fibers? Do you know what to expect when you work with or clean them? Are you aware you can buy sheer, heavy, stretchy, or firm fabrics all made of the same fiber, such as cotton, nylon, or polyester? What makes the differences?

Over the years, many changes have been made in the fabrics accepted as part of everyday life. The use to which a fabric will be put determines how it is manufactured. People's needs and tastes change constantly, and the cloth manufacturers try to satisfy them. The industry changes so fast it is almost impossible to keep up with the newest developments. In fact, more changes have been made in fabrics in the last 50 years than in the 2,000 years before that.

Ch. 4: Learning About Fabrics

A few basic principles about how fabrics are made can help you. By understanding these principles, you can work with fabrics more easily and will know what to expect from them. These principles are discussed very briefly in this chapter. You may want to read a more detailed book about fabrics. A number of excellent references are listed in the back of this book.

## FIBERS

Fibers are hair-like strands from which all yarns are made. Those that come from nature are called natural fibers. Those that are made by man are called synthetic or man-made fibers.

All natural fibers, except silk, are short in length and must be twisted together to make a usable yarn.

Man-made fibers are made in long, continuous strands called *filaments*. They can be grouped together with very little twist to make yarns. To help make man-made fibers look, feel, and blend more like natural fibers, they are often cut into short lengths called *staple*.

Fabrics made of filament fiber yarn have a shine or sheen. They feel soft and smooth to the touch when you hold them in your hand. Thus, they are often used for dressy fabrics. When a less smooth, bulkier fabric is desired for more warmth and stretch, staple fibers are used in the yarns. Recently manufacturers have developed new yarns with a rougher texture. These yarns are called *texturized*. They are made from filaments that look and handle like staple.

### Natural Fibers

For many centuries, the only fibers available for making cloth were found in nature. Today, as you know, natural fibers are still popular. Both *animal* and *vegetable* fibers are used.

The most commonly used vegetable fibers come from cotton and flax plants. Linen is made from the flax plant. Other plant fibers are used, such as ramie, hemp, jute, pina, and sisal, but they are not as common.

Cotton and linen are both strong fibers. They absorb moisture easily and are cool to wear. They launder easily and withstand high temperatures in both water and ironing. They can be bleached with chlorine bleaches. (Cotton with a resin finish, see p. 63, should not be bleached with chlorine as it will turn yellow.) They are not bothered by moths but will mildew if left in a warm, dark, damp place. They both shrink and

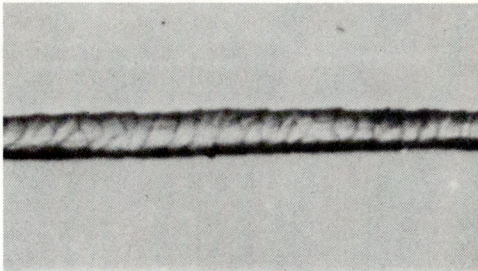

Celanese Fibers Marketing Co.
*Natural fibers, like this wool fiber, are limited in length and irregular in shape. Notice the scales on the wool fiber.*

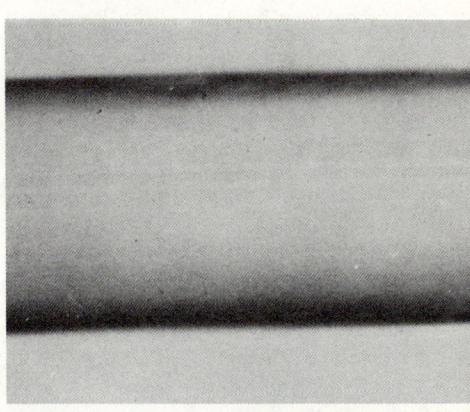

Celanese Fibers Marketing Co.
*Synthetic fibers are smooth, regular in shape, and can be made any length desired.*

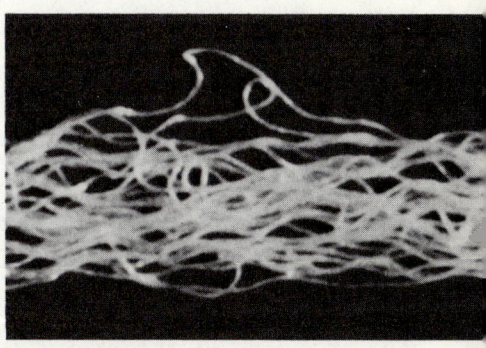

Celanese Fibers Marketing Co.
*Synthetic fibers are often texturized to give greater bulk, more stretch, improved wrinkle resistance, and an appealing soft feel. To achieve this effect, the fibers are twisted together, heat-set, and then untwisted.*

## Altering Ready-To-Wear Fashions

must be treated with preshrinking processes to keep their shape. Neither fiber is elastic so they wrinkle easily. They must be pressed to remove the wrinkles unless treated with a special finish.

The most common animal fibers are silk, produced by the silk worm, and wool from sheep. The hair from several other animals is used in making expensive, good-quality clothing. Some of these are alpaca, camel hair, vicuna, cashmere, mohair, angora, and kievet. If any of these fibers are listed on a label, the fabric is rare and expensive and should be handled carefully.

Wool and silk have some similarities. They are both absorbent. Silk is affected by perspiration, deodorants, and sunlight. Wool is attacked by moths and carpet beetles. Silverfish will eat both of them. Both are damaged and even dissolved by chlorine bleaches or other alkaline products. Silk and wool give better service if drycleaned. They can be washed, but very carefully, and should be pressed with a fairly cool iron. Wool can shrink when washed because the fibers "felt" together. This means the tiny scales along the hair fibers open and interlock with each other to form a tight, compact mass. Silk can be damaged if washed because the dyes used for it are often not fast to laundering.

### Man-Made Fibers

Man-made fibers are also divided into two kinds: *cellulosic fibers,* sometimes also called *"regenerated,"* and *synthetic* fibers, sometimes called *"non-cellulosic."*

### CELLULOSIC FIBERS

Cellulosic fibers are made from cellulose, the fibrous substance found in all plants. Spruce or other soft woods, and cotton linters are common sources of cellulose for textile fibers. This cellulose is dissolved into a liquid form and then rehardened into a solid form again.

Like cotton and linen, rayon is a pure cellulosic fiber and has many of the same characteristics. Acetate and triacetate are cellulosics that have been chemically changed with acetic acid to take on different qualities.

See the chart on this page and page 55 for special handling of these fabrics.

## TEXTILE FIBERS

| Natural Fibers | | | |
|---|---|---|---|
| Fiber | Chief Uses (Home & Apparel) | Characteristics | Care |
| Cotton | Lightweight apparel—general. Household fabrics—general. | Versatile and durable. Endures frequent laundering. Easily ironed at high temperatures when damp. Inexpensive. | Limited only by finish, dye, and construction of item. Special for durable press. May be machine laundered. Avoid risk of mildew. |
| Linen | Women's and children's dresses and blouses. Summer suiting. Table linens and other household fabrics. | Endures frequent laundering. Does not shed lint. Wrinkles easily unless treated. Resists dye-type stains. More expensive than cotton. | Limited only by finish, dye, and construction of item. Iron at high temperatures. Avoid pressing in sharp creases. Avoid risk of mildew. |
| Silk | Light- and medium-weight clothing. Accessories. Some expensive upholstery and drapery fabrics. | Strong, with natural luster. Moderately resilient. Resists wrinkling. More expensive than man-made (filament) silky yarns. | Drycleaning usually preferred. May be hand laundered in mild suds. Avoid overexposure to light. Can be attacked by insects. |
| Wool | Outerwear. Medium-weight clothing. Blankets. Upholstery. | Springs back into shape. Requires little pressing. Great versatility in fabrics. Insulating capacity which increases with fabric thickness. | Drycleaning usually preferred. Will shrink and felt in presence of moisture, heat, and agitation, as in laundry. Can be attacked by insects. |

## TEXTILE FIBERS (Continued)

### Man-made Fibers

| Fiber | Chief Use (Home & Apparel) | Characteristics | Care |
|---|---|---|---|
| Acetate<br>　Acele[1]<br>　Estron[1]<br>Triacetate<br>　Arnel[1] | Light- and medium-weight clothing.<br>Drapery and upholstery fabrics.<br>Fiberfill. | Drapes well.<br>Dries quickly.<br>Subject to fume-fading.<br>Inexpensive.<br>Triacetate is wrinkle resistant. | Will glaze and melt if ironed or pressed at higher temperatures.<br>Drycleaning preferred.<br>Triacetate is washable. |
| Rayon<br>　Bemberg[1]<br>　Coloray[1]<br>　Avril[1]<br>　Nupron[1]<br>　Zantrel[1]<br>　H.W.M.[2] | Light- and medium-weight clothing.<br>Drapery and upholstery fabrics.<br>Some blankets, throw rugs, and table coverings. | Absorbent.<br>Lacks resilience; wrinkles easily.<br>Flammability a danger in brushed or napped fabric.<br>Inexpensive.<br>H.W.M.—strong and resists laundry damage. | Drycleaning often required.<br>Can be laundered.<br>Tends to shrink and stretch unless proper chemical finish is applied.<br>Washable. |
| Rubber<br>　Lastex[1] | Foundation garments.<br>Swimwear. | Stretch and recovery rate is high.<br>Damaged by oils and light.<br>Discolors. | Frequent washing in mild suds.<br>Avoid constant overstretch and high temperatures. |
| Spandex<br>　Clospan[1]<br>　Lycra[1]<br>　Vyrene[1] | Foundation garments.<br>Swimwear.<br>Surgical hose.<br>Ski pants and other sportswear. | Stretch and recovery rate is high.<br>Resists abrasion and body oils.<br>Discolors. | May be machine laundered with warm water.<br>Dry on lowest heat, shortest cycle. |

General characteristics of the following man-made fibers:
Moderate to high strength and resilience:
Abrasion, moth, and mildew resistant.
Sensitive to heat in ironing.
Resists stretching and shrinking.
Completely washable.
Tends to accumulate static electricity.
Nonabsorbent; easy to wash; quick drying.
Resists non-oily stains, but body oils penetrate the fiber and are hard to remove.
Holds pleats because of thermoplastic qualities.

| Fiber | Chief Use (Home & Apparel) | Characteristics | Care |
|---|---|---|---|
| Acrylic<br>　Acrilan[1]<br>　Creslan[1]<br>　Orlon[1]<br>　Zefran[1]<br>　Zefkrome[1] | Tailored outerwear.<br>Knitted wear.<br>Pile fabrics.<br>Blankets.<br>Carpets. | Resists wrinkling.<br>High bulking power.<br>Wool-like texture, if desired.<br>Soft hand.<br>Very resistant to effects of sunlight. | Remove oily stains before washing.<br>Waterborn stains easily removed.<br>Washable or drycleanable.<br>Use medium ironing temperatures. |
| Modacrylic<br>　Dynel[1]<br>　Verel[1] | Deep-pile and fleece fabrics.<br>Carpets (in combination with acrylic). | Soft and resilient.<br>Resists wrinkling.<br>Nonflammable. | May be ironed at extremely low temperatures only.<br>Hand washable. |
| Nylon<br>　Antron[1]<br>　Blue C[1]<br>　Cediela[1] | Hosiery.<br>Lingerie.<br>Sweaters.<br>Windjackets.<br>Dress fabrics.<br>Carpets. | Exceptional strength.<br>Excellent elasticity.<br>Retains shape.<br>Woven fabrics often uncomfortable in contact with skin; textured yarns are less so. | Remove oily stains before washing.<br>Washes easily; wash with care to maintain whiteness.<br>Press at low temperatures.<br>Drycleanable. |
| Olefin<br>　DLP[1]<br>　Herculon[1]<br>　Vectra[1] | Seat covers for automobiles and outdoor furniture.<br>Carpets—indoor and outdoor. | No water absorption.<br>Low melting temperature.<br>Strong and abrasion resistant. | Shampoo with mild detergent and lukewarm water. |
| Polyester<br>　Dacron[1]<br>　Fortrel[1]<br>　Kodel[1]<br>　Tough Stuff[1]<br>　Trevira[1] | Wash-and-wear clothing—often in combination with other fibers, especially cotton.<br>Curtains.<br>Carpets.<br>Fiberfill. | Sharp pleat and crease retention.<br>Some are pill resistant.<br>Exceptional wrinkle resistance.<br>Reinforces cotton in durable press fabrics. | Remove oily stains before washing.<br>Washes easily; wash with care to maintain whiteness.<br>Needs little ironing or pressing.<br>Use steam iron at warm setting. |
| Saran<br>　Rovana[1]<br>　Saran[1] | Seat covers.<br>Screening and awnings.<br>Luggage. | Resists soil, stains, and weathering.<br>Flame resistant. | Blot stains; rinse with clear water.<br>Sensitive to heat. |
| Vinyon | Mixed with other fibers for heat bonding. | Resistant to chemicals and light.<br>Nonflammable.<br>Low melting temperature. | Choose care practices suitable for fabrics which have been bonded with Vinyon. |

Each natural and man-made fiber has unique physical and chemical properties which translate into the special use, and preformance properties of interest to the consumer. However, these desirable properties are only achieved if the fibers are properly used in fabrics and if selected dyes and finishes are used to enhance the finished product performance.

[1]Trademark name　　[2]High wet modulus

Textile Handbook/American Home Economics Association—Adapted by Celanese Fibers Marketing Company

## SYNTHETIC FIBERS

Synthetic fibers are made wholly from chemicals obtained from coal, air, water, sulphur, and/or natural gas. They are thermoplastic, which means they are softened by the application of heat. This sensitivity means they will glaze or melt from too much heat. It also means they can be heat-set to hold designs, creases, and pleats. They can be set to hold their shape, so knitted clothes do not need to be blocked back into shape as wool does.

They have low moisture absorbency. Thus they absorb little water and dry rapidly. The more moisture present in a fiber, the more it will swell and stretch, or pull together and shrink or wrinkle. Fibers with low moisture absorbency have greater wrinkle resistance, are as strong when wet as they are when dry, and hold their shape. However, because they cannot absorb water, they hold body perspiration next to the skin. This makes them hot and clammy to wear in warm weather. Some fibers, like the polyesters, have the ability to *wick* moisture to the surface, where it can evaporate. This means body moisture travels up the fibers to the outside rather than staying close to the skin.

Synthetic fibers collect static electricity in cold, dry weather. This electricity makes them crackle and cling. It attracts lint and dirt particles that do not brush or shake off. You have probably had clothes of synthetic fibers that clung to your undergarments and would not hang free. You may have also noticed these fibers tend to gray or discolor fairly easily. One of the reasons is that the static electricity holds on to soil particles. Another reason is they have a tendency to pick up dye from other colors when they are washed. White and pastel synthetics, especially nylon, should always be washed separately.

All synthetic fibers are lightweight and strong, so they wear well. They are versatile and can be made in many forms and textures. They no longer have as much tendency to "pill" or produce small balls of fuzz.

Like the natural fibers, the synthetics have both advantages and disadvantages. No one has, as yet, produced a perfect fiber. By blending different fibers together so the advantages of one offset the disadvantages of another, some wonderful fabrics have been developed.

## YARNS

When you look at a piece of cloth, notice the individual yarns from which it is made. As described earlier, yarn is made from fibers. The way they are twisted together determines the appearance of the yarn. The amount of twist influences the smoothness, stretch, shrinkage, and appearance of both the yarn and the fabric.

Loosely twisted yarns are used for smooth, lustrous fabrics like satins. Crepes are made from tightly twisted yarns. Most fabrics are made from yarn twists somewhere in between low and high twist.

An easy way to understand the twisting of fibers into yarns and the way these yarns behave is to experiment with a small cotton ball. Take a small ball of cotton and pull some of the fibers loose. See how tiny and fine they are?

Now twist some of those fibers together. They will hold together and form a yarn. Twist some loosely. Pull to see if they will break apart. Now twist some fibers very tightly. Pull to see if they will break apart. Do you notice how much stronger the tightly twisted yarn is? Do you see how it kinks up? Try twisting some parts of the yarn tighter than other parts. Those uneven places are called slubs. Did you ever see a fabric with slubs in it? These experiments will give you a basic idea of how different types of yarns are made.

Manufacturers use endless variations of twists to produce a great number of different kinds of yarns.

When two or more simple yarns are twisted together, they make a "ply" yarn which is stronger than the single yarn. Sometimes one ply will be made with slubs, loops, or other irregularities to add interest to the finished fabric.

Blends of two or more kinds of fibers are made by twisting different fibers into a single yarn. Great progress has been made in developing desirable characteristics in fibers. They all have good points. By blending an absorbent fiber such as cotton or rayon with a non-absorbent fiber like polyester, the finished fabric has the advantages of both fibers. It is absorbent and cool like the cotton, and wrinkle-resistant like the polyester.

Some fibers must be present in a large proportion to be effective in achieving a specific purpose. For instance, cotton fabric must have at least a 50 percent polyester blend to be wrinkle resistant. With some fibers, such as spandex, even 2 percent will add stretch to the finished fabric. Small amounts of nylon added to wool or cashmere can increase the wear resistance at points of stress such as elbows, cuffs, collars, and buttonholes.

To understand what each fiber can be expected to do in a blend, study the fiber characteristics in the charts on pages 54, 55.

## CONSTRUCTION OF FABRICS

Most fabrics are made by either weaving or knitting yarns together. A much smaller percentage is made by other processes, such as knotting, crocheting, or braiding. Some are

*A bouclé fabric made from yarns that have occasional curls and loops to give a rough, nubby effect.*

*The yarns used in this pile fabric are short and loosely twisted to give a smooth, fluffy look and feel to the fabric.*

## Altering Ready-To-Wear Fashions

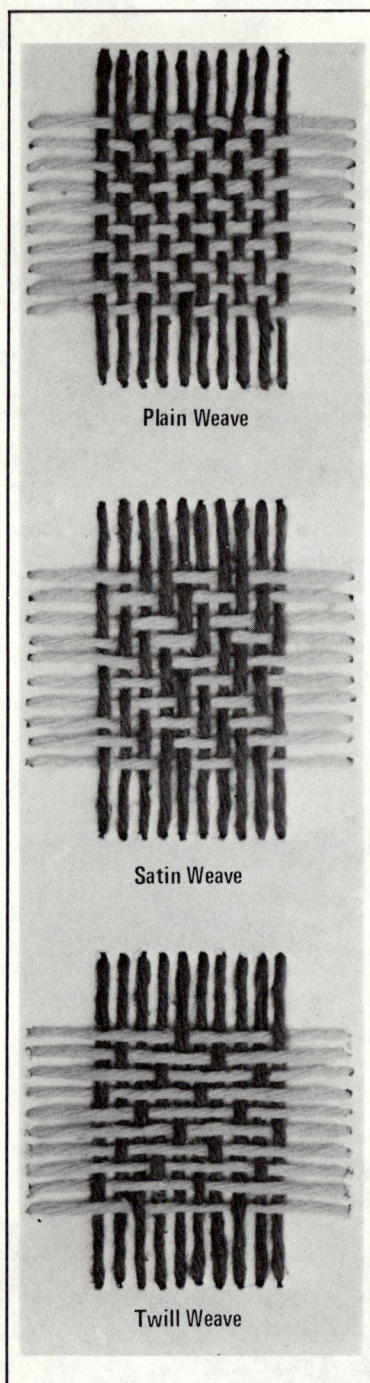

Plain Weave

Satin Weave

Twill Weave

Educational Bureau Coats & Clark Inc.

*Woven fabrics are the result of interlacing yarns over and under each other in a definite pattern. The warp yarns run lengthwise while the filling yarns run across the fabric.*

even made directly from the fibers by felting or bonding the fibers together.

### Weaves

One of the oldest methods of making fabrics is by interlacing two sets of yarns together in a process known as weaving. One set of yarns is stretched on a frame (loom) and is called the *warp* or *lengthwise* yarns. The other set is inserted so that they go over and under the warp yarns to form a fabric. Since these yarns travel back and forth from one side to the other, they are called *crosswise* or *filling* yarns. As the filling yarns go back and forth, they go around the warp yarns on the edges and form a self edge or selvage. Since this edge is woven and smooth, it does not ravel or stretch.

In clothing design and construction, the yarns are referred to as grain. Thus the warp yarns are known as the *lengthwise grain* and usually run lengthwise on the body. The filling yarns are called *crosswise grain* and usually go crosswise or around the body.

Another direction of fabric often referred to as grain is the bias. *Bias* is the exact diagonal of a square of fabric. If you fold the lengthwise grain on top of the crosswise grain of an even square, the folded edge will be the *true bias*. Bias has a great deal of stretch and is used when it is desirable to make a fabric piece curve. Always be sure to use the true bias rather than just any diagonally cut piece. True bias gives maximum stretch and allows the fabric to lie smooth and flat.

Since the warp yarns are stretched on the loom as the material is woven, these yarns do not usually stretch in the finished fabric. The crosswise or filling yarns are *not* stretched on the loom, so they *will* stretch in the finished product. You can always tell which is the warp or lengthwise grain of a piece of woven fabric by testing to see if it will stretch. If a straight grain stretches, it is crosswise grain. If it doesn't stretch, it is lengthwise grain. If there is a great deal of stretch, it is probably bias and not true grain.

Designers make use of the way the lengthwise, crosswise, or bias grain stretches or holds its shape and the way it hangs on the body. If a garment is designed to have the grain go in a certain direction, it will not hang the same or look the same if the grain direction is changed. For this reason, all garment pattern pieces are marked with arrows indicating the direction of the grain.

### Ch. 4: Learning About Fabrics

The placement of the grain on the body is the most important consideration in fitting or refitting clothes. If you see a bulge or wrinkle when a garment is worn, it usually means the grain needs to be raised or lowered at that point. Variations in body curves may have caused the fabric to stretch tightly or hang loosely in the wrong places. Thus, the grain was pushed or pulled out of line. Side seams that do not hang straight may mean the grain is not in the correct position over the hips, abdomen, or buttocks.

### Knits

In today's clothing market, the majority of clothing fabrics used are made by the knitting process. In this process, the yarns are looped together to form the fabric. The lengthwise lines of loops or *wales* are used in sewing and fitting the same way as woven grain.

Knit fabrics can be plain or ribbed or come in fancy patterns. They can be used for most any type of clothing, from delicate underwear and nightwear to fleece coats. They have the great advantages of being almost wrinkleproof, and stretching with the body for greater comfort. Another important advantage is that they are less expensive to produce.

### FILLING KNIT

In filling knit, a single yarn travels round and round to form

Educational Bureau Coats & Clark Inc.

*The grain, or yarns, of a fabric greatly influence the way the garment hangs or drapes. Lengthwise grain yarns are firm and do not stretch. Crosswise yarns may stretch slightly. The bias of a fabric stretches easily.*

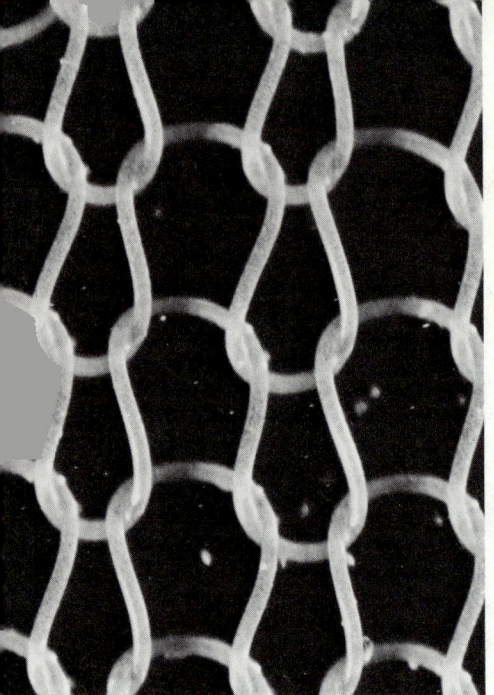

*Filling knit fabrics are made from a single yarn and are similar to hand-knitted fabrics. They stretch easily and can develop runs.*

USDA

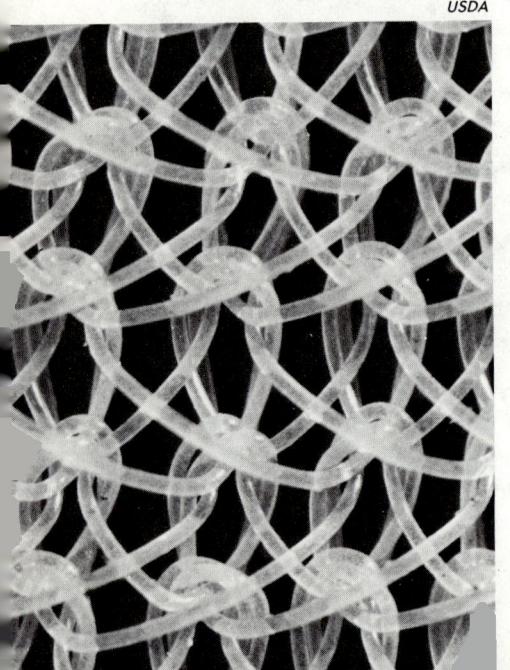

*Warp knit fabrics are made from several yarns on separate needles so the yarns are interlaced together. These fabrics are run-proof and will not ravel.*

USDA

a tube. It may also go back and forth to make a flat fabric. Hand knitting is an example of this kind of knitting. These fabrics are very elastic, stretch in any direction, and are used mainly for hosiery and sweaters. However, they will run or ladder, and they may stretch too much or sag.

## WARP KNIT

In warp knit, a set of yarns is placed on separate needles and the yarns are carried lengthwise in a zigzag fashion. These fabrics stretch primarily in the crosswise direction. The most familiar use of this kind of knit is in the tricot fabrics used for underclothing. These knits are run-proof, snag-resistant, and non-raveling. However, they are less elastic than the filling knits.

## DOUBLE KNIT

When two sets of needles are used on a knitting machine, a heavier fabric with a finished appearance on both sides is produced. These fabrics are non-clinging, firm, and hold their shape better than the usual knits made with single yarns. Double knits have become so popular they now make up a very large part of the fabric market.

## Interlocking Fibers

Some cloth is made by a simple matting together of fibers without making yarns first. By applying heat, moisture, and pressure to a sheet of wool fibers, a fabric called felt is formed. Felt is not as strong as a woven or knitted fabric but it does not ravel, is less expensive, and can be easily shaped.

Only wool fibers will mesh together and hold their shape by themselves as felt. Other fibers need an adhesive to make them stick together. Fusing fibers into cloth by adding an adhesive to the fibers is a process similar to felting. Nonwoven interfacing is a familiar example of this type of fabric.

### Lace and Net

Openwork fabrics are made by a method known as knotting. The yarns are tied together where they cross to form an open, usually delicate fabric.

Since the yarns are tied together, they do not ravel.

### Crochet

From time to time, crocheted fabrics enjoy popularity. In this method of construction, a single yarn is worked into a series of interlocking loops with a special hook. Sweaters, vests, shawls, and dresses are often made by this method. Since crochet work does not have a grain, it does not hold its shape as well as other fabrics. Most fitted garments must be attached to an underlining with special built-in controls. Such garments can be expensive and difficult to alter.

Ch. 4: **Learning About Fabrics**

### Bonded Fabrics

Although not a basic fabric construction method, bonding two fabrics together to form one is a large-volume business. In this process, two different types of fabrics are fused together. Fabrics of any type may be used for both backing and face.

The fabrics are joined together in one of two ways. An adhesive substance may be sprayed on the surface of the underlining fabric. The underlining is placed on the facing fabric. Heat and pressure from large rollers cause the two fabrics to stick together. With some underlinings, such as urethane foam, the surface of the foam is melted slightly with a gas flame before it is applied to the facing fabric. Either method works.

When bonding was first developed, the fabrics had a major problem—drycleaning fluids and wear caused the adhesive to give way. The two fabrics separated, and the clothes were ruined. This problem has been largely overcome.

Most bonded fabrics have an acetate tricot underface. Since tricot is a warp knit and will only stretch in width, it gives stability to the face fabric. Acetate is relatively inexpensive, dyes easily, drapes well, and can be heat-set into pleats. It gives added desirable characteristics to the face fabric. Remember though, that acetate is extremely heat sensitive. See Chart page 55. A bonded acetate

Educational Bureau, Coats & Clark Inc.

*Lace fabrics are made by knotting the yarns together in a patterned effect. Though lace is usually quite delicate, it will not run or ravel.*

## Altering Ready-To-Wear Fashions

tricot fabric must be handled much like an all-acetate fabric.

In working with bonded fabric, it is most important to check the grains of the face and underface fabrics to be sure they are aligned straight. If the grain on either surface is crooked, it can affect the way the entire fabric handles.

### FINISHES

Fabrics made with various fibers, yarns, and construction methods would still lack interest and some of the qualities desired in clothes if it were not for the final finishing processes. Many kinds of finishes may be applied to fabrics before they are ready to be sold. As a consumer, you should be familiar with all of them. However, only a few finishes will affect your work as an alterationist.

### Dyeing

Color is applied to fabrics by dyeing or printing. Cloth may be dyed in many ways.

Synthetic fibers sometimes have the color added in the liquid solution before the fibers are formed. This is called *solution* dyeing and is very colorfast.

The fibers can be dyed before they are twisted into yarns in a process called *stock* dyeing.

Yarns can be dyed after they are made but before they are woven or knitted into cloth. This is *yarn* dyeing.

The fabric can be dyed in one piece, called *piece* dyeing.

The way the fabric receives its color can affect how well the color will last but has little to do with any alterations you might be asked to do.

### Designs

Designs are produced by weaving them into the fabric or printing them on.

The only way the design can affect an alteration is if it is printed on the fabric off-grain or crooked. Then you have to decide whether to make the grain lie straight and let the design be crooked or make the design straight and allow the garment to hang oddly or bulge in the wrong places. You and your customer have to make a choice as you cannot have both. This problem rarely happens with a well-made garment.

### Luster Finishes

A luster or sheen is often desired in cloth. Finishes such as beetling, mercerizing, calendering, or glazing all produce various kinds of luster.

Mercerizing and glazing are chemical processes. Beetling and calendering are mechanical methods.

In working with fabrics with any of these finishes, you can preserve the shine better if you press them on the right side.

### Shrinkage Control

You may be asked to release or let out a garment that a customer has suddenly found to be too small, even though there has been no weight gain. How can that happen? Perhaps the label even states that the garment was preshrunk. The point is, how much shrinkage was left?

*Preshrunk* merely means that some shrinkage has taken place, but it does not tell you how much may still occur. The amount of shrinkage left after preshrinking is called *residual shrinkage*. A statement that the fabric has been preshrunk should also tell you how much more shrinkage is possible. If less than 1 percent shrinkage is left in the garment, it will not affect the fit too much. More than 2 percent can make a big difference. The process called *Sanforizing* guarantees that not more than 1 percent residual shrinkage is left in the garment.

Sometimes a garment can be washed several times without any apparent shrinkage and then suddenly it becomes too small. This could be caused by improper washing in too-hot water, which removed a resin finish that was protecting the garment. Sometimes a high dryer temperature will cause garments to shrink. This is true even with some of the synthetics such as polyester.

Caution your customers to check labels to see how much shrinkage is left in garments before they buy them. Also, warn them about improper laundering practices. Other than that,

**Ch. 4: Learning About Fabrics**

Easy care label.

Special finish label.

Permanent press label.

you can only release the seams as far as possible.

### Easy-Care Finishes

The terms *wash and wear, wrinkle-resistant,* and *easy care* on a label indicate the garment has been chemically treated to reduce wrinkles. It does not mean that it will not wrinkle at all. Usually only a touch-up pressing instead of ironing is needed after laundering.

The chemicals are usually resins which actually combine with the fibers in the cloth. As long as the resins are present, the garment resists wrinkles. When the resin is removed, as it can be by improper washing, the garment loses its wrinkle resistance.

These finishes have some disadvantages, such as weakening the fibers and lowering the absorbency. Sometimes they may even have an unpleasant odor. However, the advantage of being so much easier to care for makes up for the disadvantages.

Usually, these finishes will not affect alterations.

### PERMANENT PRESS

The crease-resistant finish that can affect you, as an alterationist, is called *permanent press*. In this process, the fabrics are treated with resins. However, the process is not finished until after the garment is completed. Then, the whole garment is treated by a baking process in a factory oven. When the garment comes out of the oven, the finish is permanent. This process also weakens the fibers and the garments do not wear as well as untreated ones. However, most people prefer the crisp, fresh appearance and lack of care to the extra wear.

For the alterationist, permanent press can be important. Garments treated with this finish have *permanent* creases set in them. *They cannot be altered successfully.* Hems cannot be lengthened, and side seams cannot be released because the original creases cannot be pressed out. Suggest to your customers that, when they buy permanent press garments, they buy only those that fit well with no changes needed. Do not try to alter them.

### Other Finishes

Many other kinds of finishes are used, but they probably will not affect your work in any way. As examples, embossing, crinkling, moiréing, sizing, and napping all affect only the finished appearance of the material. Water-and-stain-repellent finishes, soil-and-stain-resistant finishes, flameproofing, and moth-resistant, antiseptic, and insulating finishes all give desirable qualities to the cloth. They do not affect the way you work with the garment.

### Tricky Textiles

As long as the fabrics you work on are made by the standard weaving and knitting methods, you probably will not have many problems. However, you may be asked to work on some fabrics that call for special handling. Such materials as metallics, sequins, crepes, fake

### Altering Ready-To-Wear Fashions

furs, chiffons, leathers, fake leathers, piles, and satins need extra care. The charts on pp. 67–71 give helpful suggestions for working with these tricky textiles.

## COMPATIBLE TRIMMING FABRICS

Sometimes, in their attempts to make medium-priced clothes look like expensive designer fashions, manufacturers make mistakes. For instance, at one time, linen dresses trimmed with leather were popular. Lower-priced copies were made with imitation leather trim. The linen needed to be drycleaned to prevent shrinking, but the imitation leather hardened and disintegrated when exposed to drycleaning fluids. These garments were a disaster. Another manufacturer made dresses that featured stitched tucking on the bodice and skirt. Unfortunately, the thread used came apart when the garment was washed, dried, and pressed. When the wearer sat in the dress for any length of time, the tucks all came out.

These are examples of what can happen when trims and notions are incompatible with the basic fabric of the garment. If you are working on a garment that must be drycleaned, be sure anything you add to it can also be drycleaned. If the garment is washable, all trims, zippers, seam tapes, and laces should be washable and *pre-*

*Many luxury fabrics such as this matelassé coat require special sewing techniques to preserve their beauty. The charts on pages 67-71 offer helpful hints for working with special fabrics.*

*shrunk* before they are attached to the garment.

Remodeling or restyling clothes often calls for the addition of another fabric to be combined with the original garment. Always be sure you combine only materials that need similar kinds of care. See Chart pages 54, 54 to compare care requirements of the various fibers.

## FABRIC LEGISLATION

The world of textiles has become so complex and confusing in recent years that even an expert cannot identify a fabric by look or feel alone. To protect consumers, Congress recently passed two laws relating to textiles.

In order to identify the different kinds of fibers, they have been classified according to their basic chemical composition. These are called *generic* families. The synthetic fibers in each generic family have the same basic chemical composition but have been developed by different manufacturers and given their own trade names. For example, the polyester *generic* family includes Dacron (Du Pont), Fortrel (Fiber Industries), Kodel (Eastman), and

Blue "C" Polyester (Monsanto Textiles). All of these are polyester fibers.

## Textile Products Identification Act

The Textile Products Identification Act requires that every textile product must be accompanied by a label or tag which states the fibers used in its construction. These fibers must be called by their generic names. The percentage of each one used must be given, with the fiber having the highest percentage listed first. Any fibers present that make up less than 5 percent of the total weight may be listed simply as *other fibers*. Such fibers are usually added more for interest and effect than wearing qualities. The trade name of the fiber may be given but only the generic family name is required.

Ch. 4: Learning About Fabrics

### Permanent Care Labeling

Permanent care labeling is a ruling of the Federal Trade Commissions. It requires that most apparel and home-sewing fabrics (both domestic and imported) carry a permanently attached label giving care and maintenance instructions. These labels can be sewn, glued, or fused onto the apparel.

Retail fabric stores have printed care labels to give the buyer when fabric is purchased. These labels should be sewn into the finished garment.

Exceptions allowed in this ruling are products that do not require routine cleaning, and hats, gloves, and footwear. Also, articles intended to be sold for $3.00 or less and which are completely washable under all normal circumstances do not need a care label.

Before you begin to alter any ready-to-wear garments, read the attached labels first. Check the fiber content so you can determine pressing care and the type of needles and thread to be used. See charts pages 67–71. Check the care required so you can decide what kind of sewing supplies and notions are acceptable.

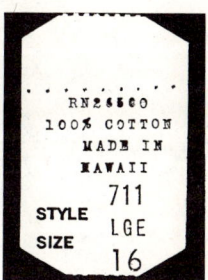
*Fiber content label.*

*Permanent care labels.*

## PERMANENT CARE LABELS

| MACHINE WASHABLE FABRICS | MACHINE WASHABLE DELICATE FABRICS | DRY CLEANABLE FABRICS |
|---|---|---|
|  1 MACHINE WASH WARM |  4 MACHINE WASH WARM DELICATE CYCLE TUMBLE DRY LOW USE COOL IRON | 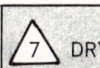 7 DRY CLEAN ONLY |
| **MACHINE WASHABLE FABRICS** | **MACHINE WASHABLE FABRICS** | **PILE FABRICS** |
|  2 MACHINE WASH WARM LINE DRY |  5 MACHINE WASH WARM DO NOT DRY CLEAN |  8 DRY CLEAN PILE FABRIC METHOD ONLY |
| **MACHINE WASHABLE PERMANENT PRESS** | **ALL HAND WASHABLE FABRICS** | **VINYL FABRICS** |
|  3 MACHINE WASH WARM TUMBLE DRY REMOVE PROMPTLY |  6 HAND WASH SEPARATELY USE COOL IRON |  9 WIPE WITH DAMP CLOTH ONLY |

*Permanent care labels for home-sewing fabrics.*

## Altering Ready-To-Wear Fashions

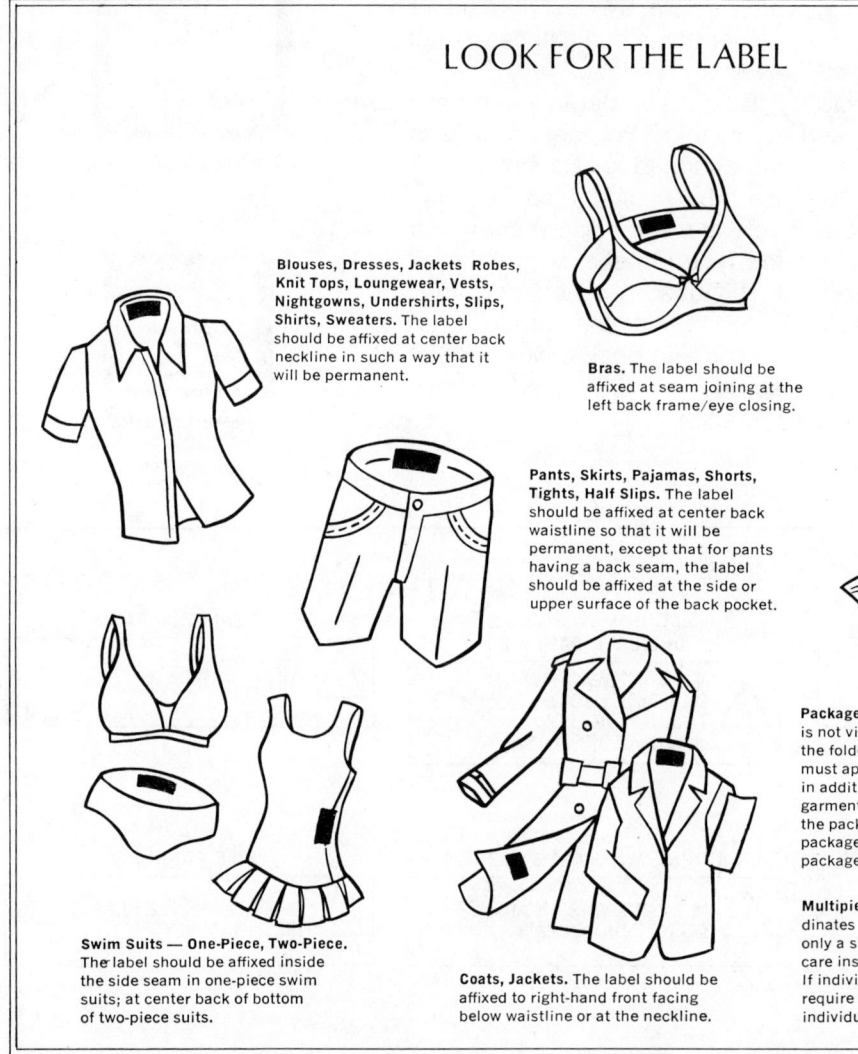

*Recommended placement of permanent care labels.*

Ch. 4: *Learning About Fabrics*

## SPECIAL TECHNIQUES FOR TRICKY TEXTILES

| Textile | Machine Preparation | Pre-sewing Preparation | Pressing |
|---|---|---|---|
| Beaded or Sequined | • Medium size needle.<br>• Average to light pressure.<br>• Light balanced tension.<br>• Mercerized cotton thread.<br>• 8 stitches per inch. | • When necessary, rip carefully to preserve as many beads or sequins as possible. | • Press as little as possible.<br>• Try finger pressing first.<br>• Do *not* use moisture or steam (may curl the backing or dull the sequins).<br>• Place right side down on pressing board, turkish towel, or needle board.<br>• Use press cloth and cool, dry iron.<br>• Do *not* top press. |
| Bonded or Laminated | • Select needle according to weight of fabric.<br>• Use medium pressure.<br>• Use medium tension.<br>• Use mercerized cotton.<br>• 8 stitches per inch. | • Springy, heavy bonded, or laminated fabrics are usually top stitched on either side of the seam line. This prevents the seam from rolling and adds a decorative trim.<br>• Reduce bulk whenever possible by grading seams, opening darts to press flat, and peeling away and trimming backing along the seam allowance edges. | • Use low iron setting and press cloth (most backings are acetate and will melt under a hot iron).<br>• If the face fabric needs a higher heat, use thicker press cloth to protect backing. |
| Chiffon | • Use new #9 needle.<br>• Use enough pressure to control cloth without leaving marks.<br>• Use normal tension.<br>• Use #60 mercerized cotton thread.<br>• 12 stitches per inch. | • Be sure the thread used matches the fabric exactly as it will show on the outside through the fabric.<br>• You may find it helpful to pin the seam to tissue paper and stitch through paper and fabric. | • Select iron temperature according to fiber in fabric.<br>• Beware of using steam as it may cause added crinkling of the fabric.<br>• Use dry iron with sheer press cloth on wrong side.<br>• Use pressing pad and seam roll. |
| Cire or highly polished fabrics | • Use sharp needles, size 9-11.<br>• Use light pressure.<br>• Use light, even tension.<br>• Use mercerized cotton thread.<br>• 8-10 stitches per inch. | • Use sharp, fine pins and do not pin beyond the seam line as the marks are not removable.<br>• Stitch with the shiny side of the fabric away from the feed dog or use tissue paper to protect the finish.<br>• Use paper clips or hair clips instead of pins and remove as soon as possible as they, too, will mark the fabric.<br>• Instead of pins, use invisible mending tape to hold hems and other folds in place as you work. | • Press with warm, dry iron.<br>• Use press cloth to prevent glazing.<br>• Use a seam roll or light-weight paper between seam and garment to prevent marking through. |

*(Continued on next page.)*

## Altering Ready-To-Wear Fashions

### TRICKY TEXTILES CHART (Continued from preceding page.)

| Textile | Machine Preparation | Pre-sewing Preparation | Pressing |
|---|---|---|---|
| Crepe | • Use fine (9-11) needles for sheer crepes, size 14 for medium weights.<br>• Use light pressure and tension.<br>• Use cotton/polyester combination thread.<br>• 8-10 stitches per inch. | • Use fine, sharp pins or ball point pins. Pin in seam allowance only.<br>• Use sharp shears to avoid catching the fabric and pulling yarns. | • Test fabric scrap before pressing to find best iron temperature.<br>• Excess moisture will cause some yarns to crinkle, creating a localized puckered effect.<br>• Steam press on the wrong side of the crepe fabric at a low iron setting with a press cloth. This maintains the texture and prevents water spotting, puckering, and glazing of the fabric.<br>• Press lightly, using a lifting and lowering motion to prevent stretching or flattening the crepe yarns.<br>• Press seams over a seam roll so they will not leave imprint on the right side.<br>• When releasing seams, an ice cube passed quickly over the old needle marks will help close the holes. Be careful not to dampen the fabric.<br>• A soft toothbrush and steam will also help remove marks. |
| Double Knits | • Use a fine (#11) ball point needle.<br>• Use fairly light pressure.<br>• Use loose, balanced tension.<br>• Use polyester/cotton thread.<br>• 8-10 stitches per inch. | • Double knits are usually very easy fabrics to work with.<br>• Stretch the seams slightly as you stitch to give added stretch during wear.<br>• If linings are added, use stretchable knit fabrics.<br>• Buttonholes should be stabilized with an interfacing. | • Select iron temperature according to the fiber in the fabric.<br>• Seams will lie flatter if a dampened press cloth and higher heat settings are used. Be careful about using the hotter iron without the damp press cloth as you may glaze the fabric. A clapper helps to set the seam.<br>• To remove creases in releasing seams or lowering hems, use a pressing pad, extra moisture, and higher heat. Sometimes white vinegar and brushing with a soft toothbrush may help restore the fabric to its original shape. |

Ch. 4: *Learning About Fabrics*

## TRICKY TEXTILES CHART

| Textile | Machine Preparation | Pre-sewing Preparation | Pressing |
|---|---|---|---|
| Fake Fur | • Use medium size (12-14) needles.<br>• Use light pressure.<br>• Use loose, balanced tension.<br>• Use polyester/cotton thread.<br>• 8-10 stitches per inch. | • Stitch in the direction of the pile whenever possible.<br>• Use a pin, a needle, or a steel fur brush to pull free any fur fibers caught in the seams.<br>• Many fake furs are made of modacrylic fibers and cannot stand heat. | • Press by fingers as much as possible.<br>• If pressing is necessary, use low iron setting.<br>• Use needle board or a piece of the pile fabric under the pile on the press board.<br>• Direct steam from iron onto dart or seam line. Press with fingers or touch lightly with point of iron only. |
| Fake Leather | • Use #14 needle for medium weight and #16 for heavy weights.<br>• Medium tension (loose enough to prevent puckering).<br>• Light pressure.<br>• Narrow needle slot plate. | • Seams cannot be pressed flat but must be top stitched or glued down with white glue.<br>• Bonded vinyls are very stretchy—handle carefully. | • Press with caution, test on an invisible part of garment first. Finger press where possible.<br>• If necessary, use a dry, slightly warm iron on the wrong side with a press cloth.<br>• Steam may remove simulated leather marks. |
| Jersey | • Use a ball point needle (9-11).<br>• Use polyester/cotton thread.<br>• Use fairly light pressure and tension. | • Use sharp or ball point pins and sharp shears.<br>• Stretch jersey slightly as you stitch to prevent seams popping during wear. | • Select iron setting for the fiber in the fabric.<br>• Press lightly, using a lifting and lowering motion to prevent stretching.<br>• Steam press on the wrong side on all but cotton jersey. |
| Lace | • Use a fine (11) needle or a ball point.<br>• Use loose, balanced tension.<br>• Use average to light pressure.<br>• Use mercerized cotton thread.<br>• 8-10 stitches per inch. | • To keep lace from getting caught in the presser foot or feed dog, and to prevent puckering at the stitching line, place tissue paper on either side of the seams. This can be torn off easily after the seam is stitched. Stitch seams on the seam line, then stitch a second time ⅛ inch (.3 cm) from the first stitching. Trim close to the second stitching.<br>• To prevent the seam from showing, the design of two pieces may be matched, laid flat on the right side, stitched around the pattern, and then trimmed close to the stitching. This gives the appearance of a continuous design and is called appliquéing the edges. | • Select iron temperature according to the fiber used in the lace.<br>• Press right side down on a pressing pad to prevent flattening the design in the lace.<br>• Use a press cloth between the iron and the lace.<br>• Do not push iron as the tip may get caught in the mesh and tear it.<br>• Steam is very helpful for lace. |

*(Continued on next page.)*

69

**Altering Ready-To-Wear Fashions**

## TRICKY TEXTILES CHART (Continued from preceding page.)

| Textile | Machine Preparation | Pre-sewing Preparation | Pressing |
|---|---|---|---|
| Leather | • Use wedge point leather machine needle. #11 for fine leather. #14 for medium. #16 for heavier skins.<br>• Use heavy duty cotton, buttonhole twist, or silk thread.<br>• Use a roller presser foot.<br>• 6-8 stitches per inch. | • Leather garments are very difficult to work on. Unless you have the proper equipment and skill, it is wiser not to agree to alter an expensive leather garment.<br>• Use rubber cement or two-faced tape for hems and for holding seams flat. | • Pressing on leather is usually done with a mallet or pounding block.<br>• If an iron is used, it should be used dry and on a low or warm heat setting. |
| Matelassé Eyelet Embroidered and other puffy fabrics | • Select needle for weight of fabric. Try ball point needle first.<br>• Use mercerized cotton thread or polyester/cotton thread.<br>• Use light pressure and light tension.<br>• 8-10 stitches per inch. | | • Use pressing pad and soft seam roll to prevent crushing texture.<br>• Press only where seams are altered, using a very light touch.<br>• Use steam iron and set for fiber used in fabric.<br>• Use tip of iron along seam to prevent crushing and snagging. |
| Metallics | • Use size 11, ball point needle.<br>• Use light, balanced tension.<br>• Use fine, strong thread. | • Metallic fabrics mark easily where pinned, creased, or stitched. Be sure it is possible before agreeing to release seams.<br>• Do not stitch before final fitting.<br>• Be sure hands are clean and dry. Perspiration contains acid which may leave marks on the metal. | • Use low heat with a dry iron to prevent discoloration and melting.<br>• Do not press before final fitting.<br>• Use sheer press cloth on wrong side. Do not top press. |

## TRICKY TEXTILES CHART

| Textile | Machine Preparation | Pre-sewing Preparation | Pressing |
|---|---|---|---|
| Pile Fabric<br>Corduroy<br>Velveteen<br>Velvet | • Use size 14 needle.<br>• Use light pressure.<br>• Use light, balanced tension.<br>• Use cotton mercerized thread.<br>• 8-10 stitches per inch. | • Avoid top stitching as it crushes the pile.<br>• Stitch in the direction of the pile.<br>• Pin in seam allowance only. | • Adjust iron for fiber used.<br>• Place garment pile side down on needle board or a piece of the same fabric pile side up.<br>• Use steam and very little pressure.<br>• To raise pile, hold steaming iron slightly above the right side of fabric without touching it. |
| Qiana<br>Nylon | • Use a fine, sharp needle (11) or try a ball point.<br>• Use fairly light pressure.<br>• Use light tension.<br>• Use polyester/cotton thread.<br>• 8-10 stitches per inch. | • When sewing, hold the fabric in front and behind the needle with a light tension to prevent puckering. Do not pull the fabric through the machine (let the feed dog do it).<br>• Use pins carefully as the fabric will mark, and the holes may not disappear. | • Use a low "wool" setting with steam.<br>• Press seam flat before opening to press open.<br>• Use paper between seam allowance and garment to prevent seam showing on outside.<br>• Open the seam with the tip of the iron on a seam roll, or send a jet of steam on to the seam line, then press flat with fingers.<br>• Or, use a damp press cloth first and then press dry.<br>• Leave fabric on board to dry before removing it.<br>• If top pressing is necessary, use a press cloth to prevent shine. |

# Chapter 5
# Pressing Altered Garments

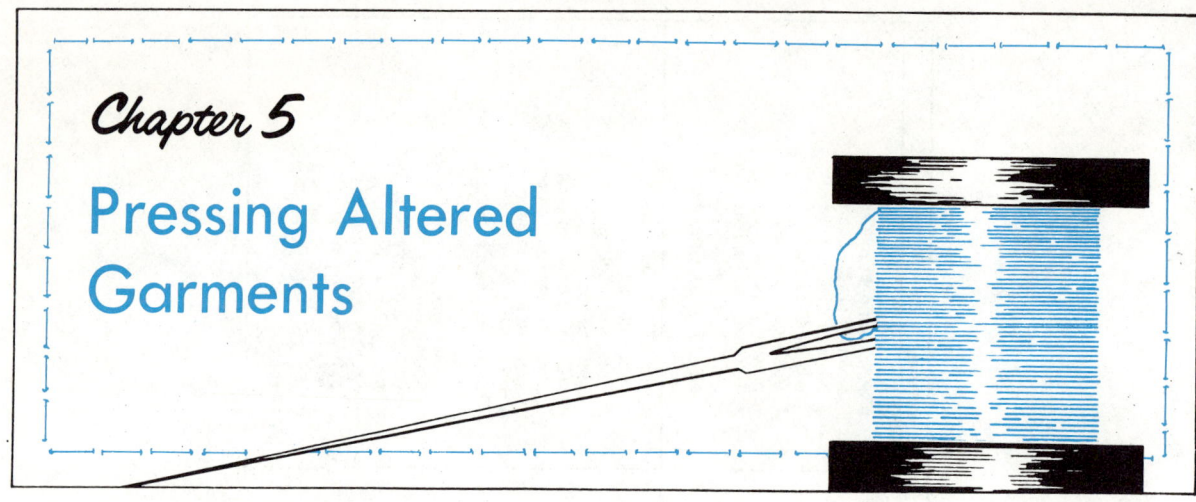

Much more is involved in pressing than putting water in the steam iron, heating it, and applying the iron to the fabric. Pressing can make the difference between a shabby, homemade appearance, and an expert, professional job.

An iron can be used to shorten and simplify some operations. It can also help remove the marks of the sewing you are replacing. In addition, it can help shape fabric so it will fit the body more smoothly.

Did you notice the use of the word *pressing* instead of ironing? Pressing differs from the usual way you do ironing. When you iron, you use a back and forth motion in moving the iron over the cloth. In pressing, the iron is lowered to the place to be pressed, than raised off the fabric and moved to the next spot. Very little pressure is needed since heat and steam do most of the work. Pushing the iron along the cloth may cause ripples, wrinkles, and stretching of the fabric.

## PRESSING EQUIPMENT AND ACCESSORIES

You will find it well worth the money and effort to have the proper pressing tools to work with. Perhaps you are accustomed to using only an iron and a standard ironing board. In that case, take time to learn about all the individual pieces of pressing equipment that can make your work so much easier and more professional.

All of the items described below can be purchased ready-made. However, many of them can be constructed easily and inexpensively at home or in a carpenter shop. If you wish to make your own, detailed instructions are included at the end of the chapter.

For an efficient alterations shop, you should have the following pressing equipment:

### Steam Iron

Second only to your sewing machine, the steam iron is the most important piece of equipment in your shop. Any good home-model steam iron with accurate temperature control can be used. Be sure it has the widest possible range of heat controls for the steam. It should also have the maximum number of holes in the sole plate for greater steam emission. A jet spray for added moisture when needed is also helpful.

If you are going to use the steam iron you already have, be sure it is working properly. Test the temperature settings on the iron on scraps of fabrics of the various fibers to see if the control is working correctly. Check to see that there are no rough

# Ch. 5: Pressing

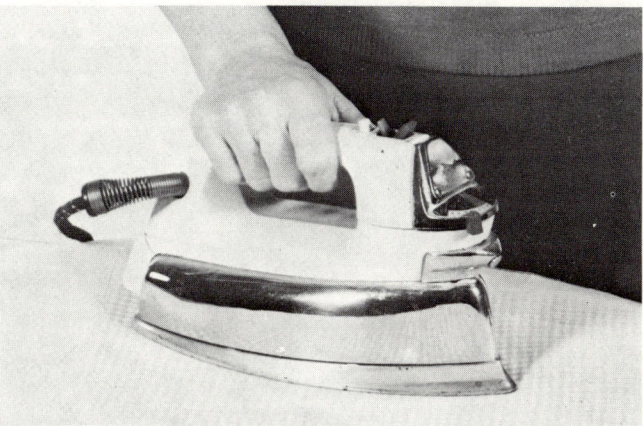

Scovill Mfg. Co.

*A properly operating home steam iron is adequate for most of the work in a small alterations shop.*

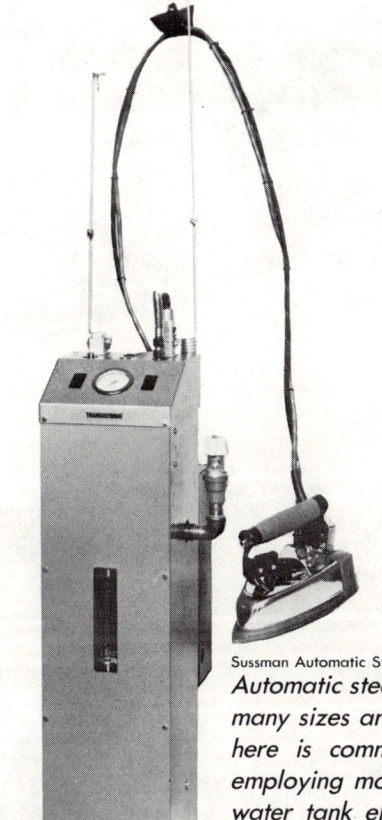

Sussman Automatic Steam Products Corp.

*Automatic steam iron systems are available in many sizes and price ranges. The size shown here is common in most alterations shops employing more than one person. The large water tank eliminates the need for frequent filling of the iron.*

places to catch fabrics, that the sole plate is clean, and that it steams properly.

## Commercial Steam Iron

As your work increases, you may wish to invest in a commercial steam iron. This type of iron comes in different weights from 5 pounds (2.3 kg) to 15 pounds (6.8 kg). It has a separate water tank with a hose attachment.

The medium-weight iron is the most desirable for alterations work.

Though this equipment is expensive, it is guaranteed to last a long time. The heavier weight of the iron, the greater steam emission, and the better heat control make it more efficient.

These irons do not require any special installation as they can be plugged into any 110-volt outlet.

Probably the most noticeable advantage to these irons is the large water tank which eliminates the need for filling and emptying the iron itself.

## Tailor's Press Board or Buckboard

The buckboard is a smaller, sturdier, more efficient version of an ironing board. It is made to be used on a table or counter top to save floor space. Because it is strong, you can use heavy pressure or even pound a garment without collapsing the board. It can and should be used for the major part of your alterations work.

Pressing formal, wedding, and other special garments often calls for a place to hang the garment while you are working on it. Notice the cloth tray under the ironing board to hold the fabric off the floor.

# Ch. 5: Pressing

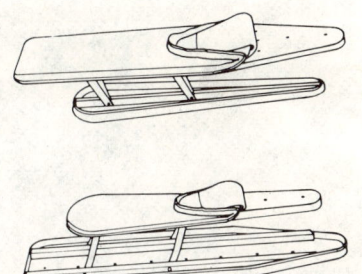

Seymour Housewares Co. Lear Siegler, Inc.

*A sleeve board is similar to a buckboard but is smaller and can be folded for easier storage.*

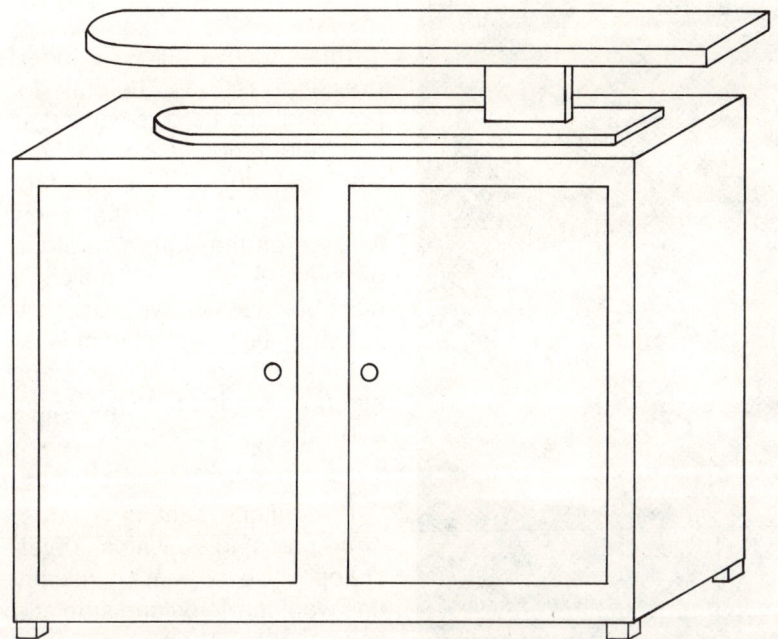

*The buckboard can be used on top of a storage cabinet for greater support and better use of floor space.*

The surface measurements of buckboards vary. The average top is about 12 inches (30.5 cm) wide at one end, tapering to about 6 inches (15 cm) at the pressing point. Lengths may vary from 22 inches (56 cm), 27 inches (69 cm), or 36 inches (91.4 cm). The 36-inch length (91.4 cm) is the most convenient for all alterations work.

### Ironing Board

You will also need a standard ironing board when pressing entire garments or long garments. Either a floor model or built-in wall model will serve, as long as it is sturdy. If possible, have a cloth-covered tray attachment under the board to support garments while you are pressing them. These trays keep garments from drooping on the floor and picking up soil. They also prevent dampened fabric from stretching while you are working on it.

### Sleeve Board

A small, collapsible, two-sided board, used for pressing sleeves and other small areas, is indispensible. One side should measure about 22 inches (56 cm) by 6 inches (15 cm) in an oval shape. The other side should be narrower and measure about 20 inches (51 cm) by 4 inches (10 cm), tapering at the open end to about 1½ inches (3.8 cm).

### Ironing or Pressing Board Covers

Cotton drill cloth or canvas make the best covers for all types of ironing boards. Many of the commercial covers available on the market have a silicone finish. This finish holds and reflects the heat of the iron back to the fabric being pressed. Sometimes the heat becomes too intense for thermoplastic synthetic fabrics and they glaze, mark, or even melt. You will run less chance of damaging your work if you use the drill cloth or canvas covers.

### Press Mitt

A press mitt is a small pressing cushion that can be slipped over the hand or the end of a sleeve board. It is useful for pressing curved or hard-to-reach areas that might not fit over a standard pressing board.

## Altering Ready-To-Wear Fashions

Press mitts are designed for pressing small hard-to-reach areas that require curved shaping.

Scovill Mfg. Company

### Seam Roll

This long, slim, padded pressing roll is helpful for pressing seams or small areas that might not fit over a conventional board. In some fabrics, seams pressed flat show through on the right side of the garment. A seam roll makes it possible to lightly press the stitching line of the seam without having to apply pressure along the edges of the seam allowance.

### Tailor's Ham

The tailor's ham is a large, firm pressing cushion, oval-shaped like a ham. It usually has wool fabric on one side and heavy cotton fabric on the other. It is used in pressing and shaping parts of a garment that need to have "shape" or curves built into them. A ham is particularly

The well-equipped pressing area will have a variety of pressing cushions and cloths as well as an iron and buckboard or ironing board. From left to right this picture shows an iron, pressing cloths, pressing mitt, seam roll, and two sizes of tailor's hams.

Scovill Mfg. Company

## Ch. 5: Pressing

helpful for pressing the bust and hip areas of clothes.

### Point Presser or Dowel Sticks

Pressing small details, such as the points of collars, cuffs, or belts, is difficult with standard pressing equipment. For such areas, commercial "point pressers" make the job easier. A common wooden dowel stick may also be used to shape points. These dowels should be about 12 inches (30.5 cm) long and from ½ to ¾ inch (1.2 to 1.8 cm) in diameter. Such sticks are inexpensive and can be purchased at most hardware stores or lumberyards.

### Pounding Block (Clapper)

Often your pressing operation may require *extra* steam and pressure. Sometimes, however, the heat of the iron can damage—shrink or melt—the fabric. Pleats, creases, or other sharp details are examples of this kind of pressing. For these details, you need a pounding block. A pounding block is a piece of hardwood about 12 inches (30.5 cm) long, 3 inches (7.6 cm) wide, and 2 inches (5 cm) thick. The wood must be free of sap

Professional pressers use a steam pressing table for speed and finish pressing. Notice the pounding block (also called a clapper) in the presser's right hand.

"Justice-ILGWU"

## Altering Ready-To-Wear Fashions

and sanded smooth on all surfaces. Edges should be rounded for easy handling. Commercially made pounding blocks often have point pressers attached to them.

### Needle Board

A needle board has a flexible backboard covered with needle-like wires. You will find it very useful in pressing fabrics with nap such as velvet, suede cloth, or corduroy. This is a piece of equipment you cannot make yourself—it must be purchased.

### Press Cloths

Your pressing equipment should include several kinds of press cloths, from heavy cotton to sheer cotton. Since the use of a press cloth requires more specific information, it is discussed later in the chapter.

### Small Supplies

In addition to larger pieces of equipment, several smaller items will be needed for specific jobs. You will find it to your advantage to keep the following items near your pressing station.
- Cleaning fluids or powders for quick spot cleaning.
- Cotton balls to apply the cleaning fluid.
- White cellulose sponges for adding moisture to press cloths by sponging.
- Hard bristle brush for removing lint.
- Soft toothbrush to restore nap and to brush together the fibers and yarns in seams that have been released.
- Fabric finish or sizing to spray on garment while pressing, to restore fabric gone limp from too much handling.

## USING A PRESS CLOTH

It is not always necessary to use a press cloth between the iron and the garment, but it is usually safer with most pressing operations. Different kinds of fabric require different kinds of press cloths. To make your own collection of different kinds of cloths, you will want:
- A piece of thin, see-through material such as organdy—for use on delicate fabrics like chiffon and single knits. Use it for light pressing or for quick *top pressing* or steaming.
- A medium-thin cotton cloth such as muslin or percale from an old sheet—for pressing medium-weight fabrics like double knits and wool.
- A heavy cotton cloth such as drill or canvas—for pressing heavy fabric or layers of fabric or pleats that need to have extra pressure and extra steam.
- A piece of cotton or wool flannel—for fabrics with a slight nap or a nubby finish.
- A piece of pile fabric such as velvet—for pressing pile or deeply textured fabrics such as velvet, matelassé, or corduroy. Lay the velvet press cloth on the press board itself with the nap side up against the nap side of the garment. Use *very little* pressure and much steam. This can be used as a substitute for a needle board (see page 79). You will find a needle board a good investment if you work with pile fabrics frequently.

Cloths that measure approximately 15 × 20 inches (38 × 51 cm) will be the most useful size. Be sure they are clean-cut with no pinked edges or seams running through them. A pressing cloth is used to prevent marks on the garment, not make them. Keep your cloths clean and store them in a box or plastic bag close to the pressing table.

## GENERAL PRESSING INFORMATION

As you do routine pressing with your work, keep in mind the general rules listed below. They can help you achieve professional-looking results in your alterations.
- Check fabric content and care label in clothing to determine the proper heat setting for the iron. Further information can be found in the charts in Chapter 4 for handling special fabrics. If in doubt as to the correct setting, use a press cloth or test the material on the edge of a seam or facing. Touch the fabric with the tip of the iron. If the fabric doesn't stick, doesn't glaze, or become shiny, you are safe. It is always safer to use a pressing cloth between your iron and the garment.

**Ch. 5: Pressing**

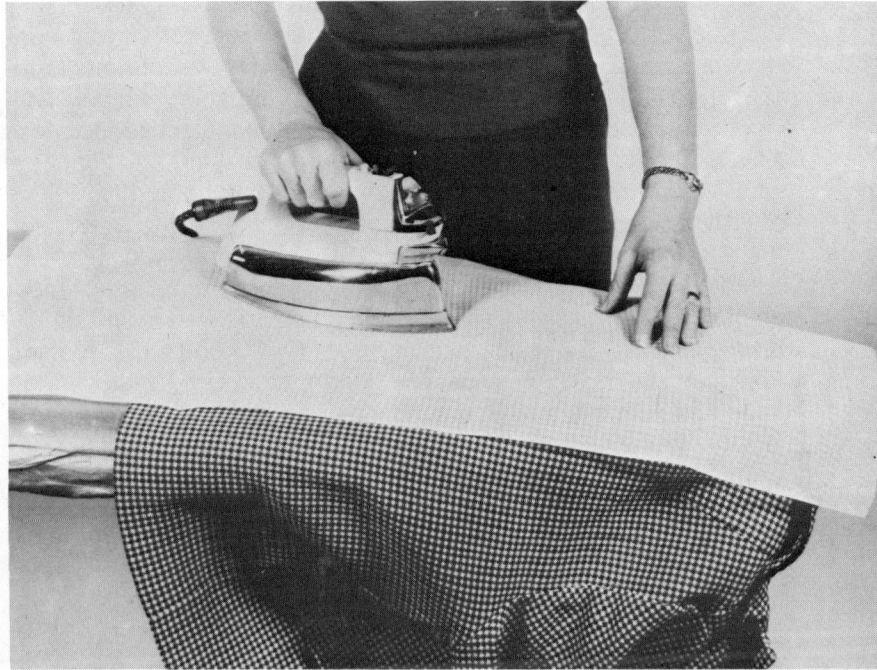

You'll need a variety of pressing cloths from sheer to heavy weights. Each type of cloth has special uses so that no one weight of cloth is sufficient for all your purposes.

Photos on this page from Scovill Mfg. Co.

*A needle board is very helpful in pressing pile fabrics. These boards increase efficiency and help you save time and energy. There is less danger of damaging the fabric as you press it.*

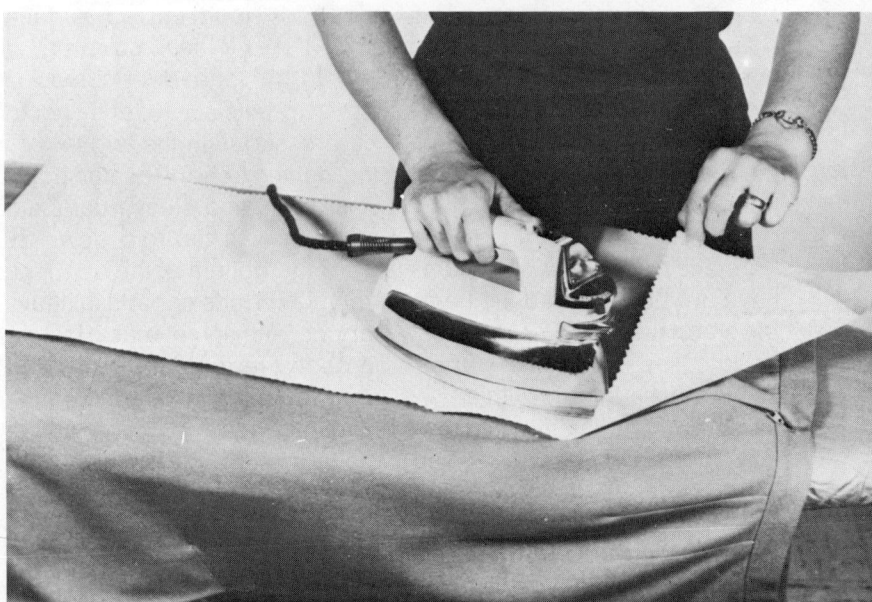

- Press on the wrong side of the garment first. This is called *underpressing*. "Finish" pressing is sometimes done on the right side last. Pressing on the right side should be done only where absolutely needed. Usually, it is used only on cotton, linen, and some rayons. Occasionally, a shiny fabric like chintz may retain its shine better if pressed on the right side. Pressing on the right side is called *top pressing*. Any other fabrics requiring top pressing should be protected by a pressing cloth to prevent glazing.
- Press by lowering the iron against the area you are pressing. Hold in place until the heat and steam have had a chance to penetrate the fabric. Lift the iron and move it to the next spot. Keep repeating the process.
- Follow the grain line in the fabric when pressing. This means moving the iron in the same direction as the lengthwise yarns of the material. Pressing across the grain or on the bias can stretch the garment out of shape.
- Press altered parts of the garment as you sew. If seams have to be released or hems lowered, the old creases must be pressed out. Most fabrics, except those treated with a permanent press finish, will press flat when the proper heat and steam are applied. For stubborn creases, try wiping your press cloth with a dampened sponge for extra steam. Sometimes wiping the crease itself with a sponge dampened in white vinegar helps. If needle marks remain, try brushing the area with a toothbrush. Continue to press over the pressing cloth until the fabric is thoroughly dry. This is one of the places a wooden clapper comes into use. To avoid over-application of heat which could cause some shrinkage (in wool) or glazing (thermoplastics), remove the iron and press cloth. With your hand, hold the wooden clapper down firmly over the steamed area until the fabric dries and the seam is flat.
- Press darts, curved seams, or small parts (such as tops of sleeves, and shoulders, chest, or bust areas) on a ham or mitt. The mitt can be held in the hand or slipped over the end of a sleeve board. Remember, the body is a curved surface and the clothes covering it should be shaped for curves.
- Up and down darts should be pressed with the fold toward the center front or center back. Bust darts and sleeve darts are pressed with the fold down toward the bottom of the garment. Very long darts or darts in heavy fabrics are sometimes slashed through the middle and spread apart or opened to reduce bulk. If you open the dart, it cannot be moved, so be sure it has been properly fitted before slashing. Slash no closer than 1 inch (2.54 cm) from the point or you'll weaken the dart.
- If long darts or curved seams will not lie flat when shaped over the pressing ham or mitt, you may need to clip them slightly. Clip with small scissors *only where absolutely necessary* to mold the shape needed in the garment. Clip no more than you must. Every clip weakens the fabric and makes further alterations difficult or impossible.
- Before you release or take in a seam, press it flat with both raw edges together. This helps prevent puckers and makes it easier to stitch. After stitching, carefully rip out the old seam. *Rip carefully so you do not cut the fabric.*

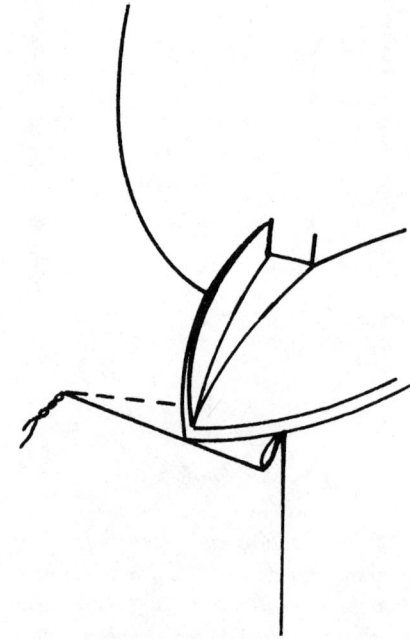

*Press bust darts with the fold toward the waistline.*

**Ch. 5: Pressing**

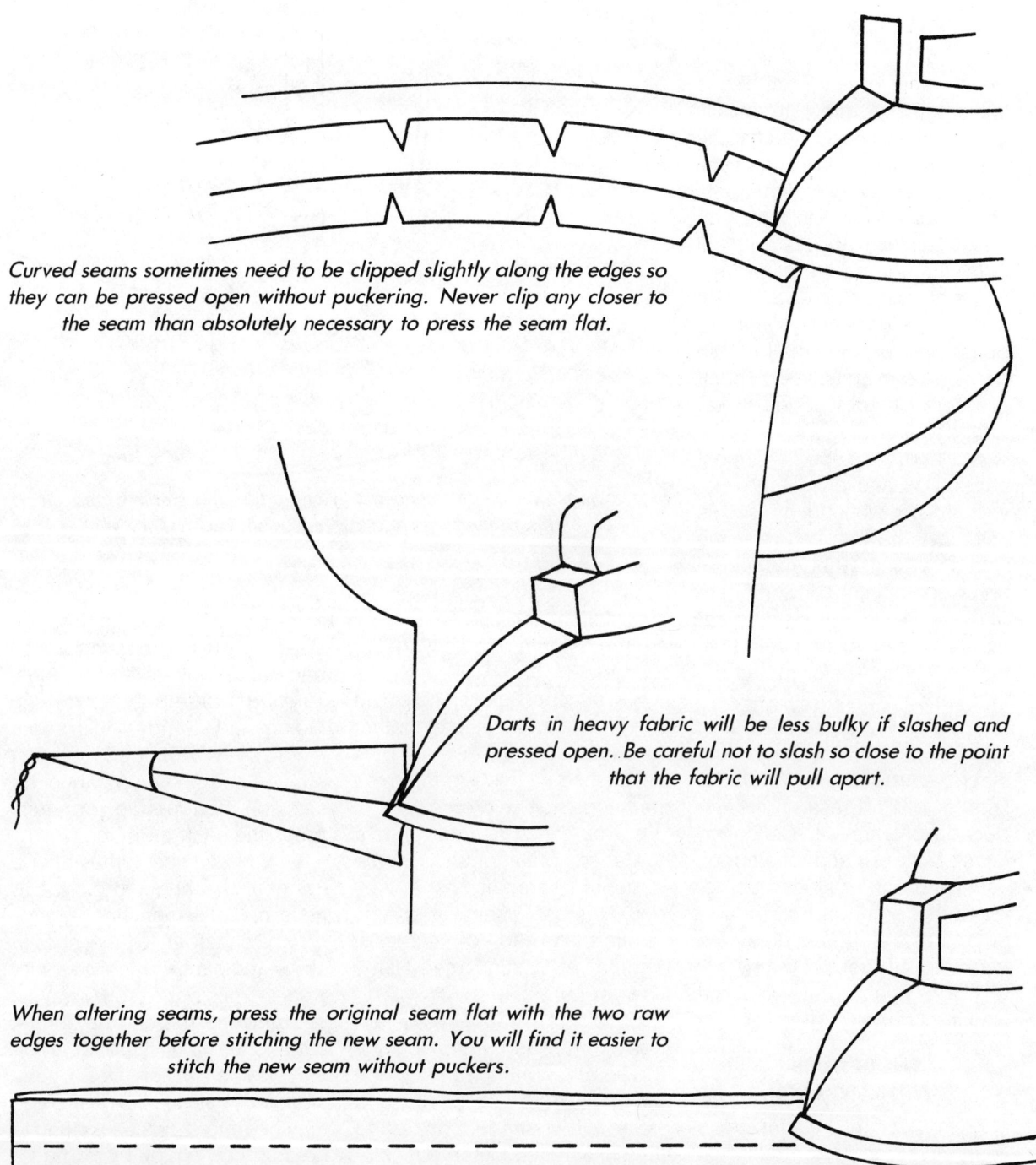

Curved seams sometimes need to be clipped slightly along the edges so they can be pressed open without puckering. Never clip any closer to the seam than absolutely necessary to press the seam flat.

Darts in heavy fabric will be less bulky if slashed and pressed open. Be careful not to slash so close to the point that the fabric will pull apart.

When altering seams, press the original seam flat with the two raw edges together before stitching the new seam. You will find it easier to stitch the new seam without puckers.

## Altering Ready-To-Wear Fashions

- Press new seams open from the wrong side of the garment, using a seam roll. Place the seam over the roll so only the stitching line is against the solid surface. Then, as you carefully press with the tip of your iron along the stitching line, the seam edges will not mark through on the other side of the garment. Some very small areas of a garment (collars or belts) may be too small to slip over a seam roll. Use a point presser or plain wooden dowel for these areas.

- Handle each garment carefully. Hang or fold it when you are not working on it. This will save having to press the whole garment when the alteration work is finished. Some fabrics should be allowed to remain on the pressing board until thoroughly dry before handling them at all.

- If the whole garment has to be pressed or freshened with steam, start at the top with the smaller parts. Press on the underside of garment. Do collar, cuffs, facings, and shoulders, using the mitt or sleeve board. Press the larger parts on a larger board last. If you press the larger areas first, they may get wrinkled again while you are working on the smaller parts.

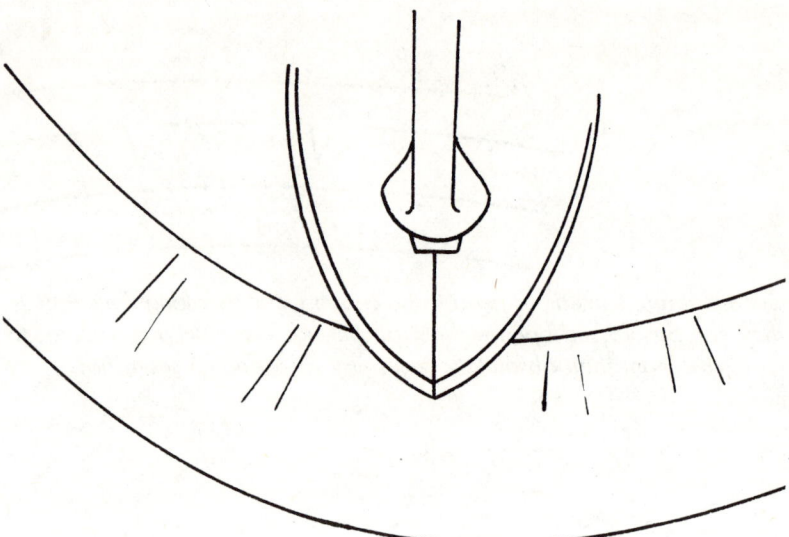

*Bias facings can be stretched along one edge and steam-eased along the other to form a curved or shaped facing.*

## SHORT CUTS WITH AN IRON

An iron can be a useful tool in your work for more than just routine pressing. In other chapters, notice references to using an iron as an aid in sewing. For example:

- You can *fuse* or help two pieces of fabric stick together for easier stitching without pins or basting. Just steam-press them together before sewing.

- You can *set* a line where a new seam, pleat, or tuck is to be made in a garment.

- You can press in a new hemline instead of marking, pinning, or basting (see Hems Chapter 10).

- You can shape bias facings, hems, and trims to fit a curved area. Pull the bias piece into the shape you desire and press with steam. Let one edge stretch and the other edge retain its original shape.

- You can use an iron instead of pins or basting to roll back undercollars and facings. Turn right side out and roll the facing side under with your thumb and forefinger. Roll just enough so the facing cannot be seen on the top side. Carefully press the seam in place.

- You can sometimes alter a garment by shrinking extra fullness out of a neckline, sleeve crown, shoulder, or the seat in skirts and pants. This works with wools, knits, and soft weaves. The amount that can be shrunk out successfully depends upon the fabric. After you have steamed out the excess, you may need to *stay* the new line to hold its new shape by adding a piece of seam tape.

## SPECIAL PRECAUTIONS IN PRESSING

One of the primary aims of good pressing is to keep the underneath construction from showing on the outside of the garment. If you press over pins, basting stitches, or thread markings, they will make marks that may not come out after the pins or thread are removed. If you press over hooks, eyes, snaps, or buttons, you may make unsightly marks on the outside of the garment. You could also scratch the sole plate or bottom of your iron. The same can happen if you press over a zipper. If it is absolutely necessary to press a seam over a zipper, use a sturdy pressing cloth and steam but very little pressure. The zipper teeth, if metal, can cut the fabric as well as make a mark through it. If it is a plastic coil zipper, the heat of the iron could damage it.

Parts of some garments should not be pressed at all. The proper look is achieved by little or no pressing. For example:

- Hems on women's dressy clothes. These garments should look soft. Even the seams on sports or day clothes should not be pressed hard.
- It is no longer considered good fashion to have a sharp crease pressed in a sleeve. Instead of laying the sleeve flat and pressing in a crease, press it over the sleeve board so it is round.
- Roll collars and cuffs are meant to have a soft, rounded look and should never be pressed flat.
- Do not press soft pleats, shirring, smocking, or gathered fullness. These construction details should hang softly without any sharp creases.

Do not press over soil marks. Perspiration, spots, or stains can be *set* by the heat so they will never come out. Also, some fibers, such as silk, deteriorate from the acids and oils in perspiration. Pressing just speeds up the reaction. For your own protection and pleasure in your work, refuse to work on garments that need cleaning.

## INSTRUCTIONS FOR MAKING PRESSING EQUIPMENT
### Buckboard

**MATERIALS TO BUY**

Two 1-inch (2.54 cm) thick hardwood boards. One board 12 inches (30.5 cm) by 33 inches (84 cm). One board 10 inches (25 cm) by 31 inches (79 cm).

Two wood blocks 1½ inches (3.8 cm) thick and 6 inches (15 cm) square.

Eight ¼-inch (.6 cm) wood screws 2½ inches (6.4 cm) long and/or industrial glue.

The pattern shown for the top of the buckboard on page 84 can be made shorter or longer to suit your own needs and space. Also, the 6-inch square (15 cm square) supporting blocks can be made higher or lower, depending upon the height of your pressing table. The base or board that will rest on the table should be cut in the same shape as the top board but should be one inch (2.54 cm) smaller all the way around than the top board.

Be sure all wooden pieces are carefully smoothed and sanded—especially the supporting blocks and the base. These parts will not be covered. The blocks should be applied at the broad end of the board (see side and end views on the pattern).

For greater strength, use both glue and screws. The screws should be put in at each end of each block on both the top and bottom. Insert them from the board side through to the blocks. Be sure the screw heads are counter sunk so they do not cause bumps. If your buckboard is well made, it will last a lifetime of pounding and pressing.

### Buckboard Cover

**MATERIALS TO BUY:**

1⅓ yards (120 cm) of 45-inch-wide (115 cm) cotton sailcloth, muslin, or flannel fabric in white, solid pastel, or pastel print. Note: This should be enough fabric for the buckboard cover as well as a pressing ham and a mitt.

1 yard (90 cm) of 36-inch wide (90 cm) cotton batting.

3 yards (270 cm) of string cord (piping cord will do).

**Altering Ready-To-Wear Fashions**

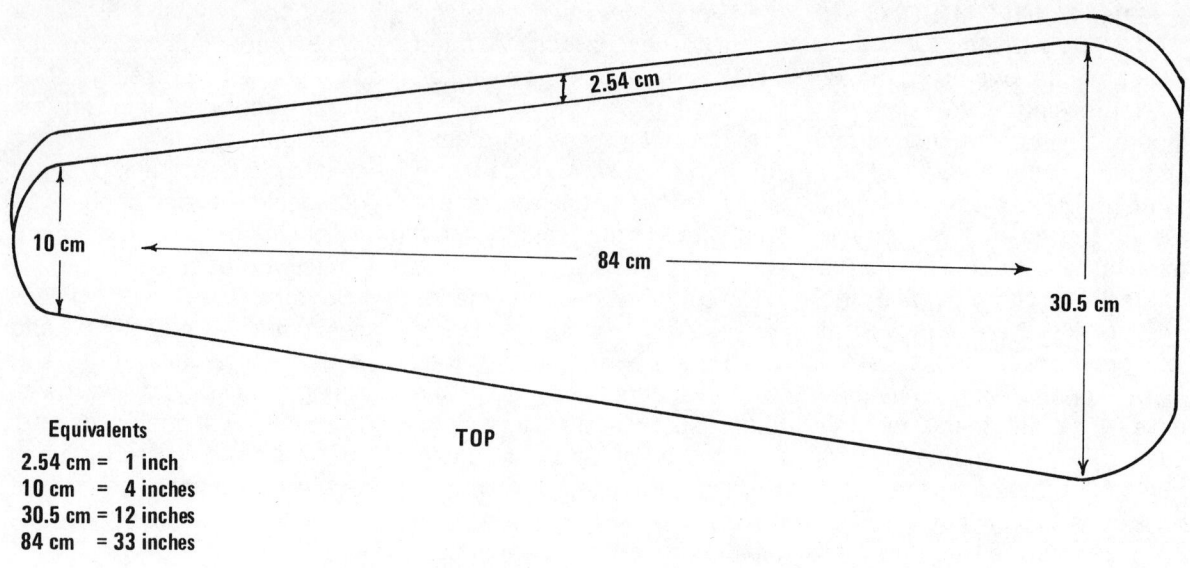

**Equivalents**
2.54 cm = 1 inch
10 cm = 4 inches
30.5 cm = 12 inches
84 cm = 33 inches

TOP

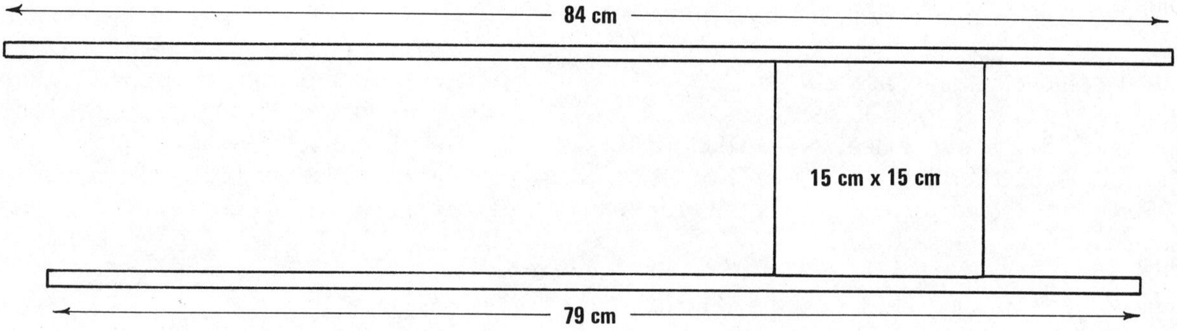

**Equivalents**
15 cm = 6 inches
25.4 cm = 10 inches
30.5 cm = 12 inches
79 cm = 31 inches
84 cm = 33 inches

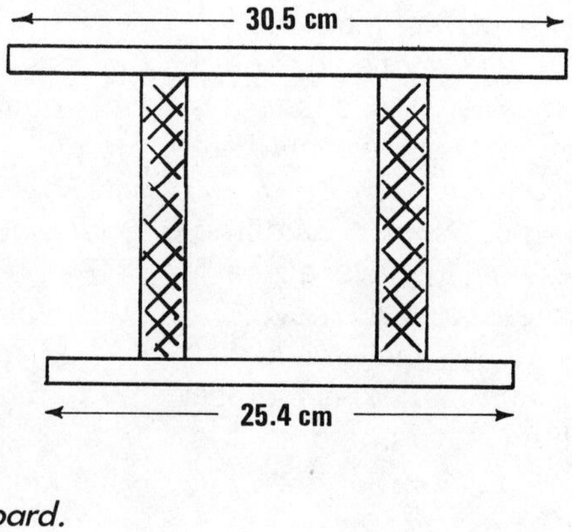

Side and back views
*Pattern for buckboard.*

Ch. 5: Pressing

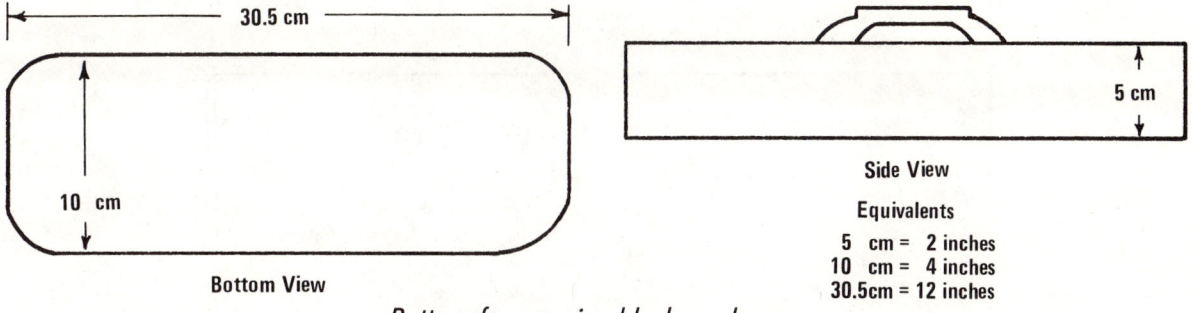

Pattern for pressing block or clapper.

1. Using the buckboard pattern, cut batting to the exact size of the top board. The batting is wide enough to cut two layers if the pattern is reversed, short end to broad end as shown in the illustration for the tailor's ham on page 86.

2. Use the same pattern to cut two covers from the fabric, but add 2½ inches (6.4 cm) on all sides. This can also be done by reversing the pattern for the second cover.

3. Cover the top board with the two layers of batting.

4. Staple or tack one cover to the underside of the top board over the batting.

5. Turn the edges of the other cover back ½ inch (1.3 cm) and stitch along this outer edge with a zigzag stitch. Leave a 1-inch (2.54 cm) opening at the broad end of the cover.

6. Pull the string cord through this casing and tie the cover tightly around the top board. This makes a removable cover that can be laundered regularly.

### Clapper
**MATERIALS NEEDED**

One 2-inch-thick (5 cm) piece of hardwood 12 inches (30.5 cm) long by 4 inches (10 cm) wide.

1. Round, smooth, and sand all edges.

2. The sides may be carved out slightly to allow the fingers to grip the clapper firmly (see the picture, page 77). If you prefer, you can screw a metal kitchen cabinet handle onto the top of the clapper to serve as a handle.

### Pressing Cushions
**MATERIALS NEEDED**

1½ yards (135 cm) of 36-inch (91.4 cm) or 45-inch (114 cm) fabric of cotton sailcloth, muslin, or flannel. The fabric may be the same as the one that you selected for your buckboard cover.

¼ yard (22.9 cm) of cotton or polyester batting. One magazine—twelve inches (30.5 cm) long. Bucket of clean sawdust (available at woodworking shop).

### PRESSING HAM

1. Cut two pieces of fabric according to the dimensions given for the ham. These may be of any firm, heavy fabric.

2. Stitch the pieces together with a ⅝ inch (1.6 cm) seam using small stitches—12–15 to the inch. Leave a space of 3 inches (7.6 cm) open across the wide end.

3. Turn right side out.

4. Pack *tightly* with sawdust. Be sure the cushion is as firm and tightly packed as you can possibly get it.

5. Close the opening by hand using small, tight stitches and heavy thread.

6. Cut two more pieces of the covering fabric.

7. Stitch together with a ½-inch (1.3 cm) seam, leaving the broad end open.

8. Turn right side out.

9. Pull this bag over the filled cushion.

10. Finish the open end with close hand stitches and strong thread.

## Altering Ready-To-Wear Fashions

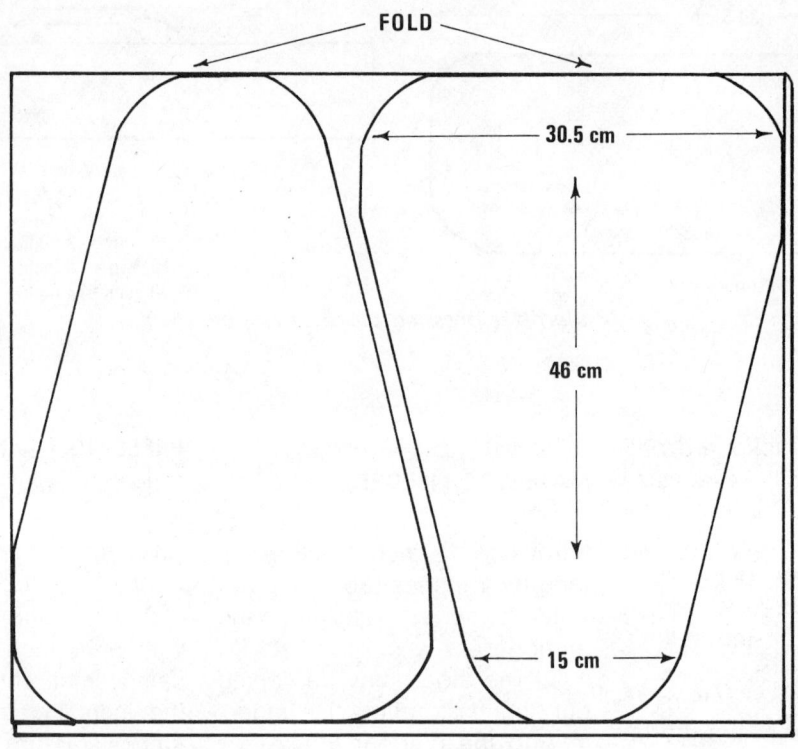

Equivalents

15 cm = 6 inches
30.5 cm = 12 inches
46 cm = 18 inches

*Pattern for tailor's ham.*

### PRESSING MITT

1. Cut all pieces as indicated in the pattern as shown on page 87.
2. Make a sandwich of the five pieces—two large pieces, the small folded piece for a "filler," and then the other two large pieces. Be sure all six rounded edges are together and even. If you are working with a printed fabric, place all layers with right sides out.
3. Starting at one straight edge, stitch a ³⁄₈-inch (.9 cm) seam all around three sides. Leave the selvage edges unstitched.
4. Turn mitt right side out.
5. Fill firmly with batting material.
6. Stitch the open end along the selvage. The short folded piece is now on the outside and forms a nice little pocket to slip over your fingers or over the end of a sleeve board. Use mitt for pressing hard-to-reach places on the garment such as shoulders.

### SEAM ROLL

1. Roll the magazine tight enough to make a firm roll, keeping the spine of the magazine on the inside. Try to leave a small hole through the center of the roll—enough to put your finger in.

2. Tape the roll together at each end and in the middle to hold it firm.

3. Take a piece of fabric about 3 inches (7.6 cm) longer than the magazine and the full width of the fabric from selvage to selvage.

4. Place the rolled magazine at one selvage end with 1½ inches (3.8 cm) of fabric extending at each end. Roll the magazine in the fabric, working the end of the fabric into the small hole you left through the center of the roll. Roll and tuck a little at a time using a blunt point to force the ends of the fabric into the center of the roll. Continue until the magazine reaches the other selvage edge. No sewing needed.

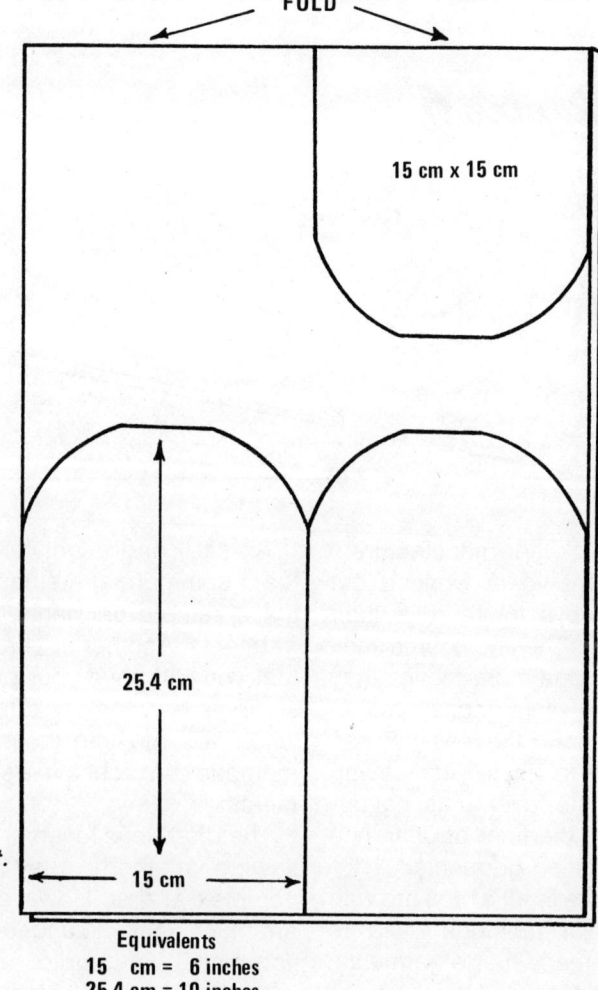

Pattern for pressing mitt.

Equivalents
15 cm = 6 inches
25.4 cm = 10 inches

# Chapter 6

# Commercial Sewing Methods

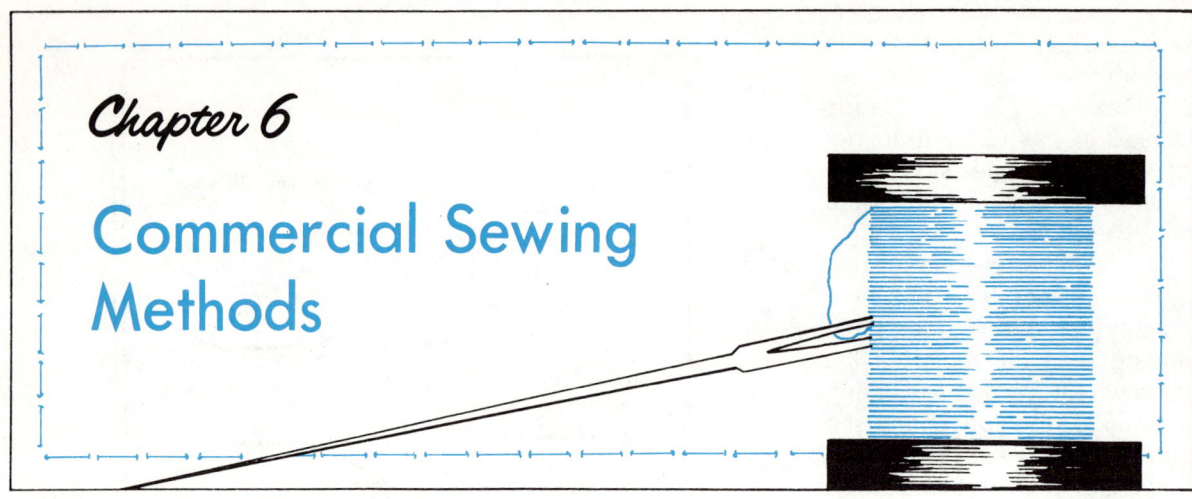

Ready-to-wear manufacturers have spent years working out special ways to improve their efficiency. The more time they can save, the more money they save. The more money manufacturers save, the less they can charge for clothes. Time-saving methods, however, must not detract from the final appearance of the finished garments.

The more familiar you are with commercial methods used to produce ready-made garments, the easier it will be for you to alter them. You may also find that these methods can save you time in custom sewing.

Do not be surprised to find that many of the methods described in this chapter are different from the home sewing methods you have already learned. For commercial work, you will have to "unlearn" some of the techniques you have been using.

An easy and effective way to learn commercial methods is to make sample garments or mini garments. Another advantage is that you will have your practice samples as memory refreshers when you run into those same methods in customers' garments.

The directions for commercial sewing methods may sound complex at first. However, they are much easier to understand if you make the sample mini garments to go along with them. As you make these mini garments, you may discover ideas for improving your home sewing methods.

## TECHNIQUES

### Marking with Clips

The most common commercial marking method is to use your scissors to cut tiny clips in the seam allowance where you want to match pieces. Occasionally you will need dressmaker's chalk. Most marking is done with little clips—they save time, are easy to find, and do not mar the garment.

Tracing carbon, tracing wheels, and tailor's tacks are rarely used commercially.

- Use clips to mark the center front and center back of the fabric piece at both the neckline and the hem.
- Clip the top of the sleeve where it matches the shoulder seam.
- Clip the collar where it matches the shoulder seam.
- Cut clips to mark the waistline.
- Clip to show where a longer seam is eased into a shorter seam as in the bustline of a princess-style dress.
- Mark the bottom of the neck opening.
- Mark the edges of darts with clips and use a piece of

dressmaker's chalk to mark just the point of the dart.

Clips may also be used to show where long seams should be matched, where inset pockets are to be placed, where hems should come on sleeves and dress edges, and where trimmings are to be placed. They are also effective in marking the opposite edges of a piece of bias to be used for a collar or other trim. As you attach the bias to the garment, be sure the corresponding clips are matched and the bias will lie flat.

### Invisible Garment Controls

You have probably had clothes in which the facing would not stay put, the jacket did not hang right, or your lingerie straps were always showing. As you read this chapter, watch for and practice the methods manufacturers use to control these and other such problems. Some of these special methods are discussed later in Chapter 11. However, you can still use your minis to practice them.

### Other Special Techniques

By making these samples, you will have a chance to:
- Practice with time-saving methods such as chain sewing.
- Use the pressing tools and techniques recommended in Chapter 5.
- Make several styles from one basic pattern.
- Practice precision stitching so that all seams and details come together the way they should.
- Apply trims and details on garments the easy way.
- Make slash openings and enlarged necklines without cutting them out first.
- Apply underlinings and interfacings and determine how and when they should be used.
- Completely line both sleeveless and sleeved garments.
- Become familiar with the difference between a lining, an interlining, and an underlining.
- Practice various types of zipper application.
- Practice the different hem finishes given in Chapter 10.

### SUPPLIES YOU WILL NEED FOR SAMPLES
#### Fabrics

3 yards (274 cm) printed material—45 inches (114 cm) wide.

3 yards (274 cm) plain lining material—45 (114 cm) inches wide.

The fabric you use for the outer garments should be sturdy, easy to work with, and easy to press. It should be firmly woven so that it will not stretch or ravel. The weight of the fabric should be similar to a bed sheet.

A printed fabric is recommended for the outer garment. By using a print, you have less chance of becoming confused as to which is the dress and

## Ch. 6: Commercial Sewing Methods

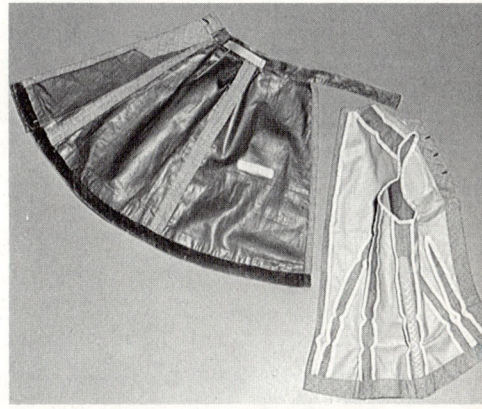

Photo by Minerva Wagner

*A-1. Making mini garments is not a new idea in learning to sew. This mini half-bodice and half-skirt were made in school in 1905 by Mrs. Lottie Hilarides of Grand Rapids, Michigan, when she was 9 years old. Notice the whalebone in the side seam for stiffening. Fine hand stitches were used to finish the garment whereas today's dressmaker uses machine stitching or fusible web.*

which is the lining. The print also makes a more attractive sample that is more fun to work on. You'll find that the 45-inch (114 cm) wide fabric will cut more pieces with less waste than other widths.

A polyester-cotton blend fabric for the lining will be easier to handle and press than acetate sheath lining fabrics. Remember that acetate ravels and must be pressed very carefully to prevent melting. See Chapter 4, "Learning About Fabrics."

**Altering Ready-To-Wear Fashions**

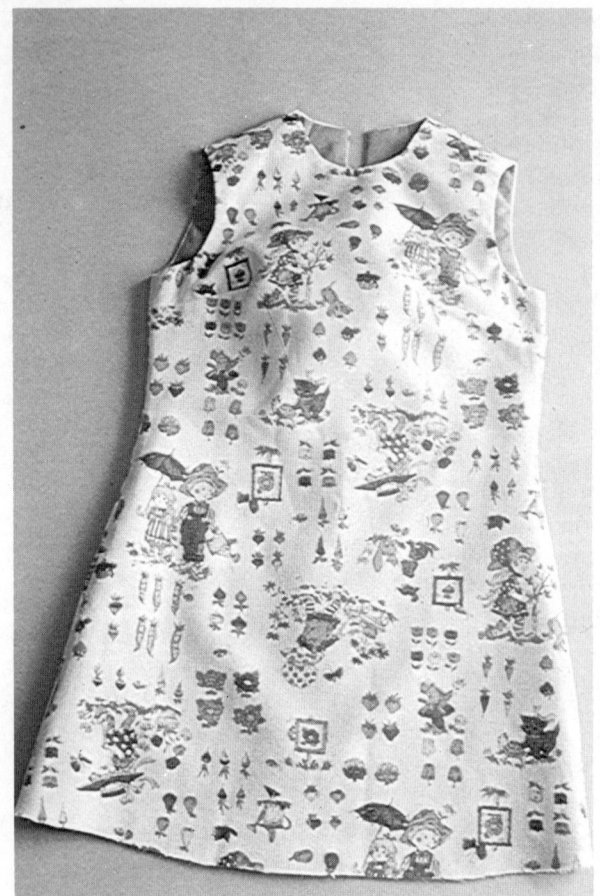
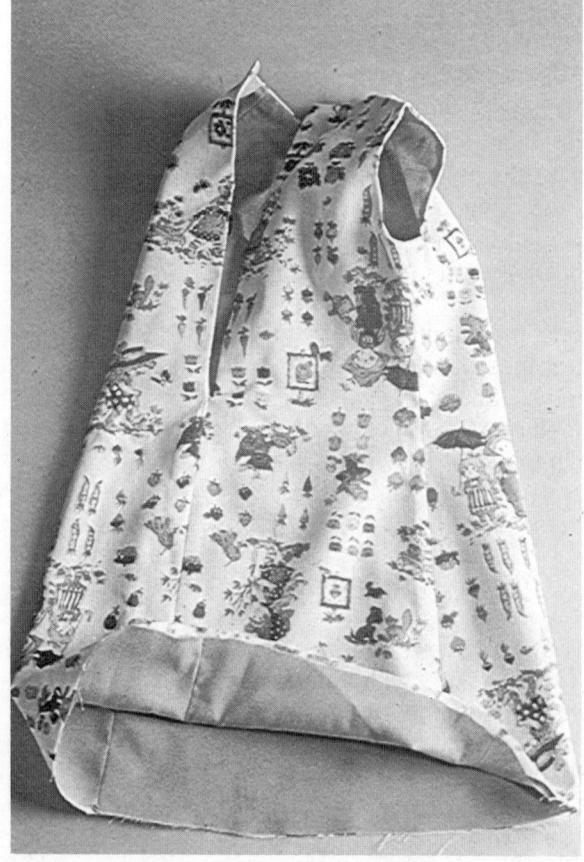

Photos by Minerva Wagner

*A-2a, b  Front and back view of Method 1 with three seams.*

## Ch. 6: Commercial Sewing Methods

These sample garments will provide invaluable learning experience for you, even if you have been sewing for years. This is *not* the time to try to save money by using up scraps and pieces of fabrics you may have around the house. Take full advantage of your opportunity to improve your skills by buying the right supplies.

### Patterns

You may wish to buy mini patterns sold by some of the large pattern companies. However, you can cut your own pattern from the scale drawings on page 384 in the Appendix. If you have children's patterns, you can use one of them. If you wish to make full-size dresses, use a basic shift pattern.

Since you will find these samples extremely good references to refresh your memory at later dates, it is preferable to make them small enough to keep handy in your sewing room.

### CONSTRUCTION METHODS

Three basic construction methods are used in manufacturing women's dresses. As you become more and more observant and experienced, you will notice that most dresses are constructed by one of these methods or a variation. This chapter gives detailed instructions for making garments by each of these basic methods as well as many variations for each. Of course, it is impossible to include every known variation. However, by practicing the methods given here, you should be able to understand any other variations you might run into in your alterations work.

*Method 1* is used for the garment that has side seams and a front-or back-opening seam.

*Method 2* is used for the garment with only side seams.

*Method 3* is used for the garment with only one seam.

Variations are given for garments that are fully lined, underlined, sleeveless, and those with one-piece facings and sleeves.

### Method 1. Figs. A-2a and A-2b

The method that follows gives step-by-step instructions for a fully lined, sleeveless dress with a back seam.

1. Lay pattern on the material so that you will have a seam down the center back. Fig. A-3. For mini garments, use 3/8 inch (.9 cm) seam allowances. Cut lining for dress the same.

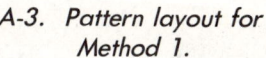

A-3. Pattern layout for Method 1.

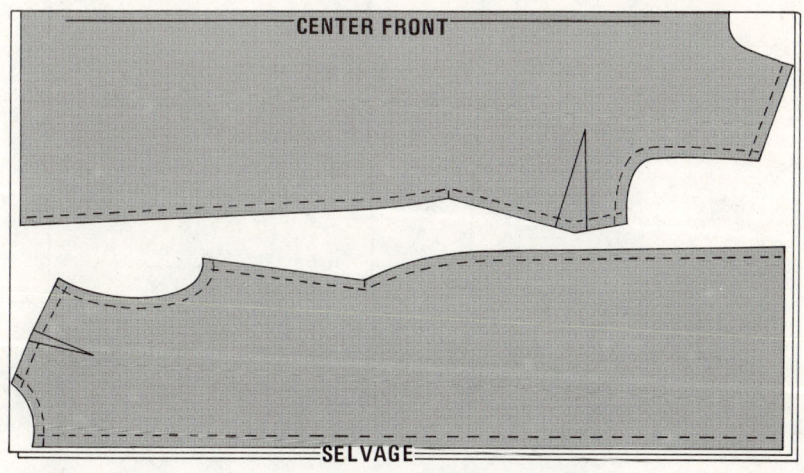

*Altering Ready-To-Wear Fashions*

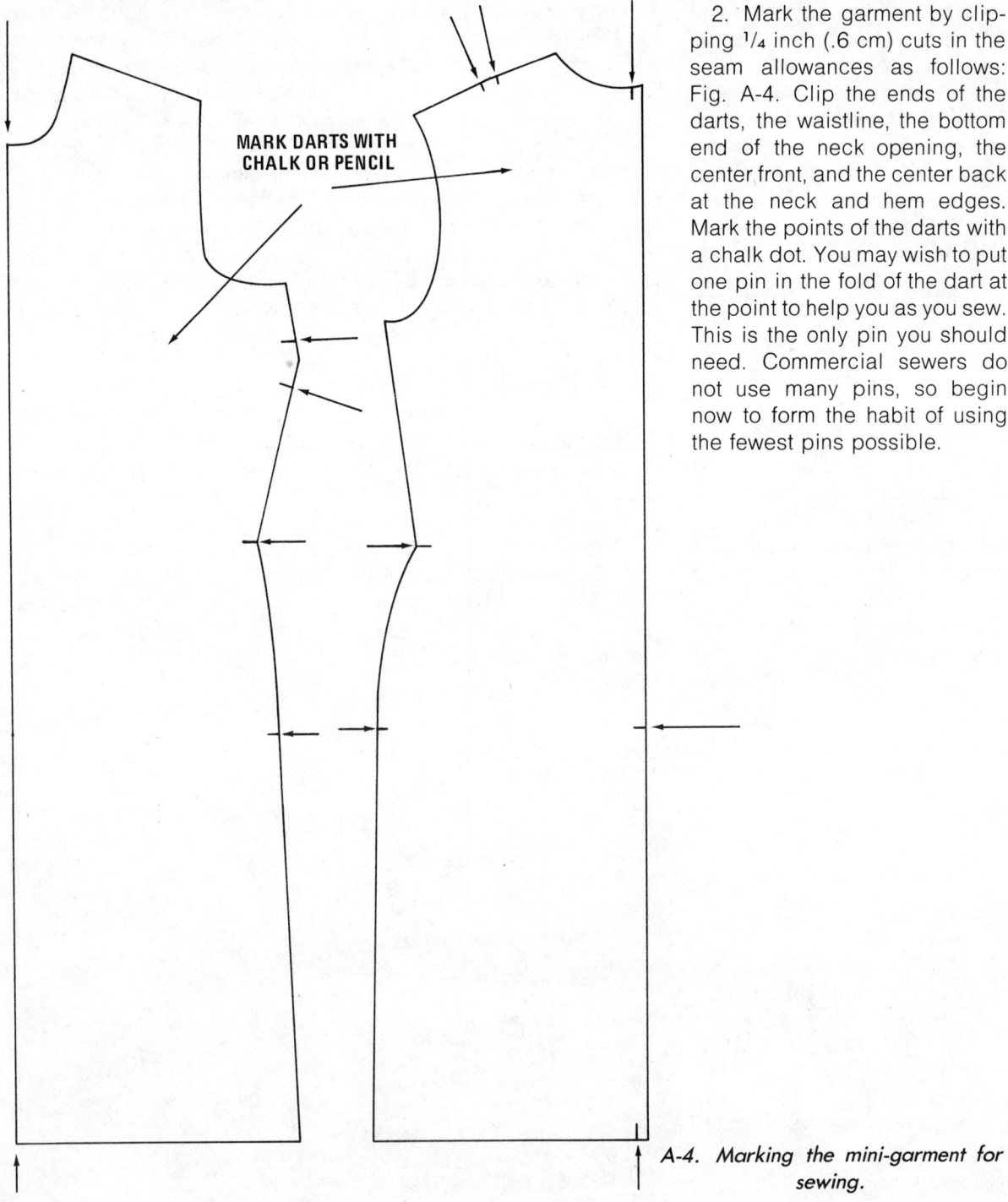

2. Mark the garment by clipping ¼ inch (.6 cm) cuts in the seam allowances as follows: Fig. A-4. Clip the ends of the darts, the waistline, the bottom end of the neck opening, the center front, and the center back at the neck and hem edges. Mark the points of the darts with a chalk dot. You may wish to put one pin in the fold of the dart at the point to help you as you sew. This is the only pin you should need. Commercial sewers do not use many pins, so begin now to form the habit of using the fewest pins possible.

A-4. *Marking the mini-garment for sewing.*

### Ch. 6: Commercial Sewing Methods

A-5. Chain sew from one piece to the next without cutting threads.

3. Chain sew the darts on all of the dress and lining pieces at one time. Fig. A-5. Stitch from the raw edge to the point of one dart, pull about an inch (2.5 cm) of thread from the bobbin and spool, and go on to stitching the next dart without stopping to cut the threads each time. Backstitching or tying knots at either end of the dart are wasted time and motion. The seam crossing the large end of the dart will keep it from pulling out and there is nothing to pull apart at the sharp point. Stitch all the darts in one continuous motion, going from one dart to the next. Then pick up your scissors and separate the pieces by cutting the threads in the center of each strand. You should have a half inch of thread left at each end of the darts.

4. Press all darts at one time. Remember, vertical (up and down) darts are pressed with the fold toward the center front or center back. Bust darts are pressed with the fold turned toward the waistline. Fig. A-6. NOTE: A hot bulb on a sewing machine light makes a handy pressing "iron" for quick touch-ups without going to the iron and press board. Open the seam or fold the dart in the proper direction with your fingers and run the stitching line over the hot bulb. This will work on most easily pressed fabrics.

5. Chain sew the four shoulder seams of bodice and bodice lining, leaving 1 inch (2.5 cm) of thread between the seams as you did with the darts. DO NOT SEW THE SIDE SEAMS. Clip the threads all at one time to separate the pieces. Leave about one-half inch (1.3 cm) of thread on each piece.

6. Press seams open and flat. As recommended in Chapter 5, press a seam with the edges together before opening it. This makes the seam easier to press open.

7. Trim 1/8 inch (.3 cm) off the straight part of the armhole edge of the lining only. *Do not* cut any of the curved area. This will make the lining slightly smaller than the garment. By doing this, the lining will not show when the garment is stitched and pressed.

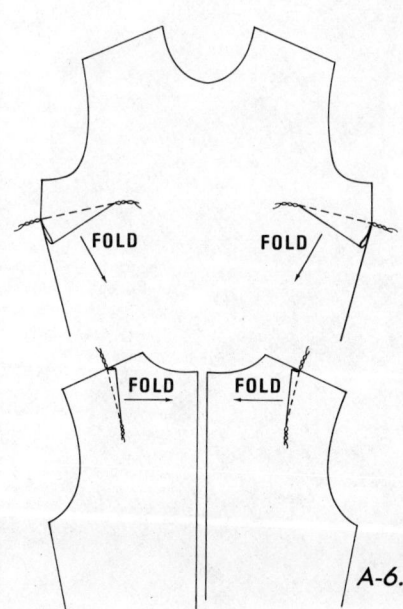

A-6. Press darts down or toward the center.

### Altering Ready-To-Wear Fashions

8. Place the dress flat on the worktable. Place the lining on the dress, right sides together. Match the shoulder seams and pin at neck edge and armhole edge. Match and pin the lower edges of the armhole openings. Match and pin the clip markings at the bottom of the neck opening. You may wish to put one more pin in each armhole edge about halfway between the shoulder seam and the lower edge. Use as few pins as possible. Fig. A-7.

NOTE: When pinning any two parts of a garment together, always pin the centers first, then each of the ends. Ease the rest of the edges together to make them fit. If you start at one end and pin around to the other end, you usually end up with one edge extending beyond the other as it is difficult to keep from stretching one edge more than the other.

NOTE: When pinning, always place the pins at right angles to the seam line, with the head of the pin toward the raw edge. The seams are easier to control and the pins will be easier to remove as you stitch. *Do not stitch over pins if you can help it.* It is too easy to hit a pin with the needle. You can blunt the needle point or break it off. Often, the broken point will fly through the air and could cause injury.

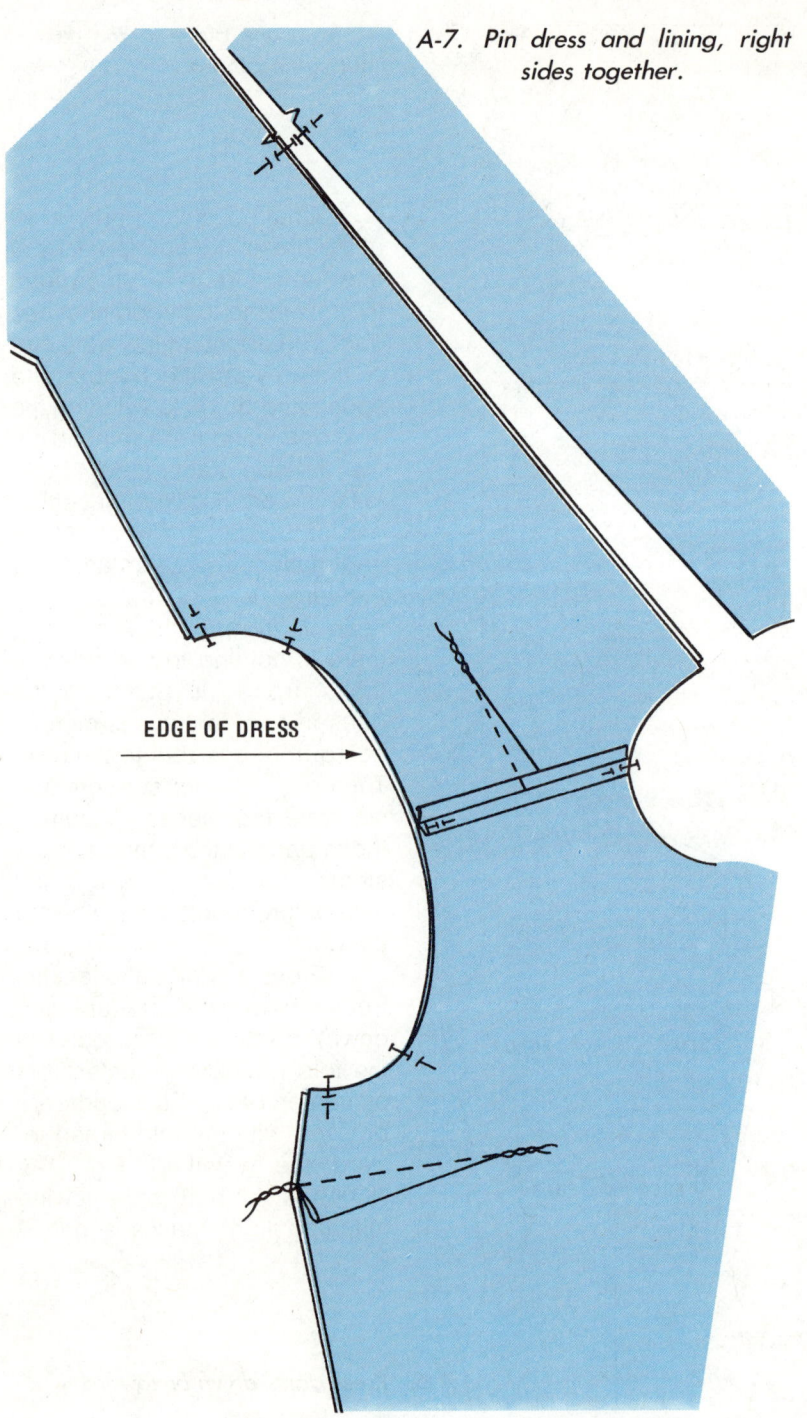

A-7. Pin dress and lining, right sides together.

**Ch. 6: Commercial Sewing Methods**

9. To finish the neck edges, start stitching at the clip marks at the bottom of the neck opening in the center back seam. Stitch in one long seam from the clip, up the back, then around the neck edge, and back to the other end of the opening in the back seam. Be sure to stitch on the seam line. Stitch with the lining side up and the dress fabric against the machine bed. It is easier to keep the edges together.

10. Again, with the lining side up, stitch around the armhole edges from one end to the other in one long seam. *Do not stitch side seams.*

11. Trim armhole and neck edges to one-quarter inch. *Do not trim the seam along the neck opening part of the back seam.* Clip to the seam line as needed to let the edge spread enough to lie flat when the garment is turned right side out. Fig. A-8. Fig. A-9 shows garment stitched and clipped and ready for next step.

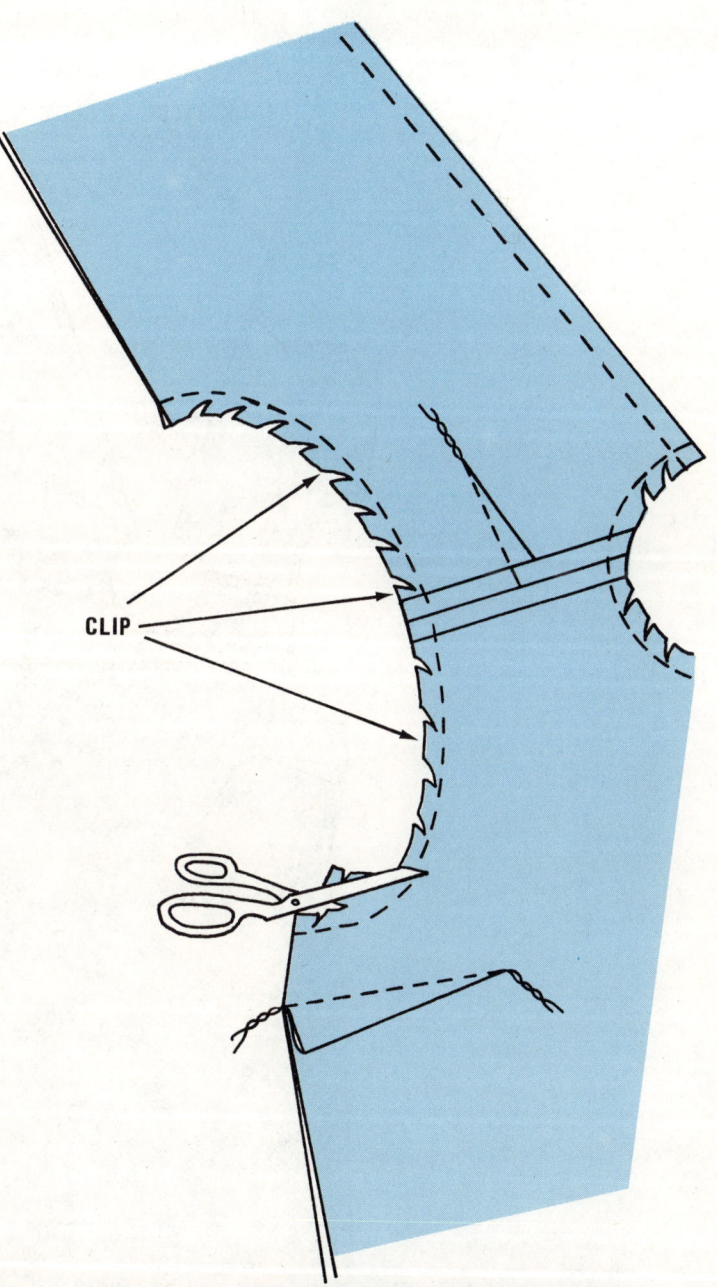

A-8. *Trim and clip armhole and neck edges.*

*Altering Ready-To-Wear Fashions*

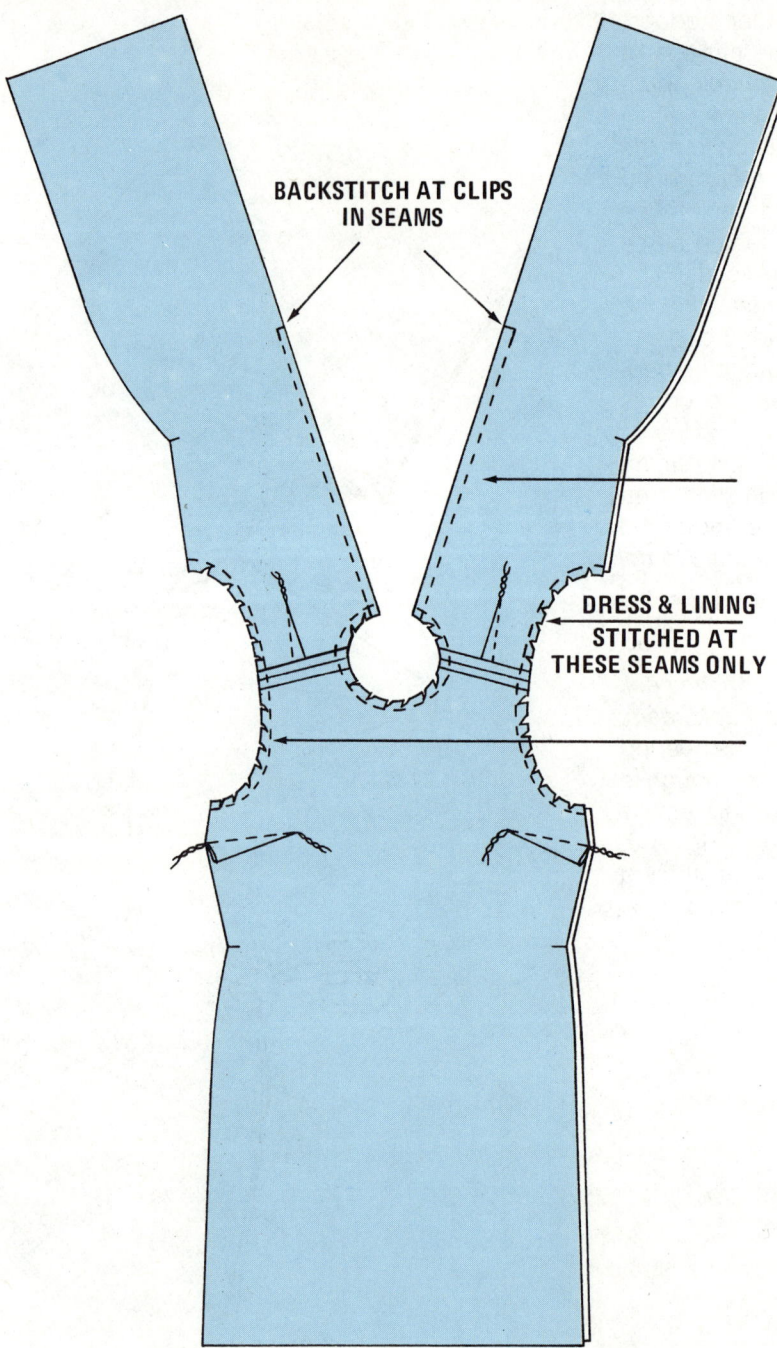

A-9. *Garment should look like this at the end of Step 11.*

**Ch. 6: Commercial Sewing Methods**

12. Understitch the facing edges. To understitch, spread the garment and lining apart. Lay the garment flat under the sewing machine presser foot with the right side of the fabric up. Be sure all the trimmed and clipped seams are turned toward the lining side. From the right side of the lining stitch through the lining and both edges of the seam with a single line of regular stitching very close to the original seamline. Fig. A-10 a, b. This helps a lining or facing stay in place. However, you will find the size of your mini sample makes understitching difficult. Just understitch three or four inches along the center front of the neck edge and along the lower curves of the sleeves if it is necessary to keep the lining in place.

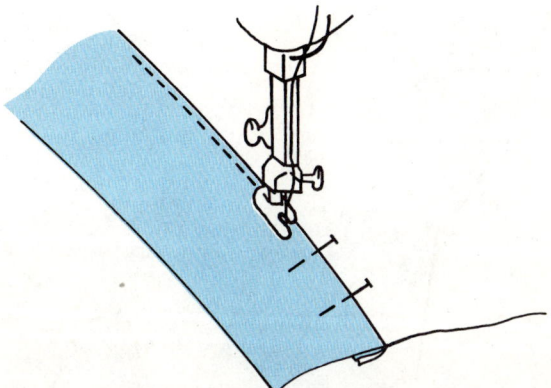

A-10a. *Understitch the facing seam.*

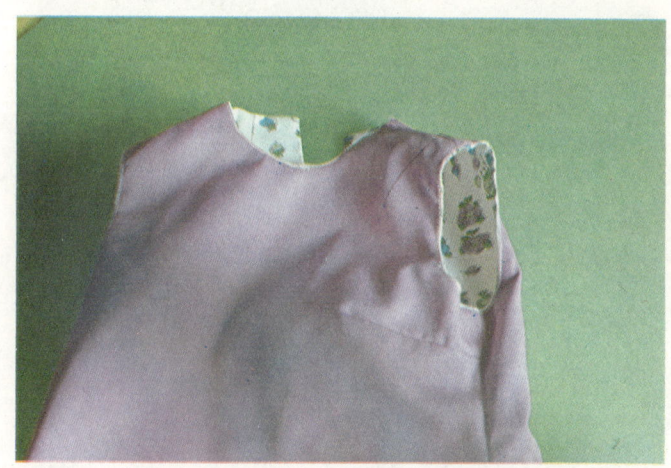

Photo by Minerva Wagner

A-10b. *Understitched facings lie flat.*

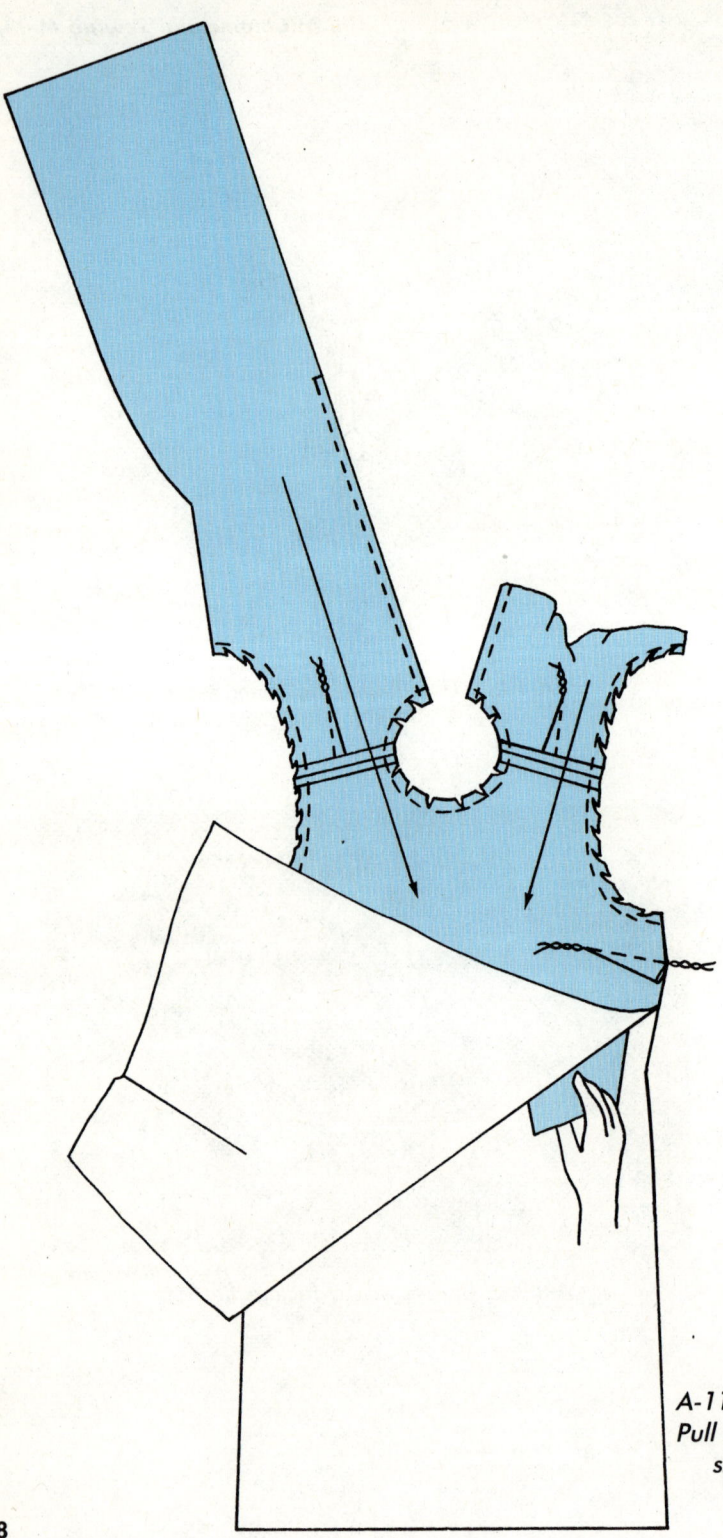

13. The dress is now ready to be turned right side out. To do this, put your hand between the lining and dress at the front hem edge, and reach through the shoulder section all the way to the back hem edge. Grasp back hem edge and pull one back half up through the shoulder section and out the front end. Repeat with the other back half pulling it through the other shoulder. Fig. A-11.

*A-11. Turn the garment right side out. Pull separate halves of garment through shoulders in direction of arrows.*

14. Pin the center back seam of the dress skirt, right sides together. Be sure to match them carefully at the clip mark at the bottom of the neck opening. Stitch the dress together down the center back to the hem edge. Lock the seam at the clip mark with careful backstitching. This seam will be strained when the garment is put on and could pull apart if this seam were not backstitched. Repeat the process on the lining. Fig. A-12. CAUTION: All four seams—skirt back, lining back, and the right and left sides of the back neck opening—must come together exactly where they meet at the clip mark.

NOTE: When making full-sized garments by this method, you would insert the zipper at this point. The machine or hand-sewn "centered" methods of zipper application may be used.

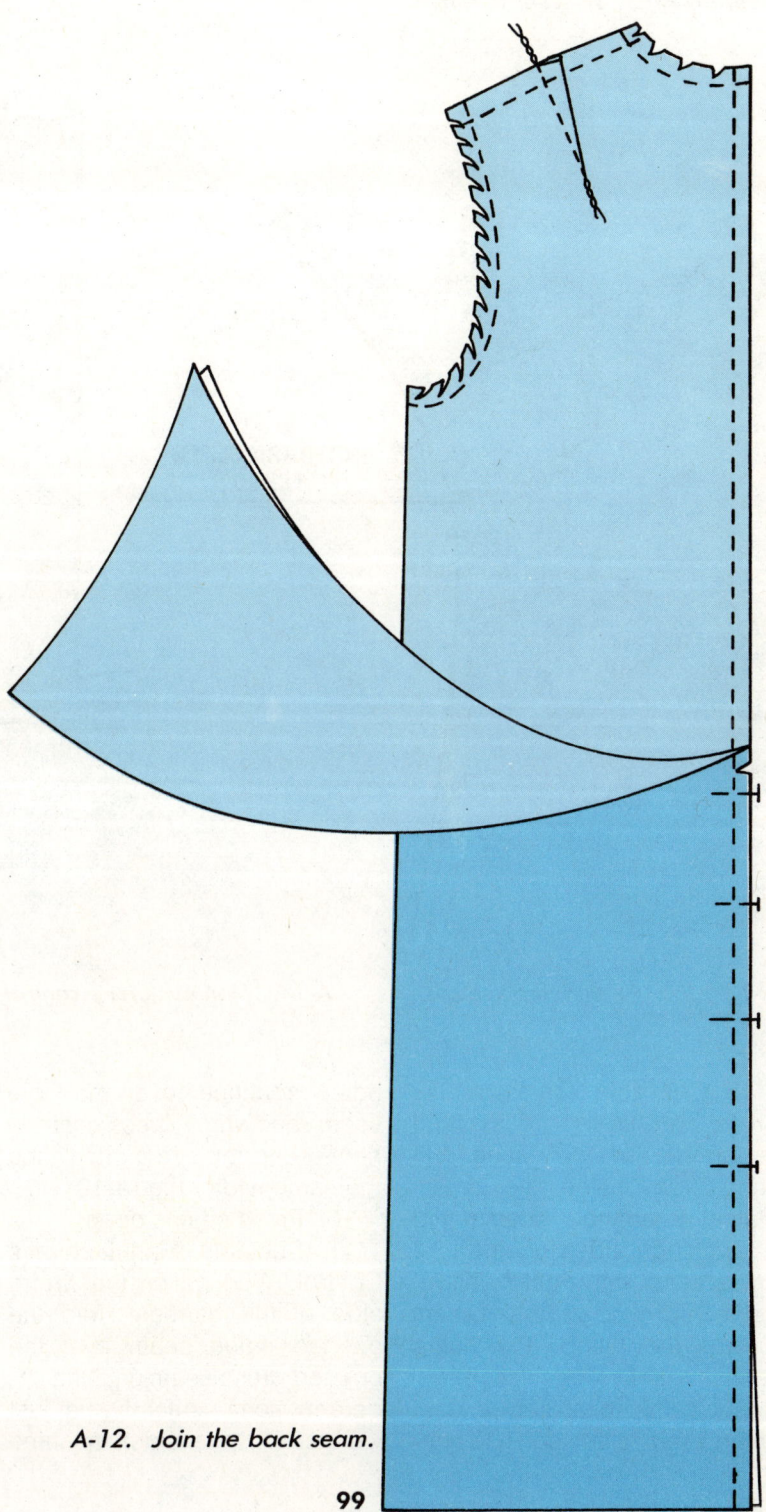

A-12. Join the back seam.

## Altering Ready-To-Wear Fashions

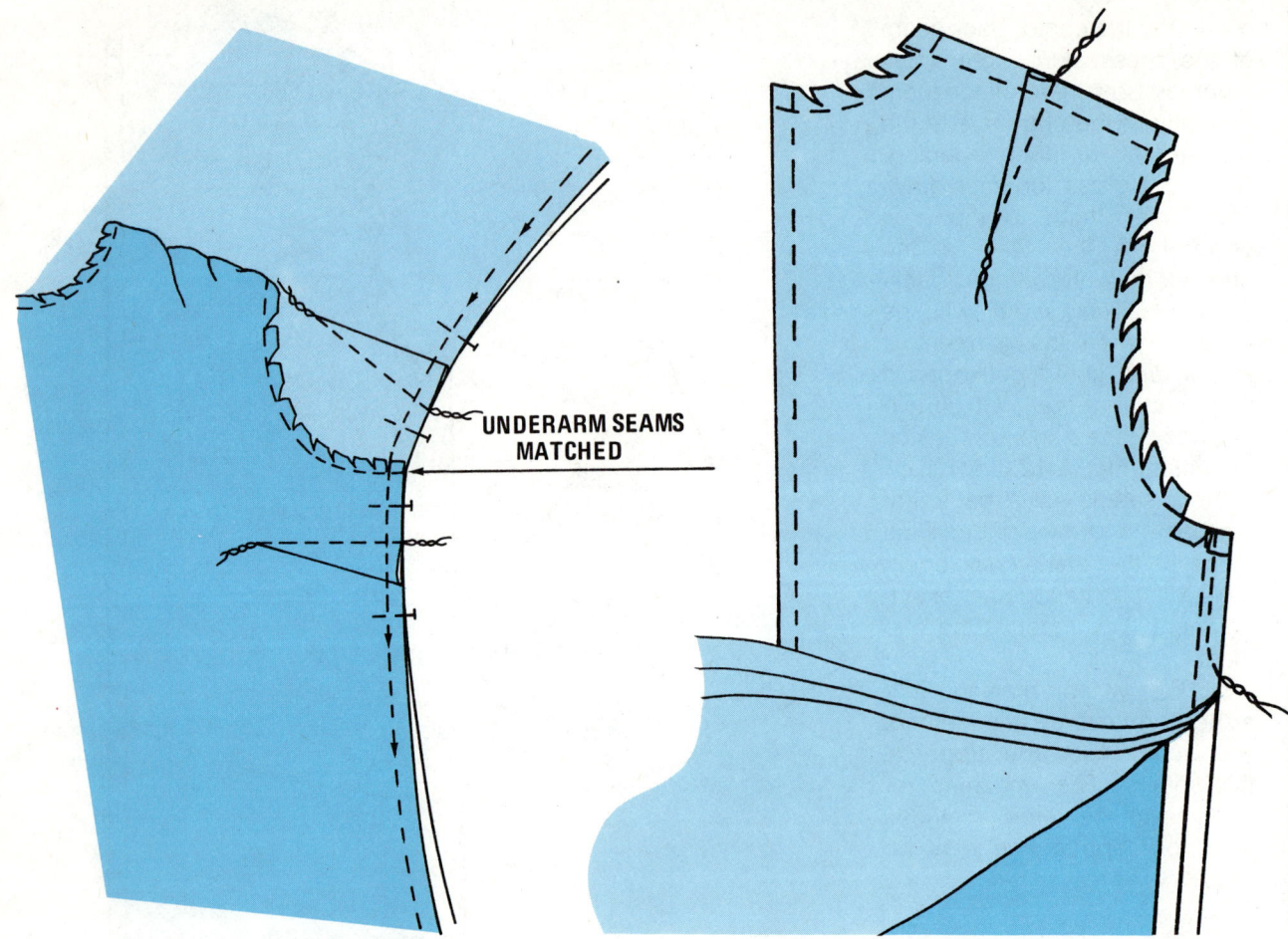

A-13. Join the underarm seams.

A-14. Manufacturer's control-stitching to hold lining in place.

15. The side seams for the dress and lining are stitched separately so the lining will hang free inside the dress. Match at armhole seams and pin with right sides together. Pin dress seam with right sides together. Turn the underarm seam toward the lining. Pin lining seam, right sides together. Begin stitching at hem end of lining seam, stitch seam to armhole, continue over armhole seam, and stitch dress seam to hem. Keep the seam allowance the same width. Fig. A-13.

16. Press seams open.

17. Special Manufacturer's Control: Working on the wrong side of the garment, fold the opened lining seam over the opened dress seam until the underarm seam stitching is just visible. On one side, machine baste the lining seam to the dress seam for two or three inches (5 to 7.6 cm). Keep the stitching next to the original seam, and run it off the edge of the seam at the lower edge. Fig. A-14. Stitching the two seams together in this way holds the lining in place and keeps it from "riding up." You will find this technique used on most sleeveless ready-to-wear garments.

## Ch. 6: Commercial Sewing Methods

### Method 2, Fig. A-15

This method gives step-by-step instructions for a fully lined garment with side seams only.

1. Cut out the dress and lining with both the center front and the center back laid on folds. Fig. A-16.

2. Mark darts, waistline, center front, and center back with the small clips as used in Method 1, Step 2. The neckline will need to be enlarged or changed so it will be large enough to go over a head. Convert the neckline to a scoop neck, V-neck, boat neck, or keyhole neck at this time. Make the necessary marks for the new neckline on the lining only. You can use chalk or pencil to draw the new neckline on the lining and will not need to mark the dress fabric. For the purposes of this sample, a 7½ inch (19.1 cm) slash neckline opening is used.

3. Chain sew darts and press as in Method 1, Steps 3 and 4.

4. Chain sew and press shoulder seams as in Method 1, Step 5. *Do not sew side seams or armhole seams.*

NOTE: Remember to join shoulder seams by matching the edges at the seam stitching line rather than the raw edges.

A-15. Method 2 with side seams only.

Photo by Minerva Wagner

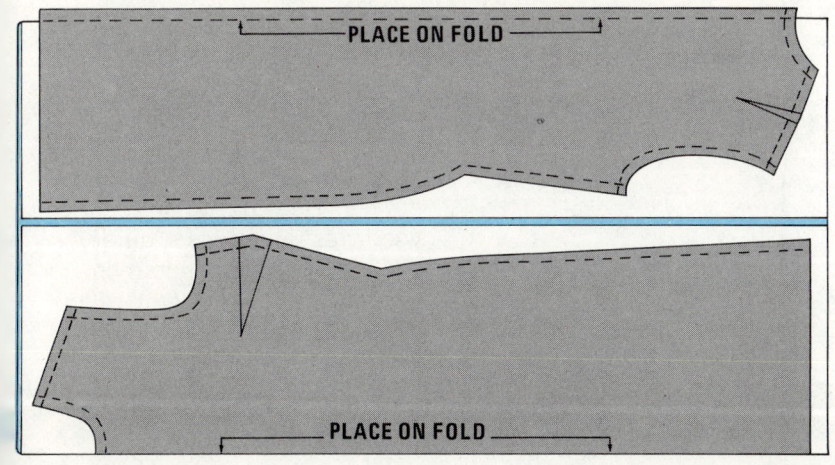

A-16. Pattern layout for method 2.

5. With right sides together, pin the lining to the dress at the neck edges, matching center front, center back, and shoulder seams. Stitch around the neck, keeping the lining fabric on top and the dress fabric against the bed of the machine.

6. To make the slash opening, fold the lining on the center front and press a light crease down the front with your finger nail. Mark the lower end of the slash with a small pencil or chalk mark. Carefully pin dress fabric to lining along the crease at the center front. Stitch a straight line from neck edge to bottom mark about 1/8 inch (.3 cm) from the center crease. At bottom mark, leave the needle down in the fabric so it will not slip, raise the presser foot, turn the material toward the center fold. Lower the presser foot and stitch across the center crease to 1/8 inch (.3 cm) on the other side. Count stitches on each side of the fold so distance is the same on each side of the center. Leave needle in the cloth again, raise presser foot, turn material, lower presser foot, and stitch back to top neck edge. Keep this stitching 1/8 inch (.3 cm) from the center crease. Use the outer edge of your presser foot as a guide.

7. Slash down the fold line to within 1/4 inch (.6 cm) of the bottom stitching. Clip carefully into each corner. Fig. A-17. Clip right up to the stitching line but do not cut the stitches.

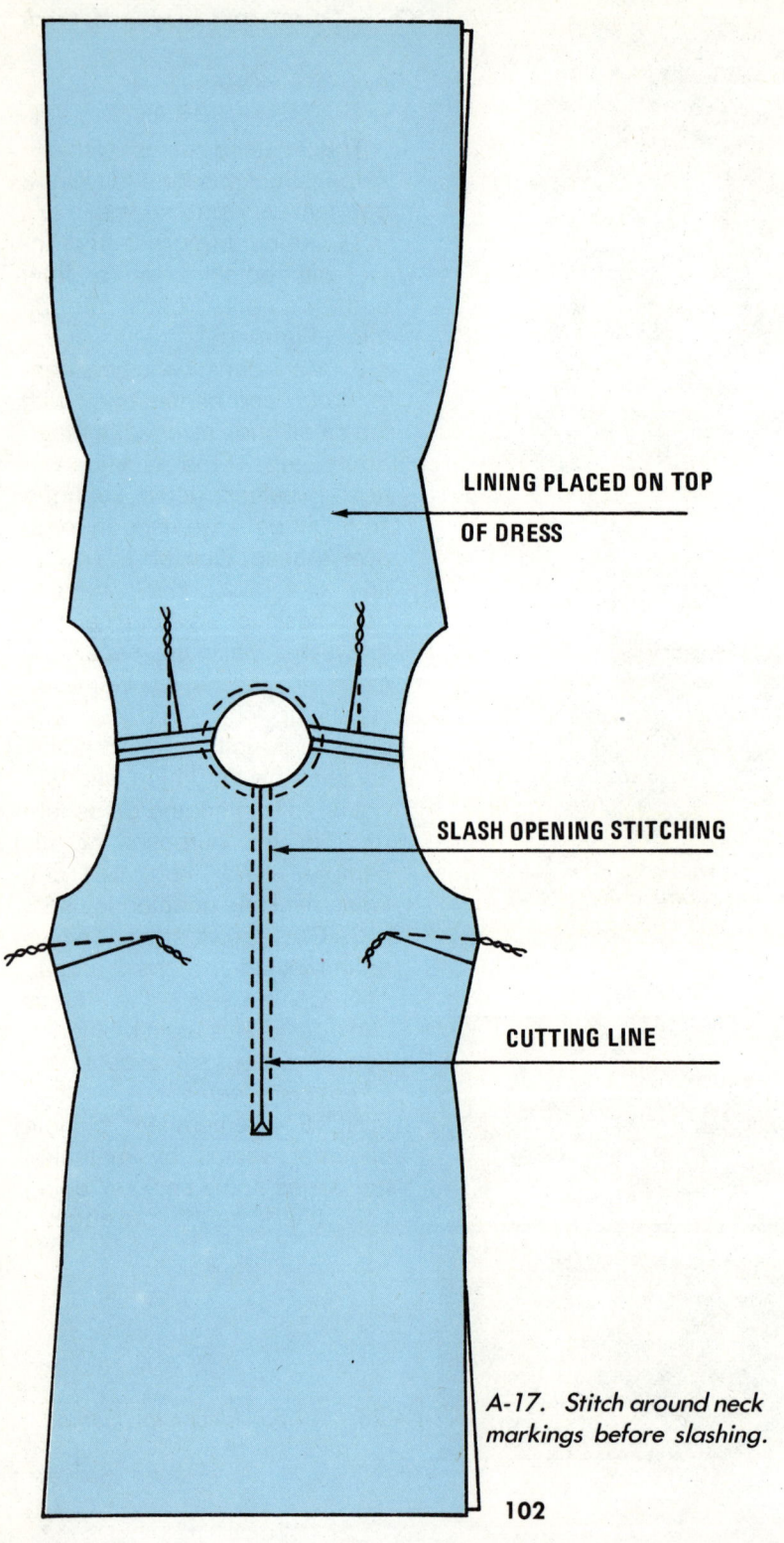

A-17. *Stitch around neck markings before slashing.*

### Ch. 6: Commercial Sewing Methods

8. Turn garment right side out and press the lining back so that you have a slot opening. As you press, you will find the lining will extend beyond the dress at the armhole almost $1/16$ inch (.2 cm). To keep the lining slightly smaller than the dress, trim away this extra lining around the top of the armholes.

9(A). Spread the garment out flat on the worktable—right sides up—as shown in Fig. A-18. Put a pin through the dress and lining at the armhole edge of the left side (A).

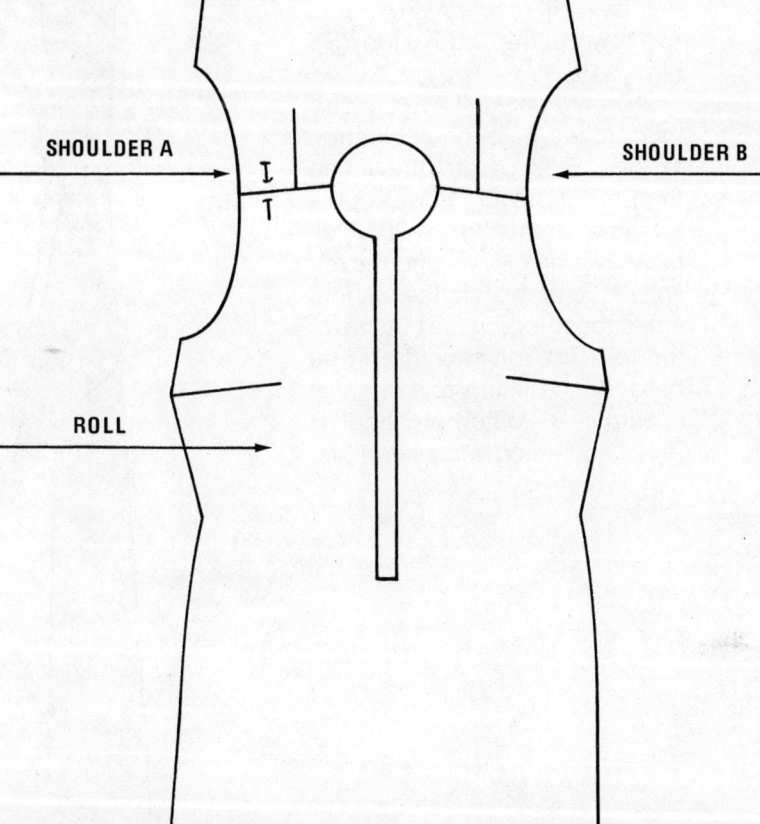

A-18. Lay garment flat and pin left shoulder to lining.

103

## Altering Ready-To-Wear Fashions

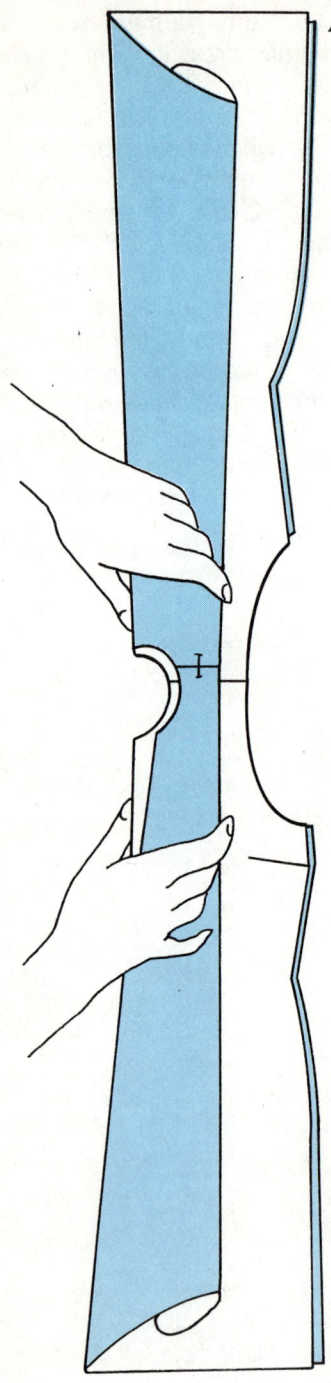

A-19. Roll shoulder A to shoulder B.

Starting with that side, pick up the armhole edges and roll the armhole section in a tight roll toward the other side (B). Fig. A-19.

9(B). When you have the garment rolled past the neck edge of side B, separate the lining from the dress on side B at the armhole area Fig. A-20. Pull these two pieces around the roll so you can match them, right sides together, on the outside of the roll. The roll should now be between the lining and dress of shoulder B. Match shoulder B dress and lining seams and pin.

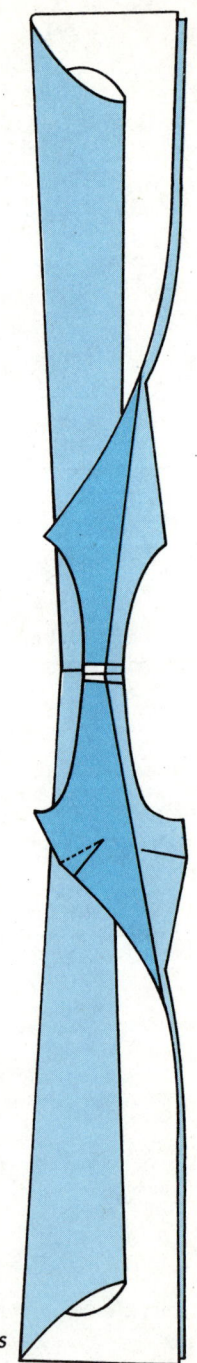

A-20. Separate lining from dress on side B at armhole area.

**A-21.** *Stitch armhole edges of side B.*

9(C). Match the underarm edges and pin. Stitch shoulder B dress and lining armhole seam from underarm to underarm. Fig. A-21. *Do not stitch side seams*. Trim and clip the seam. Reach inside shoulder B and pull the garment out so it is flat again. Fig. A-22.

10. Remove pin from shoulder A. Repeat entire process by rolling side B over to side A. Stitch armhole A. Trim and clip seam. Pull garment through shoulder A.

11. If zipper is to be inserted, do it at this time before stitching side seams. See directions for zipper page 301.

12. Stitch side seams following directions in Method 1, Step 15. Do manufacturer's control as in Method 1, Step 17.

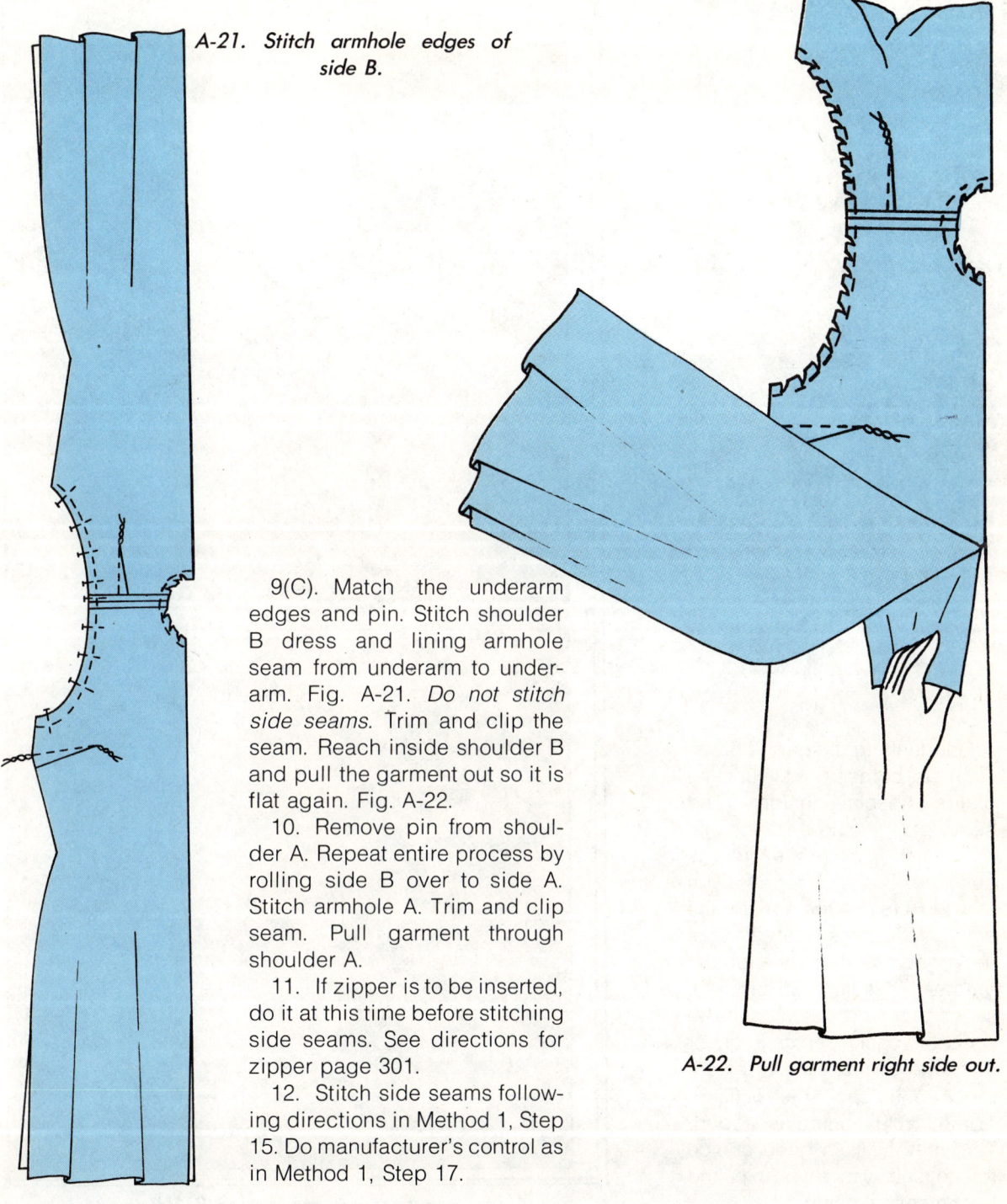

**A-22.** *Pull garment right side out.*

Photo by Minerva Wagner

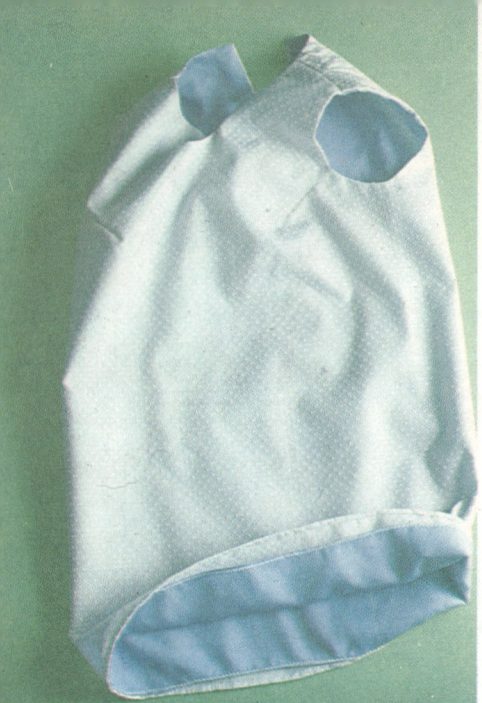

*A-23. Method 3, Version A. Note armhole darts and one seam with neck opening.*

## Method 3, Version A. Fig. A-23

Garments from some fabrics, such as border prints, uneven plaids, special designs, and heavy pile, should be made into styles using as few seams as possible. For such fabrics, you may wish to change a pattern to eliminate seams that are not necessary to the style of the garment. Method 3 has one seam only. This seam could be a center back, center front, or one side seam. For this example, a center back seam is used. Again, a full lining is added. This method is a good choice for anyone with equal hip and bust measurements.

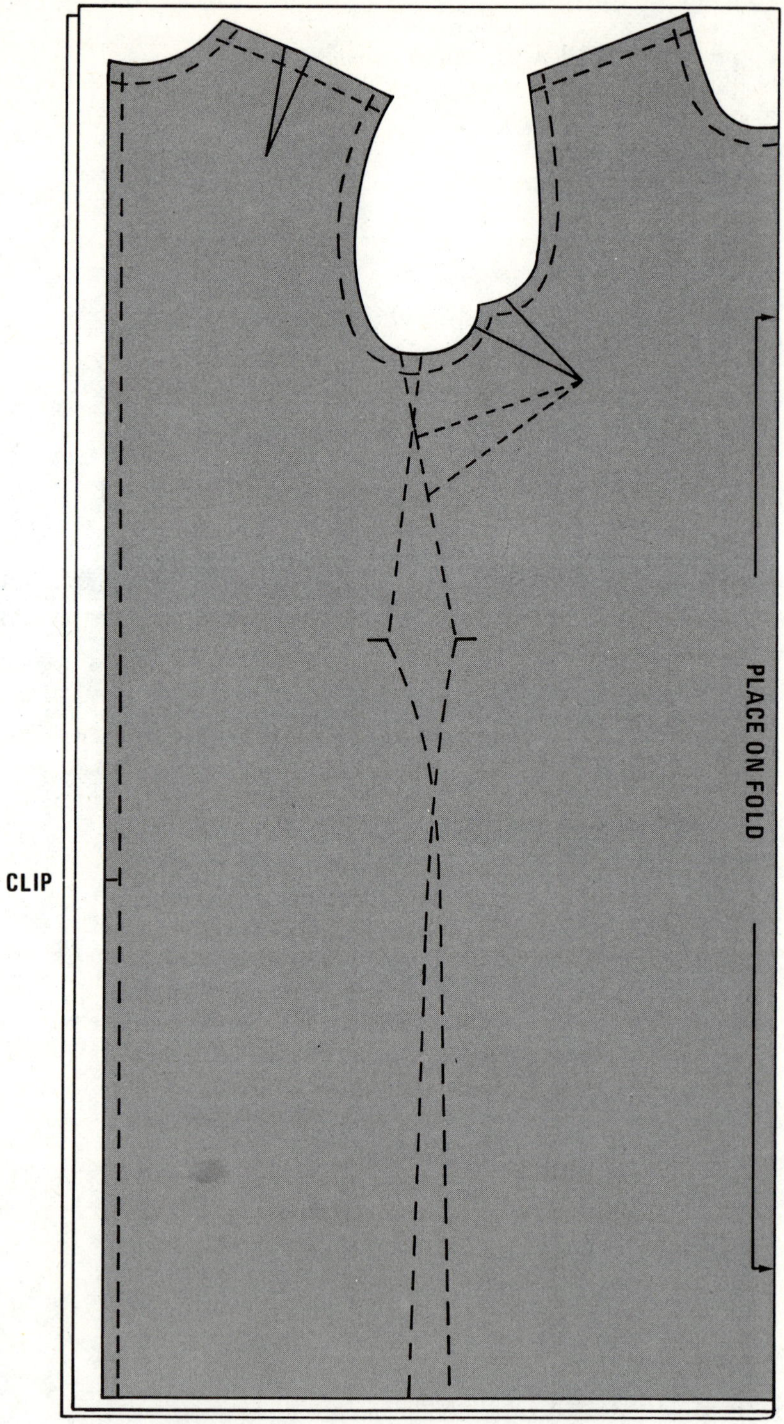

*A-24. Pattern layout for Method 3, Version A.*

**Ch. 6: Commercial Sewing Methods**

If the hips are larger than the bust measurement, use Version B of Method 3. If the bust measures more than 2 inches (5 cm) more than the hips, you will find Method 3 will not fit with either version.

To make a dress by Version A of Method 3, follow these steps:

1. If the front pattern piece has a bust dart (as in the mini pattern), change that dart to an armhole dart. To do this, fold and pin the pattern bust dart closed. Where the armhole curve starts to straighten out, cut the pattern straight down to the point of the bust mark. Fig. A-24. This is the dot where the bust dart ends. Smooth the pattern until it lies flat. The area where the pattern spreads apart forms your new armhole dart. On a normal-sized dress or jacket, you may find you will need to shorten this dart to end an inch above the point of the bust. For your mini sample, use the whole area as your dart.

2. Lay the back pattern piece over the front piece so that the skirt sections of the front and back overlap. Keep the grainline arrows in each piece straight. Line the pattern pieces up so that the underarm and hem edges are even. Pin the two pieces together so the measurement across the hip area measures the same as the bust area. Fig. A-24. In a regular-size garment, be sure to allow for the necessary ease in the hip measurement.

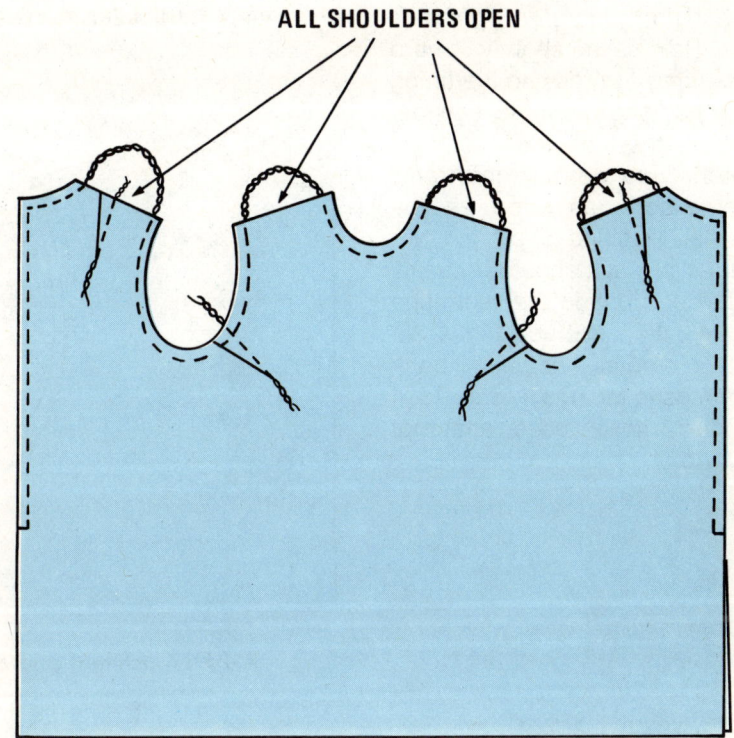

*A-25. Chain sew neck and armhole edges.*

3. Handle the two pattern pieces as one. Place pattern on the material with the center front on the straight fold. Cut the dress out as one piece. Cut lining the same way.

4. Mark the darts, center front, center back, and end of neck opening with small clips in the seam allowance as in Method 1, Step 2.

5. Chain sew darts on both the lining and the dress. Clip threads and press. For less bulk, press the lining dart up and the dress dart down.)

6. Place lining on dress, right sides together. Trim 1/8 inch from the *straight edges* of the armhole edges of the *lining only*. Do not trim the curved area under the arm. Pin the neck and armhole edges of the dress and lining together. Chain sew carefully around the neck and armholes on the seam line. Be *sure* seam allowances are even on all edges. Start and stop neck seam at the clips marking the neck opening as in Method 1, step 8. *Do not stitch across the tops of the shoulders.*

### Altering Ready-To-Wear Fashions

7. Trim, clip, *turn right side out*. Roll seam slightly toward the lining to press so the lining will not show on the outside. Check the shoulder sections carefully to be sure the fronts are exactly as wide as the backs. Machine baste the two edges of back shoulder seams together close to the seam line to keep them in place. Fig. A-26.

8. Complete center back seam as in Method 1, Step 13. If zipper is to be used, attach at this point.

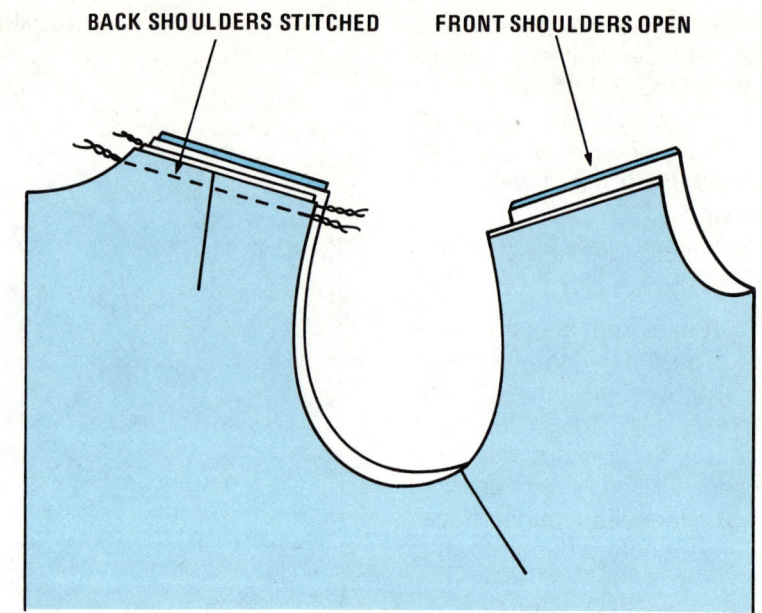

A-26. Machine baste back shoulder edges together.

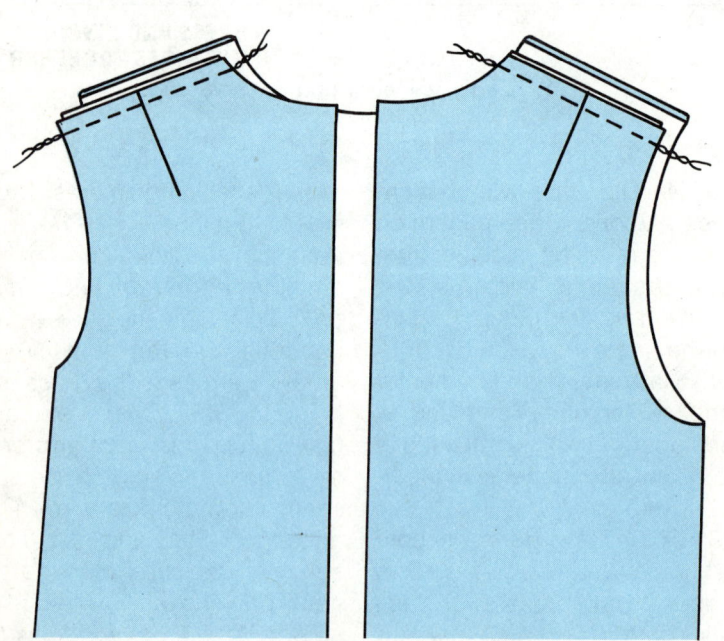

A-27. Match front shoulders to back shoulders, right sides together.

9. Put back shoulder to front shoulder, right sides together. Fig. A-27. Put your hand inside front shoulder of garment between the lining and the dress. Grasp back shoulder dress and lining edges against dress side of front shoulder and pull all three edges through to the wrong side. Fig. A-28. Pin at neck and armhole seams to hold in place.

**Ch. 6: Commercial Sewing Methods**

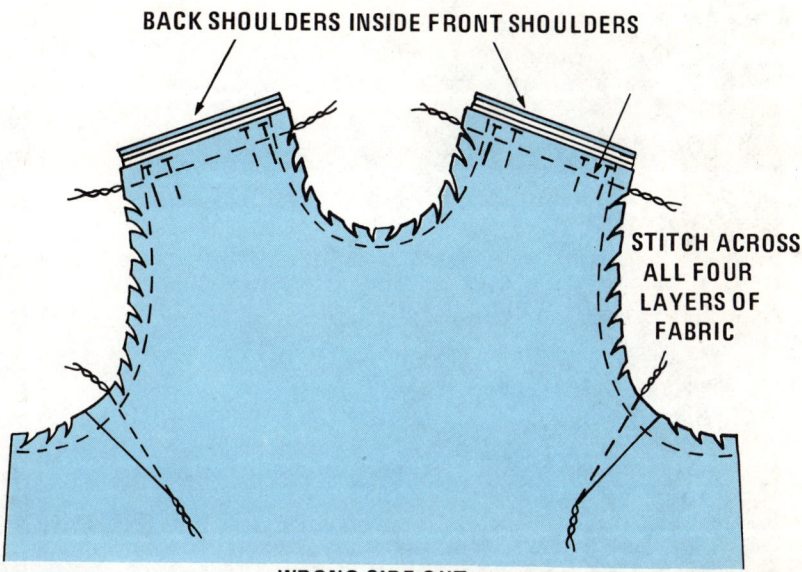

A-29. Stitch across all four layers of fabric at shoulders.

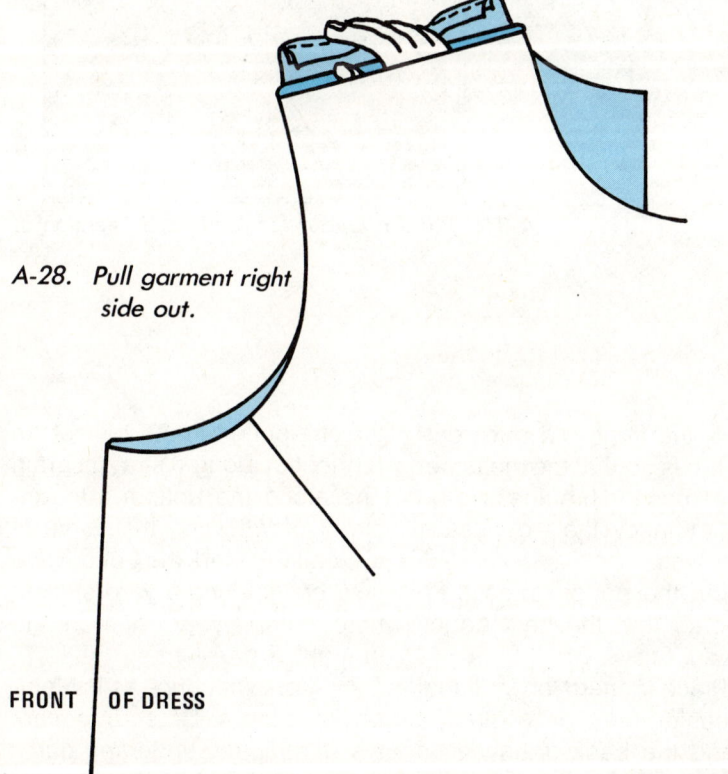

A-28. Pull garment right side out.

10. Stitch all four edges together in one seam. Fig. A-29. Trim seam only if necessary.

NOTE: To make any kind of alteration easier, get in the habit of trimming seams only when necessary to make the seam lie flat or to remove bulk that will mar the appearance of the finished garment on the outside.

11. Again, reach inside between the lining and the dress. Grasp the back shoulder section and pull the garment right side out. Press.

## Altering Ready-To-Wear Fashions

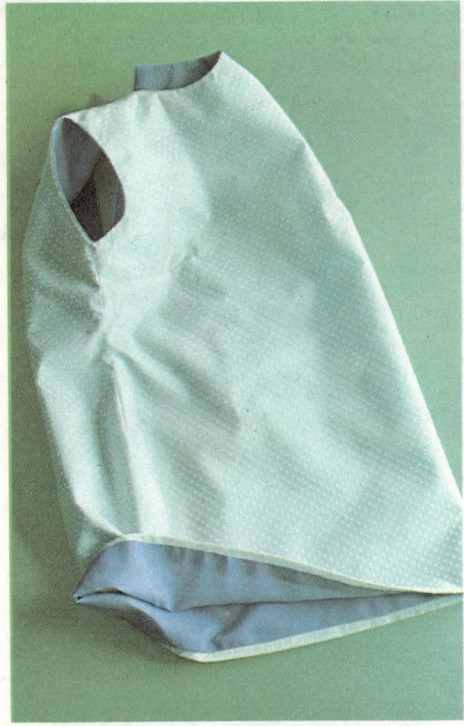

A-30. Method 3, Version B. Note long underarm dart in place of side seams and one seam in center back with neck opening.

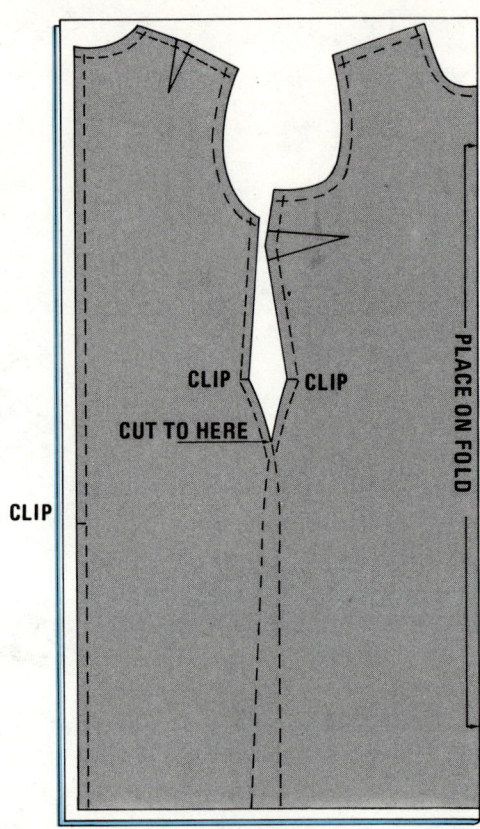

A-31. Pattern layout for Method 3, Version B.

### Method 3, Version B, Fig. A-30

This method can be used when making a one-seam dress, jacket, or vest for the figure that measures up to 2 inches larger in the hips than through the bust. It involves the following steps:

1. Leave the original bust dart as it is. Lap the skirt sections of the front and back pattern pieces so that the measurement across the hip line is large enough to allow the proper ease for the hips.
2. Pin the pattern pieces together so that the hem edges are even. Fig. A-31.
3. Place pattern on material with center front on a straight fold and the back grainline on the straight grain. As you cut the fabric, cut along a straight grain line along the bottom edge instead of following the curve of the pattern. Mark the bottom line with chalk along a yard stick to help keep your hem edge straight. Fig. A-31.
4. Mark with clips as in Method 3A, Step 4. Be sure to mark waistline in the underarm dart.

Ch. 6: Commercial Sewing Methods

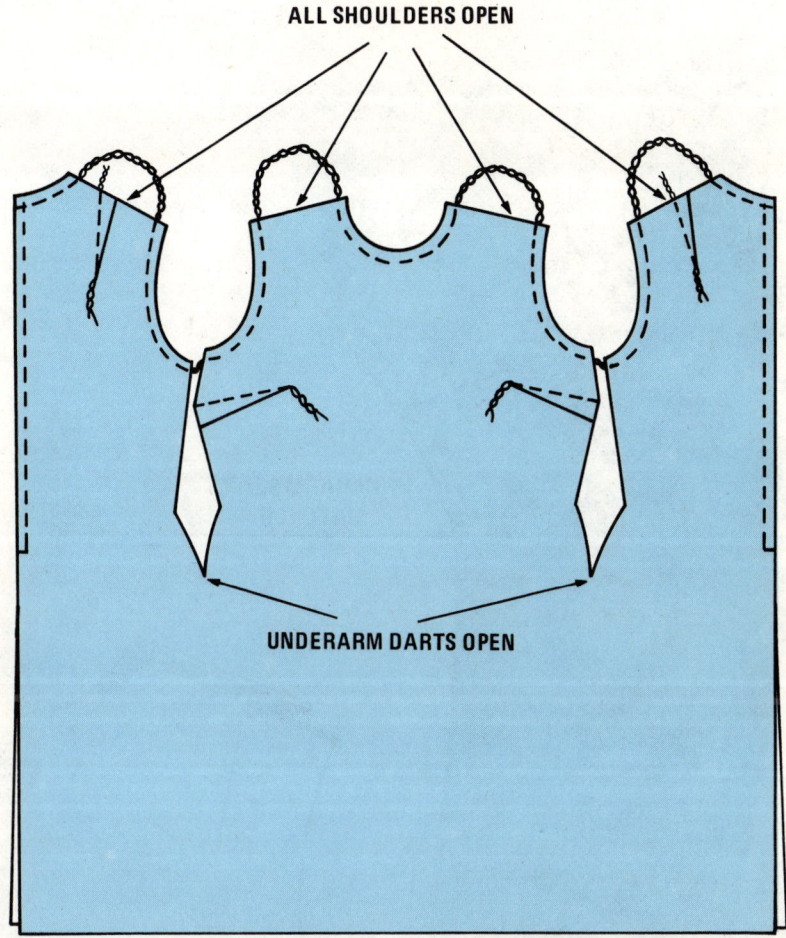

A-32. Stitch neck, armholes, and back neck opening seams.

5. Chain sew all darts *except the long underarm dart*, which is now side seam. Press darts.

6. Match right sides of lining and dress at shoulder seams, neck edges, and back opening clips. Trim lining 1/8 inch (.3 cm) on straight edges of armholes as in Method 3A, Step 6.

7. Chain sew neck and armhole edges from the back neck end clip on one side back to the end clip on the other back. Go from one piece to the other without cutting the threads until the end. Fig. A-32. *Do not stitch underarm dart.*

8. Trim and clip seams. Turn right side out. Press as in Method 3A, Step 7. Check shoulders to be sure front and back match in width.

9. Complete back seam as in Method 1, Step 13. Insert zipper, if desired.

111

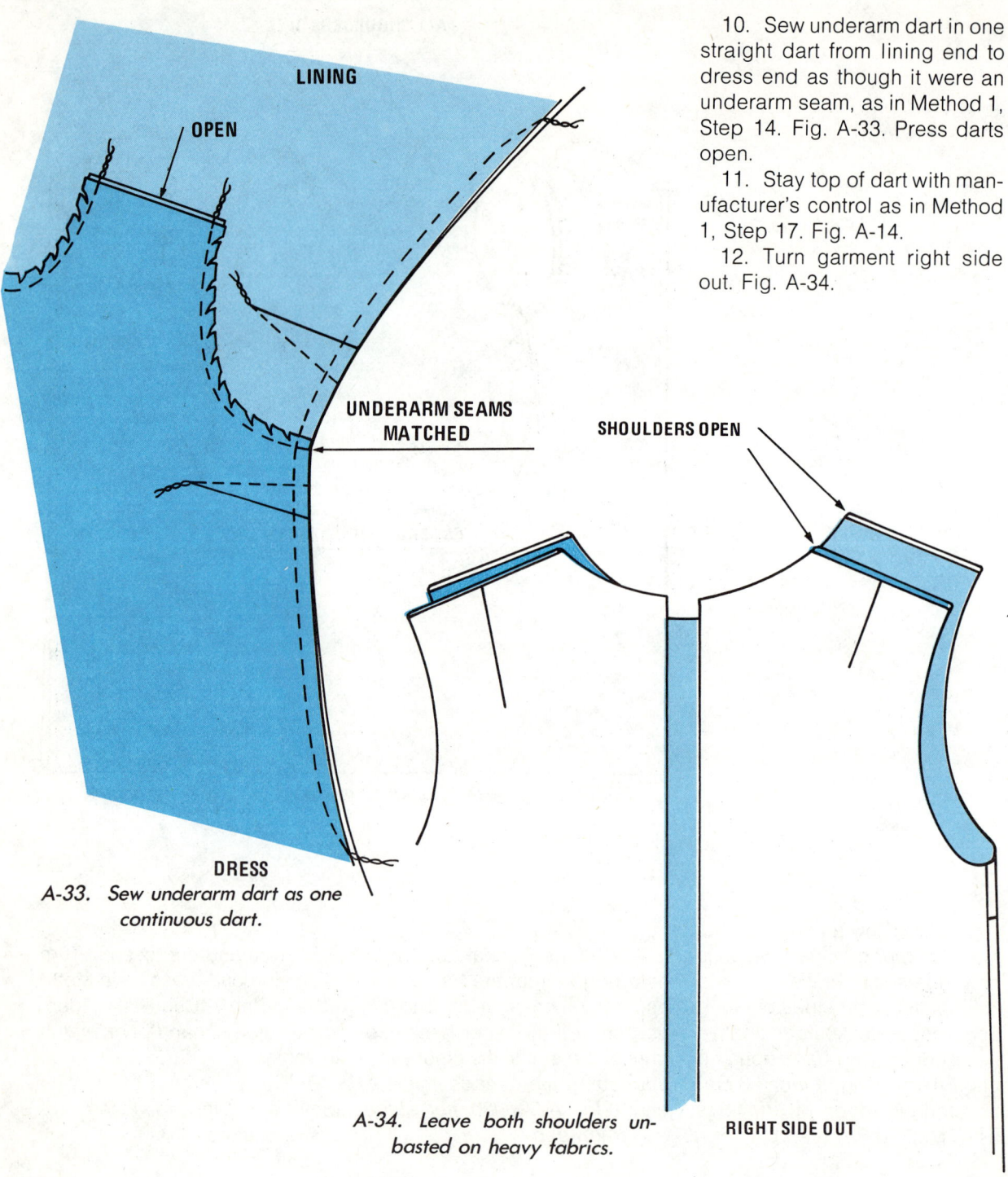

10. Sew underarm dart in one straight dart from lining end to dress end as though it were an underarm seam, as in Method 1, Step 14. Fig. A-33. Press darts open.

11. Stay top of dart with manufacturer's control as in Method 1, Step 17. Fig. A-14.

12. Turn garment right side out. Fig. A-34.

A-33. Sew underarm dart as one continuous dart.

A-34. Leave both shoulders unbasted on heavy fabrics.

## Ch. 6: Commercial Sewing Methods

13A. Shoulders may be finished as in Method 3A, Steps 9, 10, and 11, or as described below.

13B. To make dresses with wide shoulders, drop shoulders, or heavy material, the shoulder seam may be put together as follows: *Do not* sew back lining and dress shoulder edges together as in Version A, Step 7. Hold front shoulder against back shoulder with hand. On front right side, slip hand between lining and dress shoulder edges. Grasp the two lining edges and the back dress edge. Fig. A-35. Pull the garment wrong side out. The four shoulder edges should be together on each side. Now, with the two linings right sides together, and the two dress edges right sides together, carefully match the neck and armhole seams. Put armhole seams exactly together. Pin. Put neck seams exactly together. Pin. Turn armhole and neck seams toward lining side. You should have a circle of fabric. On the *inside* of the circle, start stitching so that the rest of the circle is on top where you can see it and keep it away from the needle. Fig. A-36. Sew completely around the circle. *Keep the neck and armhole seams together.* If necessary, stitch over pins.

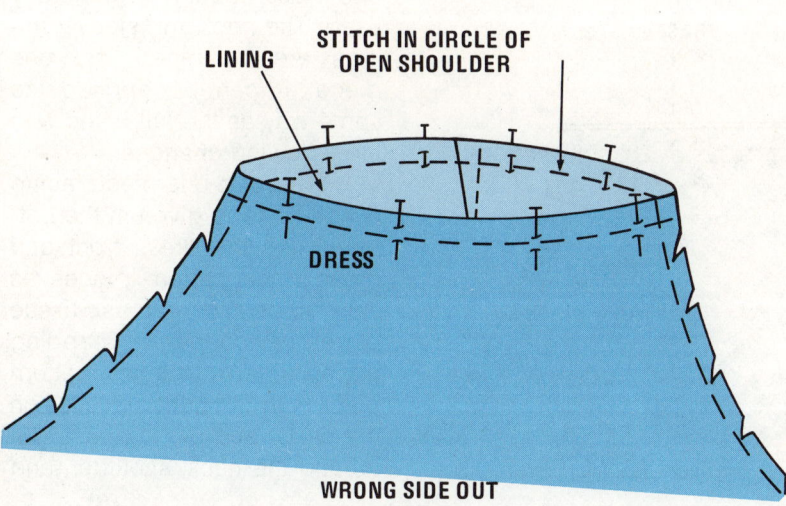

A-35. Reach inside dress front and pull garment wrong side out.

A-36. Sew shoulder in a circle.

## Altering Ready-To-Wear Fashions

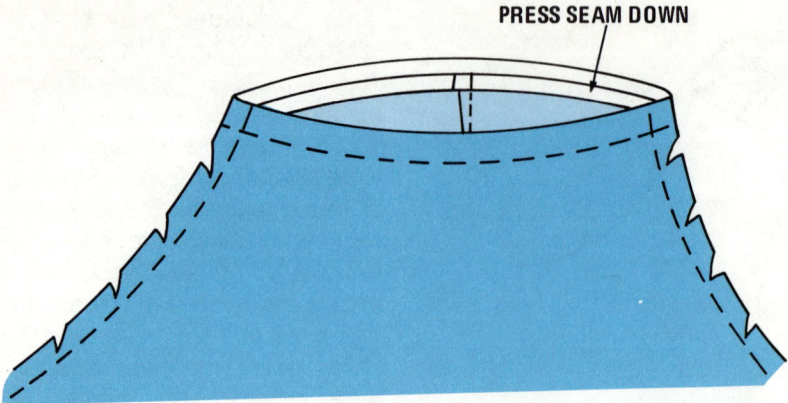

A-37. Press dress side of new seam down into the shoulder area.

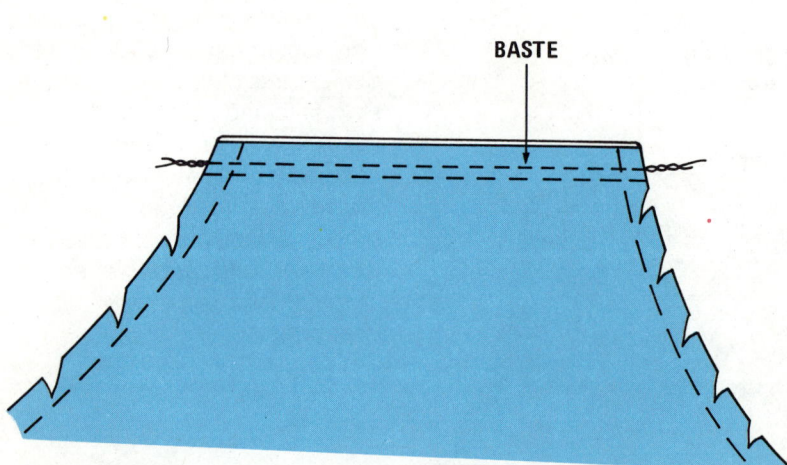

A-38. Machine baste next to original shoulder seam.

14. Using a point presser or dowel stick, press the shoulder seams open. Fig. A-37.

15. Stay this seam so it will not slip out of place during wearing or washing. To stay the seam, tuck one side of the new seam down into the shoulder. Holding the other two edges together (one lining and one dress seam), machine baste along the length of the shoulder seam right next to the original seamline. Do not back stitch or tie the threads at either end. Repeat process on other shoulder. Fig. A-38.

### VARIATIONS
### One Piece Facings
### Fig. A-39

These variations may be used with Method 1, Method 2, or Method 3.

Many garments do not need a full lining but need only some kind of facing or edge finish. With sleeveless garments, a one-piece facing is generally used. The neck and sleeve facings are combined into one piece. It can be applied the same way as the full lining with the following changes:

1. To cut a one-piece facing (when none is given in the pattern), use the dress front and dress back pattern pieces as your guide. You can use tissue paper, newspaper, or wrapping paper to make your new pattern piece. Lay the pattern pieces on the paper and pin in place. Cut around the neck, shoulder, and

## Ch. 6: Commercial Sewing Methods

A-39. One-piece facing. Photo by Minerva Wagner

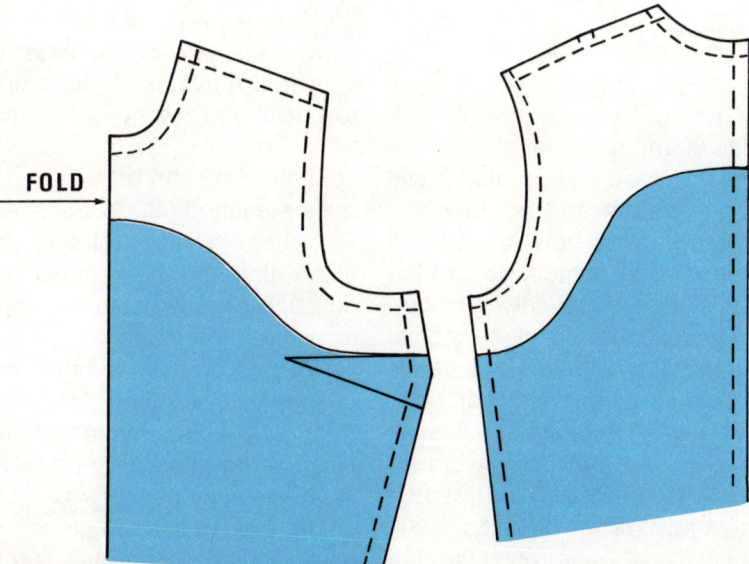

A-40. Shape of one-piece facings. When interfacings are used, they would be sewn to the garment as shown here.

armhole edges the same as the pattern piece. Then remove the pattern. To determine how deep or wide the facing should be, look for the top edge clip of the bust dart. Start cutting across the bottom of the front from that point. Cut straight in for at least an inch (2.54 cm). Then start curving upward so that the facing will clear the bust area of the garment in the front. Fig. A-40. For the back, cut the facing to come about 1 inch above the bottom of the shoulder blades. Keep it the same width at the underarm as the front piece. Always cut in straight for at least an inch at the side seam edge.

2. To cut down on bulk in the facing, ease the back shoulder edge with a slightly gathered ease-stitch line rather than putting in the dart.

3. If you are using either Method 1 or Method 2, chain sew the shoulder seams of the facings together, keeping the back or eased side up so you can be sure you are keeping it smooth. Stitch close to the ease-stitching. Chain sew the dress shoulder seams. Press open all the shoulder seams.

4. Finish the bottom edges of the facing with a line of stitching, lace, or clean-finish, depending upon the type of fabric used. To clean-finish the edge, place facing right side up under presser foot. Turn under 1/4 inch (.6 cm) along the bottom edge. Stitch close to the folded edge all the way around the bottom of

### Altering Ready-To-Wear Fashions

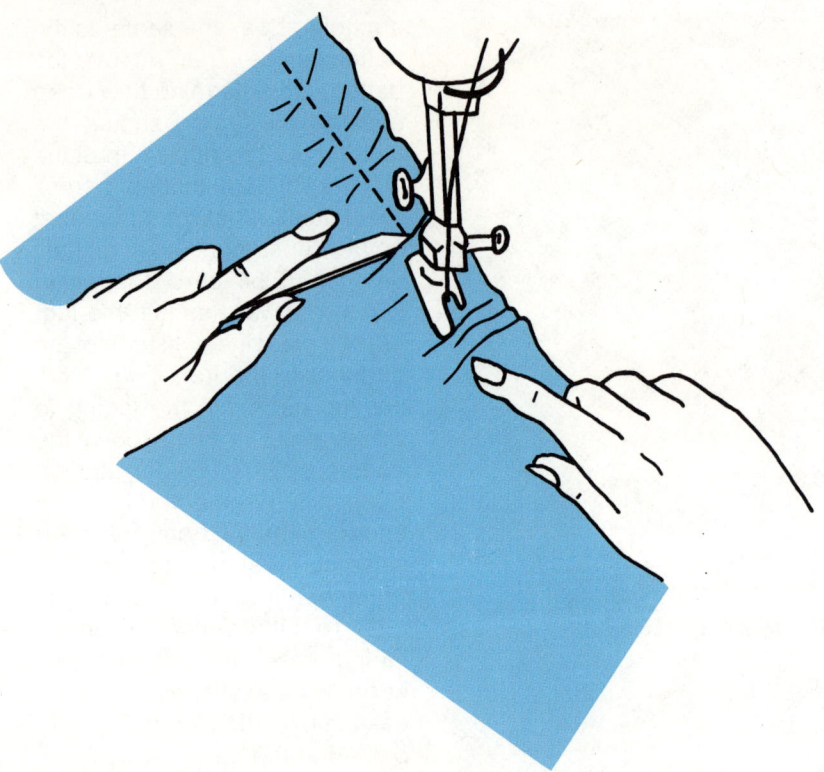

*A-41. Ease-stitching.*

the facing. The machine bed will hold the folded fabric in place for you. It is not necessary to pin or press the edge in place.

5. Apply to dress according to the directions given for the full lining at neck and armhole in each method. Method 1, Steps 8 and 9 or Method 2, Steps 5, 9, and 10.

#### Dresses with Sleeves

Alterationists often have to remove and reset sleeves to change a shoulder line. A sleeve cap must have extra fullness or ease in it so that it will hang straight and not bind the arm. Knowing how to attach a sleeve to a garment so that the cap fullness is evenly distributed across the top of the sleeve without any wrinkles or tucks is one mark of professional work. In fact, puckered sleeves scream loudly that they were set in by an amateur. Study ready-to-wear garments—you will never find lines of gathering stitches across the top of a sleeve unless it is meant to be a puffed sleeve. If there is a control stitching at all, it is the kind of ease stitching described below.

The purpose of *ease-stitching* is to force more yarns of the fabric into each machine stitch than would normally be fed by the feed dog. It is used where a slightly longer part needs to be joined to a shorter part, as in sleeves, waistlines, bustlines, and flared hems.

To ease-stitch, push the fabric toward the presser foot from both behind and in front of the foot as you stitch. Also press the blades of your scissors or the end of a metal measuring gauge against the bed of the machine at the back of the presser foot *on top of the fabric*. This keeps the material from feeding through freely. Be careful not to damage the fabric with the scissors. Now, using the index finger of your free hand, push the fabric toward the presser foot from the front. Fig. A-41. The material will "bunch up" as the needle makes each stitch. About every 2 inches (5 cm), release the material being held down behind the presser foot so it does not gather too much.

Practice on a scrap of material until you can feed the fabric through so you achieve a slightly gathered effect with no tucks or pleats stitched in.

This type of stitching is sometimes called "off-grain" stitching and works best on seams that are not straight grain.

**Ch. 6: Commercial Sewing Methods**

### A Fully Lined Dress with Sleeves. Fig. A-42

Certain materials need a full lining to protect either the wearer or the garment. Some fabrics might irritate the wearer's skin, such as scratchy wools or metallics. Colors sometimes rub off on the skin or undergarments. Materials ravel or shed pile. All of these problems can be minimized by attaching a full lining.

Manufacturers frequently use a flat method of setting sleeves into less expensive clothes. This same method makes it easier to make a fully lined garment with sleeves.

To learn this trick, follow these steps:

1. Prepare the dress and lining, following the steps used for the sleeveless samples in Method 1, Steps 1-6. *Do not join the lining to the dress.* In addition, cut sleeves from the lining and dress fabric. Clip mark the sleeves with a small clip at the top of the cap where it will join the shoulder seam. Mark the sleeve, dress front, and dress back with small clips where the sleeve will join the dress.

2. Ease-stitch across the sleeve caps of all four sleeves—2 lining, 2 dress.

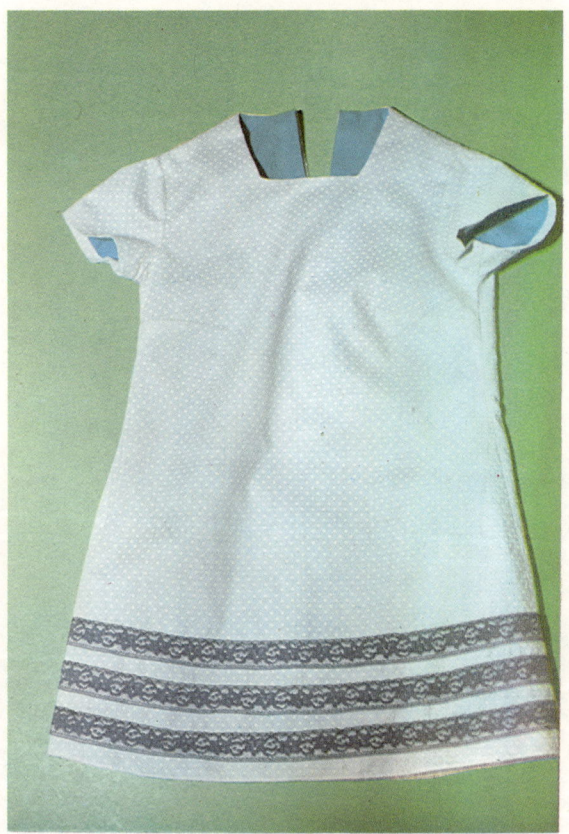

Photo by Minerva Wagner

*A-42. Mini-garment with sleeves. Sleeves may be added to any of the three methods.*

117

## Altering Ready-To-Wear Fashions

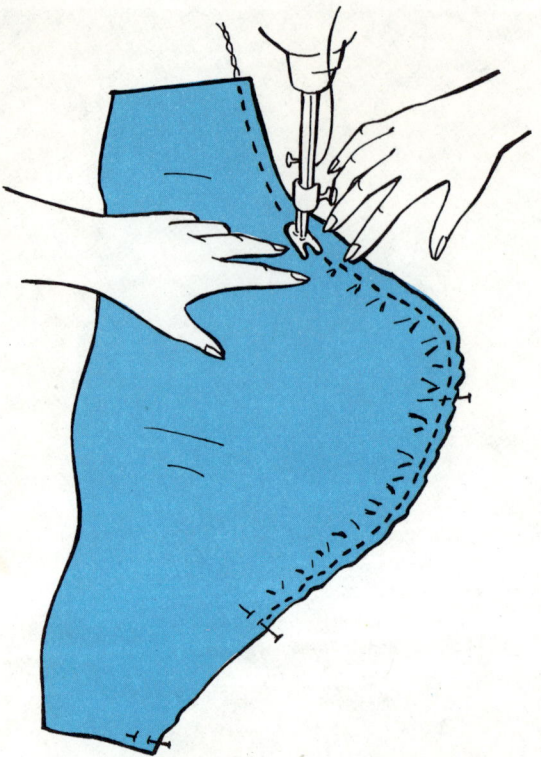

*A-43. Attaching sleeves by the flat method.*

3. Pin sleeves to dress and lining with as few pins as possible. One pin where the clip in the top of the sleeve matches the shoulder seam, one pin at the front sleeve clip, and perhaps one in each end of the sleeve should be enough.

4. As you chain sew the sleeves into the armholes, stretch the fabric smooth horizontally with your fingers where the fabric goes under the presser foot. Hold the fabric tight with the index and middle fingers of each hand. Keep two fingers on the seam allowance and two on the sleeve cap. Fig. A-43.

NOTE: For neatness, comfort, and strength, ready-to-wear dresses usually have a second line of stitching around the armhole. This stitching is 1/4 inch (.6 cm) toward the raw edge from the first seam. Seam allowances are then trimmed close to the second stitching. After trimming, *do not* clip the seam. *On a standard-size garment, check fit of sleeve before trimming.*

7. Trim 1/8 inch (.3 cm) from bottom of lining sleeve edges.

8. Place lining on garment, right sides together. Match and pin shoulder seams and center front or back (whichever was placed on the fold as you cut out your sample).

9. Stitch just around the neck edges. *Do not* stitch down the sides of the open seam as you did in your Method 1 sample. That finish is not always desirable or necessary. Trim and clip seam.

10. Stitch bottom edge of lining sleeves to bottom edge of dress sleeves, keeping edges even. Press bottom of sleeves toward the lining. *Do not stitch underarm or side seams.*

11. Turn garment right side out as in Method 1, Step 12.

12. Finish lower part of back or front seam from the clip down as you did in Method 1, Step 13. You could now insert a zipper by the centered method if you were using this method on a full-sized dress. Apply zipper to outer garment and hand sew lining to back of zipper. See zippers in Chapter 11.

13. Pin front lining to back lining, front dress to back dress at underarm, right sides together. Pin dress underarm seams toward the sleeve. Pin lining underarm seams toward sleeve. Pin bottom of sleeve seam toward lining. Stitch from bottom of lining to dress bottom across underarm seams in one long seam. Keep seam allowance

## Ch. 6: Commercial Sewing Methods

even. Sleeves may be applied in this manner in Method 2, using the "rolling" technique described in Steps 9A and 9B. Instead of stitching the armhole edges together, you would stitch the bottom of the sleeves to the bottom of the sleeve lining.

### Underlinings, Fig. A-44

Many garments are made with an extra fabric on the inside of the entire garment that looks much like a lining. This fabric is called an underlining. An underlining is cut the same as the dress but is sewn to each piece of the garment separately. Then the two fabrics are handled as one piece of material. Lining differs from underlining in that a lining hangs free of the outer garment.

Underlinings are used in dress manufacturing when extra body or stiffness is needed in the fabric, when the fabric may stretch, or when the fabric is easy to see through. Seams and hems can be hidden better with an underlining added. Sometimes underlinings are added just to change the appearance of the outer fabric, as when satin is used to underline chiffon.

The choice of underlining fabric depends upon the effect desired, the purpose for which it is used, and the kind of material used for the garment.

Make another mini sample to practice the manufacturer's methods for speed and control

Photo by Minerva Wagner

A-44. An underlined garment with one-piece facing.

in underlinings. This will help you understand how and why each step is done. As you move darts in altering a ready-made garment, you will know why you must remove the stitching used to mark and control the original dart on the underlining.

To apply the underlining, follow these steps:

1. Cut and clip the pieces exactly the same as the outer garment. Mark darts and any other pattern markings on the underlining rather than the garment fabric.

2. "Fuse" each two matching pieces together by steam pressing each underlining piece to the wrong side of the outer piece. This helps the pieces cling together and makes them easier to handle. Pin with as few pins as possible.

119

## Altering Ready-To-Wear Fashions

3. Using a medium stitch, sew the two pieces together just outside the seam line. Start at the hem edge with the underlining side up. On the front section, stitch up to 1/8 inch (.3 cm) past the lower clip of the bust dart. Stop with the needle in the fabric. Raise presser foot, turn material on the needle. Lower presser foot. Stitch slightly inside the dart line to the point of the dart. Stop, leave needle in the material at the point of the dart, raise presser foot, turn material so you will be stitching back toward the edge, lower presser foot. Continue stitching down *center fold* line of dart back to the seam line. Again, turn the material as before and continue on around the arm, across the shoulder, neck edge, shoulder and other armhole down to the second bust dart. At second dart, proceed as on the first one. The stitching this time will be just inside the top bust dart marking. Stitch to point of dart, return on center fold of dart. Continue down side to hem. Fig. A-45.

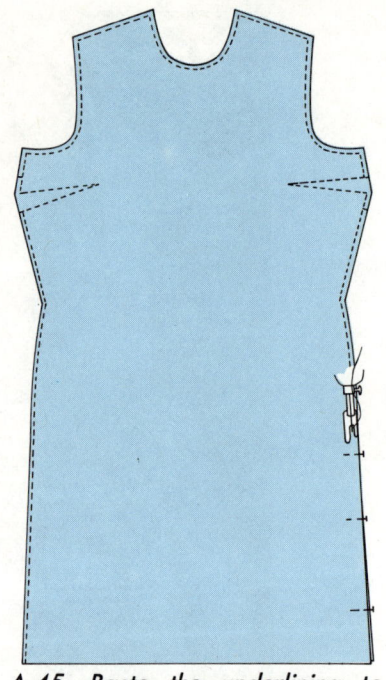

*A-45. Baste the underlining to the garment piece with one continuous line of stitching.*

4. On back pieces, again start at the bottom and stitch all the way around in one operation. With narrow shoulder darts, stitch just inside one side of dart to point (from clip) and back up inside other side of dart (to clip).

5. Stitch across the bottom of each piece last after you have again smoothed the two pieces of fabric.

6. Follow the same procedure for sleeves if they, too, are to be underlined. Many times the sleeves are not underlined, even though the rest of the garment is.

NOTE: When a garment with body darts in the waistline area is to be underlined, sew a single line of stitching through the center fold line of the dart. This will hold the two fabrics together as you make the dart. A pencil or chalk dot marking the widest part of the dart on one side only will guide you in stitching the finished dart. Fold the dart on the stitching line, pin together at the dot. With the dot side up, stitch from the sharp point at one end to the dot. Slant the material back toward the other end and continue stitching to the other sharp point. Learn to do this in one continuous operation.

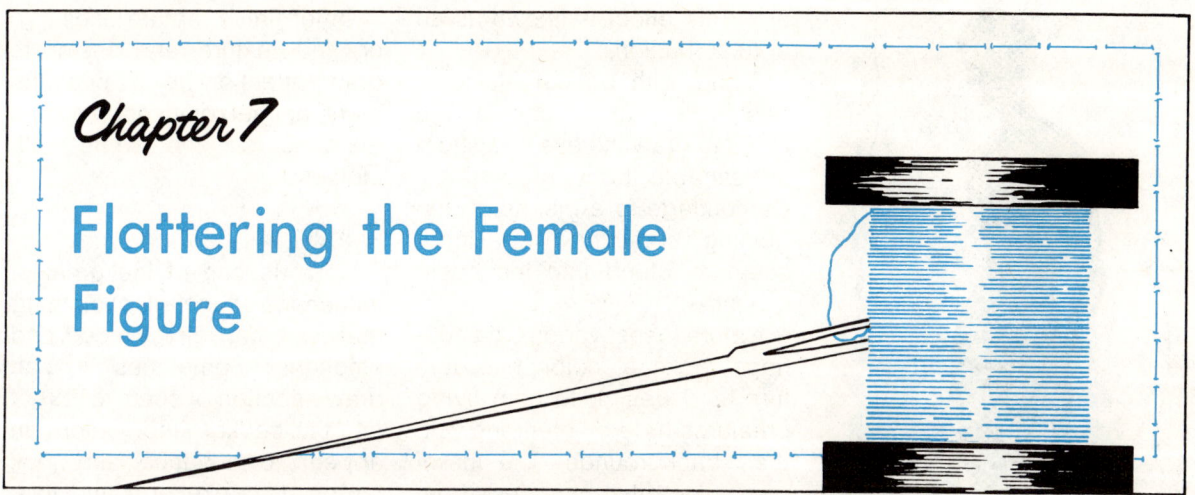

# Chapter 7

# Flattering the Female Figure

Very few female figures are perfect. Most have one or more areas that are either larger or smaller, longer or shorter than desired. One of the greatest services clothes can do, besides provide warmth and protection, is to help hide figure problems and make the most of good features. Clothing designers have been working with this principle for many years. Few of the fashion trend-setters have perfect figures. It is the skill and "know-how" of the designers they patronize that make them look so perfect.

## BODY PROPORTIONS

Body proportions involve length as well as width. Ideal proportions are considered to have two-fifths of the total height from the top of the head to the waist. Three-fifths of the height should be from the waist down. Half of the total length should come at the hipline. The top quarter comes to the underarm line. The bottom quarter is from the knees down. See illustration on page 122.

The ideal female figure is one that is well proportioned all over. Since people vary so much in height and bone structure, it is nearly impossible to give a set of measurements for an ideal figure.

In general, the figure that measures nearly the same in the bust and hips and is approximately ten inches smaller in the waist, is well-proportioned. Of course, an overweight woman with these proportions would have measurements too large for her height and bone structure. Another figure could be too slim all over.

## SELECTING CLOTHES

As a fitter and alterationist, you may be asked by your customer for an opinion on whether or not a garment is right for her. To help her, you will need to know the effects of lines, colors, textures, and designs on the overall appearance. You may already be aware of what looks best on you. However, review this chapter with an idea of learning how to apply these principles to your customers. Then you can help them to make wise choices of fitting, alteration, and accessory changes which will help enhance their appearance.

### Creating Optical Illusions and Camouflage

The human eye can be tricked into seeing things quite differently from the way they actually

### Altering Ready-To-Wear Fashions

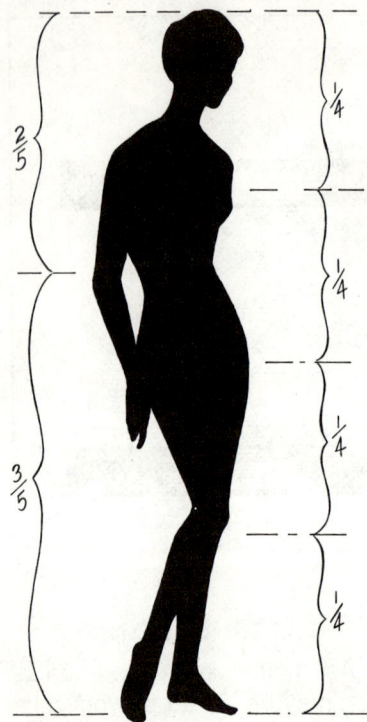

*Pleasing body proportions.*

are. This effect is known as an optical illusion.

Along with optical illusions, designers use camouflage tricks to draw the eye away from undesirable body proportions. Camouflage is a means of disguising something by making it seem to blend into the background.

Nature uses various camouflage tricks of color, line, texture, and design to help living creatures hide by blending with their backgrounds. The fur of some rabbits changes from brown in the summer to white in the winter. Thus, the rabbit blends with the forest and brush in the summer and with the snow in the winter. An enemy may look so much like the plants it lives among that an unwary victim may not see it.

Other times, nature uses color, line, texture, and design to draw attention to a beautiful plant, animal, or insect. You can learn to do the same with clothes.

### COLOR

Color is one of the greatest influences on the effect clothing makes. It can affect mood and emotions. Sometimes it can draw attention or seem to retreat into the background. Color can appear to advance and look larger. It can recede and look smaller and farther away.

Colors can be divided into different categories to help you remember what effect you can expect for each group. Bright reds, yellows, and oranges—the colors of flames, fire, and sunlight—are *warm* or *advancing*

John Meaders
*Nature uses clever camouflage to help her creatures blend into their surroundings so they will be less easily seen. Selecting clothing carefully can do the same thing for human figure problems.*

colors. They usually look and seem warmer, brighter, and larger. Blues, greens, and purples—colors of water, trees, grass, and mountain shadows—are cool or receding colors. They look calmer, cooler, and are less conspicuous.

Colors also vary in brightness and lightness or darkness. *Tints* of colors are made by adding white to the pure color. The more white a color has added to it, the lighter it will be. *Shades* of colors are made by adding black to the pure color. The more black added, the darker the shade will be.

White, bright, and light colors reflect light and appear nearer and larger. Black, dull, and dark colors absorb light and appear farther away or smaller. They also outline the body and can emphasize body contours.

If you wish to make a figure or part of it look smaller, use black, dull, or receding colors. On the other hand, if you wish to enlarge or draw attention to a figure or part of it, use white, bright, light, or warm colors.

For example, a woman with narrow shoulders, a small bust, and large hips could help balance her proportions by wearing a dark- or dull-colored skirt or pants with a bright- or light-colored blouse or jacket. A woman with a generally heavy figure but a pretty face could make her figure look more slender by wearing darker and grayed colors. She could draw attention to her pretty face by wearing a white or brightly colored scarf, collar, or necklace.

In general, concentrate on bright, light, and warm colors on areas to be emphasized. Use dark, dull, and cool colors on areas to be hidden.

Often, the rules for using color in clothing emphasize the colors each type of person— blonde, brunette, redhead—can or cannot wear. In reality, almost everyone can wear every color. It is just a matter of finding the right shade or tint of that color.

*Notice how the bright, clear, warm yellow of the blouse on the left stands out in sharp contrast to the pale tint of cool blue in the blouse on the right.*

Sears, Roebuck and Co.

The color of the skin is more important than the color of the hair or eyes in choosing colors that are becoming. People change hair color and even use colored contact lenses to brighten the color of their eyes. Skin tones, too, can be changed by sun tan, different shades and types of make-up, or age. Skin constantly reflects the colors of the clothes worn near it.

Learn to experiment with color. Don't confine yourself to any one group of colors. Learn to enjoy and use many.

### Altering Ready-To-Wear Fashions

J. C. Penney Company

*Light colors tend to reflect light and appear nearer and larger than darker hues and shades of colors.*

Sears, Roebuck and Co.
*The width and line of the lapels on these coats add width across the shoulders. The finger-tip length would cover a bulging hip problem. Notice how the contrasting scarf draws attention to the model's pretty face. The buttons form vertical lines and tend to draw the eyes to the center of the figure rather than to the outer edges.*

**Ch. 7: Flattering the Female Figure**

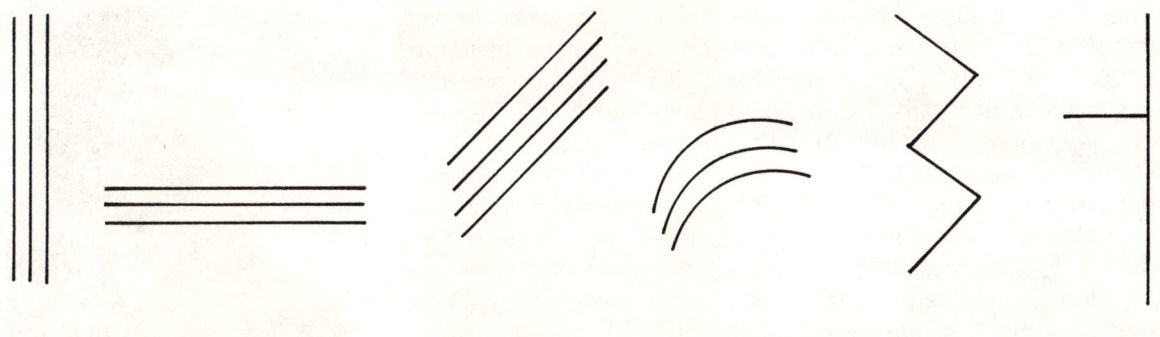

Vertical  Horizontal  Diagonal  Curved  Zigzag  Perpendicular

Lines are basic elements of all designs. They help create optical illusions as well as moods. Notice how your eye follows the direction the lines take.

Remember though, colors look different in different kinds of light. If you are helping to select a garment to be worn in daylight or bright sunlight, be sure to check it in bright daylight. If it is a garment to be worn in artificial light, check it in that light. That is, look at the person with the color held close to the face to see how it affects the complexion. Use the kind of light in which the garment will usually be worn.

Look closely at the skin. Does it look too white, too pink, too yellow, or too ash grey? Then try another color or another shade or tint of the color you had. Does it make the skin look attractive? If so, that could be a good color for the individual.

Practice this with all your own clothing. Observe your friends in the colors they wear. Notice people on the streets as you do your shopping. Become aware of the effect colors have on the overall appearance of the person wearing them, especially on the skin, hair, and eyes. What part of the figure do the colors draw your attention to? Does the color enhance or detract from the overall appearance of the wearer?

As you become more conscious of the use of color, you will probably become more aware of the effect it has on individual appearance. Thus you can help yourself and your customers in making wise color choices.

Sears, Roebuck and Co.

*Many people can wear colors they didn't think would be flattering. Wearing white or a becoming scarf or collar next to the face helps to make most colors wearable with many different skin tones.*

## LINE

Lines in clothing can also create mood and optical illusions.

Lines divide space into separate parts. They form outlines, give direction, connect parts, and suggest movement.

125

## Altering Ready-To-Wear Fashions

The most common lines are *vertical* or up and down, and *horizontal* or crosswise. Two other common lines are *curved* and *diagonal* or slanting. All other lines are created by combinations of these four.

In clothing, some lines are essential to the construction of the garment and are called *structural*. Other lines are purely for the sake of decoration and are called *decorative*.

The outline of a body is called the *silhouette*. When you look at a figure with a bright light behind it so you see only the outside lines you are seeing the silhouette.

In clothing, the silhouette is formed by structural lines. The shape and length of the skirt or pants, the line of the shoulders, the sleeves, and the waistline all contribute. Fashion silhouettes change from time to time from full, rounded lines to slim, body-hugging lines. The overall silhouette can conceal many body irregularities or call attention to body assets.

Vertical lines carry the eye up and down the body and give an impression of height and slimness. They can give a feeling of dignity. Structural vertical lines in clothes are created by straight silhouettes, darts, panels, seam lines, long straight sleeves, and slim pants. Decorative vertical lines can be formed by rows of buttons or trimmings, up and down stripes, and the use of all one color.

Horizontal lines carry the eye back and forth across the figure. They give the impression of width and can make the body look heavier and shorter. These lines also give the feeling of ease or rest since people associate them with lying down. Structural horizontal lines are formed by full skirts, cape or puffed sleeves, wide belts and cummerbunds, yokes, peplums, tunics, square or straight necklines, contrasting belts, wide collars, and midriffs. Decorative horizontal lines may be created by wide vertical or horizontal stripes, constrasting-color sleeves, cuffs, trimming lines, and pockets or flaps.

Diagonal or slanted lines usually carry the eye up or down and give an effect similar to vertical lines. However, they seem to be softer and less severe than purely vertical lines. The more slanted the diagonal is, the more nearly horizontal it becomes. The effect then is more broadening.

Curved lines are graceful and soft and add a more feminine look to clothes. Most clothes look better with a combination of curved and straight lines. Curved lines appear in round necklines, rounded collars, full skirts, scallops, and trimming lines.

Few clothes are designed with only one type of line. Most designs employ a combination of two or more kinds of lines with one being dominant. Combina-

J. C. Penney Company

*Vertical lines in clothes come in many forms. Sometimes they may be created by buttons or closings or simply by the fabric design itself.*

tions of lines can create definite optical illusions, as shown on page 127. Notice how added horizontal lines tend to shorten the effect of the vertical lines.

The neckline of a garment also creates an effect in the overall picture. It can flatter the face as well as the figure.

An oval face can usually wear any kind of neckline.

Ch. 7: Flattering the Female Figure

Sears, Roebuck and Co.

Diagonal lines may be structural, as in this wrap-around sweater knit dress. The longer the diagonal, the more vertical the effect of the line.

J. C. Penney Company

Horizontal lines may be created by fabric designs, as in the color bands in this skirt, or by the use of contrasting colors in the bodice and the skirt. They may also be created by structural parts such as the shape of the collar, a belt, or gathers in a skirt.

J. C. Penney Company

Curved lines are usually considered to be softer and more feminine than other lines. They are usually used in combination with straight lines. The collar line on this dress creates a zigzag line rather than repeating the curve of the edge of the peplum.

Most clothes have a combination of several different kinds of lines.

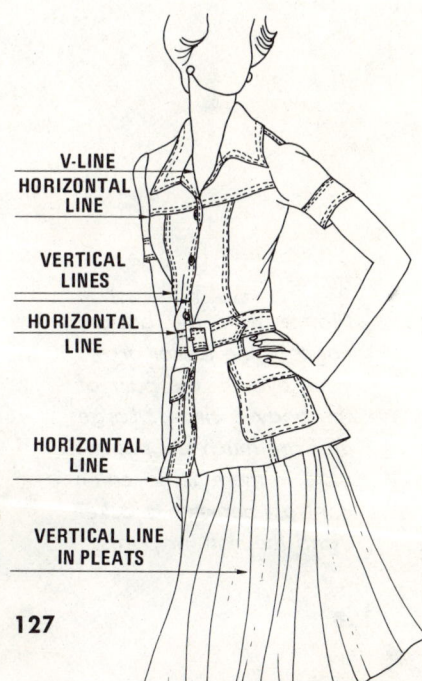

127

**Altering Ready-To-Wear Fashions**

J. C. Penney Company

Sears, Roebuck and Co.

*Long oval or rounded necklines add length and make a round face look longer. V-necklines create lines that can be very flattering to a round, full face.*

Sears, Roebuck and Co.

*Notice how the bottom edge of the jacket draws your eye to the part of the body it circles. Large hips are much less noticeable if there is no color contrast between a jacket and the skirt or pants.*

Sears, Roebuck and Co.
*Shiny textures like leather or vinyl reflect light and emphasize the curves they cover.*

A round face looks longer and less round when a long oval or V-neckline is worn. Sometimes a woman prefers to keep her neck covered but would still like to have her face appear longer and less rounded. Long necklaces or lapel lines could be used to introduce the longer lines.

Rounded necklines or high, choker-type jewelry tend to emphasize the round lines and make the neck appear thicker and the face rounder. The same illusions work in reverse for the long, too-thin face. Rounded, high necklines cut the length of the long neck and face and are more flattering. Long ovals, or V-necks, emphasize the length and are less flattering.

Study the lines in the clothes you have in your own closet. Do you see the dominant lines in each?

As you move through your daily life, observe the lines in the clothing you see on other people. Look at your customers the same way. Look through pattern books or at clothes in stores. Do horizontal lines used on the widest part of the figure give the impression of even greater width? Do you see garments that obviously make the people look much heavier than they really are? Do you see lines that make the wearers look taller and slimmer?

The dominant line catches the gaze. Thus it is possible to attract the eye to one area and at the same time, draw it away from another.

For example, a jacket hem forms a horizontal line and draws the eye to the area it encircles. If the abdomen is large, but the hips narrow, the jacket should cover the stomach. It could, however, circle the hips and draw attention to this area. When the hips are too large, a very long jacket which completely covers them and draws the eye below the hips is more flattering. Bands of contrasting colors on the bottom of a jacket add inches to the optical impression of that area.

If you understand what lines in clothes can do, it can increase your confidence in dealing with your customers.

## TEXTURE

The texture of a fabric refers to its shininess, dullness, smoothness, or roughness. The feel of the fabric or *hand* is also considered part of the texture. The *hand* can refer to the stiffness, softness, bulkiness, or crispness.

Texture is important in carrying out the intent of a designer. For example, a design that was meant for a clinging, soft fabric would look very different made

**Altering Ready-To-Wear Fashions**

Bulky textures in fabrics add width and bulk to the figure.

Padded or crisp fabrics do not mold to the figure and may add apparent size.

in a stiff, crisp fabric. Pleats that are meant to be sharply pressed would never work in a bulky, fuzzy fabric that would not stay creased.

The texture of a fabric can also create definite optical illusions for the figure. Shiny fabrics, like satin, vinyl, and taffeta, reflect light as the fabric fits over curves. Thus those curves become more noticeable. This can add width to the appearance. Dull fabrics absorb light and usually make the figure less noticeable. For this reason most people can wear dull textures better than shiny ones.

Heavy, bulky, or fuzzy fabrics seem to add to the apparent weight of the figure.

Stiff or crisp fabrics tend to stand away from the body and may give an overall impression of greater bulk. However, if used carefully, they may also help to hide figure imperfections.

J. C. Penney Company
*Large, bright-colored designs stand out and usually make the figure look larger.*

Ch. 7: Flattering the Female Figure

J. C. Penney Company
*The strong zigzag lines in the blouse fabric tend to create a horizontal movement across the body. The plain white shirt with blue pants and halter top create a more vertical impression because the eye travels up and down the figure.*

## FABRIC DESIGN

The design of the fabric can also create optical illusions in a garment. Designs may feature stripes, plaids, floral prints, geometric shapes, and natural or stylized prints.

Designs with strong vertical or horizontal movement have the same effect as vertical or horizontal lines. Indefinite outlines break up the space and can make the figure look smaller. Large or prominent design patterns usually make the figure appear larger. Designs that are "spotty" or scattered invite the eye to jump around the figure and usually seem to add pounds to the appearance.

In general, the heavy or short figure looks best in solid colors, vertical stripes, designs with curves or dots, and rather indefinite all-over designs. The more slender or well-proportioned figure can look well in horizontal stripes or movements, larger prints, and plaids.

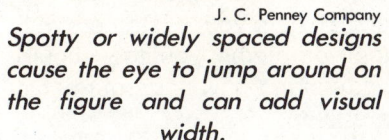

J. C. Penney Company
*Spotty or widely spaced designs cause the eye to jump around on the figure and can add visual width.*

## Altering Ready-To-Wear Fashions

*Small, all-over designs are usually easy to wear and flattering to most figure types.*

J. C. Penney Company

### Undergarments

Almost every woman has a figure problem or thinks she has. Many of these problems can be helped by wearing the right undergarments.

You may find it nearly impossible to achieve a proper fit in outer wear if bras and body shapers do not fit the customer properly. Even the most expensive garment can look out of shape if worn over improperly fitting undergarments.

Undergarment manufacturers make a wide variety of bras and body shapers. These shapers may be girdles, all-in-one foundations, panty briefs, control-top panty hose, or waist-to-calf firmers to go under pants. Every woman can find the right styles and sizes for her if she will take the time and effort to look. If bras and shapers do not give comfortable support and gentle fit, they are not right.

People usually do not buy clothes or shoes without trying them on. It is even more important to be properly fitted in undergarments. The sales personnel in lingerie, bra, and shaper departments are trained to fit various figures. They know their stock and the special purposes of each bra and body firmer. They know how to take measurements to determine the correct size and style for each figure. To help your customers with their problems, you, too, should understand how undergarments are fitted.

### BRAS

There are almost as many styles of bras as there are different body shapes. Some of the types available are: halter style: straps that cross in back to eliminate visible straps on the shoulders; strapless; cut low in front; underwired for greater support for the fuller bust; seamless to give a soft line under clinging garments. Your customer should find a style suited for her figure and the dress she plans to wear it with.

If the dress you are fitting has a low back, a low front neckline, or a cut-out shoulder line, the customer should wear the proper bra *before* you do the fitting. Then you will both be sure the bra will not show when the dress is finished.

### Finding the Proper Bra Size

To find the proper body size for a bra, measure around the rib cage directly under the bust. Add 5 inches and you will have the correct body size. If the total measurement is an uneven number, choose the next larger size. For example, if the body measures 29 inches plus 5 inches, it means the customer needs a size 34 bra. If she measures 30 inches plus 5 inches, it means she should have a 36 bra.

To find the cup size, take a second measurement over the fullest part of the bosom. This measurement indicates the cup size. If it is 1 inch more than the body size, it is a B cup. Add one cup size for each additional inch the bust exceeds the body size. The chart below is standard for most bra sizes.

Body size less than bra size . . . . . . . . . . . . . . . . . . . . . . AA cup
Body size same as bra size . . . . . . . . . . . . . . . . . . . . . . A cup
Body size 1 inch (2.5 cm) more than bra size . . . . . . . . . B cup
Body size 2 inches (5 cm) more than bra size . . . . . . . . . . C cup
Body size 3 inches (7.6 cm) more than bra size. . . . . . . . . D cup
Body size 4 inches (10 cm) more than bra size . . . . . . . . E cup
Body size 5 inches (12.7 cm) more than bra size . . . . . . . F cup

Another method of determining the body size is to take the chest measurement high up under the arms. Keep the tape straight across the shoulder blades. Use this measurement as the body size without adding anything to it.

To determine cup size using the high-chest measurement, the following chart is used.

Bust size same or less than body size. . . . . . . . . . . . . . AAA cup
Bust size ½ inch (1.3 cm) larger than body size . . . . . . . AA cup
Bust size 1 inch (2.5 cm) larger than body size . . . . . . . . . A cup
Bust size 2 inches (5 cm) larger than body size. . . . . . . . . B cup
Bust size 3 inches (7.6 cm) larger than body size . . . . . . C cup
Bust size 4 inches (10 cm) larger than body size. . . . . . . D cup
Bust size 5 inches (12.7 cm) larger than body size . . . . . DD cup
Bust size 5½ inches (14 cm) larger than body size . . . . . . F cup

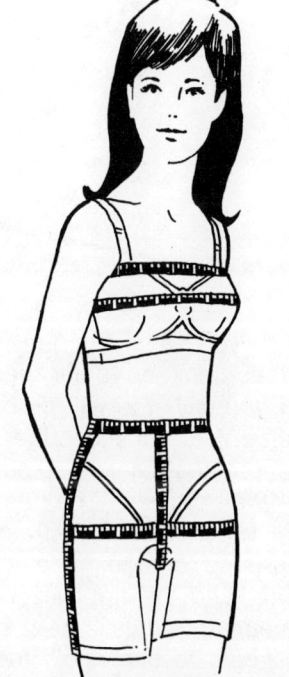

Sears, Roebuck and Co.
*Measuring for foundation garments.*

## GIRDLES

Girdles are available to control most figure problems—protruding abdomen, large hips, full thighs, or heavy waist. When you fit your customer, suggest that she wear the girdle she will usually wear with the dress. If it is apparent that the girdle does not fit properly, gently suggest to her that she wear the right kind of girdle before you do the fitting. You will both be more satisfied with results.

### Finding the Proper Girdle Size

To find the right girdle size, measure the waist, the fullest part of the hip, and the length to where you want the girdle to end.

Girdles are sized according to the waist measurement. Most of them are designed to fit hip measurements from 8 to 11 inches larger than the waist. However, this will vary with the style of the garment and with the amount of control it has. If the hips are more than 11 inches larger than the waist, a larger size may be required.

All-in-one undergarments are sold according to the bra size. Measurements for these should be taken the same as for a bra.

# Chapter 8
# Fitting Women's Clothes

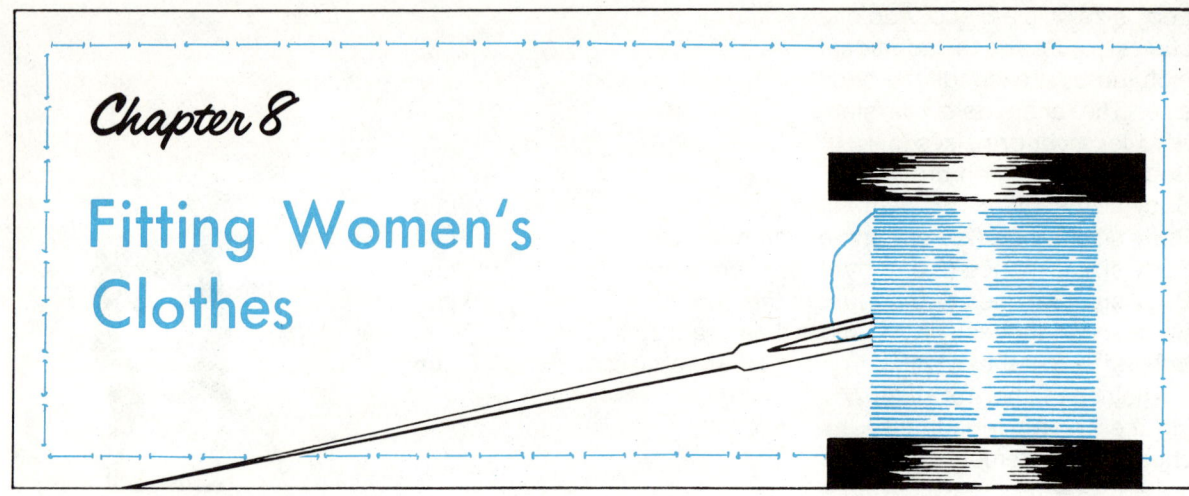

As you analyze the way clothes look on other people and yourself, you will probably realize it is not the price of a garment that makes a person look well dressed. The garment may be in fashion with good color and design, in a lovely fabric, and the right size. But, something is missing—it does not seem to be "right" for the wearer. It just doesn't fit as it should.

To look right, a well-fitted garment has:

. . . enough ease over the full parts of the body, such as the bust, hips, or stomach, so the garment hangs straight from these parts. There are no areas where the fabric pulls across the figure to distort the grain. The wearer can make all necessary movements comfortably.

. . . the grain line following the body's crosswise lines around the bust, hip, and hem.

. . . the lengthwise grain line falling straight down the center front with all other lengthwise grain lines parallel to that.

. . . waistline darts pointing toward the fullest part of the bust and ending about 1½ inches (3.8 cm) below the crown of the bust.

. . . underarm darts forming fullness in the bust area, not above or below it. The darts end about 1½ inches (3.8 cm) from the point of the bust.

. . . skirt darts shaping the fullness where needed over the hip and stomach areas. These darts end where the fullness begins.

. . . fashion lines, such as the seams in a princess style, falling true to the design. The line is not distorted by being too tight over the bust or hips.

. . . side seams falling in a straight line from the underarm. They do not pull toward the front or the back. There is no strain showing at the stitching line.

. . . center front and center back seams straight in the center. These seams do not shift or pull to either side of the body.

. . . back shoulder ease or darts—just enough to allow a flat fit over the shoulder blades.

. . . a waistline or belt line which sits right on the waist of the body. When a belt is worn, it does not slip above or below the waistline seam.

. . . the bodice meeting the waistline without bulging or blousing excessively in front or back.

. . . buttonhole closings lying smoothly without any pull or strain on either the buttons or between buttons.

. . . zippers lying flat against the body without bulging out away from it.

. . . the armhole seam lying along the line of the outside

# Ch. 8: Fitting Women's Clothes

edge of the shoulder bone. The sleeve cap rolls easily from this bone without pulling.

. . . sleeve fabric grain line falling straight in a lengthwise line from the shoulder. The crosswise grain runs in straight lines around the upper arm.

. . . full-length sleeves ending at the wrist bone with the elbow ease or elbow darts at the elbow.

. . . short sleeves or style lengths in between, such as bracelet sleeves, in proportion to the length of the arm.

. . . neckline lying flat and smooth. It does not gap or ride up the neck. If cut low in back or front, it hugs the body.

. . . collar rolling softly from the neckline and sitting well on the garment. It does not fall flat or pop up and away from the garment.

. . . hem line falling into an even line around the bottom. If skirt is circular, full, or draped, the folds fall into place in an even line.

. . . hem length suitable for the style of garment, following current fashion trends, and in proportion to the individual's body lines.

## READY-TO-WEAR SIZES

Manufacturers know their customers will be more satisfied with clothes that fit well. However, the problem is that people come in many shapes and sizes. To accommodate these variations, ladies' ready-made clothes are manufactured in many different size ranges. Even within size categories, measurements may differ from one brand of garment to another.

Size ranges are made to fit many figure types. The most common classifications are:

- *Misses sizes*—even-numbered sizes 6 through 20. Scaled for the average figure proportions of women between 5 feet 3 inches (160 cm) to 5 feet 7 inches tall (170 cm).
- *Junior sizes*—uneven-numbered sizes 3 to 15. Scaled for the shorter woman between 5 feet 2 inches (158 cm) and 5 feet 6 inches (168 cm).
- *Half sizes*—even-numbered sizes from $12\frac{1}{2}$ to $24\frac{1}{2}$. Scaled for the short, full figure with a high or short waistline and full, low bust. These clothes are for those 5 feet 4 inches (163 cm) or less.
- *Women's sizes*—even-numbered sizes 38 to 52. Scaled for a mature, heavier-proportioned figure with a full bust and long waistline. For those from 5 feet 3 inches (160 cm) to 5 feet 7 inches (170 cm).

Even within these groups, there are many who still cannot find garments to fit them. To further serve the public, these major groups have been broadened to include:

- *Petite Misses*—same even numbers as the Misses size range but with shorter waist and skirt lengths. They are scaled for shorter women with bust, waist, and hip measurements near the corresponding Misses size.
- *Tall Misses*—numbered the same as Misses sizes but with waist length and skirt lengths longer than the standard Misses size.
- *Petite Juniors*—numbered the same as the Junior sizes. Scaled for the same proportions as Junior sizes except for shorter waist and skirt lengths.

Note the measurements used for these various size ranges in the charts on pages 137, 138.

In spite of the variety of size ranges, there are still many people who cannot find a ready-made garment that will fit them. Manufacturers are constantly trying to find answers to these figure variations, but it isn't easy. The fuller-bodied garment may be fine for the full-busted figure, but it may be too large in the waist or skirt. The longer-waisted garment may fit the taller figure in the overall length of the garment—*if* she is not short waisted. The short person may want a shorter dress but find she is too long-waisted for the shorter-proportioned sizes.

Since no manufacturer can hope to meet the needs of all the possible figure variations, most of them keep their garments within the standard sizes. The individual who cannot find a size that is right for her needs to have her garments altered to fit.

## CLOTHING SIZES—METRIC CONVERSIONS

### MISSES' SIZES

| Sizes | 6 | | 8 | | 10 | | 12 | | 14 | | 16 | | 18 | | 20 | |
|---|---|---|---|---|---|---|---|---|---|---|---|---|---|---|---|---|
| | in | cm | in | cm | in | cm | in | cm | in | cm | in | cm | in | cm | in | cm |
| Bust | 30½ | 78 | 31½ | 80 | 32½ | 83 | 34 | 87 | 36 | 92 | 38 | 97 | 40 | 102 | 42 | 107 |
| Waist | 23 | 58 | 24 | 61 | 25 | 64 | 26½ | 67 | 28 | 71 | 30 | 76 | 32 | 81 | 34 | 87 |
| Hip | 32½ | 83 | 33½ | 85 | 34½ | 88 | 36 | 92 | 38 | 97 | 40 | 102 | 42 | 107 | 44 | 112 |
| BWL* | 15½ | 39.5 | 15¾ | 40 | 16 | 40.5 | 16¼ | 41.5 | 16½ | 42 | 16¾ | 42.5 | 17 | 43 | 17¼ | 44 |

### WOMEN'S SIZES

| Sizes | 38 | | 40 | | 42 | | 44 | | 46 | | 48 | | 50 | |
|---|---|---|---|---|---|---|---|---|---|---|---|---|---|---|
| | in | cm | in | cm | in | cm | in | cm | in | cm | in | cm | in | cm |
| Bust | 42 | 107 | 44 | 112 | 46 | 117 | 48 | 122 | 50 | 127 | 52 | 132 | 54 | 137 |
| Waist | 35 | 89 | 37 | 94 | 39 | 99 | 41½ | 105 | 44 | 112 | 46½ | 118 | 49 | 124 |
| Hip | 44 | 112 | 46 | 117 | 48 | 122 | 50 | 127 | 52 | 132 | 54 | 137 | 56 | 142 |
| BWL* | 17¼ | 44 | 17⅜ | 44 | 17½ | 44.5 | 17⅝ | 45 | 17¾ | 45 | 17⅞ | 45.5 | 18 | 46 |

### HALF-SIZES

| Sizes | 10½ | | 12½ | | 14½ | | 16½ | | 18½ | | 20½ | | 22½ | | 24½ | |
|---|---|---|---|---|---|---|---|---|---|---|---|---|---|---|---|---|
| | in | cm | in | cm | in | cm | in | cm | in | cm | in | cm | in | cm | in | cm |
| Bust | 33 | 84 | 35 | 89 | 37 | 94 | 39 | 99 | 41 | 104 | 43 | 109 | 45 | 114 | 47 | 119 |
| Waist | 27 | 69 | 29 | 74 | 31 | 79 | 33 | 84 | 35 | 89 | 37½ | 96 | 40 | 102 | 42½ | 108 |
| Hip | 35 | 89 | 37 | 94 | 39 | 99 | 41 | 104 | 43 | 109 | 45½ | 116 | 48 | 122 | 50½ | 128 |
| BWL* | 15 | 38 | 15¼ | 39 | 15½ | 39.5 | 15¾ | 40 | 15⅞ | 40.5 | 16 | 40.5 | 16⅛ | 41 | 16¼ | 41.5 |

### JUNIOR SIZES

| Sizes | 5 | | 7 | | 9 | | 11 | | 13 | | 15 | |
|---|---|---|---|---|---|---|---|---|---|---|---|---|
| | in | cm | in | cm | in | cm | in | cm | in | cm | in | cm |
| Bust | 30 | 76 | 31 | 79 | 32 | 81 | 33½ | 85 | 35 | 89 | 37 | 94 |
| Waist | 22½ | 57 | 23½ | 60 | 24½ | 62 | 25½ | 65 | 27 | 69 | 29 | 74 |
| Hip | 32 | 81 | 33 | 84 | 34 | 87 | 35½ | 90 | 37 | 94 | 39 | 99 |
| BWL* | 15 | 38 | 15¼ | 39 | 15½ | 39.5 | 15¾ | 40 | 16 | 40.5 | 16¼ | 41.5 |

## JUNIOR PETITE SIZES

| Sizes | 3 jp | | 5 jp | | 7 jp | | 9 jp | | 11 jp | | 13 jp | |
|---|---|---|---|---|---|---|---|---|---|---|---|---|
| | in | cm | in | cm | in | cm | in | cm | in | cm | in | cm |
| Bust | 30½ | 78 | 31 | 79 | 32 | 81 | 33 | 84 | 34 | 87 | 35 | 89 |
| Waist | 22½ | 57 | 23 | 58 | 24 | 61 | 25 | 64 | 26 | 66 | 27 | 69 |
| Hip | 31½ | 80 | 32 | 81 | 33 | 84 | 34 | 87 | 35 | 89 | 36 | 92 |
| Back waist length | 14 | 36 | 14¼ | 36.5 | 14½ | 37 | 14¾ | 37.5 | 15 | 38 | 15¼ | 39 |

## YOUNG JUNIOR/TEEN SIZES

| Sizes | 5/6 | | 7/8 | | 9/10 | | 11/12 | | 13/14 | | 15/16 | |
|---|---|---|---|---|---|---|---|---|---|---|---|---|
| | in | cm | in | cm | in | cm | in | cm | in | cm | in | cm |
| Bust | 28 | 71 | 29 | 74 | 30½ | 78 | 32 | 81 | 33½ | 85 | 35 | 89 |
| Waist | 22 | 56 | 23 | 58 | 24 | 61 | 25 | 64 | 26 | 66 | 27 | 69 |
| Hip | 31 | 79 | 32 | 81 | 33½ | 85 | 35 | 89 | 36½ | 93 | 38 | 97 |
| Back waist length | 13½ | 34 | 14 | 36 | 14½ | 37 | 15 | 38 | 15⅜ | 39 | 15¾ | 40 |

## MISS PETITE SIZES

| Sizes | 6 MP | | 8 MP | | 10 MP | | 12 MP | | 14 MP | | 16 MP | |
|---|---|---|---|---|---|---|---|---|---|---|---|---|
| | in | cm | in | cm | in | cm | in | cm | in | cm | in | cm |
| Bust | 30½ | 78 | 31½ | 80 | 32½ | 83 | 34 | 87 | 36 | 92 | 38 | 97 |
| Waist | 23½ | 60 | 24½ | 62 | 25½ | 65 | 27 | 69 | 28½ | 73 | 30½ | 78 |
| Hip | 32½ | 83 | 33½ | 85 | 34½ | 88 | 36 | 92 | 38 | 97 | 40 | 102 |
| Back waist length | 14½ | 37 | 14¾ | 37.5 | 15 | 38 | 15¼ | 39 | 15½ | 39.5 | 15¾ | 40 |

## CHUBBIE SIZES

| Sizes | 8½c | | 10½ c | | 12½ c | | 14½ c | |
|---|---|---|---|---|---|---|---|---|
| | in | cm | in | cm | in | cm | in | cm |
| Breast | 30 | 76 | 31½ | 80 | 33 | 84 | 34½ | 88 |
| Waist | 28 | 71 | 29 | 74 | 30 | 76 | 31 | 79 |
| Hip | 33 | 84 | 34½ | 88 | 36 | 92 | 37½ | 96 |
| Back waist length | 12½ | 32 | 13¼ | 34 | 14 | 36 | 14¾ | 37.5 |
| Approx. height | 52 | 132 | 56 | 142 | 58½ | 149 | 61 | 155 |

*Back waist length

*American Metric Journal*

## CLOTHING SIZES

### Chart 1—Proportioned Misses Sizes (and Junior/Misses)
For all Misses-Size Clothing. Some knit tops are excepted—read below.

Petite Misses: 5'3" or under. Average Misses: 5'3½"-5'7". Tall Misses: 5'7½"-6'.

| CHART 1 | | | | | | | | | | |
|---|---|---|---|---|---|---|---|---|---|---|
| Misses Sizes (and Junior/Misses) | If Your Bust Measures | 31-31½ | 32-32½ | 33-34 | 34½-35½ | 36-37 | 37½-38½ | 39-40½ | 41-42½ | 43-44½ | 45-46½ |
| | If Your Waist Measures | 22-22½ | 23-23½ | 24-25 | 25½-26½ | 27-28 | 28½-29½ | 30-31½ | 32-33½ | 34-35½ | 36-37½ |
| | If Your Hips Measure | 33-33½ | 34-34½ | 35-36 | 36½-37½ | 38-39 | 39½-40½ | 41-42½ | 43-44½ | 45-46½ | 47-48½ |
| | Your Size is | 6 | 8 | 10 | 12 | 14 | 16 | 18 | 20 | 22 | 24 |

### Chart 1A—Misses Knit Tops. Order by bust size, not bra size.

| CHART 1A | | | | | | | | | |
|---|---|---|---|---|---|---|---|---|---|
| Misses Knit Tops | If Your Bust Measures | 32-32½ | 33-34 | 34½-35½ | 36-37 | 37½-38½ | 39-40½ | 41-42½ | 43-44½ |
| | Your Size is | 5/6 | 7/8 | 9/10 | 11/12 | 13/14 | 15/16 | 17/18 | — | — |
| | | 28 | 30 | 32 | 34 | 36 | 38 | 40 | 42 | 44 | 46 |

### Chart 2—Proportioned Junior Sizes
For all Junior-Size Clothing.

Petite Juniors: 5'1½" or under. Average Juniors: 5'2"-5'6". Tall Juniors: 5'6½"-5'11".

| CHART 2 | | | | | | | | | | |
|---|---|---|---|---|---|---|---|---|---|---|
| Junior Sizes | If Your Bust Measures | 28½-29 | 29½-30 | 30½-31 | 31½-32 | 32½-33½ | 34-35 | 35½-36½ | 37-38 | 38½-39½ |
| | If Your Waist Measures | 19-19½ | 20-20½ | 21-21½ | 22-22½ | 23-24 | 24½-25½ | 26-27 | 27½-28½ | 29-30 |
| | If Your Hips Measure | 30½-31 | 31½-32 | 32½-33 | 33½-34 | 34½-35½ | 36-37 | 37½-38½ | 39-40 | 40½-41½ |
| | Your Size is | 1 | 3 | 5 | 7 | 9 | 11 | 13 | 15 | 17 |

### Chart 3—Half Sizes: 5'4" and under.
For all Half-Size Clothing.

| CHART 3 | | | | | | | | | |
|---|---|---|---|---|---|---|---|---|---|
| Half Sizes | If Your Bust Measures | 35-36½ | 37-38½ | 39-40½ | 41-42½ | 43-44½ | 45-46½ | 47-48½ | 49-50½ |
| | If Your Waist Measures | 27-28½ | 29-30½ | 31-32½ | 33-34½ | 35-37 | 37½-39½ | 40-42 | 42½-44½ |
| | If Your Hips Measure | 36-37½ | 38-39½ | 40-41½ | 42-43½ | 44-45½ | 46-47½ | 48-49½ | 50-51½ |
| | Your Size is | 12½ | 14½ | 16½ | 18½ | 20½ | 22½ | 24½ | 26½ |

### Chart 4—Women's Sizes: 5'4"-5'7".
For all Women's-Size Clothing EXCEPT skirts and pants.

| CHART 4 | | | | | | | | |
|---|---|---|---|---|---|---|---|---|
| Women's Sizes | If Your Bust Measures | 37-38½ | 39-40½ | 41-42½ | 43-44½ | 45-46½ | 47-48½ | 49-50½ | 51-52½ | 53-54½ | 55-56½ |
| | If Your Waist Measures | 29-30½ | 31-32½ | 33-34½ | 35-37 | 37½-39½ | 40-42 | 42½-44½ | 45-47 | 47½-49½ | 50-52 |
| | If Your Hips Measure | 38-39½ | 40-41½ | 42-43½ | 44-45½ | 46-47½ | 48-49½ | 50-51½ | 52-53½ | 54-55½ | 56-57½ |
| | Your Size is | 34 | 36 | 38 | 40 | 42 | 44 | 46 | 48 | 50 | 52 |

### Chart 4A—Women's Skirts and Pants.

| CHART 4A | | | | | | | | |
|---|---|---|---|---|---|---|---|---|
| Women's Skirts and Pants | If Your Waist Measures | 32 | 34 | 36 | 38 | 40 | 42 | 44 | 46 |
| | If Your Hip Measures | 43 | 45 | 47 | 49 | 51 | 53 | 53 | 55 |
| | Your Size is | 32 | 34 | 36 | 38 | 40 | 42 | 44 | 46 |

JCPenney

## Ch. 8: Fitting Women's Clothes

The only size range that can be said to be *average* is the Misses size. The largest number of clothes manufactured and sold in the stores falls into that group. Thus, a greater variety of styles, colors, and fabric choices are available in Misses sizes.

The measurements used for Misses sizes are the *average* for that size. Many people buy these average ready-made clothes and wear them without change. Sometimes they don't even realize their clothes do not really fit. Often, they are unhappy because something is not right but they do not know what it is. They have tried the various size ranges and proportioned sizes and have finally settled on a size they feel is theirs.

Figs. B-1a, b, c show five women who all buy a size 14 dress. In spite of the differences in heights, weights, and body proportions, these women have found a Misses size 14 is their best size.

As you can see, all the dresses need some adjustment or alteration. Study the front, side, and back views and see if you can find the places that need to be fitted and changed for each woman. Review the points listed earlier in the chapter for judging a well-fitted garment. Can you see where each woman's problems lie? Would you know how to remedy the problems?

To continue to sharpen your awareness of the way clothes fit, study fashion magazines. The clothing ads in these publications are carefully staged with the clothes fitting the models perfectly. The details are sharp so it is easy to see how the garment hangs.

It should not be long before you are *mentally fitting* the clothes on everyone you come in contact with. The awareness of the fit of garments will be your greatest asset in your new career. When you learn to see what is wrong with the fit of a garment, you can learn to correct it.

### PREPARING FOR THE FITTING

Knowing where the fitting problems exist is the first step. Next you must know how to correct them.

As with any trade, the proper working area and equipment increase efficiency. The same is true for fitting clothing. Practice your fittings in the best setup you can manage. Reread Chapter 3 on the fitting room and equipment.

### The Fitter's Tools

Fitting tools are rarely left in the fitting areas in the larger stores. They are easily mislaid and valuable time can be lost looking for them. Each fitter carries her own tools in a purse-size cosmetics case. A case measuring about 5 by 8 inches should be large enough. In your case, carry:

- Pins—make sure they are smooth, sharp, and rust-free. They may be in a box or in a pin cushion—wrist or regular.
- Tape measure—in case body measurements are necessary.
- Six-inch hem gauge—to mark long gowns.
- Pencil and small writing pad or alteration ticket—to record the details of the alterations to be done and any measurements taken. Always record the time and date the garment is to be finished or fitted again. Write the customer's name, phone number, address, and changes to be made.
- Small appointment book—again write down the date and time the garment is to be finished along with the customer's name. A careful record of garments to be finished or fitted again will help avoid confusion and customer disappointment. A quick look in one book saves going through all the individual alteration tickets on the garments to be sure everything is ready on time.
- In addition, carry a hem marker or yardstick for pin-fitting hemlines on street-length garments.

### READY, SET, GO

Now that you have your fitting space and fitting tools organized, you are ready to practice fitting. To help you build confidence and good fitting habits, ask your family, friends, or classmates to be customers or models.

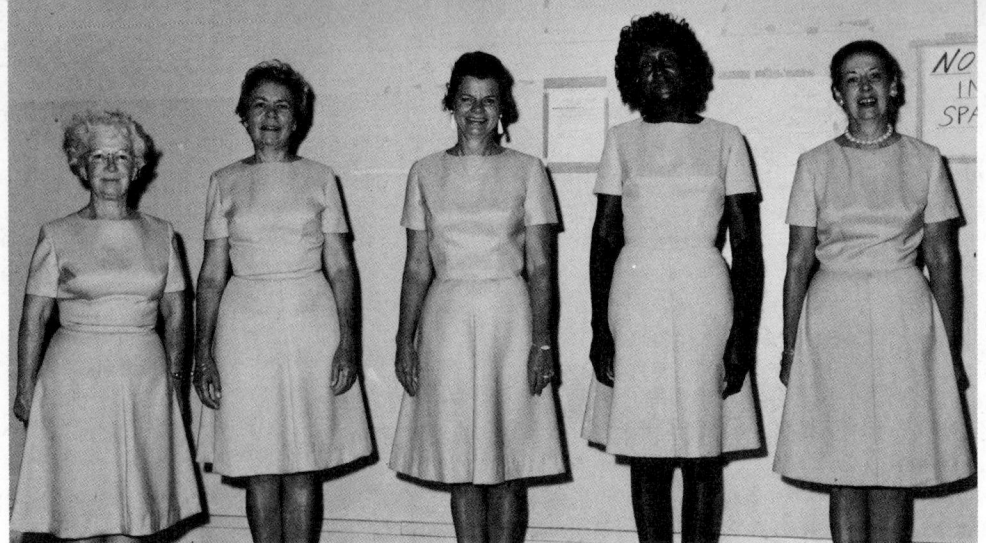

Photos by Dorothy Loudy taken in workshop given by Kitty Rotruck

B-1a, b, c. These five women are all wearing the same size 14 dress. Note the differences in height and body proportions. Can you see where each woman's garment needs to be altered so the dress will fit her own figure? Would you know what to do?

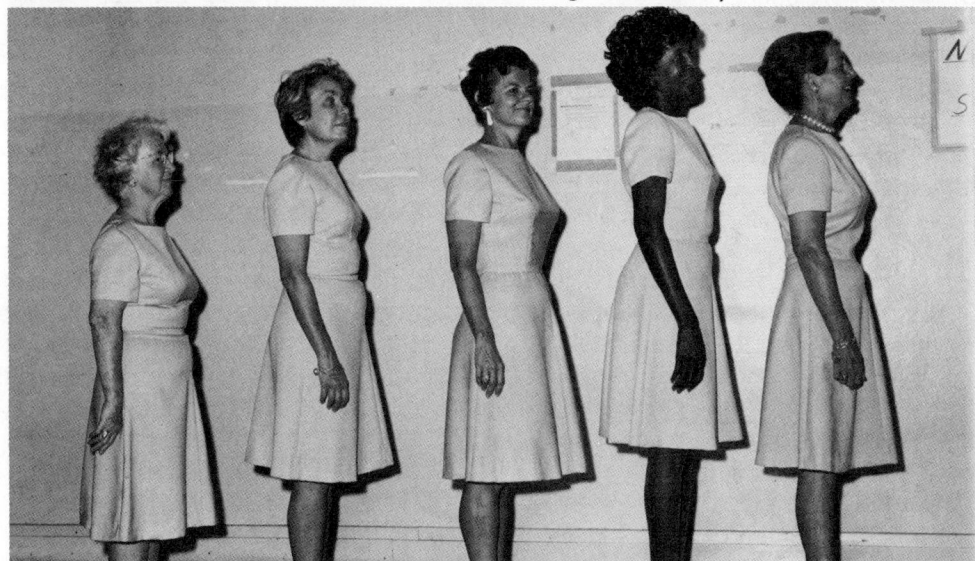

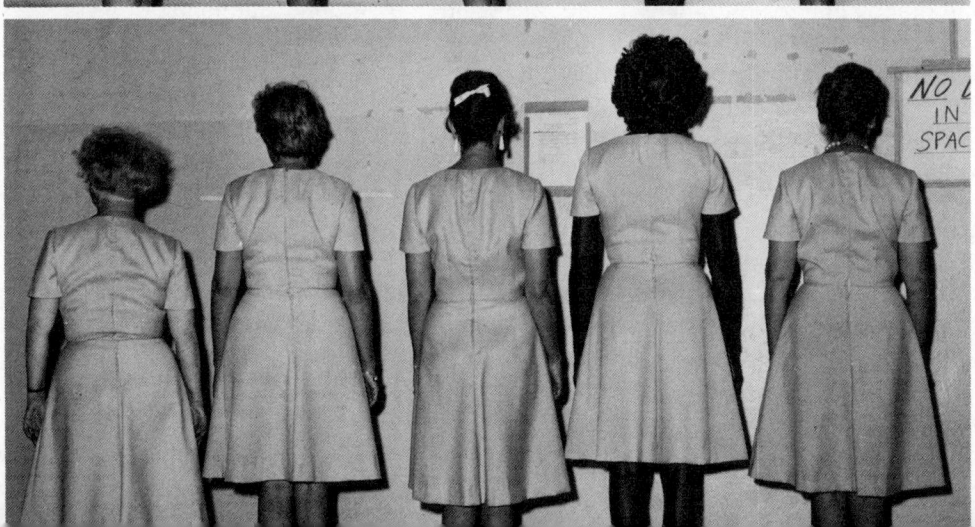

Be businesslike and professional with them and use the following fitting steps:

- Garments should always be tried on right side out for several reasons. Needed alterations are easier to determine. Many people have figure problems that may differ from one side of the body to the other. Also, it is easier to get an idea of how the garment will look when it is altered.
- If the garment has a belt, it should be placed and fastened as the customer will wear it. If a sash or scarf is part of the garment, it should be tied or adjusted in position.
- All garment openings should be closed before fitting—all buttonholes buttoned, zippers zipped, and hooks, eyes, and snaps fastened. As the fitter, you should do this for your customer. When the fitting is over, you should help her unfasten and step out of the garment.
- Check to be sure the garment neckline and shoulders are sitting properly on the neck and shoulders. Many people have a habit of pulling their clothes too far forward or back. This is especially true with coats and jackets.
- When the garment is adjusted on the client, stand back and study the changes to be made. Check *in this order*: neckline, shoulders, bodice, waistline, hips, skirt lines, and hems. If any changes are to be made, start pinning from the top down. For instance, if the neckline is to be changed or the shoulders are to be raised or shortened, start there. Then, check the bodice and so on. This is a logical order for pinning. What you do at the top affects the next part of the garment and determines how it is to be changed. The hem length and sleeve adjustments are pinned last. If a drastic change in the body of the garment has been made in the fitting, it may even be wise to pin the hem length after the other alterations have been made permanently.
- Only the changes absolutely necessary for the comfort and fashionable appearance of the customer should be suggested. Avoid overfitting. If the client requests only a hem fitting and is happy and comfortable in her garment, do not suggest other changes. She may resent the advice, or, may not want to pay for extra work. You must know your customer well or she must indicate she may need more than a hem adjustment before you suggest extra work.
- As mentioned in Chapter 7, a pin fitting is more successful if the customer is wearing the right size and style of undergarment for the particular garment being fitted. This is especially true with clothes that have low-cut bodices or that cling to the figure. Different styles require different figure controls. Many customers may not know what kinds of undergarments they need, or what kinds are available.
- The same kind and height of heels the customer plans to wear with the garment should be worn for the fitting. The effects of flat heels or 3-inch-high heels can be very different in determining the hem length. Often, shops keep sandals with many heel heights on hand to be used for fittings. If you are fitting in your own home, try to offer this service. If shoes are not available, do not make an issue of it. Just go ahead and fit.

Remember, practicing on garments for family and friends will help you know whether

B-1d, e. Note the difference in the appearance of this woman before (B-1d) and after (B-1e) her dress was properly fitted and altered.

## Altering Ready-To-Wear Fashions

you are fitting correctly. Pages 134, 135 discussed how to recognize the fitting problems. Soon you are going to learn how to pin them and describe them for your records. In Chapter 9, you will learn how to *do* the alterations.

### Measuring for Garment Fit

Usually, pin fittings for the garment a customer is wearing do not require taking measurements. However, in some situations, having the customers' measurements will aid you. Learning and practicing to take proper measurements now will help you to understand what makes clothes fit well.

Only one or two basic measurements for a particular garment are usually required for most fittings. They serve as a guide or a means of double-checking the finished alteration. It is, however, good practice to have a record of the measurements for regular clients. Often a steady customer will want a style that is not in stock in her size. The sales person may persuade her to buy the next larger or smaller size. Much fitting time is saved if you can make the necessary changes from her measurements before the first fitting.

Bridal and formal wear shops need records of measurements for special orders. Some specialty shops will "special order" garments for groups, such as large singing or dance groups. These are cut to order from basic measurements sent in by the shop.

For normal ordering or fitting purposes, you will need the measurements for bust, hips, waist, skirt length, back bodice length, and sleeve length.

When measuring, keep in mind you are not taking *body* measurements, but *garment* measurements. Therefore take easy measurements that will allow the person to move inside the garment. You may take the measurements over a lightweight, close-fitting dress.

Tie a string, ribbon, or tape around the waistline of the client. This helps mark the natural waistline and guides your other measurements in relation to the waistline.

Use a soft, 60-inch (152 cm) tape measure for all body measurements.

- *Bust*: Hold one end of tape over fullest part of bust. Pull the tape around to the back along the bottom of the shoulder blades. Bring to front again over the fullest part of the bust. Check to be sure the tape is straight across the back. Keep the tape tight enough to stay in place but loose enough so it does not squeeze the body.
- *Waist*: Wrap tape around waistline where it is marked by the string mentioned above. Pull to a snug fit with one finger underneath the tape to give the needed ease. Release tape if the client indicates she needs more ease for comfort. The waistline measurement often is determined by the customer's special needs. This measurement changes more than any other and can even change within a period of a few hours. People with this problem usually tell you. The client who has a narrow waist will often want to *feel* the waistline and will ask for a snug fit.

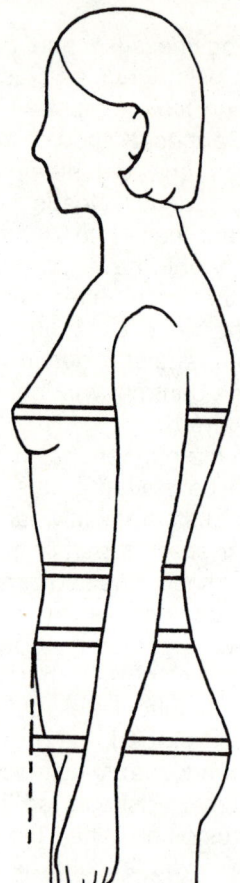

B-2a. *Taking measurements for bust, waist, abdomen, and hips.*

### Ch. 8: Fitting Women's Clothes

- *Upper hip*: Measure 3 inches (7.6 cm) down from the waistline. This measurement helps determine the fit and hang of the skirt over the stomach and upper hips. Wrap your tape around the body and lightly pull to an easy measurement.
- *Lower hip*: Measure the fullest and lowest part of the hips. Study the hip contours from the side. Measure down from the waist, along the side seam, to where the fullest part of the hips shows in a side view. Record this measurement. It may vary from 7 to 10 inches (17.8 to 25.4 cm) from the waist. At this point, wrap the tape around the fullest hip area. Hold overlapping tape in one hand. With your free hand, pull the tape loose enough under the stomach area so the tape is even with the fullest part of the stomach. This adds to the hip measurement, but gives the extra ease needed to prevent the skirt from pulling in under the stomach. It also give "sitting room."
- *Back bodice length*: Measure from the large bone at the base of the neck in the back to the waistline string. Hold tape at the neck bone and measure flat along the spine to the waist.
- *Front side bodice length*: Start with tape end at the center of the shoulder seam. Guide the tape over the fullest part of the bust to the waistline marker directly under the point of the bust.

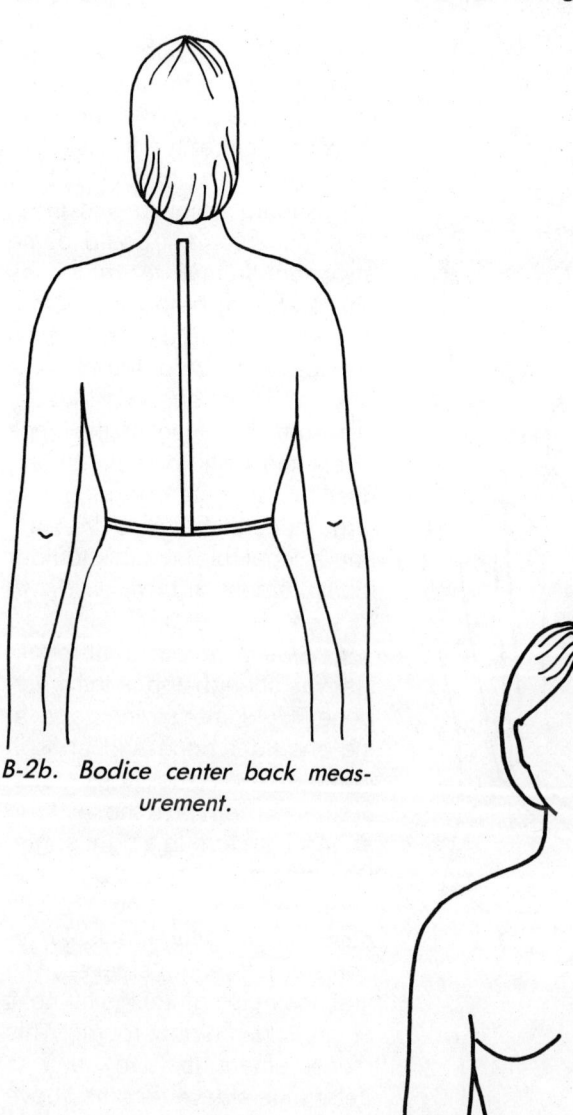

B-2b. Bodice center back measurement.

B-2c. Bodice side front and shoulder measurements.

143

## Altering Ready-To-Wear Fashions

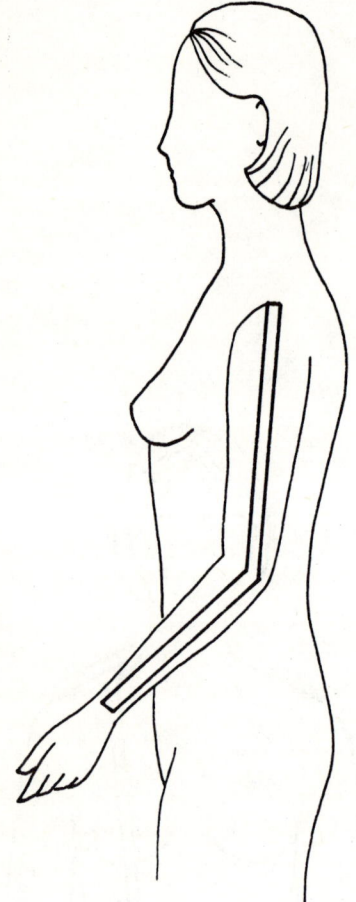

B-2d. Measuring for a long sleeve.

- *Point of bust*: As you measure for front side bodice length, note and record the measurement at the fullest part, or crown, of the bust. The bust dart should point to this area. This measurement could come anywhere from 8 to 14 inches (20 to 26 cm) below the center of the shoulder depending on the age and size of the client.
- *Width of shoulder*: Measure from the base of the neck where the neck joins the shoulder, to the outer edge of the large bone at the top of the arm. For a coat or jacket shoulder measurement, add about $1/4$ to $3/8$ inch (.6 to .9 cm).
- *Sleeve length*: Full-length sleeves should stop at the wristbone. Hold measuring tape at the shoulder bone and bring it to the elbow. Record this measurement. Then have the customer bend the arm to a right angle. Continue measuring around the elbow to the wristbone. You will have two measurements to record for full-length sleeves. The first one helps place the fullness or darts for "elbow room." This measurement is also used to determine sleeve lengths above the elbow.
- *Skirt length*: Daytime skirt length is taken from the waistline to the length the customer wishes. This measurement can vary slightly with different styles or fabrics. To measure a long narrow skirt length, start at the waistline marker. Measure to the top of the heel to be worn with that dress. A long, full skirt is measured from the waist to the desired length. If the dress is to be worn with high heels, it should come from 1 to $1 1/2$ inches (2.5 to 3.8 cm) below the top of the heel to be worn with the skirt.
- *Pants length*: For flared or straight pants legs, measure from the waist to the top of the foot where the toes start and the shoe bends. Hold your tape along the center crease of the trouser leg. For narrow pants, the hem should come at the instep of the foot. Add $1/2$-inch (1.3 cm) drop at the back of the straight pants legs. This makes the length slightly longer in back than in the front and is more attractive.

All or any of the above measurements can help you prepare a garment for a first fitting for steady customers or for special orders. When the customer is wearing the garment, you proceed as follows.

### PIN FITTING

As you practice pin fittings on family and friends, work in an organized manner. By applying the pins carefully as outlined below, you will be less apt to stick your customer while you fit. You will also avoid getting the pins caught in her undergarments, which will make it easier to get the garment off. Making alterations will be easier; you will always know where to find the head of the pin.

Ch. 8: Fitting Women's Clothes

NOTE: The manner in which the pins are applied does not necessarily indicate the method to be used to do the alteration. For example, the fact you have pinned tucks in a neckline does not mean you will always alter with tucks. You are merely using the pins to hold the fit.

• When pinning vertical seams, such as side seams or sleeves, the pins should be placed with the points down toward the hem.

• When pinning shoulder seams, the pin points go away from the neckline and point out toward the shoulder.

• When pinning hems in sleeves or skirt, insert pins with the points directed toward the floor. This way, the stiffness of the pin does not interfere with the way the garment will roll and hang.

## FITTINGS TO AVOID

Some types of fittings and alterations cannot be done successfully. Specific problems have been pointed out as they would occur. Generally, try to avoid the following:

• Garments more than one size too large or too small. An alterationist must be highly experienced to resize more than one size successfully.

• Garments made of permanent press fabrics. Since the original creases can never be completely removed and reset, the work will not have a finished look.

• Soiled or spotted garments. Tactfully explain that the pressing of the altered garments will "press" the soil into the garment, making it permanent. It is especially important to have garments cleaned or washed before the hemline is lowered.

• Avoid releasing the seams of garments made of the following fabrics or finishes:

Vari-colored silk screen prints.

Velvet, corduroy, and suede cloth.

Satin or moiré finish.

Single-knit jersey of any fiber.

Leather, vinyl, or any plastic finish.

Sequin or bead trimmed—unless the trim is available to fill in the seams that have been altered.

In most of these fabrics, the holes made by the machine needle are almost impossible to remove. In some cases, the fabric has been weakened by the machine stitching.

## NECKLINE FITTINGS

Some necklines do not "sit" well on the neck after the garment has been fastened and the shoulders squared on the client. This can happen frequently with many different kinds of neckline styles.

### Back Neckline Fullness

The garment stands away from the back of the neck as in Fig. B-3a.

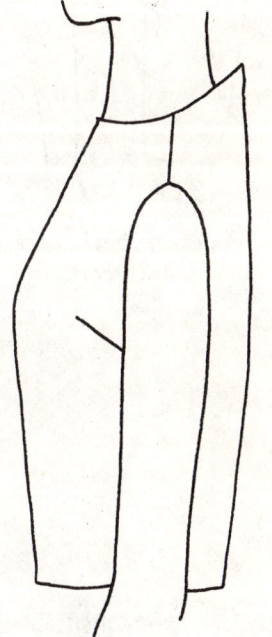

B-3a. Neckline too large in back.

## Altering Ready-To-Wear Fashions

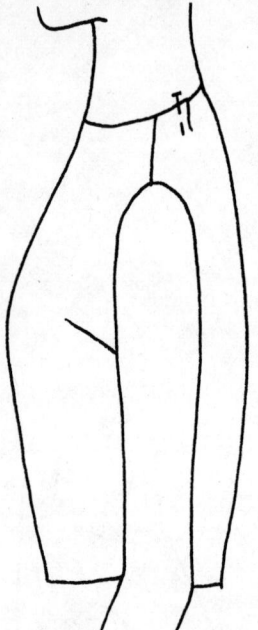

B-3b. Reducing back neck fullness with darts.

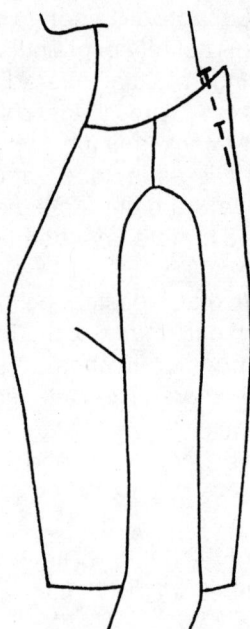

B-3c. Reducing back neck fullness in the zipper seam.

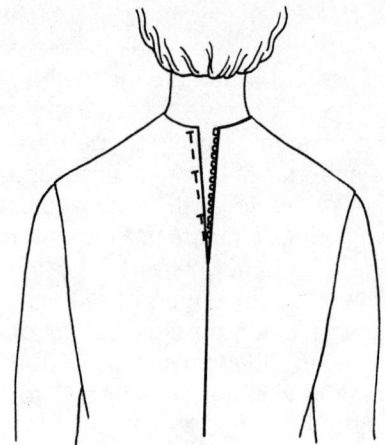

B-3d. Pins indicating zipper seam is to be taken in.

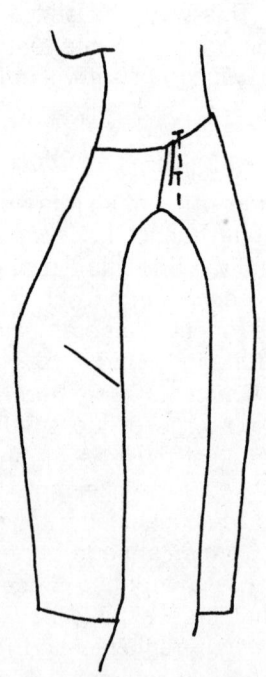

B-3e. Reducing back neck fullness in back shoulder seam.

TO FIT: When the back fullness is slight, about 1 inch (2.5 cm), pin ¼ inch (.6 cm) tucks about 2 inches (5 cm) from the center back on each side of the neckline as in Fig. B-3b.

When the back fullness is more than 1 inch (2.5 cm) and there is a zipper opening, pin out the excess fullness as shown in Fig. B-3c. To enable the client to get out of the garment after the fitting is over, remove pins one by one. Replace each pin on one side only of the zipper seam. The new sewing line will be marked and the zipper will open. See Fig. B-3d.

When there is no seam in back, the excess fullness may be removed at the back shoulder seam. Pin as shown in Fig. B-3e.

Ch. 8: Fitting Women's Clothes

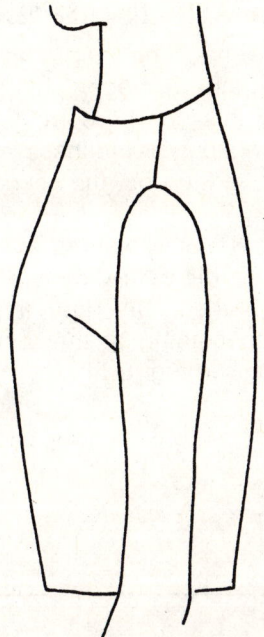

B-4a. Front neckline fullness.

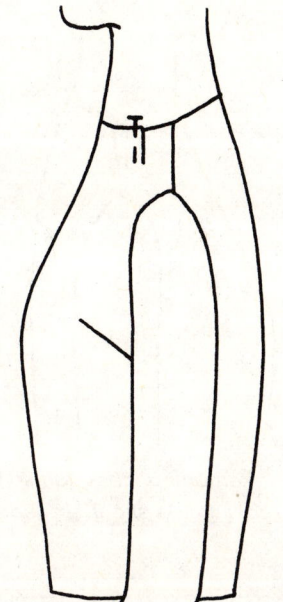

B-4b. Reducing front neck fullness with darts.

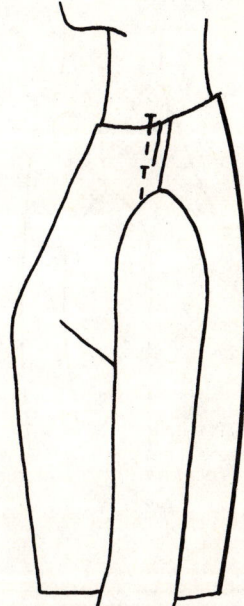

B-4c. Removing front neck fullness in the front shoulder seam.

## Front Neckline Fullness

The front neckline will not "rest" on the client, as shown in Fig. B-4a.

TO FIT: If the extra fullness is 1 inch (2.5 cm) or less, pin small tucks on each side of the neck as shown in Fig. B-4b.

If fullness is more than 1 inch (2.5 cm) pin the extra fullness out in the front shoulder seam as in Fig. B-4c.

If a V-neck or a scoop neck gaps, pin out the excess as shown in Figs. B-4d and e.

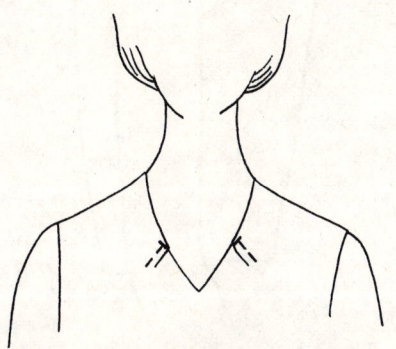

B-4d. Removing fullness from a V-neckline.

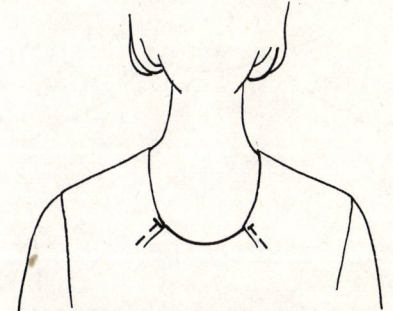

B-4e. Removing fullness from a round or oval neckline.

**Altering Ready-To-Wear Fashions**

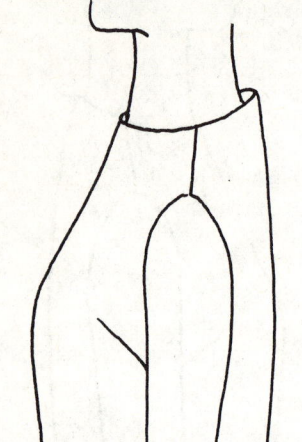
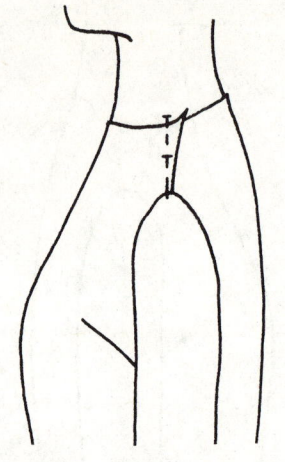

### Entire Neckline Too Large

The neckline gaps both in front and in back, Fig. B-5a. Often this can be corrected by pinning out the fullness at the neck edge of the shoulder seam.

TO FIT: Start pinning an equal amount off both the back and front of the seam. Taper this pin line to nothing at the armhole seam. See Fig. B-5b.

B-5a. Neckline too large all around.

B-5b. Removing neck fullness by increasing the shoulder seam.

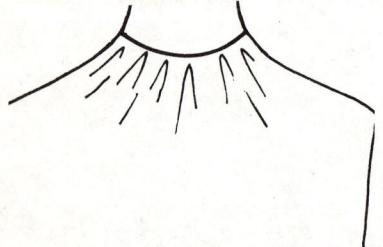

B-6a. Neckline too tight.

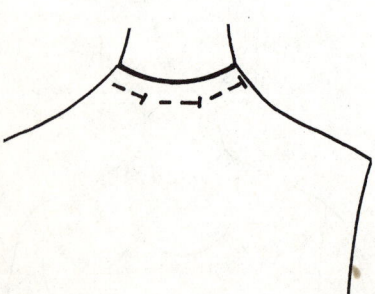

B-6b. Lowering the too-tight neckline in the front.

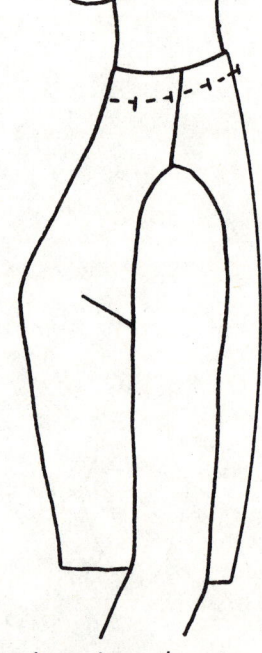

B-6c. Lowering the too tight neckline all around.

### Neckline Too High

This is the neckline that "grips" the neck and causes discomfort, as shown in Fig. B-6a. The client's own need for comfort will determine where the pin line goes. This is not restyling. You are merely fitting the neckline to the client's particular need for comfort or appearance.

TO FIT: If only the front of the neckline is too tight, start pin line from the shoulder seam and gradually lower the line toward the center front of the neck, as in Fig. B-6b.

If neckline grips front and back, start the pinline from the center back of the neckline, continue across the shoulder, and gradually lower the line toward the center front. Fig. B-6c.

Ch. 8: Fitting Women's Clothes

### Neckline Fitting with Collar

This problem could involve any collar style—lapel, shawl, roll, or mandarin. The pin fitting would be the same for all the styles.

#### COLLAR AND NECKLINE TOO LARGE IN BACK

This means the neckline does not "hug" the back of the neck. See Fig. B-7a.

TO FIT: Raise the collar and pin out the excess to bring the collar to rest on back neckline, as in Fig. B-7b.

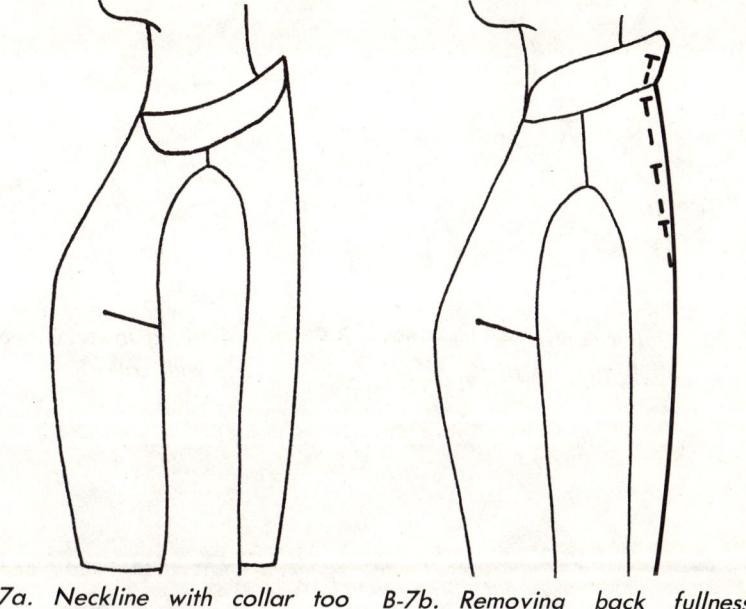

B-7a. Neckline with collar too big in back.

B-7b. Removing back fullness with a collar.

### Collar and Neckline Too Large All Around

This collar stands away from the neck front and back, Fig. B-8a. It must be brought back to the base of the neck.

TO FIT: Lift the collar, pin a tuck at each shoulder seam. Take an equal amount on each side of each shoulder seam at the neck edge. See Fig. B-8b.

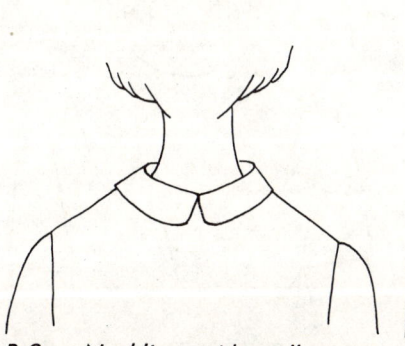

B-8a. Neckline with collar too big all around.

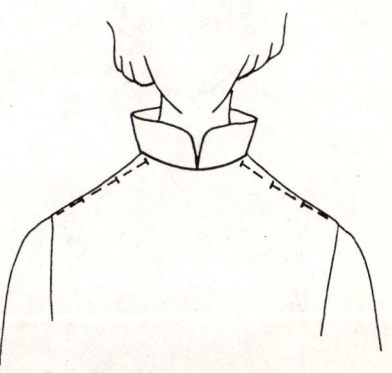

B-8b. Removing fullness on the too-big neckline with collar.

Altering Ready-To-Wear Fashions

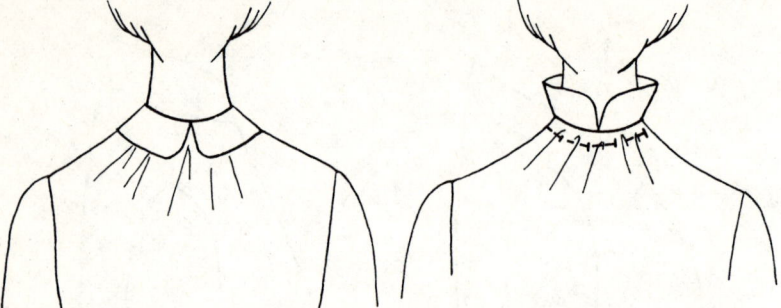

B-9a. Collar and neckline too high and too tight.

B-9b. Establishing lowered neckline with collar.

### Collar and Neckline Too High and Tight

This is a common problem for people with short thick necks and is most uncomfortable. The collar must either be worn open or replaced on a lower neckline. You can recognize this problem by the "pull" lines at the neckline when the garment is fastened front or back. See Fig. B-9a.

TO FIT: Apply a pin line around the base of the client's neck where the new collar line should be. See Fig. B-9b.

---

## SHOULDER FITTINGS

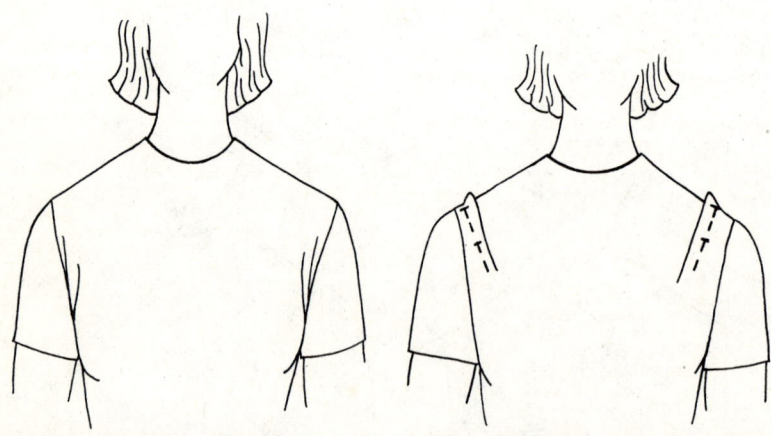

B-10a. Garment shoulders too wide.

B-10b. Reducing excess length on wide shoulders.

### Garment Shoulder Too Wide

This problem is indicated when the sleeves fall or droop from the top of the arm instead of rolling over the top. The armhole seam does not fall into the client's underarm curve. See Fig. B-10a. Note poor fit of sleeves, with folds at underarms. The same folds are found at the back underarms.

TO FIT: Start at the shoulder seam and pin a tuck close to the armhole seam. Bring the sleeve up on the shoulder bone so the sleeve rolls over the arm. Pin up only enough to bring the armhole seams to the underarm curves on the client. See Fig. B-10b. Only the front view is shown, but the same line would be pinned in back.

Ch. 8: Fitting Women's Clothes

### Garment Shoulders Too Wide in Back Only

Sometimes the shoulder fits well in the front but forms folds at the back armhole seam, as in Fig. B-11a.

TO FIT: Start at the shoulder seam with a very small tuck. Increase tuck along armhole seam until all surplus material is pinned into this fold. See Fig. B-11b. The back of the garment will be smooth across the shoulders. Now ask your customer to cross her arms in front of her. If there is a pull across her shoulders, release enough of the tuck to eliminate the pull. The back fit of the shoulders is important. People need more ease and room for movement there—especially in sportswear.

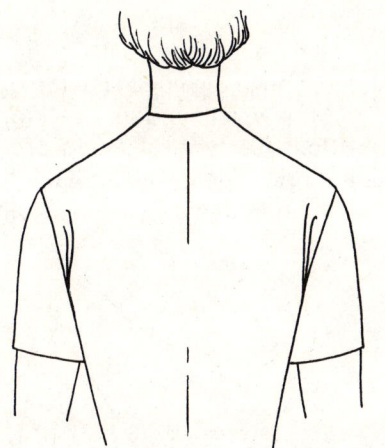
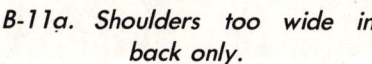

B-11a. Shoulders too wide in back only.

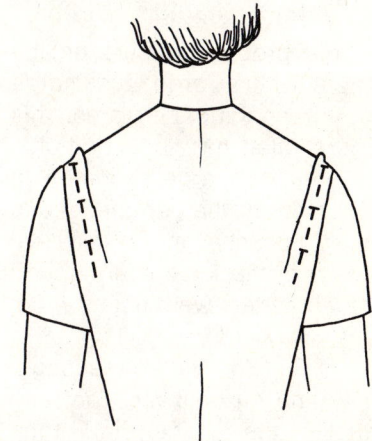

B-11b. Reducing shoulder width in back.

### Shoulders Too Wide in Front Only

Note excess folds in Fig. B-12a at front armhole seam.

TO FIT: Pin a tuck in the same way the back fullness was removed in Fig. B-11b. Follow the line of the front armhole curve. The garment should rest flat across the chest without the extra ease needed for back shoulder movement. Fig. B-12b shows garment with front fullness removed.

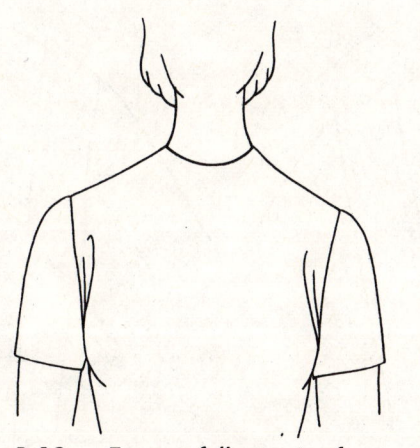

B-12a. Excess fullness in front shoulder area.

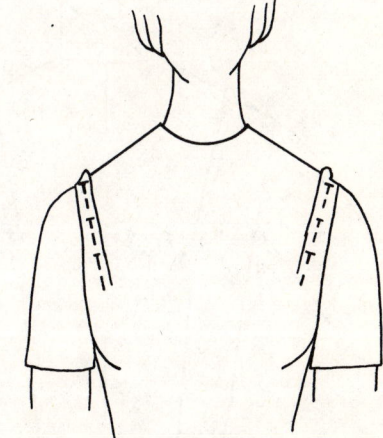

B-12b. Reducing front shoulder width.

## Altering Ready-To-Wear Fashions

### Extreme Shoulder Width

This problem occurs on the figure with a large bust, large midriff, and upper hip area. This figure often has the additional problem of a large abdomen. In other words, the garment had to be purchased in a size that would fit the torso even though the shoulders were not as wide. See Fig. B-13a.

TO FIT: You will be creating a new line on both the front and back of the bodice. Start at the back shoulder dart. Increase the dart enough to bring the shoulder to the correct width for the customer. Continue this pin line to the top of the waistline dart. Taper the tuck to nothing at the top of the dart. Fig. B-13b. Repeat on opposite shoulder dart. On front of shoulder, continue the back dart to pin out the same amount. Taper this dart to 0 at the point of the bust. Continue to mark a pin line to the top of the front waistline dart. See Fig. B-13c. This type of fitting creates new lines without taking anything from the fit over the full areas.

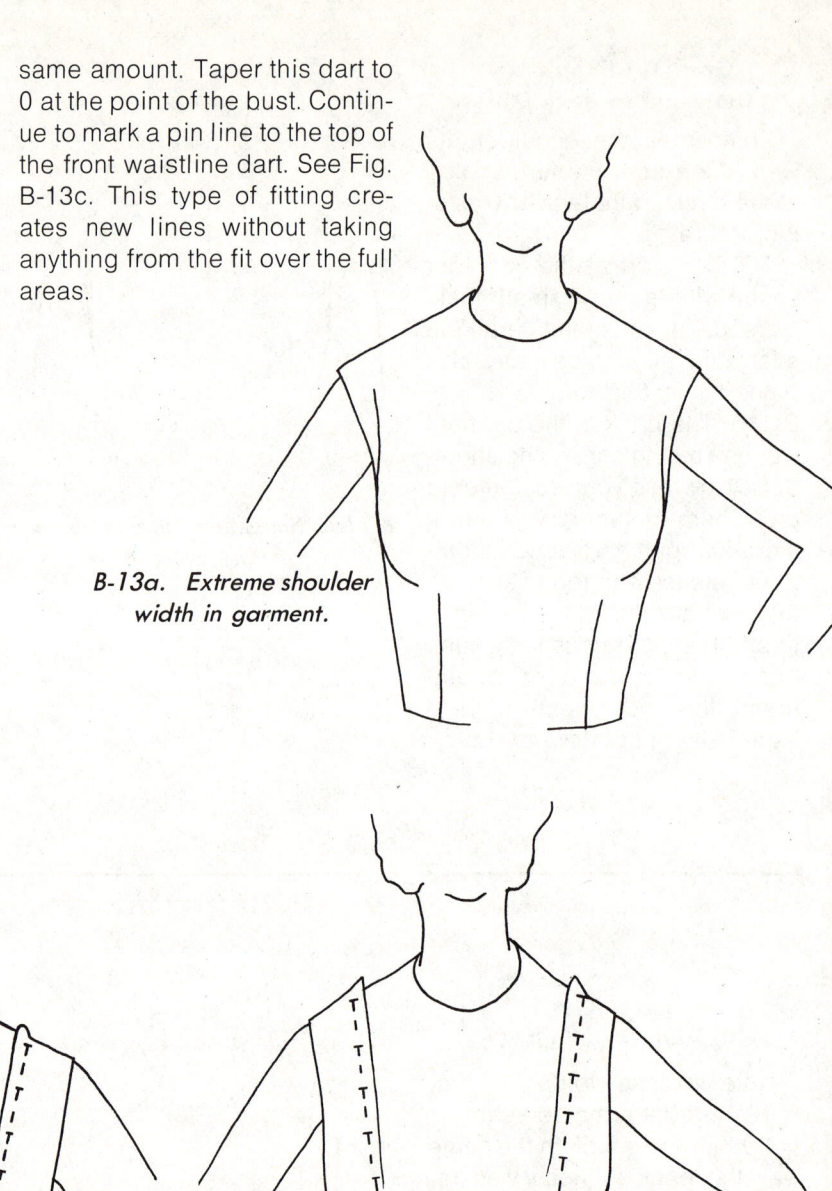

B-13a. Extreme shoulder width in garment.

B-13b. Establishing new mock seam in back.

B-13c. Establishing new mock seam in front.

### Garment Shoulders Too Narrow

This problem causes the top of the armhole seam to pull too close to the neck. The narrow shoulder of the garment pulls the top of the sleeve snug across the upper arm. See Fig. B-14. There is no ease for action across the shoulders. As a fitter, you must analyze and note what you have to work with to know if the shoulder can be widened enough. To make this alteration possible, one of the following must be present:

- The fabric is an east-west (crosswise) stretch knit.
- There are style seams in side front and side back of bodice, starting at the shoulder seams, as in a princess style line.
- Garment has a center back seam or opening and shoulder darts.
- The shoulder fit is no more than 1/4 inch (.6 cm) too narrow.

When none of these conditions exist, do not attempt the fitting because there will not be enough fabric to work with. If there *is* something to work with to extend the shoulder line, make a note of this on the work ticket.

TO FIT: Take the shoulder measurement from the edge of the neckline to the outside shoulder bone where the seam should be. Write this measurement on the same work ticket. Place crossed pins on top of the sleeves where they join the shoulder seams to indicate a change is needed.

B-14. Garment shoulders too narrow.

Ch. 8: Fitting Women's Clothes

Altering Ready-To-Wear Fashions

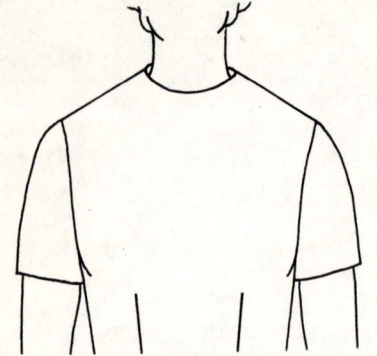

B-15a. Garment shoulder line too high at neck.

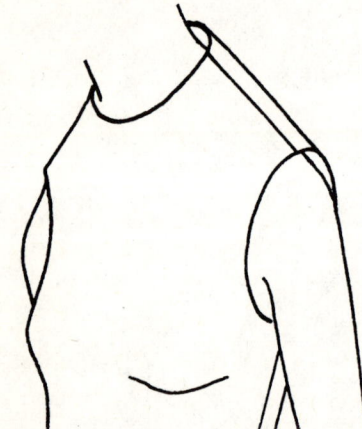

B-15b. Garment shoulder line too high at neck and armhole.

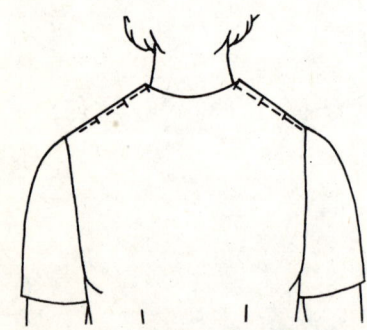

B-15c. Increasing shoulder seam to lower garment shoulder area equally front and back.

## Garment Shoulder Line Too High

There is a definite gap at the neckline as well as a droop at the armhole seam. However, the bodice darts, waistline, and other parts of the garment fall into their proper place on the body. If the garment is sleeveless, the gap is also noticeable at the armhole. See Figs. B-15a and 15b.

When the excess is the same on both the front and back of the shoulder line, increase the shoulder seam.

TO FIT: Place pins so the same amount is taken out of front and back of shoulder seams. Fig. B-15c.

If shoulders lie flat and in place across the back but there is a gap in front, pin out fullness on front of shoulder seams only. See Fig. B-15d.

Often, a full-busted person will fill out the front of a bodice but there will be a gap at the back of the shoulder seams. Then the fullness should be pinned out of the back of the bodice shoulders only. Fig. B-15e.

NOTE: If garment neckline has a trim or collar of any style, the shoulder line pinning would still be the same. The fitting of the collar or trim to the new fit is adjusted in the actual alteration of the garment.

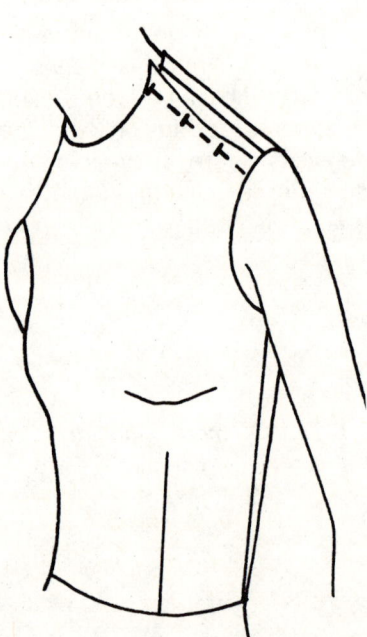

B-15d. Lowering shoulder seam in front only.

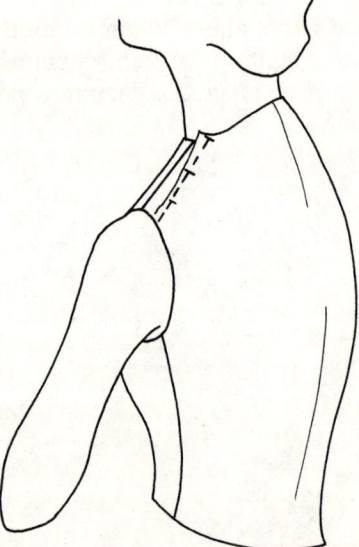

B-15e. Lowering shoulder seam in back only.

Ch. 8: Fitting Women's Clothes

### Body Shoulders Slope

Many people have sloping shoulders. The slope may be very slight or a definite droop. You can detect this problem by the unnatural folds at back and front armholes. Otherwise, the neckline sits well and the bodice is in place and fits. See Fig. B-16.

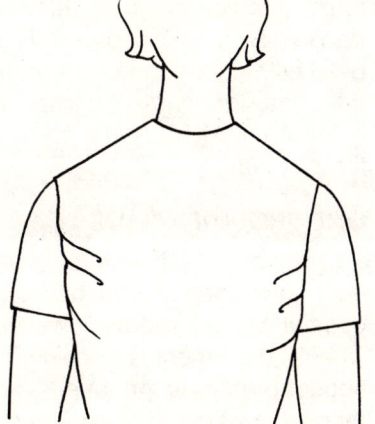

B-16. Sloping shoulders.

## SLIGHT SHOULDER DROOP

TO FIT: Pin a line through the shoulder seam from 0 to the amount needed at the armhole seams to take the folds out of the top of the bodice. Fig. B-17a. The total amount of fabric pinned out at the armhole should be no more than 3/4 inch (1.8 cm). If the garment is a coat or jacket, do not pin out the excess. Instead, insert a pair of thin shoulder pads and pin in place. Extend the pads beyond the top of the armhole seam just enough to square off the shoulders. Fig. B-17b shows shoulder pad placement *inside* jacket or coat. Pins are inserted on the outside of garment to hold the pads in place.

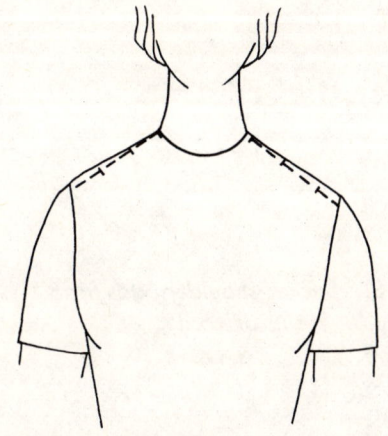

B-17a. Increasing shoulder seam at armhole only.

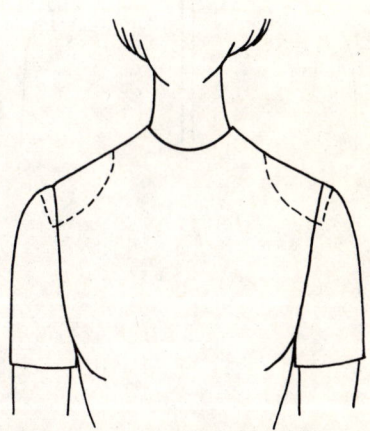

B-17b. Adding shoulder pads to a dress.

## Altering Ready-To-Wear Fashions

### PRONOUNCED SHOULDER SLOPE

This is a definite figure fault and the client needs help in a way that will not bring attention to her problem. Here the droop of the shoulders forms even more folds above the bustline as shown in Fig. B-16.

TO FIT: Use a combination of alterations. Take out half the extra fabric by pinning, as in Fig. B-17a. Then insert a pair of soft, slightly padded shoulder pads, as in Fig. B-17b. The combination of the two methods should correct the shoulder line without exaggerating it with heavy padding. Study Figs. 17a and b for combination fit. If this particular shoulder problem is found in a coat or jacket, thicker pads may be inserted as in Fig. B-18 with no alteration made on the shoulder seams. The heavier padding should take care of the problem.

### ONE SHOULDER SLOPE

Many people have this figure fault and often it can be successfully ignored. However, when the garment is thrown into noticeable folds on one side, follow the above procedures for that one shoulder only. This will make the sloped shoulder come in line with the straight shoulder. If the garment is a coat or jacket, the extra padding in the one shoulder should be all that is necessary to "square off" the shoulders.

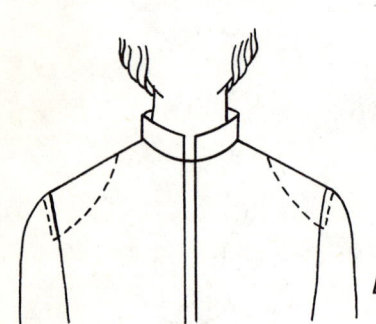

B-18. Thicker shoulder pads for a suit or coat.

### BODICE FITTINGS

The bodice is the top part of a dress from the shoulders to the waistline. It may be attached to a skirt or be a separate part of a costume. In any case, the fit of the body of the bodice should be checked after adjusting the neckline and shoulders. For a bodice fitting, check to see if:

• The bust and front waistline darts are in line with the fullest part of the bust.
• The length of the bodice is below or above the natural waistline.
• The bodice pulls across the bust or back.
• The waistline darts back or front pull across rolls of flesh at the midriff section.
• The side seams of the bodice at the underarm are so far away from client's body line that the figure is completely lost.

Ch. 8: Fitting Women's Clothes

### Bodice Too Loose

It is usually the small-busted, narrow-backed person who has this fitting problem. The garment is the correct size for her and fits well in the waist, hips, and shoulders. However, the underarm seams are much too loose at the sides. Fig. B-19a.

B-19a. Bodice too loose at underarms.

## BODICE EQUALLY FULL FRONT AND BACK

TO FIT: Pin out the fullness beginning at the top of the underarm seams. Taper pin line to nothing at waistline. Fig. B-19b. Pin each side and check fit over fullness of bust and back shoulders. There should still be ease in the bodice in those areas. Be sure the customer has room to move easily.

B-19b. Removing fullness on underarm seams.

## BODICE TOO FULL IN FRONT ONLY

This means the figure is well fitted in back but has too much room in front.

TO FIT: Pin out the extra fullness along the front side of underarm seam only. Taper to nothing at the waistline. Fig. B-20.

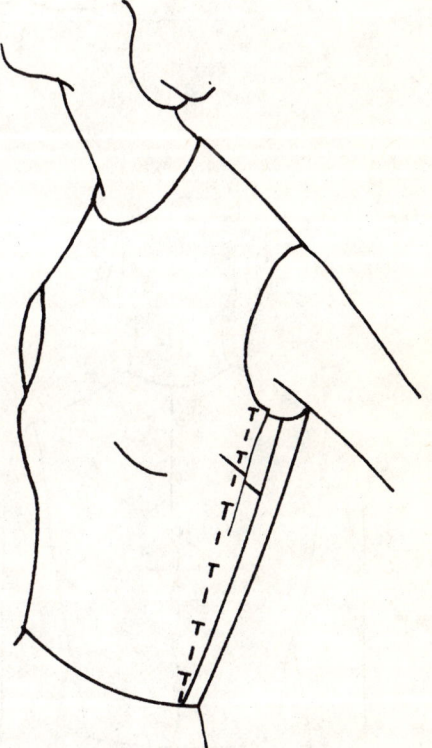

B-20. Bodice too full in front only.

**Altering Ready-To-Wear Fashions**

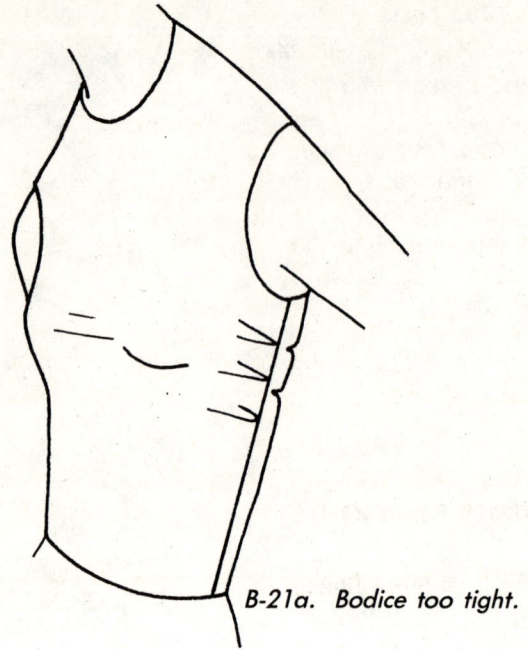

B-21a. Bodice too tight.

### Bodice Too Tight

This shows up as pull lines at underarm seams, over the bust and back shoulder areas. Fig. B-21a. If the garment has button closing, there will be gaps between the buttons or fasteners. Fig. B-21b. Here the side underarm seams should be released enough to create the easy fit needed. Moving buttons or fasteners will not be sufficient.

TO FIT: Indicate seams to be released by inserting a pin line along the seam line. This line of pins will show the amount to be released. Fig. B-21c. This is not a fold line and no material is pinned out in the fitting. Write instructions clearly for release of the bodice seams on the work ticket to prevent the possibility of a mistake.

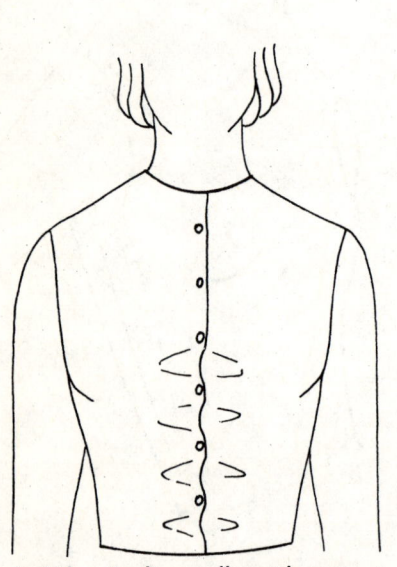

B-21b. Bodice pulls and gaps at buttons.

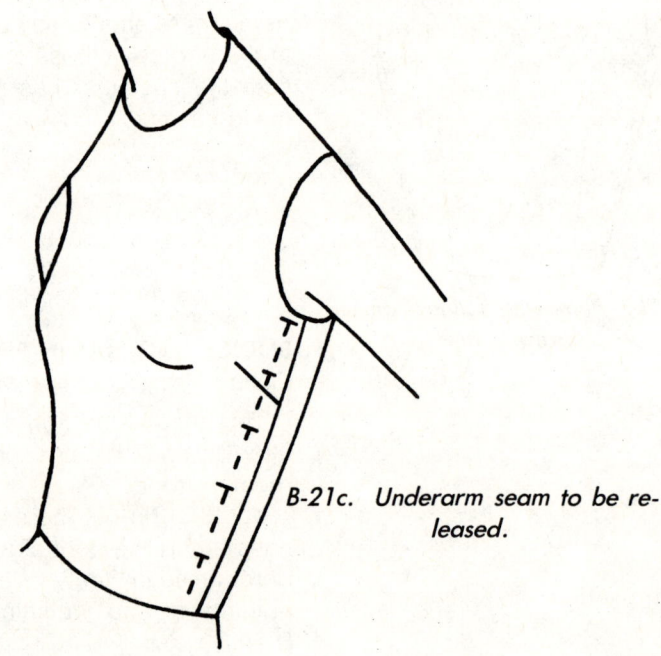

B-21c. Underarm seam to be released.

Ch. 8: Fitting Women's Clothes

### Bodice Too Long

This problem of short-waisted figures shows up in different ways. If the waistline is a loose fit, the bodice will fall below the belt or tie. Fig. B-22a. If waistline is tight, the bodice will bunch up and show an excess of fabric above the waist. Fig. B-22b.

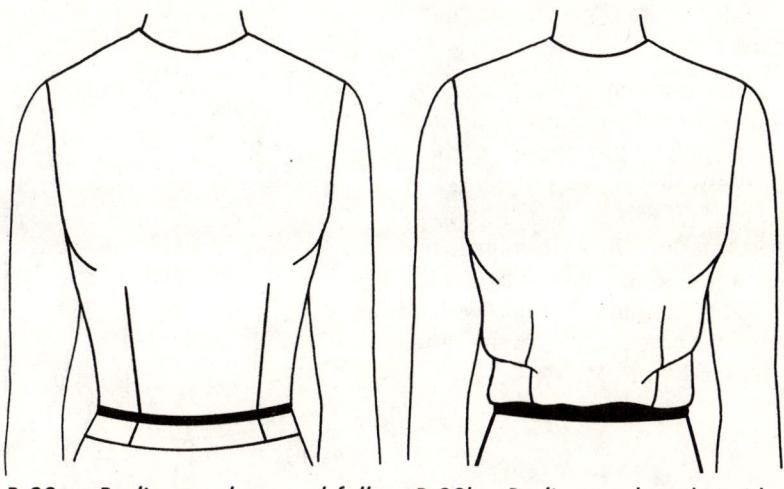

B-22a. *Bodice too long and falls below waist.*

B-22b. *Bodice too long but rides above waist.*

## BODICE TOO LONG FRONT AND BACK

TO FIT: Remove belt or tie. Replace with a piece of seam tape tied in place at the customer's true waist. Insert pins in a horizontal line around the waistline immediately below the seam tape. Put pins at the side seams, center front, center back, and one pin between each of these marks. Fig. B-23a. Now bring the top of the skirt to this pin line with the extra bodice tucked inside. Pin the skirt to the bodice along the marking pin line. Insert these pins diagonally to distinguish this line from the marking pins. Fig. 23b.

If the waistline is tight and doesn't fall below it's normal position, tuck the extra bodice fabric down into the skirt and apply pins as in Fig. B-23b.

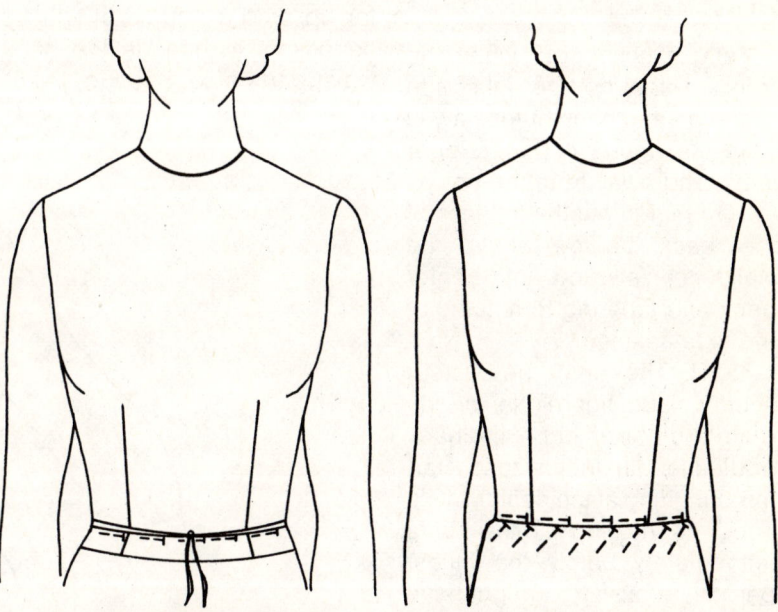

B-23a. *Establishing new waistline on too long bodice.*

B-23b. *Pinning skirt up to new waistline.*

**Altering Ready-To-Wear Fashions**

## BODICE TOO LONG IN FRONT ONLY

This problem usually occurs with the small busted figure. The back of the bodice comes to the waistline as it should.

TO FIT: Pin out the extra fullness as in B-23a. This time the pins would be inserted first at the center front. The line would then taper to nothing at the side seams. Fig. B-24.

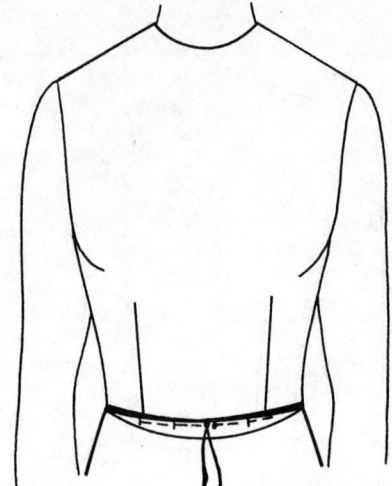

B-24. Bodice too long in front only.

## BODICE TOO LONG IN BACK ONLY

This is noticeable when the front of the bodice falls into place but the back bulges away from the figure. A back zipper will stand away from the body.

TO FIT: Pin out the fullness of the back bodice along the waistline, starting at center back and tapering to nothing at the side seams.

NOTE: The very-large-busted, short-waisted figure often needs quite a bit taken out of the back bodice length. In this case, start the pin fitting at the center back. Taper to nothing at the darts immediately below the fullest part of the bust. You might have to take as much as 3 inches (7.6 cm) out of the back bodice. When you have had to go that far up on the bodice, it will be necessary to change the back waist darts also. See Fig. B-25.

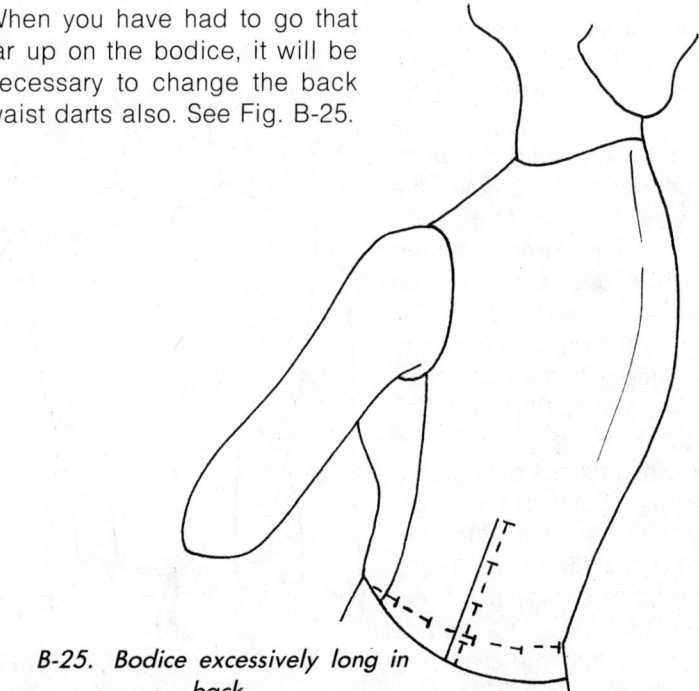

B-25. Bodice excessively long in back.

## Bodice Too Short

In this problem, the waistline will show above the seam tape tied around the waist. The top of the skirt will not sit well on the upper hipline of the body. Fig. B-26a. If the bodice is only slightly above the tie line—no more than ³⁄₈ inch (.9 cm)—the alteration is possible. It is a rare ready-made dress that would have a waist seam allowance of more than ⁵⁄₈ inch (1.5 cm). Therefore it is impossible to drop the waistline more than ³⁄₈ inch (.9 cm) and have at least a ¹⁄₄-inch (.6 cm) seam allowance left. If more length is required, you will have to go into more than a waistline fitting. This involves restyling the bodice.

TO FIT: Mark the lower line needed with a pin line on the upper part of the skirt. Fig. B-26b. Be sure to describe on the work ticket that the waistline is to be dropped and no change is to be made along the top of the skirt. If a hemline adjustment is needed, it should be fitted after the waist adjustment has been made.

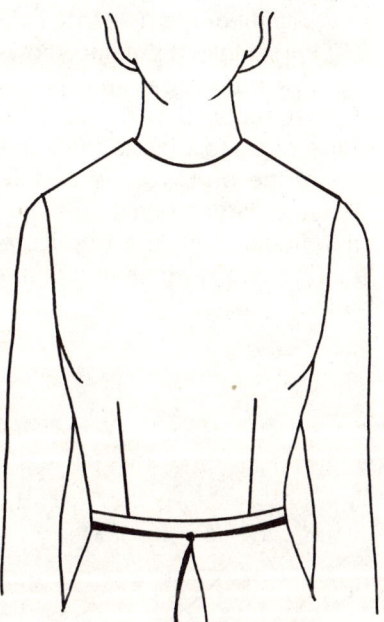

B-26a. Bodice too short.

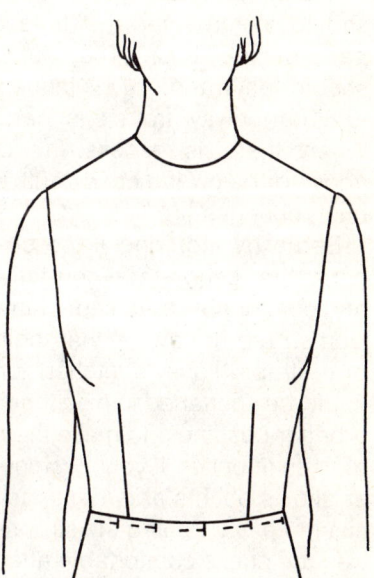

B-26b. Establishing new waistline on too short bodice.

## Altering Ready-To-Wear Fashions

### Bodice Dart Placement

Many bodice fittings are accomplished simply by changing darts. Darts can be shortened, lengthened, reshaped, released, or taken in to conform to the figure being fitted. That is true, of course, only if the darts have been left uncut by the manufacturer. You must first check to see how much fabric is in the darts to determine just how much you can do in the fitting.

**BUST DARTS**

The front fullness in a bodice should come over the fullest part of the bust. The darts should end about 1½ inches (3.8 cm) away from this part. When there is excess fabric above or below the crown of the bust, changes are needed.

Begin by inquiring if the client's bra straps are correctly and comfortably adjusted. Many women are not aware that their bra straps have stretched or could be shortened to give them a better bustline and make their clothes fit better. If your customer shows doubts about this, assist her in shortening the straps. Be sure she is comfortable after the adjustment. If you are diplomatic, you can be of great service to your customers by suggesting they try different styles and sizes the next time they shop for a bra. When you are sure the bra is adjusted correctly, check the location of the darts.

### Underarm Bust Dart Too High

The dart may be in the right place for the manufacturer's model but the client has a lower bustline. This fitting problem is very common. Fig. B-27a.

TO FIT: Make a pin line showing new placement and length of bust darts. See Fig. B-27b. Place crossed pins to mark the end of the dart. You need only mark the dart on one side as the alterationist will just duplicate this line on the other side of the bodice.

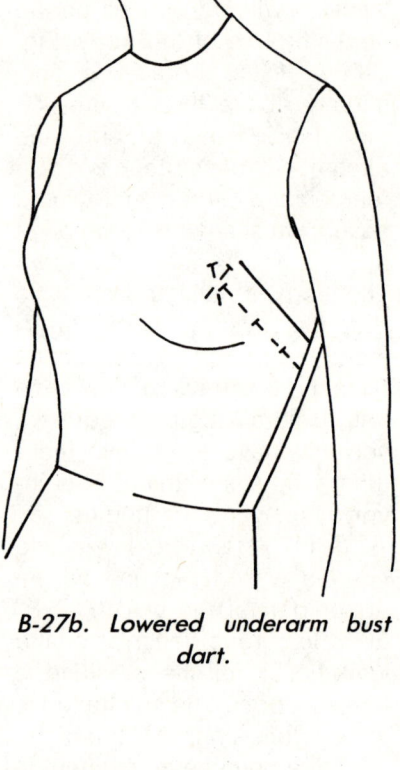

B-27b. Lowered underarm bust dart.

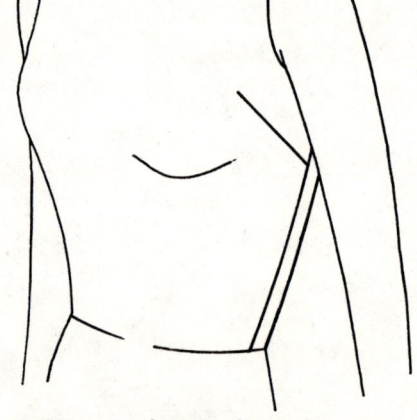

B-27a. Underarm bust dart too high.

## Ch. 8: Fitting Women's Clothes

### Bust Darts Too Low

This fitting is very rare, but can happen. Fig. B-28 shows the original bust dart and the new pin line to indicate the change required.

### Bust Darts Too Long

Darts need to be shortened and reshaped to allow for bust fullness. Fig. B-29 shows the new line and the crossed pins that indicate where the dart should end.

### Bust Darts Too Deep and Long

This problem shows up on the full-bosomed figure where the fullness starts close to the underarm seams.

TO FIT: The deep dart should be replaced with two narrower, shorter darts on each side of the bodice. Fig. B-30. Broken lines in Fig. B-30 show depth of divided darts.

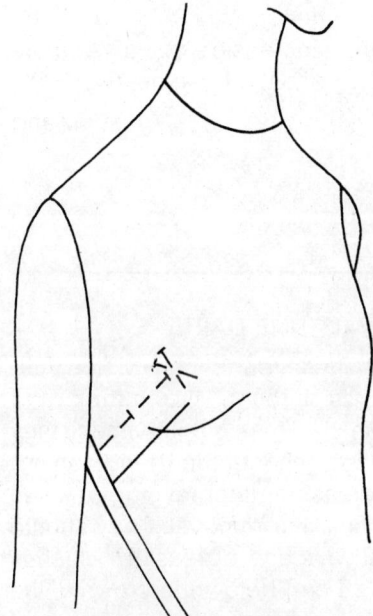

B-28. Underarm bust dart too low.

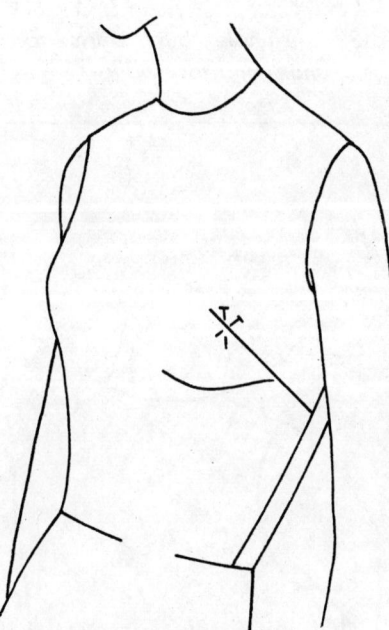

B-29. Underarm bust dart too long.

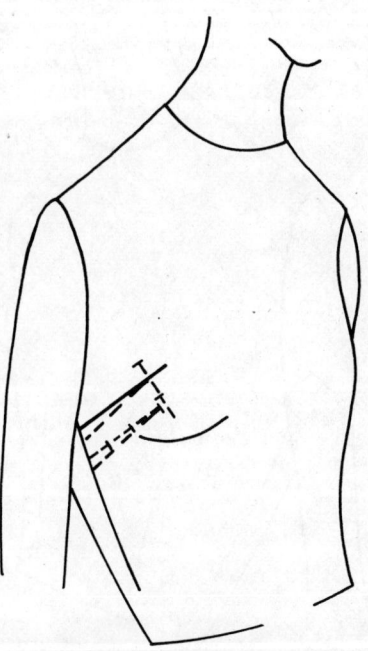

B-30. Underarm bust dart too long and too deep.

*Altering Ready-To-Wear Fashions*

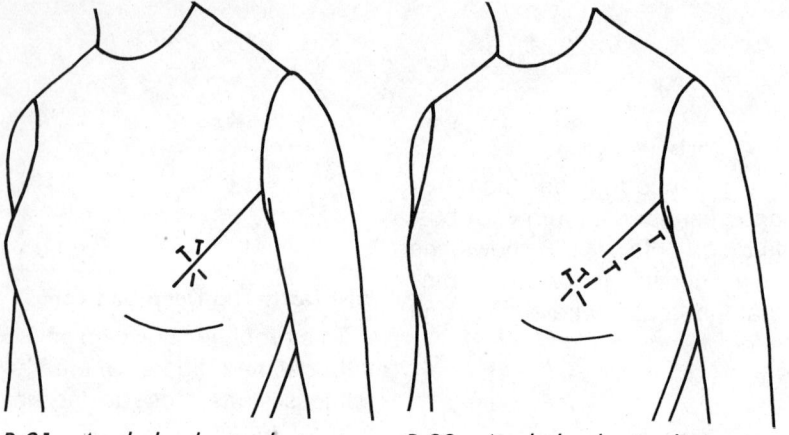

### Armhole Bust Darts Too Long

TO FIT: Place crossed pins at point where bust dart should end. See Fig. B-31.

### Armhole Bust Darts Too Short and Shallow

The small-busted figure usually needs this dart extended and increased to give more shape to the bustline. Fig. B-32.

B-31. Armhole bust darts too long.

B-32. Armhole bust darts too short and too shallow.

### WAISTLINE DARTS

These darts control the fullness through the midriff and waist areas. Sometimes they need shortening, lengthening, releasing, increasing, or even complete removal. They should always end at least 1½ inches (3.8 cm) below the crown of the bust in front or the lower edge of the shoulder blades in back.

### Waistline Darts Too Long Front and Back.

The bodice fits well except that the waistline darts extend over the bust or shoulder blade fullness. Figs. B-33a and b.

TO FIT: Place crossed pins to show where the darts should end. These pins will indicate a certain amount of reshaping as well. The darts must be re-tapered to the new point. This change is made in the altering process.

B-33a. Waistline darts too long in front.

B-33b. Waistline darts too long in back.

## Ch. 8: Fitting Women's Clothes

### Waistline Darts Tight across Front Midriff and Lower Back

This is a common fitting as many people gain weight in the midriff and waist before they expand elsewhere. The problem can be recognized by the way the fabric pulls across this part of the body. Dart seams are stretched and rolls of flesh are obvious. In this fitting, the darts nearly always have to be shortened and released. The extra room or ease will help considerably in flattering the figure and hiding the "rolls."

TO FIT: Place a pin line on one side of the dart seam to show how much the dart must be let out. Place crossed pins to show where the darts should end. It is only necessary to pin fit one dart in back and one in front. Be sure to write on the work ticket that all waistline darts are to be released and shortened. If still more fullness is needed, release the side seams, too. There should be at least one inch of ease in the waistline. Measure the midriff and waist carefully and record on work ticket so the alterationist will know how much to release. Fig. B-34a and b.

Sometimes you will find it best to completely remove the darts. Some figures with low, full bust lines and rolls of fat that protrude below the bra band in back need all the space you can give them. Suggest removing all waistline darts and carefully easing the extra fabric into the waistline seam under the bust area. The back will look best if the ease is distributed evenly all the way across. You may also need to release the side seams through the same area. This fitting is not pinned. It is simply written on the work ticket. Place crossed pins on each dart as a symbol or reminder.

NOTE: This can only be done if the dart fabric has not been cut away during manufacture.

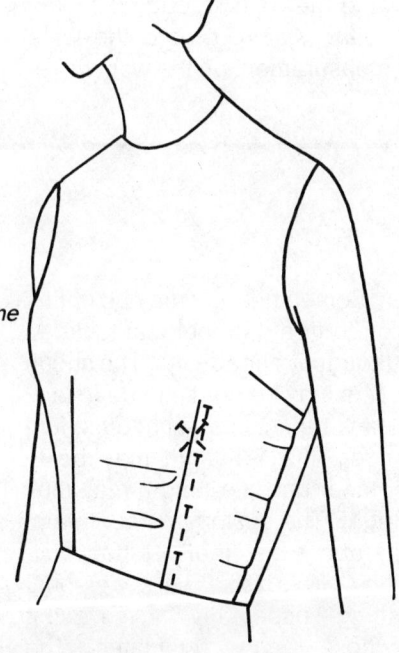

B-34b. Release back waistline darts.

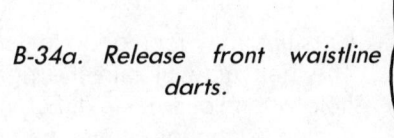

B-34a. Release front waistline darts.

**Altering Ready-To-Wear Fashions**

**Waistline Darts Too Loose across Midriff and Lower Back**

This problem occurs for the full-busted figure with a small rib cage and narrow back. The fitting can be done by increasing and reshaping the four darts enough to give a good fit and flatter the figure.

NOTE: When taking in a garment on darts or seams, it is best to pin both sides of the garment. Otherwise you cannot judge whether you are taking in too little or too much.

The comfort and appearance of the client after pinning will tell you if you have fitted correctly. Fig. B-35a and b.

With the above problem, the waistline is usually also too large. If the client wants the waist tightened, continue pinning the darts through the waist seam. Again, record the waist measurement on the work ticket.

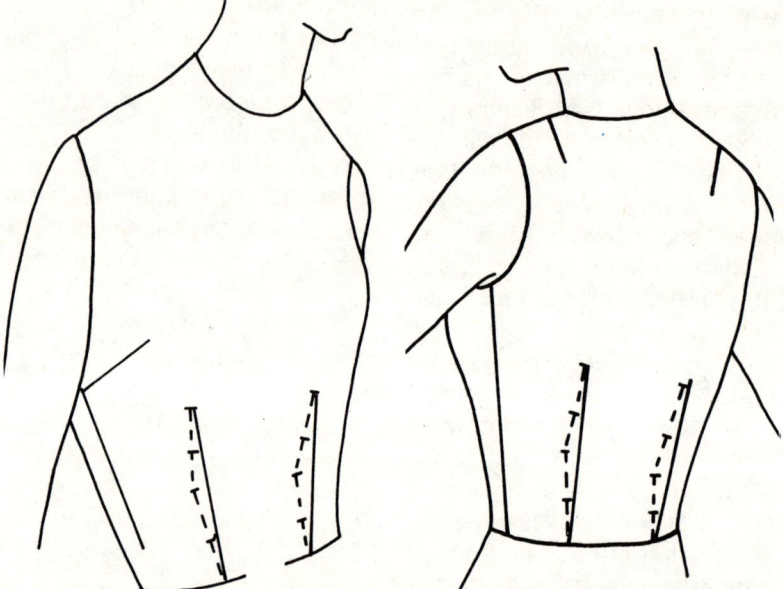

B-35a. Increase front waistline darts.

B-35b. Increase back waistline darts.

---

## WAISTLINE FITTINGS

Sometimes you may be called on to fit a garment that looks as though it already fits. The shoulders may be right, the bust darts may be in line with bust fullness, the waistline may be in place, and the length may look right. The customer's complaint is about the "feel" of the waistline. This is a very personal thing—especially for the client whose figure fluctuates. The waistline may look good to you. The belt may fit into the right hole when *you* buckle it. For the customer, though, it may be too tight or too loose depending upon how *she* wants to feel in *her* garment.

### Waistline Too Tight

This is a common complaint for mature women. The waistline can be from 1 to 4 inches (2.5 to 10 cm) too tight even though the dress is the right size for the woman.

If 1 to 2 inches (2.5 to 5 cm) are all that is required for comfort, there will always be enough ease and seam allowance to give this extra release. When a belt is involved, it is usually made so it can be adjusted an inch or two (2.5 to 5 cm) in either direction.

TO FIT: Take the client's waist measurement with your tape. Keep releasing the tape until she tells you it "feels good." Record this measurement on the work ticket. Indicate in writing that only the waistline is to be altered.

If more than 2 inches (5 cm) is needed, check to see what can be released. As the fitter, you will have to recognize the details that will give the extra waist measurement. Check the inside of the bodice and top part of the skirt for any gathers, tucks, seams, or darts that may be let out.

NOTE: Keep in mind that when you stitch one dart 1/4 inch (.6 cm) narrower than it was, you gain 1/2 inch (1.3 cm) in width.

Thus, two pairs of darts on both back and front of a bodice or skirt released 1/4 inch (.6 cm) each will add 2 inches (5 cm) in measurement. Releasing 3/8 inch (.9 cm) on the same number of darts will give an additional 3 inches (7.6 cm).

Sometimes the waistline is so tight it cannot be fastened at all. To solve this problem, pin each side to a piece of seam tape to hold the garment together comfortably. Measure the gap in the opening and make a decision as to whether the alteration is possible. If a belt is part of the garment, it, too, would have to be enlarged to the new waist measurement.

TO FIT: Take the waist measurement as described before and record on work ticket. Place crossed pins at all details—darts, seams, gathers—to be released. Write the amount to be released on the ticket along with a reminder that the belt will have to be made longer. Put crossed pins at the tip of the belt as an additional reminder about the belt.

NOTE: If the client's figure shows that most of the waist gain has been in the front, write this on the work ticket. Record the front waist measurement and the back measurement separately. Releasing the waist where it needs it most will help balance the fit of the garment. As a result, the side seams will be kept in line with the body contours.

### Waistline Too Loose

This is easy to recognize with or without a belt. With a belt, the dress will fall into pleats or gathers in the waist. A beltless garment will have no shape in the waist area and the garment lines will be spoiled.

TO FIT: Remove belt and insert pins through all thicknesses at each side seam. Be sure pins go through the waistline seam, too. This is all the fitting that will be needed if the waistline is only one or two inches too large. Fig. B-36a.

Take waist measurement and record on work ticket. Write down that the belt may have to be altered, though for this small amount it rarely is.

If more than 2 inches (5 cm) needs to be removed, additional pinning of the back waist darts will be needed. After pinning the side seams as before, pin back darts through the waistline enough to make the client feel comfortable. Continue pinning these darts as far down the skirt as needed to shape into the upper hipline. Fig. B-36b. Record waist measurement on work ticket. Also write that the belt may need to be shortened. Place crossed pins on the belt as a double reminder to change it.

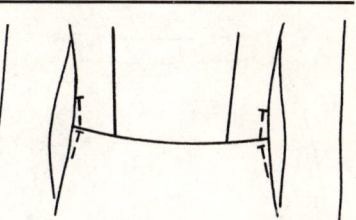

B-36a. Waistline too loose.

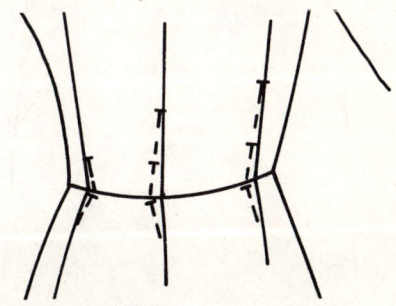

B-36b. Waistline more than 2 inches (5 cm) too large.

Altering Ready-To-Wear Fashions

## SKIRT FITTINGS

If she has a choice to make, the wise shopper will buy a garment that fits through the shoulders and bust areas as these sections are more difficult to alter. This may frequently mean that the skirt will be either too large or too small. However, adjusting a skirt is one of the easiest and most successful alterations.

The skirt should fall in place over the hips with the darts and style lines following the contours of the figure. Seams and darts should fall straight and true to grain with no pulling or distortion over the hips and abdomen. Fig. B-37. The style of the skirt or the body proportions of the client will determine whether or not any seam alterations required should continue through the hemline or stop above the hem.

Skirt hem lengths may vary from mini to maxi or any length in between. Since about 75 percent of all alterations involve a hem change, skirt length fittings are discussed separately in Chapter 10, which deals only with hems.

B-37. *Properly fitting skirt.*

### Skirt Too Large

The skirt may be too large all over.

TO FIT: Pin the excess out down both side seams equally. If necessary, pin through the waistline and hemline. Fig. B-38.

### Skirt Too Large in Waist

All the darts fall into place over the hips, front and back, and the side seams are straight. However, the waistband or waistline is loose. This often indicates full rounded hips and a proportionately small waist measurement.

TO FIT: Pin only through the waistband or waistline of the garment. Take the client's waist measurement and record on work ticket. Just as you did in the bodice above the waist, pin through the waistline at the side seams on each side. Taper pin line back into the hip line.

B-38. *Skirt too large in hips and waist.*

Ch. 8: Fitting Women's Clothes

### Skirt Too Large in Upper Hips

This may show up in bulges over the hips on the side seams.

TO FIT: Pin out the needed amount on the side seams. Taper the seam to nothing at the point where the skirt starts to hang smooth. Fig. B-39a.

The extra fabric may also show up in a bulge across the upper back where the darts are placed.

TO FIT: Increase the back darts, starting below the waistband or waistline, and ending where proper fit begins. Fig. B-39b.

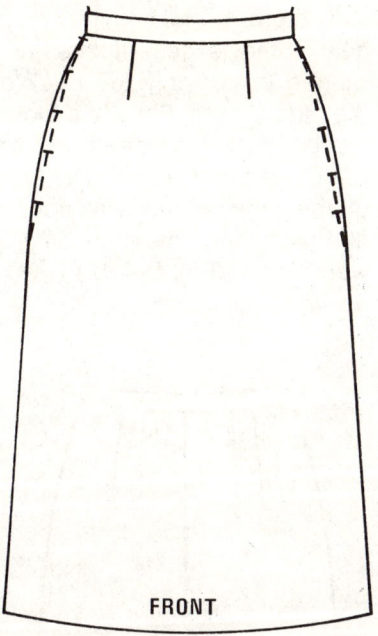

B-39a. Skirt too large in upper hips.

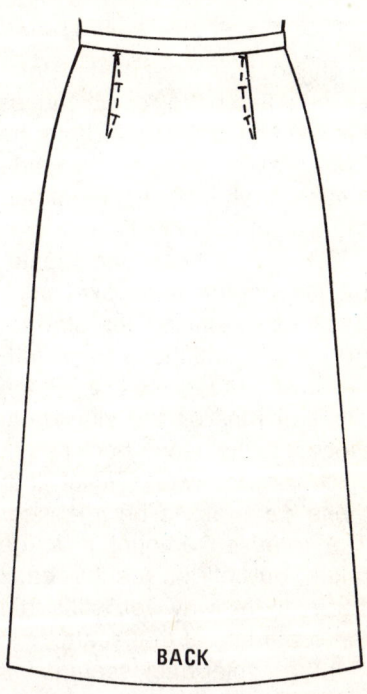

B-39b. Increasing back darts for skirt too large in upper hips in back only.

---

### Skirt Too Large in Lower Hip

This appears on the high, full-hipped figure with distended abdomen tapering to thin thighs. The skirt falls into unflattering folds over the lower hips.

TO FIT: Pin out extra folds at side seams. Start the pin line where the fullness begins and continue pinning through the hemline. Fig. B-40.

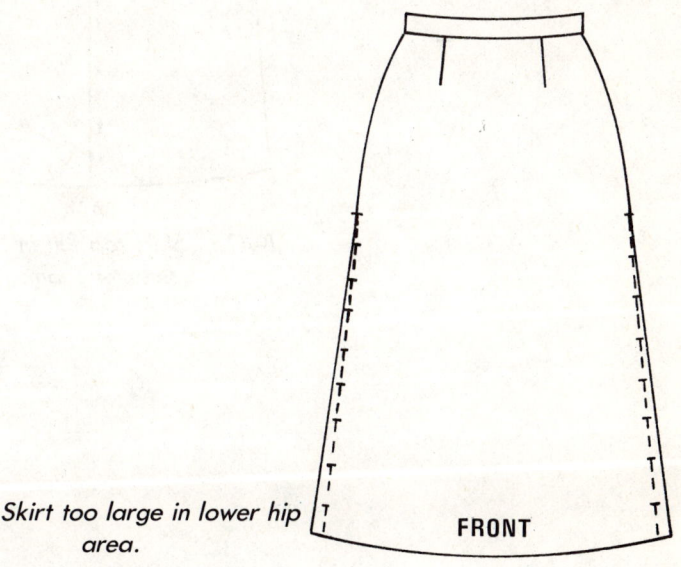

B-40. Skirt too large in lower hip area.

Altering Ready-To-Wear Fashions

## Skirt Too Full in Back Only

This occurs when the customer has flat buttocks. It causes the skirt to fall into folds in the back, even though the side seams are hanging straight and the waistline fits well.

TO FIT: Check the center back seam first. If the skirt has a back seam cut on the straight grain, pin out the excess fullness as in Fig. B-41a. Place crossed pins on the skirt darts closest to the center back seam. Write on the work ticket that these darts are to be released. The released amount is to be taken out of the center back seam. In this way, you will retain the grain line of that seam.

If the center back seam is cut on a slant, there is no need to be concerned about the grain line. Consequently, the darts are left alone but the center back seam is pinned the same as shown in Fig. B-41a.

If there is no center back seam, the excess fullness is pinned out of only the back of the side seams. Pin a fold along the back of the side seams on both sides of the skirt. The front of the side seams will not be changed. Indicate this on the work ticket. (Fig. B-41b.)

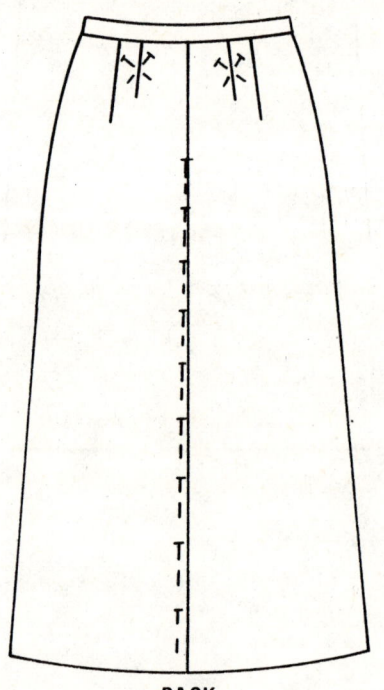

BACK
B-41a. Skirt too full in back with center seam.

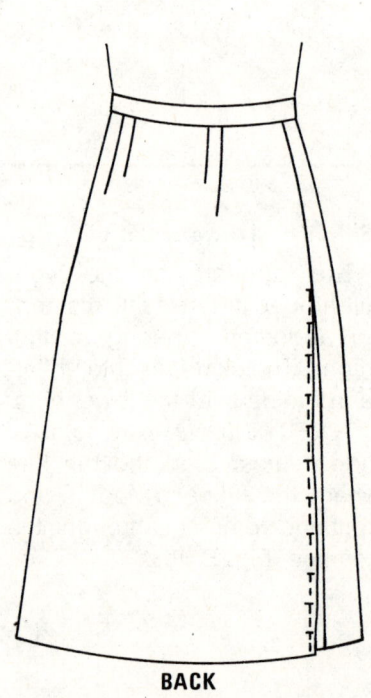

BACK
B-41b. Skirt too full in back without center seam.

## Ch. 8: Fitting Women's Clothes

### Skirt Too Small

Since the average female figure is larger in the waist and hips than in the shoulders and bust, this is a common problem. The garment may fit well through the bodice but be too tight over the waist, hips, and abdomen.

The amount of extra room needed plus the number of seams and the seam depth determine whether you can do this alteration successfully.

Keep in mind that 1/4 inch (.6 cm) on the double on any seam or dart will give an extra 1/2 inch (1.3 cm) of room. So if you have two seams, you can gain a full inch (2.5 cm) by releasing each seam just 1/4 inch (.6 cm). If the seams are 5/8 inch (1.6 cm) wide, they can be successfully released as much as 3/8 inch (.9 cm) apiece. You will still have 1/4 inch (.6 cm) seams, which can easily be reinforced in most fabrics. You may have to practice figuring in small fractions in order to make quick decisions on accepting this type of alteration. A too hasty "No" can cost a sale, a customer, or even a job!

TO FIT: Study the garment on the figure. Determine which darts may be released or removed to get the best results in the upper-hip fitting. On the front, the darts closest to the center front of the skirt are usually the best ones to release or remove. On the back of the skirt, the darts nearest the side seams are the ones that should be changed. Indicate the darts to be changed with crossed pins. The same kind of marking, used on the skirt seams, shows where to begin and end releasing seams. If seams are to be released only from the waist through the thigh area, put crossed pins at these points. If the releasing is to continue through the hemline, place crossed pins at the waist and the bottom of the hemline. Fig. B-42a. To guide alteration, record on work ticket all the measurements necessary for the skirt fitting—waist and upper and lower hip.

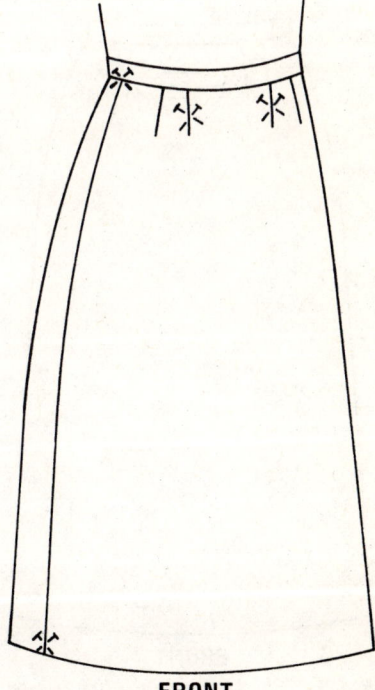

**FRONT**
B.42a. Skirt too small all over.

## Altering Ready-To-Wear Fashions

### Skirt Tight in Waistline Only

This is also a common fitting problem and one of the easiest to do.

TO FIT: First take and record the client's waist measurement. Indicate with crossed pins which darts can best be released to give the extra room needed. Write this information on the work ticket. Refer to waistline fittings earlier in this chapter for more information.

### Skirt Tight in Upper Hipline Only

The figure with a "tummy" or a fatty muscle across the upper back area often has this problem with a fitted skirt. The skirt rolls up and bulges below the waistline instead of resting on the upper hips.

TO FIT: Study the figure to see if the roll is all the way around the body. If so, indicate the darts to be removed, shortened, or reshaped with crossed pins. Fig. B-42b. Describe in detail on work ticket what is to be done. Be sure to take and record the upper hip measurement.

If the roll is across only the back or the front of the skirt, indicate this on the ticket and apply crossed pins on the darts to be changed.

NOTE: There are usually eight darts in a fitted skirt—four in back and four in front. Even if there are only four darts in all, you will still have the same amount of fabric to shift and reshape. As in the bodice darts, you can move skirt darts around to suit the shape of the individual figure. The only limitation in doing this would be if the darts have been cut away underneath. In that case, other solutions must be worked out. See Chapter 9.

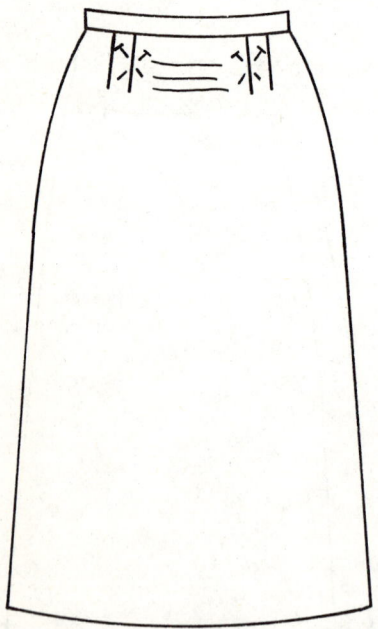

**FRONT**
B-42b. Skirt too tight in upper hip area.

Ch. 8: Fitting Women's Clothes

### Skirt Too Tight Through Lower Hipline

Sometimes a skirt will fit well at the waist, roll nicely over the upper hips, and then pull tight across the lower hipline. This will show up in distorted side seams and an unflattering profile. The skirt will cup in under the abdomen and lower hipline or buttocks. Fig. B-43a.

TO FIT: Take the lower hip measurement and record. Add the necessary ease to the measurement, as described in the section *Taking Measurements* on page 143. Be sure to record how far down from the waist along the side seams the full hip measurement was taken. Apply crossed pins on the side seams where the stress or pull on the seams appears. For a straight line or tube skirt, put crossed pins at the bottom of the hem. Write on the work ticket that the seams are to be released from the top crossed pins through the hemline.

For an A-line skirt, apply the crossed pins on the lower skirt where the seam pull or stress ends. Write on the work ticket that seams are to be released only to these pins. It is usually undesirable to add width to the bottom of an A-line skirt. Fig. B-43b.

### Skirt and Pants Waistbands

When separate skirts or pants require an alteration in the waistline to make the garment larger or smaller, the waistband will be marked to indicate the changes needed. Be sure the client's waist measurement is recorded on the work ticket. If the band is to be enlarged, place crossed pins at one end to call attention to the need for change. If the band is to be made smaller, pin a tuck to indicate the amount to be removed.

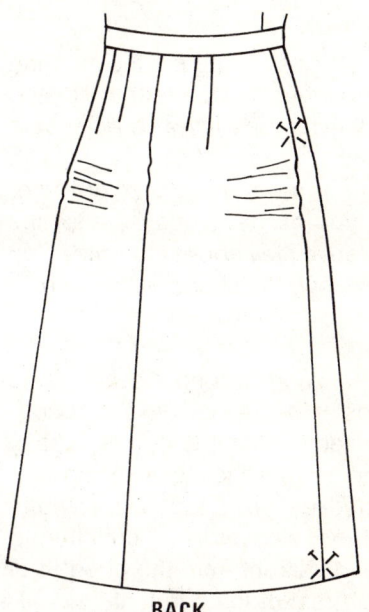

**BACK**
B-43a. Skirt too tight in lower hips (back).

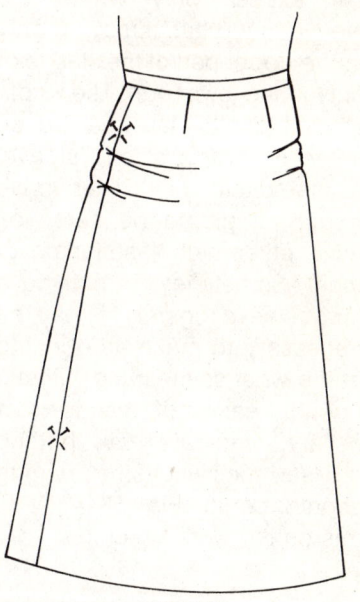

**FRONT**
B-43b. Skirt too tight in lower hips (front).

*Altering Ready-To-Wear Fashions*

## SLEEVE FITTINGS

After all fitting but the hemline has been completed, check the sleeves. See if they are in scale with the rest of the garment in width and length. After other changes have been made, the sleeve may appear too wide, too narrow, too short, or too long.

### Sleeves Too Wide

A short or long sleeve that is too wide is not always recognized by the client. It is usually up to the fitter to note that the sleeves have too much width. Such sleeves are unflattering and detract from the good fit of the rest of the garment.

TO FIT: Insert the pins along the sleeve seam with the pins pointing toward the hand. Pin out excess only where the sleeve is too full. It may be only in the upper part of the sleeve or only in the lower part. The whole sleeve length may need to be taken in. If it is a long sleeve, ask the client to bend her arm to a right angle to be sure you have left enough ease for movement. Sometimes, in making a long sleeve tighter, it may be necessary to make an opening at the wrist so the hand will slip through easily. If this is necessary, indicate by putting crossed pins where the opening should begin. Fig. B-44. Note this on the work ticket.

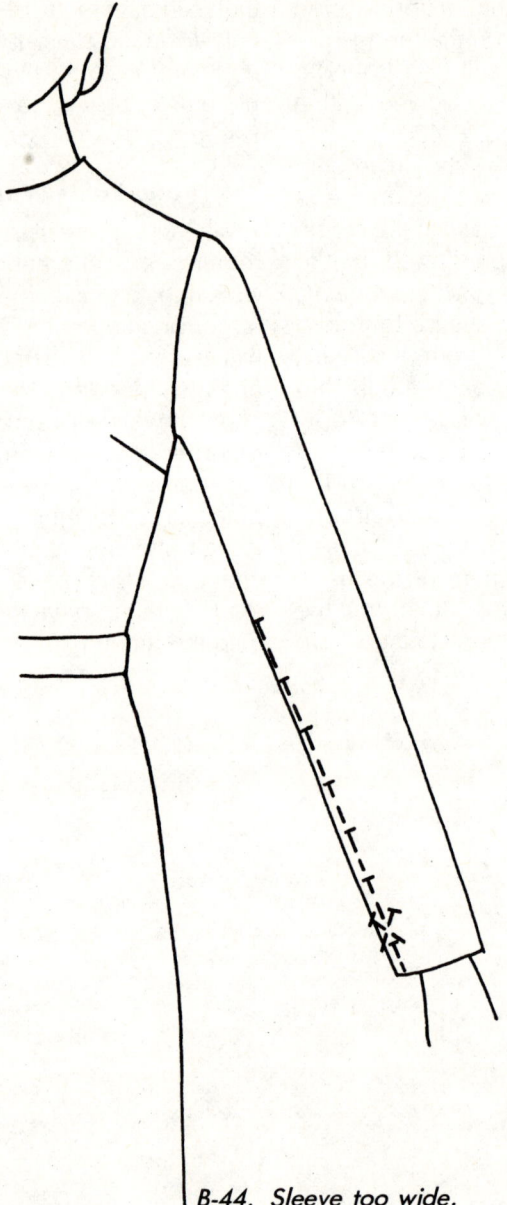

B-44. *Sleeve too wide.*

Ch. 8: Fitting Women's Clothes

### Sleeves Too Tight

Many women—because of overweight, surgery, or occupation—have extremely large upper arms, making this a common fitting problem. You will recognize the problem by the way the fabric pulls across the arm. Check a long sleeve with the arm bent as the tightness may only show up then.

TO FIT: Place crossed pins at each end of the part of the seam to be released. With the client's arm hanging loosely against the body, take and record the measurements of the areas that need the extra ease. If the needed release is minor, this is all you will need to note. Fig. B-45a.

Often the required increase is greater than can be accomplished just by releasing the sleeve seam. In such cases, you will need to investigate the possibility of adding a gusset to the sleeve. If the problem is only in the upper arm, enough material for short gussets can usually be found in the garment facings. If the entire sleeve must be widened, you may have a problem finding enough matching material to make a long gusset. You may have to suggest that the sleeve be changed to a bracelet length or short sleeve so the extra sleeve fabric can be used for the gussets. Such decisions must be made during the fitting. Fig. B-45b.

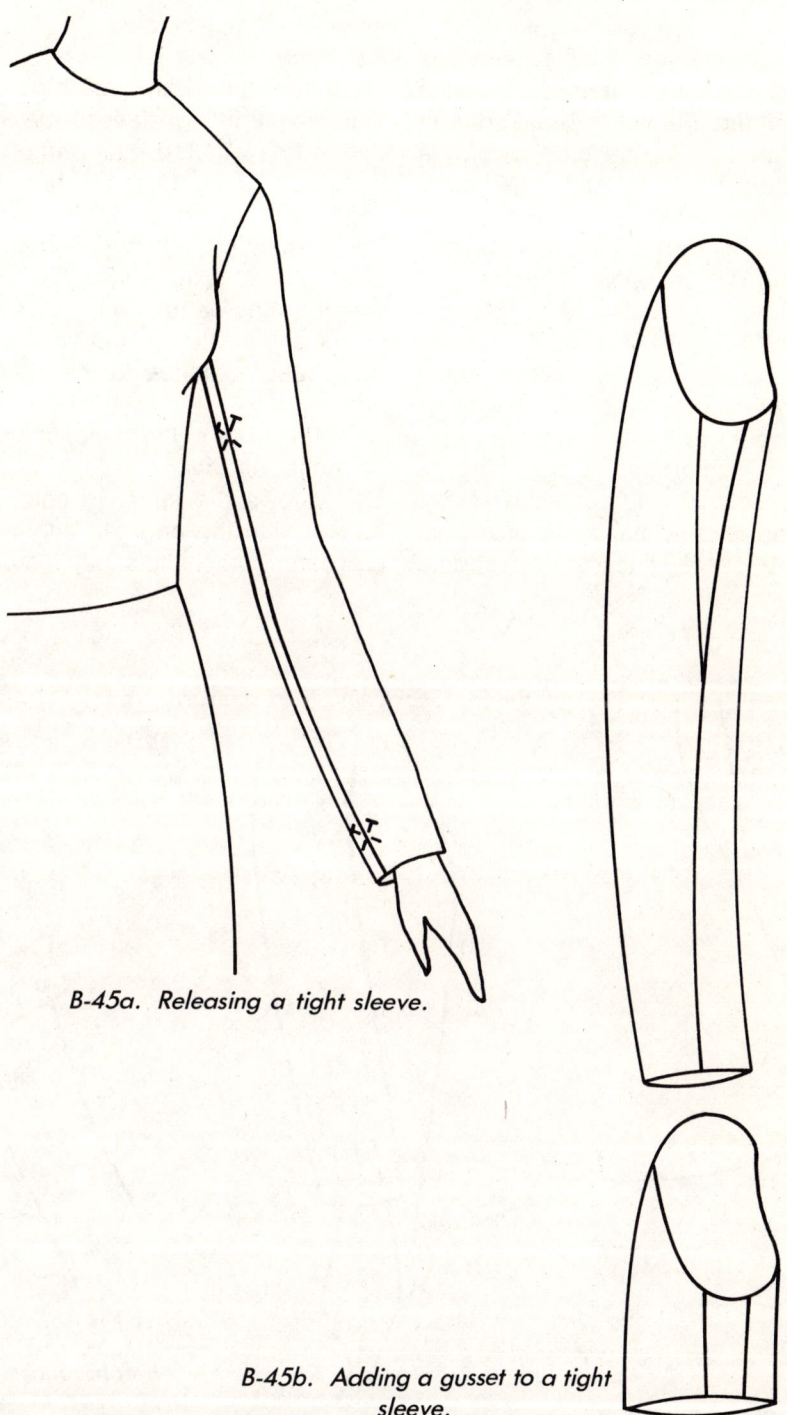

B-45a. Releasing a tight sleeve.

B-45b. Adding a gusset to a tight sleeve.

## Altering Ready-To-Wear Fashions

### Sleeve Length

The length of the sleeve is important to the proper balance of the garment. The end and fullness of the sleeve form a horizontal line and draw attention to that area of the body.

For example, on a full-busted figure, the sleeve should end above or below the bust line and should fit close to the arm. Sleeves that billow or stand away from the arm add undesirable width.

A small-busted figure needs the extra width a short sleeve adds by ending at the bust area. A loosely fitted sleeve adding extra width may be desirable for this figure.

On the figure with large hips, long, loose-fitting sleeves may end in line with the wide part of the body and add even more width. This is especially true if the garment has any trimming at the hip area. Fig. B-46a. Such sleeves may need to be made narrower and/or shortened to give better balance to the figure.

TO FIT: Make the necessary changes on one sleeve only. This allows the client to compare it with the original length and helps with the final decision on the length desired. Turn the extra length under and pin in place. Place the pins vertically with the heads at the top and the points toward the hand. This allows the sleeve to roll around the arm freely without puckers. It also makes the garment easier to remove after the fitting is finished. Fig. B-46a.

If the sleeves have a cuff or trim, they cannot be turned under. For this alteration, pin a tuck just above the cuff or trim. These pins will have to be inserted in a horizontal line to hold the tuck in place. Fig. B-46b.

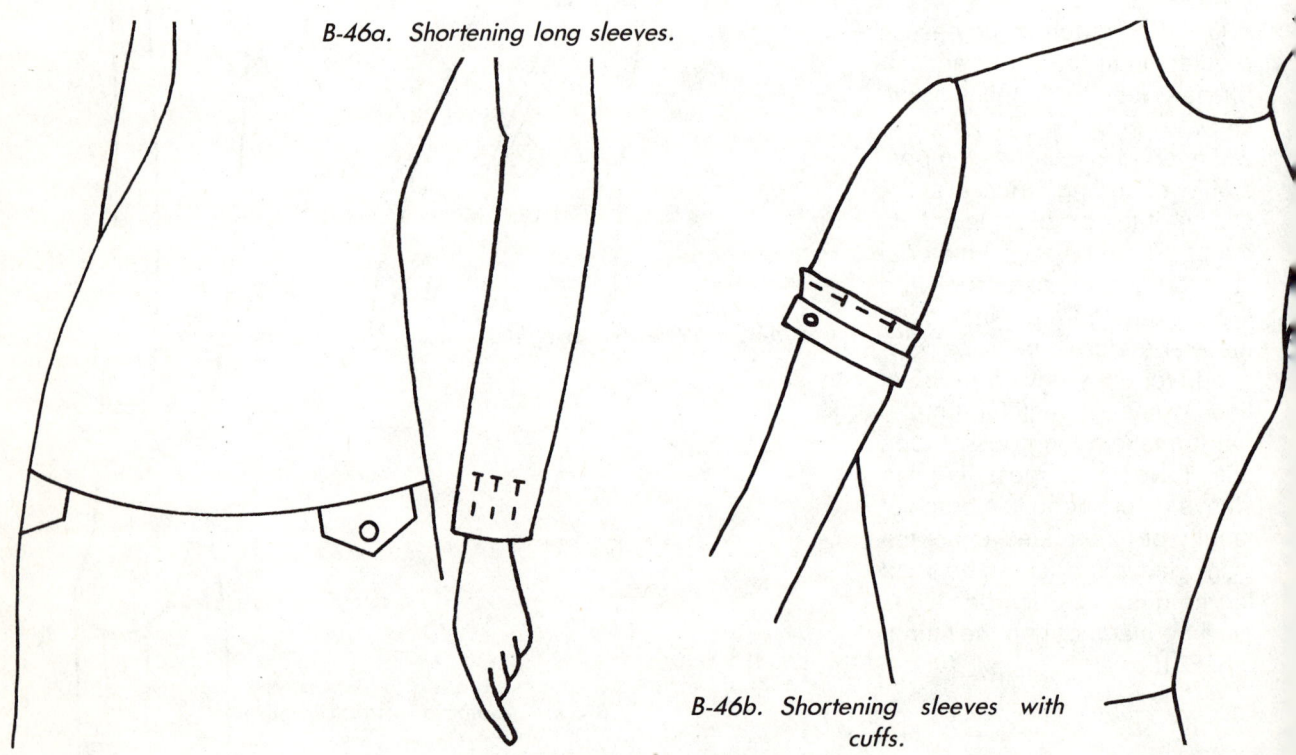

B-46a. Shortening long sleeves.

B-46b. Shortening sleeves with cuffs.

Ch. 8: Fitting Women's Clothes

## Sleeves Off-Grain

This problem occurs frequently enough for you to be prepared to cope with it. You will detect sleeves that are off-grain by the way they twist and do not hang "true" on the arm. In short sleeves, the bottom of the sleeves will stand away from the arm instead of resting on it. You may find the problem with one sleeve or both.

TO FIT: Put crossed pins on the crown of the sleeve and make a note on the work ticket that the sleeve or sleeves need to be removed and reset. Fig. B-47.

If both sleeves are off-grain, it might be that the sleeves were reversed when the garment was made. They may need to be switched to the opposite arm holes.

If sleeves are actually cut off-grain—rare in ready-made garments—there is little you can do.

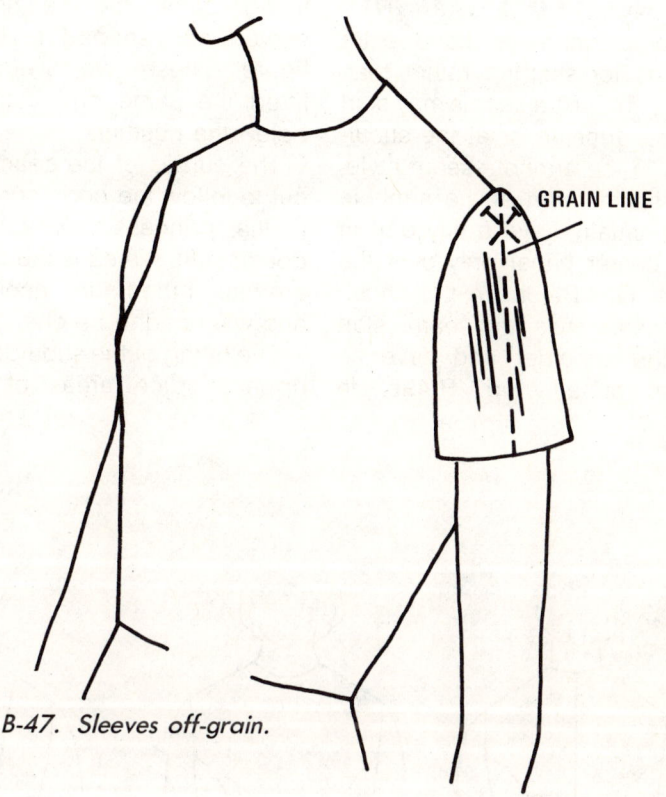

B-47. Sleeves off-grain.

## Sleeves Too Full at Armhole

Sometimes the top or cap of a sleeve will have too much fullness in the front or back. This shows up in a roll or puffiness on the sleeve at the armhole seam.

TO FIT: Tuck the extra fullness under the shoulder at the armhole seam and pin in place. Insert the pins perpendicular to the seam. Fig. B-48.

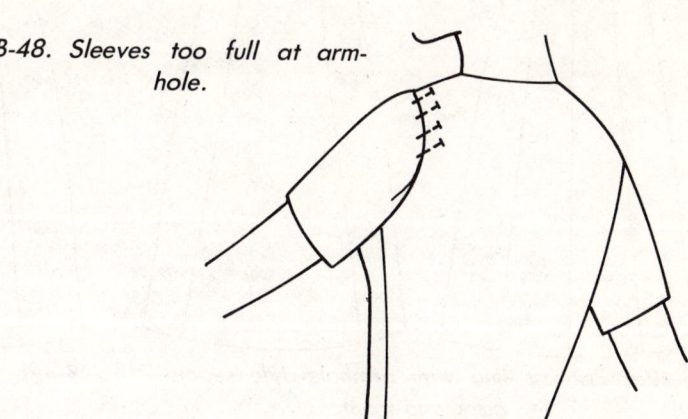

B-48. Sleeves too full at armhole.

*Altering Ready-To-Wear Fashions*

## FITTING THE PRINCESS STYLE GARMENT

Some garments have extra seams for shaping rather than darts. The extra seams may start at the armhole or at the shoulder. In the armhole-seam style, the seams start at the armhole and usually have a tiny dart in the center panel only over the bust. Fig. B-49a. In the shoulder-seam style, the seams start at the shoulder and have no darts at all. Fig. B-49b. In either type instead of waistline-fitting darts, the seams are curved and shaped to fit the figure. These two styles are fitted the same on all fittings below the bustline.

The curves of the seams are cut to follow the body contours. If the princess-style garment does not fit, it means the curves are hitting the figure incorrectly and will need to be changed.

The fitting of the shoulder and upper bodice areas of each type of princess style varies slightly, depending upon the location of the seams. Each type is described separately when the fitting method differs.

### Princess Neckline Fittings

The neckline fit is not affected by these style lines. Any changes to be made in the neckline area would be fitted according to the directions already given under "*Neckline Fittings*," pages 145–150.

B-49a. Princess line with armhole-style seams—back and front.

B-49b. Princess line with shoulder-style seams—back and front.

Ch. 8: Fitting Women's Clothes

## Princess Shoulder Fittings

### ARMHOLE-SEAM STYLE

The garment shoulders may be too wide both front and back, in front only, or in back only. The fitting is the same in each instance. If the extra fabric is in front or back only, the fitting tuck would be tapered to nothing at the top of the shoulder.

TO FIT: Make a tuck along the top of the shoulder near the armhole seam, taking out the amount needed to bring the armhole seam to the shoulder bone. This change will probably require increasing the underarm style line seams both front and back. Pin these seams in just enough to bring the armhole closer to the body. Fig. B-50a and b.

If the shoulders are too narrow, you will have to use your own judgment as to the advisability of attempting an alteration. Reread the section of "Garment Shoulders Too Narrow," page 153.

All other types of shoulder fittings for the armhole-seam style are handled the same way as they would be without the style lines. Refer to the first part of the chapter.

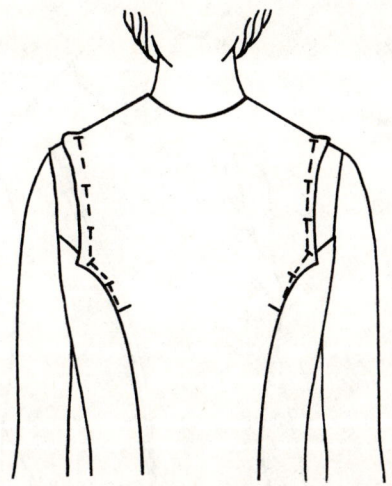

B-50a. Shoulders of garment too wide in front (armhole-style seams).

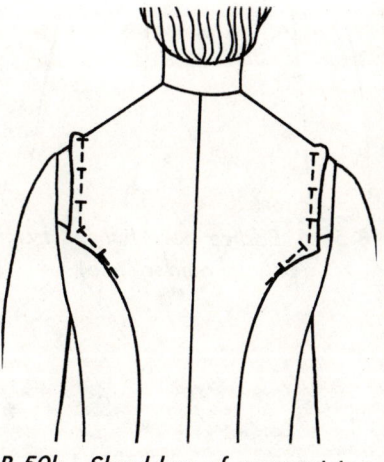

B-50b. Shoulders of garment too wide in back (armhole-style seams).

### SHOULDER-SEAM STYLE

For too-wide shoulders in this particular style, you have the great advantage of being able to use the style seams.

TO FIT: Pin out the extra shoulder width in the style seams—front and back—starting at the shoulder seams. Pin out only enough to bring the crown of the sleeve up to the shoulder bone and the front and back armholes closer to the body. Fig. B-50c. On the front seam, the pinning usually ends in the bust area or at the point of the bust. The back seam pin line usually ends at the bottom of the shoulder blades.

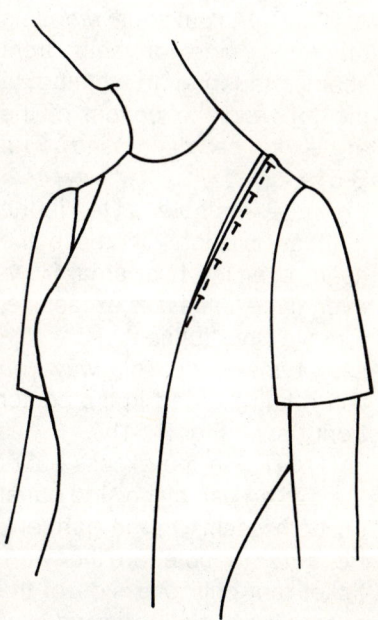

B-50c. Shoulders too wide (shoulder-style seams).

## Altering Ready-To-Wear Fashions

### Princess Bodice Fittings

The bodice of a princess style garment should fit basically the same as any bodice. The dart tips and bust ease should come to the fullest part of the bust—neither above nor below. There should be enough ease for comfort and appearance without being loose.

#### PRINCESS BODICE TOO LOOSE

TO FIT: Pin along the underarm seams in the same manner described earlier under *Bodice Equally Full Front and Back*, page 157.

#### PRINCESS BODICE TOO FULL IN FRONT ONLY

In the shoulder-seam style, increase the seam over the bust area.

TO FIT: Pin out equal amounts on each side of both front seams, tapering to nothing at the top and the bottom of the areas to be decreased. Fig. B-51a.

In the armhole style, if the fullness is slight, increase the seam over the bust area. However, if the fullness is excessive, remove the fullness from the side panel only. This way you will retain the dart in the center front panel. Fig. B-51b.

TO FIT: Pin the excess out of the curved part of the side panel on both seams of the garment. Be sure to note on the work ticket that only one side of the seam should be increased.

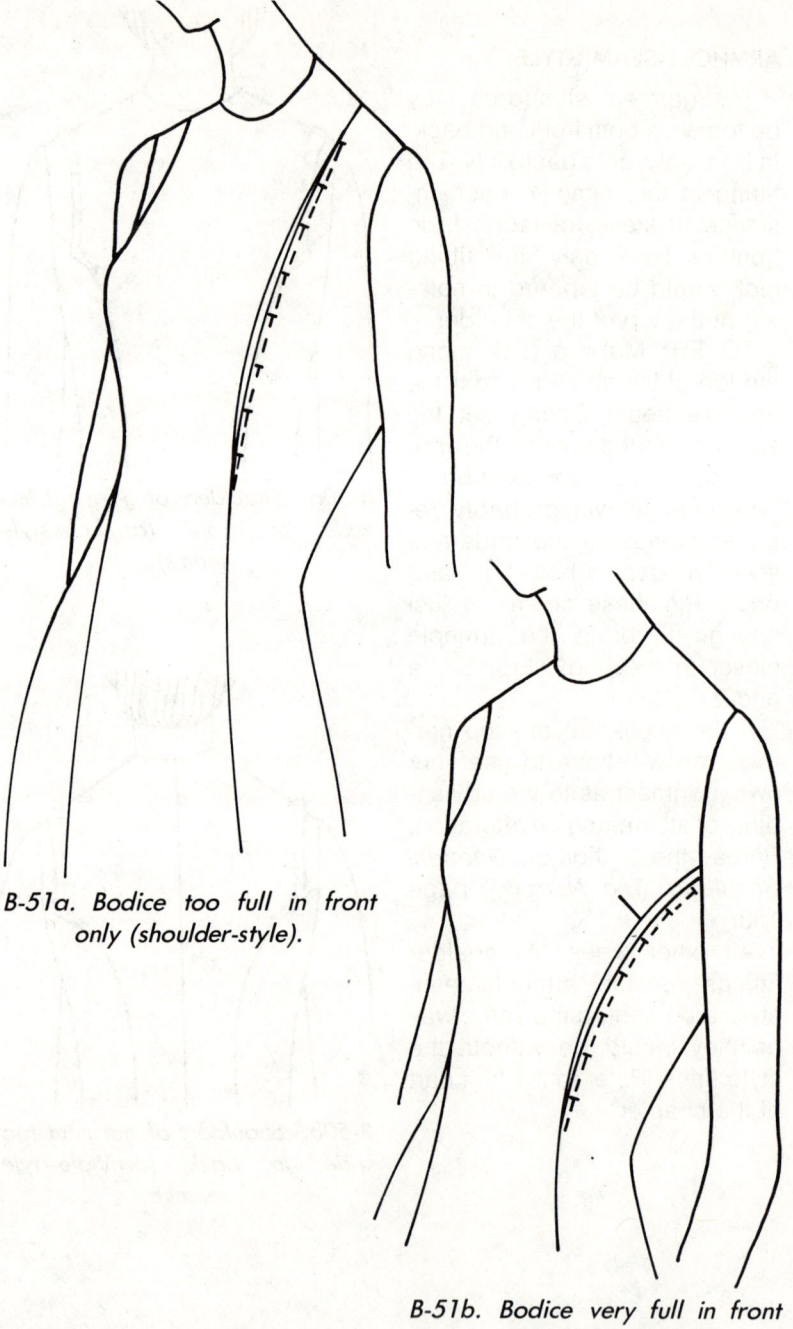

B-51a. Bodice too full in front only (shoulder-style).

B-51b. Bodice very full in front (armhole-style).

## Ch. 8: Fitting Women's Clothes

### PRINCESS BODICE TOO FULL IN BACK ONLY

Any extra fullness across the back of the bodice can easily be removed by increasing the style lines over the area.

TO FIT: Pin out the fullness along the style line, taking the same amount on each side of the seam. Pin both seams to be sure you are not overfitting.

### PRINCESS BODICE TOO TIGHT

If possible, release the side seams just as described for a basic bodice under *Bodice too Tight*.

*B-52. Princess bodice too tight.*

If more ease is needed than can be gained by releasing just the side seams, you may need to release the style seams also. If a wide back is causing the problem, release the back style lines only. If a large bust is causing the garment to pull tight over this area, the front style lines must be altered.

TO FIT: Insert a line of pins along the seams to be released, showing the amount the seam should be let out. Put crossed pins at the top and the bottom of the area to be released. Be sure to write directions for the change clearly on the work ticket. Fig. B-52.

For the armhole-style seam, do not release the style seams all the way to the armhole. If you do, you will increase the size of the armhole but will not give the ease across the bust or back where needed.

### PRINCESS BODICE TOO TIGHT THROUGH MIDRIFF

The bodice may fit through the bust and shoulders but pull across the midriff, either front or back. In this case, the style lines would be released only through this area. The pins are placed in the same manner as described before. Put crossed pins where the releasing should start and stop with a line of pins along the side of the seam to indicate how much the seam should be released. Write directions on the work ticket.

## PRINCESS BODICE TOO LONG

In princess lines, note that the waistline is cut or shaped into the curves of the seams. On the inside of a ready-made dress, you will find clip marks on all the seams at the normal waistline. If you made the mini-dresses (Chapter 6), you made these clips to show where the waistline is placed. It is important to be aware of these clips in the alteration of the princess style garment.

When the bodice is too long, fold lines will form across the midriff front and back. Fig. B-53a. These folds form because the waistline on the dress is sitting on the upper hips instead of falling into place at the waist. The narrowest part of the dress—the waistline—is pulled tight across the upper hip area. There isn't enough room to accommodate the hips so the vertical seams are pulled and distorted. Since there is no waistline seam, the changes will be made in the vertical seams. They will need to be released below the waistline to give more room for the hips.

TO FIT: Start by tying a cord around the client's natural waistline. Pull the folds of fabric in the bodice down under the cord so the bodice above the cord is smooth. Place crossed pins at the cord line. If only the side seams are pulling, place the crossed pins at the sides only. If the upper hips are large, it may be necessary to alter all the seams. In that case, place crossed pins at the cord on the style seams also. These crossed pins will mark the new waistline.

Take the client's upper hip measurement and record on the work ticket. Place pin lines along the seams that must be released to allow for the stomach and hip measurement. Place another set of crossed pins at the point on the seams where the releasing will end. Write clear instructions on the work ticket to tell the alterationist what must be done. Fig. B-53b.

Sometimes with this type of alteration, you will run into another problem. When the waistline is pulled down below the cord, you may find that the bodice will be too loose around the midriff. To indicate this, pin out the excess on the seams where needed, just as you would to fit any bodice at the waist. Insert crossed pins to indicate where the increase will taper back to the original seams. Fig. B-53b.

If the bodice is too long in front or back only, the same procedure for fitting is followed. Indicate changes only where needed.

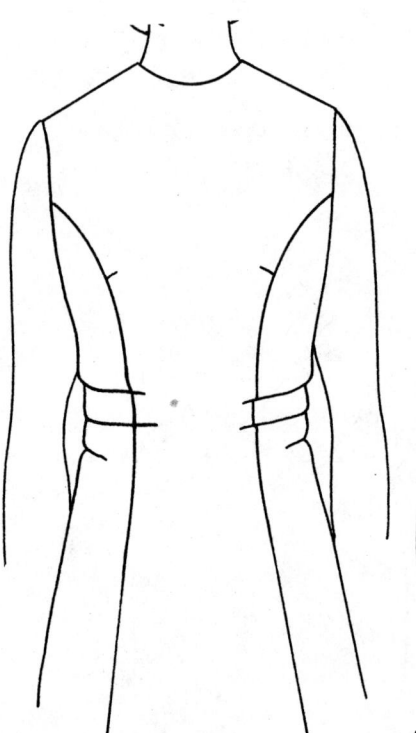

B-53a. Princess bodice too long.

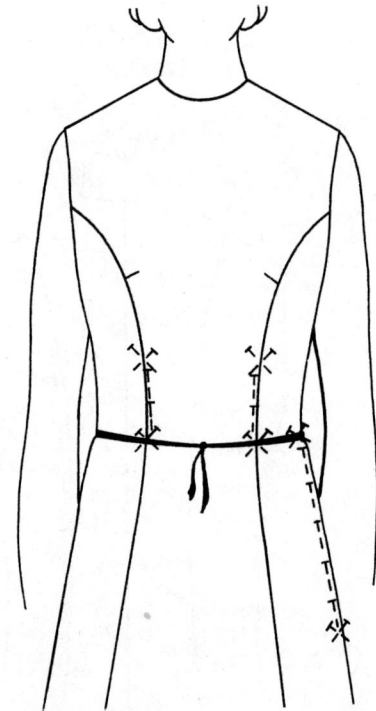

B-53b. Shortening the princess waistline.

## Ch. 8: Fitting Women's Clothes

### BODICE TOO SHORT

This fitting problem will show up on the extremely long-waisted figure. It can be recognized by the way the seams fall away from the figure at the waistline and upper hipline. The garment does not shape to the figure. If the problem is slight, the fitting may be done on the side seams only. Often the problem is severe enough that the front or back style seams must also be fitted.

TO FIT: Tie a cord at the client's waistline and pin out the fullness at the side seams. Insert the first pins at the waistline cord. Taper from there up the lower part of the bodice and down over the upper hipline. Do not take in side seams at waistline more than 1 inch (2.5 cm) on each side seam. If more fitting is needed in this area, it should be pinned in the same manner on the front or back style lines. Fig. B-54.

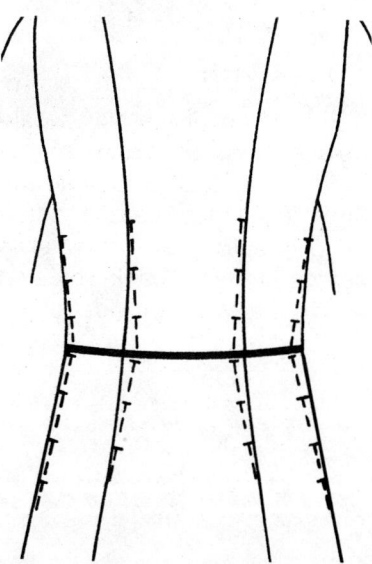

B-54. Princess bodice too short.

### BODICE TOO SHORT IN FRONT ONLY

The garment may sit well on the figure in back and the side seams may be in line with the figure contours everywhere but in the front. The dress may hang away from the figure at the waistline in front. This is usually caused by a high, full bosom that has pulled up the hidden waistline.

TO FIT: Tie a cord at the waistline and pin out the fullness on the front style seams only. Start at the waistline and pin up to the bust crown on the bodice. Pin down over the upper hipline. Fig. B-55.

### BODICE TOO SHORT IN BACK ONLY

This is the garment that fits well, except for falling away from the figure in back. The back waistline is too high for the figure. This is usually the sign of large shoulder blades or very rounded shoulders that hike the garment up in back.

TO FIT: Pin out the extra fullness on the back style seams only, following the instructions given for the front. Fig. B-55.

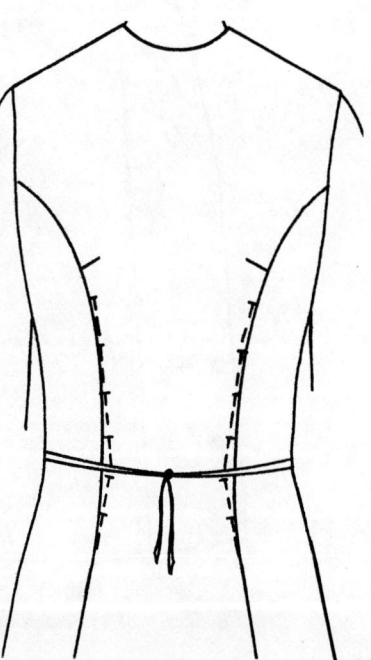

B-55. Princess bodice too short in front only.

183

*Altering Ready-To-Wear Fashions*

## Skirt Fittings for Princess Lines

The fitting of the skirt would be the same as shown on the regular hip and side seam fittings for skirts. The only difference would be if the style seams—front or back—created a skirt that was too wide for the client's figure. The style lines can add height and give a slimming effect if they are fairly straight. Sometimes this style is cut at an angle on the lower skirt to give extra flair. The extra fullness may be unbecoming to the customer buying the garment.

TO FIT: Pin out fullness, starting with the flare just below the hipline. Continue pinning on the grainline through the skirt hem. Fig. B-56a. This may need to be done in front only as the back may not be cut with the same fullness. The figure with the flat derriere may need the back flare straightened and also reduced in the same manner. Fig. B-56b.

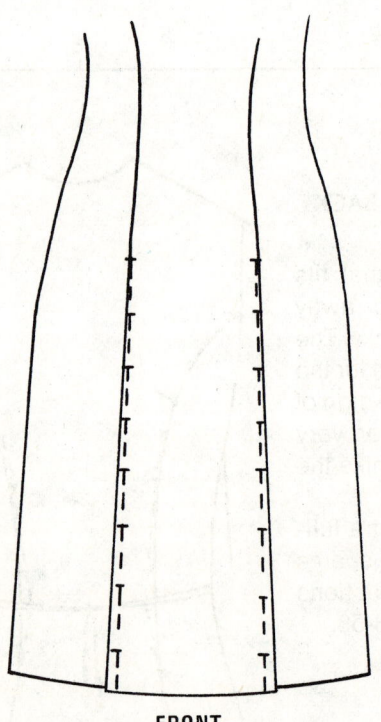

**FRONT**
B-56a. Skirt too full in front.

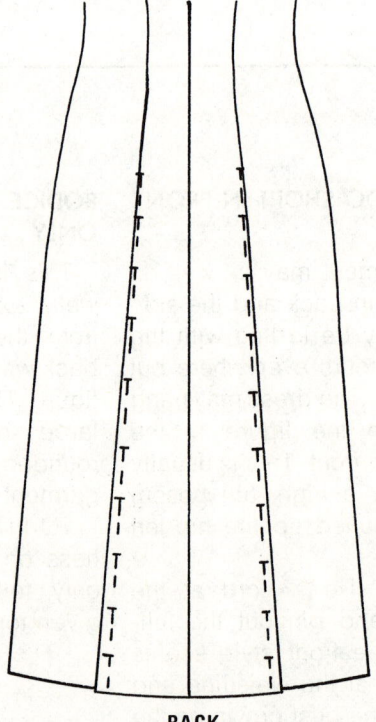

**BACK**
B-56b. Skirt too full in back.

## FITTING THE BASIC SHIFT

There have been many names for the shift garment in the past, and there will be more in the future. These names have been coined by designers, fashion writers, and sometimes by the public. When first introduced, this style was referred to as the "sack." The public scoffed, so designers worked hard at substituting other names, such as *chemise, skimmer,* or *sheath.* Since then, variations of the basic shift style have been with us almost constantly. Fig. B-57.

Basically, like the princess line, the shift has only vertical seams. They may include center front, center back, and side seams or any combination of these. The shift differs from the princess line in that it does not have a center panel with side style seams. Neither style has a waistline seam. The fitting for the body contours may be accomplished either by the use of shaping darts *or* tapered seams. Some shifts are meant to hang loose with no real waistline fitting. The skirt area is usually cut on straight lines though it can be flared through the use of center front and center back seams. In any case, the object is to have an easy-fitting, one-piece garment.

A shift may be sleeveless or have almost any style sleeves added. It may also have almost any style of neckline. These changes do not have much to do with the basic lines or fit.

Since the waistline area is the only part of the garment that would have specific fitting instructions, this is the only area to be discussed separately. For neckline, shoulder, bustline, back, and hip adjustments on a shift style garment, refer to the corresponding section in the early part of this chapter.

B-57. Variations of a shift style.

Altering Ready-To-Wear Fashions

### Shift Bodice Length

Because the basic shift pattern has a very easy fit, it does not mean the long- or short-waisted figure can fit into just any shift. The waist may fall to the hip line on a short-waisted person or may ride too high on a long-waisted figure. In either case, some adjustments must be made.

### SHIFT BODICE TOO LONG

The fabric bunches up at the waistline and midriff. If there is a back or front zipper, it may stand away from the body in an ugly bulge. The garment is resting on the upper hip area instead of sliding down into place on the hips.

Your immediate reaction may be that the garment is too large through the waist and midriff and should be taken in. In reality, the garment is too tight through the upper hip area. It should be released, letting the garment slip down to retain the easy fit of the shift style.

TO FIT: Insert crossed pins on the side seams at the client's waistline. Make a pin line along the side seams as far down the hipline as release is needed. Release enough so the garment will slide easily into place. Fig. B-58. Carefully indicate on the work ticket that these seams are to be *released* where pinned. This fitting applies to all the shift styles shown in Fig. B-57.

### SHIFT BODICE TOO LONG IN FRONT OR BACK ONLY

The figure with a small bust or a high stomach may force folds into the front of the midriff only. The back of the garment may rest in place perfectly. The full-busted figure may fill out the front of the bodice so that only the back part is too long.

TO FIT either problem, use the same technique given above.

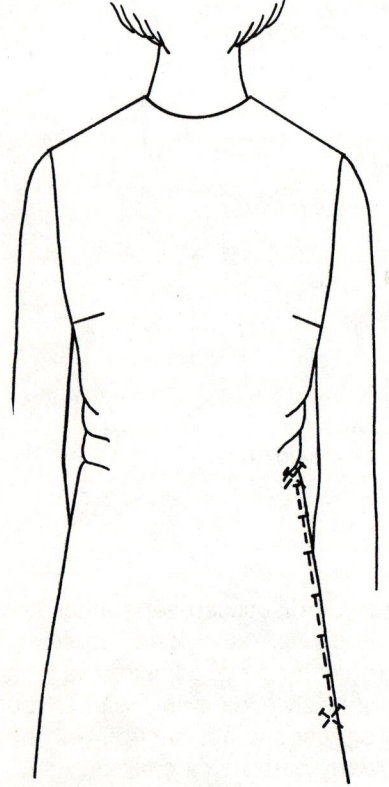

*B-58. Shift bodice too long.*

**Ch. 8: Fitting Women's Clothes**

## SHIFT BODICE BACK EXCESSIVELY LONG

If the folds in the back bodice are excessive, the preceding instructions will not be adequate. You will probably have to create a simulated waistline seam in the back to remove the excess.

TO FIT: Pin out the excess folds into a tuck, starting at the waistline on the side seams. Do not take anything out of the seams, but start there. Gradually deepen the tuck toward the center back, curving the line slightly downward. Fig. B-59. The curved back waistline is more flattering than a straight seam and creates back interest.

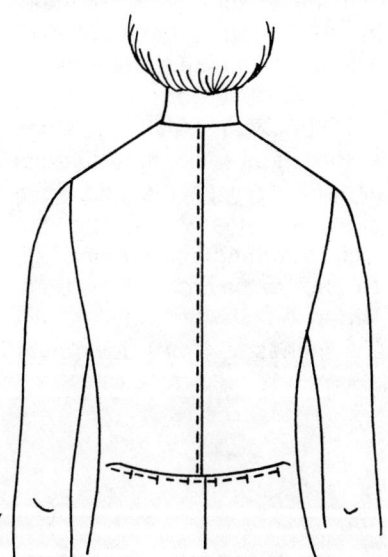

B-59. Shift bodice excessively long in back.

## SHIFT BODICE TOO SHORT

This rarely shows up in the easy-fit shift except on extremely long-waisted figures. It can happen when a client buys the shorter-scaled Junior size when her body proportions require a Misses size. The garment will hang away from the body and will not lie smoothly over the hips or follow the body contours.

TO FIT: Increase the side seams, forming a new waist shaping. Insert the pins at the client's natural waist, taking in a maximum of about ½ inch (1.3 cm). Taper seams off above and below this first pin. Pin both sides of the garment to avoid overfitting. Fig. B-60.

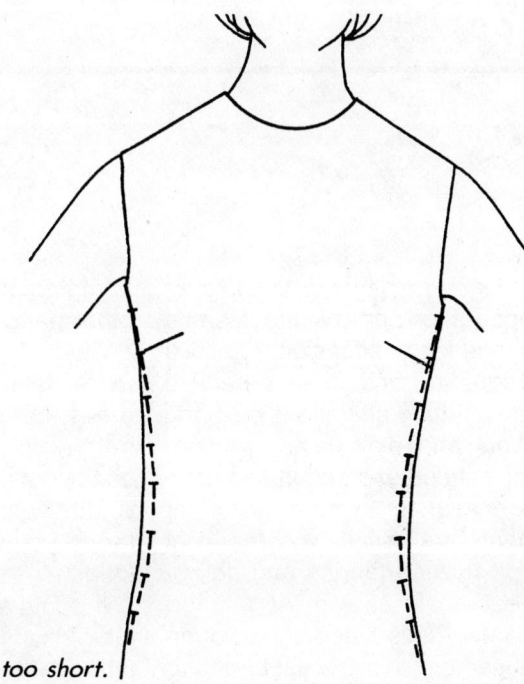

B-60. Shift bodice too short.

## Altering Ready-To-Wear Fashions

### Shift Waistline Shaping.

If the client's figure requires more shaping for the waist, do it with the addition of front and/or back waistline darts.

TO FIT: Start with a small tuck at the client's waistline directly under the point of the bust. From this pin at the waist, taper the tuck to nothing about 1 inch (2.5 cm) below the crown of the bust. Taper below the waist about 2½ inches (6.4 cm) down over the hips. Make a matching dart on the other side of the garment. Pin out only enough for a slight waist shaping. Fig. B-61. If extra shaping is needed in the back, follow the same procedure. Start at the client's waist and taper up to 1 inch (2.5 cm) beneath the shoulder blade and down to 3 inches (7.6 cm) below the waist over the hips. Do not overfit and spoil the casual style of the shift.

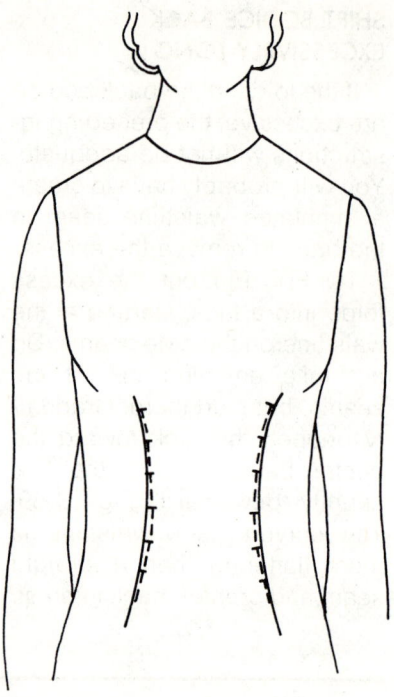

B-61. Adding darts for waistline shaping.

### FITTING PANTS

Since pants have become an accepted part of the fashion scene for all occasions, you will frequently find it necessary to make fitting alterations on them. Work and play pants are worn for comfort and action and have a casual fit. Evening or formal pants are usually loose and of soft flowing fabrics and do not need to fit as well as tailored pants. Pants that are part of an ensemble or suit must fit well to complement the figure and the other parts of the outfit.

Study Fig. B-62a to become more familiar with the pants areas that require fitting. It can help you remember what to check on the customer. Fig. B-62b will help explain the terms you will find used in the fittings.

If pants are to be worn with a tuck-in shirt or blouse, do the fitting with the customer wearing such a blouse. You will be more sure your fitting will be correct.

The fitting suggestions given here are for the pants that must fit for comfort and appearance. This is the basic, straight-leg pants with a waistband or elasticized waistline.

As usual, the fittings will be discussed starting at the top of the garment and working down to the bottom.

*Ch. 8: Fitting Women's Clothes*

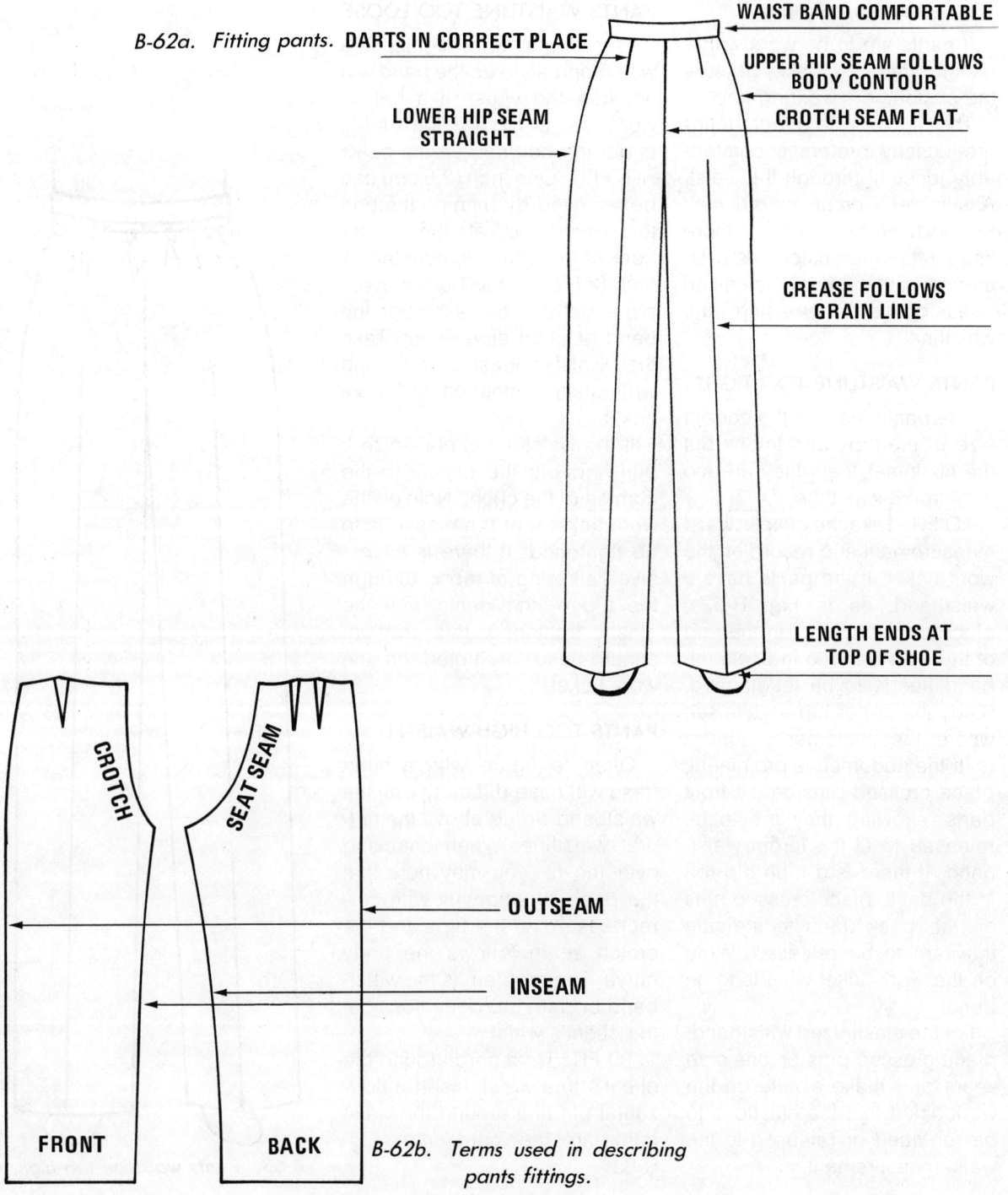

B-62a. Fitting pants. DARTS IN CORRECT PLACE — WAIST BAND COMFORTABLE — UPPER HIP SEAM FOLLOWS BODY CONTOUR — LOWER HIP SEAM STRAIGHT — CROTCH SEAM FLAT — CREASE FOLLOWS GRAIN LINE — LENGTH ENDS AT TOP OF SHOE

B-62b. Terms used in describing pants fittings.

## Altering Ready-To-Wear Fashions

### Waistline Fittings

If pants are to be worn with a tuck-in shirt or blouse, be sure the customer is wearing one.

The person with a mature figure usually prefers a comfortably loose fit through the waist. A slimmer woman or girl may like to have her pants fit more snugly. Let the customer's preference guide your decisions on releasing or increasing the waistline.

### PANTS WAISTLINE TOO TIGHT

The pants may be the correct size in the hips and thighs but the customer feels they are too tight in the waistline.

TO FIT: Take the client's waist measurement and record on the work ticket. If the pants have a waistband, as in Fig. B-62a, place crossed pins on the end of the waistband to indicate the band needs to be lengthened. Study the upper hip area to see where the customer's fullness is. If the abdomen is prominent, place crossed pins on the front darts, showing they are to be released to fit the larger waistband. If there is a high hip roll in the back, place crossed pins on the back darts to indicate they are to be released. Write on the work ticket what is to be done.

For the elasticized waistband, place crossed pins on one side seam and make a note on the work ticket that the elastic is to be replaced or released to the waist measurement.

### PANTS WAISTLINE TOO LOOSE

This is easy to recognize in a waistband style as the band will not hug the waist. If a belt is worn, the band will form folds under the belt and create bulk.

TO FIT: One inch (2.5 cm) can be removed by pinning through the waistband at the center back of the pants. If more than 1 inch (2.5 cm) is to be removed, pin equal-size tucks through the band at each side seam. Take the waist measurement and write instructions on the work ticket.

If the waistline is elasticized, pull and pin the elastic to the comfort of the client. Note on the work ticket that the elastic is to be tightened. If there is excessive gathering of fabric through the top of the pants with the elastic tightened, this problem should also be noted on the work ticket.

### PANTS TOO HIGH-WAISTED

Often, a figure with a short torso will have difficulty with the waistband riding above the natural waistline. When checking over the fit, you may note that the pants fit smoothly with correct ease over the hips and the crotch seam follows the body curve. The problem is the waistband or pant top does not sit at the client's waist.

TO FIT: Tie a cord around the client's true waist. Insert a horizontal pin line around the waist following the cord line. Fig. B-63.

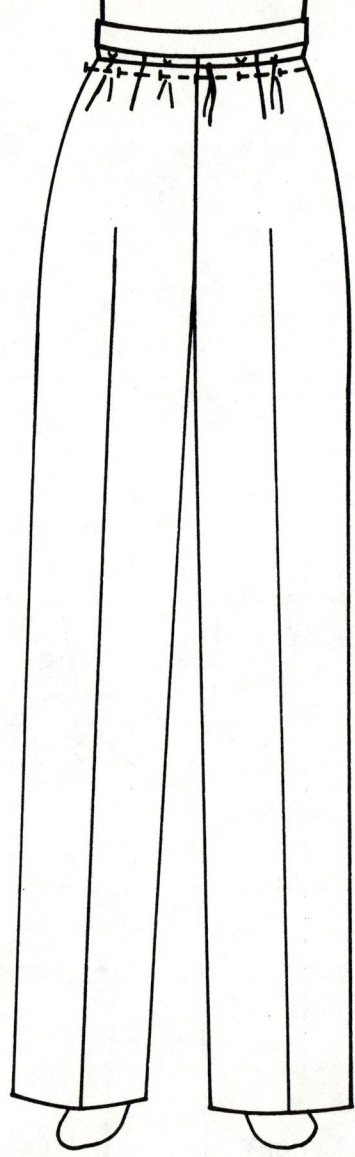

B-63. Pants waistline too high.

**Ch. 8: Fitting Women's Clothes**

**PANTS TOO HIGH-WAISTED IN BACK OR FRONT ONLY**

The front or back may fit well but the other part of the waistline rides above the waist or a roll forms just under the waistband.

TO FIT: Pin a tuck under the band. Insert the first pin at the center back or center front (whichever is too high) and taper off to nothing at the side seams. Fig. B-64.

*B-64. Pants waistline too high in back only.*

## Altering Ready-To-Wear Fashions

### Pants Hip Fittings
#### PANTS TOO TIGHT

This fitting problem will show up in distorted side seams. Sometimes a roll may form just under the waistband. If the pants have side pockets, they will gap open instead of laying flat along the seams. Fig. B-65a.

Before attempting this alteration, study the pants carefully. You cannot release successfully if:

- All the seams have been serged (cut to ¼ inch [.6 cm] with a machine overcast finish).
- There are pockets in the side seams, which means the seams have been clipped and cannot be released.
- There are only front and back crotch seams (some pants are made without side seams).
- A fly front zipper opening eliminates the front crotch seam.

You need at least two side seams of average width—⅝ inch (1.6 cm)—to give a 1-inch (2.5 cm) release through the body of the pants. If still more is needed, you will have to use the front and back crotch seams also. However, the crotch seam release is not effective through the curve of that seam. If extra room is needed below the crotch curve, it has to be obtained by releasing the inseams.

TO FIT: Insert crossed pins on the seams where the release is to begin and end. Make a pin line along the seams between the crossed pins. Fig. B-65b. If the inseam is to be released, write this on the work ticket along with the other instructions. After the client removes the pants, place crossed pins at the top of the inseam as an additional reminder that it is to be released.

#### PANTS TOO TIGHT IN UPPER HIPLINE

This fitting problem shows up only in form-fitting pants. An elasticized waist allows extra fullness in this area, which eliminates this hip fitting. The too-snug fit shows in a roll just under the waistband. This roll indicates a full abdomen or high hips in back which keep the pants from sliding smoothly into place.

TO FIT: Study the figure profile and decide whether the problem is in front or in back or both. Since the top of fitted pants and a fitted basic skirt are shaped with the same kind of waist darts, reread and follow the instructions under *Skirt too Tight*, pages 171, 172. The fitting and the solutions are the same. Also refer to the pictures

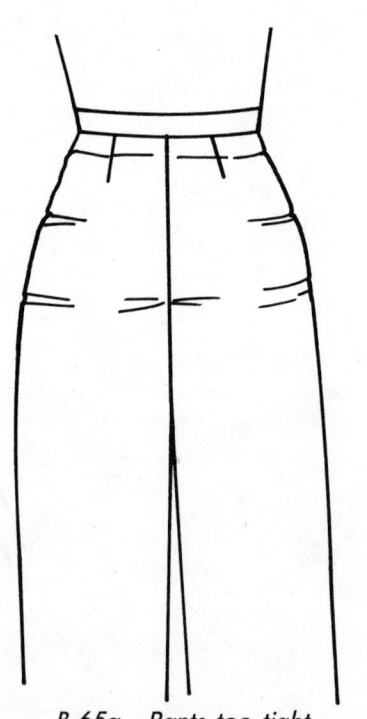

B-65a. Pants too tight.

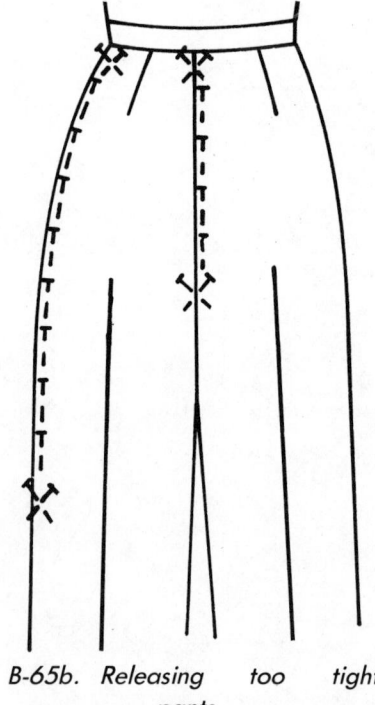

B-65b. Releasing too tight pants.

### Ch. 8: Fitting Women's Clothes

and pinning methods used on the skirt.

#### PANTS TOO TIGHT IN LOWER HIPLINE

This will show in distorted outseams and inseams near the crotch line. Check the seam allowance as the success of this alteration depends entirely on the width of these seams. If the seams have been cut away, nothing can be done.

TO FIT: Insert crossed pins above and below where the release is needed. Add a pin line along the seam to be released, between the crossed pins. When the customer has taken off the pants, place crossed pins at the top of the inseams. Be sure to write instructions on the ticket for releasing the necessary seams.

---

#### PANTS TOO LARGE

The pants droop over the hips and the crotch seam is low. Often this does not involve the waist fit, for some flat-hipped figures have a large waistline in proportion to the hips. If the pants waistline is too large, start the pin fitting in this area, following the instructions given earlier. Then go on to the rest of the fitting. If the thighs and legs are extremely thin, it may be necessary to take in the leg seams all the way down through the pants bottom for figure balance.

TO FIT: Study the way the pants hang front, back, and side. Pin out only where it is absolutely necessary and only as much as is needed for comfort and appearance. Starting with both outseams, pin from the upper hipline down. Taper back to the original seams near the knee. If, after this pinning, the pants legs still look too wide in proportion to the hip fitting, you will have to repin the fitting to the bottom of the outseams. Take out no more than 1/2 inch (1.3 cm) on the double of each seam in order to keep the center crease or grain line in place. If pants legs must be made even narrower, divide the amount between the inseams and the outseams and pin all four seams. Fig. B-66. Remember to insert the pins with the points down as you pin these seams. When the pin fitting is completed, ask the client to sit so you can be certain you have not pinned out all the ease she needs for comfort. Check the crotch seam carefully in this fitting. If the crotch seam is smooth and does not droop, the inseam can be pinned from below the crotch seam only. If the crotch seam droops, taking in the inseams across the crotch seam will help to raise it.

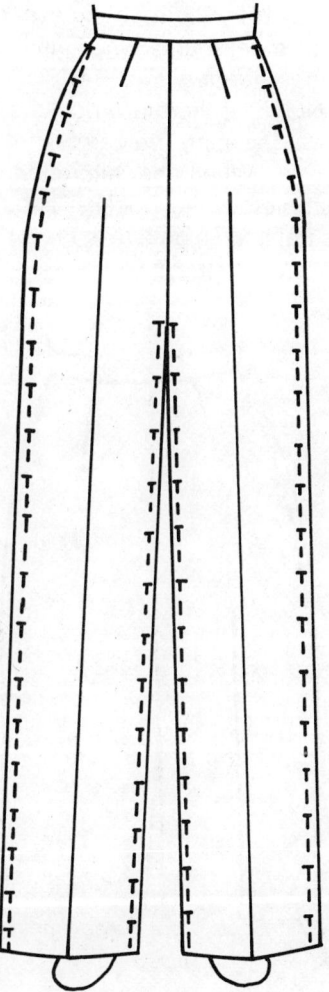

*B-66. Pants too loose all over.*

## PANTS TOO LARGE THROUGH THE HIPS

If the problem is in the upper hip area, fit as you would for a skirt that is too large in this area.

However, there are times when pants fit well through the waist and upper hipline but the side seams poke out over the lower hips. This could be due to the cut of the pants or to a hipline that is very flat in this area.

TO FIT: Pin out excess on both side seams where the fitting is needed. Fig. B-67.

NOTE: If there are pockets in the side seams, be careful not to overfit. When the alteration is completed, the pockets should lie flat and smooth over the hips.

## PANTS TOO LARGE IN SEAT SEAM

This problem can be recognized by loose folds in the seat area. The side seams are smooth and the front crotch line is in place but the seat seam droops.

TO FIT: Pin out the excess folds along the seat seam as far as the seam curve. Do not pin into the curve line of the seat seam as that curve is not changed for this fitting. If the seat seam is too long, pin out the extra length on the back of the inseams at the crotch seam. Taper back to the original seam line above the knee. Fig. B-68.

## PANTS FRONT CROTCH TOO LONG

The pants may be fine in the seat seam, but the front crotch seam droops and the line falls below the body curve. This may be due to an extremely flat figure or the cut of the pants.

TO FIT: Pin a fold to increase the front side of the inseams only. After pinning, check the crotch length to be sure you have not over-fitted. Fig. B-69. The client should sit down to be sure of comfort and fit in this area.

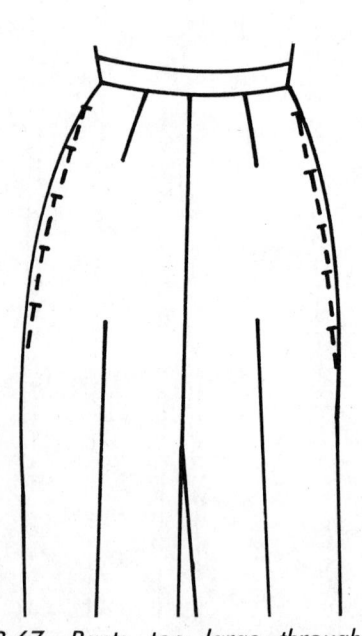

B-67. Pants too large through hips.

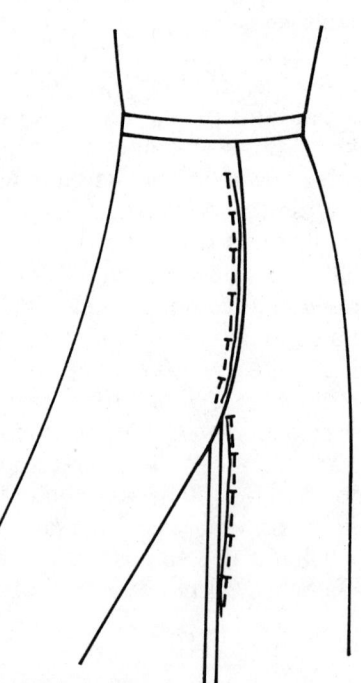

B-68. Pants too long in seat.

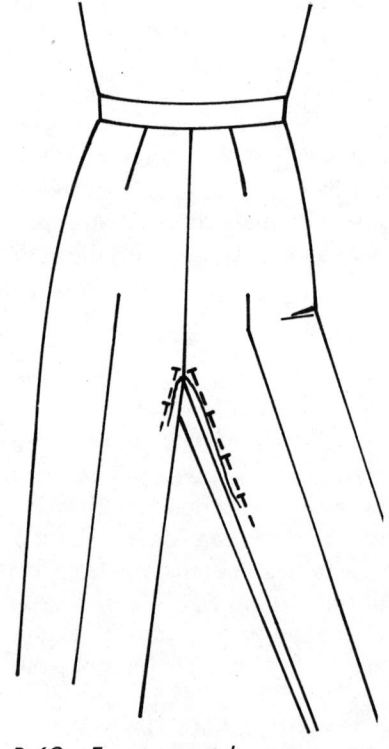

B-69. Front crotch seam too long.

**Ch. 8: Fitting Women's Clothes**

## PANTS TOO LARGE IN FRONT

The pants fit well in the seat and the side seams are in place, but the front is not smooth.

TO FIT: Pin out excess folds on the *front* part of the *side* seams only. Pin along both seams until the amount needed to make the front fit smoothly is removed. The front crotch seam is rarely used for this fitting as it is cut on the straight grain almost to the crotch curve. (Observe ready-made pants or pants patterns.) Disturbing the center front seam line can distort the grain line and spoil the flat fit desired.

### Pants Leg Width

Pants legs may vary in style from straight and tapered seams to flairs and bell-bottoms. Since there is rarely any need to change the width of full-legged pants, the following directions are given for the straight or tapered trouser leg. Make the necessary changes on one leg only as the other leg will be altered to match the one marked.

## PANTS LEGS TOO NARROW

Again, it is only possible to release the leg seams if they are full-width seams and have not been serged. Both inseams and outseams should be altered to effect enough change to make the alteration worthwhile.

TO FIT: Place crossed pins where the releasing of the seam should begin. Indicate on the work ticket that release should be the maximum amount the seams will allow and should continue through the hem of the pants.

## PANTS LEGS TOO WIDE

Some small figures need pants legs scaled narrower to give a taller appearance or better balance to the figure.

TO FIT: Begin to pin out the excess seam just below the hipline. Reduce the inseam and the outseam the same amount to keep the grain and crease lines in place. Pin all the way to the bottom of the leg.

### Pants Lengths

At one time women wore pants only for work, play, or sports and only with flat heeled shoes. Styles have changed. Today pants are worn with shoes of many different styles and heel heights. Adjusting the correct length of the leg depends greatly on the height of heel to be worn with it. If the customer plans to wear 2-inch (5 cm) heels with the pants, she should be wearing the same height when you adjust the length. If she has neglected to bring the right shoes with her and you do not have any available for her to borrow, just do the best you can.

To fit pants lengths, see Chapter 10 on Hems.

### FITTING COATS

The same general principles for proper fit and procedures given for the other garments will apply to coat fittings. You may wish to reread the first part of the chapter to refresh your memory on what to look for in the fitting.

Before attempting to fit a coat, remember:

• A coat should be fitted over the type of garment with which it will be worn.
• A coat with a zip-in lining should be fitted with the lining inserted.
• A coat that is part of an ensemble should be fitted over the rest of the ensemble.
• A coat with long sleeves and full length should completely cover the garment worn under it. This is especially true of raincoats.
• A coat should always have more ease of fit than any garment worn under it. It should not bind or bunch up the clothes worn underneath.

In general, neckline, waistline, hip, and skirt fittings would be the same or similar to those given earlier. The only area to require special treatment is the shoulders.

### Coat Shoulder Fittings

The correct fit of the shoulder is the most important part of a coat. The shoulders on a coat should never be fitted as close to the shoulder bone as the garment underneath. In fact, it is usually desirable to extend the shoulders slightly beyond the natural shoulder. The amount of extension desired would depend upon the type of coat. A coat to be worn over other jackets and suits would need more room in the shoulder than one to be worn over unpadded dresses and lightweight garments. Shoulders too narrow will make the coat uncomfortable and make the whole garment look too small. Shoulders too wide will droop and make the whole coat look too large.

TO FIT: Check the shoulder padding first. Many coats do not have sufficient padding. Sometimes the padding used is not well placed. Often the only change needed to alter a poor shoulder fit is to change the shoulder padding. This is one good reason a fitter should always keep a pair of shoulder pads nearby.

If the shoulder cannot be adjusted satisfactorily by adding or changing shoulder padding, turn to the section in this chapter on fitting shoulders, pages 150–156. Adapt the techniques suggested there to the problem.

## FITTING JACKETS AND SUITS

Jackets are often purchased separately to be worn with shorts, pants, dresses, or skirts. Therefore they do not have to be fitted over any specific garment. However, the customer should be wearing a typical garment to be sure the fit is accurate.

All the checkpoints for coat fittings apply to jacket fittings, except for the length. A separate jacket can be any length the client wants or looks best in.

A suit jacket, on the other hand, must be fitted over the skirt, pants, or dress it will be worn with. If the jacket is meant to be worn over a blouse or sweater, that garment should be worn during the fitting of the jacket. The jacket should be fitted in proportion to the other parts of the costume, allowing the extra ease needed to fit over the matching items.

NOTE: If the pants, skirt, or dress need adjusting, pin-fit these garments first. The jacket is fitted last.

TO FIT A JACKET: Refer to the other sections of the chapter that cover the area in which the problem occurs. For example, if the jacket is too wide through the back shoulders, refer to *Garment Shoulders Too Wide*, page 150.

# Chapter 9

# Standard Alterations for Women

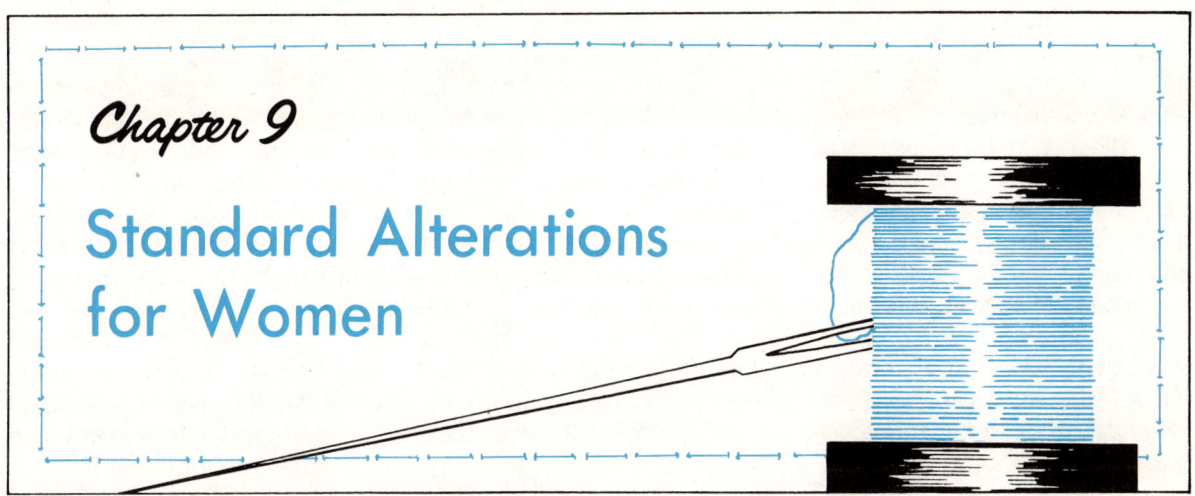

A successful alteration depends on your knowing where to begin and how to organize the job step-by-step so the garment is completed without too much handling. Alterations to be made will be indicated by the pins and instructions from the fitter. These are described in Chapter 8.

To make the work easier for you, each sub-heading in Chapter 9 corresponds to the fitting instructions in Chapter 8. For easy reference, the titles are the same. In addition, the number of the illustration showing the fitting is repeated for each alteration. To help you build your speed to a profitable level, the amount of time the alteration should take is included for each job.

When you alter a ready-to-wear garment, you start with a finished product and work backwards. This is why clothing alterations involve completely different skills from custom dressmaking or tailoring. You may have to break lifelong habits and rules along the way. You will be making changes you thought impossible and even thinking up new ways of breaking old rules and habits.

## HELPFUL HINTS

• Read the fitter's instructions on the alteration ticket and study the garment before starting to work. The instructions may be the only way you will have of knowing what needs to be done. The way the garment was made originally will guide you as to how the work should be re-finished.

• Check and organize the materials and tools you will need.

• Stitch new seam lines *before* ripping out the original seams—whether releasing or taking in seams. The original seam will hold the garment pieces in place while restitching so there will be no slipping or puckering.

• When seams are being altered, you can get a better line if you press the seam to be altered before starting to work. Press the two raw edges back together and flat rather than leaving the seam pressed open.

• When seams are taken in, do not trim back to the original 1/2 or 5/8 inch (1.3 or 1.5 cm) seam. Always leave a more generous seam allowance when possible, in case the seam must be let out.

• Stitch new seams outside of the marked fitting line so the final fit of the garment is not tightened.

- Place pins at right angles (perpendicular) to the new seam line so the seams do not shift as you stitch.
- When changing only part of a seam, always overstitch the beginning or ending of the new seam over the remaining original seam. Then there will be no gap when the original stitch line is removed.
- When taking in or releasing a new seam, it is only necessary to mark the new line on one side of the seam. This would be the top side of the seam when stitching.
- Use eight to ten stitches to the inch (2.5 cm) for most machine stitching. This is faster, easier to rip if necessary, and gives less chance of the stitches cutting the fabric. Use a shorter stitch only when necessary for narrow seams or places that have been clipped or slashed close to the seam line.
- Stitch seams to be changed from the top of the garment down. It is easier to follow the body contours. You can make better use of the manufacturer's marking clips to guide you. It is also easier to pick up the line to be straightened or joined.
- When releasing or reshaping darts, stitch the new line before ripping out the original stitching. If the darts are to be increased or taken in, there is no reason to rip out the old dart. It will not show on the right side of the garment. If the customer should gain weight and need to have the dart let out again, the old one will still be there. Of course, if the dart location must be moved, you will rip the original dart first.
- When increasing the width of a hem, apply the new finish—lace or tape—along the top of the new hem allowance before cutting the excess fabric away. This will give you greater control and make it easier to get a straight line.
- Whenever possible, work *inside* the circle of a garment section. Armholes, sleeves, waistline, pants legs, and hems are all a series of circles. When you stitch around these circles, keep the open part of the circle above the part you are stitching rather than underneath. The work is easier to guide and there will be no danger of getting the underneath part caught in the stitches.
- Avoid basting when pinning will give the same control. Avoid pinning if pressing will do the same job—turning up a hem or holding back a facing. The fewer pins you use, the less you will abuse the fabric.
- Avoid hand work as much as possible. Use machine basting or "stitch-in-the-ditch" (See Chapter 11, page 291) for inside controls of facings, linings, or waistbands. By doing this, your work will go faster and look more professional.
- Learn the different marking methods and make use of them before taking a garment apart or removing the fitter's pins. These marking methods are discussed in detail later in this chapter.
- When doing several alterations of the same type, such as hems, get your work organized for the greatest efficiency. Do all the ripping at once. Mark all the new hemlines at one time. Stitch all of the new hems. Then press them all. You will save yourself valuable time and energy.
- If you are doing a large volume of work, you can organize yourself even further. Separate all the light-colored clothing from the darker colors. Often you will be able to use the same thread or bobbin for several garments and can save time rethreading the machine.

Keep in mind that new fabrics, styles, equipment, and methods of working are always being developed. It is never safe to think you have learned all you need to know. You can keep yourself abreast of new developments by reading the newspapers, magazines, pamphlets, and other materials suggested in Chapter 2.

## TRANSFERRING PIN MARKINGS TO USABLE MARKINGS

There are several ways to transfer the fitter's pin markings to help make the required alteration. You can use thread,

## Ch. 9: Standard Alterations for Women

chalk, scissor clips, or pins. Tailor's wax or lead pencils are not recommended for reasons discussed below.

### Thread Markings

Thread markings are safest and will stay in until the alteration is completed. Thread is also the best method to use for lace, sheer fabrics, and white or light colors. Use white or light-colored cotton threads since dark colored threads often "bleed" and leave a permanent smudge on the fabric. Baste with long stitches along the line of pins placed by the fitter. Then remove the pins. This type of marking is especially helpful when parts of a garment are to be separated and put back along a new line such as sleeves into a changed armhole line.

### Tailor's Chalk

This is a special type of chalk that comes in several colors. Use only the white and light colors. Use with care and a light touch as too much chalk may show through on the right side of the fabric and is sometimes difficult to remove. Chalk along the pins on the inside of the garment where the pins are holding a new dart or seam line. *Never use chalk on the right side of the fabric.* After marking their placement, remove the fitter's pins. Repin the new line on the inside before stitching. Chalk markings are also used to mark the depth of a new hemline so you will know where to trim away the excess fabric.

### Tailor's Wax

This type of marking material is used mainly on dark colors or men's wear. It should not be used on light colors as the wax will melt when pressed and may leave a stain on the fabric. If you do use wax, follow the directions for the chalk markings.

### Clip Marking

Often small, 1/4 (.6 cm) clips, made with scissors in the edge of the seam, will aid in matching parts of the garment to be altered. For example, make a clip marking in the top of a sleeve where it meets the shoulder seams when sleeves must be removed and reset. Clips are also useful for marking the center front or center back of garments. If seams are to be ripped apart and restitched on a different line, small clips help show where the pieces will be rematched. This assures that the seam will come back to the same grain line. Clips are one of the fastest and most accurate means of marking you can use.

### Pin Marking

Pin markings are fast and professional but require skill and experience. Since pins slip out of the fabric easily, they should only be used as markings when the work can be completed quickly and at one sitting. Otherwise, the pins may fall out and the fitting line lost.

To mark with pins, put a new pin on the inside of the garment right under the marking pin used on the right side. Remove the pins from the right side. Then proceed as you would with any other type of marking.

### Pencil Markings

Some people are in the habit of using a lead pencil rather than chalk to mark fabric. Pencil marks show through on the right side of the fabric easily and are difficult to remove. Chalk is much more satisfactory. Get in the habit of using professional methods.

### DOING THE ALTERATION

After the garment has been fitted and the markings transferred to the inside, you are ready to proceed with the changes to be made.

The directions in this book have been written in a step-by-step format to make them easy to understand. It is recommended strongly that you do each step as it is discussed before reading on to the next direction. You will find it much less confusing and easier to follow if you do not read too far ahead before proceeding to do each step. In many instances, you may need to move just one step at a time.

*Altering Ready-To-Wear Fashions*

## BASIC DRESS ALTERATIONS

### Neckline Alterations

The neckline will need to be altered if it is too large and gaps, bulges away from the neck, or is so tight it is uncomfortable for the client to wear. Too-large necklines are corrected by adding darts, increasing the shoulder seam, taking in a seam, or adding a fitted tape and shrinking out the extra fullness.

### SLIGHT BACK FULLNESS

**Neckline Darts (Chapter 8, Fig. B-3b) (Time: 15 minutes)**

Slight back neckline fullness may be removed by adding short neckline darts. These darts should be no more than 2½ inches (6.4 cm) long and ¼ inch (.6 cm) deep. This type of alteration is usually only used on the back.

1. If the facing has been tacked down, remove the necessary stitches to free the facing so it can be turned back.

2. Measure and mark the halfway point between the center back and the shoulder seam on each side.

3. On the wrong side of the garment and facing, draw 2½-inch-long (6.4 cm) chalk lines along the straight grain of the fabric where you made the halfway point marks. Make a slight cross mark at the end of each line to guide your stitching. Fig. C-1a.

4. Fold the fabric along these lines to form the new darts. Place one pin at the neck edge to hold each dart in place for stitching. You will have a 5-inch-long, (12.7 cm) two-pointed fold going through both the garment and the facing.

5. Start stitching the dart on the facing to ¼-inch (.6 cm) width at the neck edge. Continue on across the seam and down to the bottom of your chalk mark, tapering the dart again to a sharp point. Repeat for second dart. Fig. C-1b.

6. Press darts toward the center back.

7. Replace the lining or facing to original position.

NOTE: If this alteration is required in a thick fabric, you may find it necessary to separate the facing and garment. Rip about 1 inch (2.5 cm) of the neck seam in the area of the new darts. In this case, mark and stitch the facing dart and neckline dart separately. Press the facing dart toward the shoulder seam and the bodice dart toward the center back. Fig. C-1c. Restitch the neckline seam. Replace the facing to its proper position. Pressing the darts in opposite directions will reduce bulk at the dart line.

**Ch. 9: Standard Alterations for Women**

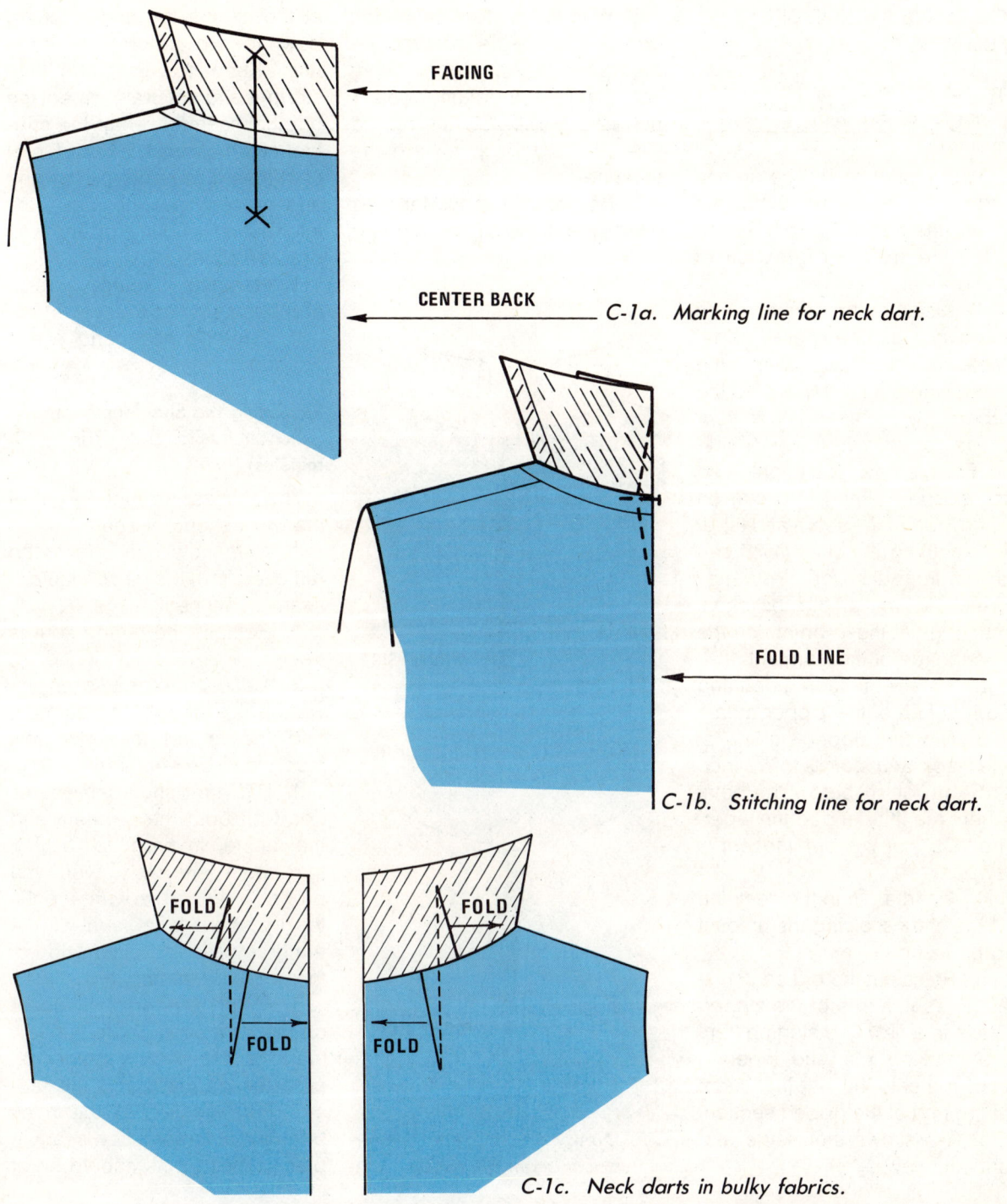

C-1a. Marking line for neck dart.

C-1b. Stitching line for neck dart.

C-1c. Neck darts in bulky fabrics.

## Altering Ready-To-Wear Fashions

### EXCESSIVE BACK NECKLINE FULLNESS

**Increasing the Zipper Seam (Chapter 8, Fig. B-3c) (Time: 20 minutes)**

Your markings will be on one side of the zipper only since the other line had to be removed to allow the customer to get out of the garment.

1. Measure the amount to be removed at the neck edge. Measure down the zipper to the point where the fitter ended the tapering of the seam. Write your measurements on the work ticket. For example, you might need to remove 5/8 inch (1.6 cm) on each side of the seam and taper it to nothing 7 inches (17.8 cm) down from the top. You may prefer to make pin or chalk markings at these points on the wrong side of the garment.
2. Untack the facing or lining so it is free of the zipper area.
3. Rip the zipper starting at the neck and going to 1/2 inch (1.3 cm) or so below the point where the fitter ended the tapering. *Do not rip out the entire zipper.*
4. Insert a pin in the neckline at the mark showing the amount to be taken in.
5. Press out the old seamline as far as it is free of the zipper. Press in a new line starting from the marking pin and tapering until it meets the original seam at the end of the ripped section. Fig. C-2 shows the inside and outside views.
6. With zipper foot on the left side of the needle, restitch the underside of the zipper seam first. Start at the bottom about 1 inch (2.5 cm) below the ripped area and stitch up toward the neckline.
7. Now stitch the overlapping seam side of the zipper, starting at the neck edge and stitching down toward the original seamline. Keep the stitching line straight and accurately meet the original seam. Overlap the original seam about 1 inch (2.5 cm) of stitching to reinforce the line and prevent raveling. For more information about zippers, see pg. 297 (Chap. 11).
8. Replace facing, press, and hand sew in place.
9. Replace hook and eye if needed.

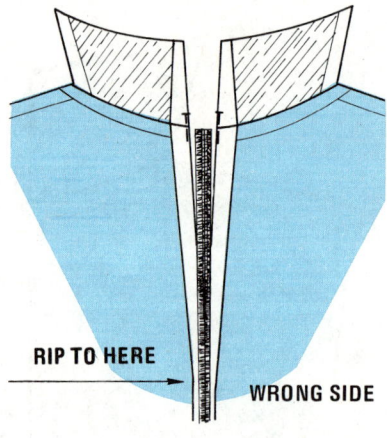
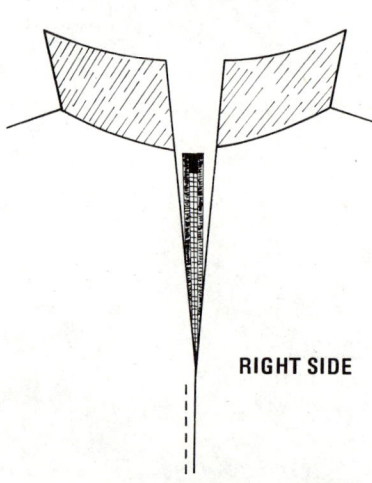

*C-2. Newly pressed seam line for zipper seam alteration.*

**Increasing the Shoulder Seam (Chapter 8, Fig. B-3e) (Time: 30 minutes)**

The fullness is pinned out of the back shoulder seam.

1. Note how much is to be removed from the back shoulder seam at the neck edge.
2. Release the facing so it is free.
3. Make chalk marks on the wrong side of both the garment and the facing to show how much is to be removed.
4. Rip the shoulder seams apart on both the garment and the facing. In order to restitch the seam smoothly, you will probably find it advantageous to rip about one inch of the armhole seam on either side of the shoulder seams. Fig. C-3a.
5. Match the original seam on the front shoulder to the new mark on the back shoulder on both the garment and the facing. Put one pin at the neck edges to hold each new seam in place. These pins should be at

### Ch. 9: Standard Alterations for Women

right angles to the new seam line. Repeat on the other shoulder.

6. Restitch all four seams—both shoulders and their facings or lining. Stitch with the front of the garment up so you can follow the original seam line. Fig. C-3b.

7. Cut away excess fabric on the back shoulders.

8. Press seams open.

9. Restitch top of sleeve seam.

10. Replace facing or lining and retack into position.

### FRONT NECKLINE FULLNESS (CHAPTER 8. FIG. B-4b,c) (TIME: 15 MINUTES)

1. Measure front of neckline from shoulder to shoulder before removing the fitting pins. Use a measuring tape and follow the neck curve to get the exact measurement the fitter intended. Write this on the work ticket.

2. Cut a seam tape or selvage strip (see note pg. 204) 1 inch (2.5 cm) longer than this measurement. Tape color should match or blend with the garment color.

3. With pencil or chalk, mark a line ½ inch (1.3 cm) in from each cut end of the tape and another mark in the center of the tape.

4. Untack facing and locate the center front of the neck edge. There should be a manufacturer's clip at the center front of the facing seam.

5. Match the center front mark on the tape to the center front clip on the *facing* side of the neck seam and pin the tape on the stitch line. Fig. C-4.

6. Ease neck fullness to the tape with additional pins between the shoulder seams and the center front. Place the pins perpendicular to the seam.

7. Machine stitch the edge of the tape along the neck seam, stitching over the pins if necessary to hold the ease. This machine stitching will come through on the facing side of the neck seam, but will not show on the right side of the garment.

8. Clip seam and tape close to the stitching line at ½-inch (1.3 cm) intervals to allow the curve to spread so the seam will lie flat.

9. Turn facing back and, using the press ham, press front neckline along the neck seam on the facing side. Use a dampened cloth to help shrink out fullness and aid shaping. Apply the clapper to "set" the pressing. Turn to the right side to finish press if necessary (with press cloth). Shrinking out the fullness is the real secret to this neck alteration.

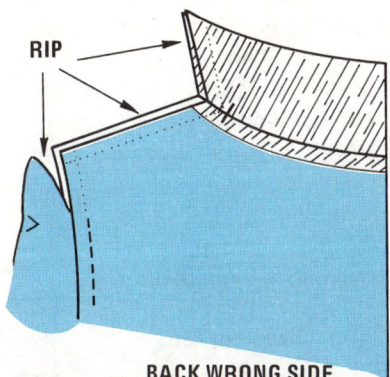

C-3a. Shoulder, armhole, and facing ripped for alteration.

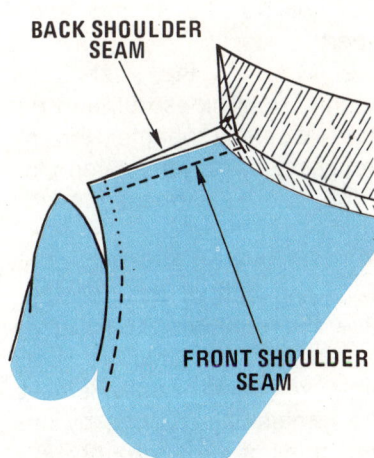

C-3b. New stitching line for decreasing neck fullness.

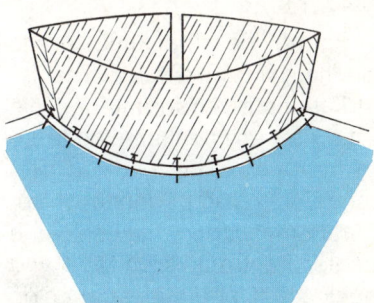

C-4. Neckline altered with seam tape.

## Altering Ready-To-Wear Fashions

10. Tack the facing back as it was before.

NOTE: Many alterations will require a control or retaining tape of some kind. Regular seam tape will do. Another idea would be to trim the selvage 1/2 inch (1.3 cm) wide off any lining material you may have and wind the different colors on spools. Keep these spools handy with your sewing supplies. The finished edge is always used at the seam line with cut edge turned toward the cut edge of the garment piece.

### Front Neckline Fullness Removed in Shoulder Seams
(Chapter 8, Fig. B-4c) (Time: 20 minutes)

Proceed with this alteration, following the instructions for the back neck fullness pinned into the shoulder seams. Just reverse the instructions to the front shoulder and use the same methods.

### Front Neckline Fullness on V-neck or Scoop Neck (Chapter 8 Fig. B-4d, e)

Both of these necklines are to be held in on a tape. The instructions given for altering pin fitting for any neckline too large in front would be followed. Remember the importance of accurate measuring, the use of the center front marks on tape and neck seam for equal balance on both sides of the neckline, and the finish pressing.

### Neckline Too Full All Around
(Chapter 8, Figs. B-5b) (Time: 20 minutes)

1. Make note of how much is pinned out of the shoulder seams at the neck seam.
2. Release the facing and rip neck seam where it crosses shoulder seams—about 1 inch (2.5 cm) on each side of shoulder seams. Fig. C-5.

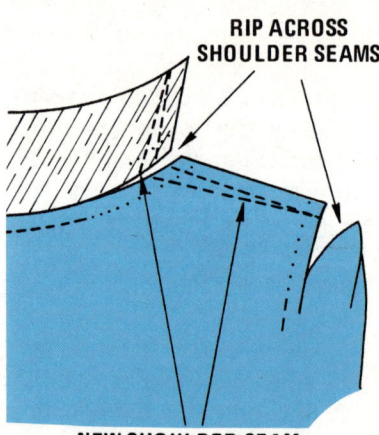

C-5. Shoulder seam increased at neck edge only.

3. Chalk mark or pin the amount to be taken in at the neck edge of shoulder seams and facing seams.
4. Machine stitch new shoulder seam from neck edge, tapering line until it meets the original seams and overlaps the stitching.
5. Trim excess seams and rip out old seam line.
6. Press seams open on shoulders and facing.
7. Stitch facing back to neck edge and press.
8. Tack facing back to shoulder seams.

NOTE: This alteration can be made a little easier if you also rip 1 inch (2.5 cm) on each side of the shoulder seams at the armhole edge at the time the neck edge is ripped. This makes it easier to stitch a neat shoulder line. It takes only a minute to restitch at the armholes when the facing seam is being restitched at the neck edge.

### NECKLINE TOO HIGH IN FRONT (CHAPTER 8, FIG. B-6b) (TIME: 20 MINUTES)

1. Untack facing or lining from around neckline. If there is an understitching around the neck seam, rip it out around the front neckline and 1 inch (2.5 cm) past the shoulder seams. Do *not* rip the facing seam apart.
2. Match the shoulder seams, right sides out, and pin the two seams together. Pin the front neckline together along the edge, folding garment at center front.
3. Remove the fitter's pins from one half of the neckline. Use the remaining pins as a pattern for the other side so both sides will be the same. Remove the remaining pins one by one and reinsert them through both layers of cloth so both sides are marked. Fig. C-6a.

## Ch. 9: Standard Alterations for Women

4. Thread mark the new neckline carefully, picking up only one layer of fabric in each stitch. (Placing your finger inside the neckline at the pin line will help to separate the fabric for easier thread marking.) Start at the shoulder line and mark toward the center front. At the center fold, make a 1-inch (2.5 cm) vertical thread mark to indicate the center front. Continue marking to the other shoulder. Fig. C-6b.

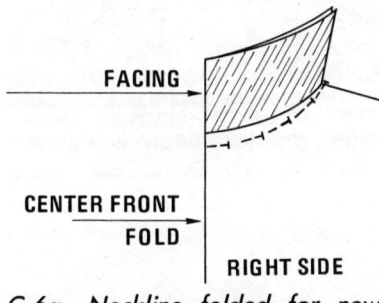

C-6a. Neckline folded for new line.

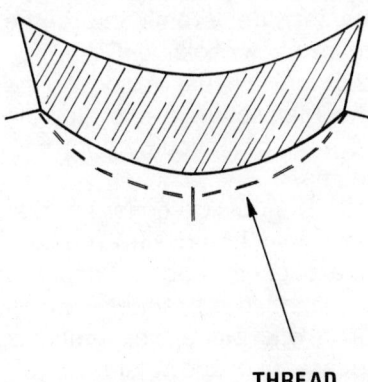

C-6b. New neckline marked with thread.

5. Fold the facing back, right side to right side of the neck front. On the wrong side of the garment, place pins—perpendicular to the thread line—to keep facing in place while stitching.

6. Stitch *on* the thread line, starting ½ inch (1.3 cm) to the back of one shoulder seam and ending ½ inch (1.3 cm) beyond the opposite shoulder seam. To keep neck line from stretching, a narrow tape may be sewn into the new seam with the same stitching.

7. Trim off excess fabric above the new seam. Closely clip the new neck seam with diagonal clips to the seam line.

8. Turn back facing to the inside and press from the facing side. If the fabric is crease resistant, you may want to replace the understitching along the front neckline. A good pressing may be all that will be needed.

9. Tack facing back into place.

### NECKLINE TOO HIGH FRONT AND BACK (CHAPTER 8, FIG. B-6c) (TIME: 30 MINUTES)

In this alteration, you will have to release the facing or lining at the zipper opening in addition to untacking it around the whole neckline. Also rip out the understitching all around the neck but do *not* rip the facing off.

1. Follow the instructions in the alteration above for marking the new neckline both front and back.

2. Turn the facing to the outside all around the neckline. Pin in place.

3. Stitch from as close to the center back as possible and pick up the new line, following the thread line around to the opposite side of the center back. As suggested before, tape may be applied with this stitching.

4. Trim and clip seam. Turn facing to the inside.

5. Press as explained in Step 8 in the preceding alteration on this page.

6. Hand sew facing back to zipper opening and tack at shoulder.

If the new neckline starts below the top of the zipper opening in the center back, you will thread mark this line the same way. All other steps will be the same except that the new neckline will start at the zipper tape. The zipper must be open for this.

1. Backstitch at the beginning and end of the new neckline seam for reinforcement.

2. Cut away excess neck seam but do *not* cut through tape of zipper.

3. Clip neck seam and press back facing as above.

4. As you sew the facing back at the zipper, fold the extra zipper tape inside—between the facing and the garment. Hand sew the facing along the zipper tape with small stitches. Zipper will lock in place when closed.

## Altering Ready-To-Wear Fashions

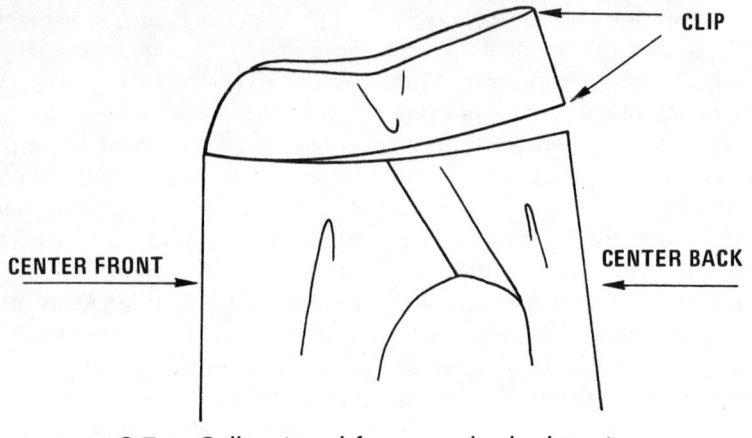

C-7a. Collar ripped for center back alteration.

### NECKLINE WITH COLLAR

**Neck and Collar Too Big in Back (Chapter 8, Fig. B-7b) (Time: 30 minutes)**

If excess fullness is 1 inch (2.5 cm) or less, this is a simple alteration.

1. Rip collar and facing from the neck edge across the back from one shoulder to the other. Note the center back clip marks on the collar, neck, and facing seams. Fig. C-7a.

2. Make new clip marks 2½ inches (6.4 cm) from the center back on each side on the neck seam.

3. Stitch ¼-inch (.6 cm) darts at new clip marks, tapering them to 2½ inches (6.4 cm) long. (See directions Fig. C-1a for more detailed explanation.)

4. Using a small machine stitch for control, ease in the 1-inch (2.5 cm) fullness on the collar and facing separately with staystitch lines along the old seam lines.

5. Press the neck darts with the fold toward the center back, shrinking in the extra fullness on the collar and facing at the same time. Use the pressing ham to aid in shaping the curved area. Place a press cloth over the collar and facing and dampen it with a sponge. Apply the iron and press carefully until the extra fullness is pressed out.

6. Stitch the collar and facing back to the new neckline, matching all the center back marking clips.

7. Tack facing to the new darts as well as to the shoulder seams to hold it in place.

NOTE: When the back fullness is more than 1 inch (2.5 cm) too much, use the instructions given in the following alteration.

**Collar and Neckline Too Large all Around (Chapter 8, Fig. B-8b) (Time: 45 to 60 minutes)**

There are two methods of doing this alteration. The one given here is the easier and simpler one. This method involves making a seam in the center back of the collar. Many collars are made with a center back seam so a seam can usually be added to a seamless collar without disturbing the style.

In the other method, the collar is removed and recut, which requires quite a bit of experience.

1. Measure the amount pinned out on one shoulder seam at the neckline. Since the other shoulder seam will be the same, writing only one measurement on the work ticket is enough to guide the rest of the alteration.

2. Separate the collar, neck, and facing (or lining) seams. Start to rip the neckline seam 1½ inches (3.8 cm) in front of the shoulder seams and rip the entire back neckline. Rip 1 inch (2.5 cm) on each side of the shoulder seams at the armhole edge to free shoulders for new seams.

3. Rip outside collar seam at least 2 inches (5 cm) on each side of center back of collar to prepare it for a seam. (If collar is all in one piece, no ripping is necessary on the outside edge.)

4. Alter shoulder and facing seams following the instructions given for Fig. C-5.

## Ch. 9: Standard Alterations for Women

5. Fold the collar with the front edges together and the fold at the exact center back. Clip mark the fold at the neck edge and the outer edge. (Since you will be making a new seam in the collar, clip marks through the collar at this point will not show when the seam is finished.) If there is an interfacing, be sure it is also marked.

6. Turn the collar wrong side out and press a sharp crease between these clips on both layers of the collar. The interfacing will be pressed along with the collar it is attached to.

7. Place pins at each end of the pressed lines to hold the fold in place. Place pins perpendicular to the fold line with an extra pin between the end pins to give added control for stitching. Fig. C-7b. Using the pressed fold as the seam edge, measure the amount of seam to be taken in and make a clip at each end of the collar and collar facing. Refer to Fig. C-7a again.

NOTE: To determine the width of the back collar seam, refer to the measurement recorded on the work ticket. Note the amount to be pinned out on the shoulder seam at the neck seam. For example, if the measurement on the work slip was 3/8 inch (1 cm), you stitch in 3/8 inch (1 cm) on each shoulder seam. When you double 3/8 inch, you have taken out 3/4 inch (1.9 cm) on each shoulder seam. With two shoulder seams, you have reduced the neckline size by 1 1/2 inches (3.8 cm). Do *not* reduce the collar this full amount. It is best to make a 1/2-inch (1.3 cm) seam in the collar. This takes 1 inch (2.5 cm) off the collar size and allows 1/2 inch (1.3 cm) ease. The ease is important for the roll of the collar.

8. Stitch new seams from clip to clip, starting at one edge of the collar seam and chain-sewing right on to the seam on the undercollar.

9. Cut seams open through the fold line. If the fabric is bulky, cut corners off ends of seams. This will help seams come together with less bulk and give more satisfactory results. Fig. C-7c.

10. Press the seams open, using the seam roll.

11. Restitch the seam at the outer edge of the collar (if needed) and press this seam flat from the under side.

12. Machine baste neckline edge of collar layers together.

13. Carefully pin the garment neckline to the collar neckline. Start at the center back clips and pin around each side of the neck toward the front.

14. Machine baste the collar and neckline together.

15. Pin the facing to the neckline in the same manner you pinned the collar.

16. With a slightly smaller stitch (8 to 10 stitches per inch), make the final stitching on the garment side of the machine-basted line.

17. Press the neckline seam (on the ham).

18. Tack the facing back at the shoulder seams.

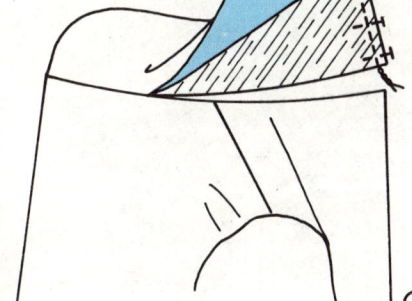

C-7b. Center back seam added to collar and facing.

C-7c. Reduce bulk by clipping away corners.

# Altering Ready-To-Wear Fashions

**Collar and Neck Too Large with Zipper Opening (Time: 45 to 60 minutes)**

To alter, follow all the instructions given for *Collar and Neck Too Large* with these few exceptions:

1. Rip the separate sides of the collar from the zipper opening to 1½ inches (3.8 cm) beyond the shoulder seams as before.

2. Alter shoulder seams as before.

3. Turn the collar ends wrong side out. Increase the collar end seams the amount necessary to make the collar fit the new neckline. Remember to leave about ¼-inch (.6 cm) ease in the collar on *both* sides of the center back so it will roll.

4. Trim seams and turn to the right side again.

5. Press seams.

6. Ease the collar back to the altered neckline following the instructions in the previous alteration. Hand sew the facing back along the zipper tape and at the shoulders.

**Collar and Neckline Too High (Chapter 8, Fig. B-9b) (Time: 45 minutes)**

1. Rip facing and collar from neckline.

2. Mark new neckline following steps 2, 3 and 4 under "Neckline Too High in Front."

3. Measure new neckline as well as neck edge of collar to determine how much to cut collar at neck seam. Usually ⅜ or ½ inch (.9 or 1.3 cm) cut away on collar neck seam will give extra ease needed to fit larger neckline.

4. Match center of collar to center of neckline and pin in place. Machine baste collar back to new neckline.

5. Restitching facing on this line.

6. Trim and clip neck seam. Turn back facing, press and tack in place.

## Shoulder Alterations

**SHOULDERS TOO WIDE (CHAPTER 8, FIG. B-10b) (TIME: 20 to 30 minutes)**

Check inside the top of the sleeve for the clip mark showing where the sleeve meets the shoulder seam (remember the mini-garments in Chapter 6?) If no clip can be found, make your own mark either with thread, chalk, or a pin. If there is enough seam allowance, you can make your own clip in the sleeve seam allowance.

**IF SHOULDERS ARE ⅜ INCH (1 CM) TOO WIDE OR LESS**

1. Rip out the sleeves about 5 inches (12.7 cm) on each side of the shoulder seams.

2. Make a mark on the inside of the shoulder seam to indicate how much is to be removed in the new seam.

3. Match the sleeve clip (or mark) to the new armhole seam mark and pin at this point.

4. Pin the old sleeve seam to the new shoulder line on each side of the shoulder seam, tapering back to the original seam in a smooth line. Fig. C-8.

5. Stitch on the inside of the armhole "circle" along the sleeve seam, overlapping the original seams at each end.

6. Trim excess shoulder width to match edge of sleeve seams.

7. There is usually no need to press this seam as the sleeves should roll softly. If there are any ripples to be steamed out, press the armhole seam on the seam roll. Press a little at a time with the point of the iron on the seam inside the circle.

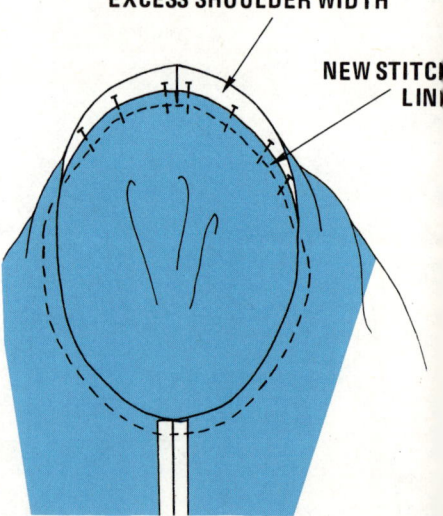

C-8. Sleeve pinned to new shoulder line.

## Ch. 9: Standard Alterations for Women

### If the Extra Shoulder Width Is in Excess of 3/8 Inch (1 cm) (Time: 60 minutes)

You will need to remove the sleeves completely. The use of the term "circle of the armhole" is a good description of it. This is the reason the term "armscye" is not used in this book. Learn to think of this opening for the arm as a hole—a round hole—so you are back to the circle!

When you shorten the shoulder line, you are making the hole larger as you stitch around the outside of the circle. Fig. C-9. When the alteration is slight, as it was in the preceding alteration, you can use the extra ease in the top of the sleeve to make the sleeve fit into this larger hole. However, the sleeve cannot be stretched indefinitely to fit a much larger hole. Therefore when the hole is made larger to fit one part of the figure, you have to make it smaller somewhere else. In this case, you take in the underarm seams on the bodice just enough to fit the sleeve back into the original hole. This is routine and is not always indicated in the pin fitting. It is a part of the alterationist's skill you should know.

1. Mark the top of each sleeve where it meets the shoulder seam. In addition, it is important to mark one shoulder and one sleeve distinctively so you will know quickly which hole each sleeve goes back into. The easiest way to do this is to put a tailor's tack or thread loop in both the sleeve and the shoulder of one side. Fig. C-10a. Leave the other side plain.

2. Carefully rip out both sleeves completely.

3. When the shoulder was fitted for this alteration, a tuck was pinned in place to raise the sleeve to the proper position. Measure the amount removed by this tuck. Remove the pins and smooth out the tuck. Reinsert the pins in a flat line showing the amount to be removed. For example, if the tuck was 1/4 inch (.6 cm) deep, the tuck will have removed 1/2 inch (1.3 cm) from the shoulder width. The new pin line will be 1/2 inch (1.3 cm) from the armhole seam line. Chalk this line on the inside of the garment. Fig. C-10a.

4. If the opposite shoulder was pin fitted also (this is optional with the fitter), remove those pins. Mark the second shoulder to duplicate the first shoulder so both will be the same.

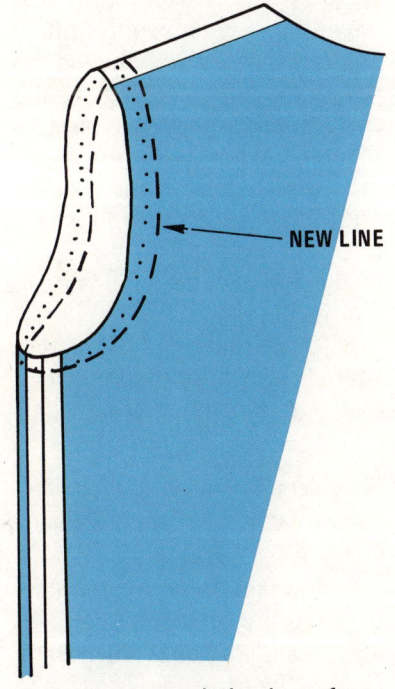

C-9. New armhole line forms larger circle.

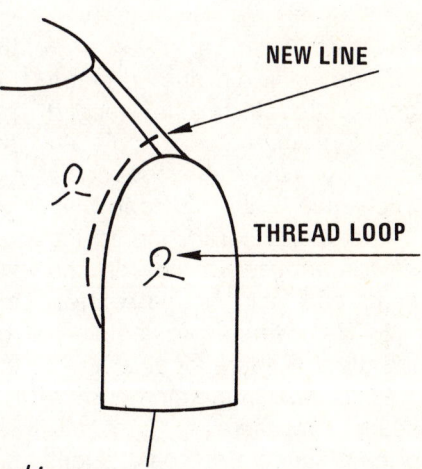

C-10a. Thread loop markings.

5. Slip the unmarked armhole inside the circle of the marked armhole, right side to right side. Carefully match the underarm and shoulder seams and the armhole seam edges. Fig. C-10b.

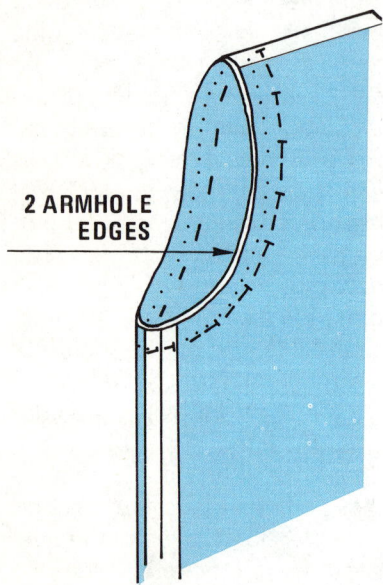

C-10b. Transferring marks from one armhole to the other.

6. Insert a pin line so that it goes through to the second shoulder and holds it in place.

7. Cut away the excess seam allowance at the changed line. Remember the pin line is the new *seam* line. Do not trim the seam allowance on the *sleeve*.

8. Remove the pin line holding the shoulders together.

9. To take in the side bodice seams, measure in from the original underarm seam about ⅜ to ½ inch (1 to 1.3 cm), as needed at the top of the seams. Stitch from this point down, tapering to the original seam in a straight line. Overlap seams about 2 inches (5 cm). Now you have reduced the armhole back to the correct size for the sleeve.

10. Rip out the original side seam stitching to the overlapped area.

11. Press seam open.

12. Check the top of the sleeves for the ease stitch. If there is none, by all means take a minute to apply it to both sleeves before attempting to replace the sleeves in the new armholes. (See Chapter 6, pg. 116 for ease-stitching.)

13. Place sleeves (check your thread loop markings) on the inside of the armhole circles, right side of sleeve to right side of the garment.

14. Match the top sleeve marks to the shoulder seams and pin. Since the new shoulder line has been cut to the correct seam allowance, you can match the sleeve and armhole edges all around. Place all the pins perpendicular to the seams and pin as necessary between the first two pins. Use as few pins as possible.

15. Stitch on the inside of the sleeve circle along the original sleeve seam. Make a second row of stitching ¼ inch (.6 cm) out on the seam allowance. If the fabric is ragged or very ravelly, this second stitching may be a machine overcast finish.

**Shoulders Too Wide in Back Only (Chapter 8, Fig. B-11b) (Time: 30 minutes)**

1. Make a chalk mark along the pin line on the inside of the garment. As in the alteration above, the pins are removed from both shoulders and the one that was marked becomes the pattern for the other shoulder.

2. Rip the sleeves from the back armhole seams between the shoulder seams and the underarm seams.

3. Match the back armhole seam edges together, right side to right side, and pin together along the chalk line. Remember this is your new *seam* line.

4. Cut away the excess seam allowance on the bodice back, leaving the same seam width at this new line as you have in the rest of the armhole. Remove the pins holding the two shoulders together.

5. Match the sleeve seam edges to the armhole edges and pin perpendicular to the seam on the inside of the circles as in Fig. C-8.

6. Stitch along the old sleeve seam line, overlapping the original seams at least 1 inch (2.5 cm).

**Shoulders Too Wide in Front Only (Chapter 8, Fig. B-12b) (Time: 30 minutes)**

Follow the same instructions given in the previous alteration for "Shoulders Too Wide in Back Only." Wherever the word *back* appears, replace it with *front*.

## Ch. 9: Standard Alterations for Women

**Extreme Shoulder Width (Chapter 8, Fig. B-13b, c) (Time: 60 minutes)**

1. Turn the garment wrong side out and make a chalk line along the pins on the front and back of the bodice. This need only be done on one side as these marks will be your guide for the other side of the bodice.

2. Remove all fitting pins.

3. On the front shoulder seams, make a clip mark where the seams meet the back shoulder darts. Fig. C-11a.

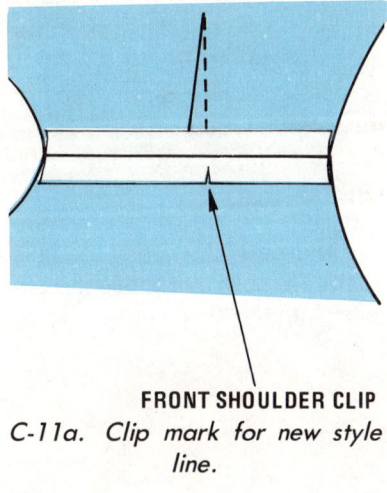

C-11a. Clip mark for new style line.

4. Rip the shoulder seams about 1 inch (2.5 cm) on each side of the shoulder darts or clips.

5. At the press board, line up the top of the back waistline dart with the bottom of the shoulder dart. Fold the garment along this line, right sides together, and press a straight line between the darts. Repeat on the back darts on the other half of the bodice. *Be careful not to erase or remove your chalk marks for the new stitching line.*

6. Still at the press board, fold the front shoulder seam at the clip mark and line it up with the top of the front waistline dart. Press this fold line. Repeat this line on the other side of the front bodice.

7. Starting at the top at the shoulder seams, stitch the new "seam" lines following the chalk markings. Stitch in a graceful curve between the top darts or clips and bottom darts. Edge stitch along the pressed lines where the garment is not to be changed in size. Figs. C-11b. Duplicate the new line on the other side of the bodice. You will have a modified princess style line.

8. Shaping the seams over the pressing ham, press the new seam lines toward the center front or center back.

9. Restitch the shoulder seams.

NOTE: The use of the steam iron to press in the curved seams between the darts before starting to stitch speeds this alteration considerably.

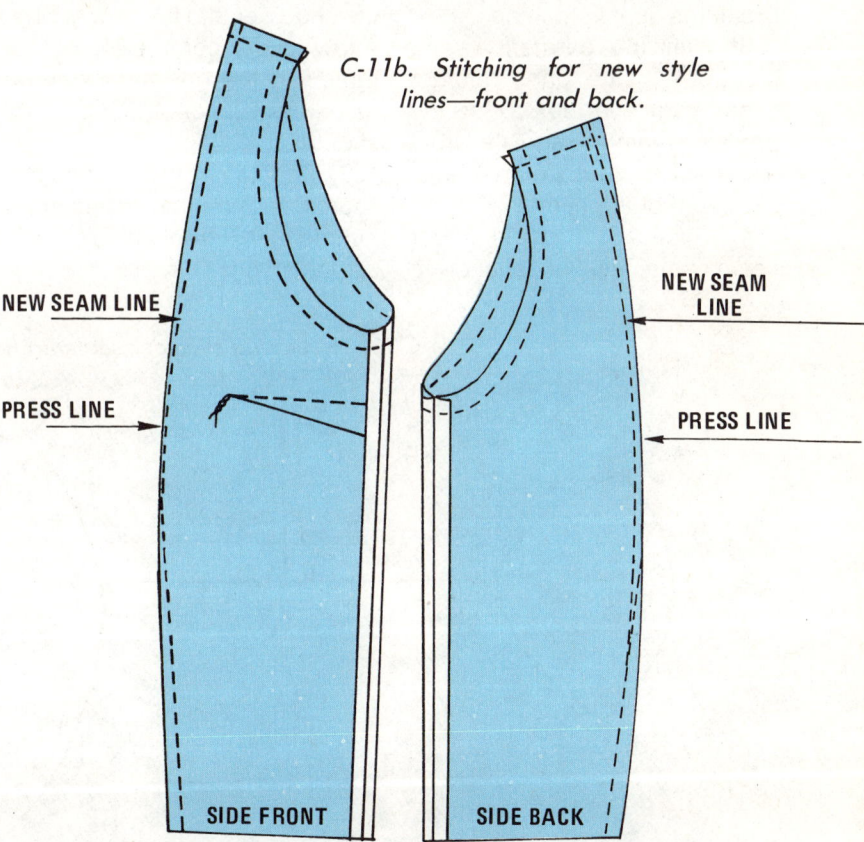

C-11b. Stitching for new style lines—front and back.

## Altering Ready-To-Wear Fashions

### SHOULDERS TOO NARROW (CHAPTER 8, FIG. B-14)

Review the section in Chapter 8 titled "Shoulders Too Narrow." Several alternate solutions are listed in that section. The alterations here are given in the order of the suggestions presented in Chapter 8.

### Fabric Has Crosswise Stretch (Time: 15 minutes)

1. Untack the facing.
2. Examine the shoulder seams. If a tape has been sewn into the seams, remove the tape. Pull the shoulder seams to break the seam stitching.
3. With the garment wrong side out, place one shoulder seam over the center of the pressing ham. Shape the front and back of the shoulder over the curve of the ham. Fig. C-12.
4. Place a pin in the shoulder seam at the neckline, anchoring the fabric firmly to the ham. Slant the pin inward toward the shoulder seam for better holding power.
5. Pull the shoulder seam to the new shoulder measurement (this should be written on the work ticket). Anchor with another pin on the shoulder seam at the armhole edge, again slanting the pin inward.
6. Shape the front and back armhole seams around the ham curve and pin in place. Smooth the fabric out over the ham.
7. Place a dampened press cloth over the seam and steam the shoulder into the new shape. Allow to dry completely before removing the garment from the ham. Repeat on the opposite shoulder.
8. Restitch the shoulder seams, pulling the fabric from behind and in front of the needle as you stitch.

### Style Seams Front and Back (Time: 30 minutes)

Refer to shoulder alterations for princess style later in this chapter.

### Garment Has a Center Back Seam (Time: 15 minutes)

1. Untack and rip facing free from the neckline 2 inches (5 cm) on each side of the center back seam.
2. Starting at the neck edge, stitch a new seam line 1/4 to 3/8 inch (.6 to 1 cm)—depending on the extra width you need—out on the center back seam allowance. About 10 inches (25 cm) down the seam, taper back to the original seam overlapping the stitching about 1 inch (2.5 cm).
3. Rip out the original stitching and carefully press the new seam. Be sure to remove the old stitch marks.

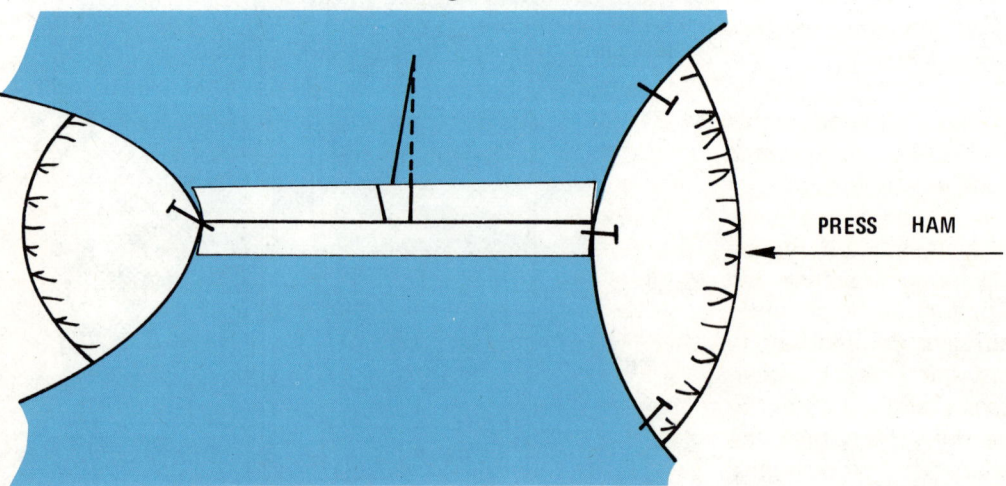

C-12. Stretching shoulder seam on ham.

### Ch. 9: Standard Alterations for Women

4. While at the press board, pull and stretch the back facing across the end of the board. Steam and press, pushing the iron across the facing. This will stretch the facing enough to fit the altered neckline.

5. Restitch the facing to the neckline.

NOTE: This alteration will give more ease across the back only, but often this is all that is needed for comfort.

**Garment Has Shoulder Darts (Time: 15 minutes)**

This change may be made in addition to releasing the center back seam for added ease.

1. Rip shoulder seams 1½ inches (3.8 cm) on each side of the shoulder darts. To make restitching the shoulder seams easier, also rip the neck and armhole seams where they cross the shoulder seams. Ripping about 1 inch (2.5 cm) of each of these seams should be enough.

2. Rip and press out the shoulder darts.

3. Put a line of ease stitching along the shoulder seam allowance just inside the old seam in the area of the old darts.

4. Restitch the shoulder seams, pulling the fabric tight both in front and behind the needle as you sew.

5. Restitch the opened parts of the neck and armhole seams.

6. Steam and press the shoulders over the ham for proper shaping.

### SHOULDER LINE TOO HIGH (CHAPTER 8, FIG. B-15c) (TIME: 30 MINUTES)

**Sleeveless Garment**

1. Measure the amount pinned out of the neck edge and write this figure on the work ticket.

2. Untack neck and armhole facings. Rip 2 inches (5 cm) on each side of the shoulder seams at the neck and armhole seams to free the facings from the shoulder seams. Be sure that you do *not* rip open the shoulder seams of the garment or the facings.

3. Measure and chalk mark or pin the new seam line on the shoulder seams of both facings and garment.

4. Stitch all the seams in a chain. Start with the facing seam, on to the garment, to the opposite facing seam, and on to the next shoulder without stopping.

5. Trim all seams and rip out the old stitching.

6. Press open all the seams (on seam roll).

7. Stitch the facing seams back to the neck and armhole seams.

8. Press facings back in place and retack to shoulder seams.

**Garment with Sleeves (Time: 30 minutes)**

Follow the same steps as above with the following changes:

1. Make a thread mark where the top of each sleeve meets the shoulder seam.

2. Rip the sleeves away from the armhole seams at least 4 inches (10 cm) on each side of the shoulder seams.

3. Alter the shoulder seams on the garment and the neck facing. Trim the seams and press them open as for sleeveless garment.

4. Trim ¼ inch (.6 cm) from the crown of the sleeves. Ease-stitch ¼ inch (.6 cm) in on the sleeve crown from the original seam line. (This will make the sleeve smaller so it will fit into the smaller armhole.) Otherwise, the sleeve may pucker.

5. Pin this new line on the sleeves to the original armhole seams, matching the sleeve shoulder mark to the shoulder seams.

6. Stitch around the inside of the armhole circle.

7. Stitch the neck facing to the neck seam.

8. Press back facing and retack to the shoulder seams.

**Shoulders Too High in Front (Chapter 8, Fig. B-15d) (Time: 30 minutes)**

1. Measure the amount to come off the front shoulder seams. Record on the work ticket.

2. Untack facings and rip apart at neck and armhole seams. Rip further on the front than on the back of these seams.

213

## Altering Ready-To-Wear Fashions

3. Rip the shoulder seams apart on the garment and facings.

4. Measure the new line on the front shoulder seams of garment and facings. Mark with a chalk line.

5. Cut away excess seam allowance on the front shoulder seams of garment and facings.

6. Match the edges of all front and back shoulder seams together.

7. Stitch all seams from the back side of the shoulder seams, following the original stitching line. Stitch chain fashion as described in the preceding alteration. Follow all other instructions given there.

8. If garment has sleeves, follow the preceding instructions for the sleeve adjustment. In this instance, only the front of the sleeves is ripped away and only the front of the sleeves is trimmed 1/4 inch (.6 cm).

9. Finish the sleeve alteration as instructed above.

NOTE: If a collar is involved, look up the instructions for adjusting the collar size to the new neckline as illustrated in Figs. C-7a, b). Follow the steps given for the collar alteration and for finishing the neckline. This work would add approximately 20 minutes to the alteration time.

### Shoulders Too High in Back

Follow instructions for "Shoulders Too High in Front," substituting the word *back* for *front*.

## SLOPING SHOULDERS

### Slight Shoulder Slope (Chapter 8, Fig. B-17a) (Time: 20 minutes)

1. Measure the amount taken out at the shoulder seam by the fitter. Record on the work ticket. Remove all pins.

2. Rip the armhole seams 2 inches (5 cm) on each side of the shoulder seams.

3. Make a chalk mark (or place a pin) at the armhole edge of the garment and the facing shoulder seams showing the amount to be removed from the original seam.

4. Start the new shoulder stitch line at the armhole seam edge and taper toward the original seam near the neck. Overlap the stitching near the neckline. Make the same tapered seam on the facing seams.

5. Trim all the seams and press open.

6. Restitch the top of the armhole seams.

7. Press back the facing and retack at the shoulder seams.

NOTE: If the garment has sleeves, follow the instructions for adjusting excess sleeve fullness given on page 213, Garment with Sleeves, step 4.

### Slight Shoulder Slope (with Pads) (Chapter 8, Fig. B-17b) (Time: 30 to 45 minutes)

To alter for sloping shoulders by adding shoulder pads, you will need pads covered in a color and fabric suitable for the garment. If the garment is "wash and wear," the pads must be completely washable. Those made of polyester filling covered with a polyester fabric or a blend of polyester are recommended. Pads may be purchased ready-made where sewing supplies are sold or you may make your own. The instructions for making the pads are given in Chapter 11, page 303.

1. The shoulder pads will have been pinned in place by the fitter as in Fig. B-17b in Chapter 8.

2. In addition to the pins attaching the pads along the armhole seam, insert a pin through the shoulder seam at the thin end of the pad (nearest the neck seam). All the *pinning* is done from the right side so you can roll the garment over the pads to insure a smooth fit. The sewing is done on the inside.

3. On the inside of the armhole circle, hand sew the pad to the armhole seam allowance, using double thread and securing it well at each end. Use basting stitches and sew along the seam through to the closest layer of fabric on the pads. Do *not* sew through the pads or you will lose the puffy effect. Fig. C-14.

4. At the thin end of the pads near the neck seams, make a 1/2-inch (1.3 cm) chain tack. Attach the tack to the shoulder seam and to the end of the pad. The pad should swing instead of pull at the shoulder seam. A

**Ch. 9: Standard Alterations for Women**

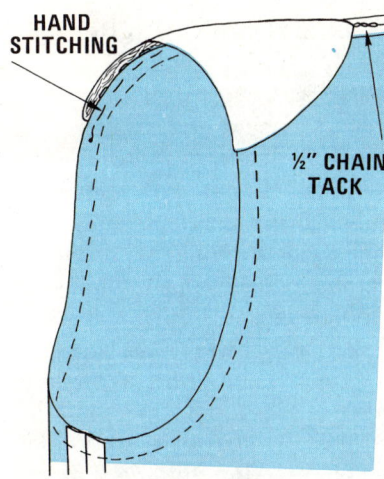

C-13. Attaching shoulder pads.

pull would destroy the overall effect of the padded shoulders.

NOTE: If the garment is a lined jacket or coat, the pad must be inserted between the garment and the lining. To do this, untack the lining or rip it away from the shoulders. Apply the pads as above and sew the lining back over the pads.

### Pronounced Shoulder Slope (Chapter 8, Fig. B-18) (Time: 60 minutes)

This alteration is accomplished by using a combination of increasing the shoulder seam and inserting pads. Follow the instructions given in the preceding two alterations.

### One Shoulder Slope (Time: 15 minutes)

Follow the instructions given for inserting the pads but on the one shoulder only.

### Bodice Fittings

### BODICE TOO LOOSE FRONT AND BACK (CHAPTER 8, FIG. B-19b) (TIME: 40 MINUTES)

**Sleeveless**

1. Transfer the pin markings to mark only one side of one seam. When seams are taken in equally on each side of the seam, you need only mark the side that will be on top as you stitch. One seam is used as the guide for altering the other.
2. Remove all pins. Untack and rip facings or lining 2 inches (5 cm) on each side of the underarm seams.
3. At the top of the marked seam, measure the amount to be taken in. Make a mark at the top of the opposite side using this measurement. Both seams will be tapered back to the original seam at the waist. Place a ruler from the mark at the top, slanting it to the seam at the waist. Mark your new seam with a pin or chalk line.
4. Mark facing seams the same way.
5. Stitch facing and side seams in a chain. Fig. C-14.
6. Trim the seams and rip out the original stitching.
7. Press seams open.
8. Stitch underarm facing back to armhole seam, press. Retack facing to side seams.

**With Sleeves**

1. Rip the sleeve seam 3 inches (7.6 cm) on each side of the underarm seams.
2. Alter side seams as above. Trim, rip, and press seams open.
3. Allow the sleeve seam to drop about $3/8$ to $1/2$ inch (1 to 1.3 cm) where the sleeve seam meets the side seams at the lower armhole.

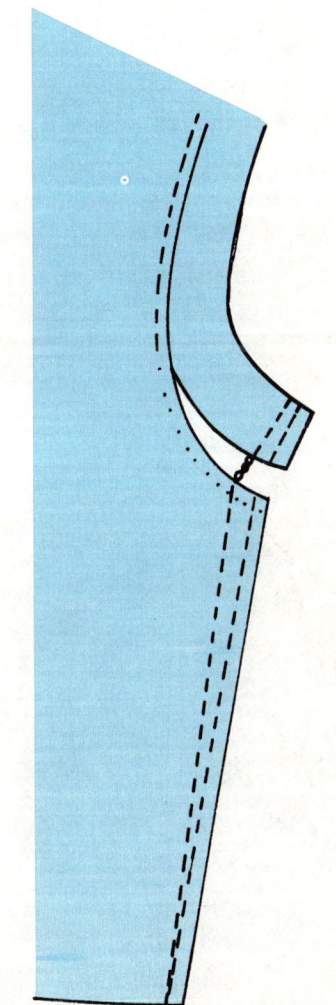

C-14. Chain sew new seam line on facing and side seam.

### Altering Ready-To-Wear Fashions

4. With the sleeve side up (inside the circle), pin the sleeve in a curved line on each side of the underarm seam so it meets the original armhole seam at each side.

5. Restitch sleeve seam and cut away the excess fabric left on the bodice armhole. Fig. C-15. Lowering the armhole in this way brings it back to the original size. This alteration is not intended to change the sleeve or armhole fit.

### BODICE TOO FULL IN FRONT ONLY (CHAPTER 8, FIG. B-20) (TIME: 40 MINUTES)

1. Mark one side of one seam as in preceding alteration. The pin fitting and work ticket instructions show that the fullness

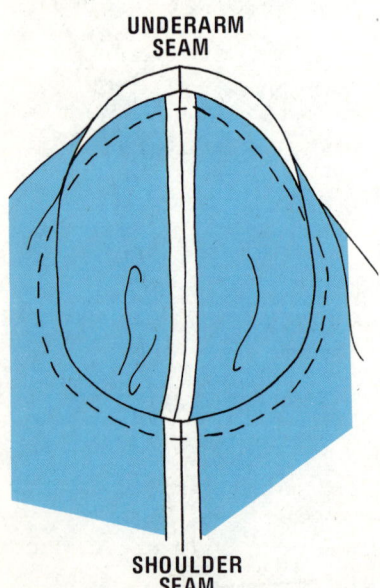

C-15. Sleeve lowered at underarm seam.

will come off the front of the underarm seam.

2. Untack and rip facing from lower armholes as instructed above.

3. Rip underarm seams apart on facing and bodice.

4. Measure the amount to be taken off the front underarm seam at the top of the seam. Use chalk or thread to mark a line tapering to the original seam at the waistline.

5. Pin the unaltered back underarm seam to the new front seam marking and stitch.

6. Make the same alteration on the opposite side seam.

7. Alter facing seams to match the underarm bodice seams.

8. Trim excess front seam allowance to match back seams and press seams open.

9. Stitch, press, and retack facing seams as above.

NOTE: For this same alteration with sleeves, follow the instructions given for restitching the sleeves in the preceding alteration.

### BODICE TOO FULL IN BACK ONLY (TIME: 40 MINUTES)

This alteration would be done following the same steps as in the preceding alteration for the front. The seam markings and alteration would be on the back underarm seam. The front seams are then pinned to the new line on the back seams and stitched. Follow all other steps as given before.

### BODICE TOO TIGHT (CHAPTER 8, FIG. B-21c) (TIME: 40 MINUTES)

1. Measure the distance of the top pin from the underarm seam. Transfer this measurement to the inside seam allowance since the seams are to be released or let out to make the bodice larger.

2. Rip away facings or sleeves 1 inch (2.5 cm) on each side of the underarm seams.

3. To help get a good line when marking the new seam, press underarm and facing seams flat or closed.

4. Mark the new line on the flat seam allowance with chalk or pins, starting at the top of the seams. Taper the line back to the original seam near the waist.

5. Stitch facing and side seams chain fashion. Do *not* change sleeve seams.

6. Rip out the original seams.

7. Before pressing the seams open, carefully steam both sides of the flat underarm seams. You must remove the former stitch marks that are now showing on the outside of the bodice seams. Then press all seams open.

8. Restitch the facing to the underarm seam and retack. Or

9. Stitch the sleeve back at the underarm seams, matching the armhole and sleeve seam edges together. Sleeves usually have enough ease to fit into the altered armhole.

NOTE: In all the above bodice alterations, the seams taper to

## Ch. 9: Standard Alterations for Women

the waist seam or just above it. Even though the waist size is not altered in any of these fittings, it would speed the alteration to rip the waist seam 1 inch (2.5 cm) on each side of the side seams. This gives a smoother line on the altered seams. It only takes a few seconds to restitch the waist seam as you restitch the armhole seams.

### BODICE TOO LONG (CHAPTER 8, FIG. B-23a, b) (TIME: 60 MINUTES)

1. Begin by removing the diagonal pins holding the skirt to the *new* waistline. Leave the horizontal pin line. If the skirt has been pinned to the bodice, remove the diagonal pins and insert a horizontal pin line on the new waistline.

2. Check the work ticket for the waist measurement. If none has been noted on the ticket, it means the waist size will not need changing.

3. Be sure garment is closed at the waist—zipper closed, buttons buttoned, snaps snapped. Place garment flat on worktable, front side up. Measure the garment along the waist seam from one side to the other. This will give half the waist measurement. Double it for the full measurement. Take the measurement before you rip the waistline seam as it may stretch and change when released from the skirt.

4. If the waistline has a seam tape in it, mark the center front, center back, and side seams on the tape. If there is no tape, cut a piece of seam tape 1 inch (2.5 cm) longer than the waist measure. Fold the tape in half lengthwise and mark the fold. Match this mark to the center front or center back of the garment—whichever does *not* have an opening—and mark the side seams on the tape. Make marks on the ends of the tape ½ inch (1.3 cm) from each end. Remove tape and pin to the work ticket to keep it handy for later.

5. If the garment has a zipper, rip it free from about 2 inches (5 cm) above the new waistline marks to the bottom of the zipper. Do *not* remove it completely.

6. Rip the waistline seam.

7. Fold the bodice in half, matching the side seams at the waist and the armholes. Check the pin line to see if the marking line matches on both sides. If one side is higher than the other, use the *lower* line as your guide (unless the fitter has made a note that the customer has one hip definitely higher than the other.) Remove the higher pins and pin the lower line through to both layers. It is better to use the lower line rather than risk overfitting by taking out too much.

8. Trim away the excess material, leaving at least a ¾-inch (1.9 cm) seam. This extra will be your insurance against overfitting. Fig. C-16.

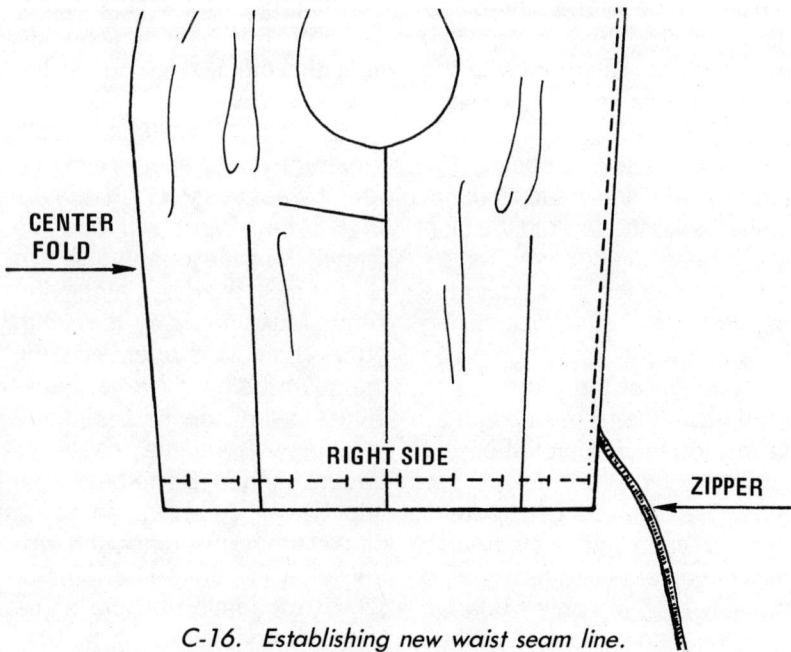

C-16. Establishing new waist seam line.

## Altering Ready-To-Wear Fashions

9. Make clip marks at the center fold of the bodice and remove all the pins.

10. If there are waistline darts front and back, take each one in 1/8 inch (.3 cm) on the double. Start at the seam edge and taper to the original points of the darts. This reduces the bodice waist to its original size.

NOTE: If the back waist has been raised much higher than the front, the back darts may have to be taken in 1/4 inch (.6 cm) to fit the back skirt waist. Press all darts toward the center front or center back.

11. If you have allowed a 3/4-inch (1.9 cm) seam allowance on the bodice waist, make a stay-stitching at 5/8 inch (1.6 cm). The stitching will be just inside the seam allowance.

12. On the wrong side of the *skirt* waist seam, match the marks on the seam tape to the matching marks on the skirt. Start with the center mark and end with the seam opening. Pin together at these marks and machine baste the tape to the skirt at the seam.

13. Leave the skirt right side out and turn the bodice wrong side out. Arrange the bodice on the outside of the skirt so you can match the right sides of the fabric together. Match the center front or center back marks, side seams, and opening seams. At the same time, match the machine basted tape line to the stay-stitching on the bodice. Pin the two pieces together,

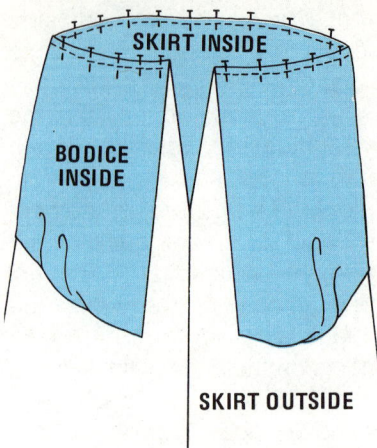

*C-17. Bodice and skirt prepared for stitching new waist seam.*

placing the pins perpendicular to the seam. Fig. C-17.

14. Working on the inside of the skirt waist circle, stitch the new line next to the tape stitching. The final stitching should hide the other stitching on the bodice and skirt.

15. Using the seam roll, press the waist seam back the way it was pressed originally.

16. The zipper will now be longer than the opening in the skirt. Lay the zipper along the seam. Make a clip on the seam edge where the zipper ends. On the seam below the clip, backstitch to the clip and continue stitching down the seam to about 2 inches (5 cm) below the clip. Rip the original seam to the backstitching. Replace the zipper following the original method of application on the same stitching lines.

### Bodice Too Long in Front Only (Chapter 8, Fig. B-24) (Time: 20 to 35 minutes)

1. Remove the pins holding the skirt to the new bodice waistline. Mark the center front of the tape. (If the dress opening is in front, there is no need to mark.) If there is no tape in the waist seam, mark one as in Step 4 in the instructions for the previous alteration.

2. Rip bodice and skirt apart across the front to 1 inch (2.5 cm) beyond side seams.

3. Match side seams of bodice and waist seam edges together and make an even pin line as in Step 7 above. Start at the center front and taper in a smooth line to the original waist seam at the side seams.

4. Trim away the excess seam allowance and make a new center front clip.

5. Increase the waistline darts as in step 10 above. Press the darts toward the center front.

6. Stay-stitch across the front bodice 1/8 inch (.3 cm) in from the seam line.

7. Machine baste the seam tape back to the inside of the skirt waist seam, matching the center front marks.

8. Pin the skirt to the bodice, matching the center front clips with the skirt seam along the bodice stay-stitching.

9. Press waist seam where altered.

10. If there is a front zipper, follow the instructions in Step 16 above.

### Ch. 9: Standard Alterations for Women

### Bodice Too Long in Back (Chapter 8, Fig. B-25)

To alter, follow the instructions given for "Bodice Too Long" and combine with the instructions for "Bodice Too Long in Front Only." Reverse the instructions given for the front to the back. Make special note of the instructions given for increasing the darts if the waistline is raised much higher than the original. This is not unusual for a back waistline alteration.

### BODICE TOO SHORT (CHAPTER 8, FIG. B-26)

Reread Chapter 8, Page 161, Fig. B-26a, 26b, as this alteration is limited by the seam allowance on the bodice waist seam. If the alteration needed is slight, follow the directions for altering in "Waistline Too Long." The procedure would be basically the same except the new seam would be restitched lower on the bodice rather than higher.

### BODICE DART PLACEMENT

**Underarm Bust Darts Too High or Too Low (Chapter 8, Fig. B-27b, 28) (Time: 20 minutes)**

1. Chalk or thread mark the new dart line on the wrong side of the bodice. Measuring carefully, duplicate the same dart line on the opposite side. Measure the length of each dart and mark across the dart line showing where the dart points end. Fig. C-18. Remember this in marking all new dart lines. It takes a second to do the cross mark but that mark insures that all darts will match in length.

2. Rip underarm seams just enough to free the bust darts. Rip the stitching on both darts.

3. On a seam roll or press mitt, press and steam out original dart lines.

4. Measure the distance between the dart clip marks to see how deep the new dart should be.

5. Using the new dart line for the center fold of the new bust darts, pin from the side seam to the new point of bust. Place the pins perpendicular to the fold line, using about three pins.

6. Start the stitching at the side seams and stitch toward the cross marks, tapering to a sharp point at the mark.

7. Press the darts toward the waist (shaping on the ham).

8. Restitch the side seams and press.

**Bust Darts Too Long (Chapter 8, Fig. B-29) (Time: 10 minutes)**

1. Make a cross mark on the wrong side at the pin that crosses the dart. Measure and make the same cross mark on the opposite dart.

2. Rip side seams just enough to free the bust darts.

3. Start stitching on the original dart line at the side seams. Gradually leave the stitch line and taper toward the new point of bust at the cross mark. Fig. C-19.

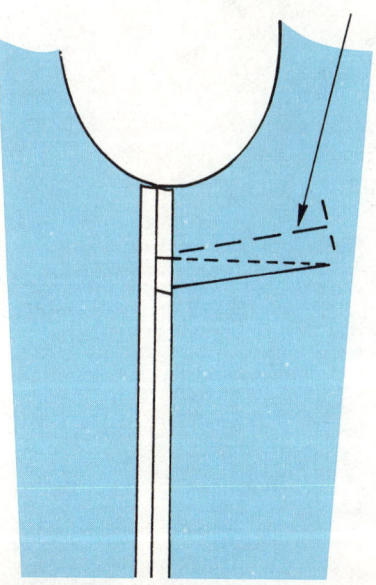

C-18. New bust dart marking line.

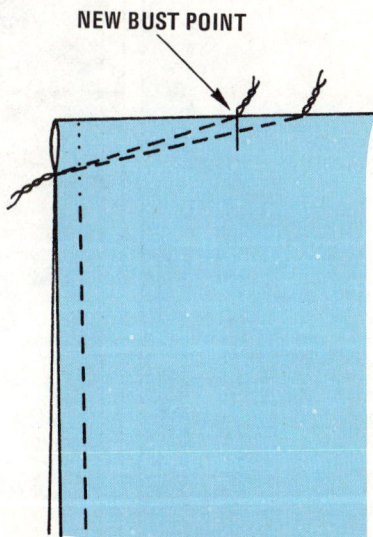

C-19. Shortened dart stitching line.

## Altering Ready-To-Wear Fashions

4. Rip out the original stitching in the dart.

5. Shaping on a pressing ham, press and steam out old dart lines.

6. Restitch the side seams and press.

### Bust Darts Too Long and Too Deep (Chapter 8, Fig. B-30) (Time: 40 minutes)

In this alteration, one deep dart will be replaced by two smaller ones.

1. Turn garment to wrong side and make the cross marks on the bust darts to be shortened. Make the *new* dart line marking below the original darts on both sides of the bodice. Make cross markings for length of new darts.

2. Rip the side seams, starting at the bust darts and ripping 1 inch (2.5 cm) past the new bust dart markings.

3. Make a new dart half the depth of the original bust darts. Taper to the cross marks for the shortened darts.

4. Rip out original dart and press out the old stitching lines.

5. Using the line marked below the original darts as the fold line for the new extra darts, insert a perpendicular line of pins along this fold from side seams to cross marks. The amount released in the upper darts will now be the depth of the new darts. Stitch the new lower darts to match the upper darts. Fig. C-20.

6. Press all the darts toward the waist (on the ham).

7. Restitch the side seams and press.

### Armhole Bust Darts Too Long (Chapter 8, Fig. B-31)

To alter, follow instructions given in preceding section for "Bust Darts too Long."

### Armhole Bust Darts Too Short and Shallow (Chapter 8, Fig. B-32) (Time: 20 minutes)

1. Mark the new shape and length of the armhole dart on the wrong side of the bodice. Make the same markings on the opposite darts.

2. Rip armhole seams just enough to free the darts.

3. Stitch the new dart line from the armhole seam to the new point at the cross mark. There is no need to rip out the original stitching since it will be covered by the new stitching.

4. Press the armhole darts toward the side seams (on ham).

5. Restitch the armhole seams.

NOTE: If the armholes are faced, untack the facing in order to rip the armhole seams to free the darts. Retack facing in place after the alteration is completed.

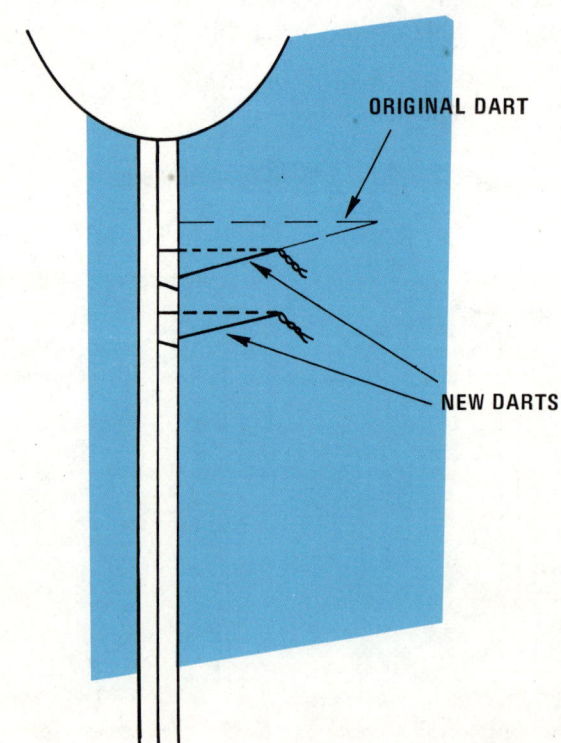

C-20. *Large bust dart changed to two smaller ones.*

## WAISTLINE DARTS

**Waistline Darts Too Long Front and Back (Chapter 8, Fig. B-33a, b) (Time: 20 minutes for 4 darts)**

1. On the wrong side of the front and back bodices, make cross marks at the new dart points.
2. Start the new stitching on the original stitch line about 1½ inches (3.8 cm) above the waist seam. Continue stitching gradually, leaving the original stitch line and tapering to the new point at the cross mark. (See Fig. C-19).
3. Rip out the original stitching to the overlap of the new stitching near the waist seam.
4. Using the ham, steam and press out the original dart lines, pressing the darts toward center front and center back.

NOTE: This alteration may involve only the *front* or only the *back* darts.

**Waistline Darts Too Tight in Midriff Front and Back (Chapter 8, Fig. B-34a, b) (Time: 30 minutes)**

1. Mark the amount to be released and cross mark for length on the wrong side of the bodice.
2. Rip bodice from skirt 3 inches (7.6 cm) on each side of the front and back darts.
3. Start new stitch line ¼ inch (.6 cm) on the inside of the original dart, stitching at the waist seam. Still stitching on the inside of the dart, follow the new dart line, tapering to a point at the cross mark. Stitch all four darts at once using the chain method.
4. Rip original stitching in all four darts.
5. Steam and press out original dart lines and stitch marks. Press darts to center front and center back.
6. Ease-stitch bodice waist seam where it was ripped from the skirt. Stitch on the inside of the bodice waist seam to insure holding the bottom ends of the darts in place.
7. Restitch the bodice to the skirt at the waist seam.
8. Press waist seam (on seam roll).

**Eliminating Waist Darts (Time: 40 minutes)**

If the darts are to be removed as suggested in Chapter 8 for an easier and more flattering fit over a full midriff, no dart marking is necessary.

1. Rip 3 inches (7.6 cm) on each side of front bust darts at the waist seam. Rip waist seam across the back, starting 1 inch (2.5 cm) from the side seams. Rip out all four darts.
2. Carefully steam and press out the lines and stitch marks on all darts.
3. Measure 1½ inches (3.8 cm) in from side seams on back bodice and clip edge of bodice waist seam at these points. The 3 inches (7.6 cm) you ripped on each side of the front darts is your guide to clip marking the front bodice waist seam. This means you will have two clips on each side of the front waist seam—one on each side of the ripped area.
4. Ease-stitch between the clips across the back bodice waist seam close to the seam allowance. Ease-stitch the front bodice waist seam between the two clips on each side of front bodice. The extra ease will be concentrated for the bust fullness in the front.
5. Stitch the bodice to the skirt waist seam, matching center back on skirt and bodice and overlapping where the seam was ripped.
6. Press the waist seam (on seam roll), taking care not to flatten the ease on the bodice.

NOTE: If there is a zipper in the center back seam, end the waist ripping 1½ inches (3.8 cm) from the zipper on each side. Ease-stitch the back waist seam between these ripped areas on each side of the back bodice. This will require a little extra ease on each side of the back bodice.

**Waistline Darts Too Loose Through Midriff (Chapter 8, Fig. B-35a, b) (Time: 20 to 30 minutes)**

1. Chalk or thread mark the new dart shape on *one* side of each dart.
2. Rip the waist seam at each dart just enough to free the bottom of the darts.

*Altering Ready-To-Wear Fashions*

3. Stitch the new dart lines from the waist seam toward the dart point, following the marks.

4. Press darts toward center front and center back (on ham).

5. Restitch waist seam and press (on seam roll).

NOTE: If the darts are pinned through the waist seam to tighten the waist fit, take in the matching skirt darts the same amount as the bodice darts. Stitch skirt darts at the same time the bodice darts are stitched and taper them to sharp points. Press darts and then restitch the waist seam as indicated above.

## Waistline Alterations

### WAISTLINE TOO TIGHT

Use this method if the difference in waist measurement is 2 inches (5 cm) or less. (Time: 20 minutes)

1. Begin by removing the inside waist seam tape. This tape is used to retain the original waist size in a ready-made garment. By removing it, the waist will sometimes stretch 1 or 2 inches (2.5 to 5 cm).

2. Measure the new waist line as directed in Step 3 under "Bodice Too Long." If more waist width is needed, pull the waist seam and really stretch it all around. As you do this, you will break the stitches holding the waist seam together.

3. Measure and mark a new seam tape as instructed in Step 4 under "Bodice Too Long." Pin the tape to the inside of the waist seam, following Step 12 under "Bodice Too Long."

4. Stitch the seam tape right on the waist seam to cover the broken stitches. Stitch as close to the opening seam as possible without disturbing the zipper or other details at the opening. Fold under and hand sew the ends of the tape to the opening seam.

*Use this method if the waistline is more than 2 inches (5 cm) too tight:* (Time: 40 minutes)

1. Check work ticket and fitting pins to see where release is most needed.

2. Make an X mark with chalk or thread on the wrong side at each crossed pin. Remove all pins.

3. Remove the inside seam tape from waistline and cut and mark a new seam tape for the new measurement (Step 4, "Bodice Too Long").

4. Rip waist seam at the marked darts. If so much room is needed that the side seams were cross marked also, rip the waist seam from front waist darts to back waist darts on each side of the garment.

5. Starting at the waist edge of both the bodice and the skirt, release the cross marked darts or seams the amount indicated by the fitter. Taper the new stitching line to the original stitching. Overlap the stitching at least 1 inch (2.5 cm).

6. Rip out old darts and seams where new stitching has been added.

7. Steam and press out original seams, dart lines, and stitch marks. Press darts toward center front and center back. Press seams open.

8. Restitch the waist seam where ripped.

9. Pin the marked seam tape to the inside of the garment waist seam, matching the center front, center back, and side seams. Since the seam tape is measured and marked exactly to the client's waist measurement, the garment waist *seam* will be pinned to fit the seam *tape*. This could mean stretching or easing the waist seam between the markings on the tape.

10. Restitch the waistline seam through the tape and along the old seam line. Sew tape ends by hand to the opening seam.

11. Press waist seam (on seam roll).

### WAISTLINE TOO LOOSE (CHAPTER 8, FIG. 36a, b) TIME: 30 MINUTES)

1. Measure the amount pinned in on the side seams and write on the work ticket.

2. Remove pins. Rip the waist seam 2 inches (5 cm) on each side of the side seams without cutting the seam tape inside.

3. Measure and chalk or clip mark the amount to be taken in on the side seams. The marking is made at the waist edge on bodice and skirt.

222

## Ch. 9: Standard Alterations for Women

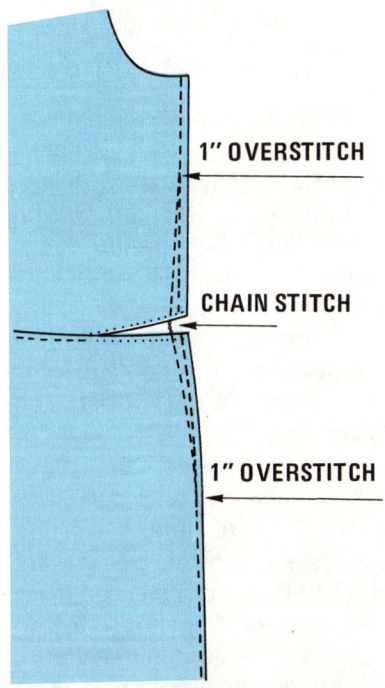

C-21. Increasing side seam to make waistline smaller.

4. Starting about 5 inches (12.7 cm) above the waist seam on the bodice side seams, stitch the new line. Overlap the original seam 1 inch (2.5 cm) and gradually taper to the new mark at the waist edge. Chain sew to the mark on the skirt side seam. Stitch from that mark down, gradually tapering to the original stitching about 3 inches (7.6 cm) down. Overlap this seam 1 inch (2.5 cm) Fig. C-21.

5. Rip seams to the overlapping stitches. Trim the excess seams or leave the extra seam allowance if the fabric is not too bulky.

6. Press all seams open (on seam roll).

7. Fold over the extra seam tape and stitch it flat as you restitch the waist seam.

### Belt Alterations
### (Time: 15-20 Minutes)

When the waistline is altered extensively, the belt will often need length added or subtracted correspondingly. In either change, the alteration is always done at buckle end of belt.

Shortening a belt is no problem. Remove the buckle, cut off the excess length, and replace the buckle.

Lengthening a belt can be another matter entirely. If the belt is made of leather, vinyl, or ribbon, it cannot be pieced successfully for lengthening. It is better to suggest the purchase of a new belt.

If the belt is made of the garment fabric, the fitter will check for facings from which to cut the matching fabric for piecing. If the garment is to be shortened, there is no problem. If no source of fabric can be found, a new belt is suggested.

If you have enough fabric:

1. Remove the buckle. If the buckle has a tongue, the piecing starts beyond the hole made for the tongue so the hole is covered. If there is no tongue, the piecing starts at the end of the belt.

2. Separate all the layers of the belt so each can be pieced separately.

3. If a belt backing is present, it must be pieced with the same type of backing. *Butt* the cut edges against each other and zigzag together with a wide zigzag stitch to eliminate bulk. Do *not* make a seam.

4. If there is an underlining, *overlap* the cut edges and zigzag together.

5. Only the outer fabric is seamed with the seam pressed open.

6. After all the layers have been pieced, carefully align all layers together and finish to match the original finish.

7. Measure new belt length and replace buckle.

### Skirt Alterations

#### SKIRT TOO LARGE (CHAPTER 8, FIG. B-38) (TIME: 30 MINUTES)

1. Mark the side seams along the pin line on the inside of the garment—from waist to hem—(if pinned through the hem). Remove all fitting pins.

2. Rip the waist seam 2 inches (5 cm) on each side of the side seams. Rip hem 3 inches (7.6 cm) on each side of side seams, if necessary.

3. Begin stitching on bodice side seams as instructed in Step 4 in "Waistline Too Loose," Fig. C-21.

4. Rip the old seams where the new lines have been stitched. Trim away excess seam allowance.

5. Press seams open on the seam roll. Use the ham for shaping the seam at the hip curve.

## Altering Ready-To-Wear Fashions

6. Restitch waist seam, folding the excess seam tape over at the waist as you stitch.

7. Sew the hem back in place and press.

NOTE: If skirt has a side seam zipper, read the instructions below.

**Skirt Too Large in Upper Hip (Chapter 8, Fig. B-39a, b) (Time: 15 minutes; 30 minutes with zipper)**

1. Mark pin line on the inside of the skirt seams.

2. Remove all pins. Rip waist seam 1 inch (2.5 cm) on each side of side seams.

3. Stitch the new line, starting on the seam at the waist and picking up the marked line as you go along. Merge back to the original seam where marked and overlap 1 inch (2.5 cm) on old seam.

4. Rip out original seams where new stitching has been sewn. Trim excess seam allowance.

5. Press seams open (on ham).

NOTE: If there is a zipper in the side seam, the procedure will be a little more complicated.

1. Rip the zipper away from the skirt only. Leave it attached at the waist seam and do *not* rip waist seam on zipper side.

2. Stitch the new line from the zipper opening down. Backstitch the beginning of the seam and merge with the original seam as in Fig. C-22.

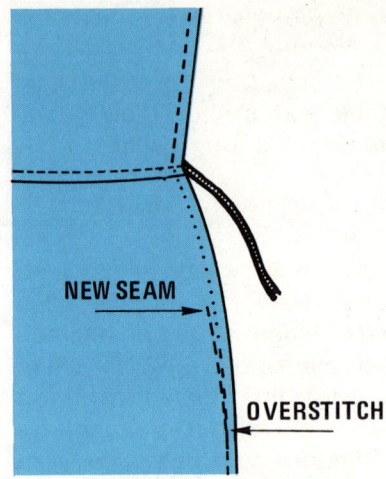

C-22. Side seam, with zipper, increased in upper hip.

3. Rip and press seam open. At the same time press the zipper opening on the new line.

4. Restitch the zipper as it was originally.

If darts are to be changed: (Time: 15 minutes)

1. Mark new dart lines on the inside of the garment and remove all pins.

2. Rip waist seam 1 inch (2.5 cm) on each side of the darts to be altered.

3. Stitch the new dart line starting at the waist seam.

4. Press all darts toward the center back (on the ham).

5. Restitch the waist seam.

**Skirt Too Large in Lower Hip (Chapter 8, Fig. B-34) (Time: 20 minutes)**

1. Mark the new pin line on inside of garment and remove pins.

2. Rip the hem about 3 inches (7.6 cm) on each side of the side seams.

3. Start the new stitching on the original seam 2 or 3 inches (5 to 7.6 cm) above the new line. Overlap 1 inch (2.5 cm). Gradually pick up the new line as you continue through to the bottom of seam.

4. Rip old stitching to the overlapped stitching.

5. Press seams open (on seam roll).

6. Replace hem and press where necessary.

NOTE: If a zipper is in the side seam, rip the zipper from the bottom of the opening only—about 4 inches (10 cm) up on the seam. Follow the instructions for the zipper given under "Skirt Too Large in Upper Hip" and shown in Fig. C-22. (Time: 35 minutes).

**Skirt Too Full in Back Only**

**WITH CENTER BACK SEAM (CHAPTER 8, FIG. B-41A) (TIME: 20 TO 30 MINUTES)**

Check work ticket and fitting pins. If there are no cross pins on the back darts, the back seam can be taken in following the steps for the side seams in the previous alteration.

If there is a zipper in the center back seam, follow the instructions for Fig. C-22 under "Skirt Too Large in Upper Hip."

If there are cross pins, it means the darts are too deep for the client's flat buttocks.

# Ch. 9: Standard Alterations for Women

1. Mark darts to be released and seam to be increased on inside of skirt.

2. Rip waist seam across the back 1 inch (2.5 cm) beyond each marked dart. Rip the hem 3 inches (7.5 cm) on each side of the center back seam. If there is a zipper opening, rip zipper from the bottom to 1 inch (2.5 cm) above the waist seam.

3. Beginning at the waist seam, stitch the new line on the skirt darts 1/4 inch (.6 cm) inside the old line. Near the end of the darts, taper to the edge and stitch to the same length as the old darts.

## Without Center Back Seam (Chapter 8, Fig. B-41b)

The extra fullness will be removed from the back of the side seams.

1. Mark the inside of the back side seams the amount to be removed and where the alteration is to begin.

2. Rip hem 3 inches (7.5 cm) on each side of the side seams. Rip side seams from the bottom to 1 inch (2.5 cm) above the beginning point for the alteration.

3. Pin the unchanged front seam to the new line on the back seam. Stitch on the front seam line, overlapping the end of the old seam 1 inch (2.5 cm) at the top of the ripped area.

4. Trim back seams to match the front seams.

5. Press seams open (on seam roll).

6. Replace hem and press.

## SKIRT TOO SMALL (CHAPTER 8, FIG. B-42a, b) (TIME: 60 MINUTES)
### Entire Skirt Too Tight from Waistline Through Hem

1. Make X marks on the inside of the garment on the darts to be altered. If the darts are to be shortened, make a small mark showing new length.

2. Measure the skirt at the waist, and upper and lower hip lines. Subtract these measurements from the new measurements on the work ticket. This shows how much release is needed in darts and side seams.

3. Rip waist seam 1 inch (2.5 cm) on each side of darts to be released and 1 inch (2.5 cm) on each side of side seams. Remove seam tape from waist seam. Rip hem 2 inches (5 cm) on each side of seams.

4. Press flat the seams to be released.

5. Stitch new lines on seams and darts. Release the bodice waistline darts that match the altered skirt darts. Overcast together the edges of the side seams with a zigzag stitch for reinforcement.

NOTE: Since the seams and darts are to be altered just a small fraction, it is usually not necessary to mark the new lines. The width of your presser foot is the only gauge you need to help stitch the new seams and reshape the darts.

6. Rip all stitching where new stitching has been made.

7. Carefully steam and press out seam marks or line. (Use the ham for upper hip area and seam roll for side seams.)

8. Cut and mark a new seam tape as instructed in Step 4 under "Bodice Too Long," page 217, using the new waist measurement.

9. Apply new seam tape to waist (Step 12, "Bodice Too Long," page 218) and restitch the waist seam.

10. Replace hem at side seams and press.

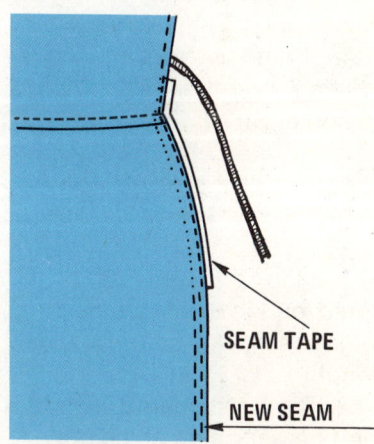

C-23. *Facing zipper seam with seam tape for side seam release.*

## If Zipper is in Side Seam (Time: 75 Minutes)

1. Rip from bottom of zipper to 3 inches (7.6 cm) above waist seam.

2. Face zipper opening seams by stitching seam tape

## Altering Ready-To-Wear Fashions

on the right side of the material close to the edge of the opening seams. This gives extra seam allowance for the zipper and also keeps the seam from stretching.

3. Stitch the new seam from the bottom of the opening, starting with a backstitch. Fig. C-23.

4. Steam and press out original lines. Re-press the opening seam on the new line before restitching zipper. Restitch the zipper *after* new seam tape has been sewn to waist seam.

### Skirt Too Tight in Waist (Time: 20 minutes)

Follow steps under "Waistline Too Tight." If there is a waistband, read instructions under "Fitting Waistbands," pg. 173 (Chapter 8).

### Skirt Too Tight in Upper Hip (Chapter 8, Fig. B-42b) (Time: 20 minutes)

1. Mark the darts to be altered on the inside of the skirt, being sure to mark the new length.

2. Rip waist seam 1 inch (2.5 cm) on each side of the darts to be changed.

3. Starting at waist seam, stitch the new dart lines, tapering to new length marks.

4. Rip out original stitching in altered darts.

5. Steam out original dart lines. Press darts toward the center front and center back (on ham).

6. Restitch waist seam.

If work ticket requests removal of darts, back or front, with the ease put into shirred fullness, follow these steps: (Time: 15 minutes for front; 30 minutes for back and front)

1. If only front fullness is needed, rip waist seam starting at front dart nearest the center front and rip to side seams. Rip out all dart stitching *carefully*.

2. Steam and press out all dart lines (on ham).

3. Clip mark edge of skirt waist seam 1 inch (2.5 cm) from side seams.

4. Make a shirring stitch on skirt waist seam, starting from new clip mark and ending at the last dart clip mark. Fig. C-24.

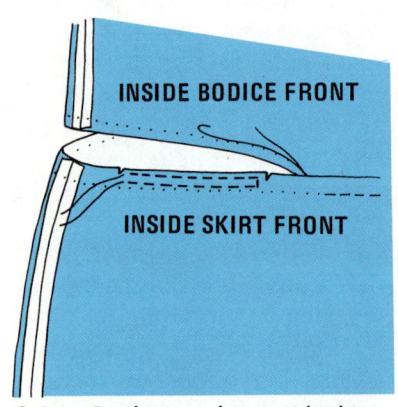

C-24. *Replacing darts with shirring.*

5. Pull shirring stitch enough to fit bodice waist seam and knot thread ends. Distribute fullness evenly.

6. Restitch waist seam. Keep shirring side up for greater control of fullness when stitching and to be sure of covering shirring stitch.

7. If fullness is needed front and back, rip waist seam front from dart nearest center front around to back dart nearest center back. Follow the same instructions for the back darts you did for the front darts.

### Skirt Too Tight in Lower Hip (Chapter 8, Fig. B-43a) (Time: 20 minutes)

1. Mark placement of crossed pins on inside of skirt seams. This indicates where release begins. The grain line determines where release ends at the bottom of the skirt.

2. Rip hem 2 inches (5 cm) on each side of side seams.

3. Press side seams flat from mark through bottom of hem.

4. Start new stitching 2 inches (5 cm) above mark—overlapping the original seam 1 inch (2.5 cm). Gradually move away from seam toward seam edge using presser foot as a guide. If the seam is straight grain, continue stitching through to bottom of hem. If seam is an A-line, pick up the grain line about 3 inches (7.6 cm) above hem fold, and then gradually come back to the original seam, and overlap 1 inch (2.5 cm). Fig. C-25.

5. Overcast seam edges with zigzag stitch if necessary.

6. Rip out original seam stitching between the new stitching ends.

## Ch. 9: Standard Alterations for Women

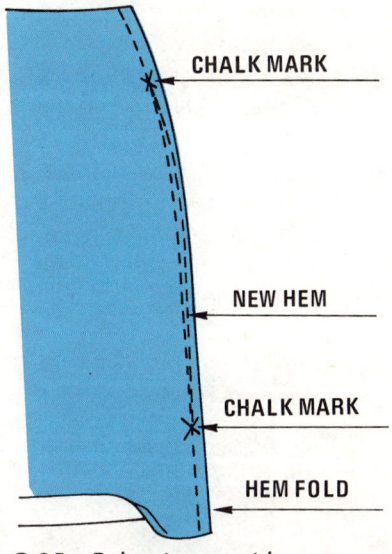

C-25. Releasing side seam through upper hip only.

### WAISTBAND TOO LOOSE
#### Side Opening (Time: 20 minutes)

1. Measure the amount the band is to be shortened from the fastening on the back side of the band. Mark the new length with a pin or thread marking. Fig. C-26.

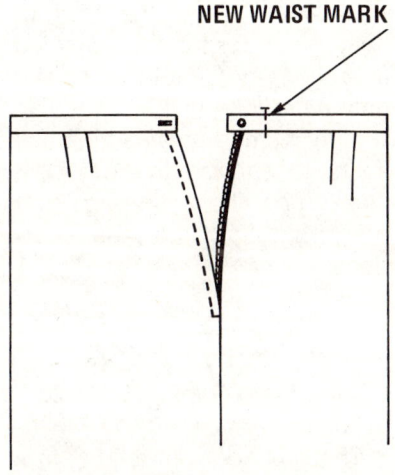

C-26. Waistband to be decreased.

2. Rip band to 1 inch (2.5 cm) beyond the back dart closest to the opposite seam.

3. Increase back darts just enough to fit new band measurement. For example, if the band is reduced 1 inch (2.5 cm), the two back darts closest to the center back may be taken in 1/4 inch (.6 cm) on the double. Or, all four darts may be taken in 1/8 inch (.3 cm) apiece.

4. Taper dart stitching to original dart line 2 inches (5 cm) below waist seam.

5. Press darts toward center back (on ham).

6. Pin new mark on the band to back seam opening and the rest of the band to the top of the skirt.

7. Stitch inside seam first and then the top stitching. Do *not* cut away or change excess waistband.

8. Sew fastening—button or hook-eye—at new mark.

9. Attach a snap so the extra waistband may be snapped to the back of the front waistband on the inside.

#### Center Front or Center Back Opening (Time: 30 minutes)

1. Measure the amount to be reduced from the fastening—button or hook-eye—at the back end of the band and mark. Fig. C-26.

2. Starting with the back end of the band, rip band from the skirt across the front—or across the back—to 1 inch past the second seam.

3. Take in the side seams enough to match the smaller size band. Taper stitching to original seam stitching 2 inches (5 cm) below the waist seam and overlap 1 inch (2.5 cm).

4. Rip original stitching and press seams open.

5. Stitch skirt band back in place and finish, following the instructions given in the preceding alteration.

7. Steam and press out original seam lines and re-press seams (on seam roll).

8. Replace hem and press.

### Waistbands on Skirts and Pants

Altering a skirt or pants waistband means working with a long, narrow, seamless strip of self-fabric. This has to be altered differently from the regular waistline alteration as you have no seams to release or take in. The exception is the man-tailored waistband that often goes with the fly-front skirt or pants. This style has a center back seam where all changes are made. Instructions for this waistband will be given last in this section.

## Altering Ready-To-Wear Fashions

### Fly-Front Opening (Time: 20 minutes)

To alter, follow the instructions for trouser waistline alterations in Chapter 12.

### WAISTBAND TOO TIGHT (TIME: 45 MINUTES)

This nearly always means piecing the band with matching fabric. Do not attempt this alteration without looking for a source for the piecing. You may find it in the hem if the garment is shortened, in facings from a matching jacket or top, or in a pocket that can be removed successfully.

### Side or Center Openings (Time: 45 minutes)

1. Follow the instructions in preceding alteration for ripping.
2. Open the back seam of the band and press the open seam flat.
3. Measure width of the band.
4. Cut the extra piece of fabric the width of the band and 1 inch (2.5 cm) longer than the extra length needed. This will give you a ½ inch (1.3 cm) seam allowance at each end of the piecing.
5. Stitch one end of piecing fabric to the open end of the band.
6. Release (as in Steps 3 and 4 in "Waistband too Loose") the side seams for center openings or the back darts for side openings. Allow enough release to fit the new band measurement.
7. Steam and press out original seam or dart lines.
8. Pin the band to the skirt, starting at the closed end and fitting the rest of the skirt to the band.
9. Stitch and finish the band, following the instructions given in the preceding alteration.

### Fly-Front Opening (Time: 20 minutes)

To alter, follow the instructions given for trouser waistline alteration in Chapter 12. The only difference is the new seam will be stitched *outside* the back seam to enlarge the waist fit. The preparation, ripping, and pressing follow in the same order.

## Sleeve Alterations

### SLEEVES TOO WIDE (CHAPTER 8, FIG. B-44) (TIME: 15 TO 20 MINUTES)

The procedure for taking in a sleeve is basically the same whether for a long sleeve or a short sleeve.

1. Mark the amount to be removed on the wrong side of the sleeve seams.
2. Rip the armhole seam where it crosses the sleeve seam. Rip the sleeve hems 2 inches (5 cm) on each side of the sleeve seams or enough so the hem can be unfolded at the seam.
3. Place a pin across each sleeve seam at the hem fold to keep the seams in place for the new stitching line. A long sleeve may require a few more pins to hold the seam securely.
4. Begin stitching on the sleeve seam at the armhole edge, gradually slanting the stitching toward the new mark at the hem. Stitch through to the bottom of the hem on a short sleeve. On a long sleeve, stitch as shown in Fig. C-27a.

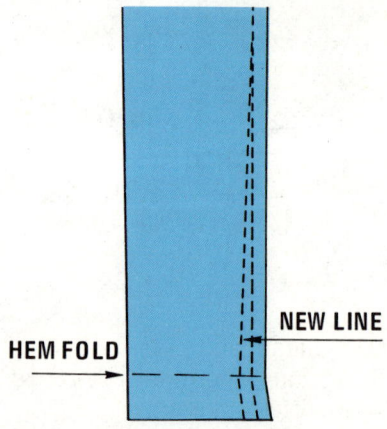

C-27a. Decreasing width in long sleeves.

5. Rip out the old stitching and trim seams.
6. Press seams open (on seam roll).
7. Resew armhole seams and sleeve hems.

### Long Sleeves with Wrist Opening (Chapter 8, Fig. B-44) (Time: 30 minutes)

1. Mark new sleeve seam on the wrong side. Make a clip mark where the crossed pins indicate the sleeve opening should start.

### Ch. 9: Standard Alterations for Women

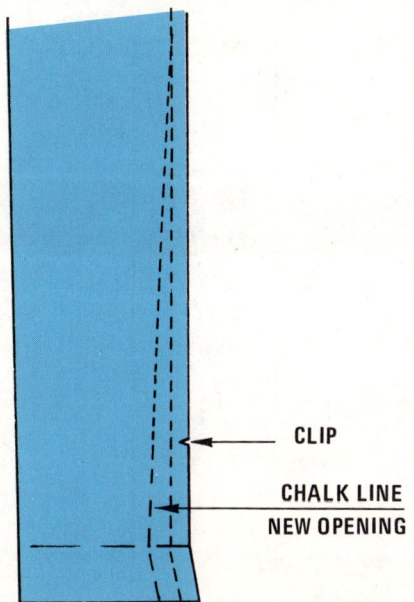

C-27b. Long sleeve stitched and marked for wrist opening.

6. Restitch armhole seams, if necessary.

7. Turn sleeve hems to the inside and press the new opening seams flat.

8. Resew the sleeve hems. After that, sew small snaps to the front and back edges of the opening sections about ¼ inch (.6 cm) from the edges. Fig. C-27d.

### SLEEVES TOO TIGHT (CHAPTER 8, FIG. 8-45a) (TIME: 15 MINUTES)

**Releasing Seams**

1. Remove the crossed pins and check the measurement given on the work ticket. If there is enough seam allowance for release, rip the armhole seam 2 inches (5 cm) on each side of the sleeve seams and 1 inch (2.5 cm) on each side of the hem.

2. Press sleeve seam flat.

3. Stitch the new seam along the old seam allowance, giving as much release as needed. Overcast the seam edges with a zigzag finish.

4. Remove crease marks from the old seams and press the new seams to one side (on seam roll).

5. Restitch the armhole seams, easing in the extra fullness in the sleeves. Replace the hem.

2. Stitch the new seam as in the previous alteration, ending at the clip mark with a backstitch. Fig. C-27b.

3. Remove old stitching and trim excess seams.

4. Press the new seam to the end of the stitching. Press the lower—or opening section—of the sleeve *front* flat. Fold the seam on the sleeve *back* in line with the new sleeve seam and press a crease line.

5. Turn sleeve hems to the outside—right side to right side. On the sleeve *back*, stitch the hem to the sleeve along the new crease line. On the sleeve front, stitch a narrow—about ¼ inch (.6 cm)—seam through the hem section. Fig. C-27c.

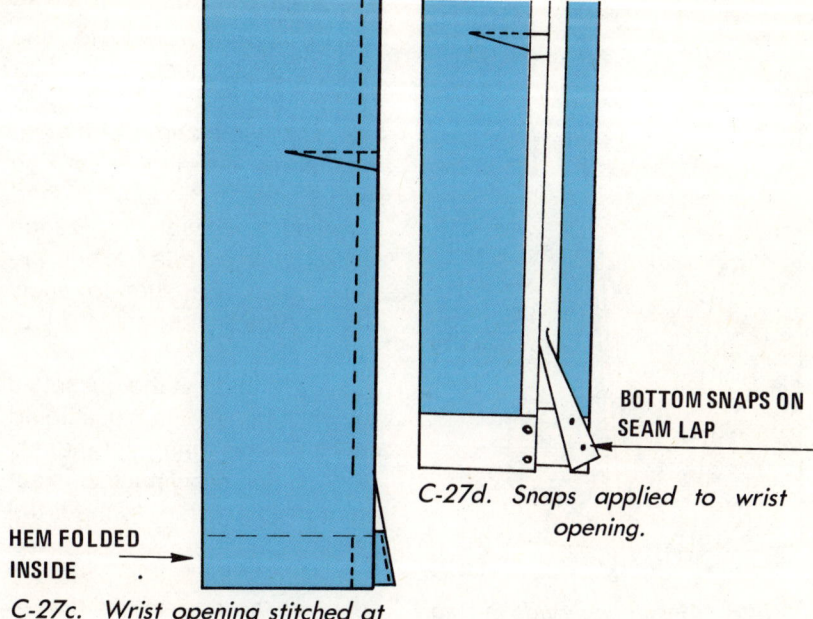

C-27c. Wrist opening stitched at hem.

C-27d. Snaps applied to wrist opening.

## Altering Ready-To-Wear Fashions

### Adding Piecings to Short Sleeves (Chapter 8, Fig. B-45b)

1. Rip the armhole seams 4 inches (10 cm) and the hems 2 inches (5 cm) on each side of the sleeve seams. Rip the sleeve seams open.

2. Cut a piece of matching fabric (gusset) the same length as the sleeve. This piece should be the width needed to expand the sleeve plus seam allowance for two seams.

3. Match the seam edges of the gusset to the edges of the sleeve seams and stitch along the old sleeve seam lines. You will now have two seams on each sleeve. Fig. C-28.

4. Ease-stitch along the underarm edge of the sleeve and gusset to aid in easing the sleeve back into the original armhole.

5. Match the center of the gusset to the underarm seam as you pin the sleeve back into the armhole. Restitch the armhole seams carefully, easing in the extra sleeve fabric as you stitch. Replace sleeve hems.

6. Press as needed, using the pressing mitt and the point of the iron to steam out any bubbles caused by the extra ease in the sleeve.

### Adding Gussets to Long Sleeves (Chapter 8, Fig. B-45b) (Time: 30 minutes)

1. Rip the armhole seam 4 inches (10 cm) on either side of the underarm seam. Rip the sleeve seam down to the crossed pins placed by the fitter to show the end of the easing.

2. Cut a rectangle of matching fabric the length of the sleeve seam opening and the width necessary to give the added inches called for on the work ticket. Be sure to allow seam allowances on all four sides.

3. Fold and cut the gusset as shown in Fig. C-29a. You should now have two triangular pieces. Mark a dot showing the exact point of the gusset to meet the sleeve opening.

4. Backstitch the sleeve seam at the end of the ripped area so it will not rip any further.

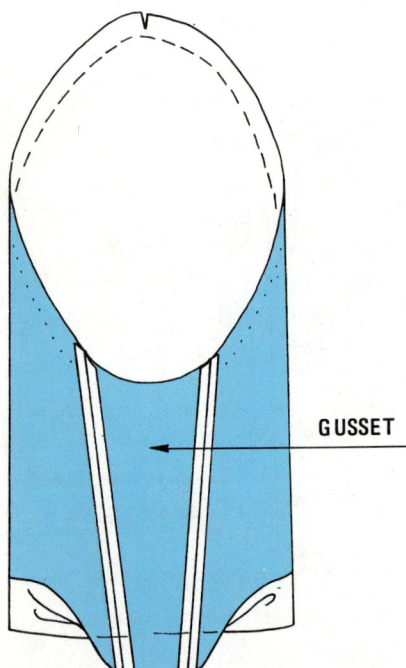

C-28. Gusset inserted in short sleeve.

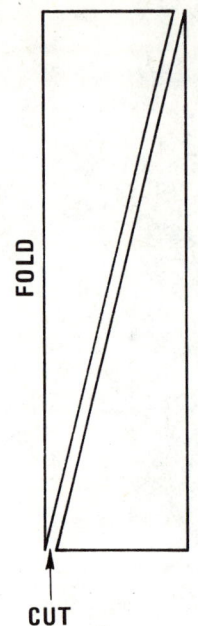

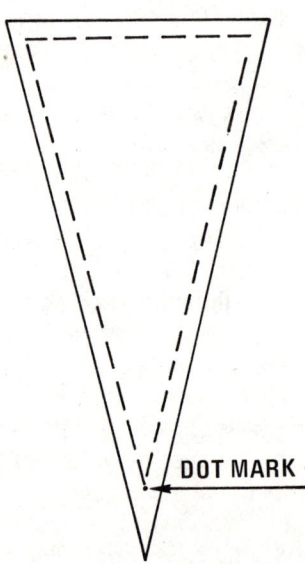

C-29a. Cutting and marking gusset for long sleeve.

## Ch. 9: Standard Alterations for Women

5. Match the dot on the point of the gusset to the end of the seam opening. With one sleeve seam side up, match and pin the edges of the sleeve seam to the edges of the gusset from the dot to the armhole edge.

6. Stitch the gusset seams as pinned. Repeat for the other side of the gusset. Be sure to start each seam at the point of the gusset, matching the new stitches exactly with the line of the original stitching in the sleeve. All three seams—the original sleeve seam, and each gusset seam—*must* meet at the same point if the gusset is to lie smooth with no bulge where it joins the sleeve.

7. Repeat the entire procedure on the other sleeve.

8. Press both gussets (on seam roll), pressing the seams open. Fig. C-29b.

9. Restitch the armhole seam, following the same directions given for short sleeves with gussets.

## SLEEVE LENGTH

### Sleeves Too Long (Chapter 8, Fig. B-46a) (Time: 15 minutes)

1. Measure the amount to be shortened as indicated by the fitter. Record on the work ticket.
2. Remove the pins. Rip out the sleeve hems.
3. If sleeves are to be shortened 1 inch (2.5 cm) or less, leave the extra on the sleeve and do not trim it off. If the sleeves are to be shortened more than 1 inch (2.5 cm), apply the new seam tape or clean finish the edge before trimming away the excess fabric (Chapter 6, page 115). It is easier to get a neat finish with the extra fabric still in place while you work.
4. With the sleeves turned wrong side out, pin new hem line in place and hem with proper stitch for type of fabric.
5. Slip the pressing mitt inside the bottom of the sleeve. Press in the new hem as you are pressing out the old crease of the old hem.

### Sleeves Too Long with Cuff (Chapter 8, Fig. B-46b) (Time: 30 minutes)

To shorten sleeves with cuffs, the cuffs must be removed and the excess fabric cut from the ends of the sleeves. Detailed directions for the alteration are given in Chapter 12 under "Shortening Shirt Sleeves."

### SLEEVES TOO FULL AT ARMHOLE (CHAPTER 8, FIG. B-48) (TIME: 15 MINUTES)

1. Measure the deepest part of the tuck pinned by the fitter. On the wrong side of the sleeve, mark the amount to be removed. Also mark the ends of the tuck as indicated by the fitter. Remove fitting pins.
2. Rip the armhole seam to about 1 inch (2.5 cm) beyond each end of the tuck. Trim away the excess fabric on the sleeve cap as marked. Taper back to the original seam allowance on either side.
3. Match the newly trimmed seam edge to the edge of the armhole at the shoulder and restitch.

## ALTERING THE PRINCESS STYLE GARMENT

Any alterations on Princess style clothes other than the ones given would be handled the same as those on basic style garments.

### Shoulder Alterations

#### SHOULDERS TOO WIDE (ARMHOLE STYLE SEAM LINE) (CHAPTER 8, FIG. B-50a, b) (TIME: 40 MINUTES)

1. Put thread markings along the pin markings made by the

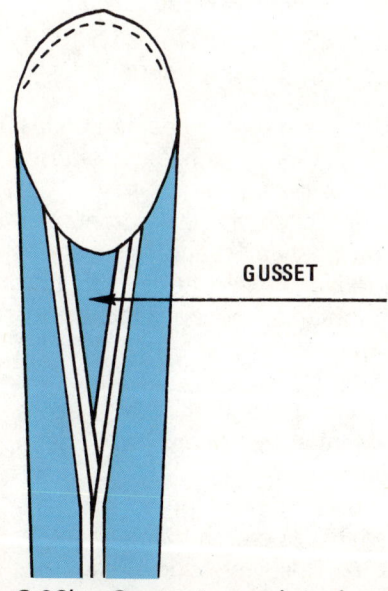

C-29b. Gusset inserted in long sleeve.

## Altering Ready-To-Wear Fashions

fitter on one armhole and one style seam. Remove the fitting pins. Duplicate the thread marks on the other shoulder. Mark tops of sleeve caps where they meet shoulder seams.

2. Rip the armhole seams across the sleeve caps to 1 inch (2.5 cm) below the style seams on both front and back.

3. Stitch the new line along the style seams, starting at the armhole edge and tapering gradually back to the original seam. The armhole edge will now be uneven. The section above the style seams over the shoulder will jut out further than the underarm section. Do not try to change the edge back to a straight line. You will notice your thread markings for the altered armhole seam will be in a fairly even line with the original, unripped section of the underarm area. Fig. C-30.

4. Rip all seams where new lines have been stitched and trim away excess fabric on style seams.

5. Press all style seams open (on ham).

6. Match the shoulder marks on the sleeve caps to the shoulder seams and pin. Pin the rest of the sleeve caps to the armhole along the thread marks.

7. Restitch the sleeve seams, following the original seams on the sleeves. Overlap the unripped part of the seams about 1 inch (2.5 cm) on each end.

8. Now trim away the excess fabric along the upper armhole edges, leaving an even seam allowance all the way around the armhole.

NOTE: If only the front or the back of the shoulder has been fitted, follow the same steps by ripping only where the shoulder lines needs to be altered.

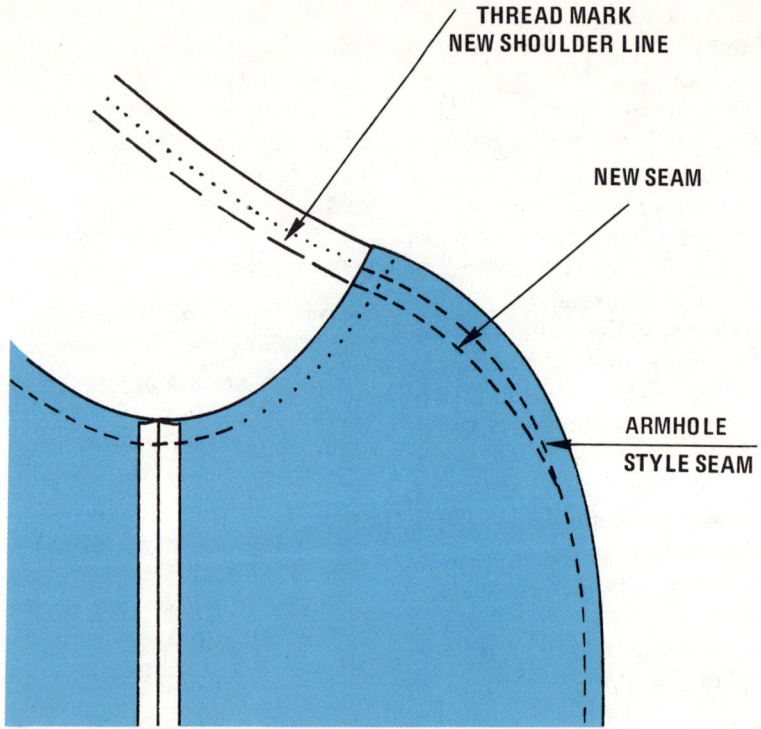

C-30. Increasing armhole style seam as part of shoulder alteration.

### SHOULDERS TOO WIDE (SHOULDER STYLE SEAM) (CHAPTER 8, FIG. B-50c) (TIME: 30 MINUTES)

1. Mark the new lines on the wrong side of the front and back style seams.

2. Remove the fitting pins. Rip the shoulder seams about 1 inch (2.5 cm) on each side of the style seams.

3. Stitch the new front and back style seams along the markings. Start at the shoulder edge and taper back to the original seam with a 1-inch (2.5 cm) overlap.

4. Rip out the old seam where new lines have been stitched.

5. Trim and press the new seams open (on ham).

6. Restitch the shoulder seams and press them open (on a seam roll or mitt).

## Ch. 9: Standard Alterations for Women

### Princess Bodice Alterations

**PRINCESS BODICE TOO FULL IN FRONT ONLY (CHAPTER 8, FIG. B-51a) (TIME: 15 TO 20 MINUTES)**

1. Transfer the pin marks along the new seam to the wrong side. Remove pins.
2. Rip the armhole or shoulder style seams about 1 inch (2.5 cm) on each side of the style seams.
3. Stitch the new seam line along the chalk marks, overlapping the original stitching about 1 inch (2.5 cm) at each end.
4. Remove the original seam along the new stitching and press the seams open (on ham).
5. Restitch the armhole or shoulder seams.

**Princess Bodice (Armhole-Style Seams) Excessively Full in Front (Chapter 8, Fig. B-51b)**

1. Transfer pin markings to wrong side. Remove pins. Mark only one side of seam.
2. Rip armhole seams as in the previous alteration.
3. Rip the style seams between marked areas only. The alteration will be easier to handle if you do not rip the style seam all the way to the underarm seams.
4. Pin the unmarked seam line along the new chalk line on the corresponding piece. Stitch the new seam in place with the unmarked seam up. Overlap the stitching 1 inch (2.5 cm) at each end of the new seam.
5. Trim the altered side of each seam and press the seams open (on ham).
6. Restitch armhole seams.

**PRINCESS BODICE TOO FULL IN BACK ONLY**

If the fullness is in the back rather than the front, the same basic procedure would be followed as given for the front. The back style lines would be changed rather than the front style lines but the steps would be the same.

**PRINCESS BODICE TOO TIGHT (CHAPTER 8, FIG. B-52) (TIME: 15 TO 30 MINUTES)**

1. Note all seams the fitter has indicated with crossed pins. Check the work ticket for the amount of release needed. Remove pins.
2. Press all seams to be released flat and with the two edges together.
3. Stitch the new lines along the seam allowances as indicated. Remove original stitching where new stitching has been added.
4. Carefully press out the original seams and stitch marks as you press the new seams (on ham).

**PRINCESS BODICE TOO TIGHT OR TOO LOOSE THROUGH MIDRIFF (CHAPTER 8, FIGS. B-52, 54) (TIME: 15 MINUTES)**

1. Check the work ticket and placement of crossed pins to find which seams are to be released or increased. Transfer the markings to the wrong side of the garment.
2. Remove marking pins and press the seams flat.
3. To release seams, stitch the new line in the seam allowance toward the raw edge from the old seam. To take the seams in, stitch the new seams inside the old ones. Overlap the old seam for about 1 inch (2.5 cm) at each end of the seam.
4. Rip out the original stitching and press the new seams open. Released seams will require careful pressing to remove the old creases and stitch marks.

**PRINCESS BODICE TOO LONG (CHAPTER 8, FIG. B-53b) (TIME: 15 TO 30 MINUTES)**

This alteration may involve two variations. Before starting to work, reread the section in Chapter 8 under "Princess Bodice too Long," page 182.

1. Transfer the crossed pins and any other markings to the wrong side of the garment and remove the pins.
2. Press the marked seams flat.

If the fitter has indicated the bodice seams are to be increased and the hip seams released:

3. Starting 2 inches (5 cm) above the new line, overstitch the old seam 1 inch (2.5 cm). Gradually pick up the new bodice seam line on the *inside* of the seam allowance. Carefully

## Altering Ready-To-Wear Fashions

stitch along this line as you gradually move toward the cross mark for the area of seam release. Pick up the new hip line on the outside of the seam allowance and taper toward the original seam at the lower cross mark. Fig. C-31.

If bodice area has not been changed and only the skirt seams require release:

3. Begin the new stitching line 2 inches (5 cm) above the first cross mark, overlapping the original seam 1 inch (2.5 cm). Gradually leave the seam and stitch the new hip line outside the old seam in the seam allowance. Taper back to the original seam as in Step 3 above.

4. Rip out the old stitching.

5. Steam and press to remove the old seam lines and stitch marks. Press new seams open (on ham).

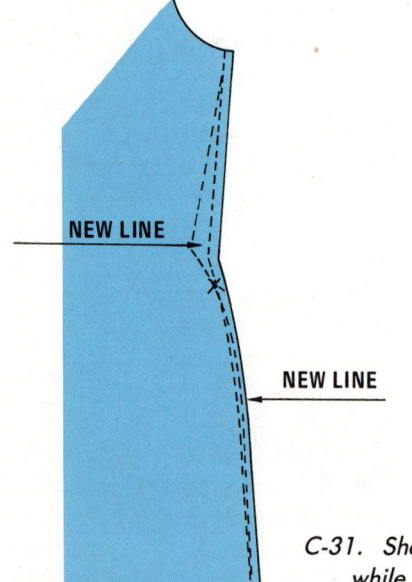

C-31. Shortening princess bodice while increasing hip line.

### PRINCESS BODICE TOO SHORT (CHAPTER 8, FIG. B-54 and 55) (TIME: 15 TO 30 MINUTES)

1. Mark the seams to be altered on the wrong side—this could be only the front or back style seams, only the side seams, or all six seams. Remove pins.

2. Stitch along the new seam markings. Overlap the original seams at each end of the new lines.

3. Rip out the old seam stitching. Press seams open (on ham).

### Princess Skirt Alterations

### PRINCESS SKIRT STYLE SEAMS TOO FULL (CHAPTER 8, FIGS. B-56a, b) (TIME: 20 TO 30 MINUTES)

1. Mark new lines on the wrong side of the seams to be altered. Remove pins.

2. Rip the hem 3 inches (7.5 cm) each side of the seams to be changed.

3. Press seams flat.

4. Begin the new stitching 2 inches (5 cm) above the mark for the new line. Overlap 1 inch (2.5 cm) and gradually pick up the new line on the inside of the original seam. Stitch through to the bottom of the hem.

5. Trim excess fabric from seams, if necessary.

6. Press seams open (on seam roll).

7. Replace hem and press.

### ALTERING THE BASIC SHIFT

#### Shift Bodice Too Long (Chapter 8, Fig. B-58) (Time: 15 minutes)

Follow the same steps given in the directions for "Princess Bodice Too Long." The only difference would be that the alteration here is limited to changing the side seams only. The alteration is the same for either a back or front bodice that is too long.

### SHIFT BODICE BACK EXCESSIVELY LONG (CHAPTER 8, FIG. B-59) (TIME: 30 TO 40 MINUTES)

1. Make a thread marking line in the fold of the tuck pinned on the outside of the garment. Mark from the center back to one side seam.

2. Measure the depth of the tuck at the center back and record the amount on the work ticket.

3. Remove pins and turn garment wrong side out. Match and pin the side seams together from the underarms to the hipline.

4. Following the thread marking on half the waist, make a pin line through to the other half. Thread (through top fabric only) or chalk mark the other side of the waist. Fig. C-32a. Remove pins.

### Ch. 9: Standard Alterations for Women

5. Starting at the center back, fold a tuck the depth of the original fitter's tuck as measured and recorded on the work ticket. From this center point, continue pinning a curved tuck to the side seams, tapering back to nothing at each side seam. Fig. C-32b.

6. Stitch the tuck in place along the pin line from one side seam to the other.

7. Press and shape the tuck toward the bodice (on ham). This tuck will be slashed and pressed open only if the fabric is excessively bulky.

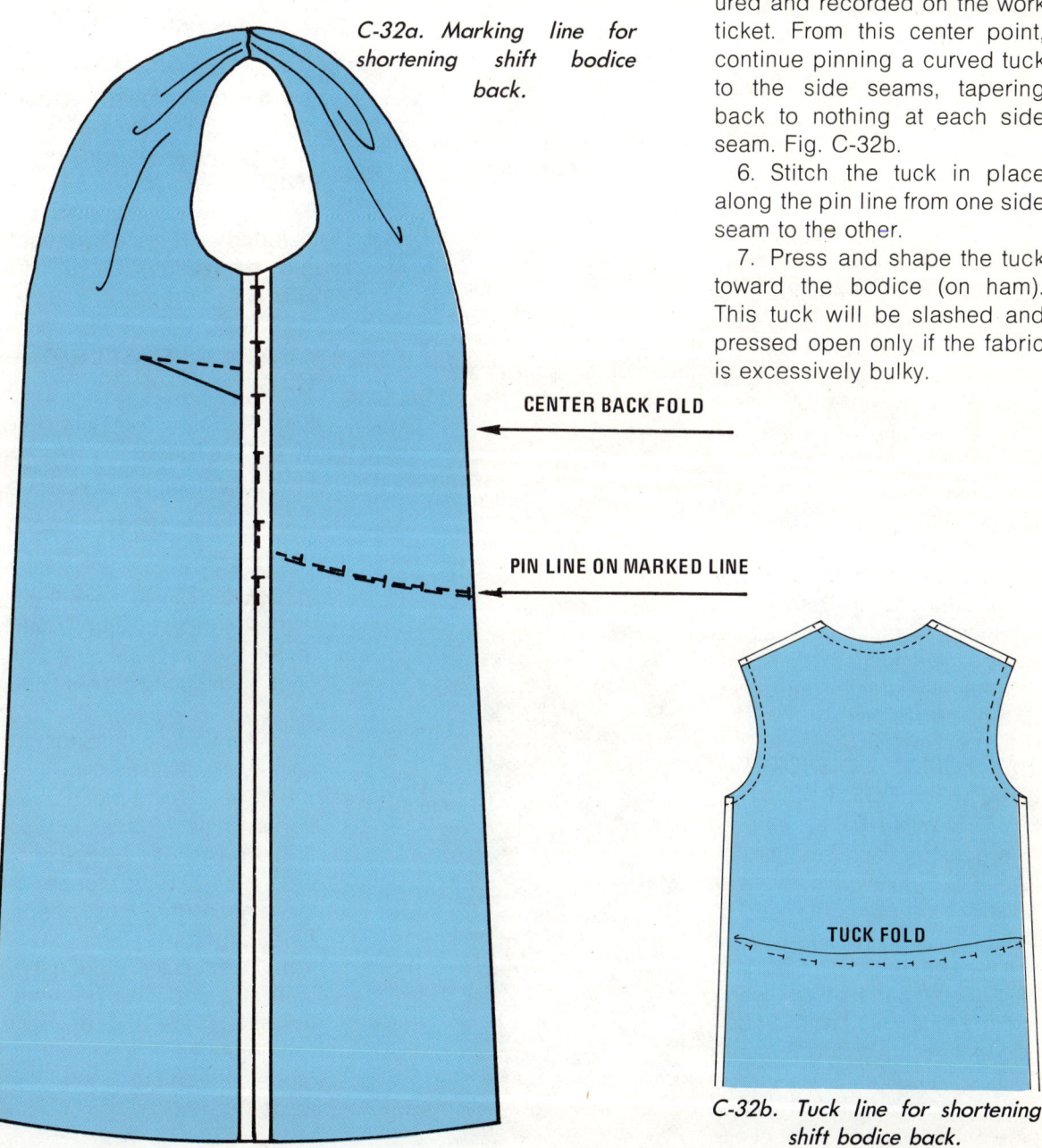

C-32a. Marking line for shortening shift bodice back.

CENTER BACK FOLD

PIN LINE ON MARKED LINE

TUCK FOLD

C-32b. Tuck line for shortening shift bodice back.

Altering Ready-To-Wear Fashions

**Shift Bodice Back Excessively Long—with Zipper**

This alteration would be done basically the same as for the bodice without a center back zipper.

1. Rip zipper free of skirt to about 2 inches (5 cm) above the waist tuck marking.

2. Establish markings for back waistline tuck the same as in the previous alteration except you will have two short tucks instead of one continuous tuck.

3. Stitch the two tucks, starting at the center back each time and tapering to nothing at each side seam.

4. Shape and press the tuck toward the bodice.

5. Increase the zipper opening in the center back seam enough to make up for the amount taken out in the tuck. Back stitch at the end of the opening. Replace the zipper using the same method used by the manufacturer for the upper part of the zipper.

**SHIFT BODICE TOO SHORT (CHAPTER 8, FIGS. B-60, 61) (TIME: 15 MINUTES)**

In general, this alteration follows the same instructions given for "Princess Bodice Too Short."

If the shift has been fitted with extra body darts at the waist, use the following steps in addition to those given for "Princess Bodice Too Short."

1. Turn the garment wrong side out. Mark the shape of one dart on one side of the garment on front or back or both.

2. Remove all pins from all darts.

3. Pin the underarm seams together from armhole to hipline. Fig. C-33.

4. Lay the garment out smooth and flat on the worktable with the dart markings up. Pin through the dart markings to the other side of the garment. Turn garment over and chalk the pin line on the other side. This insures getting the darts to match in length and shape on each side of the back or front.

5. Stitch the darts carefully, following the chalk markings.

*C-33. Marking new waistline shaping darts.*

6. Press darts toward the center front or center back (shaping on ham).

## ALTERING PANTS

### Pants Waistline Alterations

If the pants have a separate waistband, follow the instructions given earlier in the chapter under *Waistbands on Skirts and Pants*. Detailed instructions are included for both increasing and decreasing those waistbands.

**PANTS WITH ELASTICIZED WAIST**

**Pants Waistline Too Tight (Time: 10 to 20 minutes)**

When elastic is not stitched to the casing seam:

1. Feel around the waist casing to find the spot where the elastic ends have been joined.

2. Rip the casing stitching about 2 inches (5 cm) at this spot. Pull the elastic out enough so you can work on it. Rip the stitching holding the ends of the elastic together.

3. Cut an extra piece of elastic the same width as that used in the pants. This piece should be 1 inch (2.5 cm) longer than the amount the waist needs to be enlarged.

4. Overlap the old elastic ½ inch (1.3 cm) over one end of the new piece and zigzag the two together. Repeat with the other end of the piecing and the other end of the waistline elastic. Fig. C-34a.

## Ch. 9: Standard Alterations for Women

5. Slip the pieced elastic back into the waist casing and restitch the ripped section.

6. Distribute the waist fullness evenly around the elastic.

7. To keep the elastic from rolling, stitch through all layers of casing and elastic at each seam. Fig. C-34b.

When elastic is stitched to the casing seam:

1. Rip elastic free across the front from side seam to side seam. Separate the ends of the elastic where it was joined together. If the elastic seam is not in the front, cut it apart at the center front.

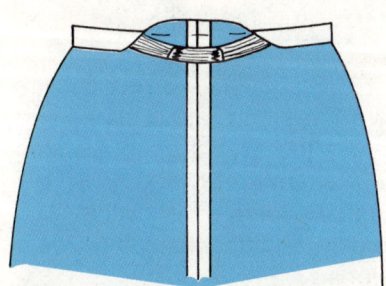

C-34a. Piecing waistline elastic.

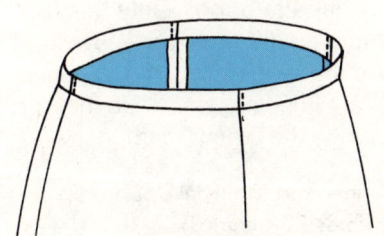

C-34b. Stitch waistline elastic to eliminate rolling.

2. Insert elastic piecing as explained in the previous section.

3. Mark the center front of the elastic. Match and pin this mark to the center front seam of the pants.

4. Restitch the elastic to the waist according to the original finish. To insure equal fullness on either side of the center front, pull the elastic and waist with one hand in front of the presser foot and the other in back while stitching. Pull with equal pressure with each hand.

5. Stitch across the elastic and the waist casing as in Fig. C-34b to prevent rolling of the elastic.

NOTE: This alteration can also be done across the back waist, but most people are larger across the front of the figure. The added elastic here is more flattering and more comfortable.

### Pants Waistline Too Loose

When elastic is *not* stitched to the casing:

1. Follow the steps given above for a tight elasticized waist. Instead of adding a piece to the separated ends of the elastic, overlap the ends to get the new measurement. Zigzag stitch the length of the overlap. Do not trim off the extra but leave all the elastic in the overlap.

2. Follow the same steps given above to refinish.

When elastic is stitched in the waist casing:

1. Follow the instructions above except that the *back* waist is ripped free from seam to seam. Overlap the elastic to fit and zigzag together.

2. Refinish the back waist. Follow steps for front waist.

NOTE: The extra fullness in back is more flattering than it would be in front.

### PANTS TOO HIGH-WAISTED (CHAPTER 8, FIG. B-63)

#### With Waistband (Time: 30 minutes)

1. Mark the new waistline on the inside of the pants. On the inside of the waistband, mark where the side seams meet the band and the center front (if opening is in back) or the center back (if opening is in front).

2. Rip waistband from pants but do *not* rip out the zipper.

3. Increase front and back darts $1/8$ inch (.3 cm) on the double, tapering to a point where the fitter has indicated the darts should end.

4. Press all darts toward the center front and the center back (on ham).

5. Match and pin all markings on the band to the new waistline markings at the side seams and center front and center back.

6. Stitch the outside of the band in place at the new line. If you stitch carefully and slowly across the zipper ends, your needle will slip between the zipper teeth without breaking.

237

## Altering Ready-To-Wear Fashions

7. Before final stitching on the band (top stitching or stitch-in-the-ditch), trim the excess fabric around the waistline to a ½-inch (1.3 cm) seam allowance. Cut off the extra zipper, leaving ½ inch (1.3 cm) above the seam.

### With Elasticized Waist (Time: 20 minutes)

1. Thread mark the new waistline.
2. Rip waist casing and remove elastic. Separate the ends of the elastic where joined.
3. Make a second line above the new waistline. Measure this line to be double the width of the elastic plus ¼ inch (.6 cm) above the first line. For example, if the elastic is 1 inch (2.5 cm) wide, the top line should be marked 2¼ inches (5.7 cm) above the first line. Fig. C-35.
4. Working on the inside of the waist circle, match the two lines, one on top of the other. Stitch with a zigzag stitch, leaving 1-inch (2.5 cm) opening at the center back.
5. Cut away the excess waist fabric.
6. Insert a large safety pin in one end of the elastic and thread the elastic through the waist casing.
7. Overlap the elastic as it was originally and zigzag together. Stitch the 1-inch opening.
8. Stitch across waistband at all 4 seams to stay the elastic. Fig. C-34b.

### PANTS TOO HIGH-WAISTED FRONT OR BACK ONLY (CHAPTER 8, FIG. B-64) (TIME: 15 TO 20 MINUTES)

For either of these changes, the preparation, marking, ripping, and finishing would be done the same as for a waistline too high all around. The only difference would be in the amount of change made. The center front or center back would be marked with the new line and the stitching would taper gradually back to the side seams.

## Pants Hip Alterations

### PANTS TOO TIGHT (CHAPTER 8, FIG. B-65b) (TIME: 20 TO 30 MINUTES)

1. Mark on the inside of the pants where the crossed pins show seam release is needed. If the inseam has crossed pins, mark at top of inseam. Make another mark about 7 inches (17.8 cm) down. Remove pins.
2. Rip waist finish stitching 1 inch (2.5 cm) on each side of the side seams. Rip crotch seam 1 inch (2.5 cm) on each side of the inseams.
3. Flat press the seams between the markings for easier stitching.
4. Stitch the new side seams by gradually picking up the new line on the outside seam allowance and tapering back to the old seam at the bottom cross mark. Be sure to overlap the seam about 1 inch (2.5 cm) at each end.
5. Stitch the inseams, beginning outside the old seam at the crotch seam and tapering to the cross mark. Overlap the original seams at the bottom. Fig. C-36.
6. Rip out all the old stitching.
7. Steam and press out the old lines and stitch marks and press the seams open (on ham and seam roll).
8. Restitch the waist and crotch seams where they were ripped.

NOTE: If the side seam has a zipper, follow the instructions for "Skirt Too Small" (shown in Fig. C-23) for that particular seam alteration. Only the ripping is different as you would rip the zipper from the bottom to the waistline *only*. Do not rip above the waist seam.

### Pants Too Tight in Upper Hip (Time: 20 minutes)

Follow the steps given for "Skirt Too Tight in Upper Hip."

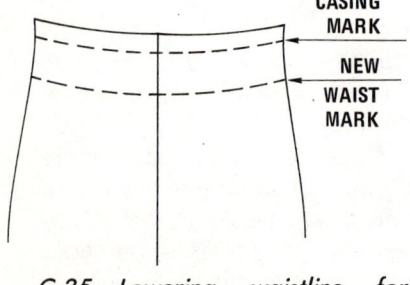

C-35. Lowering waistline for elastic casing.

## Ch. 9: Standard Alterations for Women

**Pants Too Tight in Lower Hip (Time: 15 minutes)**

Follow the instructions for "Pants too Tight" in all steps except ripping the waist stitching. Since the releasing starts well below the waistline, there is no need to change the waist. Fig. C-36.

### PANTS TOO LARGE (CHAPTER 8, FIG. B-66) (TIME: 30 TO 45 MINUTES)

1. Mark seams to be changed on wrong side of pants and remove all pins.
2. Rip the waist 1 inch (2.5 cm) on each side of the side seams. Rip the crotch seam 1 inch (2.5 cm) on each side of the inseams. Rip out the hems only if the fitter has indicated the seam increase is to go all the way through the hems.
3. Stitch new seams following markings.
4. Rip old stitching on the four altered seams. Trim seams, if necessary, and press them open, using a ham in the hip area and a seam roll on the leg seams.
5. Restitch waist and crotch seams. Rehem if hems have been ripped. Press hems with "finish" press.

NOTE: If waistline has been taken in, follow the instructions for "Waistband Too Loose" or for "Elasticized Waist Too Loose." This alteration would then be combined with the other alteration in the same sequence of marking, ripping, stitching, and pressing. Be sure that you add the time needed for this additional work to the time given above.

**Pants Too Large in Upper Hip (Chapter 8, Fig. B-67) (Time: 15 to 45 minutes)**

To alter, follow all instructions for "Skirt Too Large in Upper Hip."

If pants have side seam zipper opening, refer to Fig. C-22 and continue on to the zipper instructions on the same page.

If waist darts have been fitted also, follow the steps for altering the darts under the "Skirt Too Large in Upper Hips" heading.

If there are pockets in the side seams, follow the instructions for "Skirt Too Large in Upper Hips," except for the following change in ripping and stitching.

1. Rip waist seam along the front, enough to free the top of the pocket that is sewn into the waist seams. If there is top stitching and bar tacking on the upper seam of the pocket, rip out this stitching but do not rip pocket seams. Fig. C-37a.

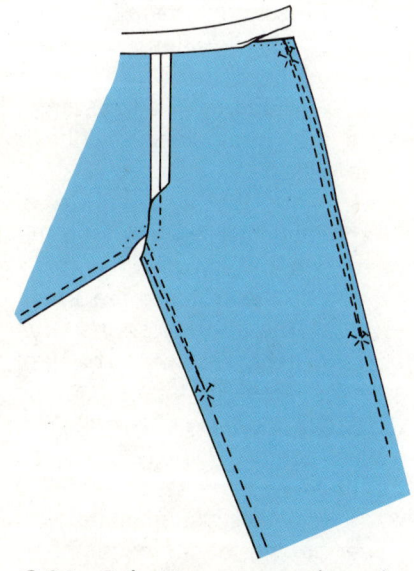

C-36. Releasing pants through hip area.

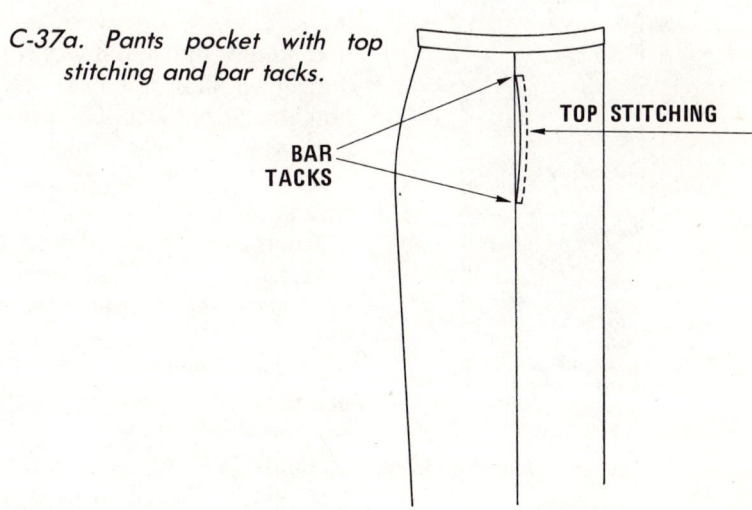

C-37a. Pants pocket with top stitching and bar tacks.

## Altering Ready-To-Wear Fashions

2. Press side seams and pockets flat.

3. Stitch the side seam above the pocket along the new line with a backstitch at the top of the pocket. Pick up the new line again below the pocket with a backstitch at the bottom of the pocket opening. Continue stitching to the bottom of the seam increase along the new seam line. Fig. C-37b.

4. Rip out the old stitching below the pockets. Press these new seams on the seam roll.

5. Press the pockets toward the front. Turn the pockets under so the original side seam is inside the pocket and the new edge of the pocket follows the altered seam line. Shape carefully (on ham).

6. Restitch the pockets into the waist seam. Finish the waist seam. Top-stitch and bar tack top pocket seam, if necessary.

### Pants Too Large in Lower Hip (Time: 15 to 30 minutes)

1. Mark new line on inside of pants seams and remove pins.

2. Begin new stitching line on the original seam line, 2 inches (5 cm) above the mark for the new line to begin. Overlap stitching 1 inch (2.5 cm). Gradually ease the new line to the inside of the seam allowance, following the chalk markings. Taper the stitching back to the original seam and overstitch 1 inch (2.5 cm).

3. Rip out the old stitching and trim seams, if necessary.

4. Press seams open (on seam roll).

NOTE: If there is a zipper in the side seam, refer to Fig. C-22 and follow the instructions for that illustration. For this alteration, the zipper would be ripped only 4 inches (10 cm) up instead of being ripped all the way to the waist.

When there are pockets in the side seams, follow the instructions as given above, with one exception. There is no need to rip the pockets at the waist seam. The only ripping would be the top-stitching and bar tacking, if the upper pocket has that kind of finish. The new seam line would begin at the bottom of the pockets and all the other steps to finish and press would be the same as instructed above.

### Pants Too Large in the Seat (Chapter 8, Fig. B-68) (Time: 10 to 20 minutes)

1. Mark wrong side of pants seat seam as indicated by fitter. Remove pins.

2. Rip waist seam 1 inch (2.5 cm) on each side of the seat seam.

3. Stitch new seam line starting at the waist. Gradually pick up the new seat seam and taper back to the original seam at the lower curve. Overstitch the original seam 1 inch (2.5 cm) at each end.

4. Rip out the old seam and trim, if necessary.

5. Press seat seam open—clip seam to flatten, if necessary.

6. Restitch the waist seam.

If the back inseams have been fitted:

1. Mark the wrong side of back inseam when marking the seat seam. Remove pins.

2. Rip the crotch seam 1 inch (2.5 cm) in front of the inseams and 2 inches (5 cm) in back of the inseams. Rip top of inseams about 7 inches (17.8 cm). Rip waist seam 1 inch (2.5 cm) on each side of the seat seam.

3. Pin *front* inseam to the *new* line on the back inseam and stitch with the front side up. Fig. C-38.

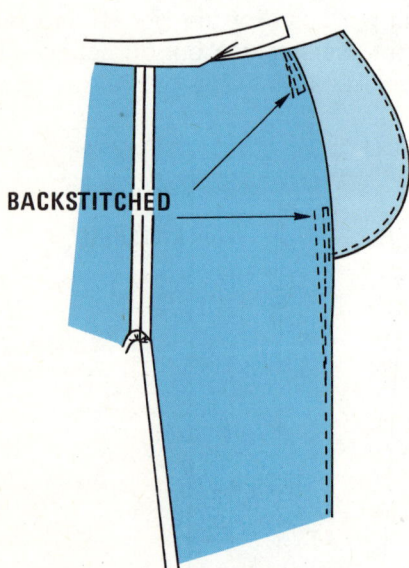

C-37b. New stitch line on pocket seam.

## Ch. 9: Standard Alterations for Women

4. Trim excess back inseams and press seams open (on seam roll).

5. Now stitch the seat seam as marked. Restitch the crotch curve across the inseams, overlapping the front crotch curve 1 inch (2.5 cm).

6. Press seams open and restitch waistline.

### Pants Too Large in Front (Time: 15 to 45 minutes)

1. Mark the new line on the wrong side of front side seams where pinned. Remove the pins.

2. Rip waist seam 1 inch (2.5 cm) on each side of the side seams. Rip side seams where new line is marked.

3. Pin *back* side seams to the new line on the *front* seams. Stitch along the original back seam line. Overlap the original seams 1 inch (2.5 cm) at each end.

4. Trim excess front seams and press seams open (on ham).

5. Restitch the waist seam.

### With Zipper Opening

Follow instructions for "Skirt Too Large in Upper Hip" for zipper alteration. The exception to the instructions would be that only the *front* of the zipper is ripped to the waist and the *back* of the zipper is ripped only 1 inch (2.5 cm) at the bottom. Stitch *back* zipper opening seam to new *front* zipper seam line and backstitch. Finish front zipper seam using the new line.

### With Pockets in Side Seams

1. When ripping the side seams apart, be careful *not* to rip the seams where the pocket pieces are attached. *Do* rip the stitching holding the two pocket pieces together.

2. Match back seams to the new line on the front seams. Front pocket will extend beyond the back pocket edge.

3. Stitch around the outer edge of the pockets as in Fig. C-39.

4. Stitch side seam as shown in Fig. C-37b.

5. Trim excess front seams and front pocket edges.

6. Press pockets toward the front. Turn the pocket edge under so the new edge of the pocket follows the altered seam line. Shape carefully (on ham).

7. Restitch the pockets into the waist seam. Finish the waist seam. Top stitch and bar tack top pocket seam, if necessary.

### PANTS FRONT CROTCH TOO LONG (CHAPTER 8, FIG. B-69) (TIME: 15 MINUTES)

1. Mark new line on front inseam on wrong side of pants. Remove pins.

2. Rip crotch seam 1 inch (2.5 cm) in back and 2 inches (5 cm) in front of inseams. Rip top of inseams about 7 inches (17.8 cm).

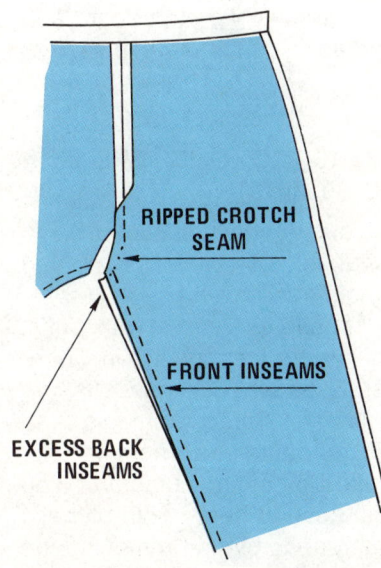

C-38. Shortening the seat seam.

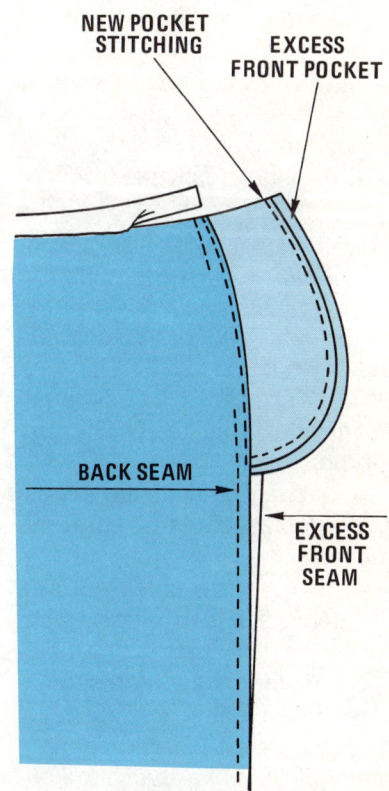

C-39. Reducing front fullness on pants with side pockets.

## Altering Ready-To-Wear Fashions

3. Pin *back* inseam to the new line on *front* inseam and stitch with the back side of seam up. Overlap 1 inch (2.5 cm) on the original seam. Fig. C-38.

4. Trim excess front inseams and press seams open (on seam roll).

5. Restitch the crotch seam.

### PANTS CROTCH SEAM TOO TIGHT (TIME: 15 TO 40 MINUTES)

If the back inseam seam allowance is wider than the front inseam allowance, follow instructions given in Chapter 12 under "Lowering the Rise."

If front and back inseam edges have equal seam allowances, proceed as follows:

1. Rip the crotch seam 1 inch (2.5 cm) on each side of the inseams.

2. Stitch the new line on the outside seam allowance from the crotch toward the original seam about 7 inches (17 cm) down. Overlap the original seam about 1 inch (2.5 cm) at the bottom.

3. Zigzag or finish the edges of the released seam to prevent raveling.

4. Steam and press out the old seam and stitch marks and press the new seam to one side.

5. Restitch the crotch seam.

NOTE: If still extra room is needed, see if there is enough material to make gussets. Follow the instructions for gussets given under "Adding Gussets to Long Sleeves" with Figs. C29a, b. Treat the inseam the same as the sleeve seam. Restitch the crotch seam after both gussets have been inserted and the seams pressed open.

### PANTS LEGS TOO NARROW (TIME: 30 MINUTES)

1. Mark location of crossed pins on wrong side of pants outseams. There is no need to mark the inseams as the releasing will start at the top of the inseams. Remove all pins.

2. Rip the crotch seam 1 inch (2.5 cm) each side of the inseams and rip out the hems.

3. Flat press all four seams.

4. Begin the new outseam stitching 2 inches (5 cm) above the cross mark on the original seam and overstitch 1 inch (2.5 cm). Gradually move to the outside seam allowance. Stitch in a slightly curving line past the cross mark. Continue stitching in a straight line through to the bottom of the pants hem. Begin the inseam stitching at the crotch edge on the outside seam allowance. Stitch a straight seam through to the pants hems.

5. Overcast or zigzag edges on all four seams to prevent raveling.

6. Rip out old stitching on all seams.

7. Steam and press out old seam lines and stitch marks. Press all seams to one side.

8. Sew hems back in place and press.

### PANTS LEGS TOO WIDE (TIME: 30 MINUTES)

1. Mark on the wrong side of the pants the seams to be taken in. Remove pins. Rip crotch seam 1 inch (2.5 cm) on each side of inseams.

2. Begin stitching new line on the outseams 2 inches (5 cm) above the marking. Overlap seam 1 inch (2.5 cm) and gradually move inside the seam allowance. Pick up the marked line and continue stitching in a straight line through the hems. Overlap the inseams 1 inch (2.5 cm) at the crotch seam. Pick up the new line and continue stitching a straight line through the hems.

3. Rip out the old stitching on all four seams and trim excess fabric, if necessary.

4. Press seams open (on seam roll).

5. Restitch crotch seam and replace hems. Press hems.

### Pants Lengths

### PANTS TOO LONG (TIME: 15 TO 30 MINUTES)

Follow the instructions in Chapter 12 under "Hemming Uncuffed Trousers."

To shorten pants with cuffs, follow the instructions in Chapter 12 under "Making Cuffs."

NOTE: Since women's and girl's pants are hemmed or cuffed by the manufacturer, you will have to begin both of these alterations by first removing the cuff or hem.

## PANTS TOO SHORT (TIME: 15 to 30 MINUTES)

If pants have to be lengthened, it usually involves the addition of a facing of some kind. Refer to "Hemming Pants" in Chapter 10.

### COAT ALTERATIONS

Coat fittings and alterations are handled the same as those in dresses of similar styles. The exceptions are due to the inside finish of the coat. If it is lined, the lining usually needs the same alteration. If the coat is unlined, the altered seams must be carefully refinished.

### Coat Neck and Collar

Follow the instructions for these problems given earlier in this chapter. These alterations do not involve lining changes.

### Coat Shoulder Alterations

If the alteration is slight, the lining may be eased back and tacked to the coat shoulders without altering the lining shoulders.

If the shoulder fitting is changed more than ¼ inch (.6 cm), the lining must be altered the same as the coat.

If the shoulder can be altered by the use of shoulder pads alone, refer to Fig. C-13 in this chapter.

### Coat Seam Alterations

Any seams that are taken in, released, or tapered on the coat should be taken in, released, or tapered on the lining. The marking, stitching, ripping, and pressing steps should be done on the coat and the lining at the same time and in the same sequence.

### Coat Sleeve Alterations

#### SHORTENING LINED SLEEVES

1. Measure the amount to be shortened and write on the work ticket. Remove pins.

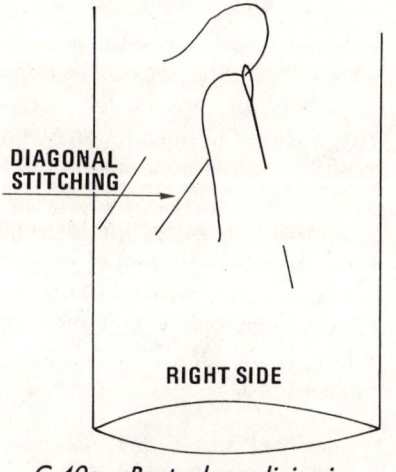

C-40a. Baste sleeve lining in place.

2. Shove your hand inside the sleeve about 8 inches (20 cm) and spread your fingers to push the lining against the outer sleeve. Sew a large diagonal basting around the entire sleeve catching the lining in the stitches. Fig. C-40a. The basting keeps the lining in place while the sleeves are being changed and it also speeds the alteration.

3. Rip the bottom of the sleeve lining free of the sleeve. Rip the sleeve hems.

4. Pull sleeve wrong side out.

5. Press out old creases in sleeves and linings (on seam roll).

6. Turn sleeve hems to the new length and sew with a large tailor's stitch (see Chapter 10). Use a close whipping stitch at the sleeve seams.

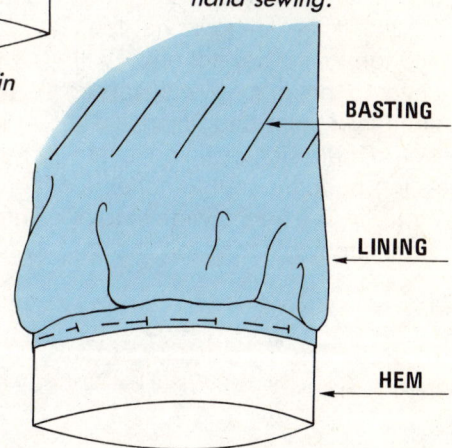

C-40b. Lining pinned in place for hand sewing.

### Altering Ready-To-Wear Fashions

7. Drop the lining down over the bottom of the sleeves and fold it under so the fold is even with the bottom of the sleeve. Place one or two pins in this fold to hold the length. Pull the lining back up the sleeve so the fold is about 1½ inches (3.8 cm) above the edge of the coat sleeve. (Fig. C-40b) Pin the lining at this length and sew the lining to the sleeve using a slip-stitch. (See Chapter 11). Remove diagonal basting.

NOTE: The above method of hemming the lining is a quick, sure way to get the required lining ease so the coat sleeves hang correctly.

### LENGTHENING LINED SLEEVES

1. Follow the same measuring, basting, ripping, and pressing steps as given for shortening sleeves.
2. Turn up the hems on the new line and hand sew, using a large tailor's stitch.
3. Check length of sleeve lining with the finished sleeve length. If the lining is not long enough for the new length, it will have to be pieced with fabric similar in color and finish.
4. Open sleeve lining seam at the bottom about 2 inches (5 cm). Stitch a 2-inch wide strip of the matching fabric on the inside of the circle of the sleeve lining. Start at one side of the opened seam and end at the opposite side.
5. Press piecing seam open (on seam roll).
6. Restitch lining sleeve seam to the bottom of the added piece.
7. Sew lining to sleeve, following instructions given for "Shortening Lined Sleeves." In this case, the sleeve hems will be less than 1½ inches (3.8 cm) and the lining will be sewn closer to the bottom.

### JACKET ALTERATIONS

Jacket alterations are so similar to coat and dress alterations that they are not treated separately. Refer to the section of the chapter dealing with the specific problem to be altered.

Jacket hem alteration instructions for a curved front style may be found in Chapter 12 under "Shortening Men's Jackets." All other hem alterations are in Chapter 10.

### PREPARING FOR A SECOND FITTING

Sometimes a drastic waistline, shoulder, or seam alteration will require another fitting before the garment can be safely finished. Often the hem fitting should be postponed until after other alterations are completed.

Though a second fitting can be time consuming and annoying to a customer, it is appreciated *if* the alteration requires it. This need is usually determined by the fitter, but sometimes a customer will ask for the second fitting.

To be sure the customer will be happy with your work even before you are finished, follow these tips:

- Use matching thread for all machine or hand basting.
- Machine baste all altered seams except for fabrics that mark easily—satin, taffeta, pile, sequinned, beaded, and hand or silk-screen painted.
- Avoid trimming altered seams unless absolutely necessary.
- Rip and press out old seam lines while lightly pressing or steaming the new seams open (on seam roll).
- Always have the hem basted in place even if the new line for the hem still has to be established. Use uneven hand basting—¼ inch (.6 cm) on the outside and 1 inch (2.5 cm) on the inside of the garment—at the top of the hem only.
- Remove all loose threads from the garment.

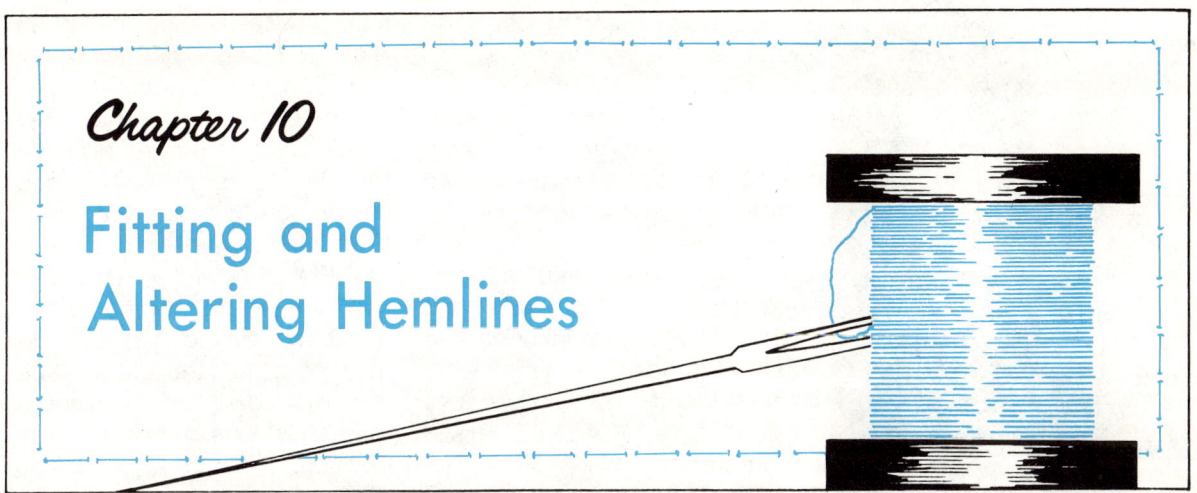

# Chapter 10
# Fitting and Altering Hemlines

When buying clothes, people often ignore or don't even notice some parts of the garment that may not fit too well. A shoulder line that is too broad or too narrow may be accepted with little comment. If the waistline is too loose, a customer may just tighten the belt. If a dress is too tight, the client may say she is on a diet. Almost no one, however, ignores a hemline or pants length that is not right. Hemlines at the wrong height can make the wearer feel uncomfortable.

Sales have been lost because shops have no fitter or alterationist to assure the customer the length can be successfully changed. Clothes are made of many different blends of fibers with linings and underlinings of still different materials. Therefore most people hesitate to alter a hemline on a ready-made garment themselves. They are willing to pay someone to do this work for them. When a shop is too small to hire a fitter-alterationist, the customer is often grateful to have one recommended to her.

About 85 percent of all clothing alterations is in the hem length (pants lengths included). This is usually the easiest alteration to make on a ready-made garment. Many people earn a living doing only hem alterations. Therefore practice and master this alteration first.

Begin by pin-fitting and altering ready-made garments of family and friends. Nearly every closet has clothes that are not being worn because the length is not right. This chapter will give detailed instructions on fitting and finishing many different kinds of hemlines—from sportswear to formals, from leather to sequinned fabric.

## PREPARING TO DO HEM FITTINGS

### Tools and Equipment Needed

Full-length mirror (preferably 3-way).
Hem marker, yardstick, and 6-inch ruler.
Dressmaker pins, coat pins, and ball point pins.
Plastic or metal hem clips.
Fitting platform (optional).

## GENERAL GUIDELINES TO REMEMBER

- Hem fitting is the last adjustment made on a garment after other changes have been made. Sometimes it may be necessary to alter a garment and have a second fitting for the hem length. (See Chapter 9, "Altering for a Second Fitting."
- The customer should be wearing shoes with the same height heel as those she will be

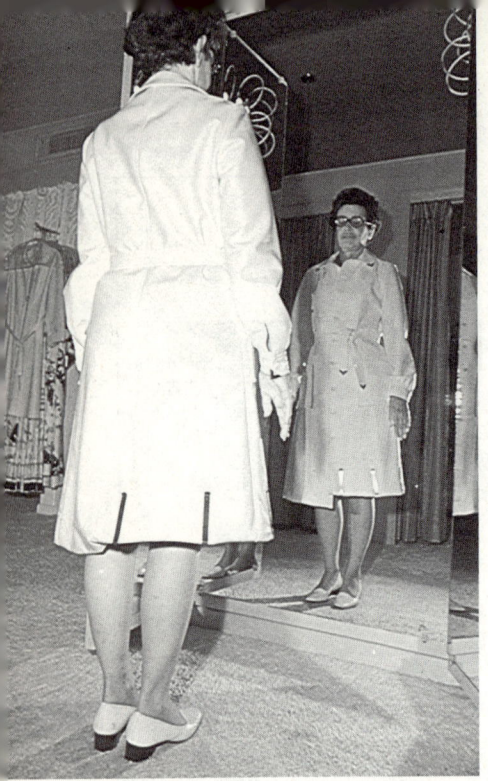

Courtesy Dagmar Fashions
Photo by Minerva Wagner

D-1. Use plastic or metal clips to hold new hemlines on fabrics that should not be pinned.

wearing with the altered garment.

• Do not rip the original hem before fitting unless the customer requests it.

• Fit quickly using as few pins as possible. Your time is money and the customer may tire from standing too long.

• If the hemline is even and only needs raising or lowering, it is not necessary to mark it all the way around. A short line of pins—approximately 5 inches (12.7 cm)—will show the alterationist what is to be done. To reinforce these marking pins and be sure they will be noticed, place another pin vertically across each pin (cross pins).

• When the fitter has placed a second pin across another one (cross pins), be sure to read the work ticket for further instructions.

• Be sure the client is standing straight with head erect while you are measuring the hem. If she tries to watch what you are doing, she may cause the hemline to drop slightly in the front.

• Ask the customer to turn slowly as you pin. Most fitting rooms are too small for the fitter to move around the customer. Also, the movement makes it easier for the client to keep her balance without tiring.

• Let the garment fall naturally without pulling on it as you pin.

• Some types of fabrics—vinyl, fake fur, and leather—should not be pinned. The pins are either difficult to put in or leave marks that cannot be removed. To fit hems in garments of these materials, note the correct measurement with a yardstick or hem marker. Fold the fabric under at this point. Keep the hem fold in place with smooth-surfaced plastic or aluminum clips such as hair clips. As soon as the hem length is decided, measure the amount folded under. Record this amount on the work ticket and remove the clips immediately. Even clips may permanently mark these fabrics if left in place too long. Fig. D-1.

• Some fabrics—velvet, suede cloth, satin, and other highly glazed fabrics—retain pin and needle holes and should be handled carefully. Use only the finest pins available. Pin mark only on the hem fold line where the marks will not show. Use the metal or plastic clips to hold the fold in place while deciding on the proper length. Remove clips as soon as possible and thread mark any pin line so the pins can also be removed immediately.

### Determining the Correct Length

*Know the current styles.* Is the trend long or short or is any length acceptable? Reading the current fashion news, especially in the daily paper, will help you stay up-to-date. If your advice is asked, you will be able to answer with confidence and assure your client she can rely on your judgment and knowledge. If she is hesitant about trying a new length, you may reassure her by taking a few extra minutes to pin the garment at different lengths to show her the effect.

Do *not* force *your* hem length on anyone. You may only make suggestions. If a client is very definite about *her* length, do not even hint that she is not "in style." However, you may suggest she try another length for that particular garment. Then, quickly pin the hem at that length for her approval. Tactful persuasion, patience, and self-confidence are essential.

*Understand body proportions.* You may wish to reread Chapter 7, especially "Body Proportions." Studying the body chart should help you to analyze a figure and apply this knowledge to your hem fittings. A person with a well-balanced figure may choose almost any length and wear it well. But, the "exceptional" figure may need your tactful, silent help. Examples would be:

• A short-waisted figure with long legs may look more balanced in a garment with a shorter hemline.

• A long-waisted figure with short legs may need a hemline that is a little longer.

*Study the lines of the garment.* Chapter 7 (under "Lines") offers a brief explanation of what lines and styles can do for a figure and how this knowledge can help you in fitting. Lines are especially important in hem fittings. Examples:

• Garments with unbroken vertical lines may be worn shorter than other garments for the same client.

• Garments with belts or other horizontal lines or trims look better if they are longer.

• Two-piece styles such as suits, tunics, and separates should be treated in the same way as garments with other horizontal lines.

• Full-length coats should be at least 1 inch (2.5 cm) longer than the longest garment in the client's wardrobe (except formal wear). Ensemble coats should be the exact same length or ½ inch (1.3 cm) longer than the matching dress or skirt. This length should be adjusted *after* the underneath garment has been fitted.

• Sportswear hem lengths should be determined by garment use and the freedom of movement needed.

• Longer floor lengths are dictated by the style of the garment. A bouffant style may go to the floor. A straight line garment should stop at the top of the shoe or top of the instep.

As you can see, there is no *one* hem length to be applied to all figures. Nor is there a length to be applied to all garments for any *one* figure. Paris, New York, London, or Rome cannot decide that all women shall wear skirts 18 inches (46 cm) from the floor. Though this might be a perfect length for some figures and styles, it could be wrong for other figures and styles.

## FITTING STREET-LENGTH HEMS

Begin by checking to see if the length is even. This can be done quickly by placing a yardstick upright alongside the skirt hemline at the side seams, center back, and center front. If the measurement is the same at all these points, you need only determine the amount to be shortened or lengthened.

### To Fit Even Hemlines

#### SHORTENING AN EVEN HEMLINE

TO FIT, use a 6-inch (15 cm) ruler to measure from the hem fold to the new pin line. Place a short line of pins above the hemline at the measurement desired. Cross each pin with another pin for a series of cross pins to catch the alterationists attention, Fig. D-2. Record the amount to be shortened on the work ticket.

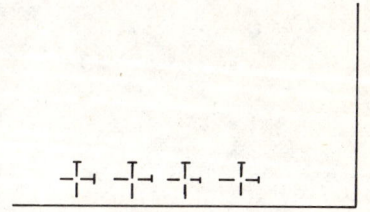

D-2. *Crossed pins as a marking symbol.*

#### LENGTHENING AN EVEN HEMLINE

TO FIT, place a short line of pins underneath the hem fold. Turn the hem back to measure on the under side. Place the cross pins as in the previous alteration. Record the amount to be let down on the work ticket. Underline the fact that the garment is to be *lengthened*.

## Altering Ready-To-Wear Fashions

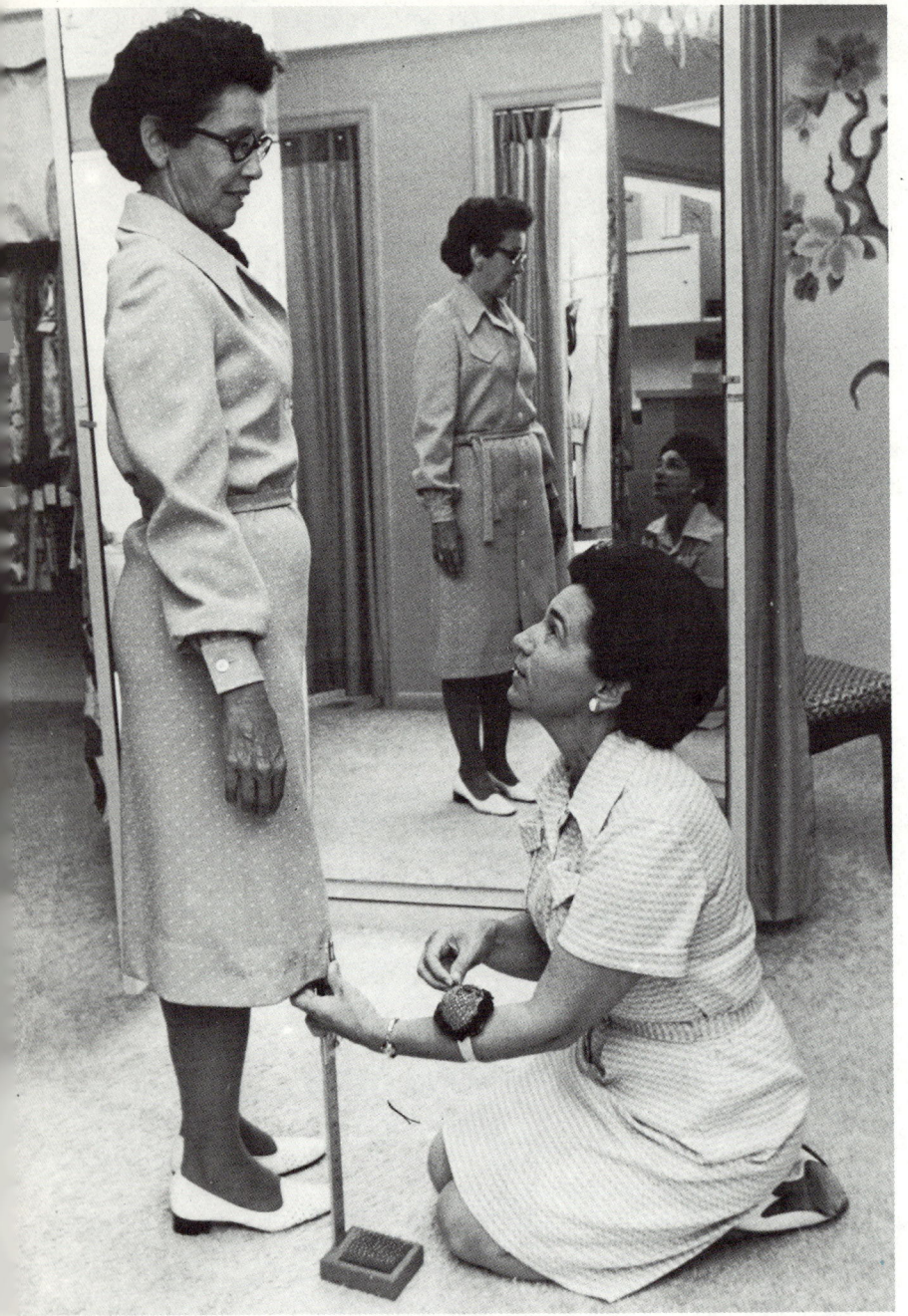

D-3. Using a hem marker.

Courtesy Dagmar Fashions
Photo by Minerva Wagner

### To Fit Uneven Hemlines

Use a hem marker for quick, professional results. Place the marker level on the floor next to the hemline. Adjust the metal clamp to the measurement desired for the new hem length. This measurement will be indicated by the bottom of the clamp. The clamp slides up and down on the wood ruler which supports it. Fig. D-3.

### SHORTENING UNEVEN HEMLINES

TO FIT, place a line of pins around the hem at the desired measurement. Using the hem marker, place pins 3 to 4 inches (7.6 to 10 cm) apart on straight skirts and 2 inches (5 cm) apart on full skirts. Ask the client to turn slowly as you work. The faster you work, the more accurate the hemline will be as the client will have less time to "fidget."

If the customer wants to see how the new hemline will look, turn the hem under along the pin line. Pin the edge of the hem to the garment with vertical pins on the right side. Pin from the center front to the center back only. She can see a front, side, and back view of the new length in the mirror. Fig. D-4.

Remove the vertical pins as soon as the customer is satisfied. If she decides she wants the skirt longer or shorter, use the cross pin symbols to indicate this. Clearly write this information on the work ticket.

### Ch. 10: Fitting and Altering Hemlines

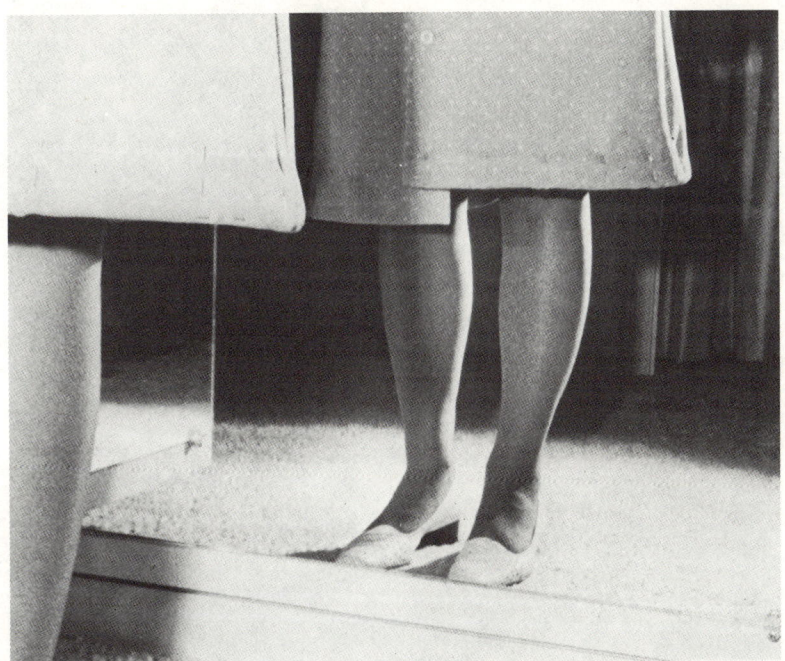

D-4. Pin half of the new hemline in place for the customer's approval.

## LENGTHENING UNEVEN HEMLINES

TO FIT, determine the amount the hem is to be lengthened. Measure and mark around the bottom of the hem as far down as possible to get an even line. Record on the work ticket the amount the hem is to be *lengthened* from that line. Place cross pins on the under side of the hem at the new length to call the attention of the alterationist.

## GARMENT WITH SEPARATE LINING

TO FIT, let the lining fall into the measuring clamp along with the garment and pin through both layers at the same time. If the lining is not cut on the same lines or with the same width as the skirt, the two layers must be pinned separately.

To do the lining separately, fold back the upper layers (outside dress) and pin them out of the way. Under sheer fabrics, measure the lining only 1/4 to 1/2 inch (.6 to 1.3 cm) shorter than the outer layer. For opaque fabrics, the lining should be 1/2 to 1 inch (1.3 to 2.5 cm) shorter.

### Garments with Trim, Ruffles, or Pleats at the Bottom

TO FIT, use a 6-inch (15 cm) ruler. Measure and pin above the top of the trim the amount to be shortened. Pin the top of the trim to this pin line, using vertical pins to hold it in place. For this type of hem, the trim will need to be pinned up all the way around the garment to get the proper effect.

### Garments to be Shortened at the Waist

Garments with scallops, embroidery, permanent pleats, or any other finish that cannot be changed at the bottom, are shortened at the waist. If the garment is princess style or shift style, the hem cannot be shortened.

TO FIT, mark a pin line at the length desired just as you would for an even or uneven hemline fitting. Clearly write on the work ticket that the garment is to be adjusted at the waist seam.

NOTE: This type of garment cannot be lengthened except by restyling.

### Uneven Hem with Overlap or Panels

TO FIT, fold the overlap or panel back out of the way and pin it up. Determine the hem length and start the pin marking at the beginning of the bottom layer. Drop the top layer back into position and pin it separately. Make the panel the same length as the rest of the garment. Occasionally you may find it desirable to let a back panel drop 1/2 inch (1.3 cm) below the length of the rest of the garment.

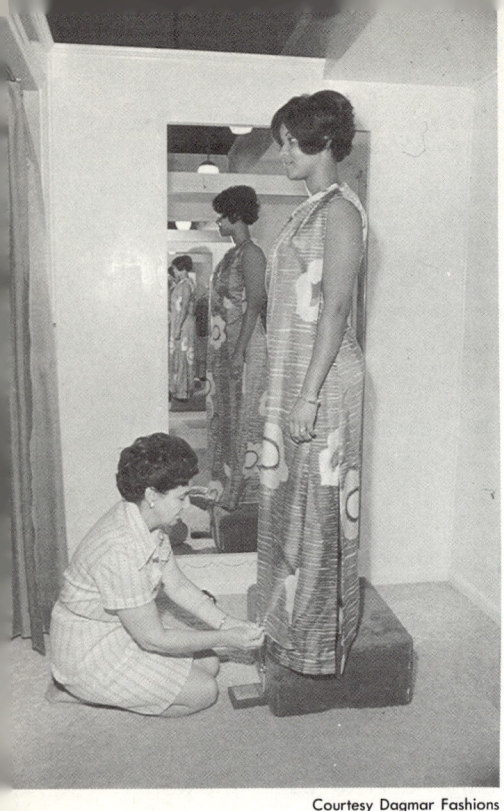

D-5a. *Use a hem marker for long gowns if a platform is available.*

Courtesy Dagmar Fashions
Photo by Minerva Wagner

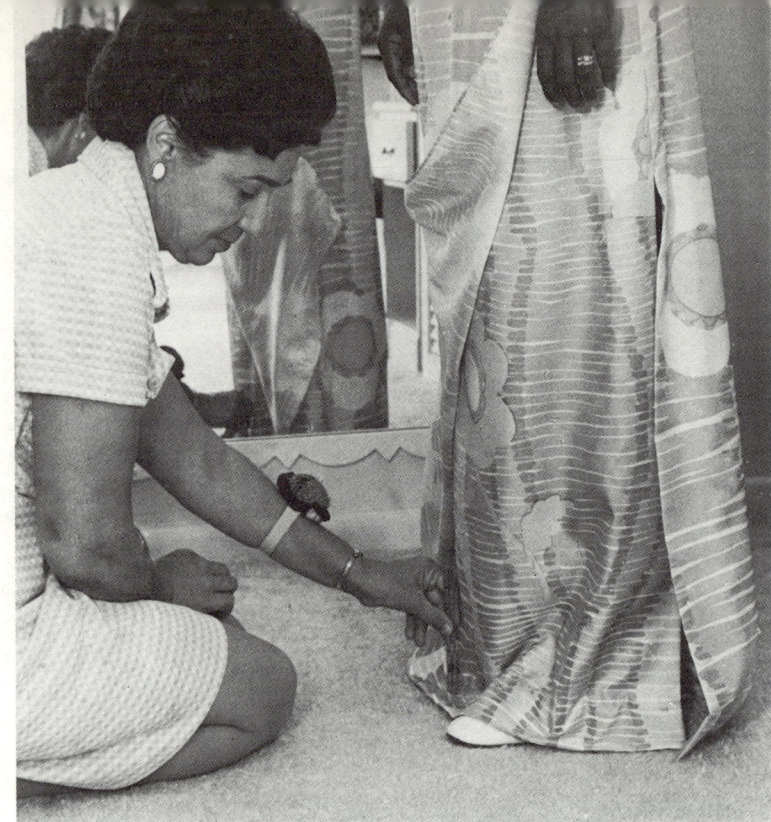

D-5b. *Use 6-inch ruler to measure long gowns if no platform is available. Notice each layer is pinned separately.*

NOTE: If the hem is to be shortened the same amount all around, you need only apply the cross pin symbols at the new length. Record the amount to be shortened on the work ticket.

Garments in this style can rarely be lengthened as the hem has usually been cut away under the panels or overlay.

### FITTING FLOOR LENGTH HEMS

Since the garment length is so close to the floor, it is important for the customer to be wearing the correct heel height. It is also desirable to use a fitting platform. Do not risk using a chair or *any* table top. When in doubt, floor level is safest.

TO FIT on a platform, have the client stand near the edge so the garment falls below the platform. Place the hem marker on the floor and adjust the clamp to the correct length for the style of gown. (See "Lines of the Garment," long floor lengths, page 247). Let the garment fall naturally between the clamps and pin. The fitter stays in one place and the customer slowly turns at the edge of the platform until the pin line is completed. See Fig. D-5a. If the garment is layered, proceed as in "Garment with Separate Lining," page 249.

TO FIT at floor level, use a 6-inch (15 cm) ruler placed upside down on the floor next to the hem. Mark pin line at correct length for that particular style. If the gown is so long it lays on the floor, work with the ruler placed on top of the excess length but do not pull on the gown. Figure D-5b.

As the client turns, let the gown "float" back into position before you continue to pin. Do not pull the skirt into place as you pin—you may stretch the fabric longer in some spots than others. Insert the pins in a horizontal line as with the hem marker.

## Bridal Gown or Formal with Train

These directions are for the train that is cut into the style of the gown, not the separate detachable train. The train may be just long enough to trail slightly behind. It may be a great sweeping train trailing several feet behind the wearer. In either case, the fitting is the same. Work at floor level with a large clean sheet or blanket spread on the floor to prevent soiling the gown.

TO FIT, use a 6-inch (15 cm) ruler to measure the new line across the *front* of the gown. Do *not* pin all the way to the side seams. At the side seam, measure *half* the amount measured for the front pin line. For example, if the line across the front has been pinned at 2 inches (5 cm), the side pin should be 1 inch (2.5 cm). With your "fashion" eye, taper the pin line from the side front to the side seam. From the side pin, taper the line to the edge of the train in a graceful curve. Turn the hem up inside the gown on the pin line and pin in place with vertical pins.

Fitting and pinning across the front and one side to the train is enough to allow you to determine suitable length and taper of the train and gown. Fig. D-6. The other side of the gown will be adjusted by the alterationist. When the correct length has been decided, remove the vertical pins.

Courtesy Gowns Unlimited
Photo by Kimio Sato

**D-6.** A gown with a train is pinned the correct length across the front and tapered back into the original length at the side.

## Altering Ready-To-Wear Fashions

NOTE: A separate, detachable train is rarely shortened. For the rare occasion when it must be, you need only decide how much of the train is to be removed and write this on the work ticket.

### Wide-Legged Evening Pants

These pants are often made of the same fabrics and with layers and linings like the gowns. The big difference will be that you will pin only one leg unless the customer has one hip considerably higher than the other. In that case, you might need to measure both leg hems.

TO FIT, measure, mark, and adjust from the inseam around the front to the side seam and then across the back. Turn the hem up along the pin line and pin with vertical pins. Check the inseam length carefully to be sure it hangs the same as the outseam. After checking, remove the vertical pins. The alterationist will adjust the other leg to the fitted one.

### Tailored Pants

Remember, the most flattering length for pants usually comes just to the top of the shoe in front with a slight drop of extra length in the back. The leg should be long enough to skim the top of the shoe without resting on it or "breaking" in a fold. In the back, the hem should come just below the top of the heel.

Adjust the hem for only one leg as the other leg will be measured to match that one. (Unless the customer has one hip higher than the other.)

### PANTS TOO LONG

TO FIT, work from the side of the client so you can determine where the pants should end in both front and back. Turn under the extra length, starting with the front crease line. Allow at least ½-inch (1.3 cm) drop in back. Insert pins vertically with the points down and use just enough to hold the new hem in place.

If pants with cuffs need to be shortened, observe the same rules about length. However, you will have to pin the excess into a tuck just above the cuff as you did with a cuffed sleeve rather than turning the fabric under. Fig. D-7.

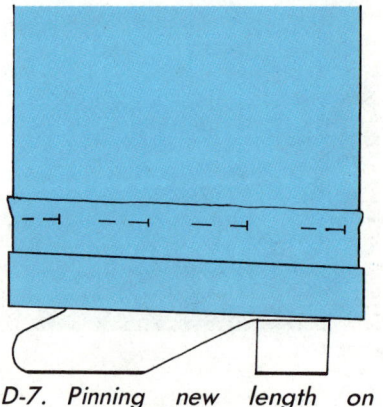

D-7. Pinning new length on cuffed pants.

### PANTS TOO SHORT

This alteration is only possible if there is enough hem to drop.

TO FIT, place crossed pins at the bottom of one leg to call attention to this part of the garment. Determine how much more length is needed both front and back to get the proper length. Write clear instructions on the work ticket.

The same instructions would be used for pants that are cuffed.

### Fitting Coats

#### FULL LENGTH COATS AND CAPES

Top coats, or lightweight coats and capes should be fitted over the kind of garment with which they will be worn. Overcoats and heavy capes should be fitted over a sweater, jacket, or bulky garment. These underlying garments affect the length and drape of the coat or cape. Remember, a full-length coat or cape should be longer than the garment that is worn underneath.

In fitting coats and capes, do not worry about marking the linings. They will be adjusted during the alteration.

TO FIT if the coat hem is even, follow the pin-fitting instructions under "Fitting Street-Length Clothes" for either shortening or lengthening.

TO FIT, if the coat hem is uneven, follow the instructions under "Fitting Street-Length

## Ch. 10: Fitting and Altering Hemlines

Clothes" for the uneven hemline.

NOTE: Raincoats, vinyl, and leather coats cannot be lengthened. The construction used on the original hems leaves marks that cannot be removed.

### COATS TO BE WORN WITH PANTS

Since the full-length coat is an awkward length with pants, there are many requests to shorten a coat to fingertip or car-coat length. The client's height or figure will determine the coat length.

TO FIT finger-tip length, ask the client to stand with her arms straight alongside her body and open her hands. Place a line of pins even with the fingertips on one side of the coat. If the client wishes to see what the coat will look like at that length, fold the extra fabric up inside and pin enough to hold it. Pin one side only. Raise or lower to suit the client and find the most flattering length.

When the length has been determined, place a short line of pins at the proper length. Cross them with vertical pins. Measure from the cross pins to the bottom of the coat. Record on the work ticket the amount the coat is to be shortened.

NOTE: The client may decide the coat should be longer or shorter than fingertip length, but you have helped her make this decision quickly by starting *somewhere*.

### FLOOR-LENGTH COATS OR CAPES

Long coats or capes should be fitted over a compatible garment. Use the same procedure you would use for fitting any floor-length garment.

### HEMMING TECHNIQUES

A truly professional-looking hem is not visible on the outside of the garment. Due to the variety of fabrics and styles used in clothing, many different techniques are required to achieve the desired results. These techniques include various ways to finish the edge of the hem and several types of hand and machine stitches. The edge of the hem may be finished with tape, lace, pinking, ease stitching, zigzag stitching, plain stitching, or a fold. The stitches may include blind stitch, tailor stitch, invisible catch stitch, or machine stitch. Some hems are even *glued* together.

If you are a relative beginner or are seeking to improve your hemming skills, you will find it to your advantage to make a series of samples of the hemming techniques described in this chapter. You will not only gain valuable practice but you can also label your samples and keep them filed for future reference.

To make the samples, cut pieces of muslin about 10 × 12 inches (25.4 by 30.5 cm) and make the hems on the 10-inch (25.4 cm) sides. You can make two hem samples on each piece of muslin. Label them clearly, and slip them into clear, plastic notebook pages for quick reference.

The use of a contrasting color thread for the hem finishes and hand stitches will enhance the value of the samples as reference material. You will be able to see at a glance which sample you have. Also, you will be better able to judge how well and invisibly you are doing your hand stitches.

### Hem Finishes

Hem finishes vary widely and serve several purposes. They may be added:

- To keep the fabric from raveling.
- To help ease in extra fullness.
- To make the edge of the hem stronger.
- To add body so the garment will hang better.
- To give a more finished appearance.
- To give added depth to the hem.

### FOLDED EDGE FINISH

This finish should be applied only to lightweight fabrics and hemmed with a blind stitch.

Fold the cut edge of the hem under 3/8 inch (1 cm). Press with a light touch so the fold is soft rather than sharp. In crease-resistant or permanent-press fabrics, you will have to stitch the 3/8-inch (1 cm) fold in place.

### Altering Ready-To-Wear Fashions

The stitching should be 1/8 inch (.3 cm) from the fold. Do *not* stitch so close to the edge that there is no room to hide the blind stitch in the fold. Press the entire hem and pin for hand stitching.

### DOUBLE HEM FINISH

This is a very successful finish for sheer or finely woven fabrics cut on the straight grain. It gives extra body to the hem and there is no danger of the fabric ravelling.

Press the hem *on* the hem line. Open the hem and fold the cut edge inside to the first press line. Press the second fold with a light touch. Turn the two thicknesses of hem back against the garment. Pin hem in place and blind stitch at the top fold. If you do this type of finish carefully, no cut edges will be visible even in the sheerest fabric. Fig. D-8.

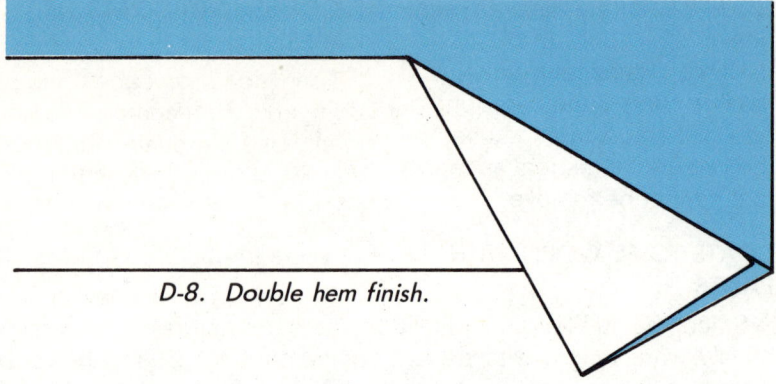

D-8. Double hem finish.

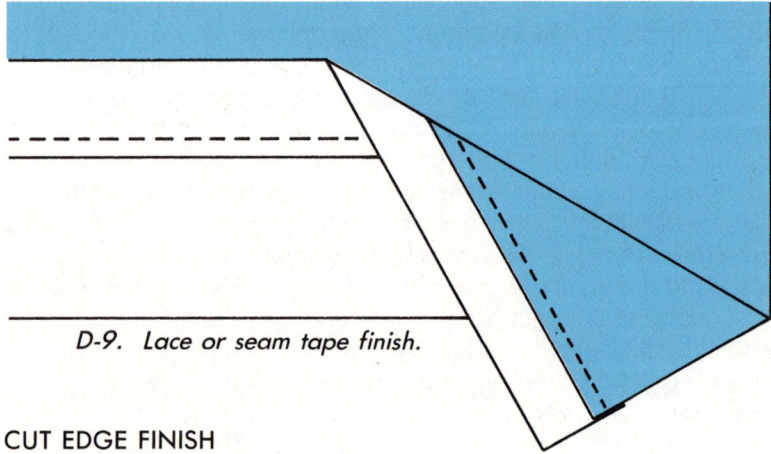

D-9. Lace or seam tape finish.

### LACE AND SEAM TAPE FINISH

This finish is applied to light- and medium-weight woven fabrics and hemmed with the blind stitch.

Lay the bottom edge of the tape or lace 1/4 inch (.6 cm) from the cut edge of the hem. Stitch along the edge of the trim through the single thickness of the hem. Fig. D-9. Use the zig-zag stitch only if the fabric ravels easily. If the lace is scalloped on one side, use the straight edge along the hem edge for the stitching.

### CUT EDGE FINISH

This finish is used only for knit fabrics with the tailor, surface catch, or invisible catch stitch. If the knit fabric does not ravel or run, no machine stitching is necessary.

Trim the edge of the hem to an even depth with dress-maker shears. If the fabric seems to ravel or run, stitch a line of regular machine stitching 1/4 inch (.6 cm) from the edge of the hem. If there is excess fullness to ease in, stitch a line of ease-stitching 1/4 inch (.6 cm) from the edge.

### CUT OR PINKED EDGE WITH MACHINE STITCHING

This finish is very similar to the preceding cut edge finish. It differs only in that some firmly woven fabrics may be trimmed with pinking shears and left without any other finish. The edge is always stitched as above for extra firmness and control of raveling.

**Ch. 10: Fitting and Altering Hemlines**

## ZIGZAG FINISH

This finish is used for appearance and to prevent runs or raveling in knit fabrics.

Use a wide zigzag stitch of about 12 stitches to the inch (2.5 cm). Stitch ¼ inch (.6 cm) from the cut edge of the hem. Either leave the extra ¼ inch (.6 cm) of fabric at the top of the hem or trim down to the zigzag line.

## HONG KONG FINISH

This finish is usually used on seams and hems in unlined coats or jackets. It received its name because of its frequent use on the finer clothes from the Orient. It is also sometimes called a bound-edge finish.

The binding is made of bias strips of matching color lining fabric that is cut 1 inch (2.5 cm) wide.

To apply, lay the right side of the binding on the right side of the hem edge. Stitch ¼ inch (.6 cm) from the cut edge of the hem. Press the bias up toward the cut edge. Then turn it down over the hem edge to the wrong side of the hem, and press again. The edge of the bias should come below the ¼ inch (.6 cm) stitching on the wrong side.

On the right side of the hem, stitch-in-the-ditch (see Finishing Touches, pg. 291) next to the bias seam, or stitch on the edge of the bias. This stitching will hold the bias edge in place on the inside of the hem. Fig. D-10.

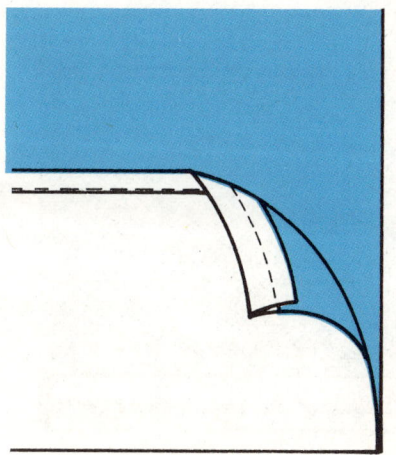

D-10. Hong Kong finish.

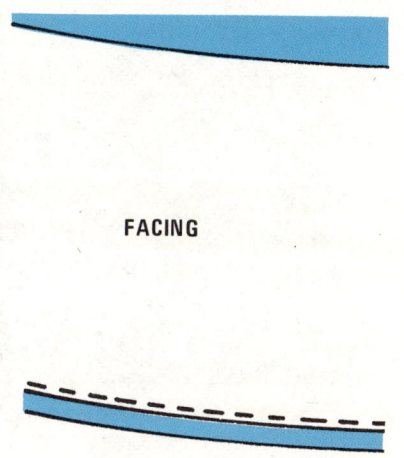

D-11. Bias facing finish.

## HEM FACINGS

Facings are applied as a finish to take the place of a hem when a garment is lengthened or a rough texture fabric needs to be covered. The fabric used for the facing should be the same weight as the garment or a lighter-weight lining fabric. If the garment is a "wash and wear," the facings should be, too. A matching or blending color is desirable. For women's wear, the 2-inch (5 cm) straight-edged facing lace has been popular as it blends successfully with all but the heavier-weight fabrics.

### Bias Facings

For full or shaped hems, a bias facing cut 2½ to 3 inches (6.4 to 7.6 cm) wide is best.

Lay the right side of the facing to the right side of the hem with the edges even. Stitch ¼ inch (.6 cm) from the edge, pulling the bottom of the bias slightly so the facing will shape to the slope of the garment. Press the seam: open on equal weight fabrics, up on heavy fabrics with light-weight facing. Finish the edge of the facing as needed. Fig. D-11.

### Straight-Grain Facings

For straight-grain hemlines, a 2½ to 3-inch (6.4 to 7.6 cm) strip of straight-grain fabric fits better and allows more control and speed.

Apply the straight facing to the hem edge in the same way you did the bias facing, with one slight change. With a straight facing, you should pull the garment edge slightly as you stitch rather than the bottom edge of the facing. This prevents the facing from becoming too tight for the garment edge.

**Altering Ready-To-Wear Fashions**

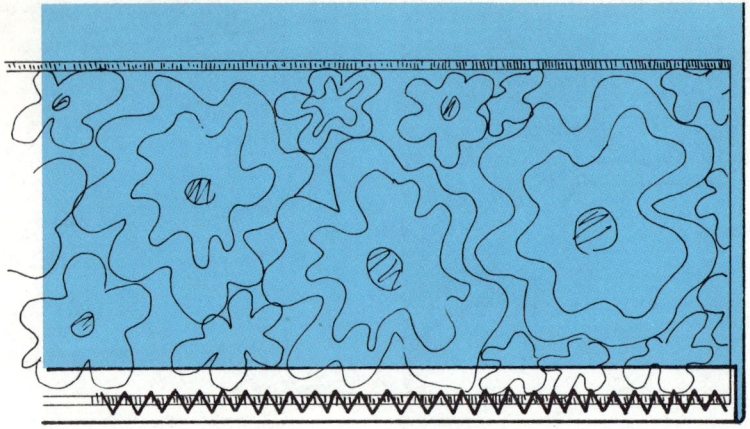

D-12. Wide lace facing finish.

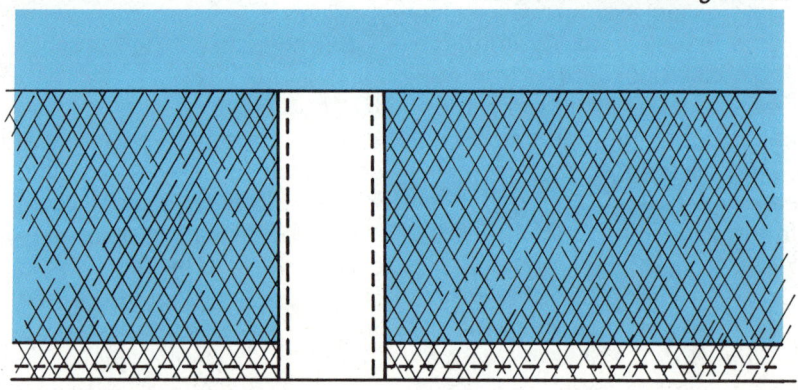

D-13. Wide horsehair facing finish.

### Wide-Lace Facing

The 2-inch (5 cm) wide commercial lace facing can blend and shape to almost any fabric or style hem. It is attractive and easy to apply and can be purchased in a wide variety of colors. The procedure for applying the wide lace is the same as for narrow lace. Fig. D-12.

### Wide Horsehair Facing

A 2-inch-wide band of stiff nylon filaments is still called horsehair braid. It is used around the bottom of full evening gowns to help keep the skirt full and bouffant. This braid is stitched in place around the bottom of a skirt in the same manner as the wide lace is applied. The only real difference is that a piece of seam binding is stitched over the overlapped seam to cover the ends of the nylon filaments. Fig. D-13.

### Facings for Rough Fabrics

Some fabrics, such as those covered with sequins or beads, may have to be shortened. The newly turned-up hem may have rough places that catch on hose and undergarments. Occasionally a novelty fabric will have an unexpected roughness on the underneath side. To protect under clothing, these fabrics may require facing the hem area. See "To Shorten Sequined or Beaded Fabrics," pg. 268.

### Hand Hemming Stitches

The purpose of putting in a hem by hand rather than by machine is to keep the finished hem as invisible as possible. This means that to make it profitable, you must develop speed. To make it invisible, you must develop skill. Keeping a light touch and a loose stitch are musts.

Stitches should be spaced no closer together than $1/2$ inch (1.3 cm) on the outside fabric. The stitch going through the outer fabric should be so small it only catches one thread of that fabric. Usually the larger portion of the stitch will be in the fold or under the edge of the hem finish where it, too, will not show. The exception to this is the surface catch stitch. Stitches should be left slightly loose and never pulled up tight.

Mercerized cotton thread is an old stand-by that still has many advantages for use with most fabrics. The polyester-cotton threads are strong and stretchable and do have an advantage for knit or stretchable fabrics. The all-polyester thread is very strong. However, this thread has more disadvantages than advantages. It cuts the threads of the garment fabric it is used on, twists more easily when doing hand sewing, and is more apt to cause difficulties with machine sewing.

To keep the thread from twisting and knotting as you hand sew, thread the needle before you cut it from the spool. Put the knot in the end you cut last. The thread will be pulling through the fabric in the same direction as its natural twist and will be easier to keep smooth. It also helps to dampen your fingers with laundry fabric softener and run them down the thread to dampen it slightly.

To keep your stitches small and inconspicuous, a sharp, slender needle—like a milliner's needle—works best. For most fabrics, use a number 9 milliner's needle with number fifty or sixty mercerized cotton or cotton-polyester thread. For heavy fabrics, use a number seven milliner's needle and number fifty cotton or cotton-polyester thread.

Hold the hem of the garment rolled over your hand and sew toward you. Rolling the hem over the hand helps keep the stitches loose.

You may begin and end your hand stitches without a knot at either end. You can take three tiny, overlapping stitches in the edge of the fabric to hold the thread. Or, you can make a *slip knot*. Take two tiny overlapping stitches. Leave a loop in the second stitch before pulling it tight to the fabric. Slip the needle through this second loop and then pull it tight. Trim the thread close to the fabric and it is secured.

When you have finished your samples of the various hem finishes, you are ready to pin the hems in place and practice the hand stitches used by skilled, commercial alterationists.

## BLIND STITCH

This is the fastest and most commonly used hemming stitch for light- and medium-weight woven fabrics. It is used with a finished hem edge such as tape, lace, or a fold—stitched or unstitched.

The stitches through the top or garment fabric are spaced ½

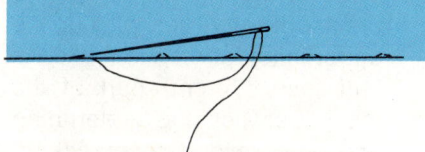

D-14. Blind stitching a hem.

inch (1.3 cm) apart and are so tiny they pick up only a single thread of the outer fabric. The longer stitch goes either through the fold at the edge of the hem or underneath the lace or binding.

To make the blind stitch, anchor the thread at a seam or the edge of the hem. Pick up one thread of the garment fabric next to the edge of the hem. At the same spot, slip the needle back into the fold of the hem or under the binding. Push it along so the needle will re-emerge ½ inch (1.3 cm) from the first stitch. Pick up another thread of the outer fabric and slip the needle back into the fold for another ½ inch (1.3 cm) stitch. Continue all the way around the hem. Fig. D-14.

To use the blind stitch on an underlined garment of sheer fabric, follow the same procedure. However, the tiny, one-thread stitch will be in the underlining fabric and will not go into the outer layer.

To use the blind stitch on an underlined garment of opaque fabric is the neatest and easiest of all. Make a stitch through the

## Altering Ready-To-Wear Fashions

edge of the hem finish. Where the needle emerges, pick up the underlining fabric and make the half inch (.6 cm) part of the stitch between the underlining and outer layer. Do *not* pick up the garment threads at all. Bring the needle back out at the edge of the hem finish. Catch the hem in a tiny stitch and go back under the underlining for the long part of the stitch.

### Tailor Stitch

This stitch is commonly used with heavier fabrics and a variety of hem finishes. It is quick and easy, and does not show on either the hem or the garment. It holds the two layers together with the weight evenly distributed on each layer and eliminates pulling. And, it lasts well because the hemming thread is protected by the outer layer of the hem. Because of this protection, it is not exposed to abrasion wear against hose and undergarments.

The tailor stitch is used on a cut edge finished with machine stitching, zigzag, or Hong Kong finish.

Turn back top edge of hem and work on wrong side of hem. Make the first stitch on the hem at the stitch line. Move the needle forward 1/4 inch (.6 cm) and pick up one thread of the garment fabric. Move forward again 1/4 inch (.6 cm) and pick up the hem fabric—through the stitching line. Repeat the 1/4-inch (.6 cm) spacing top and bottom,

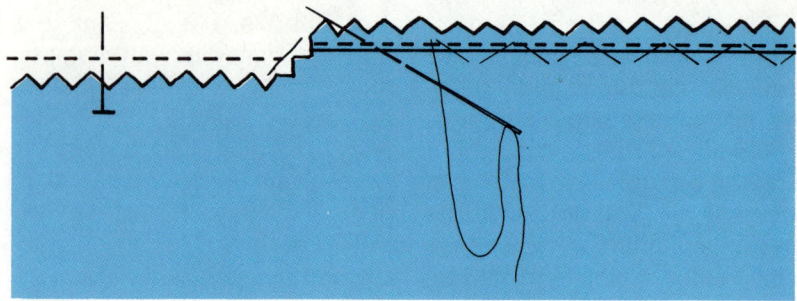

D-15a. Tailor stitched hem.

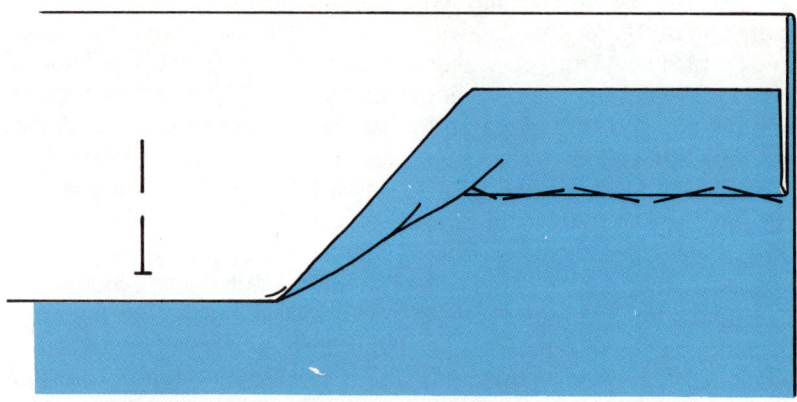

D-15b. Tailor stitched basting used on deep hems.

using a very light touch. Fig. D-15a. Notice that the 1/4-inch (.6 cm) spacing of each stitch results in a total of a 1/2-inch (1.3 cm) stitch.

NOTE: Tailor stitch basting is useful in holding a hem in place for deep hems. Turn the hem back half way and run a tailor stitch of 1/2 inch (1.3 cm) spacing around the center of the hem. Smooth the hem back into position and finish the top edge with the 1/4 inch (.6 cm) spaced tailor stitch. Fig. D-15b.

### CATCH STITCH

This stitch is used as a "finish" stitch to control raveling in unfinished hem edges and for "stretch" with knits. It is never used with a taped or lace finish since the stitch itself is a finish.

When making this stitch, always point the needle away from the direction in which you are sewing. If you sew from left to right, point the needle to the left. With the hem edge held toward you, anchor the thread and make the first stitch 1/4 inch

## Ch. 10: Fitting and Altering Hemlines

(.6 cm) below the hem edge. Move the needle ¼ inch (.6 cm) away to the garment at the hem edge. Pick up one thread of the garment fabric. Pull the stitch through. Move forward and down to ¼ inch (.6 cm) on the hem and pick up several threads of the hem fabric. Repeat the ¼-inch (.6 cm) spacing forward and up and down for an evenly spaced finish. Use a very light touch and never pull the stitches tight. Fig. D-16.

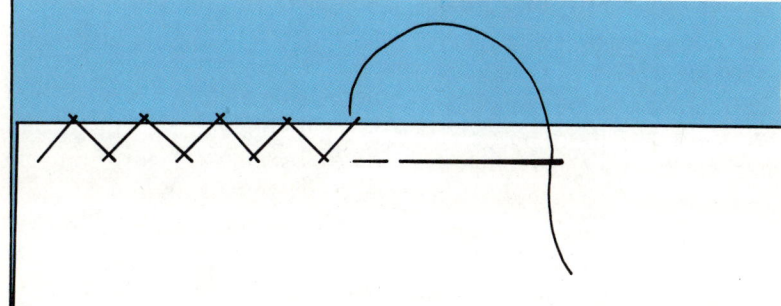

D-16. Catch stitch.

### INVISIBLE CATCH STITCH

This stitch is used for fine single, double, or bouclé knits. It combines the "meshing" effect of the tailor stitch with the stretch quality of the catch stitch.

Turn back the hem edge as for a tailor stitch. Make the first stitch in the hem ¼ inch (.6 cm) from the hem edge. Make the same ¼-inch (.6 cm) spaced stitches as for the tailor hem but with the needle pointing in the opposite direction each time as in the catch stitch. This is what forms the little loop that creates the stretch needed for knits. Use a very light touch and do *not* pull the stitches tight. Fig. D-17.

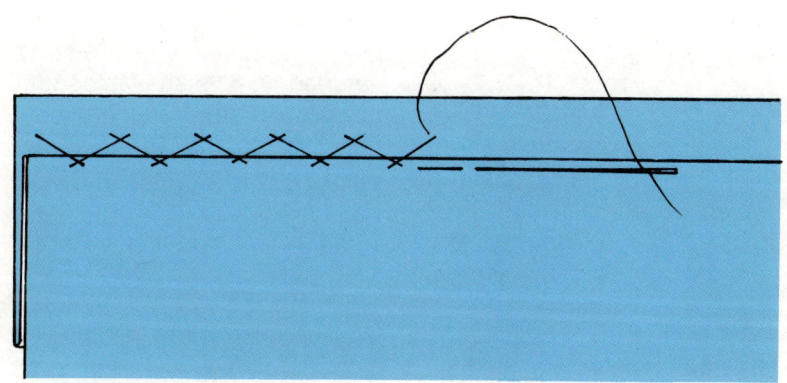

D-17. Invisible catch stitch.

#### Invisible Catch Stitch Basting

This stitch is used for the same purpose and in the same way as the tailor stitch basting. Fig. D-15b. NOTE: Make your sample of the catch stitch on knit fabric so you can test the stretching quality of the stitch.

### Machine Hem Finishes

Many hems can be finished entirely by machine. With the right equipment and skill, you can do a large volume of hem alterations with very little hand stitching.

### MACHINE BLIND STITCH

Some models of home sewing machines have an attachment for blind stitching. However, if you plan to do a lot of hems, you may wish to invest in a blind stitch sewing machine as shown on page 36 in Chapter 3. Either of these machine finishes can be applied to any kind of hem with any of the previously mentioned hem finishes. You will be limited only by your machine and your ability to operate it efficiently.

Always test the stitch on a piece of similar fabric before working on a garment. NOTE: It is not advisable to use this kind of machine finish in place of handwork on better garments made of finer fabrics.

## Altering Ready-To-Wear Fashions

### SINGLE-EDGE STITCHED HEM

This type of finish is usually used for very full, bouffant, or accordion-pleated hems. Such hems are cut off-grain or on the bias so there is no raveling of the cut edge.

Fold the hem to the wrong side of the hemline. Stitch on the edge of the fold with a small stitch (12 stitches per inch). Cut away the excess fabric close to the stitching.

This finish is used by many designers to give a floating effect to the skirt.

### DOUBLE-EDGE STITCHED HEM

Sometimes a second line of stitching may be necessary to control raveling if the edge-stitched hem is desired for a garment cut on the straight grain.

Fold the hem under 1/4 inch (.6 cm) below the hemline. Stitch on the edge of the fold and cut away the excess fabric as for the edge-stitched hem above. After trimming to the stitching, turn edge again close to the stitching. Stitch close to the first line of stitching so only one stitching line shows on the right side.

### Edge-Stitched Hem with Horsehair

This finish is used to give extra stiffness to the bottom of long, sheer gowns.

Trim edge of hem to 1/2 inch (1.3 cm) below the hemline. Fold this 1/2 inch (1.3 cm) to the inside of the garment. Pin one edge of 1/2-inch (1.3 cm) horsehair braid to the inside of the hem fold. Stitch through horsehair and hem fold (on the wrong side) 1/8 inch (.3 cm) from the edge, using a medium-length stitch. The horsehair will cover the cut edge of the hem and the stitching will keep the braid in place. No other stitching is necessary. Fig. D-18.

### ZIGZAG EDGE-STITCHED HEM

This hem is used on the same types of garments as the edge-stitched hem finish. It is popular because it gives a decorative finish with no possibility of raveling.

Adjust the stitch length the same as for an edge stitch finish and combine with a narrow zigzag stitch. Fold the fabric to the inside on the hemline. Stitch along the edge so the zigzag stitch wraps around the hem edge. Then trim away the excess fabric on the inside to the stitch line.

It would be wise to make several samples using different combinations of stitch lengths and zigzag widths and identify each for reference. Different stitches are required for different weights and types of fabrics.

NOTE: The single-edge and zigzag-edge stitching can be successful with knit fabrics. However, great control must be used to prevent rippling or stretching of the edge. Feed the folded hem edge into the sewing machine with scissor or ripper point and do not pull front or back.

### RIPPLE-EDGE STITCH (LETTUCE LEAF)

This finish can be used with dramatic effect on very lightweight tricot knits.

Adjust the machine for a short, narrow, zigzag stitch. Cut the fabric on the hemline. Stitch along the edge stretching the fabric in front of the presser foot while pulling the fabric from behind the presser foot. The fabric should ripple and feed evenly into the sewing machine. As you stretch the fabric, it will roll to the right side and the zigzag stitch will wrap around this roll. Fig. D-19.

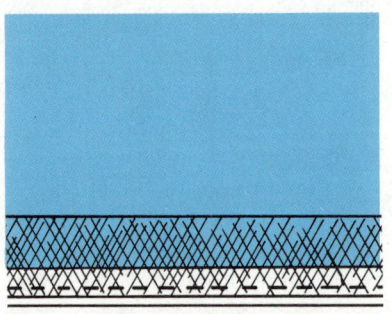

D-18. Edge stitched hem with horsehair.

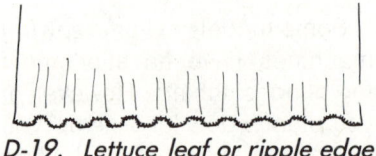

D-19. Lettuce leaf or ripple edge hem.

## Ch. 10: Fitting and Altering Hemlines

Make several testing samples on tricot knit fabric before attempting to use this finish on a garment. Label your samples with the stitch used for easy reference later.

### TOP-STITCHED HEM

Many sportswear manufacturers and designers use top stitching to outline and accentuate seams and details in their garments. If the garment you are altering has top stitching, you can make use of this finish to add to the looks of the hem. If the garment does not have top stitching, you might suggest it be top-stitched to improve the appearance. The stitching can be used on collar, cuffs, or pockets. To top stitch, use same stitching, thread, and stitch length as in rest of garment.

To hem the garment, if the fabric is bulky, use seam tape. Stitch the seam tape 1/4 inch (.6 cm) from the raw edge of the hem. Press the tape to the inside, rolling the hem back 1/8 inch (.3 cm) so the tape won't show. Use the clapper to get a hard press. Fig. D-20a. On the right side of the garment, stitch 1/8 inch (.3 cm) from the fold. Make a second stitching 1/4 inch (.6 cm) from the first stitching. Fig. D-20b. If only one top-stitch line is desired, it should be the same distance from the hem edge as any other stitching on the garment. Use the stitching gauge on your machine for precision stitching.

For *lightweight* fabrics, press in a hemline 3/4 inch (2 cm) from the cut edge. Fold the cut edge to meet the inside press line (see double-hem instructions) and press top fold. Stitch 1/8 inch (.3 cm) from hem fold on the wrong side of the hem. Make the second stitching on the top hem fold (still on the wrong side). Precision pressing will result in precision stitching. If only one stitch line is needed for effect, stitch only on the top fold of the hem.

NOTE: If the garment is of a knit fabric, you need only press a 1/2-inch (1.3 cm) fold to the inside of the garment. Stitch on the wrong side of the garment as above.

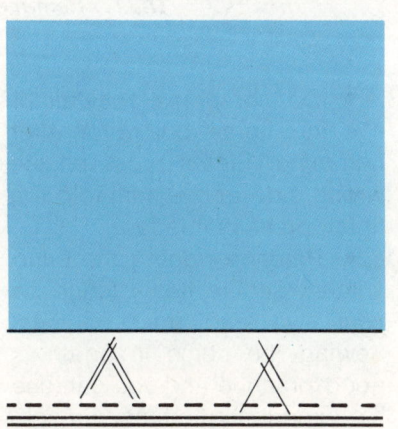

D-20a. Seam tape finish for top-stitched hem.

**RIGHT SIDE**

D-20b. Machine stitched hem.

### Finishes To Control Hem Fullness

Apply an ease-stitch on the hem-depth marking line. Fold the hem to the inside and check the fit of the top of the hem to the garment. If the hem is too tight, snip the machine stitching where release is needed. If too loose, pull the thread with a pin to tighten where needed. After adjustment of fullness, trim the excess hem to 1/4 inch (.6 cm) beyond the ease-stitching.

If fabric is *woven*, apply seam tape, lace, or Hong Kong finish. If fabric is knit, leave the clean-cut edge. With the tip of the iron, steam and shrink out the fullness at the top of the hem. Hand sew with a blind stitch for woven fabric and the tailor's stitch for knits. You can also use a machine blind stitch for either.

For a folded-edge hem finish, follow the above steps for ease-stitching and adjusting the hem fullness. After adjustment, trim excess hem 3/8 to 1/2 inch (1 to 1.3 cm) beyond the ease-stitching. Press this allowance to the inside of the hem *on* the stitching line. Shrink out the hem fullness at the same time. Sew with a hand or machine blind stitch.

### HEM ALTERATIONS
#### General Pointers

• Before altering, rip the original hem and press out all the old stitch marks and hem creases.

## Altering Ready-To-Wear Fashions

- Begin and end all machine and hand stitching at a side or back seam. On pants, begin and end at the inseam.
- Use seams as "pillars of support" for the widely spaced hand stitches by making tiny whip stitches on *top* of the seams. Never sew through the seams to the outer fabric.
- Gather and steam out fullness at the top of the hem before sewing. Pull and stretch (with steam) the top of a too-narrow hem before sewing. (The too-narrow problem is usually found when shortening straight pants.)
- Keep the hem depth to 2½ to 3 inches (6.4 to 7.6 cm) for straight or slightly A line skirts. A very full skirt should have a hem of about 1 inch (2.5 cm).
- Make several cardboard measuring gauges from seam tape cards. These are 5 by 2 inches (12.7 by 5 cm) and can be notched for different measurements. Have a clearly marked gauge for each measurement. Fig. D-21.
- On opaque fabrics, free hanging linings should be ½ to 1 inch (1.3 to 2.5 cm) shorter than the garment. For sheer fabrics, the lining should be only ¼ inch (.6 cm) shorter.
- Press new hemline in woven fabrics—but not in knit garments—before finishing. The loose catch or tailor stitch used in knits allows the hem to shift a little after the hand work is completed so it is better to press after the shift.

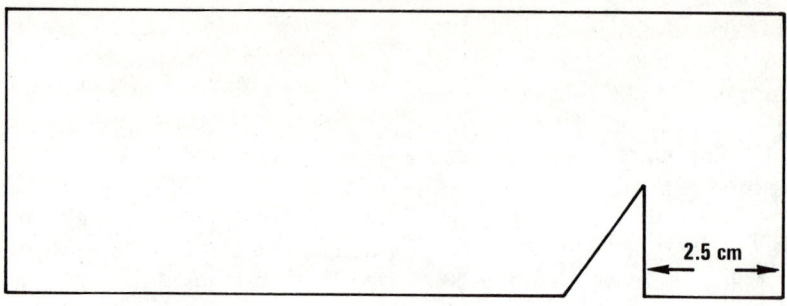

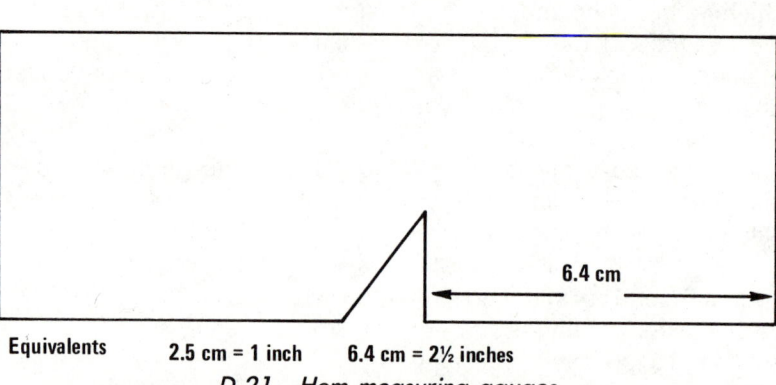

**Equivalents**  2.5 cm = 1 inch  6.4 cm = 2½ inches

*D-21. Hem measuring gauges.*

- Do *not* press cocktail or evening hems before or after hemming. Steam press on the wrong side *above* hem fold if a finish press is needed.
- Practice ripping the blind stitch machine hems found on your own ready-made clothes. Sewing the hems in again is good practice and you can use the experience to time yourself. To rip the machine blind stitch, hold the hem fold in your left hand and, with the scissor points, clip through the top loop and the thread under it. Pull the next thread loop toward you.
- Work on a garment lining at the same time you are working on the outer layer. Rip both hems at the same time, and press at the same time.

### Altering Even Hemlines
### (Time: 30 to 40 minutes)

**TO SHORTEN EVEN HEMLINES**

1. Remove all pins after noting the amount to be shortened.
2. Rip out the hem stitching.
3. Press out hem crease, leaving a slight line as a guide for the new hem. Steam out old stitching marks on the wrong side.
4. Lightly press in the new line, using a notched hem

**Ch. 10: Fitting and Altering Hemlines**

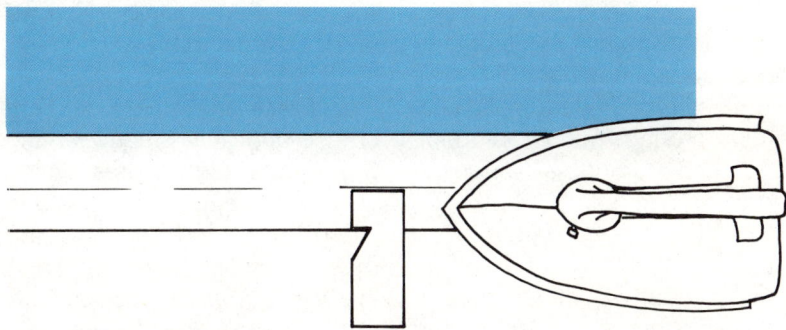

D-22a. *Pressing new hem line using hem gauge as a guide.*

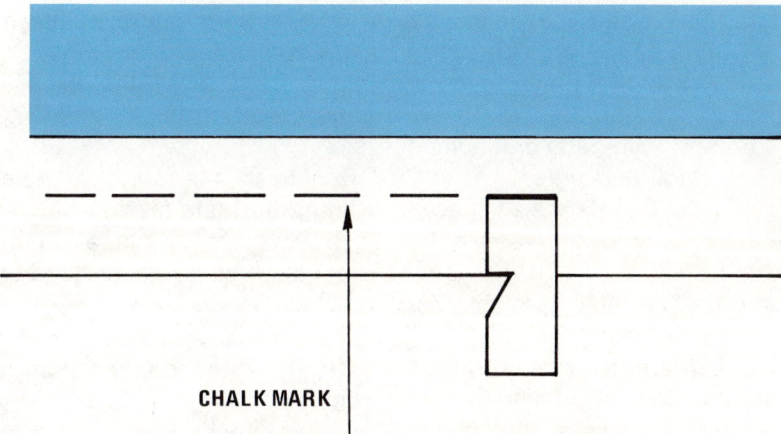

CHALK MARK

D-22b. *Measuring and marking hem depth.*

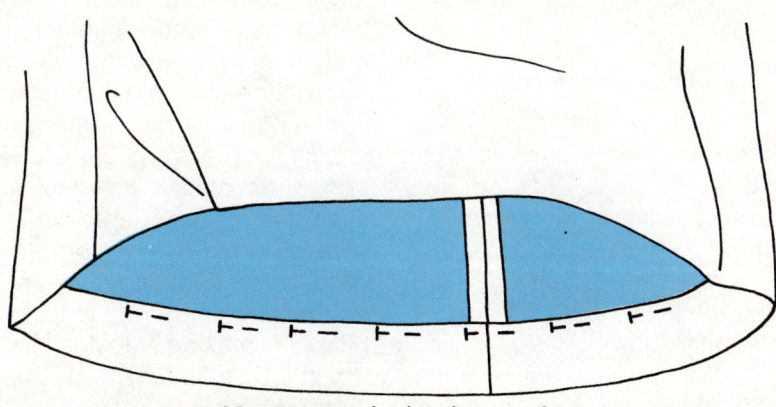

D-23. *Pinning the hemline in place.*

gauge to measure from the original hemline. Fig. D-22a. If the new line is to be left unpressed (dressy styles), mark the new line with pins or thread.

5. Prepare the edge of the hem with the appropriate hem finish. If the top of the hem is to be a folded edge, measure the hem depth plus ½ inch (1.3 cm) for turn back. Make a chalk line as you measure and trim through this line. Fig. D-22b. If top of hem is to be a clean-cut finish with no control stitching, chalk mark *at* the hem *depth* and cut through marking. If top of hem is to be finished with any of the other hem finishes, mark hem depth very lightly with chalk but do *not* cut away excess hem.

6. With garment wrong side out so you can work inside the hem circle, apply the hem finish chosen. Cut away the excess fabric leaving ¼ inch (.6 cm) under tape or lace or above machine finish.

7. If the new hem will not make the total hem depth too deep, leave the original finish in place.

8. Turn garment right side out and spread hem on work table. Fig. D-23. If hemline has been pressed, you need only pin hem in place at the top. If unpressed, fold at marked line and pin in place at the bottom and again at the top of the hem.

9. Finish the hem with the correct hand stitch or the machine blind stitch.

263

### Altering Ready-To-Wear Fashions

NOTE: If the garment has a separate lining, rip and press out the original hemline. Press in new hemline, removing the same amount you did on the outer garment. Press cut edge of hem to the inside of the hem fold, making a double hem (see page 254). Pin hem at top and machine stitch along edge of top fold.

### TO LENGTHEN EVEN HEMLINE

1. Remove all pins after noting amount of hem depth left when the "drop" (amount to be lowered) is subtracted. For example, if the hemline is dropped 1 inch (2.5 cm) and the original hem depth is 3 inches (7.6 cm), subtracting 1 inch (2.5 cm) from this will leave a 2-inch (5 cm) hem. Write 2-inch (5 cm) hem depth on work ticket.

2. Carefully steam out all stitch marks and the hem fold.

3. *If there is adequate hem depth*, press or pin hem along the new line and again at the top of the hem. Finish with the correct hand stitch or machine blind stitch. Press.

*If there is little or no hem left*, turn garment to wrong side and apply fabric or lace facing to hem edge.

NOTE: To finish the ends of the lace at the seam, fold under ½ inch (1.3 cm) of lace and lap it over the lace where you started. Stitch to the end of the overlap, lift presser foot, pivot, lower presser foot and stitch on to the edge of the lace.

When applying a fabric facing, open bottom of side or center back seam 1 inch (2.5 cm). Begin stitching at edge of seam, stitch around bottom of hem, and end facing at opposite edge of the same seam. Restitch the ripped seam overstitching 1 inch (2.5 cm) of the original seam. Continue through to the bottom of the facing and back stitch. Press seam open and finish edge of facing as instructed for the samples.

4. Press new hemline and turn garment to right side.

5. Pin hem in place at top of facing.

6. Sew with hand or machine blind stitch and press.

NOTE: If the garment has a separate lining, lengthen it the same amount and at the same time as the outer garment. Machine sew hem in lining.

If the hem has been dropped "all the way," the lining should be finished with a ¼-inch (.6 cm) machine hem. You may also apply ½-inch (1.3 cm) lace to right side of the cut edge with a fine zigzag stitch.

### Altering Uneven Hemlines (Time: 30 to 40 minutes)

This is the hemline that has been pin-fitted all the way around with a horizontal pin line.

### TO SHORTEN UNEVEN HEMLINE

1. Rip out the hem stitching.
2. Remove and re-insert each pin into a single layer of fabric, releasing the hem underneath.

3. Press and steam out hem crease and stitch marks on the wrong side. Lightly press in the new hemline by folding along the pin line and removing the pins one by one before applying the iron. Do *not* press in new line if garment is "dressy". In that case, be sure to leave the pin line or a thread line as a guide.

4. With hem gauge, chalk an *even* hem depth. See Figs. D-22a,b. Trim away the excess fabric through chalk marking line.

5. Finish the edge of hem with appropriate finish.

6. Pin hem in place. Complete the hem by either hand or machine sewing.

7. Press.

NOTE: If the garment has a separate lining, rip and press out hem crease in lining. While at the press board and with garment still on wrong side, pull the lining down over the garment hem. Lightly chalk lining at garment hem fold. Now, turn lining wrong side out. Fold lining hem 1 inch (2.5 cm) shorter than the chalk line. Press the fold. Measuring from this fold, chalk an even line for hem depth. Leave hem as deep as possible. Cut excess fabric along this line. Fold cut edge of hem to inside hem fold, making a double hem. Pin at top and machine stitch at edge of top fold.

## Ch. 10: Fitting and Altering Hemlines

### TO LENGTHEN UNEVEN HEMLINE (TIME: 40 TO 50 MINUTES)

This hem fitting may have been ripped and quickly pressed out for the pin-fitting. An even pin line may have been marked close to the bottom of the unripped hem. In addition, cross pin symbols were put under the hem to indicate the amount to drop the hem below the even pin line.

If hem has been fitted with the cross pin drop, rip hem. Remove and re-insert each pin into a single layer of fabric. Measure and make a thread line below this pin line the amount indicated by the cross pins.

If hem has been ripped and fitted, replace the pin line with a thread marking.

1. Carefully steam and press out all stitch marks and hem fold.
2. Measure an even chalk line for hem depth below the thread line. Use the narrowest part of the remaining hem to get this measurement. Fig. D-24.
3. If there is adequate hem depth, apply appropriate hem finish and trim excess fabric.
4. If no hem depth is left, apply facing to chalk line as directed under "To Lengthen Even Hemline."
5. Pin or press hem fold at thread line. Pin at top of hem and sew with hand or machine blind stitch.
6. Remove thread marking and lightly press hem.

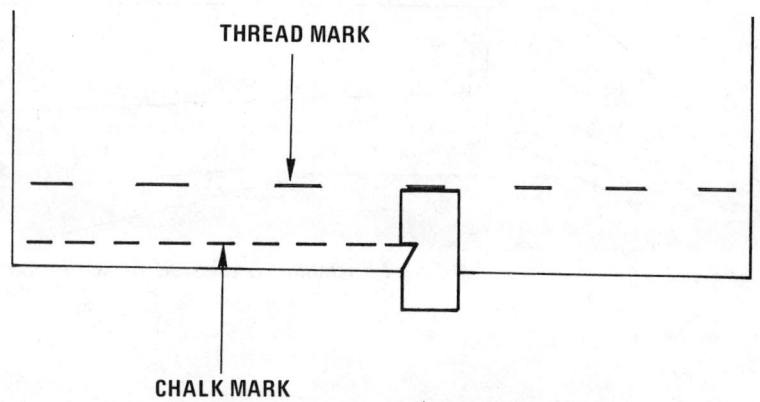

D-24. Marking new hemline for lengthening garment.

NOTE: If garment has a separate lining, rip and press out hem. Finish garment hem and press. Pull lining over garment and pin to skirt close to bottom of lining. Pin all around, spacing the pins about 6 inches (15 cm) apart. Measure and make a chalk line on the lining 3/4 inch (2 cm) from the garment hem fold. If the lining is shorter than 3/4 inch (2 cm) above hem fold, you will have to increase this measurement accordingly. Cut lining on chalk line and make a 1/4-inch (.6 cm) machine hem. If lining had to be measured shorter than 3/4 inch (2 cm), apply 1/2-inch (1.3 cm) lace to the chalk line with a fine zigzag stitch and trim excess fabric under the lace.

### TO SHORTEN HEM WITH TRIM ATTACHED (TIME: 30 MINUTES)

This hem has been fitted with a tuck pinned at the top of the trim.

1. Remove vertical pins holding the tuck in place. Make a thread line along the horizontal pin line. Remove those pins also.
2. Rip trim from bottom of skirt.
3. Mark a chalk line 1 inch (2.5 cm) below the thread line on the skirt. Cut along chalk line with pinking shears.
4. Rip bottom of center back or one side seam 3 inches (7.6 cm) and separate trim where it has been joined.
5. Turn garment wrong side out. Apply right side of trim to right side of garment with trim seam *on* the thread line. Start and end at the open seam of skirt.
6. Pin the trim to the skirt. Ease it gently to prevent the trim from pulling in the bottom of the skirt. Place pins perpendicular to the trimming seam.
7. Stitch on trim seam, inside the skirt circle.

## Altering Ready-To-Wear Fashions

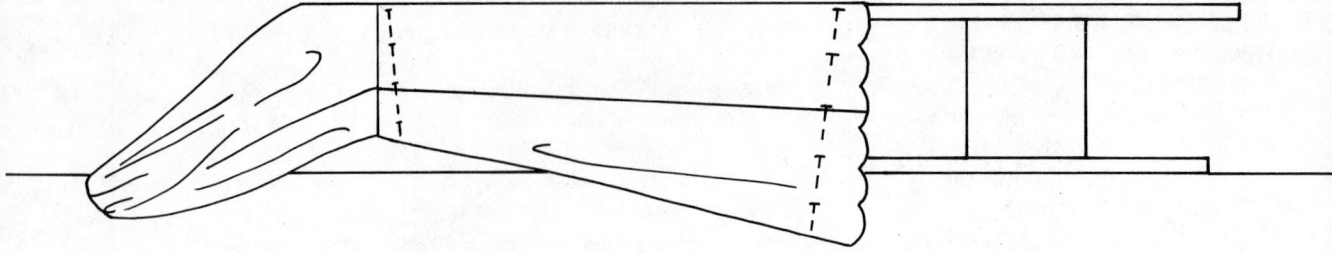

D-25. *Shortening a pleated or scalloped hemline.*

8. Press seam toward skirt on wrong side (on seam roll).

9. Restitch the skirt seam, including the trim, and backstitch at the bottom of the trim.

10. Press seam open (on seam roll).

### TO SHORTEN LENGTH AT WAIST

This method is for the permanent-pleated, scalloped, or design-bordered skirt that cannot be changed at the bottom. Although the hem has been fitted along the bottom part of the skirt, the alteration is made at the waistline.

### Skirt Is an Even Length

1. Measure where the cross pins indicate the new length desired and record on work ticket. Remove pins.

2. Measure the amount to be shortened from the waist seam at the top of the skirt. Make a thread marking around the top of the skirt at this measurement, starting and ending at the garment opening.

### Skirt is Uneven Length

1. Leave pin line marking around the bottom of the skirt in place.

2. Place full length of skirt on the press board. Begin at the opening seam at the top of the skirt. Transfer the amount to be shortened to top of skirt with a pin line. Fig. D-25. Measure only at the center back, side seams, and center front. Transfer those measurements from the bottom to the top of the skirt. With your "fashion" eye, make a pin line between these key points. Remove pins at the bottom. Replace pins at the top with a thread line.

### For Either Even or Uneven Alteration

3. Make a vertical thread mark on skirt and bodice at center back or center front. If skirt has no side seams, make a thread mark where skirt meets side seams of bodice. Mark the inside seam tape with pencil dots at side seams, and center front, or center back.

4. Measure garment waist size and write on work ticket.

5. If there is a zipper opening, rip zipper from bottom to 2 inches (5 cm) above waist seam.

6. Rip skirt from bodice.

7. If top of skirt is fitted with darts, increase size and length of darts at the new waist seam to match original darts. Press darts toward the center (on ham). If skirt is pleated, stitch pleats flat on right side with an ease stitch, 1/8 inch (3 cm) above the new line. Check waist measurement on the work ticket to see how much needs to be eased in. If skirt is gathered at the top, machine baste a new shirring line 1/8 inch (.3 cm) above the new line.

8. Pin seam tape to the inside of the skirt 1/8 inch (.3 cm) above the new waistline. Match center front, center back, and side seam markings. Pull the shirring to match the size of the seam tape. Machine baste tape to skirt.

9. Cut away excess skirt

## Ch. 10: Fitting and Altering Hemlines

above seam allowance at top of skirt.

10. Pin skirt waist seam to bodice waist seam, matching center mark and side seams. Pin waist seams together between these markings.

11. Stitch inside the skirt waist circle. Make the final stitching on the new line just below the seam tape to hide all previous stitching.

12. Press the waist seam toward bodice (on seam roll).

13. Rip seam of skirt at zipper opening the same amount taken off the top of the skirt. Backstitch to reinforce opening.

14. Replace zipper following original method and on the same stitching lines.

### TO SHORTEN FLOOR-LENGTH CLOTHES

If gown has a hem, check the fitting pins. If the line is even, follow instructions for altering given under "Shorten Even Hem" and apply original hem finish. Sew with appropriate hand stitch or machine blind stitch.

If hemline is uneven, follow the instructions given under "Shorten Uneven Hem" and use the appropriate finish.

If gown has been finished with machine stitching at the hem edge, it should be redone by machine. Reread the instructions under "Machine Hem Finishes." Often it will be up to you to decide on the best finish for the fabric.

1. If the hem is to be shortened evenly all around, measure and make a pin line or thread line for the new hem. If the new hem length has been pinned, leave the pins in place or replace them with a thread line. A thread marking is advisable if the hem is extremely wide or the fabric is so sheer the pins won't hold. Do *not* cut hem yet.

2. Test needle, thread color, and stitch size on the folded edge of similar fabric.

3. Beginning at a side or center-back seam, fold the hem to the inside on the pin or thread line. Edge stitch bottom of hem fold with straight stitch or fine zigzag.

4. With sharp scissors, cut away the excess hem *close* to the stitching. Keep the rounded point of the scissors next to the garment fabric for smoother cutting. Hem is finished.

5. If a double edge-stitched finish is desired, fold the hem to the inside ¼ inch (.6 cm) below the new line. Follow the instructions given for the double edge-stitched hem in your sample under "Machine Hem Finishes."

### With Horsehair Braid

If hem has been finished with ½-inch (1.3 cm) horsehair braid, it should be refinished with braid.

1. Carefully rip off the horsehair braid, keeping it intact.

2. Cut away excess hem ½ inch (1.3 cm) below the new hemline. (See Step 1 in preceding alteration).

3. Read instructions under "Machine Hem Finishes" for the edge-stitched hem with horsehair. Follow the steps given, remembering to start and finish at a seam. Overlap the ends of the horsehair ½ inch (1.3 cm).

4. A "finish" press may be necessary to set the braid in place.

### WITH RIPPLE OR LETTUCE EDGE

If the gown has a ripple or lettuce edge, the same edge should be replaced.

1. Carefully cut away excess hem *on* the new hem line.

2. Practice and test needle, thread color, and stitch size on similar fabric or hem scraps before applying to garment hem. The hem is finished when last stitch is done. Do *not* press.

### With Train

This is the garment that has been fitted across the front and on one side.

1. Replace the pin line with thread line on the side that was pinned. End thread line at the center front of the skirt.

2. Remove pins. Spread garment on work table.

3. Match side seams and edges of original hem.

4. Pin hem edges together from beginning of thread line on the train to the center front of skirt.

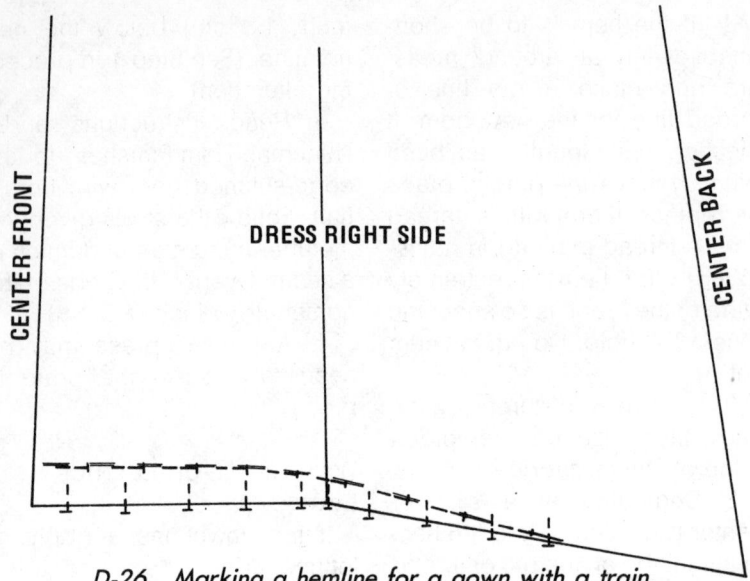

D-26. Marking a hemline for a gown with a train.

5. Insert a horizontal pin line through the thread line to the other side of the garment. Fig. D-26.

6. Turn garment over and carefully thread-mark along the pin line on the other side of the skirt. Be careful to pick up only one layer of fabric in the marking stitches.

7. Remove pins. Apply hem finish to match the unchanged hemline in back.

8. Press hem only if necessary.

## TO SHORTEN SEQUINED OR BEADED FABRICS

1. Use a medium- to heavyweight lining fabric in a matching or blending color. Measure the full depth of the hem from the new hem line to top of hem. Cut the facing strip this measurement plus 1/2 inch (1.3 cm) for seam allowance. Make it long enough to go around the skirt plus 1 inch (2.5 cm) for seam allowance. Join the ends with a 1/2-inch (1.3 cm) seam and press seam open.

2. Turn under one edge of facing 1/2 inch (1.3 cm) and lightly press this fold.

3. With garment right side out, slip bottom of hem over the press board. Place circle of facing over the hem—right side of facing to right side of skirt. Match the facing seam to a skirt seam and the pressed fold of the facing to the hem line marking. The hem should be open and flat with the facing *on* the skirt *above* the hemline marking. Fig. D-27.

4. Pin facing to new hem line across the facing fold.

5. Hand stitch in the facing fold line with a fine running stitch. Take a back stitch about every inch (2.5 cm) for reinforcement.

6. Pull facing down over hem. Pick-baste facing in place at bottom of hem. See Chapter 11 for these hand stitches.

7. Machine baste tops of facing and hem edges together 1/4 inch (.6 cm) from hem edge.

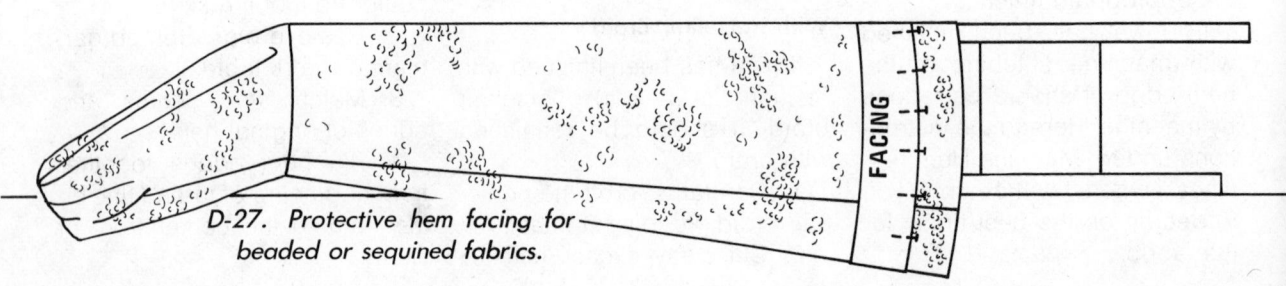

D-27. Protective hem facing for beaded or sequined fabrics.

### Ch. 10: Fitting and Altering Hemlines

Apply seam tape or lace finish along this stitching or overcast edge with a zigzag finish.

8. Fold hem along bottom fold of facing. Pin in place. Pin top of hem and finish with a hand blind stitch or tailor stitch.

### SHORTEN WIDE-LEGGED EVENING PANTS

This fitting has been done on one leg only.

1. Make a thread line on the new pin line all around the one leg. Remove all pins.
2. Pull opposite leg wrong side out. Slip it down inside the fitted leg. Match inseams and outseams at bottom. Fig. D-28. Match hems along bottom edges and pin together.
3. Insert a horizontal pin line at the thread line through both layers of fabric (both legs).
4. Pull inside leg to the outside and carefully thread-mark the pin line. Again, be careful to pick up only one layer of fabric. Remove all pins.
5. Duplicate the original hem finish on the new hem line.
6. Press the new hems only if necessary.

### Tailored Pants Lengths

#### TO SHORTEN TAILORED PANTS (TIME: 15 to 30 MINUTES)

Follow the instructions given in Chapter 12 under "Hemming Uncuffed Trousers."

To shorten pants with cuffs, follow the instructions in Chapter 12 under "Making Cuffs."

NOTE: Women's pants are hemmed or cuffed by the manufacturer while men's are not. Before following the instructions in Chapter 12 for these alterations, rip out the cuffs or hems. Press out all the lines.

#### TO LENGTHEN TAILORED PANTS (TIME: 15 TO 30 MINUTES)

1. Measure what is left of the hem after subtracting the amount the hem is to be dropped. Record this amount on work ticket. Remove pins.
2. Rip out hems and 2 inches (5 cm) of lower inseams.
3. Turn pants inside out. Stitch a facing to the bottom edge of the pants, beginning at the edge of the open inseam. Stitch inside leg circles with facing side up. Finish at the other edge of the matching inseam. Fig. D-29.

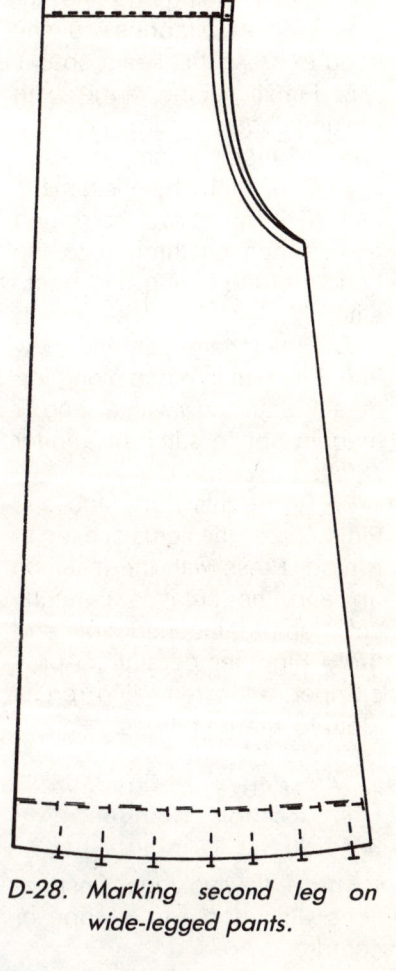

D-28. Marking second leg on wide-legged pants.

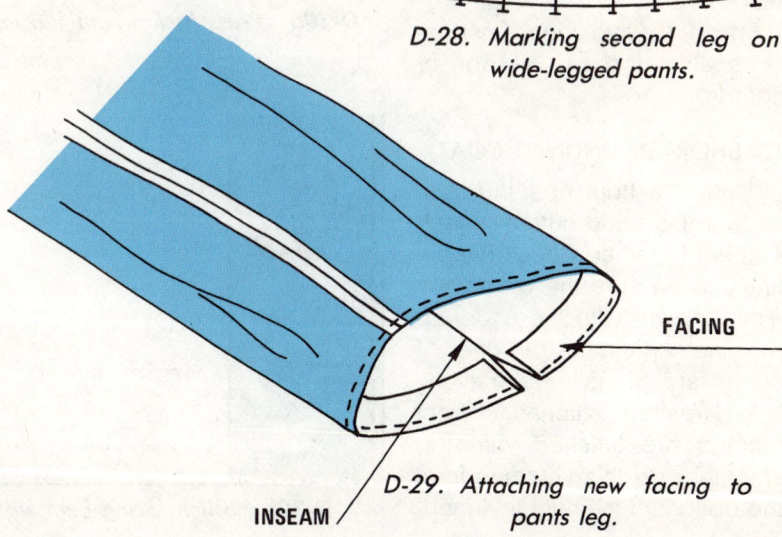

D-29. Attaching new facing to pants leg.

## Altering Ready-To-Wear Fashions

4. Press facings to the inside. (For heavy fabrics you may need to press this seam open.)

5. Finish facing edge with pinking shears or turn under the edge 1/2 inch (1.3 cm). Press.

6. Overstitch the inseams 1 inch (2.5 cm) above the ripped area. Stitch on through to the bottom of the facing and backstitch.

7. Press hems on the new line. Pin hem in place along top of facing and sew with a hand or machine blind stitch or a tailor stitch.

8. Turn pants right side out. Finish press the hems one leg at a time. Press with the inseams up and the creases carefully set. Use a dampened cloth and fairly high temperature. Apply clapper after removing press cloth to sharpen press.

### Altering Coat, Cape, or Coatdress Hemlines (Time: 45 minutes)

The following coat instructions also apply to a cape or coatdress.

### TO SHORTEN UNLINED COAT

1. Match front opening from neck to hem and button or fasten coat together. Check the pin lines to be sure the overlap is exactly even with the underlap pin line. Adjust the pin lines, if necessary, to make them even.

2. Rip hem stitches. If front facings are finished with top stitching, rip this stitching from the bottom of the hem to 4 inches (10 cm) above the new hemline. Do *not* rip facing seams.

3. Replace the pin line with a thread marking through the outer layer of the fabric. This releases the hem and facings.

4. Press and steam out the hem fold and old stitch marks.

5. Lightly press in the new hem on the thread line, starting with facing seam or fold. Remove thread line.

6. Turn up the hem on the facing. Fold the facing over the coat hem. Line up the facing hem with the coat hem, making the facing 1/8 inch (.3 cm) shorter than the coat hem. Press each facing hem. Fig. D-30a.

7. Reverse hem facings at hem (right side of facing to right side of coat) and pin across the hem fold with the facing side up. The facing hem fold will be 1/8 inch (.3 cm) above the hem fold on the coat.

8. Stitch along the facing hem fold from the front seam to the end of the facing. Backstitch. Fig. D-30b.

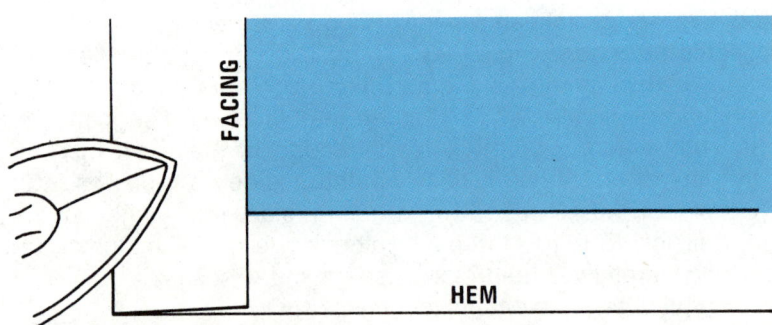

D-30a. Press facing hem 1/8 inch (.3 cm) shorter than coat hem.

D-30b. Stitch facing hem with facing turned wrong side out.

## Ch. 10: Fitting and Altering Hemlines

9. Using a hem gauge, chalk mark a line for hem depth.

10. Apply new hem finish at chalk line. Start 1 inch (2.5 cm) behind facing edge. End 1 inch (2.5 cm) beyond facing at the other end.

11. Cut away excess hem, leaving even hem depth under facings, if possible. (Some readymade coats have no hem under the facings. Do *not* repeat this practice in altering a coat hem except for raincoats.)

12. With the facings still reversed, fold facing hem back toward the right side along the new hem fold until the facing hem stitching shows slightly. Match seam edges exactly. Machine baste along the seam stitching. Stitch from top of hem to hem fold. This is another "invisible" control used to keep the hem in place under the facing. Fig. D-30c. This control is similar to the underarm control stitching explained in Chapter 6, Method 1, page 100.

13. Turn facings right side out. Force the points out sharp at the corners of the facings. Use the corner of your ruler to push the corner out in place.

14. Lay the coat out on a worktable. Pin the hem in place at the top. Pin facings to the hem.

15. Whipstitch the facings to the top layer of the hem. Sew hem with hand tailor stitch or blind stitch or a machine blind stitch, depending upon the fabric and hem finish.

16. If facings were topstitched, replace this stitching. Stitch on the right side of the coat, matching stitch length and thread color. Overstitch the original stitching about ½ inch (1.3 cm).

17. Press coat hem on the wrong side, using the clapper on the facings to sharpen the press.

### TO SHORTEN LINED COAT (TIME: 60 MINUTES)

1. Check front overlap and straighten pin lines as in Step 1 for unlined coats.

2. Replace pin line with thread marking, picking up one layer of fabric. Do not thread mark lining or facings.

3. Spread coat out on worktable. Adjust the lining so it does not sag from the shoulders and back neck. (A quick way to do this is by pressing the backs of your hands inside the coat neck and shoulders and pushing the lining against the coat in this area.)

4. About 12 inches (30.5 cm) from the new hemline, make a large diagonal basting through coat and lining to hold the lining in place. Begin and end at the front facings. Fig. D-31a.

5. Rip stitching in coat and lining hems. Rip the lining from

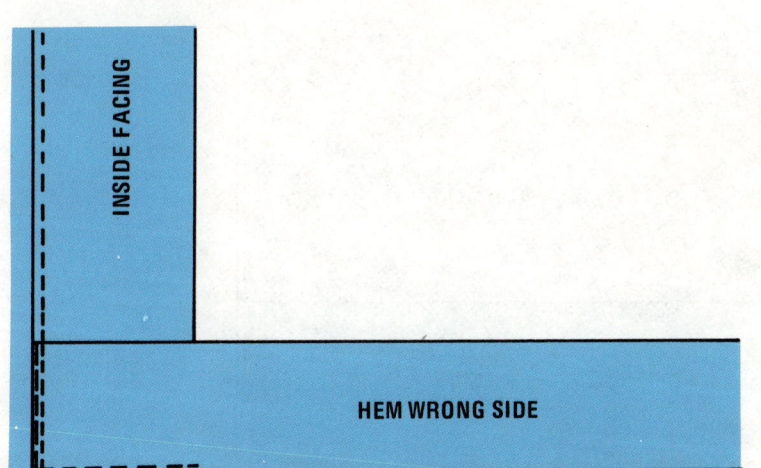

D-30c. Invisible control for hem facing.

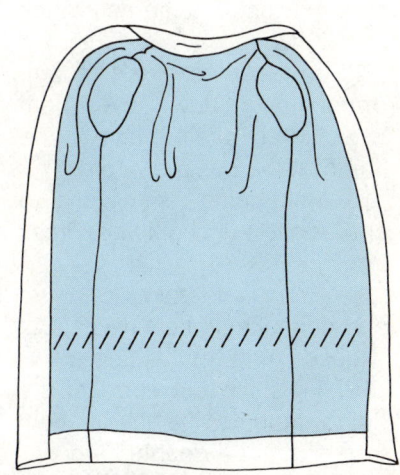

D-31a. Diagonal basting to hold lining in place.

## Altering Ready-To-Wear Fashions

the facing edge to 4 inches (10 cm) above the new hem line. If facings are top-stitched, rip stitching from bottom of hem to 4 inches (10 cm) above new hemline. Do *not* rip facing seams.

6. Press and steam out hem folds and stitch marks on coat and lining. Lightly press in the new hem on the thread line, starting with front facing seam or fold. Remove thread line.

7. Turn up hem on facing and fold facing over coat hem. Line up hem folds, adjusting facing hems so they will be 1/8 inch (.3 cm) shorter than coat hem. Do not worry about the lining yet.

8. Using a hem gauge, chalk a line for the hem depth.

9. Apply new hem finish at the chalk line, starting and ending at the edge of the facings.

10. Cut away the excess hem on both coat and facings.

11. Pin hem in place on the coat but just fold the hem back on the facings.

12. Spread coat out again. Bring lining down over hem fold. Lightly chalk a line on the lining at the coat hem fold.

13. Fold lining hem 1 inch (2.5 cm) above the chalk line. Press lightly.

14. From this fold, measure and chalk lining hem depth. Cut excess lining on this line.

15. Fold the cut edge of the lining hem to the inside hem fold, making a double hem.

16. Sew lining hem with hand or machine blind stitching.

17. Restitch edges of lining hems to edge of facings in line with the rest of that seam.

18. Turn edge of facings back at the hem fold, right side to right side. The lining hem should be between the layers of the facing hem and should be 1 inch (2.5 cm) shorter than the coat hem.

19. Place one pin across the turned back facing hem to hold the hem in place in the seams. Stitch seam from 1 inch (2.5 cm) above hem edge to bottom of fold. Fig. D-31b.

20. Cut through lining and facing seam at top of hem to seam stitching.

21. Turn facing to right side. Pin hem in place at top of hem.

22. Sew coat hem from facing edge to facing edge with appropriate hand stitching or machine blind stitching.

23. Press coat hem. Fold facings back over coat hems, and press. Use the clapper to sharpen front fold.

24. Turn the corner back about 3/4 inch (2 cm). Make a 1/2-inch (1.3 cm) long thread tack 1/2 inch (1.3 cm) from the edge of the facing and the hem fold edge at each side. Make 2-to-3-inch (5 to 7.5 cm) chain tacks at coat and lining side seams to attach the lining to the coat. Anchor these chain tacks at the tops of the hems. Fig. D-31c.

NOTE: Sometimes in a very full-style coat, the lining will be cut narrower than the coat at the bottom. In that case, make the chain tacks long enough so the coat "floats" away from the lining without any pull.

25. Remove the large, diagonal basting stitches.

### If Coat Fabric Is Bulky

For bulky fabrics it is not desirable to turn back the edge of

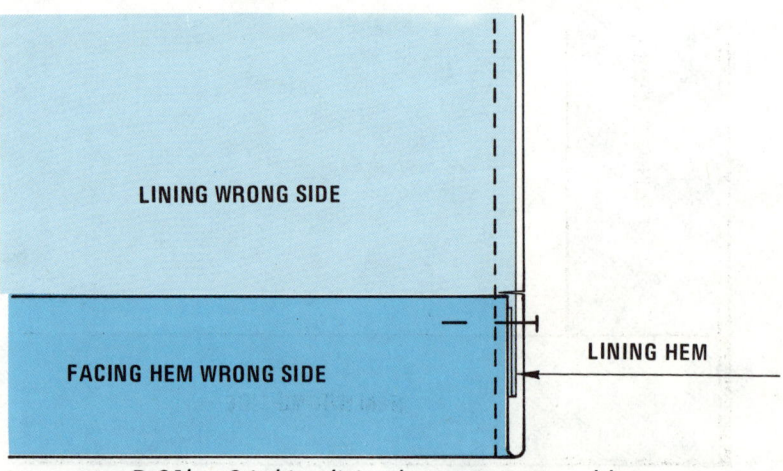

D-31b. *Stitching lining between coat and hem.*

### Ch. 10: Fitting and Altering Hemlines

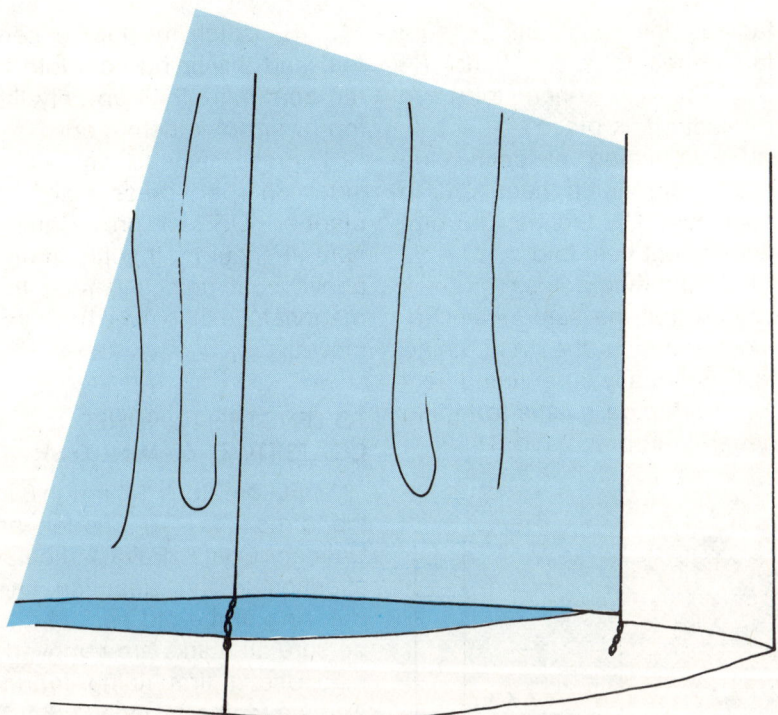

D-31c. Chain tack lining to coat hem.

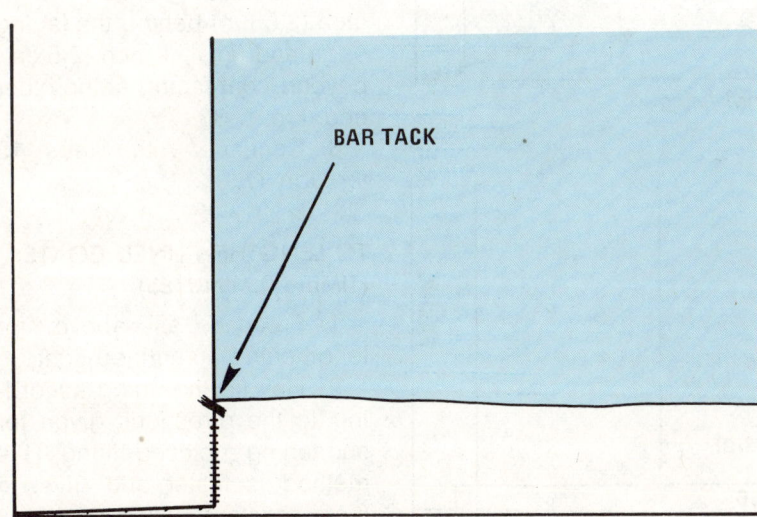

D-31d. Bar tack corner of hem for added reinforcement.

the facing to make a finished seam, as in Fig. D-31b. This creates too much bulk inside the coat overlap. For this type of hem, restitch the edges of the lining hem to the edge of the facings, as in Step 17. Sew the coat hem. Press the hem and facings, as in Steps 21, 22, 23.

1. Pin edge of facing seams to coat hem with the facing hem fold 1/8 inch (.3 cm) above the coat hem fold.

2. Slipstitch the hem folds together at the bottom. Whipstitch the edge of the facing to the coat hem.

3. Make a bar tack (Chapter 11, pg. 288) at the bottom corner of the lining where it is attached to the facing to reinforce the lining edge. Fig. D-31d.

4. Apply chain tacks at side seams as instructed in Step 24.

5. Press front facings on the wrong side, using the clapper to sharpen the press. Remove diagonal basting.

### TO SHORTEN COAT WITH CLOSED LINING (FRENCH LINING) (TIME: 60 MINUTES)

1. Follow all instructions given in "To Shorten Lined Coat" up to Step 8.

2. Do not apply any finish along the chalk line of the coat. Instead, cut excess hem on this line.

3. Follow Steps 11 and 12 under "To Shorten a Lined Coat."

4. Make another chalk mark on the lining below the first line.

## Altering Ready-To-Wear Fashions

Make it the same depth as the coat hem.

5. Cut excess hem away along the second chalk line.

6. Fold lining hem so it is ½ inch (1.3 cm) shorter than coat hem. Pin along fold of lining only. Restitch edge of lining to edge of facing.

7. Sew hems with a wide-spaced tailor stitch or machine blind stitching.

8. Press hem and facings.

9. Spread coat out and fold facings into position. Be sure facing-hem folds are ⅛ inch (.3 cm) above coat-hem fold and pin facings in place.

10. Beginning at each side seam, pin lining hem fold to coat hem 1½ inches (3.8 cm) above coat hem fold.

11. Pin lining across the back of the coat the same way. Remove pins in the front lining fold. Gradually taper lining hem fold from side seams to facing hem. Pin in place. Fig. D-32.

12. Slipstitch the facing hem fold and the lining hem fold to the coat hem. Pick up only the top layer of the hem fabric.

13. Press facings on wrong side. Sharpen press with the clapper. Do *not* press lining hem. It should fall softly in line above coat hem fold after the diagonal basting has been removed.

### TO LENGTHEN UNLINED COATS (TIME: 60 MINUTES)

1. Follow steps 1 through 8 in the directions "To Shorten an Unlined Coat." Pay particular attention to the steaming and pressing of the old hem fold to be sure all marks are removed.

2. Use a firm lining fabric. Apply a facing ½ inch (1.3 cm) above the hem marking line. Follow the directions under "Hem Finishes" for these facings. Hem facing should start 1 inch (2.5 cm) behind the facing edge and finish 1 inch (2.5 cm) beyond coat facing at the other end. Fig. D-33.

3. Continue with Steps 13 through 17.

### TO LENGTHEN LINED COATS (TIME: 70 MINUTES)

1. Proceed as above for lengthening an unlined coat.

2. Handle the lining according to the directions given for shortening a closed lining. This method is faster and gives a more satisfactory finish. It hides most of the hem facing and the

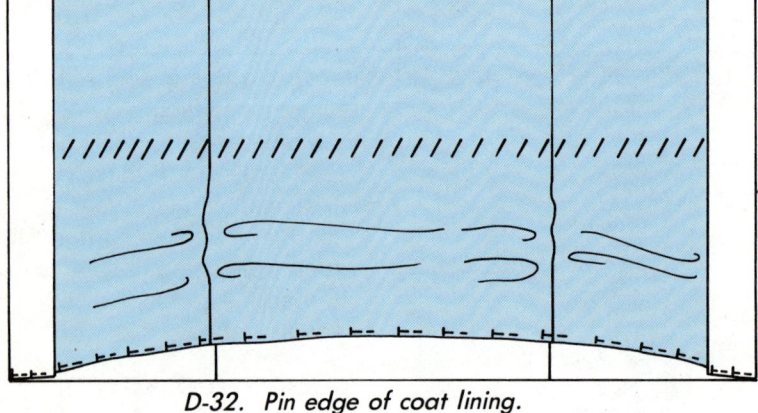

D-32. Pin edge of coat lining.

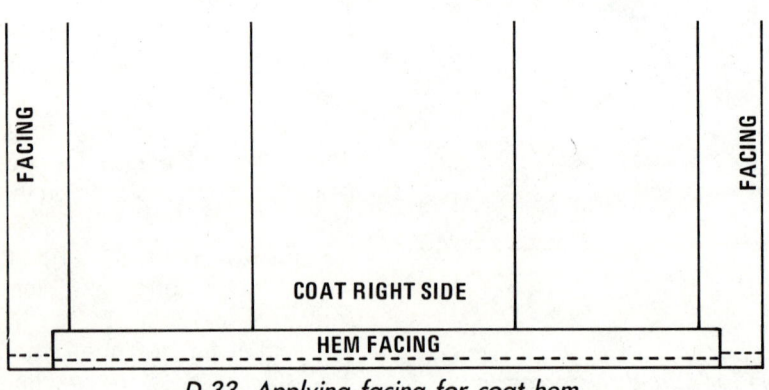

D-33 Applying facing for coat hem.

## Ch. 10: Fitting and Altering Hemlines

lining need not be faced. Simply turn bottom edge of lining under ½ inch (1.3 cm). Pin to coat hem facing as instructed in the *closed lining* directions. Finish with the same slipstitch.

3. Remove diagonal basting and press facings (using the clapper). Do *not* press lining.

### TO SHORTEN RAINCOAT HEM (TIME: 30 MINUTES)

This is the basic straight-line coat with the 1-inch (2.5 cm) machine-stitched hem. The facings are top-stitched ¼ inch (.6 cm) from the seam edges. This is often referred to as the "London Fog" finish, after the well-made coats of this brand name. Note the even stitching that makes the hem finish and is a trademark for this type of coat. These hems are always shortened with an even measurement.

1. Measure up from the bottom of the coat. Lightly chalk a line at the new hemline.

2. Mark another line 2 inches (5 cm) below the first line. Cut away excess hem *on* the second line. If the second line is below the machine stitching of the original hem, rip the stitching and then cut.

3. Rip the top stitching on the facings 2 inches (5 cm) above the new hem line.

4. Sharply press the new hemline. Press the facings to line up even with the new hem. Fold the cut edge of the hem to the inside hem fold, making a double hem. Sharply press this fold, starting at the edge of the facings.

5. Unfold the hem under the facings. Starting ½ inch (1.3 cm) from where the edge of the facing laps over the coat hem, cut away the second layer of the double hem along the press line. Fig. D-34a.

6. Turn facings to the outside at the hem folds. Match the hem folds right side to right side. Pin across the folds. Stitch the facings to the coat along the hem fold. Turn facings right side out and make a sharp point at the corners of the facings. Use the corner of your 6-inch ruler to push the corners out.

7. Insert one pin through the edge of the facings at the top of the hem. Then pin through the top of the hem and coat at each side seam and the center back.

8. Use matching thread and stitch length. Begin stitching on the inside of the coat 1 inch (2.5 cm) above where the top-stitching was ripped on the facing. In one continuous line, stitch down the facing, across the bottom of the facing, back up to the hem edge, and on to the hem. Pivot and make right-angle turns at each corner. Fig. D-34b. Use the point of a ripper to keep the hem in place while stitching. Apply the same finish on the other facing.

9. Sharply press hem and facings.

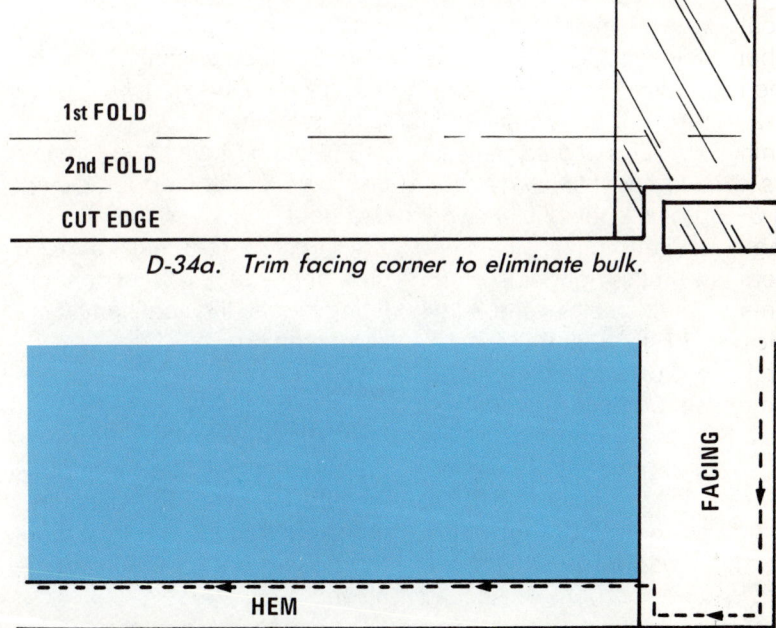

D-34a. Trim facing corner to eliminate bulk.

D-34b. Top stitching for "London Fog" finish.

## RAINCOAT WITH LINING (TIME: 45 MINUTES)

1. Rip lining from edges of coat facing to about 4 inches (10 cm) above the new hemline.

2. Measure, press, and cut lining, using the same measurements used for the coat hem. This will keep the lining hem shorter than the coat, as it was originally.

3. Stitch lining hem along the top fold. Restitch lining to edges of coat facing before finishing the coat hem.

## TO SHORTEN FAKE FUR COAT HEM (TIME: 60 MINUTES)

The amount the coat is to be shortened will have been written on the work ticket. There will be no pins left in the coat.

1. Rip out hems on lining and coat. Free lining from facing about 4 inches (10 cm) above the new line.

2. Press out hem creases in lining *only. Do not press fake fur as it is very heat sensitive.*

3. Spread coat out on work table. Lightly chalk the new hemline on the right side of the lining. Chalk another line 3 to 4 inches (7.6 to 10 cm) below the first line. Cut away excess lining on the second line.

4. On the wrong side of the coat, chalk the new hemline. Make a second chalk line 2½ to 3 inches (6.4 to 10 cm) below the first. Use large shears and cut excess hem on the second chalk line.

5. Lightly press lining hem on chalk line. Fold cut edge of hem to inside hem fold. Press second fold, making a double hem.

6. Pin lining hem up and sew with a hand or machine blind stitching.

7. Restitch edges of lining hem to edge of facings.

8. Turn hem up along inside chalk mark and hold hem in place with large metal or plastic clips. Turn hem on facings ⅛ inch (.3 cm) shorter than coat hem. Clip in place.

9. Sew hem with heavy-duty thread and a tailor stitch or catch stitch.

10. Fold facings back over hem, and hold in place with clips.

11. Slipstitch hem folds together at the bottom and whipstitch facing edges to coat hem.

12. Bar tack bottom corners of lining where it is attached to the facings. See Fig. D-31d.

13. Pound hem and facing corners with the clapper. *Do not use heat.*

14. Make 2-to-3-inch (5 to 7.6 cm) chain tacks to attach the lining hem to the coat hem at the side seams.

## TO SHORTEN VINYL COAT HEM (TIME: 60 MINUTES)

This hem was fitted with clips instead of pins. The measurement was recorded on the work ticket before the clips were removed.

1. Follow the instructions given for fake fur for ripping, marking, and cutting the new hems on the lining and the coat. If there is top stitching along the edge of the facings, rip to 4 inches (10 cm) above the new hem line.

2. Follow the fake fur instructions for pressing and finishing the lining hem. *Do not press vinyl.*

3. To finish the edges of the facings where the lining is to be restitched, follow instructions and illustrations under "To Shorten Lined Coat" in Steps 17 through 21, page 272.

4. Turn hem up and hold in place with the clips. Sew with a tailor stitch.

5. Tack edge of facings to coat at top of hems with ½-inch (1.3 cm) chain tacks in addition to the side seam chain tacks. Fig. D-35.

6. After new hem has been completed, restitch facing top stitching with matching thread and stitch length. Before restitching, lightly spray the machine bed with silicone spray or talcum powder and loosen the pressure on the presser foot.

## TO SHORTEN SYNTHETIC SUEDE COAT HEM (TIME: 60 MINUTES)

This hem is fitted with clips instead of pins. The measurement is recorded on the work ticket.

1. Rip out hems on lining and coat. Rip bottom of lining free from facings to 4 inches (10 cm) above the new hemline. If coat

## Ch. 10: Fitting and Altering Hemlines

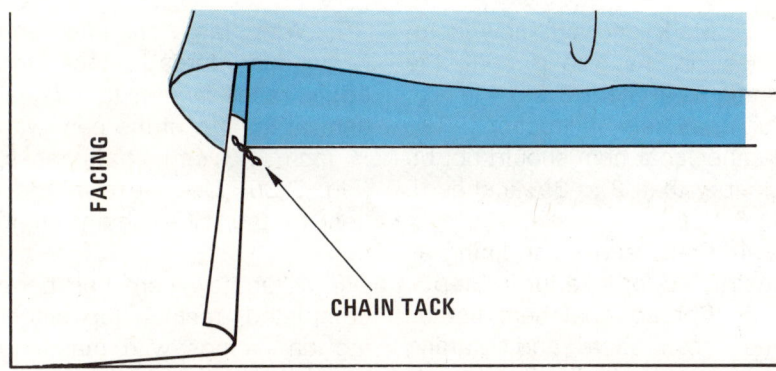

D-35. Chain tack lining and facing to coat hem.

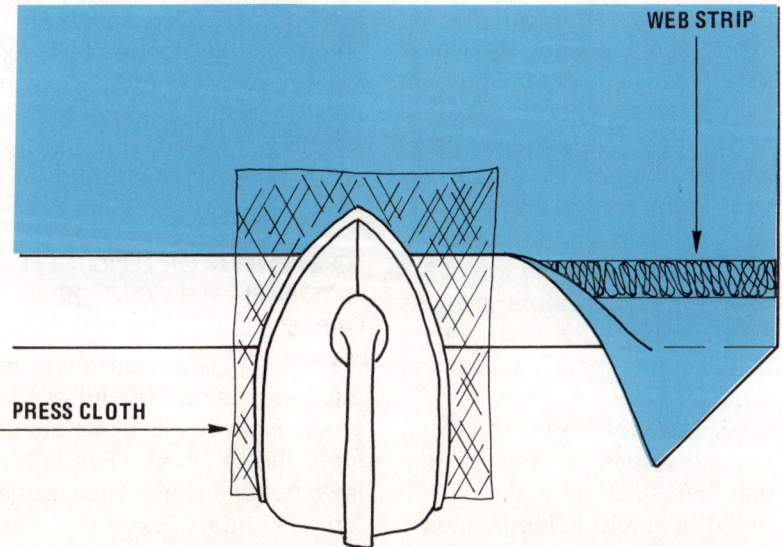

D-36. Apply heat to loosen hem held by fusible web.

hem has been put in with a fusible web material, the hem must be separated with heat. Cover hem with thin cloth and apply heat to soften adhesive. Pull hem apart. Fig. D-36.

2. Press out hem creases in lining and coat, using a thin press cloth. Press on wrong side of coat.

3. Spread coat out. On the right sides of coat and lining *lightly* chalk the new hemline. Chalk a second line for the hem depth. On the coat this should be 2½ inches (6.4 cm) and on the lining 3 to 4 inches (7.6 to 10 cm) below the first line.

4. Trim coat and lining along the second chalk lines.

5. Press lining hem. Sew as instructed in Step 5, 6 under "Shorten Fake Fur."

6. Fold coat hem on new line. Cover with thin press cloth, and press hem fold on hem side with low heat. Apply clapper to set the press. Press facing hem ⅛ inch (.3 cm) shorter than coat and apply clapper to sharpen press.

7. Cut 1 inch (2.5 cm) strips of fusible web material. Cut enough strips to equal the measurement of the coat hem from edges of facings. The strips should be fairly short (about 10 inches, 25 cm) for ease of application.

8. Spread hem out on the press board with hem folded in place. Begin at the end of the facing on one side. Pick up top layer of hem and lay web strip just below the hem edge. Replace hem. Set iron on low, steam temperature. Cover the hem with a thin press cloth and apply iron on hem edge. Press 10 seconds in one place and then set with the clapper. If the web has not melted enough, apply heat a little longer than 10 seconds. Do *not* move iron back and forth. Repeat pressing in small areas, slightly overlapping ends of web strips, to end of opposite facing. Fig. D-36.

9. Restitch ends of lining hem to edge of facings. Run the machine stitching to the bottom of the hem fold of the facings.

10. Tack edge of facings to the coat at the top of the hem

## Altering Ready-To-Wear Fashions

with ½-inch (1.3 cm) chain tacks in addition to the side seam chain tacks. Fig. D-35.

11. Check right side of hem. If press marks show, remove with a clothes brush.

NOTE: If facings have been top-stitched, follow the instructions under Step 6 for vinyl coats.

### TO SHORTEN LEATHER COAT (TIME: 60 MINUTES)

This coat has been fitted with clips and the measurement recorded on the work ticket.

1. Rip out the hem on the lining. Rip bottom of lining free from facings to 4 inches (10 cm) above the new hemline.
2. Spread coat hem out on press board, wrong side up. Lay a thin press cloth over hem and apply low temperature heat to hem with a dry iron. Leave iron on hem long enough to soften the glue which holds the hem together. Carefully pull hem apart after each application of heat.
3. Mark and cut new hemlines on lining and coat, the same as in Steps 3 and 4 in fake fur coat hem instructions. The leather coat hem should not be deeper than 2 to 2½ inches (5 to 6.4 cm).
4. Press and finish lining as instructed for fake fur in Step 5.
5. Spread coat hem flat on the press board and, starting with edge of facing hem, apply rubber cement or fabric glue evenly on hem allowance. Spread with a small brush to the inside hem marking. Allow glue to get "tacky." Fold facing hem ⅛ inch (.3 cm) above hem fold and "press" fold with hard pressure of clapper. Do small portions of the hem at a time. Try to use just enough glue to hold and not spill over the top of the hem edge. Remember to press with clapper after each portion of hem has been glued and folded.
6. Restitch ends of lining hem to edges of facings. Run machine stitching to the bottom of the hem fold in the facings.
7. With large needle and heavy-duty thread, tack the edges of the facings to the coat hem at the top of the hem with ½-inch (1.3 cm) chain tacks. (Fig. D-35). Use these in addition to the side seam chain tacks.
8. After new hem has been completed, restitch top stitching on facings with matching thread and stitch length. Before stitching leather, spray machine bed with silicone spray or talcum powder. Use special machine needle for leather and rolling presser foot. Do not backstitch at the end of the top stitching. Instead, pull the last stitch through to the wrong side, tie a knot, and trim thread.

### TO SHORTEN OR LENGTHEN FLOOR-LENGTH COAT OR CAPES

Follow instructions given for altering hems in full-length coats. Floor-length coats are altered the same way. Fabric and style determine the finish of coat facings and hems.

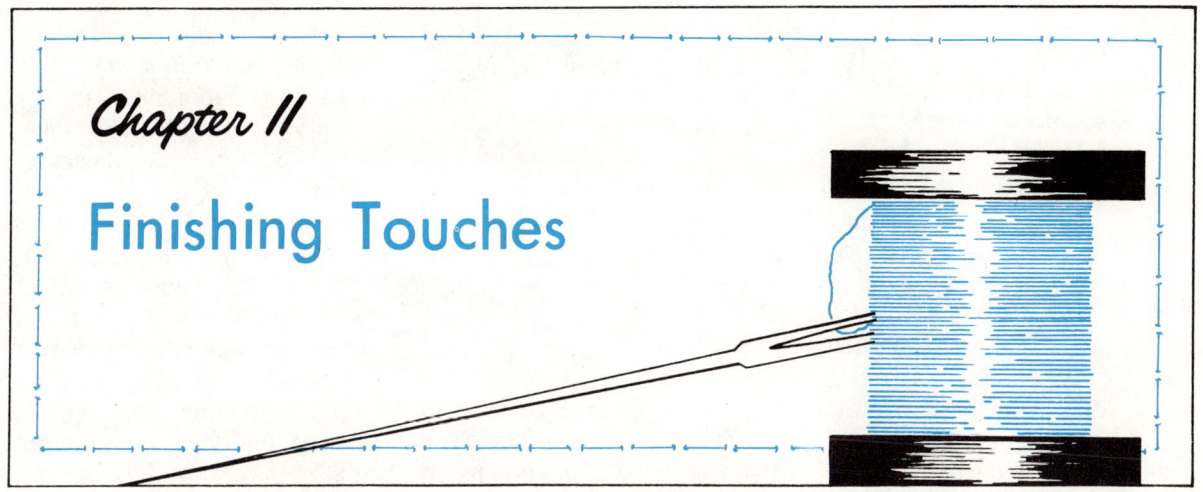

# Chapter 11
# Finishing Touches

Many people can "sew a fine seam," follow directions, and make beautiful garments. However, they often are not completely satisfied because something just doesn't look the way they want it to. Some part of the garment does not hang "just right" or lie in place without constant adjusting.

The same can be said about ready-to-wear garments. Did you ever wonder why the more expensive garments look so much better than the less expensive ones? There is more involved than clever lines and handsome fabrics. These clothes have special stitches, controls, and inside touches that make the difference.

If you are going to work on clothes containing these "secrets," you will need to know why each special touch is used and how to replace it. You may also need to add some type of control to a garment to give it that special look.

The techniques described in this chapter are designed to help you learn to gain speed in your work and to give garments that special couturier look.

You will find it to your advantage to practice these techniques on samples. Then, when you run into them on finished clothes, you will understand what needs to be done and will have the skill to do it. Also, the samples will be available for quick and easy reference to refresh your memory.

To make your samples, use pieces of muslin cut to about 7 by 10 inches (17.8 to 25.4 cm). This size fits neatly into 8-by-10½-inch (20 by 26.7 cm) see-through plastic envelopes that can be put into a 3- or 5-ring notebook. You may also want to write the directions directly on the muslin so you don't have to bother to look them up each time you need to use the techniques. You may, if you wish, apply your practice stitches to the mini dresses you made following the instructions given in Chapter 6.

## HAND STITCHES

Unless otherwise instructed, a Milliner's needle and a single strand of matching thread are used for all hand stitches. Use a No. 9 Milliner's needle for small stitches and a No. 7 needle for heavy fabrics and longer stitches.

### Thread Markings

The marking stitch is an uneven basting stitch used to mark new lines for a garment alteration. The stitch is spaced so 1 inch (2.5 cm) shows on the top

## Altering Ready-To-Wear Fashions

E-1. Marking stitch.

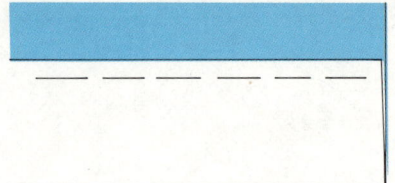

E-2. Uneven basting.

of the fabric and ¼ inch (.6 cm) on the underneath side. Fig. E-1. Pick up only one layer of fabric when marking and do not go through seams, darts, zipper tapes, or pockets. Leave the thread loose with only a large knot at each end to keep it from pulling out as you work with the garment.

NOTE: A 1-inch-long (2.5 cm) thread marking is sometimes used instead of clips or notches to re-match parts of garments that must be separated for altering. For example, center front markings on skirt and bodice to be ripped apart for alteration.

### Basting Stitches

In today's "instant sewing," very little use is made of basting. When it is necessary, however, it is important to use the correct stitch and basting thread in matching color.

### UNEVEN BASTING

Uneven basting is used to hold up two thicknesses of fabric as in sleeve or skirt hems or to control facings for a second fitting.

Make the same stitch as for a marking stitch. However, space it closer together—½ inch (1.3 cm) on the inside and ⅛ inch (.3 cm) on the outside. Fig. E-2.

### SLIP BASTING

This stitch is used to baste details or restyled seams, as pinned. The basting is done on the right side of the garment but when turned over and laid flat, it is ready for the machine stitching. For example, a plaid or striped fabric may be matched easier using the slip basting.

Fold the seam allowance of one piece to the inside. Lay the fold along the seam line of the matching piece carefully lining up the design. Slip baste together.

The stitches are spaced ½ inch (1.3 cm) equally top and bottom of the seam or detail. The needle goes into the top fold at the point where it comes out of the bottom layer. Slide the needle into only the bottom layer of the fold and do not come through the top layer. Although the sewing is done on the right side of the garment, no stitches will be seen on the right side. Fig. E-3.

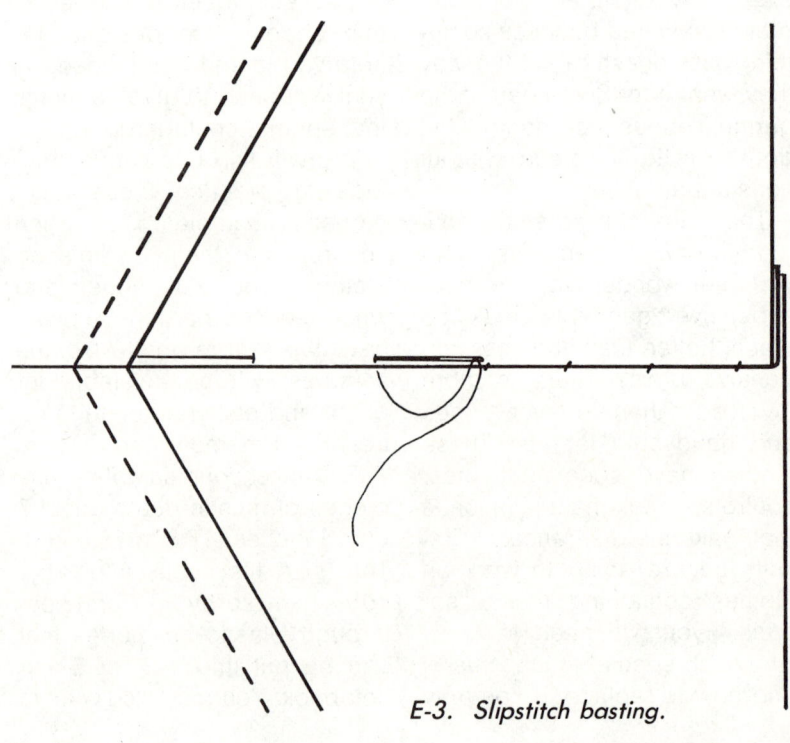

E-3. Slipstitch basting.

Ch. 11: Finishing Touches

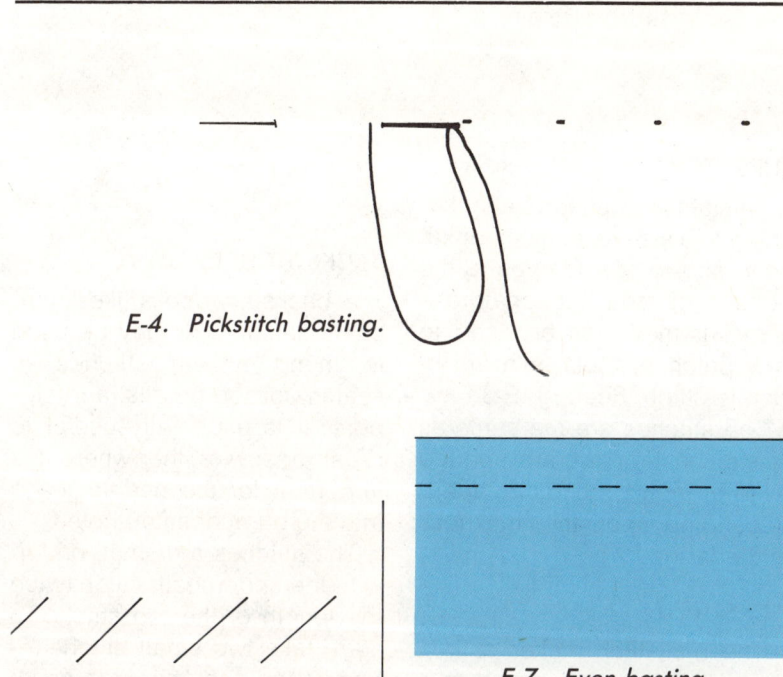

E-4. Pickstitch basting.

E-7. Even basting.

E-5. Diagonal basting (large).

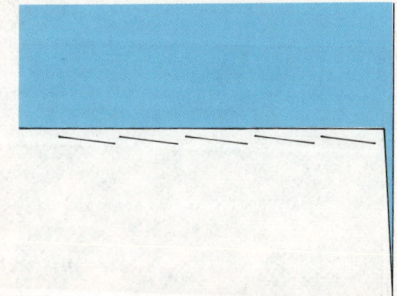

E-6. Diagonal basting (small).

side. The needle should go back in just one thread of fabric back of where it came to the surface. The result is a line of tiny, even dots of thread on the top of the seam. Fig. E-4.

## DIAGONAL BASTING

This is very fast and is used for a greater area of control while working on a garment. For example, the large diagonal stitch is used to hold linings to the outer garment to speed the final finishing of alterations.

This stitch is an even 1 inch (2.5 cm) on top and 1 inch (2.5 cm) underneath in a slanting line. Use large knots at each end. Fig. E-5.

A smaller diagonal basting is used in place of pins to hold hems or facings in place for hand finishing in fabrics that pin-mark. For this purpose, the stitch should be 1 inch (2.5 cm) on top and ¼ inch (.6 cm) underneath. Apply loosely with a knot at each end. Remove carefully as soon as the work is finished. Fig. E-6.

## PICK BASTING

This is a very secure, almost invisible basting stitch, used to baste in zippers or surface details for second fittings. If neatly done and evenly spaced, it need not be ripped out after use. Instead, another pick stitch may be inserted between the original basting stitches to give a final finish. Machine stitching can be made on top of the pick basting. The pick stitch basting should be done *on* the line to be stitched for finishing the seam after fitting.

Pick basting is spaced ½ inch (1.3 cm) apart with a tiny backstitch on the top and a ½-inch (1.3 cm) stitch on the in-

## EVEN BASTING

This stitch is used to prepare altered seams for a second fitting on fabric that would be marked by a machine basting.

The stitches are even and short—¼ inch (.6 cm)—and should be firm. The basting should be done *on* the seam line for a true fit. Secure with a back stitch at each end of thread or seam. Fig. E-7.

281

*Altering Ready-To-Wear Fashions*

## Finishing Stitches

### RUNNING STITCH

This is basically the same stitch used for even basting except the stitches are much closer together—as close as the fabric will allow. This stitch can be used instead of machine stitching to mend seams, to ease one seam to another, and for fine, controlled, shirring. Combined with a tiny backstitch every 1 inch (2.5 cm) or so, it becomes a strong control stitch to hold a stretched seam inside a neckline or pocket finish. Fig. E-8.

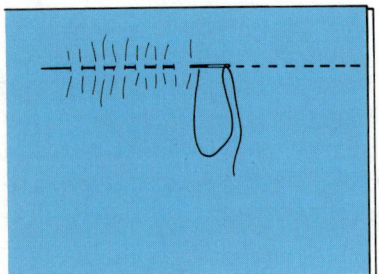

E-8. Running stitch.

### SLIPSTITCH

This stitch is used to attach a lining to a sleeve, coat, or jacket hem, and to sew facings to the bottom of coat or coatdress hems. It may also be used to sew patch pockets with an invisible stitch. See Fig. E-3.

The stitches are the same as in slip basting but are spaced $1/8$ to $1/4$ inch (.3 to .6 cm) apart, depending upon the thickness of the fabric.

### PICKSTITCH

The pickstitch makes a firm, decorative stitch. It can give a high-fashion look when used for zipper insertion or pocket application in place of machine stitching.

This stitch looks the same on the surface as the pick basting. Underneath the stitch is closer together—$1/4$ inch (.6 cm) apart. See Fig. E-4.

### BACKSTITCH

A backstitch looks like a machine stitching. It may be used to mend broken stitches in seams, for top details, and zippers. It is especially useful to repair or sew leather where it is important for the needle to go into the original stitch holes.

The stitches are small on top with the underneath stitch twice the length of the top stitch. To start, take two small stitches—one on top and one underneath the fabric. Bring the needle back to the top at the end of the second stitch and pull the needle and thread through. Reinsert the needle exactly at the end of the first stitch. Push it forward to one stitch length beyond the point where the thread came out. Pull needle through again. Fig. E-9.

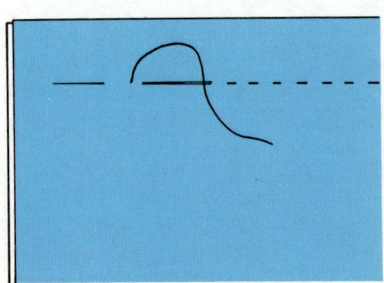

E-9. Backstitch.

## FELLING OR OVERHAND STITCH

Use a No. 9 Sharp needle.

The fell stitch is used to sew the undercollar to a tailored top collar, especially in menswear. It is also used to sew coat and jacket linings to inside facings and fur pieces. The stitches should be 1/4 inch (.6 cm) or less apart.

When the felling stitch is used on a man's jacket collar, the undercollar will be a single thickness of felt. Lay the cut edge of the felt just below the fold of the top layer. Insert the needle between the layers of the fold in the top-collar seam, and come up through the cut edge of the felt. In a straight line from the spot where the needle came through the felt, move to the fold of the upper collar and reinsert needle through the one layer of the seam allowance. Take the longer part of the stitch in the collar seam allowance and re-emerge through the felt edge again. Fig. E-10.

To sew a lining to a facing or hem, handle the folded edge of the lining the same as you would the cut edge of the felt undercollar. Follow the directions above for the stitch. The folded edge of the lining will be flat against the edge of the facing or hem it is to be attached to.

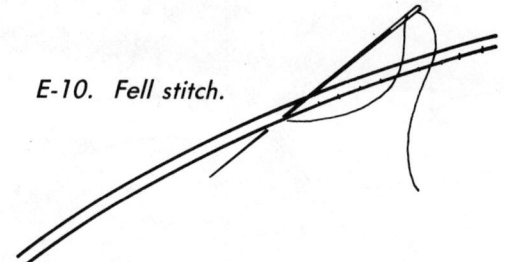

E-10. Fell stitch.

## WHIPSTITCH

This stitch is used for lace and design appliqué and to apply bands of ribbon, lace, beads, or sequins. It is also used for hemming sweater knits. The stitches will stretch and are so fine they will be lost in the knit.

The whipstitch differs from the felling stitch in that the stitches are much closer together and go a little deeper into the edge of the fold. Fig. E-11.

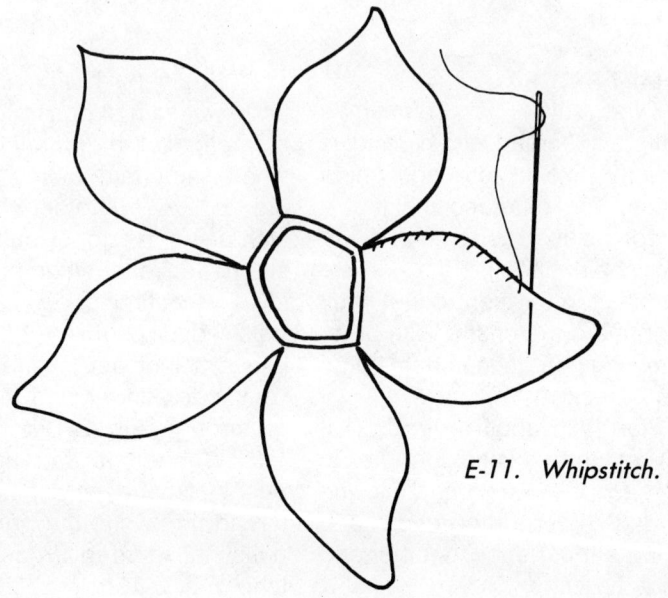

E-11. Whipstitch.

## Altering Ready-To-Wear Fashions

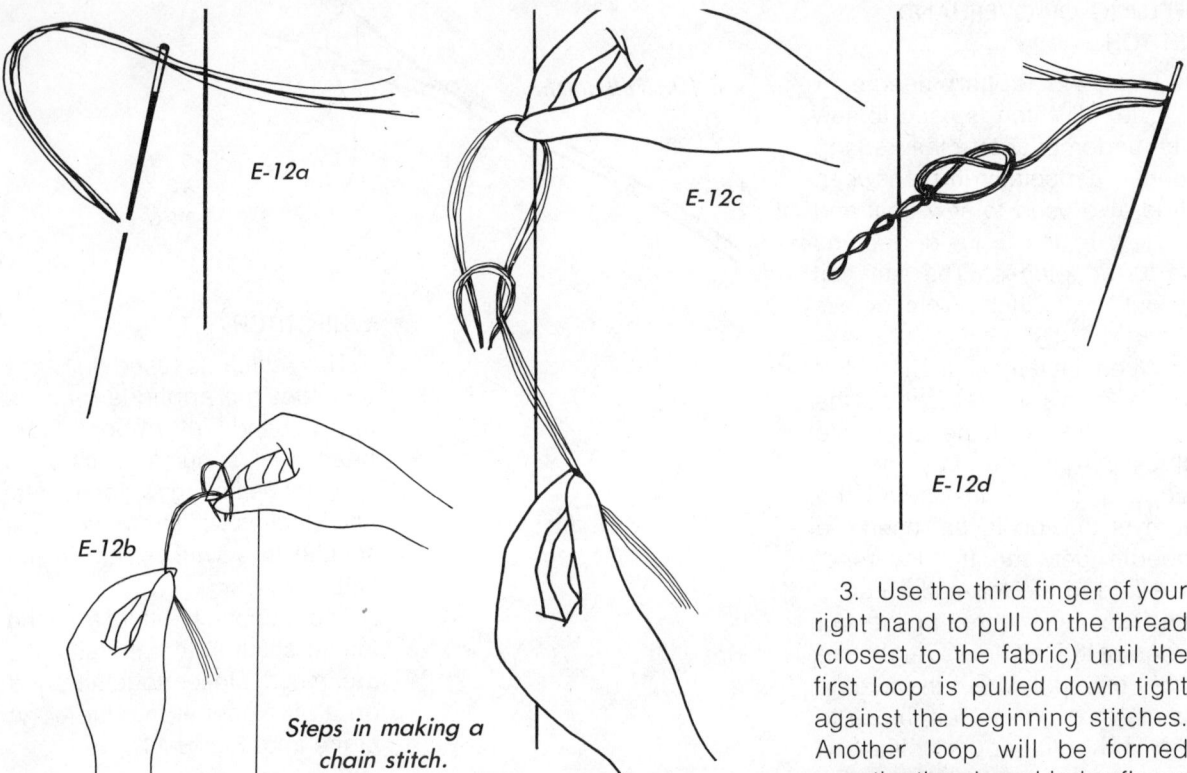

Steps in making a chain stitch.

### CHAIN STITCH

This stitch is sometimes called a "thread chain" and is exactly like a crochet chain stitch. The difference is that a needle is used to begin and end the chain and the fingers are substituted for the crochet hook in forming the chain. With practice, you can do the chain stitch very quickly.

Start with about 2 yards (1.8 m) of thread and double it. Thread the two ends of the thread through the needle and bring all four ends together and knot the ends.

1. Begin by hiding the knot under a seam, if possible. Make a small stitch through the fabric where the chain tack is to start. Fig. E-12a. Reinforce this stitch with one slip knot or buttonhole stitch. Make another stitch on top of the first one but do not pull it down tight to the fabric. Leave a loop large enough for your index finger and thumb to go through. Fig. E-12b.

2. With thumb and index finger of left hand, hold the straight thread firm while the right hand pulls the thread through the loop. Fig. E-12c.

3. Use the third finger of your right hand to pull on the thread (closest to the fabric) until the first loop is pulled down tight against the beginning stitches. Another loop will be formed over the thumb and index finger in the meantime.

4. Continue pulling loops through and down tight to the other loops to the desired length for the chain. On the last loop needed, pull the needle through the loop and pull tight. This will lock the last loop so the chain will not pull out. Fig. E-12d.

5. At the point on the garment where you want the other end of the chain to be anchored, use the needle to fasten several small stitches. This second end of the chain may also be sewn to a snap rather than fastening it to the garment. This will be explained further in the explanation of "Lingerie Keepers."

## Uses for Chain Loops

*Belt Carriers* made of chain loops are used on most ready-to-wear clothes to hold belts in place. The chain should be at least 1/4 inch (.6 cm) longer than the belt width. Divide the chain equally above and below the waist seam or waist clip (if shift style). Fig. E-13. This will help the belt stay in place.

*Bra Carriers* are used on low-backed garments to control the neckline and prevent the bra from sliding into view. The chain should start on the inside center back neckline, 1/4 inch (.6 cm) below neck edge and end 2 to 3 inches (5 to 7.6 cm) below neck edge. It should be just loose enough to allow one end of the bra back to slip through before fastening. If there is a zipper opening in back, sew the chain on one side of the opening seam. Fig. E-14.

*Hanger Bar or Loops* are used on wide-necked garments to keep clothes on a slotted hanger. Make a 1-inch (2.5 cm) chain loop across the shoulder seam 1/4 inch (.6 cm) from the neck edge. Reinforce at each end with extra stitches. When the dress is hung on a slotted hanger, the slots are caught in the loops. Fig. E-15a.

To help keep a skirt on a hanger, 3-inch (7.5 cm) loops may be attached to the sides of the skirt. The chain should begin and end at the same spot forming a long, loose loop. Fig. E-15b.

Ch. 11: Finishing Touches

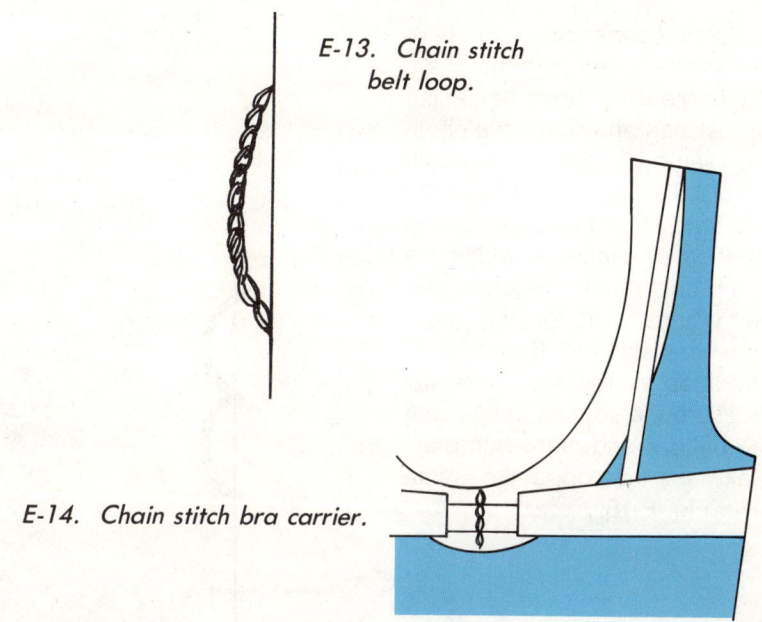

E-13. Chain stitch belt loop.

E-14. Chain stitch bra carrier.

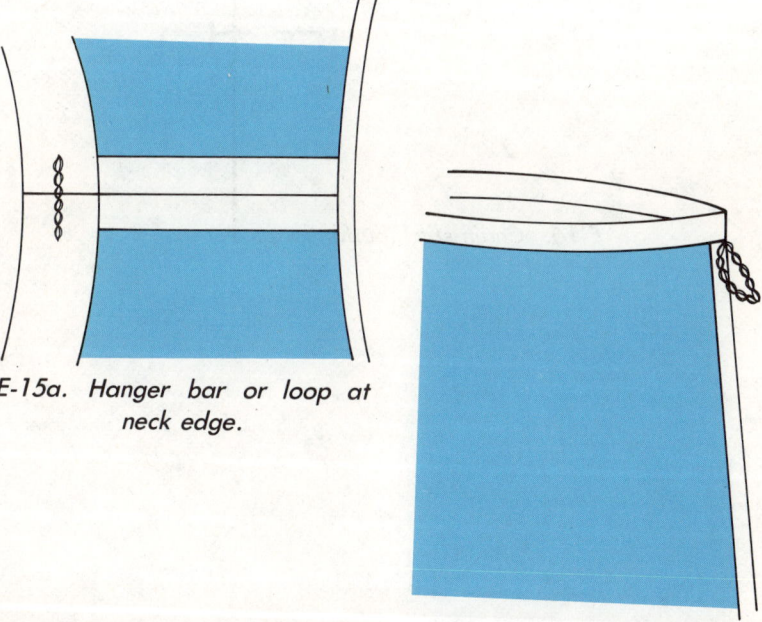

E-15a. Hanger bar or loop at neck edge.

E-15b. Skirt hanger loop.

### Altering Ready-To-Wear Fashions

*Button Loops* can be made or replaced quickly with the chain stitch. Measure the button at the widest part and make the chain the same length. The chain should start on the edge of the fold with three tiny overlapping stitches to anchor it. Make the chain the length desired and end it back at the fold with three more tiny stitches. If more than one loop is needed, carefully measure the spaces in line with the buttons and mark with pins. Make all the loops the same size. Fig. E-16.

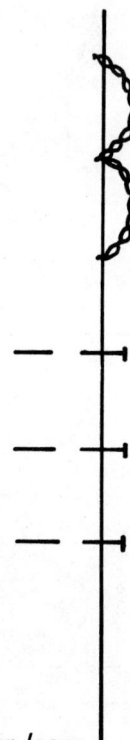

E-16. *Chain stitch button loops.*

*Hook Loops* made from thread rather than metal are considered a "custom" touch. If neatly made, the loops are practically invisible and do not mar the outward appearance of a garment. They are usually used on jackets that are to be worn open. The hook is sewn to the overlapping edge of the jacket. The thread loop goes on the underlap side in line with the hooks.

These small loops may also be used on formal or bridal wear to attach removable panels and trains.

The hook loop should be flat, firm, and tight. It must be reinforced at each end as in button loops. It should be just long enough to catch the metal hook and hold it—not more than 1/4 inch (.6 cm).

Ch. 11: **Finishing Touches**

*Lingerie Keepers* or strap holders are attached to the inside shoulder seams to control slip and bra straps. They also help to control the neckline.

For normal shoulder width, begin the chain on the shoulder seam 2 inches (5 cm) from the armhole seam. Make the chain about 1¼ inches (3 cm) long. Finish off the chain and thread the needle through one hole of the ball part of the snap. Make several stitches to secure snap to chain. Sew socket part of snap to the seam at this point. You will have ¼-inch (.6 cm) ease for the straps. The keeper is snapped over the lingerie straps after the garment has been put on and the shoulders are in place on the figure. Fig. E-17a.

If the garment shoulders are narrow, the snap will have to be placed closer to the neck seam and the chain will begin near the armhole seam.

Lingerie keepers may also be applied to the lower sides of low-cut necklines for more control. Fig. E-17b.

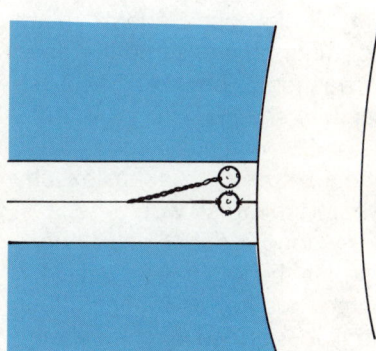

E-17a. *Chain stitch lingerie keeper.*

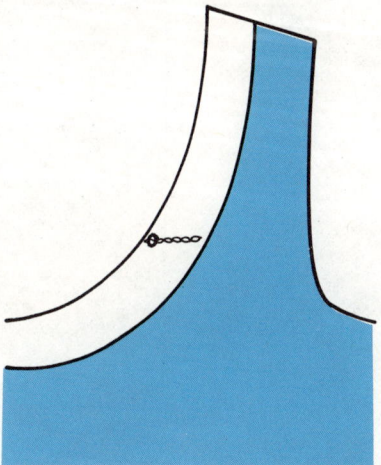

E-17b. *Chain stitch lingerie keeper for scoop neckline.*

*Chain Tacks* are used to hold two parts of a garment together while allowing for movement or "swing." These tacks may be from ¼ to 3 inches (.6 to 7.6 cm) long. Common uses of chain tacks are:

• To tack collars and cuffs to a garment.
• To attach a cloth belt to a garment when belt carriers are undesirable.
• To control "floating" panels or free-hanging jacket and coat linings.
• To allow "play" in shoulder pads and keep them from pulling.

NOTE: If garments are bulky or subject to hard wear, such as sports and winter clothes, use two strands of buttonhole twist or heavy-duty thread to make the chain tacks.

### Altering Ready-To-Wear Fashions

## HONG KONG STITCH

This is a smooth, satin-finish loop or tack found on the better garments imported from the Far East. This stitch may be used instead of the chain stitch for a finer custom finish. It is also used for decorative bartacking at points of stress.

Use four strands of thread for greater speed and strength. Work on the right side of the garment but with the beginning thread knot on the underneath side. Make two stitches—one right on top of the other—so you will be working with eight strands of thread at once. These are your base stitches. The length of the base is discussed below. Pull the stitches flat against the fabric but do not allow any pucker. Slip the needle under the stitches on one side. Pull it up and over the base stitches and back under from the first side again. The thread will be wrapped around the base stitches. Keep wrapping the thread until the base stitches are entirely covered with a smooth, tight, satin-like, cover. Finish with a slip knot on the wrong side. Fig. E-18a.

NOTE: For greater speed and ease, slip a smooth-surfaced, firm object under the base stitches before wrapping them. You can use a short, narrow strip of cardboard for a bartack or a pencil for a button loop.

The length of the base stitches is determined by their purpose.

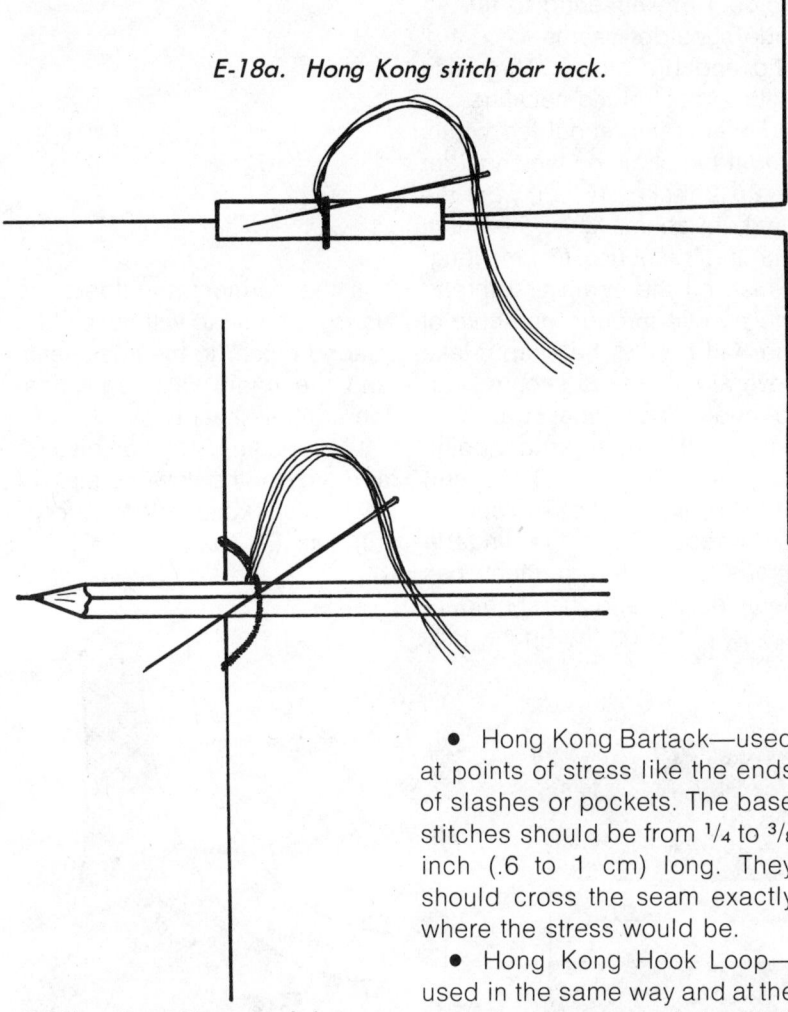

E-18a. Hong Kong stitch bar tack.

E-18b. Hong Kong stitch button loops.

- Hong Kong Bartack—used at points of stress like the ends of slashes or pockets. The base stitches should be from $1/4$ to $3/8$ inch (.6 to 1 cm) long. They should cross the seam exactly where the stress would be.
- Hong Kong Hook Loop—used in the same way and at the same location as a chain stitch hook loop. Base stitches should be from $1/8$ to $1/4$ inch (.3 to .6 cm).
- Hong Kong Button Loops—used in place of chain stitch button loops. Base stitches should be the same length as the widest part of the button. Begin and end the same as a chain button loop. Fig. E-18b.

Ch. 11: Finishing Touches

## BUTTONHOLE STITCH

Use a No. 7 Sharp needle and two strands of mercerized cotton thread treated with fabric softener.

Except for those with bound buttonholes, most manufactured garments have machine-made buttonholes. You will need to use the hand buttonhole stitch to make extra buttonholes, to mend frayed buttonholes, and for eyelets in a belt. The stitch is also used as another way of making button loops.

The stitch is made by looping the thread around the needle and then pulling the stitch up in a straight line with the raw edge of the hole. This forms a small loop or "purl" along the cut edge for the finish.

### Buttonholes

Thread mark the length and placement of the button hole. Machine stitch 1/16 inch (or .2 cm) on each side of the placement mark and across each length mark. Use a stitch length of 12 stitches to an inch (2.5 cm). Fig. E-19a. Cut through the center of this stitching and remove the thread markings.

Insert the needle from the underside. Do not knot the end of the thread. Leave about an inch of thread underneath so you won't pull it all the way through as you sew. Work the buttonhole stitch on the right side, starting at the straight or inside end. Insert the needle toward you at the outside stitching line and

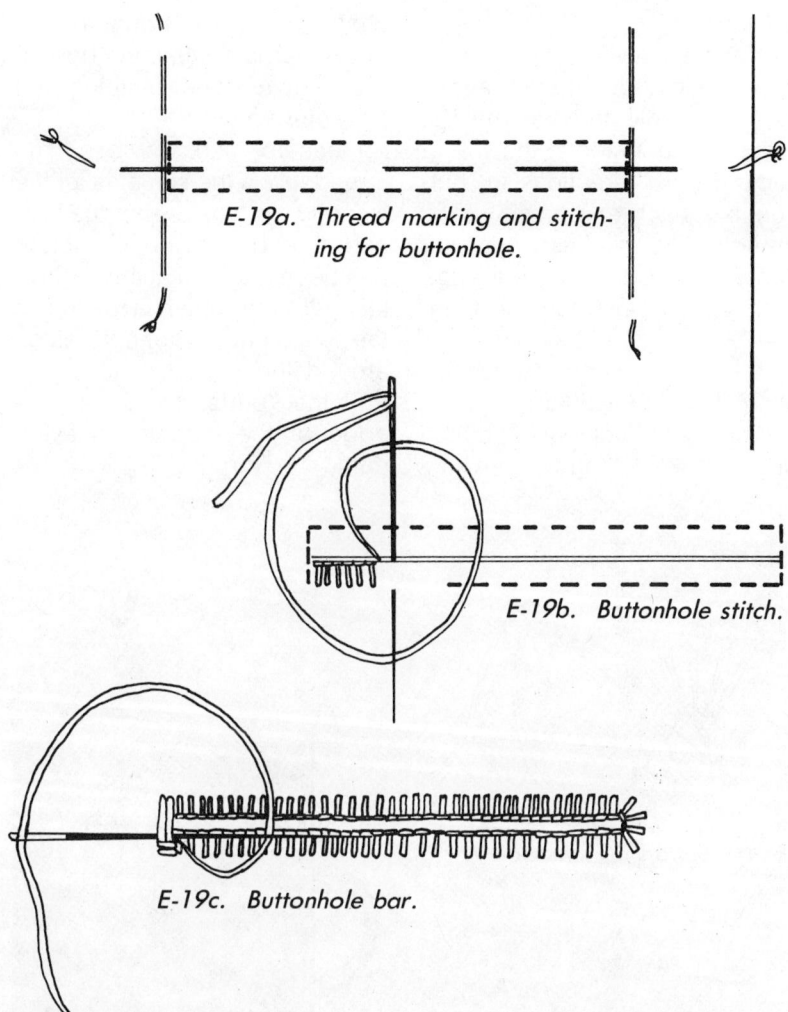

E-19a. Thread marking and stitching for buttonhole.

E-19b. Buttonhole stitch.

E-19c. Buttonhole bar.

loop the thread in a complete circle under the needle. Pull the stitch through so the purl forms right on the cut edge. Fig. E-19b. Continue in this manner all the way around the buttonhole, back to the straight end. Keep your stitches as close together as possible and of uniform length. At the curved end (nearest the open edge of the garment), fan the stitches out at the outside. Fig. E-19c. Finish the straight end of the buttonhole with a Hong Kong bartack. See Fig. E-19c.

If the buttonholes are going up and down on the garment instead of crosswise, make bartacks at each end.

### Altering Ready-To-Wear Fashions

**Eyelets**

Make a dot where the eyelet is to be made. Use a steel awl to pierce a hole through the dot from the right side to the wrong side. Follow directions for buttonhole stitch and finish edges of hole. The stitches will all be fanned out at the outside edge rather than close together. Fig. E-20.

**Buttonhole-Stitched Button Loops**

This method of making button loops takes longer than the chain or Hong Kong button loops but is sometimes desirable. It gives stiffer shaping and a fancier finish.

Measure, mark, and begin the thread loops the same as for the Hong Kong loops. After the second thread loop (base stitch) has been secured at the edge of the garment, insert a pencil in the loop, and buttonhole stitch around the thread of the loop. Pull the "purls" to the outside edge of the loop in an even, tight, line. Fig. E-21.

**FLAT TACK**

This is a quick, simple method of holding two parts of a garment in place, such as facings to seams and darts.

Work on the wrong side of the garment. Begin the first stitch with the knot hidden under the seam or dart at the edge of the facing. Pick up only the top of the seam or dart—be especially careful not to go through to the outer garment. Make three overlapping stitches. End with a slip knot. Fig. E-22.

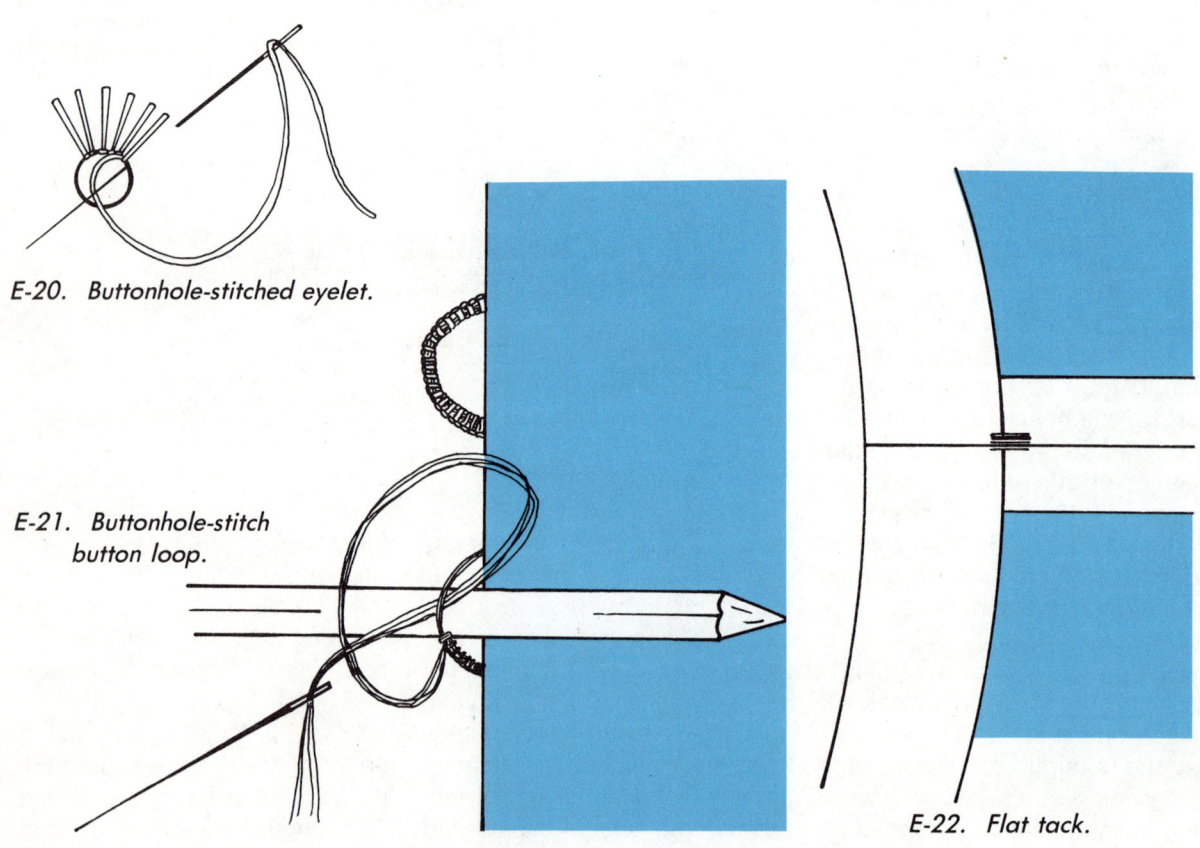

E-20. Buttonhole-stitched eyelet.

E-21. Buttonhole-stitch button loop.

E-22. Flat tack.

## MACHINE STITCHES

The regular straight stitch on any machine can be used for many tasks formerly done by hand. You can gather or shirr, tack facings, ease in fullness, baste, and sew invisibly from the top.

### Stay-Stitching

Stay-stitching is one of the easiest and fastest ways to keep fabric from stretching out of shape as you work on it. This is a single line of stitching through a single thickness of fabric. The stitches should be from medium to small. They are stitched near the seam line, between the seam line and the raw edge. Stay-stitching keeps fabric from stretching, raveling, or pulling apart at points of stress. It is especially useful for curved or bias edges of a garment. The stitches are permanent and will not be removed.

### Ease-Stitch

This control stitch has many different uses and is referred to frequently in Chapters 9 and 10. Follow the instructions given in Chapter 6 for "Dresses with Sleeves."

### Stitch-in-the-Ditch

This is an almost invisible stitch applied to the right side of the garment. It is used to stitch neck, armhole, and skirt waist facings at the seams or darts in active sportswear and children's clothes.

Pin facing in place. With right side up, stitch right on top of the seam stitches to the end of the facing. Backstitch. You may also continue stitching 1 inch (2.5 cm) below the end of the facing and trim the thread without backstitching. Fig. E-23.

Stitching *in* the seam on the right side—stitch-in-the-ditch—is also used as the final stitching for waistbands and bias trims. For this use, press the seams to one side so the band or trim will drop below the seam on the inside at least $1/4$ to $3/8$ (.6 to 1 cm). Baste or pin in place. Using a zipper foot on the left side of the needle, stitch as close to the seam as possible.

### Shirring or Gathering

During an alteration, a section of the garment may occasionally have to be shirred or gathered to control the fullness. For example, when bodice darts are removed, shirring gives extra fullness through the midriff.

If the shirring is to be done on a seam, clip mark where the stitching is to begin and end. Using the largest machine stitch, begin $1/4$ inch (.6 cm) from the seam edge at the clip mark. Stitch to the next clip, leave needle in fabric, raise the presser foot, and pivot the fabric on the needle to turn a right angle. Stitch two stitches. Pivot again so you are going back toward the first clip. This will bring the second shirring stitch near the seam line and the edge of the presser foot along the first stitching. Continue stitching back to the first mark. Pull the material away from the machine and cut the threads leaving from 2 to 3 inches (5 to 7.6 cm) at the end. Fig. E-24.

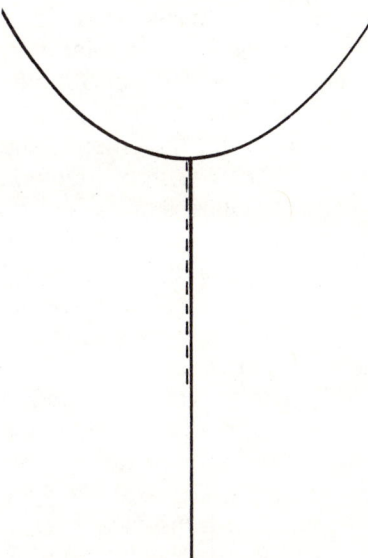

E-23. Stitch-in-the-ditch.

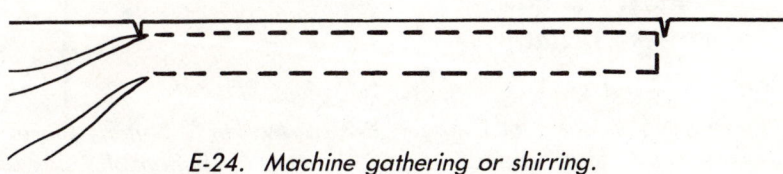

E-24. Machine gathering or shirring.

## Altering Ready-To-Wear Fashions

Pull *both* bobbin threads at the *same* time until the fabric is gathered to the desired measurement. Pull the top threads through to the underneath and knot all four strands together. Distribute fullness evenly as you pin the seam together and stitch the seam. Keep the shirred side up as you stitch so you can control the fullness and cover the shirring stitch.

Sometimes you may find it necessary to add shirring to the body of the garment where there is no seam. For example, you might improve the fit of a shift-style dress by using shirring stitches at the waistline instead of darts.

If the shirring is *not* on a seam, thread-mark the line and length of shirring. Work on the right side of the garment. Stitch ⅛ inch (.3 cm) on each side of the marked line, beginning and ending as in the instructions above. Working on the wrong side of the garment, pull the bobbin threads to the desired measurement and knot as before. Distribute the fullness evenly. Reinforce the shirring with a seam tape backing to hold it in place. Sew the tape securely at each end of the shirring with a tiny whipstitch.

### FASTENERS AND OTHER CONTROLS

#### Buttons

Use a No. 7 Sharp or Darner needle and four strands of matching cotton mercerized thread. For heavy fabrics, use heavy-duty thread.

Some alterations require the realignment of the buttons. To mark the placement for buttons, lap the buttonhole side over the button side. The end of the buttonhole nearest the edge of the garment should meet the closing line marked on the other side. Place a pin in the end of each buttonhole until all are marked. Fig. E-25a. Carefully lift away the buttonhole side of garment, leaving pins in line underneath. Anchor the marking pins securely. If buttonholes are vertical, lap the buttonholes over until the *length* of the holes is *on* the marked line. Place the marking pins in the top edge of the buttonholes.

To mark placement of buttons for button loops, lap edge of seam to meet the marked line and place pins at outer edges of loops. Fig. E-25b.

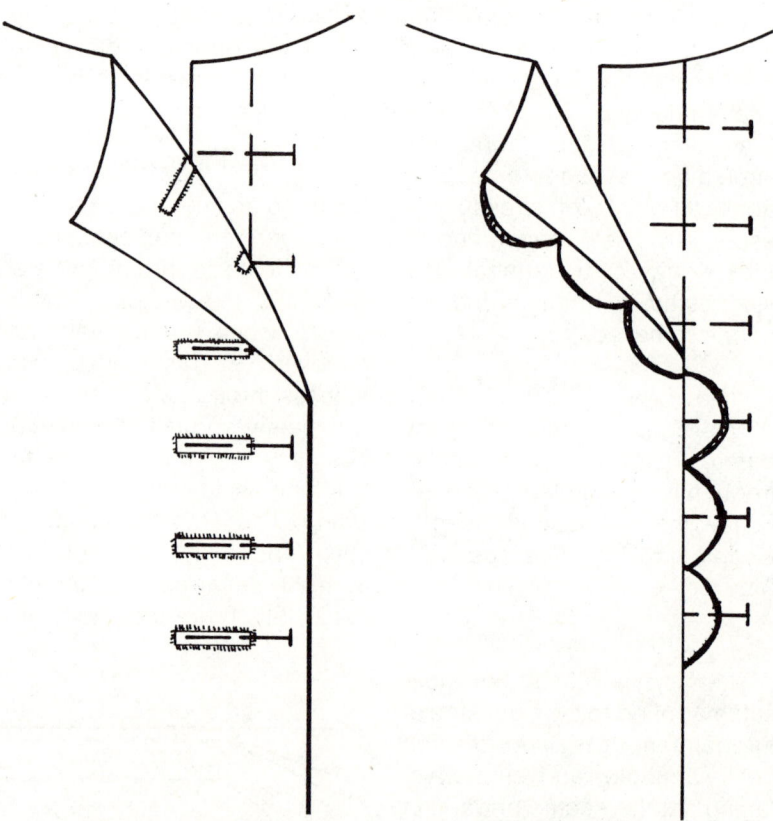

E-25a. Marking button placement for buttonholes.

E-25b. Marking button placement for button loops.

## Ch. 11: Finishing Touches

Buttons should never be sewn flat against the fabric. There should always be room or "play" under the buttons to accommodate the thickness of fabric around the buttonhole. Some buttons have metal or plastic "shanks" on the underneath which supply this room. Buttons with holes must be sewn loosely enough so the thread of the stitches forms a thread shank.

### BUTTONS WITH SHANKS

Make a short stitch on the right side of the garment, picking up all the layers of the fabric. Pass the needle through the shank and make another stitch on top of the first one. Repeat stitch once more and finish with a slip knot through the stitches on the side of the shank. (Remember to use four strands of thread.)

### BUTTONS WITHOUT SHANKS

For a two-hole button, make the first stitch at the mark the same as for a shank button. Pass the needle through the holes in the button. Bring the needle up from underneath, over the top of the button, and down through the other hole. Make another short stitch over the first one. Hold the button 1/8 inch (.3 cm) above the garment or place a toothpick between the button and the thread on top of the button. Fig. E-25c. This will keep the thread loose enough to form a shank. Repeat the stitches twice, still holding the button away from the garment. Bring the thread out between the garment and the button. Wrap it tightly around the stitches under the button, forming a firm shank. Finish with a slip knot. Fig. E-25d.

To sew a four-hole button, you have a choice of making crossed or parallel lines to finish the top of the button. Whatever finish is selected, all the buttons on the garment should be applied the same way. Follow the instructions for a two-hole button for sewing and making the shank.

NOTE: If the garment is bulky, a longer shank is necessary, even for buttons with a shank. Make the first stitch holding the button 1/4 inch (.6 cm) above the fabric and secure it with one more stitch. Test shank length by buttoning one buttonhole. If the garment is smooth and shows no pull, the shank is long enough. Make additional stitches and finish shank so the button "stands up" firm and straight and does not droop.

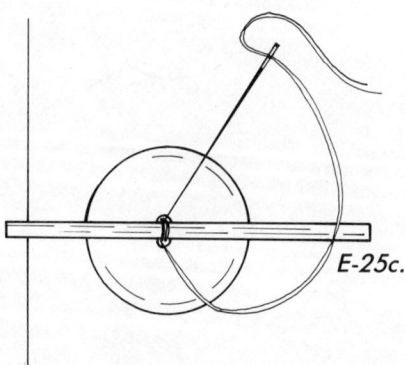

E-25c. Sewing buttons with a thread shank.

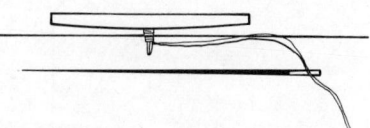

E-25d. Thread shank under button.

## Altering Ready-To-Wear Fashions

### Snaps

Use a No. 7 Sharp needle and four strands of mercerized cotton thread in a matching color.

The snap is divided into two parts, referred to as the ball (top) and socket (bottom). The ball part of the snap is always sewn on the top part of an overlapping seam. It should be placed 1/8 inch (.3 cm) from the edge of the seam.

To apply, sew the ball part of the snap in place first. Make two stitches in each hole going under the top layer of fabric between the holes. Finish with a slip knot through the last stitches. Rub the ball with chalk and press the snap on the opposite side to mark the location of the socket snap. Sew socket over this mark. Fig. E-26a.

### Covered Snaps

These snaps are used as a custom touch where snaps are needed for control but may show. The snaps between buttons on jackets or coats are one example. Use a size No. Four snap. Use opaque lining fabric in a color matching the garment. Cut a circle of fabric for each section of the snap 1/4 inch (.6 cm) larger than the snap. Make a running stitch 1/8 inch (.3 cm) from the edge of the circle. Place the snap right side down in the middle of the circle. Pull the thread to gather the fabric tightly around the snap. Secure with several overlapping stitches. Sew the snap to the garment through the holes the same as a plain snap. Repeat for the other half of the snap. When snapped, the ball part will penetrate the fabric in the socket part and make the hole. Fig. E-26b.

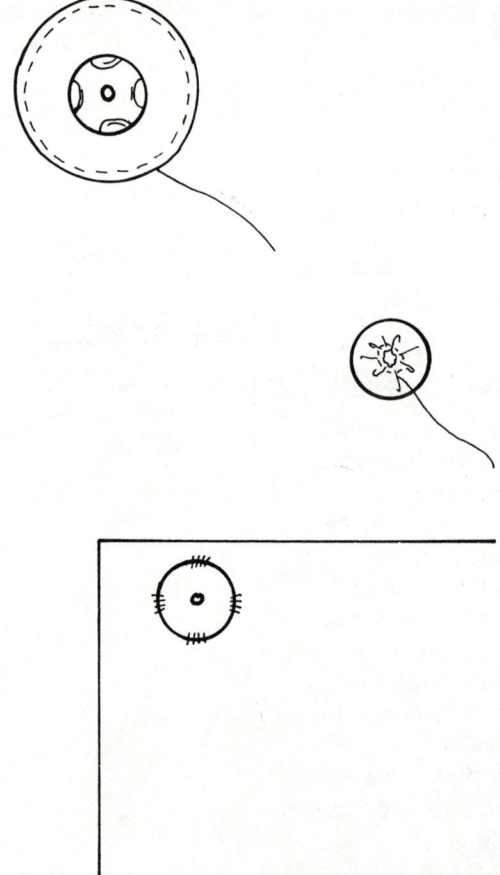

E-26a. Snap placement.

E-26b. Steps in covering snaps with fabric.

## Ch. 11: Finishing Touches

### Hook Fasteners

Use a No. 7 Sharp needle and four strands of mercerized thread in a matching color.

Hook fasteners come with two parts on a card—the hook, and two styles of eyes. The bar, or straight eye, is for use opposite the hook on the bottom side of an overlapping seam. The eye, or loop eye, is to use opposite the hook on openings that meet.

Position the hook so the end is 1/8 inch (.3 cm) from the edge of the seam. Sew two short stitches in each circle. Pick up only the top layer of fabric. After the circles have been sewn down, push the needle under the fabric to the head of the hook. Make two stitches across the metal part under the curve of the hook. These stitches hold the hook flat to the fabric for a smoother closing. Slip the needle under the top layer of fabric and back to the circles to finish with a slip knot. Fig. E-27.

Sew the bar eye 1/8 inch (.3 cm) inside the matching line, opposite the hook. Sew with two short stitches in each circle. Finish under the seam with a slip knot.

To apply the loop eye, extend the loop 1/8 inch (.3 cm) beyond the seam edge, opposite the hook. Sew under the seam. Sew through the two circles in the same way the hook circles were sewn, picking up only one layer of fabric.

### COAT AND FUR HOOK FASTENERS

Use a No. 7 Sharp and two strands of buttonhole twist in matching color.

These are extra-large hooks and eyes that may be purchased already covered with buttonhole twist and ready to apply. They are attached to the garment in the same manner as the regular dress hooks. The only difference would be for a coat with a lining.

For application on fur garments, the lining is sometimes ripped just enough to slip the hook and loop circles under the lining. The circles are sewn inside, under the lining and only the actual hook and loop show.

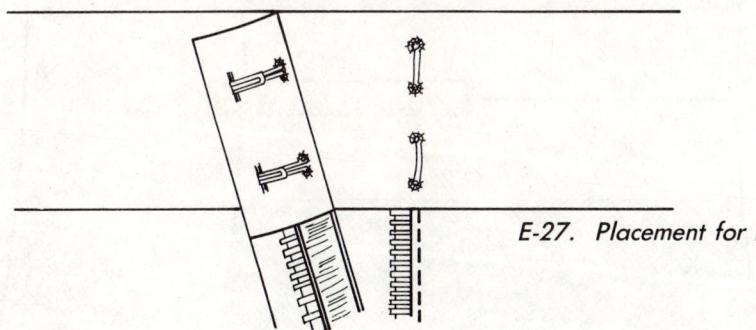

E-27. Placement for hooks and eyes.

*Altering Ready-To-Wear Fashions*

### Lingerie Keepers (strap holders)

Use a No. 7 Sharp needle, four strands of matching cotton mercerized thread, and matching color seam tape.

These lingerie keepers are placed and used the same as the chain-loop lingerie keepers mentioned earlier. They give firmer control and are more durable than the chain variety.

Cut a 6-inch (15 cm) length of seam tape. Fold the tape in half lengthwise and machine stitch near the finished edge of the tape. Cut the strip in half giving you two 3-inch (7.6 cm) strips. Fold each of these in half. Sew the folded end with a whipstitch across the shoulder seam 2 inches (5 cm) from the armhole seam. Turn the end of the bottom tape under ¼ inch (.6 cm) and place socket part of snap over the end of the tape. Sew snap and tape to the top of the shoulder seam at the same time. Fold the end of top tape under ¼ inch (.6 cm) and sew ball snap to the tape. Finish with a slip knot at the last hole. Fig. E-28.

### Zipper Fastenings

There are several methods of applying a zipper—lapped, centered, slot, fly, and invisible. All of these methods may be stitched by machine or sewn by hand with a pickstitch or a backstitch. If zippers are inserted by machine, a zipper foot, adjustable for right or left side stitching, is used. Industrial machines have separate right- and left-hand zipper feet. Invisible zippers are applied with a special foot adjustable to your machine.

Since you will be working with ready-made clothes, you will have to ignore all the zipper instructions that start with a machine-basted seam for the zipper opening. Once you have learned the open seam application, you will find it faster, more accurate, and more professional.

You can get valuable practice by making zipper samples or applying 7-inch (17.8 cm) zippers to the mini-dresses (Chapter 6). You may use any plastic or metal zipper you have on hand.

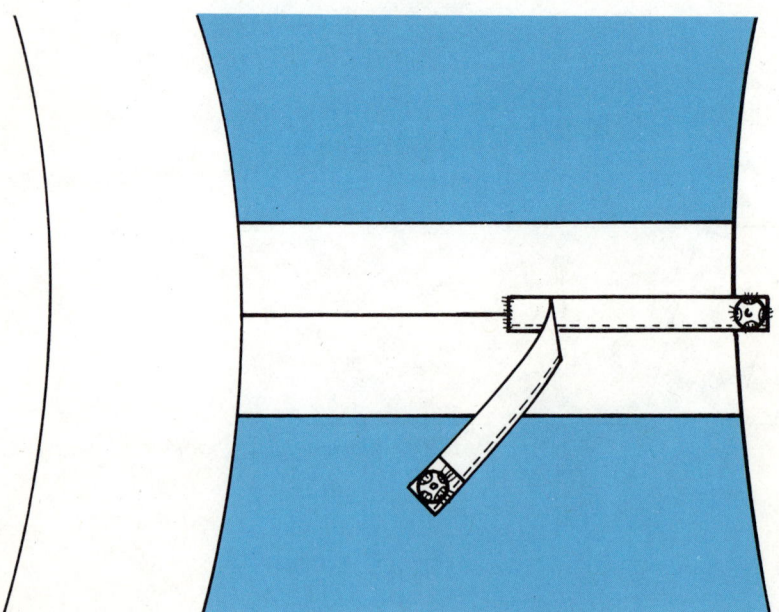

E-28. Fabric strip lingerie keeper.

## LAPPED ZIPPER

The zipper seam opening should be the length of the zipper plus a seam allowance.

1. Backstitch the beginning of the seam at the bottom of the zipper opening.
2. Press overlapping seam *on* the seam line. Press a fold in the bottom seam allowance 1/8 inch (.3 cm) outside the regular seam line. Fig. E-29a.
3. Pin the bottom seam fold to the zipper tape close to teeth of the zipper. Have the zipper slider 1/8 inch (.3 cm) below the seam at the top of the opening. With the zipper foot on the left side of the needle, stitch the bottom seam to the zipper tape close to the zipper teeth.
4. Lap the top seam over the zipper just enough to cover the stitching on the underneath seam. Pin it in this position along the folded edge of the lap. Then place a row of pins across the line to be stitched, holding the zipper in place under the seam. The bottom cross pin should be just below the zipper stop to indicate the end of the zipper and the place to pivot. Fig. E-29b.
5. Remove the pins on the outer folded edge of the lap and open the zipper all the way. With the zipper foot still on the left side of the needle, stitch from the top to the bottom of the zipper. Stitch from the right side of the garment, removing the pins as you sew. Pivot at the bottom, stitch across bottom to seam, and backstitch. The stitching line should be 3/8 to 1/2 inch (1 to 1.3 cm) from the seam edge, depending upon the thickness of the fabric. Fig. E-29c.

NOTE: Either the pickstitch or the backstitch may be substituted for all machine stitching, following the same steps for the application of the zipper.

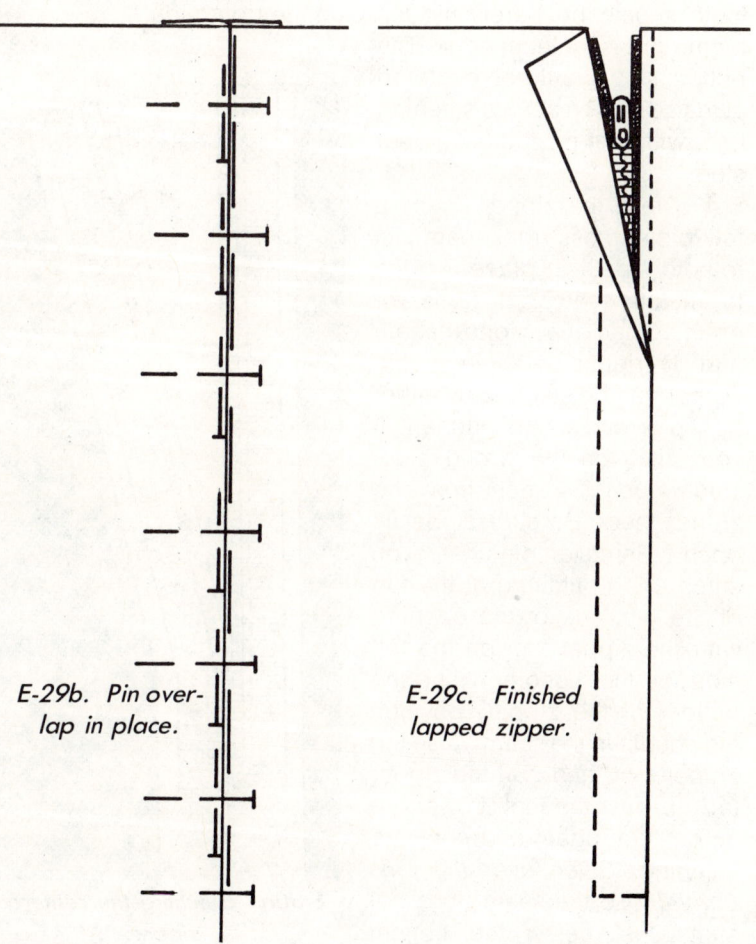

E-29a. Press crease in underneath seam allowance 1/8 inch from seam.

E-29b. Pin overlap in place.

E-29c. Finished lapped zipper.

## Altering Ready-To-Wear Fashions

### CENTERED ZIPPER

The stitching around the zipper should be about 1/4 inch (.6 cm) away from the center seam on each side.

1. Follow the first step as given for a lapped zipper.

2. Press *both* sides of the seam opening on the seam allowance.

3. Open the zipper. From the right side of the garment, place the left side of the zipper under the left seam fold. The zipper teeth should be barely hidden by the pressed seam edge. The bottom stop should be centered at the seam. Pin across stitching line, with last pin below zipper stop.

4. Close the zipper. Place a few pins across right seam just to hold zipper in place enough to match seams, designs, or grain. Open the zipper again and pin right side same as left. Zipper can be stitched on either right or wrong side of garment. If you stitch on the wrong side, stitch about 1/8 inch from the zipper teeth. Be sure zipper is open. Remove pins as you stitch. Start stitching at the top of the left side of the opening with the zipper foot on the left side of the needle. Near the bottom of the zipper, position the needle in the seam, raise the zipper foot, and pull the zipper tab up past the foot. Lower the zipper foot again and continue stitching. *Stitch over the pins carefully* so the seam does not shift. Just below the bottom stop, pivot and stitch across the zipper tapes and seam to the other side of the zipper. Pivot and stitch up to the tab. Leave the needle in the seam, and again raise the zipper foot. Open the zipper all the way. Continue stitching to the top of the opening, removing pins as you go. Figs. E-30a,b.

NOTE: Either the pickstitch or the backstitch may be substituted for the machine stitching. Handstitching is always done on the right side.

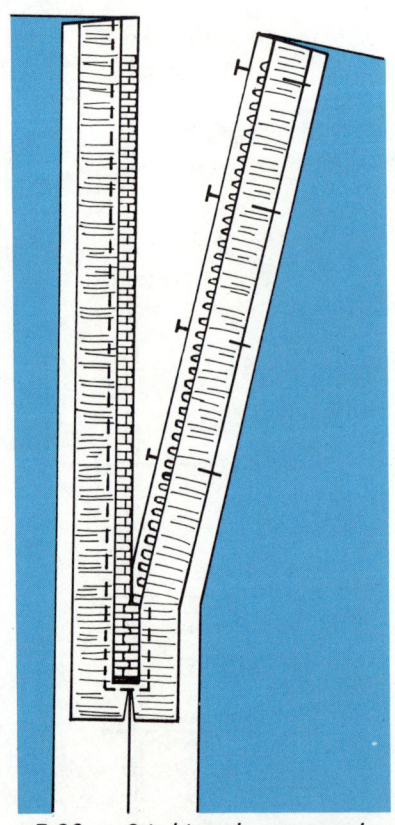

E-30a. Stitching the centered zipper.

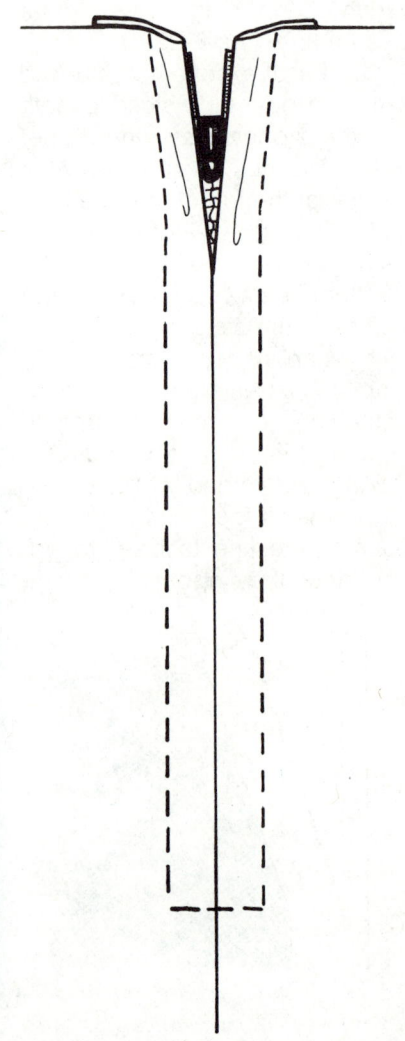

E-30b. Finished centered zipper.

Ch. 11: Finishing Touches

## SLOT ZIPPERS

### Slot Zipper in a Seam Opening

1. Follow the first two steps given for the centered zipper.

2. Turn the garment wrong side out. Open the pressed seam out flat. Place the open zipper face down on top of one side of the seam. The pressed seam line should be along the tape edge of the zipper teeth. The zipper tape should be within the seam allowance.

3. Pin the zipper tape to the seam.

4. With the zipper foot on the right side of the needle, stitch from the top to the bottom of the zipper tape. Keep the foot close to the zipper teeth. Remove the pins as you stitch. Fig. E-31a.

5. Rearrange the fabric so you can open the left side of the seam out flat on the bed of the machine. Lay the left side of the zipper along the left seam allowance. Pin as you did for the right side. Fig. E-31b.

6. With zipper foot still on the right side, stitch from bottom of tape to top, staying close to zipper teeth. Fig. E-31c.

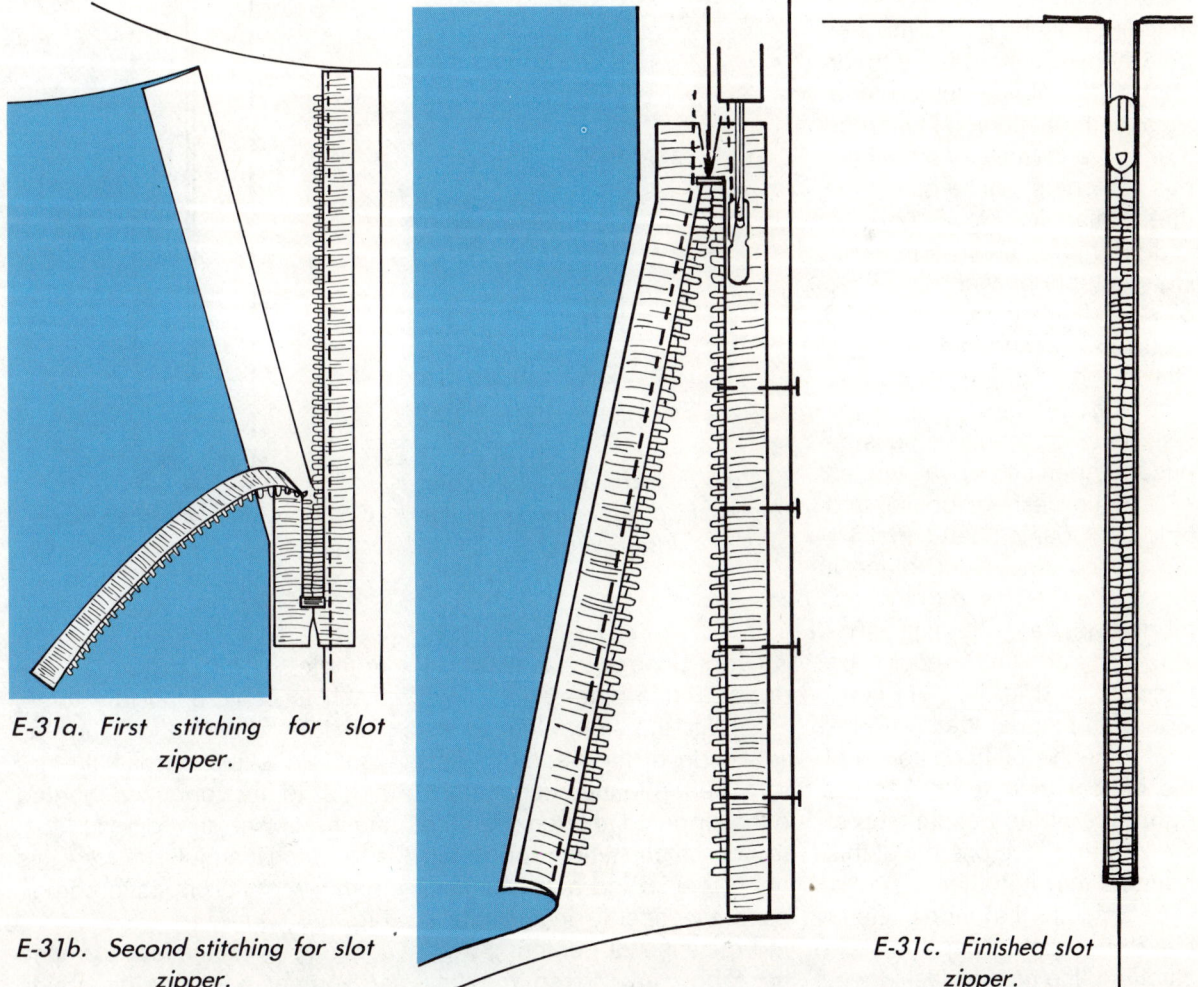

E-31a. First stitching for slot zipper.

E-31b. Second stitching for slot zipper.

E-31c. Finished slot zipper.

### Altering Ready-To-Wear Fashions

#### Slot Zipper in a Slash Opening

The slash opening should be the length of the zipper plus a seam allowance.

1. Make a thread-marking where the zipper is to be inserted in the garment. Cross the bottom of the line with a thread mark to indicate the end of the slash opening.

2. Stay-stitch the fabric so it will not stretch as you work on the zipper. Stitch a line of small machine stitching (15 stitches per inch) 1/8 inch (.3 cm) on each side of the thread line. Pivot at the bottom of the thread marking and make one continuous stitching all around the thread marking. Fig. E-32a.

3. Remove marking threads. Carefully cut between the lines of stay-stitching to 1/4 inch (.6 cm) above the bottom stitching. Cut to the stitching at the corners. Fig. E-32b.

4. With garment wrong side out and open end up, lift the left side of the slashed opening and hold it in your left hand. Pick up the closed zipper and place it face up under the edge of the fabric you are holding. The stay-stitching line should be lined up next to the right hand side of the zipper teeth.

5. Line the left hand corner of the bottom triangle up with the right side of the bottom stop of the zipper. Place one pin at this point to hold it in place.

6. Smooth the fabric along the zipper tape. Keep the stay-stitching line on the slash open-

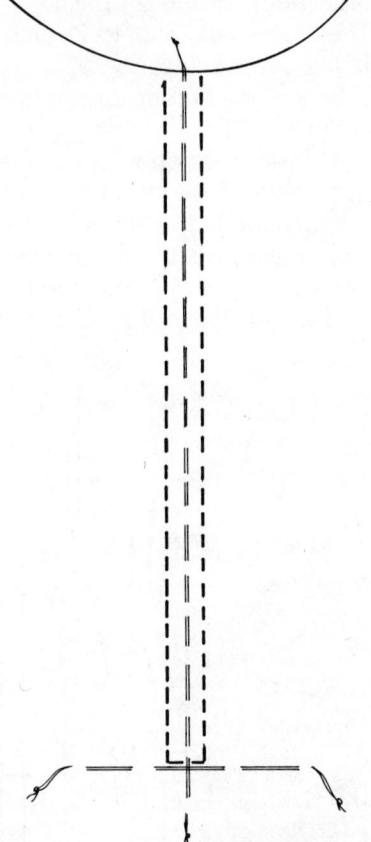

E-32a. Thread marking and stay-stitching as preparation for slash opening.

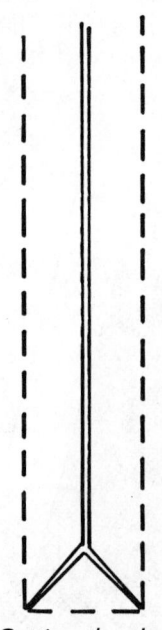

E-32b. Cutting the slash opening.

ing very close to the teeth of the zipper. Pin in place.

7. With the zipper foot on the right side of the needle, stitch from the top to the bottom close to the zipper teeth. Remove pins as you stitch. When you reach the corner of the bottom slash, leave the needle in the fabric and raise the zipper foot. Swing the fabric around so the tiny triangle of the bottom of the slash is centered on the tape. Turn the zipper and fabric so you can stitch across the triangle to the opposite angled slash. Lower the presser foot and stitch carefully across this triangle to the opposite corner. Fig. E-32c.

Again swing the fabric around so you can stitch the other side

### Ch. 11: Finishing Touches

of the opening. Lay the zipper flat on the bed of the machine and smooth the stitched seam back away from the face-up zipper. Carefully line up the stay-stitching on the free side of the seam, next to the zipper teeth. Pin in place. Lower the presser foot and stitch along the zipper teeth to the top of the zipper.

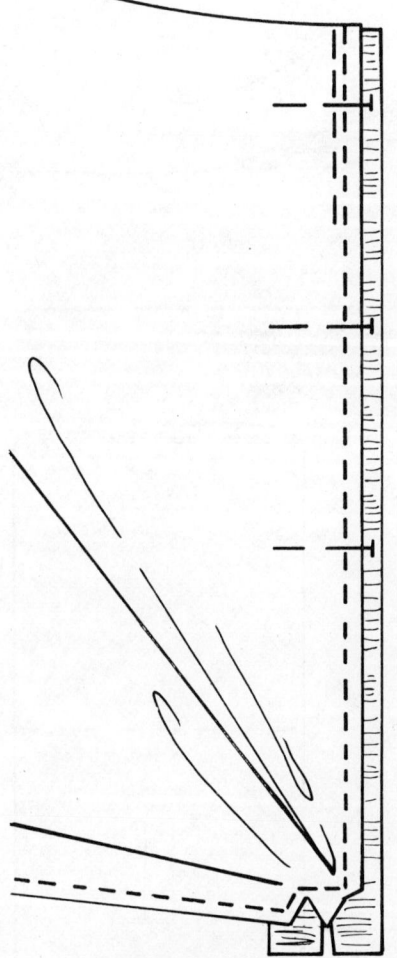

*E-32c. Stitching the zipper in a slash opening.*

### Slot Zipper with Top Stitching

The slot type of zipper opening can also be made with top stitching rather than hidden stitching.

1. To top stitch a slot-type zipper in a seam opening, press the seams on the seam line.

To top stitch a slash opening zipper, follow the first three steps given for the slash opening with hidden stitching. Fold the edges of the slash back just enough so the stay-stitching does not show on the right side. Press the edges flat.

2. Place the top stop of the zipper 1/8 inch (.3 cm) below the seam at the top of the opening.

3. With the garment right side out, pin the fold on one side to the zipper tape close to the zipper teeth. Pin the bottom of the opening just below the bottom stop. Pin the other side of the opening fold to the zipper as you did the first side.

4. Open the zipper. Stitch the left edge of the seam fold to the zipper from the top to the bottom (with the zipper foot on the left side of the machine needle). Pivot the fabric on the needle and stitch across the bottom. Pivot again and stitch the right side up to the top. Your stitching will be in one continuous line.

NOTE: If you make the Method Two mini-dress with the slash opening, apply the zipper following these instructions. Since the neck seam is already finished in this garment, fold the excess zipper tape under to the inside of the neckline at the top before stitching.

### FLY ZIPPER

A fly zipper placket can be made in a variety of ways. Manufacturers use several different methods for this type of opening. Your job will be to study carefully the manufacturer's method before removing and replacing a fly zipper. There are too many variations to explain them all.

A fly zipper sample made with muslin would be a valuable learning experience and addition to your other samples. Follow the instructions for the fly-front zipper given in men's or women's pants pattern with this opening. Replacing a fly-front zipper in men's trousers is explained in Chapter 12.

### INVISIBLE ZIPPER

This zipper is applied exactly as instructed and illustrated in the zipper package. Be sure to purchase the special foot needed for both the invisible metal *and* invisible plastic zipper. They are slightly different but each one is important to the successful application of the metal *or* plastic zipper.

### TO SHORTEN A ZIPPER AT THE BOTTOM

This may be necessary if the bottom stop of the zipper falls well below the opening and it is not desirable to enlarge the opening.

### Altering Ready-To-Wear Fashions

1. Place the metal bar eye from a hook fastener card across the wrong side of the zipper teeth where the zipper should end. Sew securely in each circle of the bar eye. Cut off the excess zipper 1/4 inch (.6 cm) below this bar.

2. Insert the zipper with the bar at the end of the seam opening. Backstitch at the bottom of the tape on each side of the zipper. Do not stitch across bottom as it will serve no purpose.

### WEIGHTS

Weights are used to control the drape or hang of a specific part of a garment that cannot be controlled any other way.

### Chain Weights

This type of weight is known as the "Chanel chain," after the designer who introduced its use. It is a decorative metal chain used to control the drape of loose jackets. The chain may be purchased at handcraft or notion shops.

Use a No. 7 Milliner's needle and double strand of matching color thread.

Place the chain at the top of the hem, just below the lining. Catch the top of every other link to the top layer of fabric. Hide the long stitch between links in the fabric. Fig. E-33. To control the drape of a "Chanel" type jacket front, sew the chain along the lining at the edge of the front facing on both sides of the jacket.

### Flat Weights

Cover the weight by making a bag with lining fabric in a matching or blending color. Cut the bag 1/4 inch wider than four times the width of the weight. The length should be 1 inch (2.5 cm) more than the size of the weight for a cowl neckline and 1/2 inch (1.3 cm) longer than the weight for a jacket hem.

Stitch the bag 1/8 inch (.3 cm) wider than the weight with the seam the same width as the bag. Fig. E-34a. Turn the bag right side out and slip the weight in between the seams. The weight will be padded with two layers of fabric on each side. Stitch across the bag close to the top of the weight. Fig. E-34b.

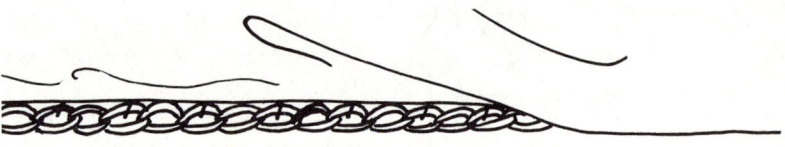

E-33. Chain weight sewn along hem edge.

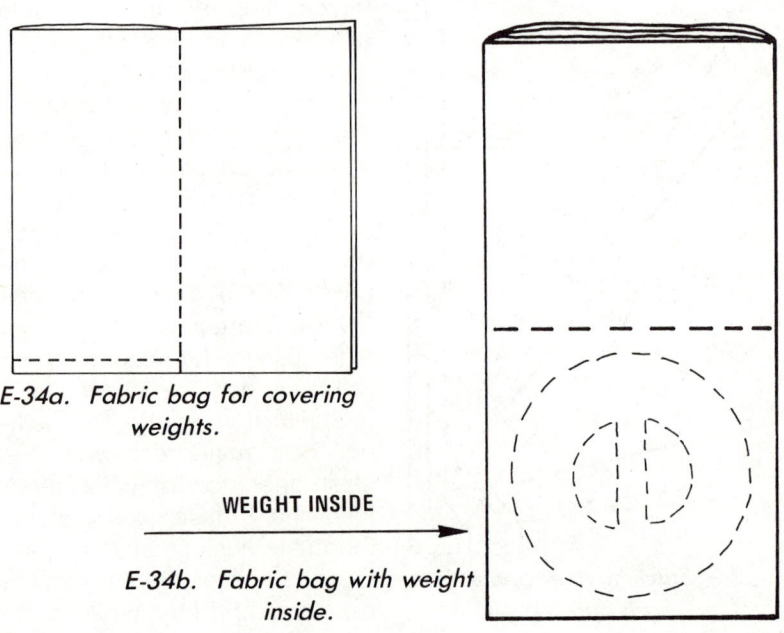

E-34a. Fabric bag for covering weights.

WEIGHT INSIDE →

E-34b. Fabric bag with weight inside.

Ch. 11: Finishing Touches

To apply to a cowl neckline, mark the center of the neck at the seam edge. Place the center of the unfinished edge of the bag under the wrong side of the neck seam. Stitch the bag to the seam allowance with a zig-zag machine stitch or a hand whipstitch.

To apply to jacket hem, rip out the lining and hem 2 inches (5 cm) on each side of the seams where the weights are needed. Sew the bag to the top layer of the seam *under* the hem and about ½ inch (1.3 cm) above the hem fold. Resew hem and lining.

### SHOULDER PADS

As you read in Chapter 8, some fitting problems can be solved with shoulder pads. You may need to increase the size of pads already present. You may need to add a new pad.

If quite a lot of padding is required—men's wear, very sloping shoulders, or shoulder irregularities—ready-made pads may be the wisest and easiest choice. These pads are available in a variety of sizes and thicknesses.

If a small amount of extra padding will solve the problem, you will want to make the pads yourself. You might only need to add another layer of batting to pads already in the garment.

To make shoulder pads, you will need polyester quilt batting and compatible lining fabric in a matching color.

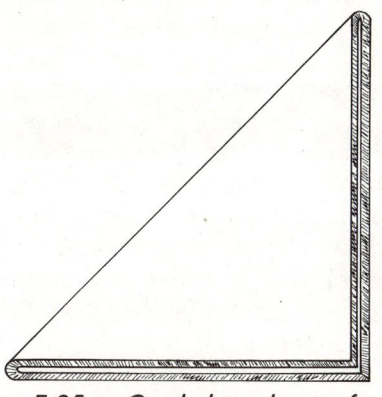

E-35a. *Graded top layer of shoulder pad.*

1. Cut two 5-inch (12.7 cm) squares of batting and two 6-inch (15 cm) squares of lining fabric. The edges should be on the straight grain of the fabric.
2. Fold the batting squares in half on the bias to form two triangles.
3. Trim ¼ inch (.6 cm) from the edge of the top layer. Hold your scissors almost flat against the pad as you cut to "shave" or "grade" the edge. Repeat the grading on the outer layer without trimming it in size. Fig. E-35a.
4. With a diagonal basting stitch, lightly baste the upper edge to the bottom layer.
5. Fold the fabric squares on the bias and lightly crease the bias line with a fingernail. Open the square and lay the folded edge of the pad along the crease line of the fabric.
6. Stitch the two outer edges of the pad to the lining fabric

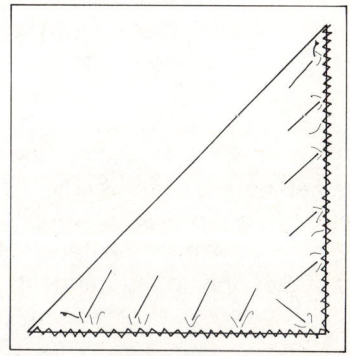

E-35b. *Padding stitched in place for shoulder pad.*

with a large zigzag stitch or machine basting. Fig. E-35b.

7. Fold the top layer of fabric over the pad, matching cut edges. Stitch around the edges with a machine zigzag stitch or a straight stitch. Stitch ⅜ inch (1 cm) from the edge and trim the edge with pinking shears. (Just like making an apple turnover.)

NOTE: You will notice the folded bias edge is soft and pliable, which helps shape the pads to the shoulders. You are now ready to attach the pads to the garment as instructed in Chapter 9 in "Shoulder Alterations."

*Altering Ready-To-Wear Fashions*

## LABELS

The importance and types of labels in clothes were explained in Chapter 2. As you may recall, many of the better retail stores prefer to have their own labels sewn into the clothes they sell. They may make arrangements to have this done by the manufacturer before delivery. On the other hand, they may have their own alterationists put the labels in the clothes.

Such labels come woven into a long ribbon with cutting lines marked between labels. The two cut ends are pressed under $1/4$ inch (.6 cm) and the label is ready to apply to the garment.

Coat, jacket, and fur labels are the largest and are used in both men's and women's wear. For men's wear, pin the label to the lining below the right front inside pocket. For women's wear, pin the label to the lining or facing at the center of the back neckline. Sew around the label with a fine catch stitch through the top layer of the fabric under the label.

Dress labels can be almost any size but are always smaller than coat labels. There are several ways to sew these labels, and all are correct.

- Catch stitch each end or all around the label.
- Tack each corner of the label down with three overlapping stitches.
- Whipstitch the pressed ends of the label.
- Slipstitch the pressed ends of the label.

To apply garment labels, sew them to the center back neck facing or neck finish. If the opening is in the center back, place the label on one side of the opening. To apply to sweaters and unlined sheer garments, sew the label along one of the side seams, parallel to the seam. On skirts or pants, the label is sewn to the band at the center back.

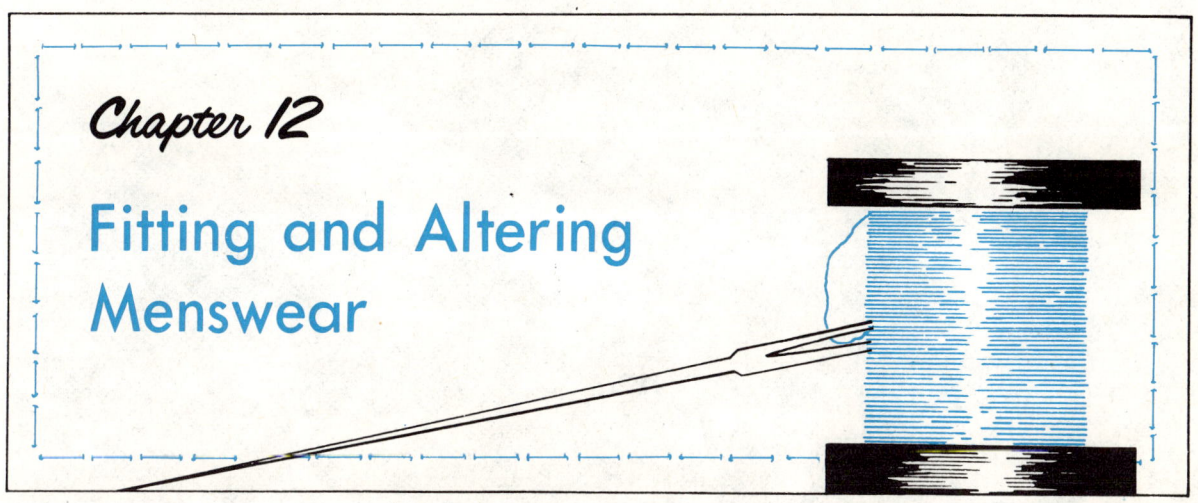

# Chapter 12
# Fitting and Altering Menswear

In recent years, men have once again become more conscious of the clothes they wear and have had more styles and colors available from which to choose. After so many years of wearing white or pastel-colored shirts, and dark, solid-colored suits, men often find the many choices available confusing.

Many men do not seem aware that colors, designs, and style lines can flatter them as well as women. Most of the principles of design discussed in Chapter 7 also apply to men's clothing. For example, like women, men find that not all colors are equally becoming to them. They have to try different ones to see how they affect the skin tones. Likewise, large checks and plaids and bulky fabrics will add width and breadth to their appearance. Stout men and short men should avoid them.

Men should be aware that patch pockets, straight lines in pocket flaps, and wide lapels create horizontal lines and add width. Belts—front or back—also form horizontal lines and call attention to the waistline. Sharply contrasting colors in jackets and trousers break the figure into two sections and make the individual appear shorter than matching trousers and jackets. Fig. F-1a.

Vertical, or lengthening and slenderizing lines, can be created through the use of one color, contrasting color thread used for top stitching, or narrow, pleated pockets. Narrow lapels and ties create vertical lines just as wide lapels, wide ties, and double-breasted styles add width. Figs. F-1b,c.

Men vary in size and shape just as women do. Fig. F-2. Few men can walk into a clothing store and buy a coat or suit that fits perfectly.

The more expensive suits usually have wider seams and can be made larger if the client needs more room. Less expensive suits, while often very satisfactory, may be more difficult or impossible to release as the seams are usually narrower.

Since the job of selecting the proper colors, lines, designs, and sizes will be up to the man and the salesman serving him, you will seldom be called upon to give advice. As an alterationist—or bushelman, as it is called in men's tailoring—it will be your job to see what changes need to be made.

Then you must determine if these changes are possible. Only a limited amount can be added or taken out of jackets or trousers without losing the shape of the garment.

**Ch. 12: Fitting and Altering Menswear**

Courtesy Sears, Roebuck and Co.

F-1a. The lines in men's clothes are created by the design of the fabric as well as the structural lines in the construction. The plaid in this suit creates strong horizontal as well as vertical lines. When the jacket is worn with matching trousers, the vertical lines carry the eye up and down the entire figure and add height. When the jacket is worn with contrasting trousers, the figure is broken into two segments.

Courtesy Sears, Roebuck and Co.

F-1b. In solid-color suits, structural lines such as the accented V-shaped yoke seam become more noticeable.

F-1c. The lines in men's clothes also have definite movement. In this jacket, the edge stitching around the collar, lapels, style seams, and opening edges creates vertical lines. The large patch pockets and flaps form horizontal lines that add width to the hip area. The wide lapels give a broadening effect over the chest area.

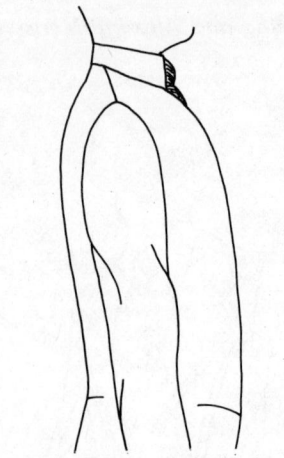
Normal figure, regular back and chest.

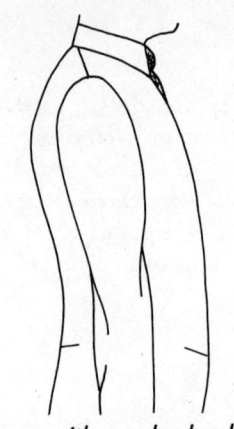
Figure with regular back and chest but head thrust forward.

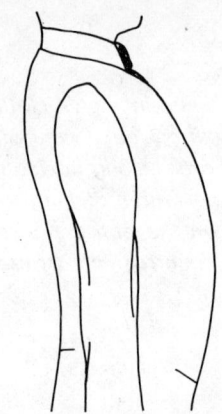
Full-chested, narrow-backed figure with erect carriage, head up.

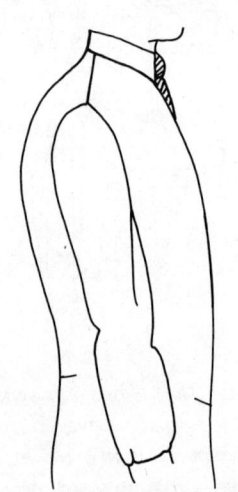
Round-shouldered, flat-chested figure.

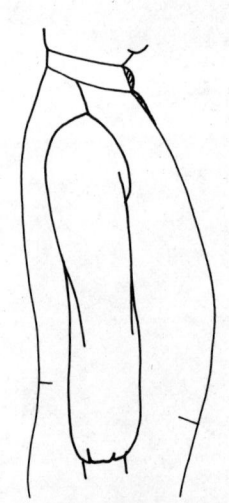
Stout figure with regular back and chest.

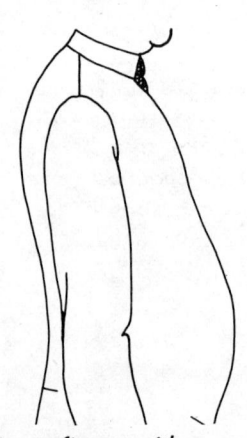
Stout figure with prominent abdomen, round back, flat chest, and head thrust forward.

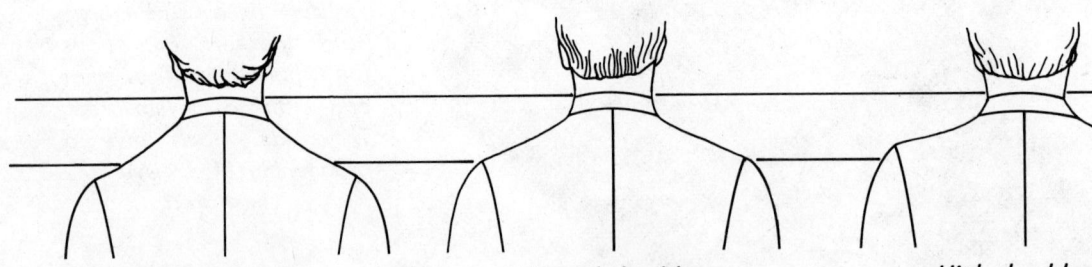
Sloping shoulders. Normal shoulders. High shoulders.

F-2 Men vary in size and shape, creating many fitting problems. These are the most common categories of male shapes.

Ch. 12: **Fitting and Altering Menswear**

Sometimes a man with broad shoulders and narrow hips and waist will find that a suit large enough in the shoulders needs to be altered in the waist of the trousers. The amount that can be taken out in the waistline is limited by the position of the back pockets. If too much has to be removed from the back seam for a small waist (28–32), the pockets may be drawn too close together. Up to 1 inch (2.5 cm) or even 1½ inch (3.8 cm) can be removed from the back seam without pulling the trousers out of line. If more than that must be removed, the side pockets will have to be taken out and reset. The customer should be informed of this so he will understand the additional charges involved. He may prefer to purchase another size or style to avoid alterations.

## JUDGING THE FIT OF MEN'S JACKETS

The general fit desired for a jacket varies from one man to another. Fitters use the terms snug, easy, or loose to describe the type of fit desired. Some men prefer to have their jackets fit so smooth and *snug* that their movements are somewhat restricted. Others want smoothness with enough room to move comfortably, or an *easy* fit. Still others may have a figure problem to hide or just like plenty of room and prefer a *loose* fit.

In a well-fitted jacket (Fig. F-3 and F-4):

Courtesy Sears, Roebuck and Co.

**F-3. The sleeve should extend slightly beyond the edge of the shoulder with no puckers at the armhole. The grain should be straight.**

- The shoulder seams should lie smoothly with no puckers. The seam joining the sleeve to the shoulder should extend slightly—¼ to ½ inch (0.6 cm to 1.3 cm)—beyond the edge of the shoulder. The extra room allows the sleeve cap or *head* to roll smoothly so the sleeve hangs straight. The biceps, or large muscles in the upper arm, should not bulge the sleeve out of shape.
- The lapels should be flat and not stand away from the chest.
- The jacket collar should lie so that ½ inch (1.3 cm) of shirt collar shows above it. This keeps the jacket cleaner as body oils and soil will not be in contact with the suit collar.
- When the jacket is buttoned, it should lie against the body smoothly without pulling or gapping.
- The shirt cuff should end at the point where the hands join the wrists. The jacket sleeves should be ½ inch (1.3 cm) above the edge of the shirt cuffs and come to the wrist bone.
- When the arms are down straight at the sides, the jacket hem should come to the midpoint of the thumbs. The coat should cover the buttocks.

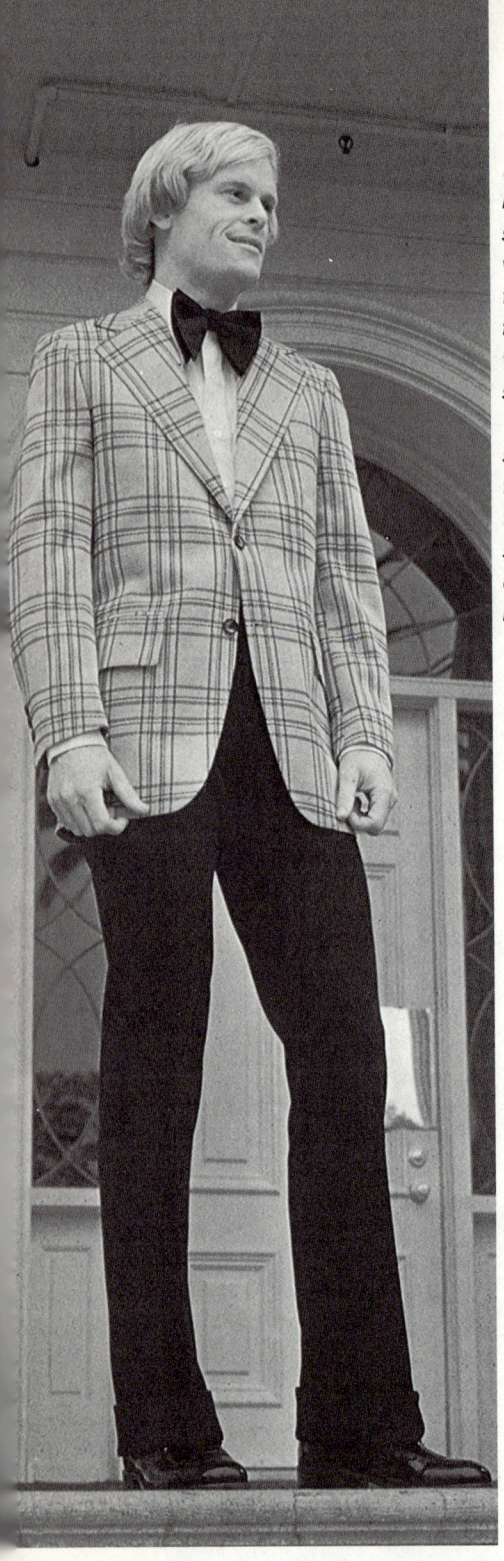

Courtesy Sears, Roebuck and Co.

F-4. A man's jacket should fit smoothly through the shoulders with no pull at the lapels or buttons. The sleeves curve slightly forward and come to the point where the hands join the arm. The shirt sleeves should show about 1/2 inch (1.3 cm) below the jacket sleeves with the collar showing 1/2 to 3/4 inch (1.3 to 2 cm) above the jacket collar. The jacket length should cover the buttocks and come to the curve of the second knuckle when the hand is slightly closed.

- Both the body of the jacket and the sleeves should lie against the body smoothly with no excess fabric to form fullness, "drape," or wrinkles. There should be enough room in the garment so no lines of "pulling" are visible.
- The area across the shoulders should lie smoothly with no excess fullness, drape, or bulge below the collar.

## JUDGING THE FIT OF MEN'S TROUSERS

The desirable fit for trousers is often dictated by fashion. Styles vary from tight to baggy and current styles affect the overall appearance desired by the wearer. Again, the man himself will determine which fit feels most comfortable. As a general rule:

- The waistline seam should rest just above the hip bone.
- The length of the pants leg should come just to the top of the shoe and hang straight. Some men prefer their trousers slightly longer so they rest on the shoe with a slight bend or "break" in the front. Usually the length looks better if it is about 1/2 inch (1.3 cm) longer in the back than in the front. Full or flared bottoms are usually worn longer that straight bottoms.
- The seat and rise should fit close enough to be smooth and not baggy without being so tight it binds and is uncomfortable when the man is seated.
- The legs should be wide enough to hang straight without pulling tight over large thigh or calf muscles. They should be loose enough to allow freedom of movement.
- The hip area should fit smoothly but be loose enough to cover bulges from articles in the pockets.

Courtesy Sears, Roebuck and Co.

F-5a, b. Men's slacks or trousers should come to the top of the shoe in front so the leg hangs straight with no "break" or bend. The back drops slightly over the heel.

**Altering Ready-To-Wear Fashions**

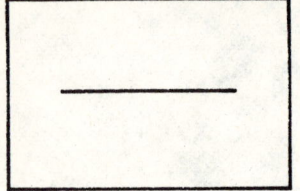

SHORTENING MARK

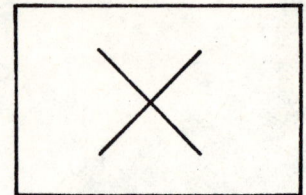

INDICATE ONE SIDE
ONLY TO BE ALTERED

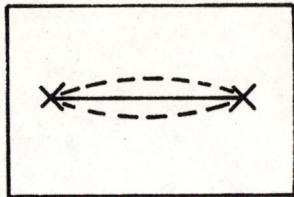

TAKE IN SPACE BETWEEN

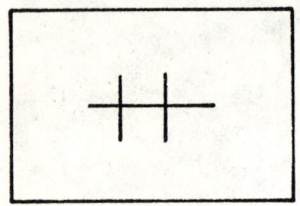

LENGTHENING MARK

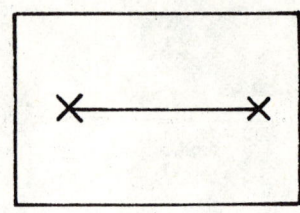

INDICATED SPACE TO BE RELEASED

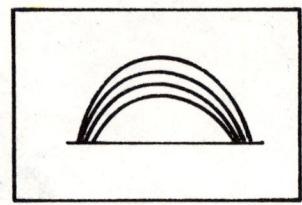

PADDING BY SHEETS

F-6. Tailors and bushelmen use symbols to indicate the changes needed rather than pinning the alterations as is done for women's clothes.

## FITTING MEN'S CLOTHES

Often the fittings required for menswear are done with the aid of measurements. The sales person or tailor may take and record measurements on the work ticket for you to use in making the alterations. They will probably use tailor's chalk to make marks indicating the changes to be made. Fig. F-6. Pins are not used as commonly as they are for women's wear.

A tape measure with a 2-inch (5 cm) long heavy fiberboard piece at one end—called a crotch piece—is used in taking measurements for men. Fig. F-7.

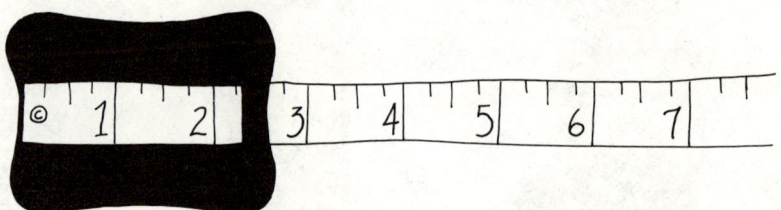

F-7. The tape measure used for men's wear has a special fiberboard piece on the end called a crotch piece.

When you are called upon to do a fitting for a man, be sure he has the garment adjusted the way he will wear it before you start.

• The trousers should be adjusted on the waistline where the man feels most comfortable and where he plans to wear them. With the aid of a belt or fitted waistband, the trousers should rest in the same position all day.

• If the trousers are to be worn with a tucked-in shirt, they should be fitted over a shirt.

### Ch. 12: Fitting and Altering Menswear

• The jacket should be buttoned and adjusted correctly on the shoulders—neither too far back nor too far forward.

The fitting will be more successful if done before a three-way mirror so the customer can watch what you are doing. Thus he will not be so apt to look down and throw the clothes out of line.

#### Measuring Trousers

When the trousers are adjusted in the proper place:

• Take the waist measurement over the shirt but not over the trousers. Hold the tape loose enough to slide a finger underneath it. Fig. F-8.

• To measure the outseam length, hold the end of the crotch piece at the bottom of the waistband and measure along the outside seam to the top of the shoe. You may wish to chalk a mark at that point on the bottom of the trouser leg. Also, record the measurement on the work ticket. Fig. F-9.

• To measure the inseam length, fit the crotch piece of the tape measure snugly into the crotch and continue measuring down the inside leg seam to the top of the shoe. Record the measurement and chalk the trousers at this point.

• To determine the length of the rise—or crotch seam—subtract the inseam measurement from the outseam measurement. Thus, if the outseam measures 42 inches (107 cm)

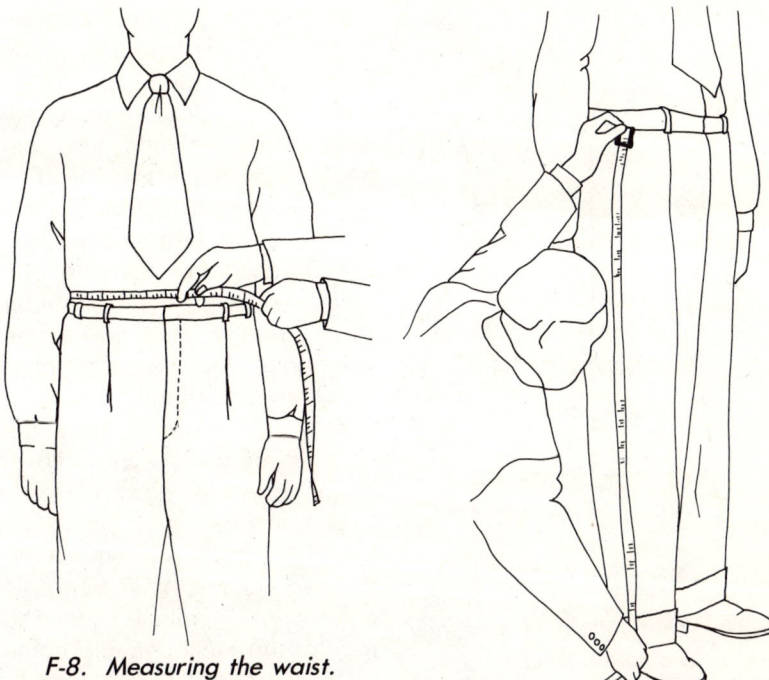

F-8. Measuring the waist.

F-9. Measuring the outseam.

and the inseam measures 32 inches (81 cm), the rise is 10 inches (25 cm). This means the area from the waistband seam in front to the bottom of the fly or fly point on the slacks front.

• Check the width of the trouser legs to see if they are too full or too tight. The outseams of most trousers are usually cut to from 1/4 to 1/2 inch (0.6 to 1.3 cm) wide and cannot be released. The inseams are usually wider. Most releasing of trouser legs will need to be done on the inseams. However, it is better if you can release or take up equal amounts on both the inseam and the outseams where possible. This helps keep the center crease and grain in place.

#### Measuring Jackets

Since the way a jacket should fit a man depends to some degree upon the way he prefers to have his jacket "feel," it is difficult to give definite directions. The fitter may take measurements, may make chalk marks, or, just record directions for the changes to be made on the work ticket.

The most commonly used measurements for a man's jacket are the jacket length, sleeve length, and chest, waist, and

313

## Altering Ready-To-Wear Fashions

F-10. Taking chest, waist, and hip measurements.

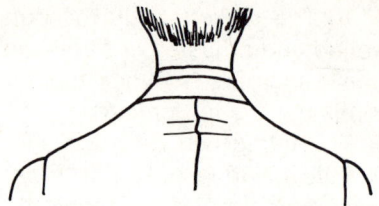

F-11. Bulge showing below the coat collar across the back shoulders.

hip. See Fig. F-10. In measuring the chest and waist, the amount of ease to be left depends upon the amount of freedom the man wants in his clothes.

- To take the chest measurement, hold the tape firmly around the body across the fullest part of the chest. Be sure the tape is straight across the shoulder blades and does not droop down. Ask the man to inhale and expand his chest to the fullest amount. Record this measurement.
- To take the waist measurement, place the tape around the waist and keep one finger underneath it as you read the measurement.
- To take the hip measurement, place the tape around the largest part of the hips.
- If the customer has a very large abdomen and the coat gaps over this area, you may need to record the measurement over the largest part.
- To take the sleeve length, measure from the shoulder seam, around the elbow to the wrist bone. Ask the customer to bend his arm slightly.
- If you need to take the measurement for the jacket length, measure down the center back seam to a point just below the buttocks. It may help to have the customer bend his fingers into a relaxed fist. The hem of the jacket should come to the bend of the second knuckles.

## FITTING JACKETS

### Fullness Under the Collar

The slope of a man's shoulders and the length of his neck will affect the way the jacket shoulders sit. Check the back of the jacket across the shoulders, directly under the collar. If the collar needs lowering, you will see a bulge, roll, or wrinkle across this area. Fig. F-11.

TO FIT: Pinch the extra fabric into a horizontal tuck at the center back seam to see how much fabric should be removed. The maximum amount that can be removed is $3/4$ inch (1.9 cm). Make a chalk mark across the center back seam to indicate how far the collar should be lowered. Record amount on work ticket.

### Shoulders Too Wide

The jacket should be adjusted on the figure so the armhole seam extends over the edge of the shoulder from $1/4$ to $1/2$ inch (0.6 to 1.3 cm). If the shoulders are too wide, the adjustment should be made in the center back seam.

TO FIT: Pull the center back seam out toward you until the armhole seams are in the proper place. When you do this, the collar and jacket will stand away from the neck in the back. Make a chalk mark along the center back seam to indicate how much the seam needs to be increased. Indicate with chalk the point where this larger seam will be tapered back into the original center back seam—about 6 inches (15 cm) down.

### Shoulders Too Sloping

If the man is very slope-shouldered and you find the

## Ch. 12: Fitting and Altering Menswear

jacket "breaks" or gathers in folds under the arm, both front and back, you will need to increase the shoulder seam and add to the shoulder pads.

TO FIT: Lift the shoulder of the jacket until the folds under the arms disappear. Estimate how much must be taken out of the shoulder seam to raise the garment that much. Record on work ticket.

NOTE: It is wisest to ask the customer to return for a second fitting to be sure your estimate is correct before pressing and cutting away any material from the shoulder seam.

### Chest Too Full

If there are folds of material across the chest between the lapels and the shoulders, the jacket is too wide across the chest area. This fullness will be taken out of the underarm dart or front underarm seam.

TO FIT: Pin up the excess by increasing the size of the dart until the coat lies flat and feels right on the customer. Mark the new stitching line with chalk. Record the amount on the work ticket.

### Coat Too Snug at Front

If the jacket is too snug across the waist and abdomen, the jacket will gap between the buttons.

TO FIT: You may either estimate the amount to be let out of the back side seams, or check the jacket against the man's measurements. Indicate on the work ticket the amount the side seams should be released.

### Coat Overlaps in Front

If the jacket is too full and hangs in folds when buttoned, you must determine how much should be removed from the jacket fronts.

TO FIT: Pull the jacket together in front to see how much overlap there is. Indicate on the work ticket how much should be removed. Check the location of the side seams to be sure whether the extra should be removed from just the front sections of the side seam or whether the back side seam should be taken in equally both front and back. Indicate on the work ticket.

### Coat Pulls Across Back

If the jacket pulls across the back of the shoulders or waist, it will need to be released. This alteration is usually done in the center back seam. The amount to be released will be determined by measurements.

TO FIT: Ask the man to raise his folded arms in front of him and shrug his shoulders forward. Record the measurement from the point where his arm joins his body on one side across the shoulders to the other arm. Indicate on the work ticket how much needs to be released from the center seam.

If the jacket is too tight in the waist in back, it is probably too tight in front also. Releasing the side seams to make the fronts larger will take care of the problem.

## FITTING TROUSERS

As in everything else, the fitting is done from the top down.

Start at the waistline and check to see that it is comfortable.

### Waistline Too Tight

TO FIT: If the waistline is too tight, indicate with a chalk mark the amount to be released from the back seam. Record on the work ticket.

### Waistline Too Loose

If the waist is too loose, the back seam will have to be increased.

TO FIT: Hold the excess fabric with one hand like a tuck. Make a chalk mark on one side to show the amount to be taken out. Fig. F-12. Make a chalk mark at the lower end of the fold to indicate where the new seam will be tapered back into the original seam. Write the directions for the change on the work ticket.

NOTE: You may need to pin the tuck in place long enough to measure length of trousers.

### Crotch Seam Too Tight

If the crotch area is too tight, write the amount to be released on the work ticket. An experienced fitter can usually estimate this amount without any

## Altering Ready-To-Wear Fashions

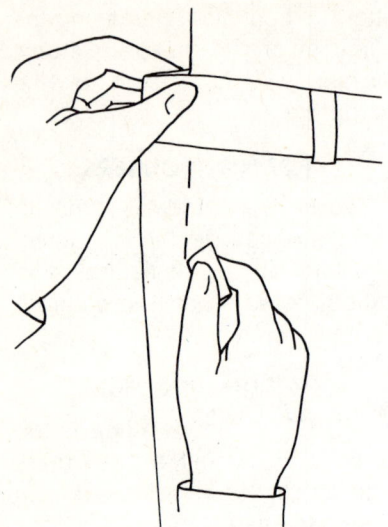

F-12. Marking the amount to be removed from the center back trousers seam.

actual fitting. If you cannot do that, the amount may be determined by subtracting the inseam measurement from the outseam measurement.

### Seat Too Long and Baggy

If the seat is too long, write the amount that should be taken up on the work ticket. This amount can be determined by the measurements of the inseam and the outseam. *No more* than 1 1/2 inches (3.8 cm) can be removed from the seat successfully.

### Trouser Legs Too Wide

Too much width in the trouser legs to suit the customer is usually taken out equally on each inseam and outseam. The customer will usually tell you how wide he wants the trouser legs to be.

### Trouser Length

To check the length of the trousers, measure and record the outseam measurement from the bottom of the waistband to the top of the shoe. Mark this point with a chalk mark, if desired. Or, fold up the excess fabric and pin in place. See Fig. F-9.

### SPECIAL POINTERS FOR ALTERATIONS

As you start to work, keep the following in mind.

• When you take in a new seam, always leave the seam as wide as possible. Trim only the amount necessary to keep the seam from pulling when you press it.

• Always remember you are sewing double when you take in or let out a seam. For example, if you release a seam 1/2 inch (1.3 cm), you are letting out 1 inch (2.5 cm).

• Never make a new seam without pressing it well. Pressing brings out the beauty in your work. Old crease lines advertise to the world that the garment has been altered.

• Always exercise extreme care in ripping out the original seam. One small slip with a ripper or scissors can ruin an entire garment. If the stitches are especially small, it may be wise to pick the stitches out one by one so you do not damage the fabric.

• Always check your measurements twice before you proceed to work on a garment. Think twice before you cut. You may be asked to alter that same garment again sometime.

• Before starting to rip or alter, study the garment to understand how it was made originally. Always try to put it back the same way after making the changes. Sometimes it is better to work on only one side at a time so you can refer to the other side to see how it was made.

### ALTERING TROUSERS
#### Waistlines

If 1 1/2 inches (3.8 cm) or less are to be removed from the waist, the entire amount can be taken out in the center back seam.

1. Untack center back belt loop and release waistband lining so it swings free.
2. Pin the back seam the amount to be taken in. Remember a 1/2-inch (1.3 cm) seam increase will remove an inch from the total measurement.
3. Start stitching at the top of the band lining and continue stitching across the waistline seam. Taper the back seam so it rejoins the original seam at the point indicated by the fitter. Fig. F-13.
4. Rip the original seam carefully.
5. Press the new seam open.

## Ch. 12: Fitting and Altering Menswear

6. Replace waistband lining to its original position. Tack back in place with same method used by manufacturer.

7. Replace belt loop.

If the amount to be removed from the waist measurement is more than 1½ inches (3.8 cm), the side pockets will have to be removed and reset.

1. Rip the belt loops and the waistband from the center back to an inch (2.5 cm) or so beyond the outseam on each side.

2. Open the side seams to the hip area and remove the side pockets.

3. Replace pockets on new seam lines which remove ½ inch (1.3 cm) from both the back and front of each side seam. Fig. F-14. Trim excess fabric from seam. Finish pocket seams as they were before.

4. Press side seams.

5. Replace waistband.

6. Take in the back seam ½ inch (1.3 cm) as in steps 2 and 3 in altering waistlines.

7. Press waistband if necessary.

8. Replace loops.

### Altering Seat and Crotch

#### LOWERING THE RISE

Sometimes trousers are too tight through the crotch seam and are uncomfortable to wear.

1. Open the seat seam 1 inch (2.5 cm) on each side of the inseams.

2. Open the inseam almost to the knee.

3. When restitching the inseam, release the back part of the seam as much as necessary, using the extra fabric on the back of the trouser leg—called the outlet. Some less expensive trousers do not have this extra fabric. In such trousers, the inseam may be too narrow to allow any releasing. If you have enough fabric from the amount cut off the bottom of the trouser legs, you could use it to piece the back of the leg. Use the same procedure as in adding a sleeve gusset. See Chapter 9, "Sleeve Alterations." This fabric may be used crosswise grain. If extra fabric is not available, you would not be able to make this alteration.

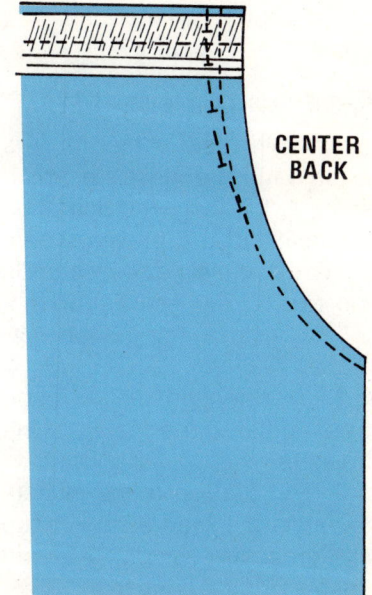

F-13. Increasing the center back seam in trousers.

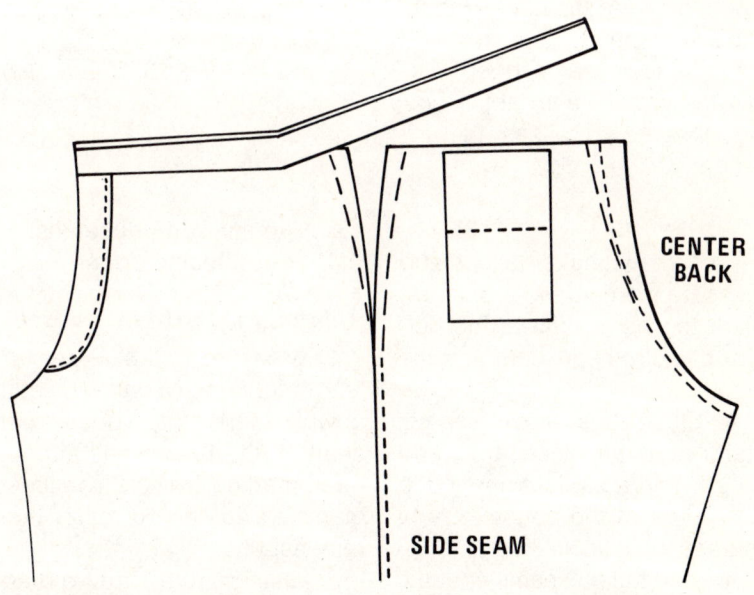

F-14. Increasing side seams after removal of pockets.

## Altering Ready-To-Wear Fashions

4. Restitch crotch seam and press.

### SHORTENING THE SEAT SEAM

When the seat of the trousers is too baggy because the crotch seam is too long, the alteration is similar to the previous one, except that the back inseam is increased. Remember, do not try to remove more than 1½ inches (3.8 cm).

1. Transfer the marks made by the fitter to the inside of the trousers.
2. Rip the top of the inseam as far as the knee area. Rip the crotch seam 1 inch (2.5 cm) each side of the inseam.
3. Pin the original front inseam line to the back leg 1 inch (2.5 cm) in from the original seam. See Fig. C-38, Chapter 9. Stitch. This will not shorten the length between the end of the fly and the inseams.
4. Press inseams open. Rejoin the crotch seam at the bottom where it crosses the inseams.

### Tapering Trouser Legs

1. Turn wrong side out and measure the new width desired. Mark the new width at the bottom of both the inseam and the outseam.
2. Stitch the new seams, starting at the knee area and tapering in a straight line to the new mark at the bottom. Try to release or take in both the inseam and the outseams equally, if possible.

3. Rip the original seams.
4. Press seams open.

### Hemming Uncuffed Trousers

1. Measure the desired length from the waistband seam down. Mark this point with chalk. If the length has already been marked for you, use those marks to guide you rather than remeasuring.
2. Using a ruler, draw a diagonal line across the bottom of the pants leg on both sides—½ inch (1.3 cm) longer in back than in front. Fig. F-15, Line 1.
3. Measure 2½ or 3 inches (6.4 or 7.6 cm) down from this line and draw another line parallel with the first line. Fig. F-15, Line 2.
4. Place the marked leg on top of the unmarked leg and mark the second leg to match the first. *Always mark the second leg from the first one rather*

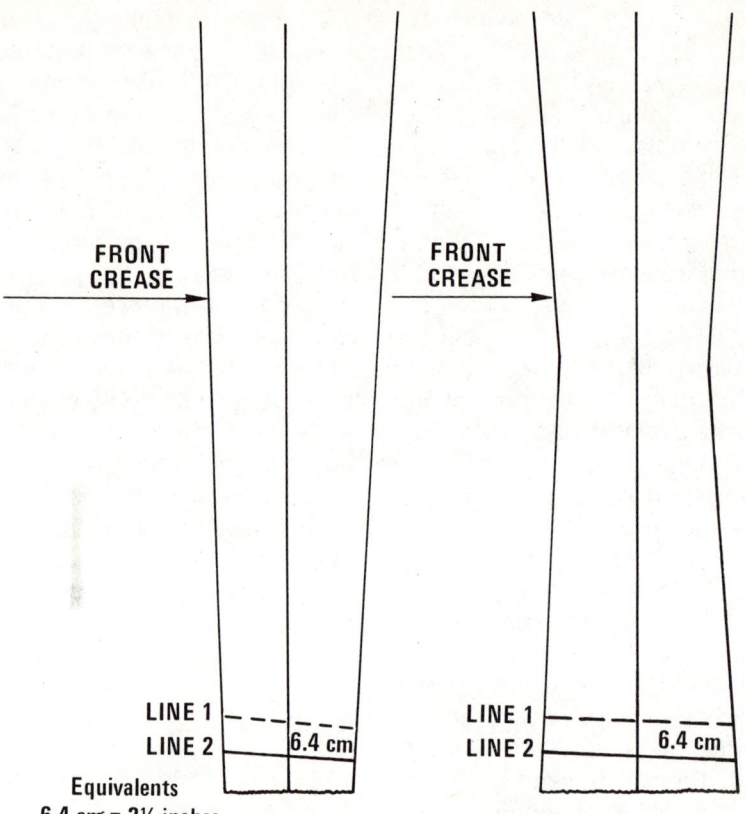

F-15. Measuring for uncuffed trousers.

### Ch. 12: Fitting and Altering Menswear

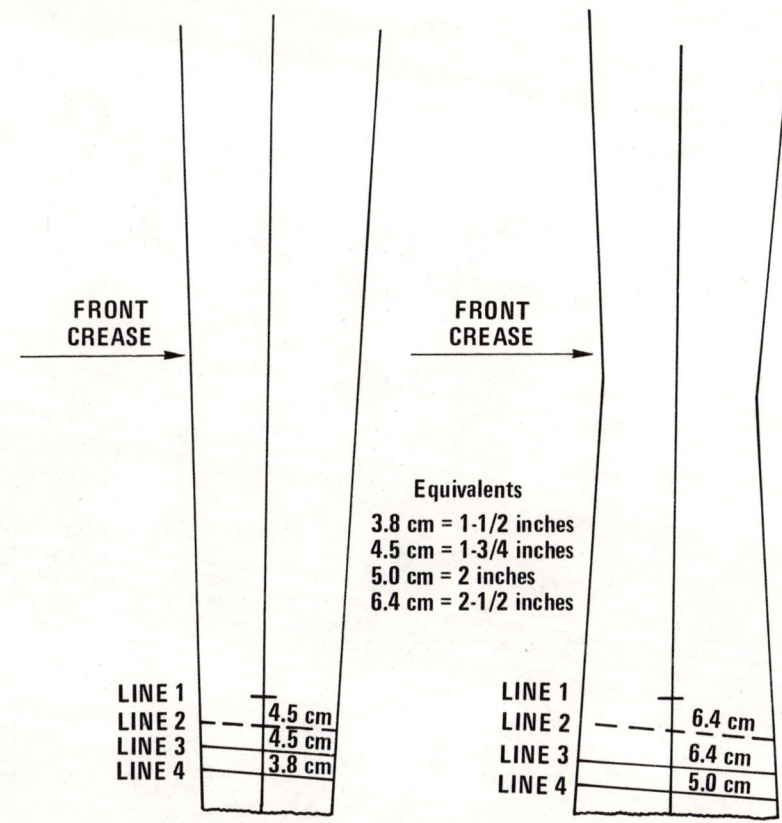

F-16. Measuring for trousers with cuffs.

Equivalents
3.8 cm = 1-1/2 inches
4.5 cm = 1-3/4 inches
5.0 cm = 2 inches
6.4 cm = 2-1/2 inches

1. Measure from the waistband seam down to the desired length, or use the fitter's marks. Fig. F-16, Line 1.

2. Measure from this line to the desired width of the cuff. Draw a diagonal line across the trouser leg on both sides at this point so that the trousers will be $1/2$ inch (1.3 cm) longer in back. Fig. F-16, Line 2.

3. Mark a third line the same distance from Line 2 as 2 is from Line 1. Fig. F-16, Line 3.

4. Measure $1 1/2$ inches (3.8 cm) down from this line for straight-leg trousers, 2 inches (5 cm) down for flares. Trim away any excess fabric left below Line 4. The extra amount is left for stitching and future alterations.

5. Fold fabric under along Line 2 and stitch at top of hem with catch stitch or machine blindstitch. *Be sure cuffs are even and matching on both legs.*

6. Fold cuff to the outside along Line 1. Press.

7. Tack cuff in place at the side seams so the tacking doesn't show on the right side. See Chapter 11 for detailed information.

NOTE: If you do cuffs on trousers frequently, you will find it to your advantage to make a set of cuffing tools or measuring guides shown in Figs. F-17 a, b,c,d. These guides are easy to make from any firm cardboard. Fig. 18 shows how to use the cuffing tool.

than measuring twice (unless the customer has one leg shorter than the other). This not only saves time, but it is also more accurate.

5. Cut off excess fabric below Line 2.

6. Turn fabric under on Line 1 and hem with a catch stitch or a hemming machine. (See Chapter 10, "Hems.")

NOTE: If the hem is too narrow to fit back into the trouser leg, steam and stretch the crosswise grain at the top of the hem to make it fit.

7. Press.

### Making Cuffs

The width of the cuff varies according to the current style and the width of the trouser flair at the bottom. You and your customer will have to decide how wide the cuff should be.

## Altering Ready-To-Wear Fashions

F-17a, b, c, d. Measuring gauges for cuffing trousers.

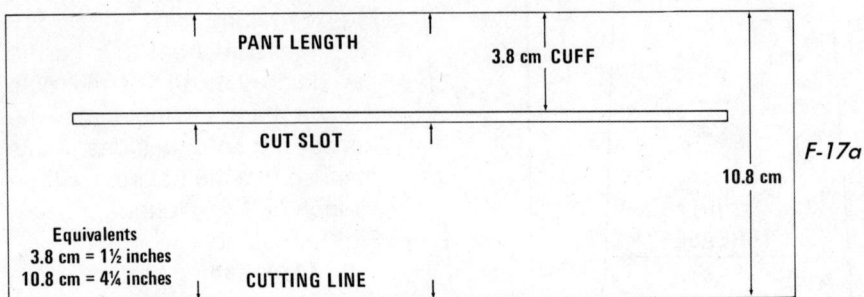

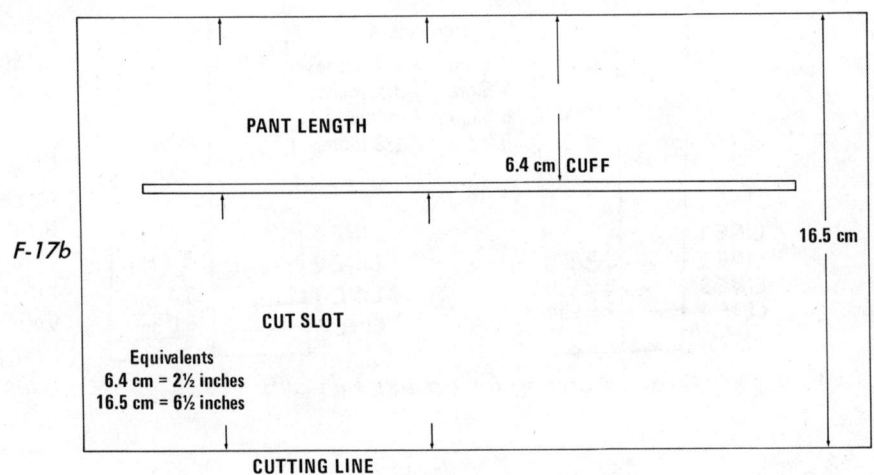

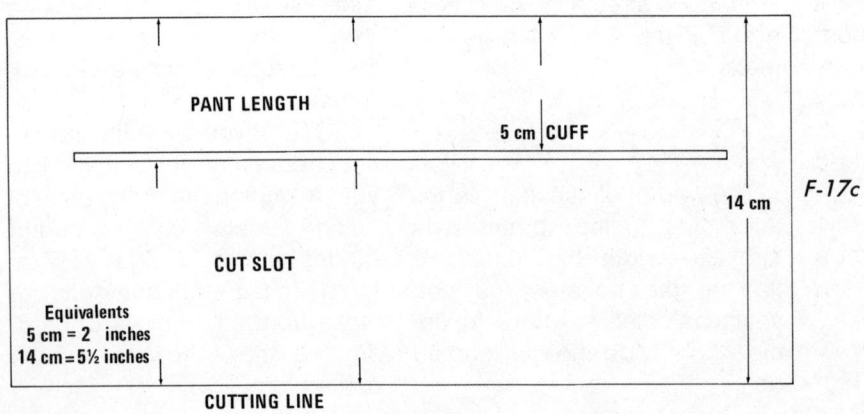

*Ch. 12: Fitting and Altering Menswear*

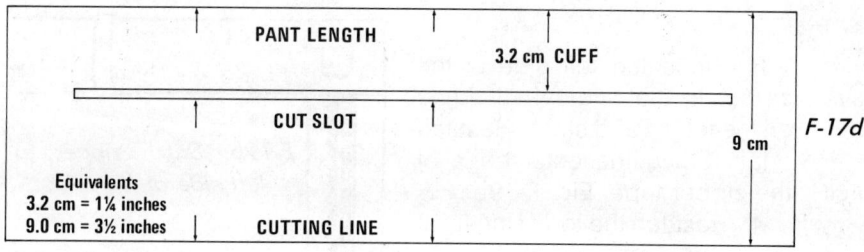

F-17d

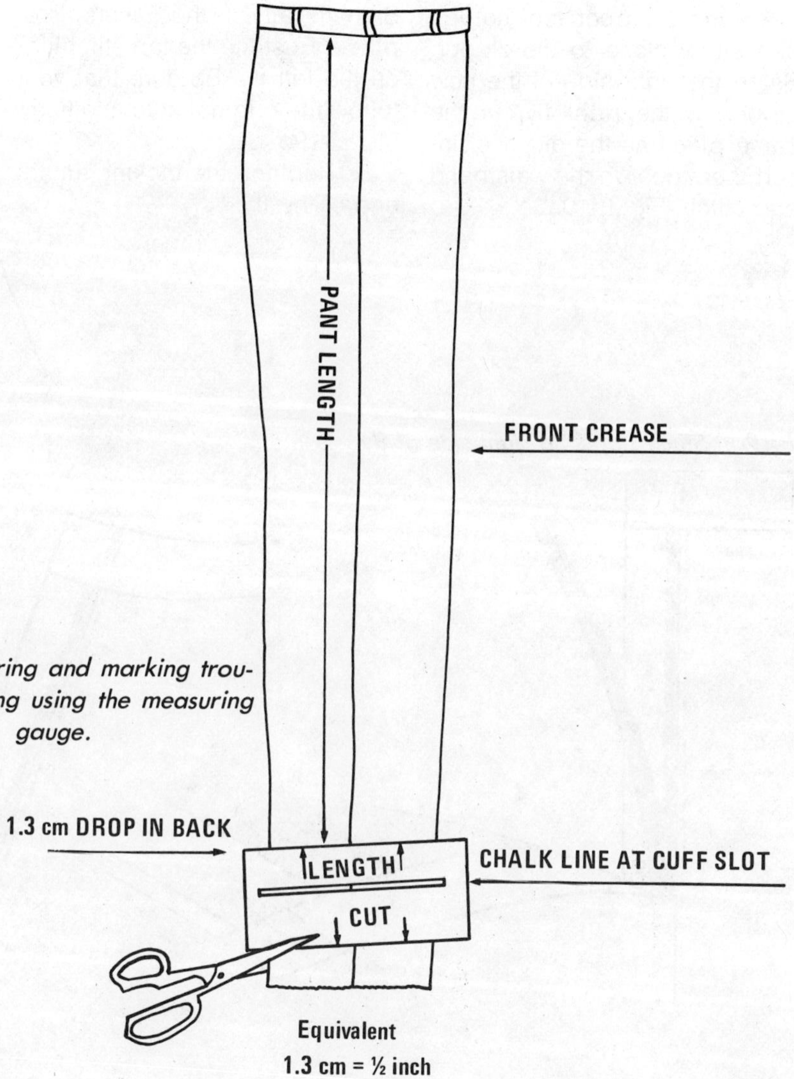

F-18. Measuring and marking trousers for cuffing using the measuring gauge.

1.3 cm DROP IN BACK

CHALK LINE AT CUFF SLOT

Equivalent
1.3 cm = ½ inch

**Altering Ready-To-Wear Fashions**

## Replacing Zippers

Often, alterations will require the replacement of a defective zipper.

1. Rip the old zipper from both sides of the fly. Rip just enough at the top of each fly to allow you to remove the old zipper. Rip out the top stitching on the left fly.

2. Use a zipper foot so you can stitch close to the zipper. Stitch the right side of the new zipper to the right fly, in the same place as the old one. Insert the zipper in the waistband and stitch. Fig. F-19a.

3. Place the left side of the zipper in the original stitchline on the left fly and stitch. Restitch again along the outer edge of the zipper tape. Fig. F-19b.

4. Restitch the top of the fly at the waist.

5. Turn the trousers right side out with the zipper open. Smooth all of the layers into place. Restitch the top stitching on the left fly. Be sure that you follow the original stitching line. Fig. F-19c.

6. Replace the tacking at the end of the fly.

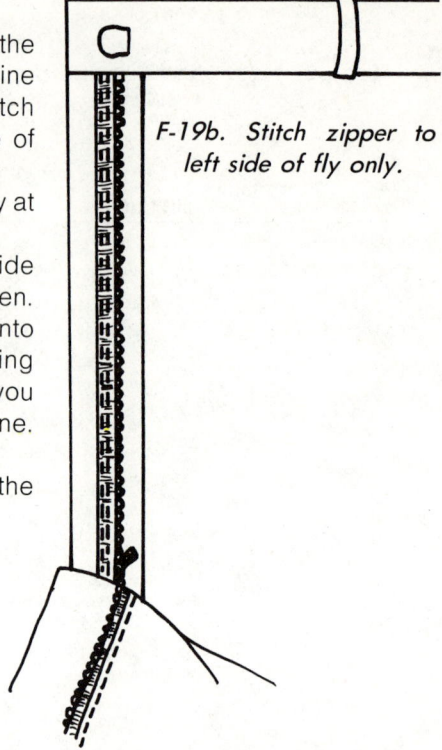

F-19b. Stitch zipper to left side of fly only.

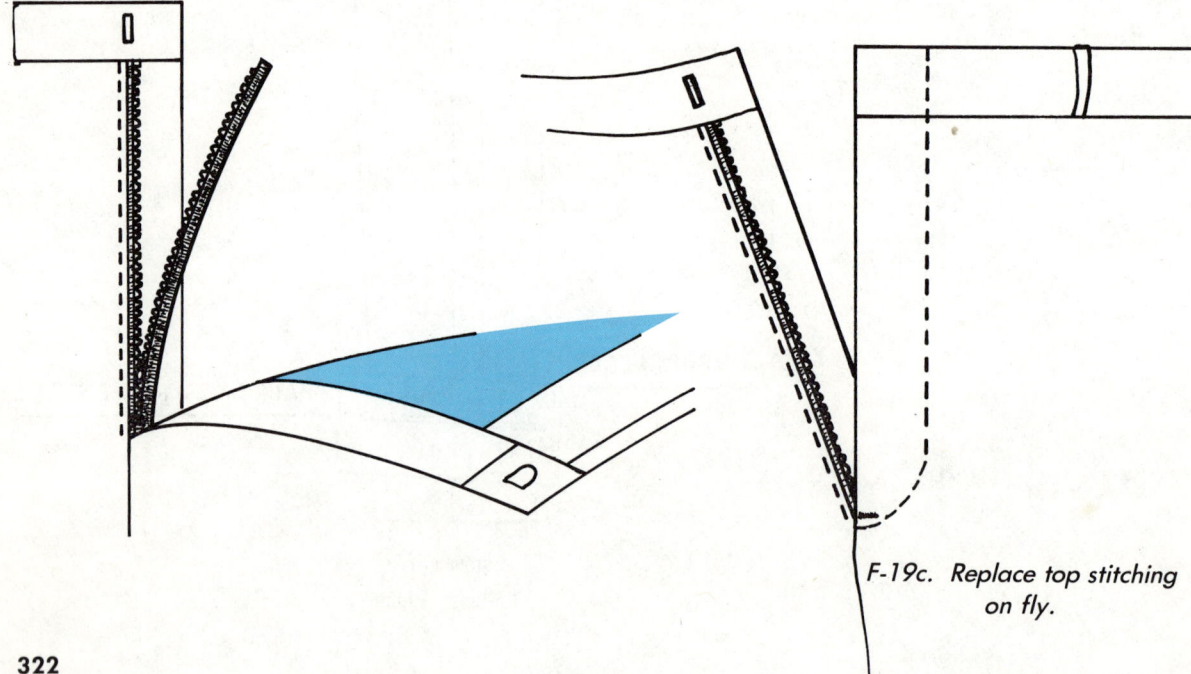

F-19a. Stitch zipper to right side of fly.

F-19c. Replace top stitching on fly.

Ch. 12: Fitting and Altering Menswear

## JACKET ALTERATIONS

Men's jackets are made one of two ways. The side seam is always slightly behind the underarm rather than directly underneath as in most women's clothes. The front section may have a long dart which ends at the lower pocket. Or, there may be a full seam going to the bottom of the jacket. This seam is referred to as the underarm or front dart. See Fig. F-20 for an explanation of the terms used.

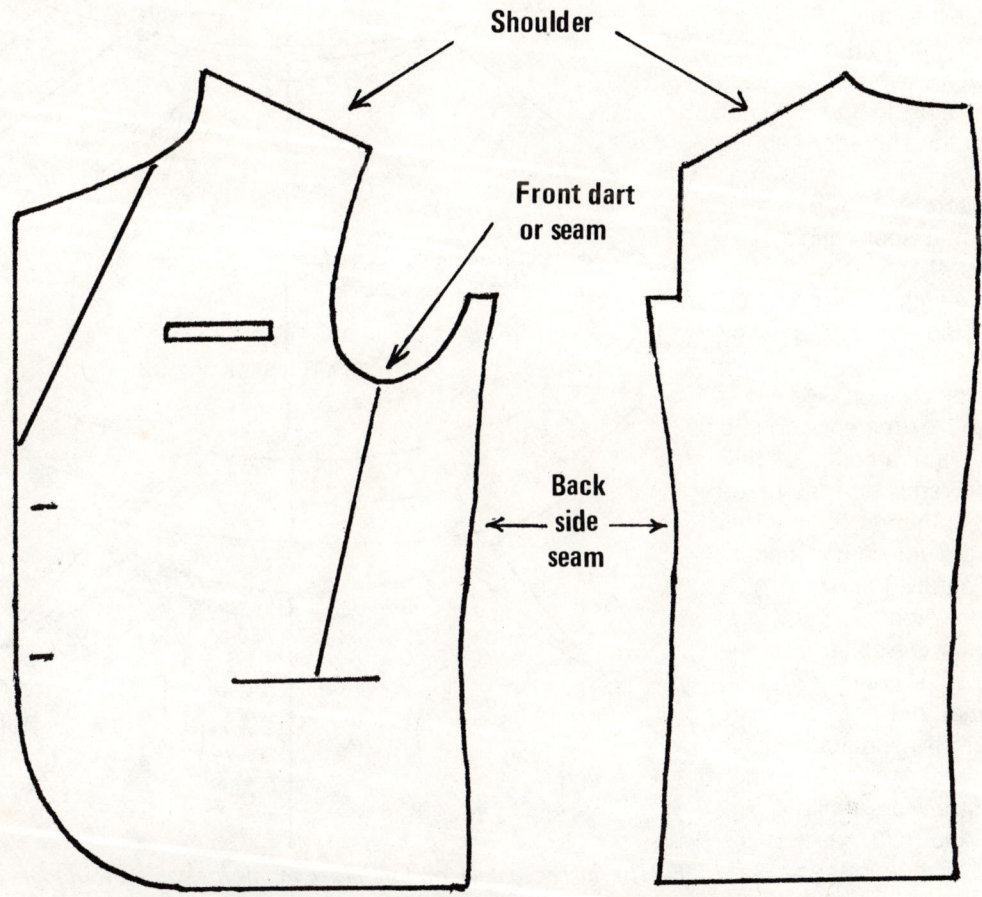

F-20. Separated jacket pieces showing seams referred to in text.

## Altering Ready-To-Wear Fashions

### Removing Fullness Beneath Collar in Back

If the bulge below the collar consists of a tuck about 1/4 inch (0.6 cm) deep, the excess can usually be removed by shrinking it out with the steam iron and extra moisture on the press cloth. Try this method first. If you find that the fabric will not shrink, then you can lower the collar slightly.

1. Detach the collar from the center back to the shoulder seams.
2. Lower the collar seam on the coat 1/4 inch (0.6 cm) at the center back. Taper the seam gradually back to the original location at the shoulder seams. Fig. F-21a.
3. Restitch the top collar along the new seam line.
4. Press.
5. Fell stitch (Chapter 11, Fig. E-10) the undercollar back in place.

If the customer has a short neck and extremely square shoulders, the amount of fullness to be removed may be as much as 3/4 inch (1.9 cm). This is about the maximum amount you can safely remove in this type of alteration.

1. Detach the collar from the neck edge to 1 inch (2.5 cm) beyond shoulder seams.
2. Open the shoulder seams from the neck to about 1 inch (2.5 cm) from the armhole. *Remember you will need to restitch the shoulder seam and may not want to disturb the seam where the sleeve joins the shoulder.*
3. Increase the shoulder seams so that you remove the same amount by which you will be lowering the collar. Fig. F-21b.
4. Trim and press the new shoulder seams.
5. Baste the collar to the coat along the chalk line the fitter made to indicate how much the collar should be lowered. Stitch as basted.
6. Fell stitch (Chapter 11, Fig. E-10) the undercollar back in place to the top collar.
7. Press.

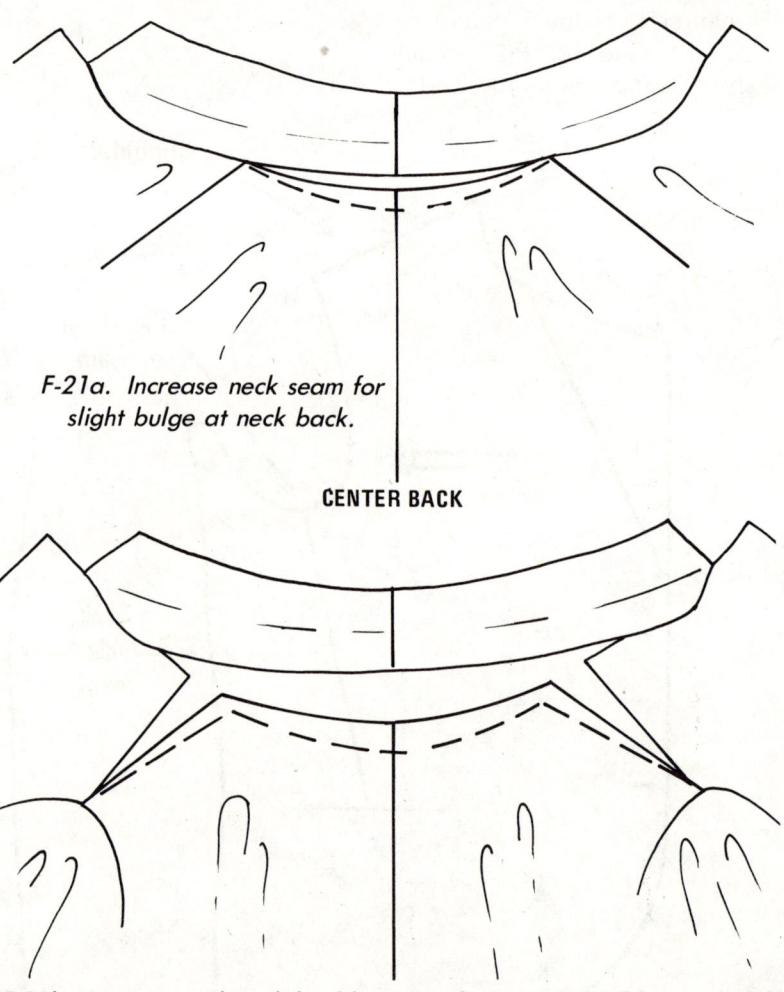

F-21a. Increase neck seam for slight bulge at neck back.

CENTER BACK

F-21b. Increase neck and shoulder seams for square shoulders and neck bulge.

## Ch. 12: Fitting and Altering Menswear

### Collar Stands Away from the Neck

If the collar stands away from the neck in back, both the collar and the center back seam will need to be altered.

1. Rip the top collar loose on the right-hand side of the coat from the front to about an inch (2.5 cm) beyond the center back seam.

2. Take in the center back seam of the coat the amount required—1 inch (2.5 cm) would be the maximum, or 1/2 inch (1.3 cm) on each side of the seam.

3. Taper the center back seam into the original seam about 6 inches (15 cm) down from the neck edge.

4. Take 1 inch (2.5 cm) out of the undercollar at the center back seam. If the undercollar is all in one piece, make a new half-inch (1.3 cm) seam. Press.

5. Trim the excess fabric on the coat back. Trim the corners of the undercollar seam. Fig. F-22a.

6. Carefully reshape the top collar to the shortened undercollar. The top collar will now be longer than the undercollar by the same amount you removed in the new seams.

7. Baste the top collar to the undercollar and trim away the excess fabric on the lapel edge of the collar. Fig. F-22b.

8. Reattach the top collar to the undercollar by the same method used in the original construction of the garment. Sometimes the collars have been machine stitched together and sometimes they have been hand sewn with the felling stitch.

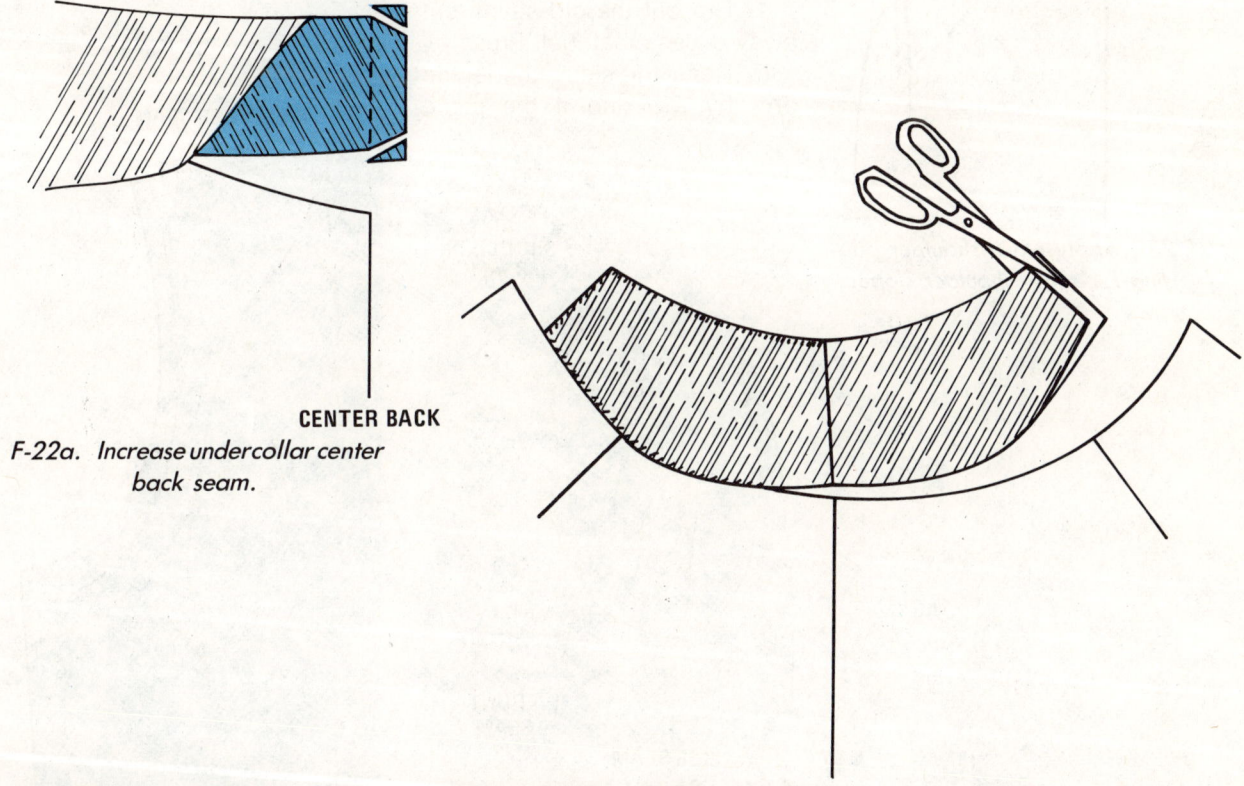

F-22a. Increase undercollar center back seam.

F-22b. Reshape upper collar to fit shortened undercollar.

## Altering Ready-To-Wear Fashions

### Sloping Shoulders

If the customer's shoulders slope more than usual, the coat will "break" or fold under the armhole in front and in back. A slight break can usually be remedied by the addition of extra shoulder padding. Increase the pad size, using the same method of application as in the original. Fig. F-23. See Chapter 11 for shoulder pads.

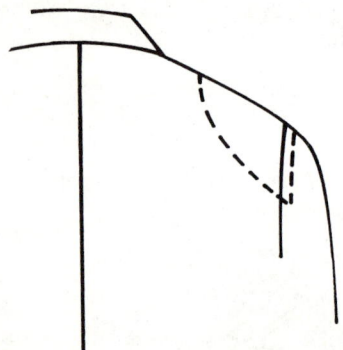

F-23. Apply extra shoulder padding for slight shoulder slope.

### Excessive Slope

To correct the fit for excessively sloping shoulders:

1. Baste around the armhole about 2 inches (5 cm) from the seam to hold the lining and interfacing firmly in place. Fig. F-24a.
2. Rip the sleeve and sleeve lining loose at the armhole.
3. Increase the shoulder seam the required amount indicated by the fitter. Taper the seam carefully back into the original seam at the collar edge. Fig. F-24b. *At this point, ask the customer to return for a second fitting.*
4. Rip out the old seam, cut away excess material. Press.
5. Reset the sleeve under the arm by lowering it the same amount you removed from the shoulder seam. For example, if you took a half inch (1.3 cm) seam in the shoulder, you would drop the underarm seam one inch. Remember, each seam has two sides, so a half inch (1.3 cm) is actually an inch (2.5 cm). Drop the sleeve notches the same amount, both front and back, to keep the sleeve in line.
6. Restitch armhole seams, trim excess seams, replace shoulder pads. Baste lining over new armhole seam.
7. Fell stitch top of sleeve lining to new armhole seam.

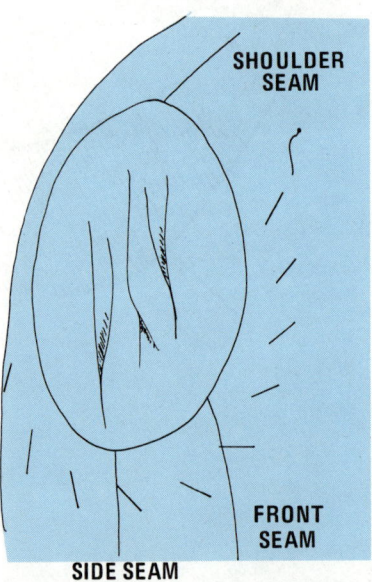

F-24a. Baste lining in place before working on shoulder seams.

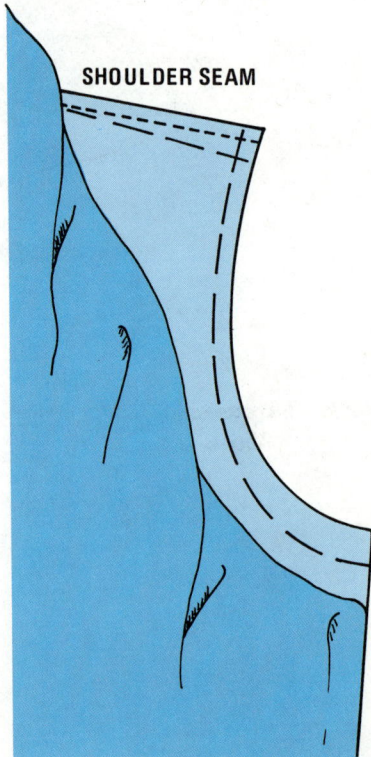

F-24b. Increase shoulder seam.

Ch. 12: Fitting and Altering Menswear

### Coat Too Snug at Front

About 1½ inches (3.8 cm) can be released successfully from the front to make the coat larger.

1. If the coat is lined, rip the lining just enough to be able to work on the seams. Open the side seams as close to the armhole as possible. Rip bottom hem 2 inches (5 cm) each side of side seam.

2. Release as much as possible from the front of the seam. Fig. F-25. If there is not enough material on the front seam to allow the increase needed, release some from the back seam also.

3. Restitch seams. Press. Resew hem and lining.

4. Slip-stitch the lining back in place.

5. Move the buttons ¼ inch (0.6 cm) closer to the front edge.

### Coat Overlaps in Front

As much as 1½ inches (3.8 cm) may also be removed from the front of a jacket without throwing it too much out of line.

1. If lined, rip lining just enough to work on the seams. Open the side seam as near to the armhole as possible and still leave room to resew it successfully.

2. Take up the side seam ¾ inch (1.9 cm) on both front sides. Keep the original position on the back side seam. Fig. F-26.

3. Press seams open and slip-stitch lining back in place.

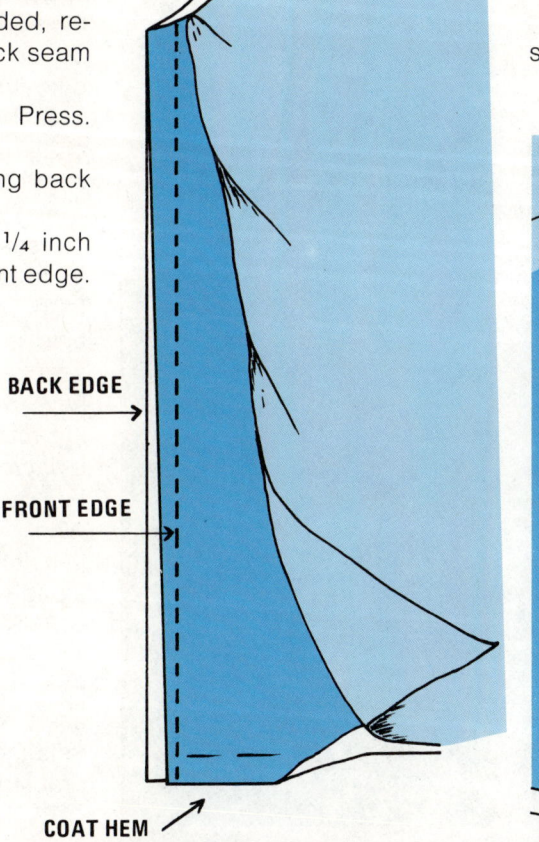

F-25. Release front edge of back side seam.

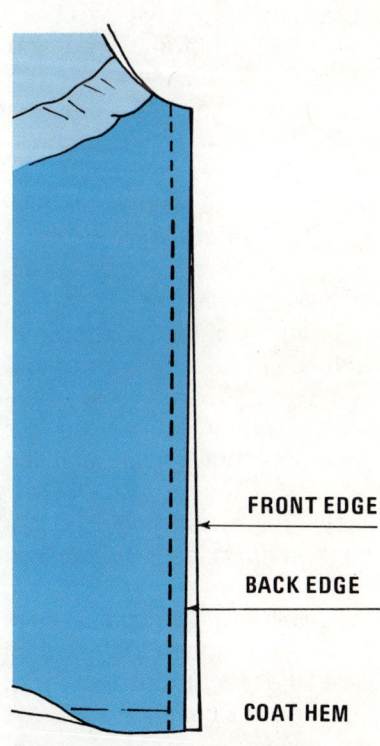

F-26. Increase the back side seam on front edge only.

## Altering Ready-To-Wear Fashions

### Chest Too Full

The coat shows too much fullness through the chest area but fits over the abdomen and waist. As much as 2 inches (5 cm) may be removed from this area.

1. Baste the lining and interfacing in place with a line of basting about 2 inches (5 cm) from the armhole seam. See Fig. F-24a.
2. Rip the front sleeve and sleeve lining seams from the shoulder seam down to about an inch (2.5 cm) beyond the front underarm dart or seam.
3. Increase the underarm dart 1/2 inch (1.3 cm) to take out a total of one inch (2.5 cm) on each dart.
4. Rip the old dart seam and press.
5. Lower the sleeve seam in front the same amount you removed from the dart. Fig. F-27.
6. Reset the sleeves and lining. Remove basting.

### Coat Pulls Across the Back

Some men have a problem with round shoulders or prominent shoulder blades. They need extra room across the shoulders but not through the rest of the coat.

1. If lined, rip lining at bottom back seam enough to work on seam.
2. Release the center back seam the required amount to give the room needed. Start stitching as near the collar as you have working room. Gradually taper the seam out to the amount needed across the shoulders and then gradually taper back in to the original seam at the waist.
3. Remove the original seam through the altered area and press. The pressing must be carefully and completely done. This is a very noticeable alteration if the crease is not completely removed.
4. Slip-stitch lining back in place.

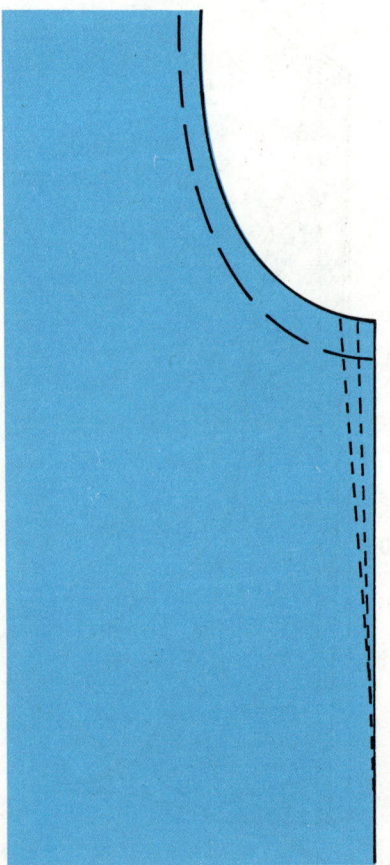

F-27. *Increase the side front seam or dart (may be either).*

### Shortening Sleeves

1. Measure the desired length for the sleeves and mark with chalk on both the inside and the outside of the arm.
2. Run a diagonal basting stitch (See Chapter 9, Fig. 40a.) around the sleeve about 6 to 8 inches (15 to 20 cm) from the bottom to hold the lining in place.
3. Remove sleeve buttons and rip out the hem of the lining around the bottom of the sleeve.
   NOTE: Observe carefully the spacing of the buttons and method used in finishing the button seam so you can duplicate the same method.
4. Turn the sleeve up on the chalk marks indicating the desired length.
5. Catch stitch the sleeve to the seam only. The sleeve hem is never sewn to the outside fabric of the sleeve. It is always held in place by tacking to the seams. Jacket sleeves usually have a narrow strip of interfacing around the bottom. This interfacing is held in place by being stitched into the seams. When you shorten the sleeve, this interfacing is turned back along with the sleeve fabric.
6. Refinish button seam as done in the original manufacture. Many different methods are used for this seam finish, so detailed instructions are impractical.
7. Replace the sleeve lining to position and fell stitch in place.

8. Press new hem.

9. Replace sleeve buttons—spaced as before alteration—and remove basting.

### Shortening Men's Jackets

Jackets that fit short, full-figured men through the shoulders and chest are often too long. The most difficult part of this alteration is to make sure the curved front edges are retained accurately and smoothly.

1. Make a paper pattern of the round front edge using the bottom edge of the jacket front as the straight grain. Fig. F-28a.

2. Release lining across the bottom and up the side seams 2 inches (5 cm) above the new hem line. Take out the old hem.

3. If jacket has top or trim stitching, remove this stitching only. *Do not rip facing seam around the curve.*

4. Turn facing to wrong side.

5. Press hem and facing seam flat.

6. Lay pattern (made in Step 1) even with the new hem line with the front edge of the pattern along the front *seam* of the jacket. Fig. F-28b.

7. Draw new curve around the edge of the pattern for your new stitching line on both jacket front sections.

8. Stitch along marking. Check to be sure both fronts are stitched to exactly the same length.

9. Starting ½ inch (1.3 cm) from the inside edge of the facing, trim seam to ¼ inch (0.6 cm). If fabric is heavy, grade the seam by trimming one side closer than the other to remove bulk. The facing edge would be trimmed closer than the coat edge. Cut small notches out of the seam to relieve the bulk.

10. Turn right side out, smooth all layers, and press facing seam carefully on the *facing* side. Turn up jacket bottom along the new hem line and press new hem edge in place.

11. Trim excess fabric to leave the new hem the same depth as the original one.

12. Replace hem with a tailor's stitch.

13. Slip-stitch lining back in place.

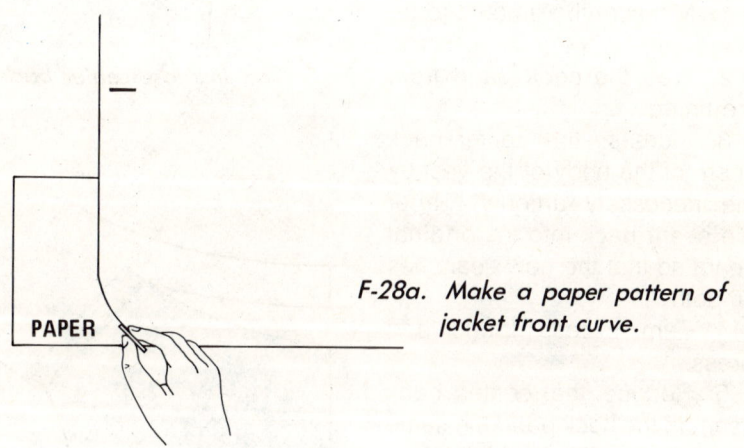

F-28a. Make a paper pattern of jacket front curve.

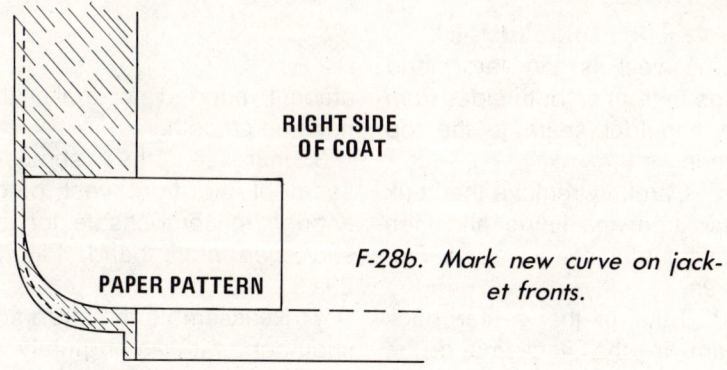

F-28b. Mark new curve on jacket fronts.

## Altering Ready-To-Wear Fashions

### ALTERING VESTS

The following adjustments may be needed to make vests fit well.

### Vest Stands Away from the Back Neck

Just as with the jacket back, the vest may be too large across the back so that it stands away from the neck. To make the neck smaller:

1. Measure the amount to be taken out.
2. Free the neck band from the lining.
3. Increase the center back seam of the body of the vest by the necessary amount. Taper the seam back into the original seam so that the new seam lies smooth.
4. Trim excess fabric and press.
5. Reduce the center back seam in the neck band the same amount you took out of the center back seam of vest.
6. Replace the neck band on the lining following the procedure used in constructing the garment.

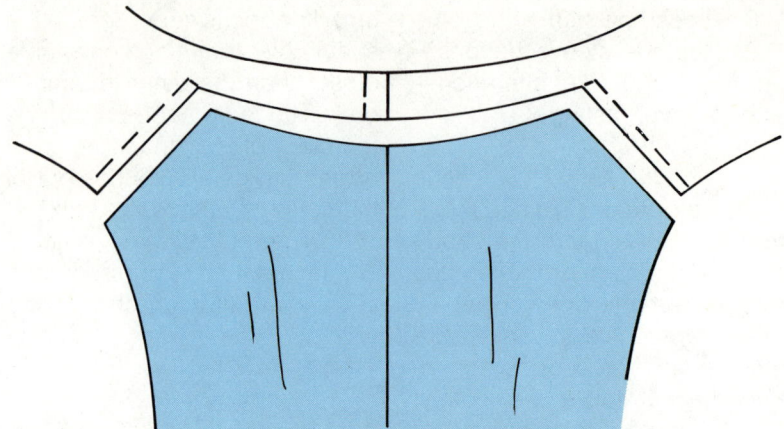

F-29a. Increase center back seam and shoulder seams on vest.

### Vest Too Large at Neck

The vest is too large and gaps in front on both sides from the shoulder seam to the top button.

1. Carefully remove the neck band from the lining and then rip shoulder seams apart. Fig. F-29a.
2. Take in the center back seam in the neck band the amount needed to make the neck lie smooth.
3. Increase the shoulder seam of the front vest piece enough to compensate for the shortened neck band. Fig. F-29a.
4. Reassemble the strap and shoulder as it was originally.

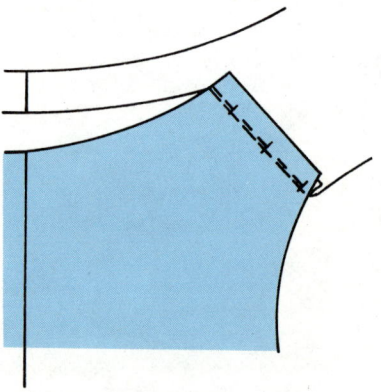

F-29b. The shoulder seam increased.

### Back Wrinkles under Neck across Shoulders

When the customer has square shoulders, the vest will often pull and wrinkle across the shoulders just below the neck. This alteration is similar to that done on a jacket for this problem.

1. Free the neck band across the back of the neck and rip the shoulder seams apart.
2. Pin the seam line on the neck band along the chalk mark made by the fitter to indicate the lowered neck seam.
3. There will be excess fabric on the shoulder seams which must also be removed. Restitch the shoulder seams, removing the extra left by lowering the neck band. Fig. F-29b.
4. Trim excess fabric on the shoulder seam and press.
5. Restitch the neck band to the back of the vest along the new seam line. Press.

6. Fell stitch the inside of the neck band to the vest back. Press.

### Vest Body Too Large or Too Small

The body of the vest may be either too snug or too loose. Either alteration is easy to make and involves similar steps. To help you understand these directions, it may help you to know how vests are constructed. Usually, vests are made by lining the fronts and backs separately before joining the two sections. When the front and back are joined, the front pieces are slipped between the two back layers. All four layers are stitched together in one operation and pressed toward the back. In releasing or increasing the vest side seams, stitch through all four layers at once.

### Vest Too Large

1. Release the lining at the back neck edge so you can turn the vest wrong side out.
2. Increase the side seams the amount needed to take out the extra fabric.
3. Leave seams untrimmed and turn right side out.
4. Fell stitch the neck band back in place.
5. Press.

### Vest Too Small

If the vest is too tight and pulls across the body, the side seams need to be released. Follow the same steps given above but make the side seams smaller instead of deeper. For this alteration, you will need to rip out the original stitching.

### SHIRT ALTERATIONS

Men's shirts come in four basic types, classified according to the occasion for which they are worn. *Dress* shirts are designed to be worn with a necktie for business, street, and semiformal wear. *Work* shirts are usually worn open at the neck. Because these shirts get such rough wear, fit is not important. *Sport* shirts are worn open at the neck, are often short-sleeved, and should be roomy enough to allow freedom of movement. *Formal* shirts are worn with some form of tie and should fit well.

Men's dress shirts and formal shirts often require some form of alteration. They are sized from 14 to 17, according to the neck measurements. The sleeve sizes run from 32 to 36 inches according to the length of the man's arm.

Sometimes a man will find that his neck size in a shirt comes with sleeves that are too long for him. He may prefer to have the shirt fit more closely around the waist.

The three most common types of alterations you might be asked to do on a man's shirt are shortening the sleeves, cutting off long sleeves to make short ones, and tapering the body for a closer fit.

### Shortening Shirt Sleeves

1. Measure the desired length so the sleeve cuff will come to the point where the hand joins the wrist.
2. Remove the sleeve cuff and the placket binding.
3. Apply ease stitching ½ inch (1.3 cm) below new sleeve length.
4. Cut the necessary amount off the bottom of the sleeve and cut placket to match original opening. Fig. F-30a.
5. Replace the placket binding as it was made originally.
6. Replace the cuff. Fig. F-30b.

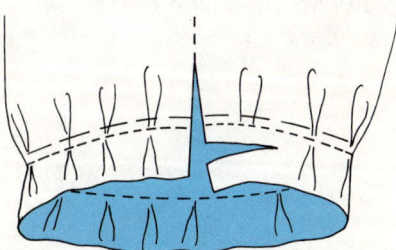

F-30a. Remove cuff and apply new ease-stitching.

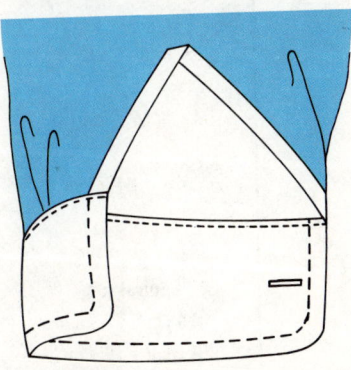

F-30b. Replace cuff.

## Altering Ready-To-Wear Fashions

### Making Short Sleeves from Long Sleeves

1. Measure the length desired plus 1 inch (2.5 cm) for a hem.

2. Measure the underarm seam 3 inches (7.6 cm) shorter than the top of the sleeve. Draw a line across the sleeve on both sides connecting the two measuring marks. Fig. F-31.

3. Cut off the bottom of the sleeve along this line.

4. Turn up the 1 inch (2.5 cm) for a hem. Turn the raw edge under ¼ inch (0.6 cm). Stitch the hem in place through all layers. This stitching will be easier if you remember to stitch around the inside of the sleeve circle.

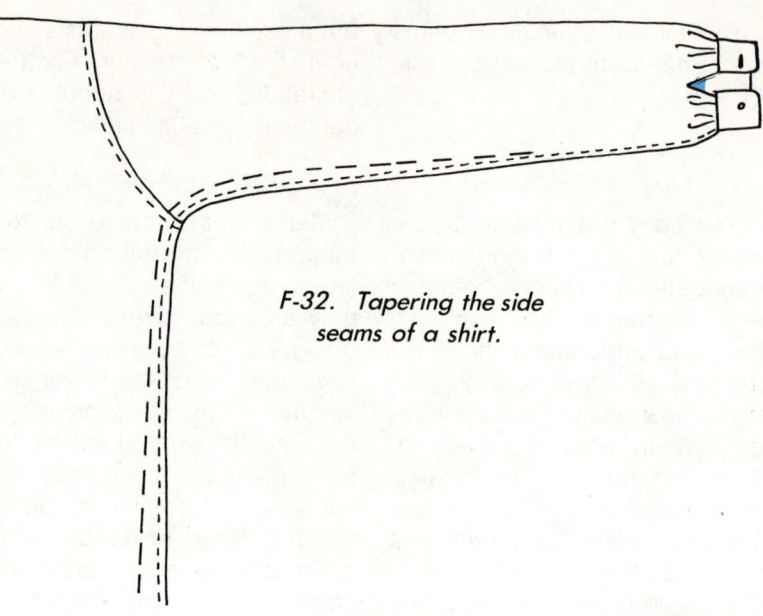

F-32. Tapering the side seams of a shirt.

F-31. Making short sleeves from long shirt sleeves.

**Equivalents**
19 cm = 7½ inches
26.7 cm = 10½ inches

### Tapering Shirt Body

1. Measure the desired amount to be taken out of each side. Make sure you take the same amount off each side seam.

2. If you have a small amount to take up, start stitching from the underarm seam of the sleeve.

3. If over 4 inches (10 cm) must be removed, the sleeve will also need altering. Start stitching the seam at the hem edge of the shirt. Continue stitching up the side, across the armhole seam and on down the sleeve seam. Taper the seam back into the original seam above the cuff so it does not have to be removed and reset. Fig. F-32.

4. In either method, trim the excess material and refinish the seams as they were originally.

Ch. 12: Fitting and Altering Menswear

Courtesy Sears, Roebuck and Co.

F-33. Many men prefer dress shirts tapered at the sides to fit smoothly into the trousers without unnecessary bulk. Shirt sleeves should come just to the top of the thumb. The collar should lie flat and fit around the neck without gapping or pinching.

# Chapter 13
# Developing Speed and Efficiency

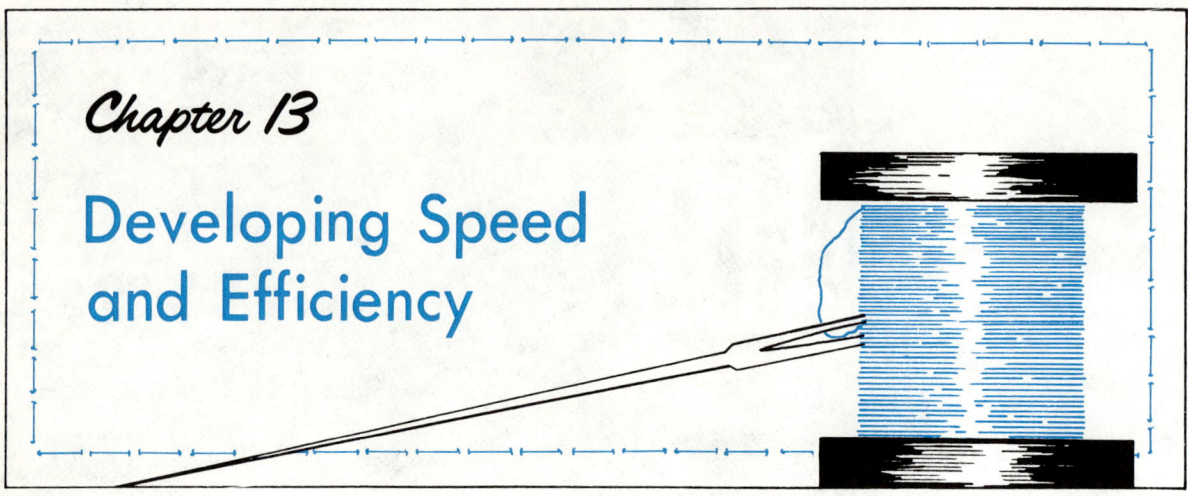

Alterations work is similar to piecework in a factory. This means you are paid a certain amount for each piece on which you work. The more you can do in an hour, the more money you make. Of course, speed is not the only consideration. You must always maintain high quality in your work to keep your customers satisfied. The secret, then, is to develop speed and efficiency while holding your standards of workmanship high. When speed causes mistakes, you lose both time and money making corrections. *Do it right the first time.*

There are several things you can do to increase your efficiency without lowering your quality of work. Most important, learn to save your energy as well as your time.

## TIME-STUDY METHODS

During World War II, it suddenly became necessary for the survival of the country to increase the efficiency of industry. Not only did the country need war materials, but there were fewer workers available to do the producing. This meant each worker had to produce more in the same length of time.

Efficiency experts were employed to study factory operations and suggest ways the output could be increased. Results showed that in some places workers' efficiency could be increased 1000 percent! As a result, production also increased.

Since then, time and motion studies have become an important part of all efforts to increase production. You, too, can increase your output by applying the same principles to alterations work:

• Keep your supplies close at hand, arranged nearest the hand with which you will use them.

• Have adequate work space, well-arranged so that you can easily go from one step to the next without having to move from place to place or hunt for supplies. This coordinated movement is called "work flow."

• Keep all your equipment in tip-top condition. This means your machine should be clean, well-oiled, and operating perfectly. Have a supply of new machine needles and bobbins on hand at all times. Always be sure to keep your shears and scissors sharp all the way to the points.

Photo by Minerva Wagner
*An efficient arrangement of equipment saves time and energy. With a posture chair on casters, you can easily roll from one station to another without jumping up and down. Notice the telephone and extra spools of thread within easy reach. The foot pedal controls the machine. The knee lever raises or lowers the presser foot and frees your hands to control the fabric.*

- Be sure the lighting is adequate to prevent mistakes, eye strain, and excessive fatigue.
- Invest in a swivel chair on free rolling wheels or casters. Instead of jumping up and down to go from worktable, to machine, to pressing board, you can roll to each.
- Plan your work space to have plenty of storage for projects. Have a place to hang customers' garments. Keep small plastic bags handy to attach to the hangers with each project. Put belts, scarves, tapes, laces, buttons, and other small items in the bags.
- Make accurate records on special time cards of:
  - Alterations to be made.
  - Time spent each time you handle the garment.
  - Supplies—tapes, laces, buttons—you use that cost money.
  - Prices charged for each job.
- Learn to use fewer motions to get work done by recognizing when:
  - to pin instead of baste.
  - to use fewer pins.
  - to use a pressing line marking instead of pinning or basting.
  - to take work directly to the machine without pinning, basting, or marking.
  - to machine baste instead of hand baste.

### TIME-AND-ENERGY SAVERS

Your time and energy are two of your greatest resources. Learn to budget them so you can make the most of each.

### Organizing Your Work

Get into the habit of planning each day so that you:
- Do the most difficult alterations first, when you are fresh.
- Save the easy work or things you enjoy doing for later in the day.
- Save some handwork to be done in the evening. This can be a time to relax with family and friends.
- Go over the work to be done and plan what you have to do in logical order.
- Do all the necessary marking at one time on all garments for the day.
- Do all the ripping needed to prepare for the machine stitching.
- Group similar fabrics; such as dark-colored, light-colored, sheer, or heavy, for one

## Altering Ready-To-Wear Fashions

work session. That way the machine adjustments, threads, press cloths, and iron temperatures will not have to be changed as often. If you have several light- or dark-colored garments, you may find you will not need to change the bobbin thread. One color may blend successfully with several garments. You may only need to change the top thread. *Every change you need to make takes time.* (Also, by grouping colors, you may prevent dark colors from "rubbing off" onto the light-colored fabrics.)

- Whenever possible, stitch all the seams by the chain sewing method given in Chapter 6.
- Clip all threads and seams at one time.
- Press several seams at one time. Jumping up and down to go back and forth between the ironing board and sewing machine takes time and energy.
- Keep the iron running at a low temperature all the time you are working. You won't waste time waiting for it to heat up when you need it. Reheating the iron may also cause it to "spit" water and make a water spot on the fabric.
- Keep a supply of different-colored threads, seam tapes, laces, and elastic on hand. Keep all supplies neatly arranged and easy to reach and find. Time spent going to the store to buy new supplies or in searching for those on hand costs money. If new supplies are necessary, shop for them at the end of the day rather than breaking into your working time. Shop for several items at once rather than running to the store for each one as needed.

### Finding Your Work Pace

Keeping records of how long it takes you to do each type of job—a plain hem, releasing the seams on a skirt, lowering a dart—will help you to know how much time you must allot for each. You can then schedule your work with more confidence. Look at the Alterations Time Schedule on pages 337, 338. Prepare a separate chart for your own use. Record how long it has taken you to do each type of alteration until you have a good idea of the average time for each.

Keep an accurate record of how many hours you actually work every day. Business calls and fitting appointments are working time. If you need to make a special shopping trip for sewing supplies, count it as working time. Do not count time taken for personal or family activities, or lunch or coffee breaks. Check the clock when you start and finish a particular job. You will soon learn how much you can do in a day.

Add up all the charges for the alterations finished that day. Divide this by your "working" time. You will know how much you earned each hour. For example, if you did several alterations that totaled $20 in charges, and you worked five hours, you made $4 an hour. As you develop efficient work habits, you will find you are increasing the amount of money you can make an hour. However, try not to overdo.

### Avoiding Tension and Fatigue

You can take the time you need to relax when you know how long the work you have to finish will take.

If a particular job is creating tension or fatigue for you—stop! Pick up a job that is routine work such as a plain hem or some handwork. Better still, just take time out to unwind in front of the television or with a phone chat to a friend. Take a walk or a nap. Time taken to relax is well worthwhile. You will make fewer mistakes, work goes more smoothly, and you will enjoy what you are doing.

There may be days when you do not feel well or family emergencies arise. If you know what you can do and how long it takes for a particular job, you can meet most situations calmly. Using time-study methods, you can gain the confidence of knowing you can get your work done.

Knowing your own *time-pace* will remove some of the tension from your schedule. It will help you to know when you can accept emergency alterations work.

## ALTERATIONS TIME SCHEDULE

| Type of Alteration | Date of Work | 120 | 100 | 90 | 80 | Minutes 70 | 60 | 50 | 40 | 30 | 15 |
|---|---|---|---|---|---|---|---|---|---|---|---|
| **Hems** | | | | | | | | | | | |
| Straight. | | | | | | | | | | | |
| Circular. | | | | | | | | | | | |
| Pleated (at bottom). | | | | | | | | | | | |
| Pleated (at top). | | | | | | | | | | | |
| Coat. | | | | | | | | | | | |
| Pants. | | | | | | | | | | | |
| **Side Seams** | | | | | | | | | | | |
| Release through hemline. | | | | | | | | | | | |
| Take in through hemline. | | | | | | | | | | | |
| Take in or release at zipper. | | | | | | | | | | | |
| Take in or release bodice. | | | | | | | | | | | |
| **Waistline** | | | | | | | | | | | |
| Raise waist or lower. | | | | | | | | | | | |
| Take in or release waist size. | | | | | | | | | | | |
| Take in or release waist with zipper. | | | | | | | | | | | |
| Raise or lower—with zipper. | | | | | | | | | | | |
| Waistline on trousers. | | | | | | | | | | | |

## ALTERATIONS TIME SCHEDULE (continued)

| Type of Alteration | Date of Work | 120 | 100 | 90 | 80 | 70 | 60 | 50 | 40 | 30 | 15 |
|---|---|---|---|---|---|---|---|---|---|---|---|
| **Sleeves and Shoulders** | | | | | | | | | | | |
| Raise shoulders. | | | | | | | | | | | |
| Raise armscye. | | | | | | | | | | | |
| Reset sleeves after taking in seams. | | | | | | | | | | | |
| Relocate darts. | | | | | | | | | | | |
| Cuffs. | | | | | | | | | | | |
| **Necklines** | | | | | | | | | | | |
| Lower neckline. | | | | | | | | | | | |
| Take in neckline (with tape or darts). | | | | | | | | | | | |
| **Linings** | | | | | | | | | | | |
| **Zippers** | | | | | | | | | | | |
| Men's or boys' trousers. | | | | | | | | | | | |
| Ladies' skirt. | | | | | | | | | | | |
| Ladies' dress—back neck. | | | | | | | | | | | |
| Ladies' dress—side placket. | | | | | | | | | | | |
| **Men's and Boys' Wear** | | | | | | | | | | | |
| Cuffs. | | | | | | | | | | | |
| Buttons and buttonholes. | | | | | | | | | | | |
| Waistline on trousers. | | | | | | | | | | | |
| Replacement of pockets. | | | | | | | | | | | |

*Minutes*

Ch. 13: Developing Speed and Efficiency

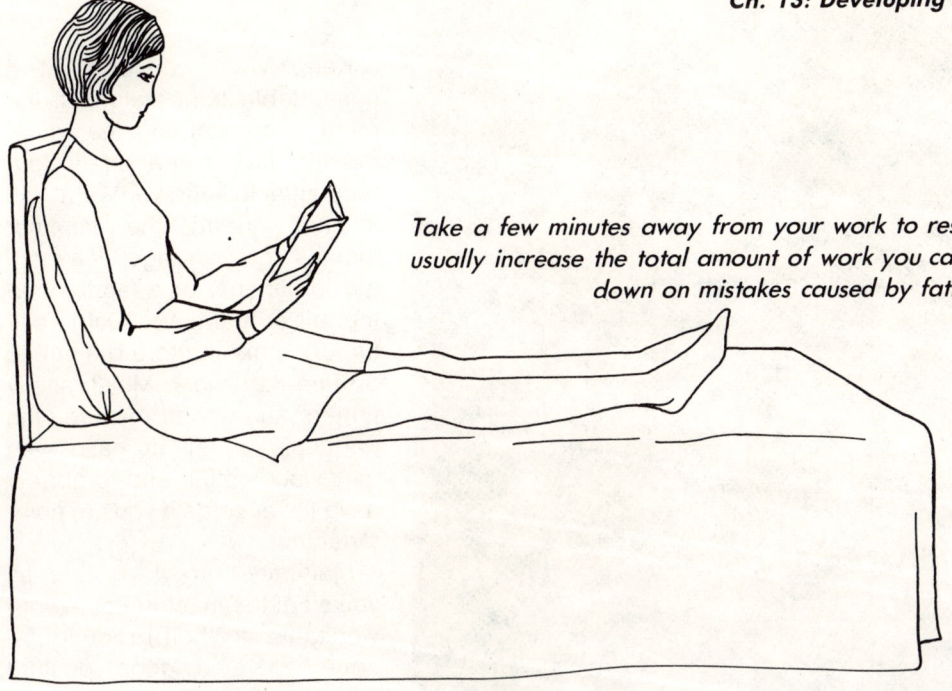

*Take a few minutes away from your work to rest occasionally. It will usually increase the total amount of work you can do and will also cut down on mistakes caused by fatigue.*

People will often need work done for special occasions and want it in a hurry. If you know you can get it done, you will find your customers grateful for this quick service. Often, they will not question the price you must ask. You should charge your maximum rates for this kind of service.

### VALUE YOUR TIME

Value your time and establish an hourly wage you expect to make. If you charge $3 for a job that takes three hours to complete, you are making $1 per hour. The minimum wage for unskilled work is more than that. *Remember, you are a highly skilled worker* and worth more money than an unskilled or semi-skilled worker. *If you do not value your own skill and time, no one else will.*

### LEARN TO SAY "NO"

If you are going to be a successful business person, learn to run your work like a business. Family and friends have been used to calling on you at any time for help. They may need to learn that things are different, now that you are working. You may have to learn not to be afraid to say "No" to:

• Projects you are not skilled enough to handle or do not have the proper tools to do, such as working with leather or fur.

• Customers who are not willing to pay the proper amount for your work.

• Friends and neighbors who want your help free.

• Family and friends who keep you from your scheduled working time.

• "Rush jobs" you cannot possibly find the time to do.

When you do find it necessary to say, "No," be courteous and diplomatic. Try to suggest someone else who might be able to offer the service.

### TAKE CARE OF YOUR HEALTH

People work their best when they are feeling well. Keeping your health and energy at top levels can increase your efficiency and output. There are several simple steps you can take to protect your health and well-being as you work.

Keep your workroom at a comfortable temperature. If the room is cold during the winter months, invest in a small electric heater to keep you warm. If it is hot during the summer months, try to arrange for a room air conditioner or a fan to keep the air circulating. Cold, stiff fingers make it more difficult to do fine handwork. Moist, sticky fingers and hands may soil the garments. In either case, you can work better and probably have fewer colds if you are comfortable.

Maintain correct posture as you sit at the machine or at your worktable to help reduce fatigue. Have a good posture chair, such as described on page 39. Be sure it is the right height for you. Keep your work on a worktable rather than in your lap. This helps keep your spine straight and prevents tiring.

Take time to eat well-balanced meals of non-fattening foods. A worker who neglects regular meals and fills

*Photo by Minerva Wagner*
**Controlled lighting and good posture help you work longer hours without strain or excessive tiring.**

*Photo by John Meaders*
**Put your work completely out of your mind and relax with your favorite recreation between work sessions.**

Courtesy Chevrolet Motor Division
General Motors Corporation

*Plan to do your family shopping only once a week to save time, energy, confusion, and money.*

up on snacks will not only gain weight but will lose efficiency.

Time to relax and renew your energy can be time well spent. Fifteen minutes used for a coffee break may help you turn out half again as much work during the hour after the break. A job that seemed difficult and stubborn before a rest may fall into place easily after a few minutes away from it.

Sometimes you can get so involved in your work that you even forget or postpone taking the necessary time for a trip to the bathroom. It seems silly, but people do. Not only can this practice be bad for your health, but it can also decrease your efficiency.

Be sure to get plenty of rest at night. Lack of sleep increases nervousness. Your hands will not be as steady and work will not go as smoothly.

When you reach the end of your scheduled sewing time, put your work out of your mind completely until the next day.

### ORGANIZE YOUR DAY'S ACTIVITIES

The lessons learned in organizing your sewing area and your work time can be carried over into organizing your "living time" and living area. You may be able to apply time management to your housekeeping duties as well as your social life.

It has often been said that a busy person can get more done in a day than someone with "nothing to do." In other words, you can take all day to do something if you have nothing else planned for that day.

Many books have been written on the subject of managing time and finding shortcuts. Here are a few typical suggestions:

• Make lists of what has to be done. Schedule your time to include everything that needs to be done by a certain time. Check off each completed

341

## Altering Ready-To-Wear Fashions

6a  Beef Ragout

6c  Chicken Stuffed Crepes

6b  Blanquette de Veau

6d  Eggplant Parmigiana

Courtesy Family Circle
Photos by George Nordhausen

Busy people can still prepare, and serve attractive, inexpensive meals. The secret is to plan ahead and have meals on hand in the freezer for rush periods.

chore as you finish it. This helps you keep yourself organized and gives you a feeling of accomplishment.

• Decide what household jobs should be done every day. Making beds and picking up family clutter before starting the day's work takes only a little time and does wonders for your morale. You can also plan to do these routine chores as part of your work break.

• Laundry can be done in the evenings or between sewing jobs when you feel the need to move around.

• Food shopping can be done in less time and in one trip if you make a careful list. Shop in one store so you become familiar with the arrangement of the departments and can shop quickly. Going from one store to another to save a few cents on bargain items may waste time and energy. The extra time it takes plus the expense of operating your car may cost more than the money you save.

• Plan meals that are easy and quick to prepare. Many cook books give recipes for instant meals. Whole menus are planned, giving a time schedule for each recipe. Keep some convenience foods on hand. Learn to use them but be sure to use fresh foods, also. A variety of foods eaten daily will insure good nutrition.

• Go on cooking "binges"

Ch. 13: Developing Speed and Efficiency

Courtesy of American Telephone & Telegraph Company
Long Lines Department

*Help your children understand there are times when they must not interrupt you unless it is a real emergency.*

during slow periods in your work schedule. When you make spaghetti, make enough sauce for three meals. Bake two cakes at the same time. Freeze the extra for future rush periods.

• Budget time during the day for special events such as a luncheon, a fashion show, a sewing demonstration, or a spectacular once-a-year sale at your favorite store.

• Refuse to take time out for social outings you do not enjoy or with people you do not like. This is time wasted.

• If you have been involved in daytime club activities or church groups, you must decide which of these are really important to you. Do not drop out of everything, but decide to limit your participation only to those you enjoy.

• If you have children who have to be taken to various activities, put this in your schedule. Try to form car pools whenever possible. Check on the public transportation. You can waste much valuable time serving as a chauffeur.

• There is no need to give up evening social activities just because you are working. If you have enjoyed entertaining in the past, continue to do so. You will find it a challenge to work this into your new time budget. Family activities will have more meaning, for this is living time well-earned and planned.

**Altering Ready-To-Wear Fashions**

Courtesy of GAF Corporation

*If you have children, be sure to allow time in your schedule for unexpected extra work and responsibilities.*

If you are always too tired or too busy for worthwhile social or family activities, it may be you have not planned your working or living time well enough.

## Management Check List

1. Do you see the big job first—do you look ahead?
2. Do you list the things you wish to do in order?
3. Do you do the important tasks first?
4. Do you leave the tasks you like till last?
5. Do you try to do some tasks ahead of time or do you put everything off until the last minute?
6. Do you organize your work to eliminate unnecessary movements?
7. Do you use good judgment and common sense and think before you act?
8. Are you orderly—a labeled space for nearly everything?
9. Do you avoid fatigue from overwork?
10. Do you allow plenty of time for completion of a job?
11. Do you follow good health practices?
12. Do you allow time for leisure and relaxation?
13. Do you budget your time?
14. Have you organized your activities so your family shares responsibilities?

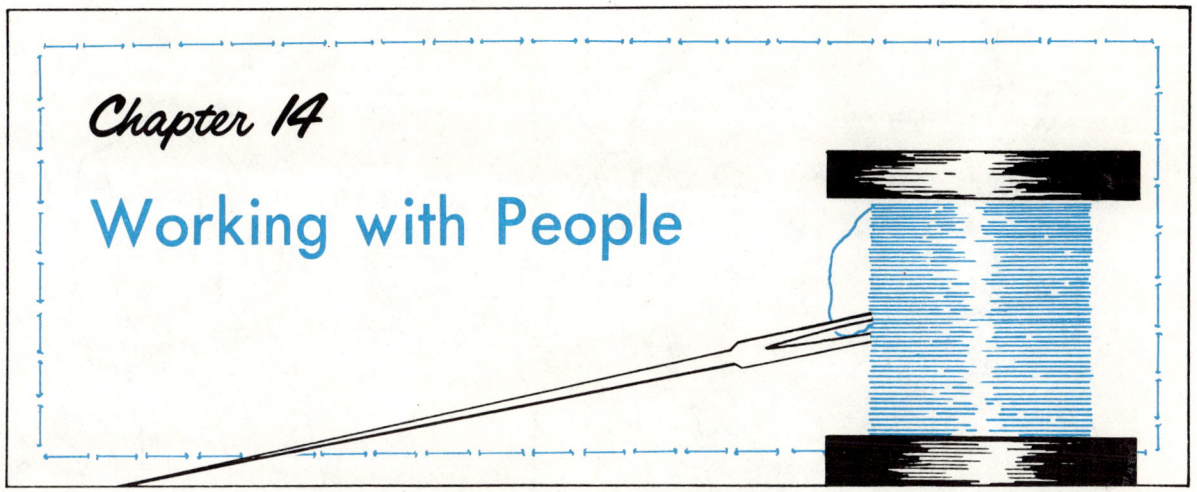

# Chapter 14
## Working with People

In any kind of employment, whether working for yourself or for others, a good part of your success depends on your ability to get along with others. Many people have lost jobs or failed to get employment, not because they could not do the work, but because they could not get along with other people. Too often, one person in an office or shop can cause more trouble and create a greater state of turmoil than all the others put together. Even if such employees are not fired, they make themselves unpopular, fail to gain advancement, and slow down the work of the others. When working for yourself, you can also lose many customers for the same reasons.

Alterations work involves dealing with all kinds of people. The ability to try to get along with everyone is a valuable asset. For instance, please your customers by helping them in a pleasant manner. Cooperate with employers, sales people, and your fellow workers in the alterations room. When seasonal pressure in the shop increases your work load, be prepared to accept the extra work and responsibility with good grace and cheerfulness.

It helps considerably if you make up your mind to be special. When your own work load lessens, be willing to look for something to do to help others. Management notices and appreciates a worker who never wastes time, never grumbles or refuses to do anything extra, and never gossips or complains about other workers. People who are cooperative and good workers may be offered the opportunity for more pay and a better job.

The suggestions in this chapter can help you become a valuable worker. They are based on surveys of employers as to what they look for in their employees. These characteristics have been divided into five groups, all of which begin with the letter "C"—confidence, competence, courtesy, cooperation, and costs. As you read each section, you will no doubt think of other things you can do that would come under each group. Each day as you work, remind yourself of the five "C's," your clues to being a good employee. The important points under each of these topics should come to your mind easily.

### CONFIDENCE

One of the best qualities you can develop is confidence—not conceit, but confidence—in your own ability.

Polish up your own appearance. Since you are working in the world of fashion, look your

**Altering Ready-To-Wear Fashions**

*One well fitting basic dress with changes of accessories can give you several different looking outfits at a minimum cost.*

best when on the job. Be suitably and fashionably dressed. You can be your own advertisement—your ability to fit and sew for others should show on *you*. Be sure your clothes are becoming to you and that they fit well and are clean. You need not have a large wardrobe. One or two plain outfits with changes of accessories can do more than a whole closet full of misfits.

Rather than worry about the impression you are making, be concerned about putting other people at ease. You will not only make them feel more comfortable, but you will also forget to be nervous yourself.

Remember, your expression is the most important thing you wear. Smile—be happy to be of service. Keep your normal facial expression frown-free and pleasant. Often, people form the habit of frowning or looking cross because of tension. Take a good look at yourself in a mirror. Are there signs of lines that are caused by negative facial expressions? Are there strong vertical creases between your brows? Do the corners of your mouth droop? You have heard of whistling to keep up your courage. A pleasant, happy facial expression and attitude can do the same for you.

Ch. 14: Working with People

Photo by Deanna Laughlin

*Your facial expression is the most important thing you wear and greatly influences how people react to you.*

Daily count your blessings. Add up all the good things that have happened to you in your life. Everyone has troubles of one sort or another. If you concentrate on your problems, you can soon make yourself, and everyone who must be around you, uncomfortable.

Be enthusiastic and enjoy your life and what you are doing. People will respond to you positively and life will become more pleasant.

Leave your problems at home when you report for work. Leave your business problems at work when you return home. Remember a smile is more contagious than a virus and can help you develop confidence.

## COMPETENCE

Competence means having the ability and knowledge to do your work well. When you create an air of confidence in yourself, you inspire other people to believe in your competence. Customers, employers, and fellow-workers respect people who always seem to be in command of the situation.

You display competence by the manner in which you carry out your activities. Everyone knows someone who is always busy rushing around. At the end of the day, however, nothing much has been accomplished. Such people seem to be spinning their wheels while they stay in the same spot. A competent person behaves in a different manner. For example, when called to do a fitting, you would:

• Be professional at all times. Be pleasant but not too personal. Beware of indulging in senseless chatter or trying to burden others with your troubles.

• Answer all calls promptly. Appear for your fittings at the time scheduled and be thoroughly prepared. Carry a small case with your tape measure, pins, pencil, alteration cards, appointment book, and thimble with you.

• Listen to the salesperson and/or customers when they tell you something.

• Be complimentary and immediately try to find something nice to say. It may be the color of the garment goes well with the customer's skin, hair, or eye coloring. It could be the fabric texture is particularly flattering to the customer's figure. Maybe the fashion lines are slenderizing. If you feel the purchase is a total disaster for that customer, be diplomatic and refrain from making any comments. After all, the customer has already made

*Be diplomatic, pleasant, and efficient when working with customers.*

Photo by Bill Snyder

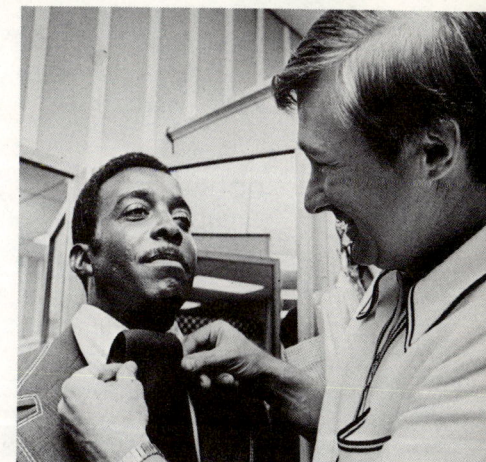

347

*Be cheerful and courteous when talking on the telephone.*

a choice so whatever you say should be encouraging and not negative.

• Keep your alterations cards handy and write down everything you need to remember. Do not depend on your memory alone. Write in detail everything that needs to be done to the garment. Make an appointment with the customer for a fitting. Write it on the card and on your appointment calendar. Write down the date you promise to have the garment ready, and have it ready on that date.

• Start to work immediately. Do not hesitate, appear unsure, or linger to gossip. Make decisions quickly, and fit with speed.

## COURTESY

You can be forgiven for other weaknesses if you are always courteous and pleasant. Many people return time after time to a hairdresser, restaurant, or men's shop just because they enjoy the people who work there. If the customers enjoy your personality, they may soon start to ask for you.

Be diplomatic when fitting or talking to the customer. Before you say anything to a customer, be sure you would not be offended to have the same thing said to you. When referring to parts of the body, use socially acceptable expressions such as hips, buttocks, or derriere. Refer to a thin person as slim or slender rather than skinny. Refer to a roll of extra fat as extra muscle. Instead of saying the garment must be "let-out," say, "Release the seam."

Be especially tactful with people who may have abnormal fitting problems or handicaps due to a crippling disease, birth defects, accidents, or operations. Displaying shock or surprise over a customer's figure problem only makes a difficult situation harder for everyone. Try to act as though you have fitted many others with the same kinds of problems and it is nothing unusual. Be especially sensitive to the customer's feelings.

Make suggestions only as to the changes to be made rather than attempting to impose your will on the customer. Remember, other people have as much right to their opinions as you have to yours.

Keep the tone of your voice loud enough to be heard easily but soft enough to be pleasant. Loud talking, loud laughter, nervous giggling, and profanity are offensive to most people. You may find it revealing to tape your normal conversations on a tape recorder and then listen carefully to yourself.

Answer the telephone pleasantly and immediately. Identify the business and person answering such as "Good morning, this is Betty Orr speaking," or, "Good afternoon, this is Fit 'Em and Fix 'Em Alterations. May I help you?" Then, listen and reply pleasantly to whatever question or information the caller has for you. Avoid indulging in unnecessary chatter, but do not be rude or abrupt. Before hanging up, thank the person for calling and say, "Good-bye."

Courtesy and good manners are based on consideration for other people. Try to put yourself in the other person's position and say or do what you would want them to do for you if they were in your place. Courtesy, kindness, and thoughtfulness are the greatest assets you will ever develop.

## COOPERATION

Think of yourself as a part of a team. Whether you work with a group of other people in a shop or by yourself at home, you are never in a position where you can consider only yourself. Remember, everyone else has the same rights, privileges, responsibilities, and number of problems you have.

Be willing to accept shop rules, even though you may not understand the reason for them.

**Ch. 14: Working with People**

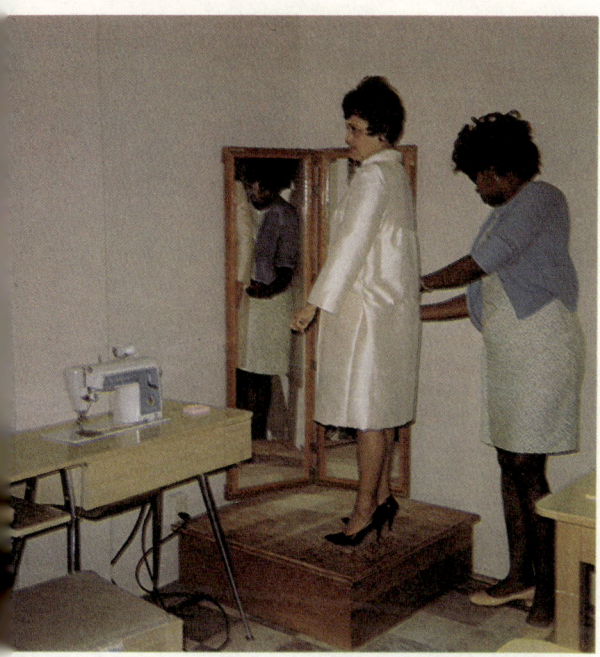

*Keep a sweater handy if you are often cold when others are comfortable.*

*Avoid habits which may be annoying to others. These include whistling, humming, chewing gum, or making other monotonous noises.*

Keep in mind that others must use the machines, worktables, and pressing equipment. Leave them uncluttered and ready for the next worker. Keep equipment in the proper place so the next person can find it easily.

Get rid of annoying habits that may be keeping others from doing their best work. Humming, whistling, drumming your fingers on a table, or any other noises may be irritating to others.

Avoid smoking except in designated areas. You will not only annoy others but the clothes will pick up the odor of smoke. You could even burn a hole in a garment.

Take your rest breaks for the exact time allowed everyone else.

Be careful not to feed discontent by spreading gossip or saying unkind things to or about others. Usually, what you say about someone else will very often be repeated to that person. If you never say anything you would not be happy to say to someone's face, you will not hurt others. You will also avoid being embarrassed by your own lack of good sense and kindness.

Consider the comfort of others. If you are always too warm but others are not, wear cooler clothes instead of insisting the windows be opened. If you are often too cold, keep a sweater handy rather than turn down the air conditioner. Of course, if you work alone, you can adjust the temperature for your own comfort.

Develop a code of loyalty to your employers and customers. If you do not like a place and find it impossible to work there, leave. While you are working and accepting your paycheck, however, be loyal. This means supporting your fellow workers instead of being critical.

## COSTS

Most employers you work for will have their own list of prices to be charged for the work you do. You will find out about their shop policies when you go to work for them.

If you are planning to operate your own business, Chapter 16 offers suggestions for determining the prices you should charge for your work.

The term *costs* as used here refers to the business expenses your employer faces because of you. Part of your loyalty to your employer will be to do your work as inexpensively as possible.

Make the best possible use of supplies and equipment. Wasting thread, seam tape, laces, needles, pins, and other supplies raises costs.

Taking things home to use for yourself, unless you have permission, raises costs. No matter how many excuses you make to yourself, taking things that do not belong to you is stealing. Because supplies are made available to you does not mean you have the right to take them home. These supplies are for use on the job only.

Make your time count. Taking extra time for a rest break or staying home when you could be at work, raises costs for your employer. Sick leave benefits provide an income for you when you are really sick. They should not be used for doing personal business or just taking time to relax or go to a ball game. These benefits help everyone, but if they are abused, they could be discontinued.

Be willing to put forth extra effort demanded by special sales, seasonal pressure, or other unusual situations. Many businesses have decided to close out their alterations departments entirely because their employees refused to make any extra effort when needed.

Sometimes employers are prevented from making the profit they should by their own employees. As a result, they are unable to give their employees a raise. They may even be forced out of business just because their employees wasted time and supplies.

If you want to work and enjoy having your own pay check, help your employer make the business a profitable one.

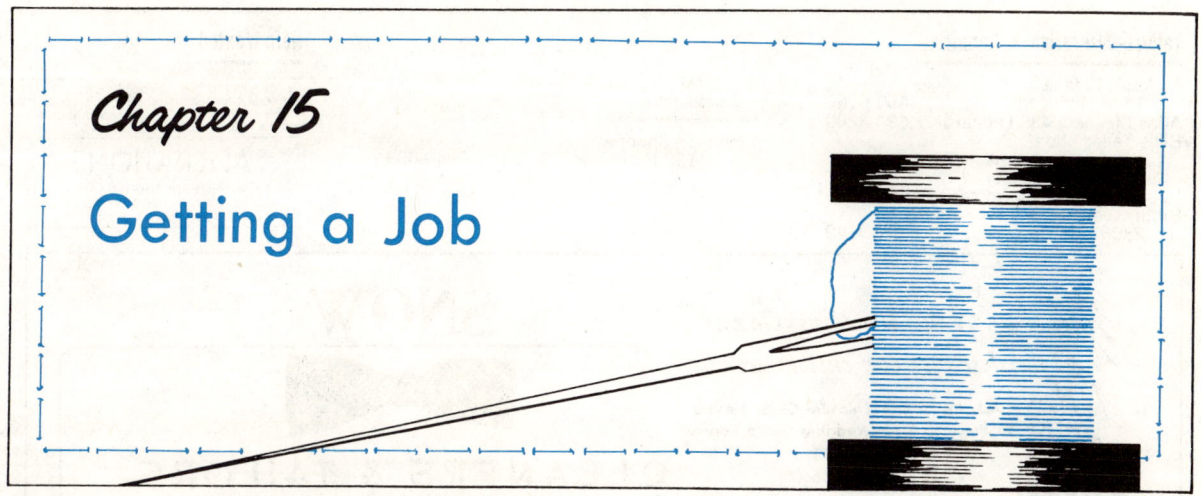

# Chapter 15
## Getting a Job

When you have completed your training program, you are ready to apply for work. Many people prefer to work for someone else rather than go into business for themselves. As employees, they know they will make a certain amount of money every week. Thus they have financial security without the responsibility of running a business themselves. They like having the company of co-workers. Even if they wanted to go into business for themselves, they might not have the needed space or equipment to work at home.

Working for a store or shop provides valuable experience. You can learn from your co-workers and can develop an understanding of good business practices.

You might want to reread the job opportunities listed in Chapter 1. Then make plans to contact businesses that offer the kinds of jobs you want.

### WHERE TO LOOK

There are several places to look for job openings you might want. Stores or drycleaners sometimes have a "Help Wanted" sign in the window when they need an alterationist. Some places put advertisements in the classified section of the community or neighborhood newspaper. Others notify local employment agencies of the openings they have. If you are in a school program, the vocational guidance counselors as well as the teachers may have information of available positions. Check all of these sources.

### Employment Agencies

There are two kinds of employment agencies in most large communities—state and private.

State employment agencies make no charge to either the employers or the applicants. They are a service of the state government. They may furnish you with leads to places that are looking for help.

Private agencies charge for their services. Some charge the employers and some charge the employees. If they find a job for you, you may be required to pay a fee based on the wages you will receive. Usually, you should be able to find a job through other sources without having to pay for it.

### Classified Ads

Newspaper "Help Wanted" ads and the telephone directory are excellent sources of job opportunities in your area. Perhaps your neighborhood has its own small newspaper that carries local advertising. Any jobs advertised would probably be

351

**Altering Ready-To-Wear Fashions**

**Tailors—Alteration & Repairing**
Andoulis Cleaners
   1238 Michigan e .........459-9160
Atlas Cleaners 436 Leonard ...694-4209
Bill's Tailor Shop
   Ladies' & Men's Tailor—Alterations & Cleaning A Specialty
   1409 Robinson Rd se .....694-4530
Bunny Cleaners & Shirt Laundry
   2806 Division s ..........241-5140

**Dressmakers**

Modiste Shoppe
   1127 Harley se ..........594-4003

**Help Wanted**

ALTERATIONIST, experienced fitter needed for exclusive women's specialty shop in northern Oregon resort. Benefits. Call Mrs. King 847-2273.

**ALTERATIONS**
Experienced fitter seamstress. KITTY RYON, 1204 S. Woodward. 635-9230. Apply in person.

*Your Wedding Gown deserves our custom service.*
Ask About Our Treasure Chest Service To Preserve Your Wedding Gown Forever

# SNOW

## CLEANERS & TAILORS
QUALITY DRY CLEANING • SHIRT LAUNDRY
COMPLETE TAILORING AND ALTERATIONS — FORMAL WEAR RENTALS

Call 451-2723          496 Snow Road

*Classified ads from newspapers or the telephone directory can give valuable leads for possible job opportunities.*

in your own neighborhood and easy to reach. City newspapers have a "Help Wanted" section that can give you leads.

Answer only the ads for jobs that interest you and that you can get to easily from your home. You only waste time if you investigage jobs you do not want or those located long distances from your home.

If none of the advertised jobs appeal to you, place your own "Situation Wanted" ad in the paper. This lets employers know you are looking for work.

The yellow pages of your local phone book may help you find places offering alteration services in your area. Check the listings under *Alterations, Dressmaking, Tailors, Drycleaners,* or *Women's Apparel.* Contact those shops within a reasonable distance from your home.

A new shopping district is a good place to make contacts. Call and ask if the business has any openings or expects any in the near future. They may not need you at the moment but may be happy to have your name to call in the future.

If you have had any sales experience or are interested in sales work in addition to alterations, be sure to mention this. Some small shops are delighted to find people who can do both.

## APPOINTMENT FOR AN INTERVIEW

Most employers prefer that you make an appointment to interview for a job. This gives them the opportunity to allow ample time for the interview,

Become thoroughly familiar with the merchandise offered for sale in any store where you are seeking employment.

When you present yourself for an interview, your grooming and manner will influence the interviewer as much as your skills.

and to introduce you to a supervisor or other workers.

When you make your first contact with a prospective employer, whether by phone or in person, you are making your first impression. Think about the reactions you have had to people the first time you have heard or met them. What makes you take an immediate liking to someone? What gives you a negative impression about them?

When you call to ask for an appointment, be businesslike, courteous, and as brief as possible. Keep your voice pleasant and speak distinctly. Explain that you would like to make an appointment for an interview. If your time is limited and you must have an appointment only during certain hours, say so immediately. It is better not to have to turn down several suggested times because you cannot get there.

## GETTING READY FOR THE INTERVIEW

Before you keep your interview appointment, there are a few things to prepare ahead of time. You will need to have your social security card, the names and addresses of people who can recommend you, and a resumé of your past work experience.

### Social Security Card

Your employer will need to know your social security number to pay regularly into your social security benefit fund. Income tax deductions are also identified by your own social security number. If you do not already have a number, apply for one at the local social security office. This is a very simple process that takes only a few minutes.

### Personal Inventory

Often people who have not worked for pay tend to underestimate what they have to offer to the business world. It may help your self-confidence if you sit

353

*Altering Ready-To-Wear Fashions*

## Personal Resumé

**Name**  Elizabeth C. Bennett
**Address**  16 Darwin Street, Alexandria, La.
**Telephone**  495-5551
**Social Security Number**  000-16-4900
**Date of Birth**  March 21, 1945
**Birthplace**  Alexandria, La.
**Height**  5 feet 3 inches
**Weight**  112 lbs.
**Educational Information:**
  Graduated from Robert E. Lee High School, 1963.
  Major:  Vocational Home Economics—occupational training in clothing alterations.
**Activities:**  Future Homemakers of America, program chairman. Career Day, exhibits committee. Class play, costume committee.
**Work Experience:**  Part-time salesgirl at Sink 'r Swim.
  Made sample dresses for Jean's Fabric Shop
  Baby-sitting in neighborhood (3 years)
**References:**
  Mrs. Betty T. Smith, Home Economics teacher, Lee High School, Alexandria, La.
  Mr. Frank P. Russo, Manager, Jean's Fabric Shop, 85 Plaza Court, Alexandria, La. Phone: 495-3321.
  Mrs. Adele Voyle, Manager, Sink 'r Swim, 116 Beach Street, Alexandria, La. Phone: 496-6710
  Mrs. Alan Patterson, 18 Darwin Street, Alexandria, La. Phone: 495-6630

down and make an inventory of all your good points. You would not take this sheet with you on an interview, but it might help your own self-esteem.

Try to think of all the good things people have ever said about you. What are your good qualities? Have others ever complimented you on your co-operation, courtesy, or dependability? Have they ever commented on your sense of style or the way you dress? Did anyone ever indicate they thought you were emotionally stable? Do people like to get you to work on committees in school, church, or clubs because they know you will do your share and carry through until the job is finished? Do you get along well with people of all ages and have many friends?

All of these qualities are important to employers. You can probably think of many more ways in which you have shown you will fit into the business world.

As mentioned before, you would not take this list to the interview with you. However, recognizing that you have these qualities can help you to feel more sure of yourself.

### References

Most employers will wish to have the names of people who know you and can comment on your character and your ability to work. These people will be your references. Be prepared to give the names of at least three to five people who know you well.

Someone for whom you have already worked makes a good reference. A satisfied customer is your best advertisement.

If you have never worked before, you can give the names of business people in the community who know your character. A minister, priest, or rabbi will often be willing to give you a reference. If you are just graduating from school, you might give the name of the teacher who trained you or a school counselor. In small towns, the school principal will often do this.

*Be sure to ask the individuals ahead of time for permission to use their names as references.* Some may have a reason for not wanting to recommend you and may be irritated to have you use their name. Such references would do you more harm than good.

### Resumés

Have a resumé or summary of information neatly typed or hand-printed and ready to hand to the interviewer. This form should give the important information about you—name, address, phone numbers, social security number, age, height, weight, educational background, work experience, and names and addresses of references. Keep it brief and readable at a glance.

If you are planning to go on several interviews, you may want to have extra copies of your resumé ready. Many public libraries and post offices have duplicating machines you can use to make photo copies for a few cents apiece.

Keep the information in the summary confined to subjects that will be important to the job you are applying for. List special training courses you have had. Give job experience and any special talents you have that will help you as an *alterationist*.

### Show Your Interest

If you are interested in working in any particular store or shop, study it before you go for your interview. Visit the shop to see what kinds of clothes they sell. Notice the customers to see what kind of people the store attracts. Check the labels on the garments displayed. Look at the way the clothes are made. Pay attention to the detail work and fabrics. If you see things you are not familiar with, do some homework to find out about them.

When you appear for your interview, you can talk easily about your ability to handle the kind of work they need. Your interest will tell the employer that you will *care* about the business.

### APPEARANCE

The day you appear for your interview, be prepared to put your best foot forward. Make the very finest impression that you can.

Your clothes and general grooming will be the first things the interviewer sees. Wear clothes that are simple, fashionable, neat, and well-fitted. Avoid clothes that are too extreme in style. Wear colors that

*During an interview, answer the questions quickly and politely and then stop talking.*

are complimentary to you and do not clash with each other. Shoes should be considered part of the total look. They should be polished and in keeping with the clothing worn for the interview. It is wise to wear hose.

Your general cleanliness and grooming will be noted immediately by the interviewer. A neat, becoming, and uncomplicated hairstyle is best. Clean hands and neatly filed fingernails make a better impression than an elaborate manicure with highly colored nails. Your clothes should be clean and spotless. Be sure to wear a deodorant.

These simple principles apply as well for dressing on the

*An application blank should be filled out as neatly and completely as possible.*

Of course, you want to avoid awkward silences and if one occurs, you might take this opportunity to offer your resumé. Perhaps you could make a brief comment that shows your genuine interest in the work you would be doing. There will be plenty of time to inquire about fringe benefits, opportunities for advancement, pay scales, and coffee breaks after you have been offered a job.

Be prepared for such direct questions as "What are your strong points?" or, "Tell me about yourself." *Now,* you can mention the qualities you put on your personal evaluation list!

Practice at home in front of a mirror. If possible, get a friend to act out an interview with you ahead of time so you can get your thoughts organized.

## APPLICATION FORMS

Tuck some sharpened pencils and a pen or two in your purse before you start out. In some stores, you may be asked to fill out an application form, so you want to be ready. *Read the directions before you start to fill in the forms.* Take the time you need to be accurate, neat, and complete. Crossed-out words, poor spelling, or improperly filled-out forms tell the interviewer uncomplimentary things about you. If you usually have trouble with spelling, carry a small pocket dictionary with you. This may show you have a weakness, but it also shows you

job. You may find later that casual clothes will be acceptable in the alterations room, but the other items remain important at all times. You may be working in a small, fairly crowded area, and body odors, unpleasant breath, heavy colognes, and noisy jewelry are always annoying to others.

When you are carefully dressed to look your best, it will increase your feeling of confidence in yourself.

## THE INTERVIEW

Arrive promptly for your interview appointment. If you are delayed or cannot keep the appointment for any reason, call and let the interviewer know.

When you arrive, looking your very best, you are "on stage." This is your brief but valuable time to sell yourself to your employer. Do not waste it. Wait until the interviewer offers to shake hands before offering yours. Wait to be seated until a chair is offered. Sit gracefully and quietly. Avoid fiddling with your hands, jewelry, or objects on the desk.

Answer the questions with the information requested and then stop talking. Too many people offer more than is asked and sometimes talk themselves out of a job they might have otherwise had. Your object is to get a job, not establish a personal relationship or charm the interviewer. This is not the time to discuss your attitudes on controversial issues like politics or religion. Neither is this the time to impress anyone with your devotion to your family.

## Ch. 15: Getting a Job

are willing to admit it and work on it. (See sample application blank on pages 358, 359.)

Remember, this application form will be placed on file as your record. It may be weeks or months before a job opening occurs. At that time, all the manager or personnel department has to remember you by is this form and any notes they may have made during the interview. Make sure the application blank is filled out neatly and properly.

If the idea of filling out an application form frightens you, perhaps you should only apply in small shops which do not require them.

### SHOW WHAT YOU CAN DO

During the interview, you may be asked to demonstrate your ability. Perhaps the interviewer and a supervisor may ask you to go directly to the work room and work for an hour or two. They will be watching to see how you go about doing the work. The way you handle the garments and equipment will be noted. Quickly check the work to be done for the kind of things you do best—perhaps a hem to be shortened. Start to work immediately and calmly. It may make you feel more comfortable if you bring your own thimble and other small tools.

This kind of demonstration is a routine request in many shops and does not reflect on your ability in any way. Instead, it means they are interested enough to give you a chance. Your willingness to show your skill can be as impressive as doing it.

### ACCEPTING THE JOB

After you have actually been offered a job, you can ask questions about the things you would like to know in addition to the information you have been given. You can now ask about base pay, raises, opportunities for advancement, and employee benefits such as group insurance. Ask if the work is seasonal or year-round, and if there are periods when you would be expected to put in extra time. Ask to see the work room if you haven't seen it.

### KEEPING THE JOB

After you have accepted the job, you are ready to put into practice everything else you have learned. Remember your five C's. Do not hesitate to ask questions about shop procedures and rules. Be sure to report to work in plenty of time every day. Be that valuable worker you know how to be.

*Remember, every employer becomes a potential reference for any other job you may want.*

*If you are asked to demonstrate your ability, get to work as quickly and efficiently as you can.*

## Application for Employment

Date of application .....................

Type of work applied for ................................................

Name ..................................................................

Address ...............................................................

      Previous Address ................ Telephone ........................

Marital status—Married ....... Divorced ....... Widow ....... Single ......

Dependents—Number ................ Children under 16 years .............

Date of birth .........................................................

Social security number ................................................

      Education—High school ...... College ................ Additional ...........

............................................................................

Language other than English ..........................................

Do you have to work? .................................................

Name of company where last employed .................................

      Address ...................... Dept. Mgr. .........................

      Position held ....................................................

      Length of employment—From ........ To. ...........................

      Rate of pay ......................................................

      Reason for leaving ...............................................

Would you accept a position in any of our shops? .....................

## Sample Application Blank

**Ch. 15: Getting a Job**

**Application for Employment (continued)**

Please name three other employers

1. ..................................................................................

2. ..................................................................................

3. ..................................................................................

Three personal references

1. ..................................................................................

2. ..................................................................................

3. ..................................................................................

Have you had experience in selling ........................... fitting .............

sewing ...........................................................................

I will ........ will not ........ submit to security guard check during my employment.

Signature ..................................

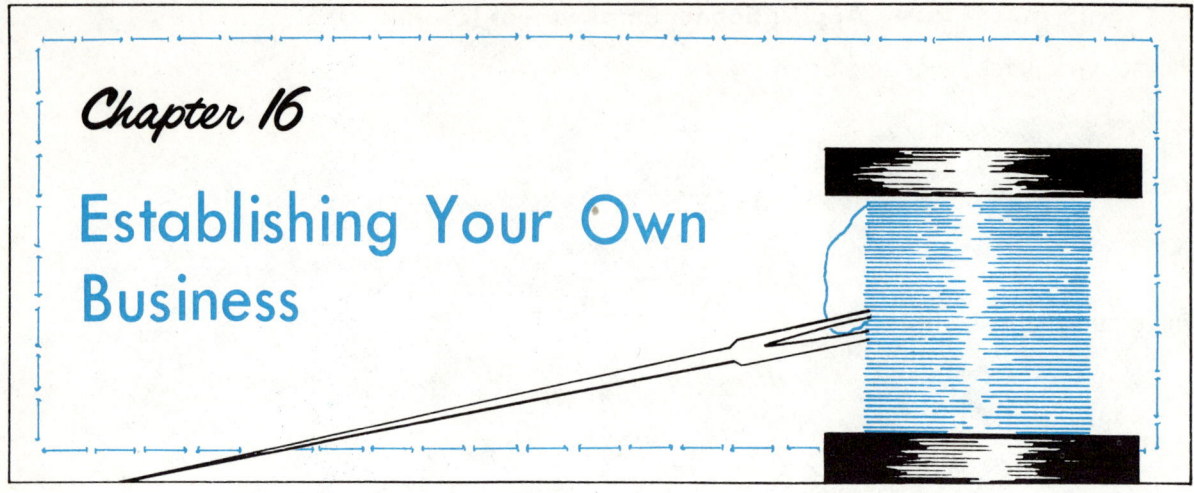

# Chapter 16
# Establishing Your Own Business

You may now be thinking about establishing your own business.

You have read, studied, and practiced the methods and suggestions given in the early parts of this book. This has given you a chance to evaluate your career possibilities. The skills you now have can give you good opportunities to earn your living or to supplement your family's income.

The ready-to-wear clothing industry is the third largest industry in the United States. A shortage of skilled workers in alterations exists in almost every community. Opportunities are numerous for competent, businesslike people to be successful on their own.

## ADVANTAGES

This field has great opportunities for you as a skilled alterationist because:

- You are offering a service that almost everyone needs. Thus there is little competition.
- Since clothes are worn by everyone, you can start a business in any community. Being close to a military post, a college campus, or a business district is helpful. However, even in the suburbs, small towns, or a city neighborhood, people need to have clothes altered.
- You are not limited by your age. If you know your work, you cannot be too young or too old. Some teenagers as well as people in their 80's earn money this way.
- Your skill and personality are your credentials. You are not limited by your ethnic background, the color of your skin, or your sex.
- You can manage this work within your own physical limitations. Many people with physical disabilities have been able to earn income by pacing the hours they work within their own capacity. By working at home, they can keep whatever routine of rest, diet, or medication is needed for their particular problem. Of course, poor eyesight or poor hand coordination would limit the type of work that could be done.
- You can make your own schedule and work the hours that suit you best.
- You can specialize and do only the kind of work you enjoy and want to do. You can concentrate on doing just men's alterations, or just women's. You could just do hems, or bridal and formal wear.
- You can work the year around or any part of the year that suits you best. You can even travel with the seasons and work in the north in the summer and in the south in the winter.

## Ch. 16: Establishing Your Own Business

- You can control the amount of business you want to handle. You can keep it small or expand until you need to hire extra help.
- You can go into business with just the sewing equipment you have been using for your home sewing plus a telephone. As your volume of business builds, you can add new equipment as needed. You do not need to make a large initial investment or need extra money to get started.
- You can work in a small corner of a room in your home or you can expand into your own shop in a separate building.
- You will be working in a clean, quiet service. You need not be a nuisance to your neighbors as you will not create smoke, odors, trash, or noise. The only visible difference will be in the number of cars in the area as your customers come to you. If parking is a problem in your area, perhaps you can arrange to go to your customers.
- You can work alone or hire help. This can be your decision. *You* are in control and *you* decide how large or small you want your business to be.
- You are providing a valuable service for which people are willing to pay. This makes you part of a community and gives you prestige and a sense of self-respect and worth. These are priceless "coins" that cannot be carried to the bank and cannot be measured in dollars.

### PROCEDURE

If you have decided you would like to establish your own clothing alterations business, you will want to go about it in a professional manner. There are, of course, several things you will need to do to get started right. There are local laws and insurance requirements to consider, social security opportunities to investigate, income tax laws to learn, and records to keep. You will want to get your working areas set up for maximum efficiency. You will want to let your public know you are offering this needed service.

### Licensing

Before going into business, find out if an occupational license is required in your community. Some places require a license for any kind of commercial service, including sewing. If so, it means your place of business must be located in a commercial or semi-commercial zone. Many homes are located in semicommercial zones. To find out if yours is, call your local city or township hall or county courthouse for the information. You can also find out if you need to have a license and if your home is in an area which permits running a private business.

If you do need to have a license, the small fee required is usually worth the advantages it offers. These advantages include:

- You may have a sign outside your place of business to help customers find you and to attract extra business.
- You can choose a name and have it legalized so no one can copy you and trade on the reputation you have built up. The name you select can be simple as in "Alterations by Rose," or catchy as in "Fit 'Em and Fix 'Em Alterations Service."
- You can have a phone listing in the yellow pages of the phone book using this name.
- You can advertise in community newspapers, organization bulletins, church bulletins, and school programs.
- Your neighbors can't object to your business since you have a license for it.
- You can expand and grow and get bank financing.
- You can add an extra room or close in a carport to house your workroom.

Suppose you find, upon investigation, that you live in a strictly residential area that is not semicommercial. Many people still conduct businesses from such areas. Many artists, authors, and tax consultants work from their homes. You probably can, too. However, you should get a lawyer's opinion so you do not run into legal difficulties. In addition, you must be even more careful not to disturb your neighbors:

- Be considerate and don't make appointments that will

## Altering Ready-To-Wear Fashions

bring clients too early or too late and disturb your neighbors.

• Provide a parking space for clients so they don't block a neighbor's place.

• Make sure you have a private phone line so your calls do not tie up the phone for anyone else.

• Make some of your fitting appointments in your clients' homes. Such a practice not only cuts down the traffic to your home, but provides an extra service. Home calls are rare these days and can be very much appreciated. Customers are often more comfortable in their own homes. Also phone calls to your home will not interrupt you. In addition, the customer may think of several other garments to be fitted or altered at the same time.

• If you're using a power sewing machine or your regular machine is noisy, you can cut down on the noise. Make sure your machine is well-oiled and in good working order. Put a foam rubber mat under it to muffle the sound and prevent annoying anyone close to you.

All in all, your home can also be your place of business if you are thoughtful and considerate of your neighbors. Many people conduct successful businesses from one- or two-room apartments in condominums, cooperative apartment houses, and retirement homes as well as in houses in residential areas. Sometimes an apartment complex or neighborhood will provide you with all the business you care to undertake. However, you may prefer to keep your business entirely separate from your neighborhood and find your customers in other areas.

### Insurance

Check with the insurance company to be sure your policy covers any problem that might arise. For instance, if you had a fire would your policy replace garments left there by your clients? If one of your customers fell or was hurt on your property or in your work room, would your insurance pay the medical expenses? This kind of liability insurance is a necessity.

### Social Security Payments

You have probably taken out a social security card by now. If you have not, you will need to get one now. Since you are going to be self-employed, it will be your responsibility to make your own social security payments and be sure you get credit for future retirement benefits. A visit to your local social security office should give you the information you need to do this.

### Income Taxes

If you are employed, your employer withholds your income tax payments for you. Since you are self-employed, you will need to do that for yourself. You will be required to estimate your income every three months and send the tax payment to the Internal Revenue Service (IRS). At the end of the year, you will have to file your yearly return.

Unless a close relative is an expert on income tax laws, you will be wise to get professional help. The local IRS office will give you free information about your responsibilities for your taxes. You may find it more to your advantage, and well worth the extra charge, to go to a tax consultant. Perhaps someone in your bank can give you the advice you need. Be sure you know what kinds of records you must have, what expenses will be deductible, and how to pay your estimated tax.

Do not rely on friends, family, or neighbors to give you the correct information unless they are experts who work with income taxes all the time. Tax laws change from year to year and most people do not have the background of information you will need. In fact, you could be given incorrect information that would cause you trouble.

Put your mind at rest about these business responsibilities before you get started. It is dangerous to assume you know what to do or not do. You could miss out on several quarters of social security credit. You might even throw away records that would have allowed you to deduct certain expenses from your income tax. Find out the correct

## Ch. 16: Establishing Your Own Business

procedures first. The peace of mind will be worth the little time and effort it takes.

### PLANNING YOUR WORK AREA

After you have the information you need to operate your business from your home, take a critical look at your work space. Some of the small equipment and the arrangement that was good enough for your personal sewing may not be suitable for volume work. You may now need a more organized area, a permanent worktable, better pressing tools, more storage space, and privacy.

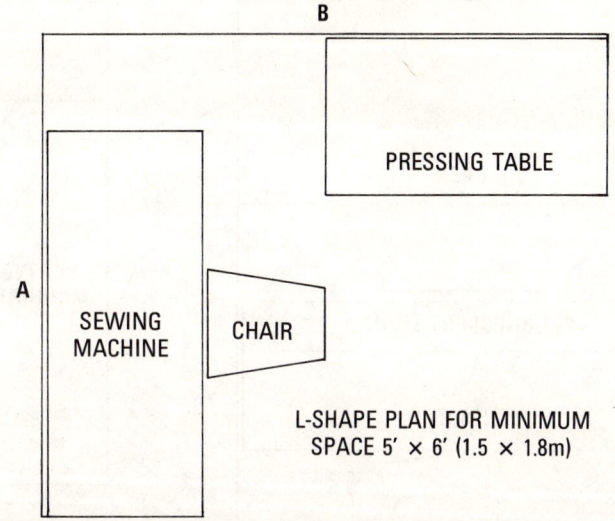

*If you have a minimum space of five feet by six feet along two walls, you could arrange your equipment in an L-shape as shown here.*

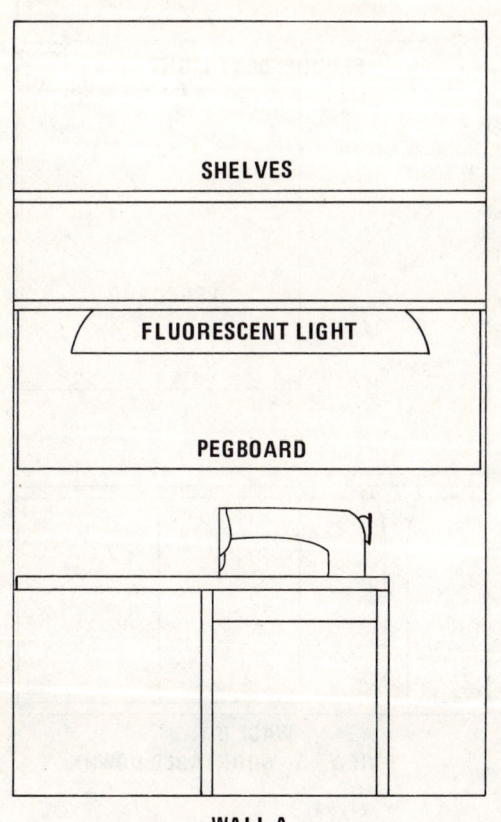

**WALL A**

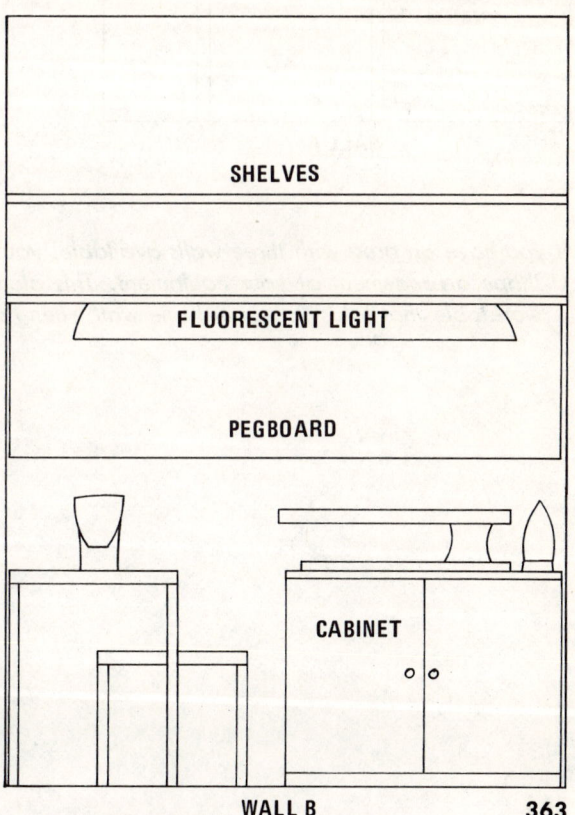

**WALL B**

**Altering Ready-To-Wear Fashions**

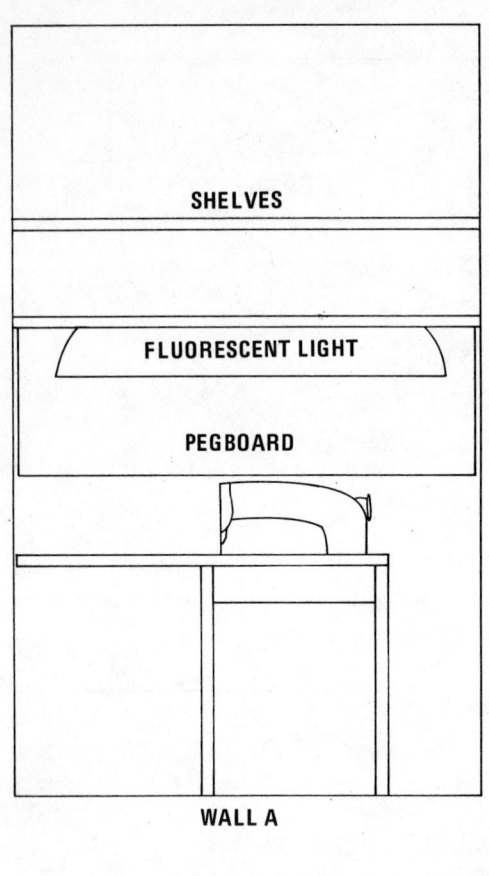

WALL A

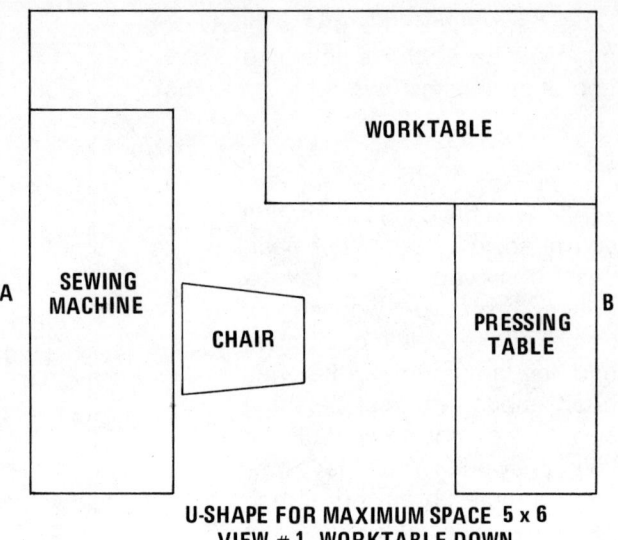

U-SHAPE FOR MAXIMUM SPACE 5 x 6
VIEW #1 WORKTABLE DOWN

*If you have an area with three walls available, you might try a U-shape arrangement of your equipment. This plan features a worktable that folds up against one wall when not in use.*

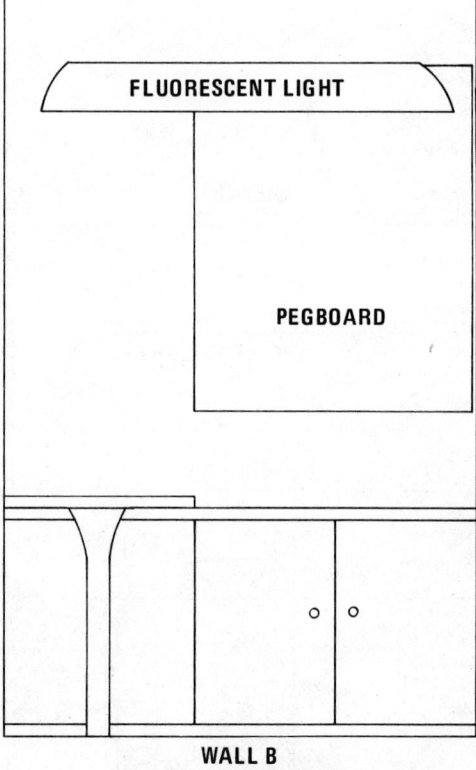

WALL B
VIEW #1 WORKTABLE DOWN

## Ch. 16: Establishing Your Own Business

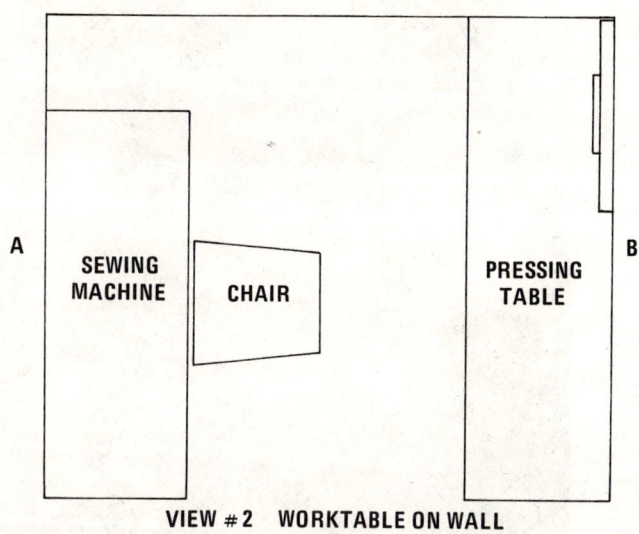

VIEW #2   WORKTABLE ON WALL

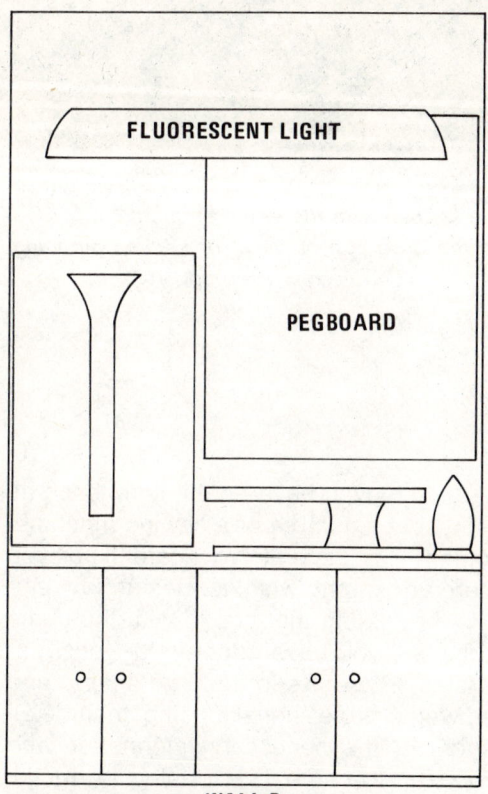

WALL B
VIEW #2   WORKTABLE UP ON WALL

Experiment with different ideas. Try to set things up so you don't have to take everything down and put it away after each work session. If the only space you have is in a corner of a room, you may be able to block that corner off in some way. You could invest in an inexpensive screen or room divider to hide the area. You could rearrange the furniture so a bookcase or high cabinet hides your area from the rest of the room. You might even be able to use a large closet. Remove the doors and hang a curtain or drapery to cover the area.

For greatest efficiency, try to get your equipment arranged in a U or L shape with the sewing machine in the center, the work table on one side, and the pressing board on the other. Storage areas can be both above and below the work surfaces. A buckboard pressing table on top of a chest of drawers is much more efficient than an ironing board that is always in your way. Use the chest for storing sewing supplies.

### CUSTOMER CONTACTS

By the time you decide to go into business, you may already have all the customers you need. There is such a shortage of capable alterationists that often people ask you to do work for them as a favor. However, if you need to find extra customers, there are several ways to go about it.

365

*An excellent sewing alcove arrangement using one end of the family kitchen for the work area.*

Courtesy Family Circle
Photo by Vincent Lisanti

*The same kitchen with the sewing equipment folded away so the area can be used for kitchen planning and record keeping.*

Courtesy Family Circle
Photo by Vincent Lisanti

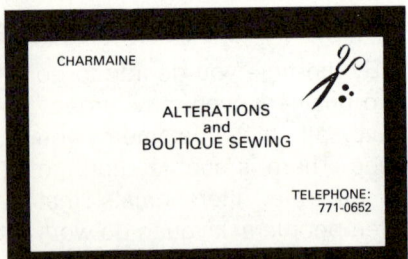

*Business cards are a worthwhile investment.*

### Business Cards

First, have your own business cards printed. Every community has at least one commercial printer. You can find one in the yellow pages of your phone book. The cost for this professional printing is small and well worth it to you. The standard 3½-inch by 2-inch, wallet-size card is best. Your printer may even have an emblem, such as a thimble or a sewing machine, to decorate your card. If not, you might wish to design an emblem that ties in with the name you have adopted for your venture. Keep the card simple and professional looking. Include all the necessary information and be sure it is printed correctly. Put as much on the card as you

Courtesy J. C. Penney Company

*Retail stores usually maintain alterations departments in their stores. Contact the personnel manager to see if they need extra help.*

want the public to know. If you don't want anyone dropping by and want to conduct business over the telephone, list only your phone number. If you prefer to have customers come to you, give your address.

While you are ordering your cards, investigate the possibility of getting a rubber stamp made with the same information on it. You can use this stamp for your alteration tickets, stationery, envelopes, and bills to customers. You can even use it to mark your pattern books and magazines. Later, you may wish to invest in printed stationery and invoice forms.

The design and information on your cards are important as they represent you to the public.

When you have your cards, you are ready to start distributing them. As you make your personal contacts, look your best and remember the suggestions for an interview given in Chapter 15.

### Retail Stores

Some of the best places to contact are retail stores which sell the kind of clothing you wish to work on. Call ahead and make an appointment with the owners or managers. If they already employ someone for their sewing, suggest they may need extra help to see them through rush seasons. Many such shops, however, do not employ their own alterationists and depend upon individuals like you to do all their work. Arrange to leave your card in person—don't mail it. When you find a shop that would like your services, discuss a schedule of pickup and delivery convenient for all concerned. Be prepared with a price list for each type of alteration, (See page 369) and come to a definite agreement about payment. Be businesslike and professional in your manner and discussions.

Even if the individual shops don't wish to enter into a definite

*Small specialty shops try to insure customer satisfaction by supplying the services of an alternationist.*

Sink 'r Swim
Lynn Photo Service

## Altering Ready-To-Wear Fashions

agreement with you to do their work, they may be happy to give your cards to their customers when alterations are required. In that case, give them a supply of your calling cards.

### Drycleaning Establishments

Most drycleaners make minor repairs to garments as a part of their service. Sometimes they also offer an alteration service as a sideline. Even if they don't offer the service themselves, their customers may ask them where they can get such help. If you decide to contact drycleaners, follow the same steps you did with the retail stores. Be sure to leave a supply of your business cards.

### Launderettes

Most neighborhood launderettes have a bulletin board where people can leave notices for the patrons. You can tack your card up in several launderettes in your area. Leave a few cards with the manager or attendant to give out. Check back occasionally to be sure your card is still in place.

### Apartment Houses, Hotels, and Motels

Managers of large residence complexes often keep a list of service people for the convenience of their tenants or guests. In some, you may even find a special place to display your card or name.

### Beauty and Barber Shops

Men and women talk about all kinds of problems to barbers and beauty operators. Many shops would be willing to have some of your cards to give to their customers when they hear them wondering where they can get the kind of service you offer.

### Clubs and Organizations

Ask to make an announcement of your business in clubs or organizations meetings in which you take a part. Give your cards to the members.

### Friends and Relatives

Give cards to your friends and relatives to pass out to their friends. A contact in a large business firm, such as a bank, hospital, phone company, or business office, can distribute many cards for you. Be generous with your cards. Each one given is an investment in your future business. You don't need a license to conduct business in this way.

### Other Contacts

Always keep in mind, once you are established, your best advertisement is a satisfied customer.

Perhaps you are thinking that most of the contact ideas given in the preceding pages are impossible for you. Maybe you have a physical handicap that makes it hard for you to leave your home. Perhaps there are small children you can't leave. Not having access to a car or being able to drive can also eliminate many of the above-mentioned possibilities. However, you can still make the same contacts, but just approach them differently.

Polish up your most charming telephone manner. Make phone calls to the places you would like to contact. Explain carefully the service you have to offer and the reason you can't call in person. Ask them to help you if they can. Contact organizations that make it a practice to help people in your situation. Often the churches in your neighborhood will help. Many civic organizations, such as women's groups, the Chamber of Commerce, Vocational Rehabilitation, and men's clubs may help. Very often teachers of sewing classes, home economics teachers and supervisors, and home economics extension agents are contacted by the public to ask if they know anyone who does alterations work. You could let them know you would like to offer this service. Mail your cards to anyone who expresses the willingness to help you.

Remember though, it is always best to present yourself in person. So don't rely solely on the telephone if it is possible for you to go yourself.

### CONDUCTING BUSINESS

People in business get paid for their expenses as well as their time. Thus you will need a

## Ch. 16: Establishing Your Own Business

### ALTERATIONS PRICE LIST

**Ladies:**
SKIRTS
   Taper and hem (zipper) . . . . . . . $6.00 & up
   Taper and hem . . . . . . . . . . . . . $5.50 & up
   Taper . . . . . . . . . . . . . . . . . . . . . $3.50 & up
   Zippers . . . . . . . . . . . . . . . . . . . . $2.00 & up
   Culottes—hem . . . . . . . . . . . . . . $4.00 & up
SHORTS
   Zippers . . . . . . . . . . . . . . . . . . . . $2.00 & up
   Zippers with fly . . . . . . . . . . . . . $2.50 & up
BATHING SUITS
   Zippers . . . . . . . . . . . . . . . . . . . . $4.00 & up
DRESSES
   Zippers . . . . . . . . . . . . . . . . . . . . $2.00 & up
   Hems . . . . . . . . . . . . . . . . . . . . . $3.00 & up
   Hems (facing) . . . . . . . . . . . . . . $4.50 & up
   Shoulders . . . . . . . . . . . . . . . . . $4.00 & up
   Waist . . . . . . . . . . . . . . . . . . . . . . $4.00 & up
   Taper . . . . . . . . . . . . . . . . . . . . . $3.50 & up
COATS
   Hems . . . . . . . . . . . . . . . . . . . . . $6.00 & up
   Shorten sleeves . . . . . . . . . . . . . $4.00 & up
SLACKS
   Cuffs . . . . . . . . . . . . . . . . . . . . . . $2.50 & up
   Taper 4 seams . . . . . . . . . . . . . . $4.00 & up
   Taper and zipper . . . . . . . . . . . . $5.50 & up

**Men's:**
SLACKS
   To shorten . . . . . . . . . . . . . . . . . $5.00 & up
   Waist . . . . . . . . . . . . . . . . . . . . . . $1.75 & up
   Cuffs . . . . . . . . . . . . . . . . . . . . . . $2.50 & up
   Cuffs (continental) . . . . . . . . . . . $2.50 & up
   Cuffs (machine continental) . . . . $1.50 & up
   Bind pocket . . . . . . . . . . . . . . . . . $1.50 & up
   Half pocket . . . . . . . . . . . . . . . . . $1.00 & up
   Three-quarter pocket . . . . . . . . . $1.25 & up
   Zippers . . . . . . . . . . . . . . . . . . . . $2.50 & up
   Taper 4 seams . . . . . . . . . . . . . . $5.00 & up
   Waist elastic retainers . . . . . . . . $1.50 & up
COATS
   Hem . . . . . . . . . . . . . . . . . . . . . . $6.00 & up
   Shorten sleeves . . . . . . . . . . . . . $4.00 & up
   Take in sides . . . . . . . . . . . . . . . . $5.00 & up
   Jacket zipper . . . . . . . . . . . . . . . $3.50 & up
SHIRTS
   Taper sides . . . . . . . . . . . . . . . . . $3.00 & up
   Sleeves with cuffs (shortened) . . $3.00 & up
   Sleeves (shortened) . . . . . . . . . . $1.50 & up
   Turn collar . . . . . . . . . . . . . . . . . . $1.50 & up
   Sport shirt, turn collar . . . . . . . . $1.50 & up

Sample price list for alterations.

schedule of prices to charge and a system of keeping records. Your overall expenses are known as *overhead*. Your overhead will include rent, utilities, gas for business trips, supplies, and equipment maintenance and replacement. The price you charge must be high enough to give you a respectable hourly wage and to cover any expenses connected with your business. This means you will need to keep careful records of everything you buy or pay out as well as the money you take in.

### Price List

Decide on your minimum prices. Study the suggested price lists shown above for both men's and women's wear. These are sample lists to be used as a guide. Note that all charges are followed by *"and up."* In other words, the $2.00 charge for replacing a zipper would vary according to the length of the zipper and type of garment. A long zipper in a hard-to-handle fabric, or a lined garment would double the charge. An underlined hem alteration or one with a separate lining would increase the charge. A hem in a full skirt or formal dress could double or triple the price. You may want to make a separate list for the different kinds of hems with a description of each and the price charged.

## Altering Ready-To-Wear Fashions

Every community differs in the standard prices charged for such service. In large cities and resort areas, people in the service industries charge higher prices than in areas where the cost of living is lower.

Find out what others are charging in your area for these services. Call local alteration shops and make discreet inquiries of the charges for basic alterations. When you or your friends are shopping in a retail shop, ask how much a hem or shoulder alteration would cost. Many women ask for this kind of information when making a decision, so don't hesitate to do the same. Ask friends how much they have paid for alterations. Knowing the charges for a few basic alterations can be a guide for all the others that come up.

Have your list typed or clearly hand printed and display it in your work area. Keep a copy folded in your appointment book to take with you to outside calls.

### Paper Work

Operating a business of any kind involves a certain amount of paper work. Yours will be no exception. You will need a few forms, calendars, and an account book.

Having the proper forms available not only makes it easier for you to work, but makes you seem much more businesslike to your customers. Keeping accurate records helps you in paying income tax, making social security payments, and figuring how much money you are making per hour and per job.

### STATEMENTS (BILLS)

A *statement* is a business term for a written bill. The stationery counter of your local variety or discount store should have several tablets of forms you can use. An office supply business will have an even wider choice. The printer who makes your business cards may also carry those forms.

Choose a simple form with enough lines for the information you need. Statement forms are usually sold in sets of two or three colored sheets with sheets of carbon paper to slide in between. The copies are necessary for your records. Keep the top one or two and give the customer the bottom copy. Be sure to put all the information you need on this form at the time the garment is received or fitted. When only one garment is accepted at a time, the statement can also serve as the work *ticket*.

Use these forms to record:

• Your business name, address, and phone number. (You can use your rubber stamp for this.)

• The date the clothing was received or fitted.

• The date and time of day the clothes are to be finished.

• Name, address, and phone number of the customer or shop for whom you are doing the work.

• Description of the work to be done, such as, "Hem shortened 1 inch," "Side seams released," or "Sleeves shortened ½ inch."

• Description of the garment, such as blue wool dress.

• The charge for the work to be done. If the customer makes a deposit, subtract that from the total of charges and record the balance to be collected. In some cases, where you are uncertain of the time and material involved, you may have to make an estimate. When the job is done, you can write in the final charge.

Attach one copy of the statement to the garment and give

*Statement forms are inexpensive and readily available.*

**Ch. 16: Establishing Your Own Business**

*Make out two copies of a small work ticket for each garment you agree to alter.*

*Make out a set of large work tickets for each individual customer or store for whom you are doing several garments.*

the customer the other copy. If you have an extra copy, file it. Keep your files in alphabetical order, using the first letter of the customer's last name. At first, you may use a shoe box as a file box if you have to keep expenses down. Later, however, you should get a fireproof metal box so your records will be safe.

When the work has been completed and your payment received, be sure to mark all copies *paid* and put your initials on each copy. The customer keeps her copy and yours goes into the file.

Some customers and shops may prefer to have you bill them monthly for the money they owe you. If so, keep a separate file box for those customers to make the billing easier for you. Any time you receive only part of the payment, record the amount received and subtract it from the amount still owed to you. This amount then becomes the *balance*. Next time you send statements, repeat the balance owed from the month before and add any new charges.

Remember, carefully kept records serve several purposes:

• They help you keep track of work finished.

371

*Alterations tickets like this are used by fitters to record the information the alterationist will need to work on a garment.*

- They show you how much money you received and how much is still owed you.

## ALTERATION OR WORK TICKET

If you get several pieces of work from one shop or one customer, you will need information on each garment. Sometimes shops are careless about specifying in writing what is to be done on the garment. This can lead to costly mistakes.

Be prepared to *ticket* each garment before you take the work. You can buy small sales books, $3\frac{1}{2}$ inches by 5 inches (9 cm × 12.7 cm) in size, to use for this. These small books can be found in any variety store at very little cost. The pages are in sets of two colors with a sheet of carbon paper. This gives you one copy for an original and one copy for the customer.

When you accept a garment, fill in the following information on the tickets for *each* article:

- Customer's name or initials and the name of the shop where you picked it up.
- Date and time the work is to be finished.
- Brief description of garment so you will know where the ticket belongs.
- Complete description of the work to be done.
- Alteration charges.

After you have filled out the work ticket, attach it to the garment. Then fill out one statement for each customer, listing the garments with the prices to be

## Ch. 16: Establishing Your Own Business

| AUGUST Business Expenses | | | AUGUST Money Received | | |
|---|---|---|---|---|---|
| 8/1 | | | 8/1 | | |
| | Notions, fabric | $5.06 | | Patrick | $ 9.50 |
| | | | | Garcia | 4.00 |
| | | 3.50 | | Poitier | 13.50 |
| 8/3 | Thread, tape, | | 8/3 | Gallo | 15.00 |
| | zipper | | | Rueben | 14.00 |

Sample of bookkeeping ledger.

charged. Total the charges at the bottom and deduct any deposit you receive. Attach all the duplicate copies of the work tickets to a copy of the statement and leave them with the customer.

On your appointment calendar, record the dates you have promised to complete the work. File the original statements along with the extra copies in your alphabetical file. As you complete the work on each garment, remove the work ticket and attach it to the statement. When the work on each statement is completed, be sure to put it where you can locate it easily. As soon as you receive payment for your work, mark the statement *"Paid in full"* and add your initials and the date the money was received.

### NOTEBOOK (LEDGER)

While the individual tickets and statements are necessary for your day-by-day work, you will also need an overall record. When it comes time to figure your income tax, social security payments, and monthly income, you can't go through every individual statement. Plan to record each day's total expenses and income at the end of the day.

For this, you may wish to have a regular bookkeeping ledger but a plain school notebook can also be used. An 8-inch by 11-inch notebook with hard covers and lined pages works very well.

To organize the book, use the first page for the name of your business and the year. On the next two facing pages, record the current month. Label the left side for *Business Expenses* and the right side for *Money Received*. Each day, record all the supplies, materials, and other expenses you paid and the date. On the opposite page record any money received for work done with the date and customer's name. You will probably want to do this at the end of the day rather than interrupting your work. Meantime, you can tuck the money and checks you receive between the pages of the book, along with the statements paid that day. After you do your bookkeeping at night, you can put the money away.

You may find it helpful to tape, clip, or paste a large envelope to the front cover of the notebook. In this envelope, keep all your payment receipts for your expenses. Each month, clip all the receipts for the month together and put them in your income tax file. Then you won't get them mixed up with your household expenses that are not deductible.

At the end of the month, total your expenses. Total your income received. Then, subtract the expenses from the income to find your net profit or how much you really earned that month. Since you have been keeping a record of the hours you worked, you can now divide the total number of hours worked into the amount of net profit. For example, if you worked 100 hours during the month and made $325, you make $3.25 an hour.

If your hourly wage is what you think you are worth, it is a great morale booster. If the amount is too low, review your work methods, organization, charges, and time management to see where you can improve.

Has all this talk about doing paper work discouraged you? Many talented people don't like to do paper work and you may be one of them. Don't give up. Perhaps a member of the family or a friend can assume this responsibility for you.

Courtesy Family Circle
Photo by Vincent Lisanti

*You can brighten your work day and make things go more smoothly by having an extension telephone, a calendar, a clock, and a radio easily available. This area even has a small mirror so you can quickly check your appearance before answering the door.*

### APPOINTMENT CALENDAR

Now that you are going into business, your time will be scheduled closely. You will have customer appointments, and work-due dates to keep in mind. The needs of your family will still be important, and you'll still want to see your friends socially. Keeping track of all the things you need to do and all the people you need to see can be impossible without planning your time ahead and writing down appointments. You will be surprised to find out how much you can accomplish if you plan well. One of the first aids to getting yourself organized is an appointment calendar.

You can buy an appointment book with the dates already in it. Business supply companies have loose leaf calendars with one page printed with the hours of the day and lines. The other side is a dated, but otherwise blank, page for any notes you might like to make. You can even use just a blank notebook in which you write the days yourself.

Keep your appointment calendar handy and always write the exact appointment time for each customer. When you fill out work tickets, transfer the date you promised to have each garment ready to that day on the calendar. For example:

Mon. Aug. 1 3:00
Patrick—3 garments finished

Or

Mon. Aug. 1 3:00
Patrick—3 garments, fittings

If several garments have been promised to the same customer, you could record it like this:

Mon. Aug. 1 3:00
Patrick—blue wool—fitting
pink silk—fitting

5 garments promised for Aug. 4

The above information is your work calendar and should be kept in the work room near your work area. Family dates need not be recorded here.

### FAMILY CALENDAR AND NOTE PADS

On the desk or wall near the phone you will need a complete calendar record of *all* your responsibilities. When a customer calls to make an appointment with you, you can tell by a glance at your large calendar whether or not you will be free at

## Ch. 16: Establishing Your Own Business

the desired time. You may have been saving that time to go to the dentist. Also, if a member of the family answers the phone for you, they will know by looking at the calendar when you will be available.

On this calendar, you only need brief notes as reminders, such as:

8/1 10:00 Brown (1 hr.)
    12:15 Lunch at Ronnie's
        with Catherine
    3:00 Patrick (45 minutes)

This type of record will also help you to keep from overloading yourself on some days so that you can't possibly finish the work in time to meet your deadlines.

Be sure all your commitments are recorded as soon as they are made. Train your family to write all messages down and record any appointments they make for you. Keep a note pad and pencil by the phone so special instructions or messages will be easy to record. You might want to set certain days for appointments only and leave other days just for sewing, free of interruptions.

## DAILY SCHEDULE

As you start to organize each working day, glance over the work to be done and make a schedule. Keep a small pad of note paper handy to your work area to help you as you make your plans.

Check your calendar to be sure you remember all your appointments and each garment you have promised to complete that day. Make a note of each garment so you can check it off as you finish it. This check list or schedule will not only keep you organized, but it will also give you a great sense of satisfaction at the end of the day. You can see how much you have accomplished and will know you are getting everything ready on time.

## CUSTOMER RECORD FILE

One more record you may want to keep is a file of personal information for each of your regular customers. This is not absolutely necessary but it is good public relations and a time-saver. You can keep this record in a small cardboard or wooden file box on 3-inch by 5-inch file cards. Both items are inexpensive and easy to find.

On the first appointment with each new customer, fill out an information card. Record name, address, zip code, and phone number. If you take measurements, record them. Note any particular fitting problem, such as sloping shoulders, large hips, or one hip higher than the other. If this customer just wants you to alter hems, you might record the length desired for skirts and/or pants. If customers have been recommended to you by someone else, record that.

These cards should be regarded as personal information that no one but you would see. When clients call for another appointment, reread the cards before the appointment time to refresh your memory. This can help you to be more gracious in greeting them. If they have been recommended to you by someone else, ask how that person is. If they have recommended you to other clients, you can thank them. You may want to put very good customers on your Christmas card list. All these activities are good public relations.

The memory prompters on cards have another big advantage. When you are familiar with the fitting problems you can expect for that customer, you can get to work more easily and quickly.

### Brighten Your Corner

How often have you gone to a particular shop or chosen a restaurant because it was attractive and had atmosphere? The same quality of merchandise or food may have been available closer to your home but the pleasure you received from being in the other place made it worth the extra effort to get there. This can be true of your work space. With small cost and a lot of imagination, you can make your fitting and sewing area colorful and inviting. A pleasant atmosphere can help you work better and attract more business.

Choose a color or theme that is personal to you. For example, you could build your color scheme around your favorite

Courtesy Family Circle
Photo by Vincent Lisanti

*This extremely well-planned work area converts in a matter of minutes to an efficient office where everything is available for your bookkeeping needs.*

color scheme in mind. For instance, look for a piece of flannel printed with a design of your favorite flower.

You could glue pieces of attractive print fabric on the shoe box you will be using for filing your bills and work tickets. If you prefer, cover them with adhesive paper or gift wrapping paper. Even your customer card file, appointment book, city phone book, and notebook can be covered with the print. You might give the same treatment to an old wastebasket and an ordinary tin can to make a pencil and pen holder. Paint your storage cabinets and shelves to blend with the other items.

Put a piece of peg board or a bulletin board on any spare wall space you might have. The peg board can hold small tools and thread or you can use it to display "boutique" items. You will have some slow periods in your work when you can make special items for which you can take orders. Picture a peg board display of evening skirts, stoles, scarves, caftans, or cloth roses. They could add color to your work area and inspire your customers to order some of the same items.

color and/or flower. Suppose you like yellow and daisies make you happy. Use tints of your favorite yellow to paint or cover old furniture or sewing equipment. Use different shades or tints of the same color or a pleasantly contrasting color for other items. If your equipment is old and battered but in good working condition, a coat of paint can do wonders. A yellow sewing machine or a yellow ironing board, for example, will fit right into the color scheme.

When making your pressing cushions (see page 85), select fabrics to cover them with your

A bulletin board painted, covered with fancy paper, or made of just natural colored cork or composition board, could be functional as well as attractive. Trim the board with your favorite artificial flowers or vines around the edges. Display your price list in the center of the board. Then surround it with colored pictures from fashion magazines. If you have room for two bulletin boards, you could use one to display some of the articles you use to show a customer how a garment would look when accessorized.

Since you would never display a customer's clothes for anyone else to see, you will want some garment bags and covered hangers. These too, can be made from attractive fabrics to match your overall scheme. Customers may want to have you make matching closet accessories for them, too. If you want this kind of business, be sure to keep a record of your materials and time so you will know how much to charge.

If you don't have enough furniture to decorate your shop the way you want to, you may need some help. Often friends, relatives, and neighbors have old pieces of furniture tucked away in attics, basements, or storage rooms. If they know you are looking for an extra chair, a chest of drawers, a magazine rack, or an extra lamp, they may have that item. Garage sales or secondhand stores often have bargains you can use. Again, your imagination, a little paint, and attractive fabric or adhesive paper can work wonders. You might want to let your family and friends get into the picture with paint brushes, scissors and paste, and ideas.

Besides the decorations you use in your very own shop, there are a few functional items that can help brighten your day. Arrange a shelf where you can have a clock and a radio. If possible, have an extension phone with its own table for your calendar and note pads. Have a straight chair where your customers can sit between fittings or while you make out a work ticket. A shelf or magazine rack where you can display current fashion magazines or pattern books will help keep your customers happy and show you are up-to-date.

If there are other items you would like to have after you have tapped all the sources you can think of, remember that you have birthday and Christmas gifts coming. Drop suggestions to those who usually buy you gifts and let them know what you'd like to have that would help you in your new business. Also, check the gift catalogs for items you can get with your trading stamps.

### Lighten Your Work Load

If you have a family, share your plans with them and invite their cooperation. They will ben-

Photo by Deanna Laughlin
*Teach your children to answer the phone courteously and write messages correctly.*

efit from your extra income and should help share the work load. You may have a close friend who would like to feel part of your new venture. There are several ways others can help you.

As mentioned before, you might like to have help with your paperwork and record-keeping. Perhaps a family member could do you a great service here. Even younger children could help address envelopes and mail bills. You could make a family project of this kind of work once a week or month.

Everyone in the home could help by answering the phone. Encourage them to use pleasant telephone manners, to know what information you need, and then to make sure they write everything down.

Teach family members to help with the business shopping. If you have a detailed list of everything you need, someone else can do most of your buying for you. Be sure they

*Even though you may not be planning to leave your shop all day, you will feel and work better if you get dressed neatly and fix your hair and make-up.*

understand the need for saving the cash register tapes for your records.

When customers are due to come for fittings, tell the family the name of the person expected. They can greet them for you, call them by name, and direct them to your workroom.

Perhaps you can train relatives or friends to help with the routine handwork. Teach them the proper hemming stitches and how to apply snaps, buttons, hooks, or belt loops. You can reward them with money or by making some special fashion item for them.

One of the best places to enlist help will be in the meal preparation and routine household chores. Now that you are working, these chores should be shared. Each person's responsibility can be included on the family calendar, if you choose.

### Getting Started

Once you are launched in a business of your own, get into a routine. Start your work day as though you are going out to a regular job. Bathe and dress and brush your hair before you start your work schedule. A woman will probably feel more dressed with makeup and cologne. A man may feel the necessity for a tie and jacket to improve his image. Perhaps your schedule may not include any customers' appointments. However, it is a great morale booster to be well groomed. Also, you never know when someone may drop in. You will have the assurance of always looking your best, which adds to your professionalism. A lightweight jacket or smock may be worn over your clothes as a working uniform.

Check your calendar and appointment book. Take a minute to write a list of work to be finished that day. Note any fittings you have scheduled.

If this is one of your sewing days, line up your work and supplies as suggested in Chapter 13. If this is one of the days you have scheduled fittings, you may want to be sure the house is neat. If the client doesn't have to enter the rest of the house to get to your shop, just be sure your own area is presentable.

Sometimes you will have to schedule a fitting on your sewing day to accommodate a customer. If so, try to schedule the appointment before or after your regular sewing hours so you can keep your work flow as smooth as possible.

Remember, during your working hours you are employed to do a job. If you were working in a shop, you couldn't take time out for personal phone calls or visiting with neighbors or friends. Now that you are self-employed, you must learn to discourage phone calls or drop-in visits. Be firm but tactful. Let people know your work schedule. Never, never allow a client to wait while you visit with a friend.

When clients call you on the phone, don't ask them to wait while you take care of family business. Ask family members to wait until you are through with your business before they interrupt you. Only in an extreme emergency would you ask the client to wait. If the doorbell rings while you are on the phone, finish the phone message first, and then answer the door. If, for any reason, you do have to leave the phone while clients are calling, give them a brief explanation and ask if you can call them back. If your practice is to call on your customers,

## Ch. 16: Establishing Your Own Business

you may wish to install a telephone-answering device.

## ENLARGING YOUR BUSINESS

If you are a skilled alterationist and have followed all the suggestions in this book, sooner or later you may have all the work you can handle. Possibly, you may have to start turning down business and recommending someone else who can do the work. On the other hand, you might want to consider the possibility of hiring help and expanding your own operation. Before you jump into an increased business venture, you should ask yourself several questions.

Do I need the extra income?

Do I really want the added responsibility a larger business requires?

Am I ready physically and emotionally for a larger operation?

Can I still take care of my family commitments? Will my family help me?

Is there room to expand at home or will I have to rent space somewhere?

Will my zoning laws allow me to expand in my own home? If not, will I have to add the expense of paying rent for a business space in a commercial zone?

Can I work with someone else? Am I organized enough in my work habits and methods that someone can work with me?

Do I have enough money or credit to finance the new venture?

Have I kept good records so I am sure I am making a good profit?

Have I made enough contacts to be sure I will have a large enough volume of work? Will this extra volume be year-round work or seasonal?

Am I willing to work a longer day or full time?

Can I find a good assistant to hire?

If you have doubts about answers to any of these questions, you probably are not ready to expand. You might want to tuck the idea in the back of your mind and wait a little longer.

### Enlarging at Home

If your business is ready to grow, you will want to explore the different possibilities for expansion.

First, decide whether or not you could expand where you are. Perhaps you are ready to invest in more sophisticated machinery, so you might investigate a commercial power machine. This one investment alone could increase your speed and volume of work by almost 50 percent. If you have room, you can leave your regular machine in place. If not, you could store it away for use during rush periods only. Look into the possibility of buying a blind-stitch hemmer power machine (page 36).

While these machines are expensive, they enable you to do much more work in the same amount of time. Since you are being paid for the amount of work you turn out and not by the hour, you can easily increase your income enough to pay for them.

Perhaps your business has increased enough so you not only need power equipment but extra help as well. You are ready to hire a helper, either part-time or full-time. If you have enough room in your present work area, your only problem is to find the right help. However, your first consideration will be whether or not you have the space for two people to work efficiently and comfortably. The corner of one room or a closet setup would not lend itself to this kind of arrangement.

Is there any possibility another room in the house could be converted from its present use to a workshop? Is there a carport, garage, basement, or porch that could be changed into a workroom for you?

The more remodeling you find necessary, the more expensive your expansion will be. However, if you plan carefully, any changes you make will improve the appearance and value of your home. Since your business has been showing a good profit, and your credit is good, you should be able to get your bank to help you finance the additional home improvement.

Courtesy Family Circle
Photo by Alan Hicks

An attached garage on a house can be converted to a valuable living or working space if your business expands. If you plan to use the space for work, you could plan an outside door opening directly into your shop.

Courtesy Family Circle
Photo by Alan Hicks

The inside of a garage may take some imagination to see the wonderful possibilities for a decorating scheme. You may have so much room you will want to share your shop with a friend. A craft shop could be a compatable partner for an alterations business.

### Ch. 16: Establishing Your Own Business

You may ask your bank about an FHA home improvement loan which has financing similar to a home mortgage. Banks usually have financial advisors you can consult for help.

If you need new power machines, the seller should be able to help you finance the purchase on a time basis so your additional income will cover the monthly payments.

The interest on your loan as well as a portion of your monthly housing expenses are deductible from your income taxes as business expense. Also, both the improvement and the new machinery are depreciable and hence deductible from your gross income. On the machines, you may also take an investment credit which is offset against your income tax. Your tax consultant will give you detailed instructions for these deductions.

Expanding your business in your own home involves the least amount of risk, change, and expense. However, suppose there is just no way you can expand in your home. Your neighbors may already be complaining about the customers you draw to the house. In that case, it may be time to think about renting commercial facilities.

#### Going Commercial

Before you sign a lease to rent a shop, be sure the location meets your needs. Since you must have a steady flow of customers to make your business profitable, you should be located in an easily accessible area with plenty of parking space. You will want to be in a location where you and your customers will feel safe. You will have to sign a lease and commit yourself to paying rent every month for a specified length of time. These are possibilities to consider if you rent a shop.

#### Sharing Space

One possibility will be to find another business where you can share space and customers.

Many successful retail clothing shops are willing to provide work space for the convenience of having a fitter-alterationist on the premises. Each of you helps attract business to the other. Financial arrangements in such situations will depend on the shop. Some might offer you the use of their space free just to have someone with your skills available. Probably, though, they would like to have you pay a part of their operating expenses, such as a percentage of the rent, electricity, and heat. Perhaps they may ask you to pay a flat sub-rental fee.

Established custom designers or dressmakers are often asked to do alterations, but very few of them want to do this type of work. They might be glad to share their facility and advertising with you to have you provide this service for their customers.

Clothing concession shops sell high-quality secondhand clothes. One of them may welcome someone to use part of the space to provide alteration service for their clients.

Drycleaners often find their customers desiring alteration service. If they are located in a prosperous neighborhood, they may be interested in having you set up a shop with them. A drycleaner in a low-income area probably wouldn't draw enough alterations business to make it profitable for you.

Small fabric shops, or knit and yarn hobby shops, often welcome someone to share rent and utilities.

Other small businesses, such as beauty shops or boutiques, may be looking for someone to share expenses.

Don't hesitate to approach any of these business possibilities. Look in a business directory for places convenient to you and call for an appointment. Use your business card to introduce yourself to the shop owners or managers. If you are businesslike in your manner and appearance, you will impress them as a successful business person who has something to offer.

Explore several possibilities, but get business and legal advice before making any final decisions. Be sure you know the exact financial arrangements that would be required of you. Does the business have any equipment they would be willing to share with you? Could you save money on pressing equipment or power machines? Will they answer your phone and take messages for you? Would they want you to do the same for them? Be sure you investigate all the possibilities thoroughly before making any commitments. You will probably want to check their credit rating and business reputation with the Better Business Bureau.

### Renting a Shop

You may have gained enough of a following and made enough profit to give you the confidence to rent your own facility. You have studied your records and know your profit is good, growing steadily, and is not seasonal. You are constantly getting new customers and would like to accommodate more. You have every reason to believe your business can continue to grow. You are prepared to take the risk of extra expenses such as rent, utilities, a business phone, extra advertising, and the salary of a helper. You are reasonably sure you can meet all of these additional expenses and still make a good profit.

Begin by investigating and exploring business areas close to your home. Spend time in these areas and study the parking, flow of business traffic, and the amount of foot traffic. Check the kinds of businesses already established there. Would they draw the same kind of customers you would? Would there be competition or would your business complement the others? Is the surrounding area prosperous enough to supply you with sufficient customers? Are costs of available spaces so high you would have to do a large volume of business just to pay the rent? Are you going to expect a large part of your extra business to come from the new contacts? Will you still be doing the regular pick-up and delivery work you've been doing for your established clients?

As you study the different business districts, drop into some of the already-established shops. Introduce yourself with your business card. Ask their opinions about the possibilities for an alterations shop in the section. They should be excellent sources of information. If the response is not favorable, try to find out why. Perhaps they can suggest other locations.

After you feel you have found just the right area, you must still consider the space to rent. How much space do you really need? Will most of your business be with clients who will come to your shop? Is most of your business pick-up and delivery work? Do you deal with many people who would find climbing stairs difficult and therefore might avoid a second-floor location?

A street level shop has some advantages, though the rent may be higher. The shop is usually easier to find so your customers can locate you easily. You will also have windows you can decorate to attract attention.

An upstairs location will normally be less expensive. It may be just what you want if you do most of your business with established shops and pick up and deliver the work yourself.

### Bookkeeping Help

No matter how you decide to expand your business, you will still have paperwork to do. In fact, it will become even more important, because you will be doing more business. This may be the time to hire a bookkeeping service to do it for you. Many communities have people who offer bookkeeping services for small businesses like yours. For a reasonable fee every month, they will keep your records, bill your customers, and do your taxes. Check into the possibilities of getting this service for yourself.

### Sewing Help

Before you were ready to even consider expanding your business, you probably found it necessary to hire extra help in your home. If you do not already have an assistant, there are several places to find such help.

Many schools have vocational training programs where students are being taught alterations skills. Perhaps you received your training in such a program. If so, you already know whom to contact to find help. If not, you might call the local school superintendent's office to find where these programs are offered. You can contact the vocational guidance personnel in these schools and ask that they send some students for you to interview. Perhaps, they have a cooperative program in which the students work part of the day and go to school part-time. Programs such as these are always looking for good places for their students to earn money and gain experience. These students have had basic training in school and are eager to learn on the job. You will find your contact with them and the vocational program most rewarding. The teachers in their program have already made them aware of the importance of their appearance and job responsibilities. They know how helpful experience in a shop such as yours can be.

Many community vocational programs have adult classes in commercial sewing. Some of these mature women are only interested in part-time work, while some are looking for full-time employment. Check into these possibilities as a source for additional help.

If such programs are not available in your community, you can find help other ways. Check with the state employment service for applicants who are looking for alterations work. Place a "Help Wanted" ad in the classified section of your newspaper. You might ask your local fabric shops if they know of anyone looking for this kind of work.

When you hire help, you become an employer. You must insure your employees, make social security payments, and withhold income taxes from their pay. Thus you will need the services of a professional bookkeeping service.

# Appendix A

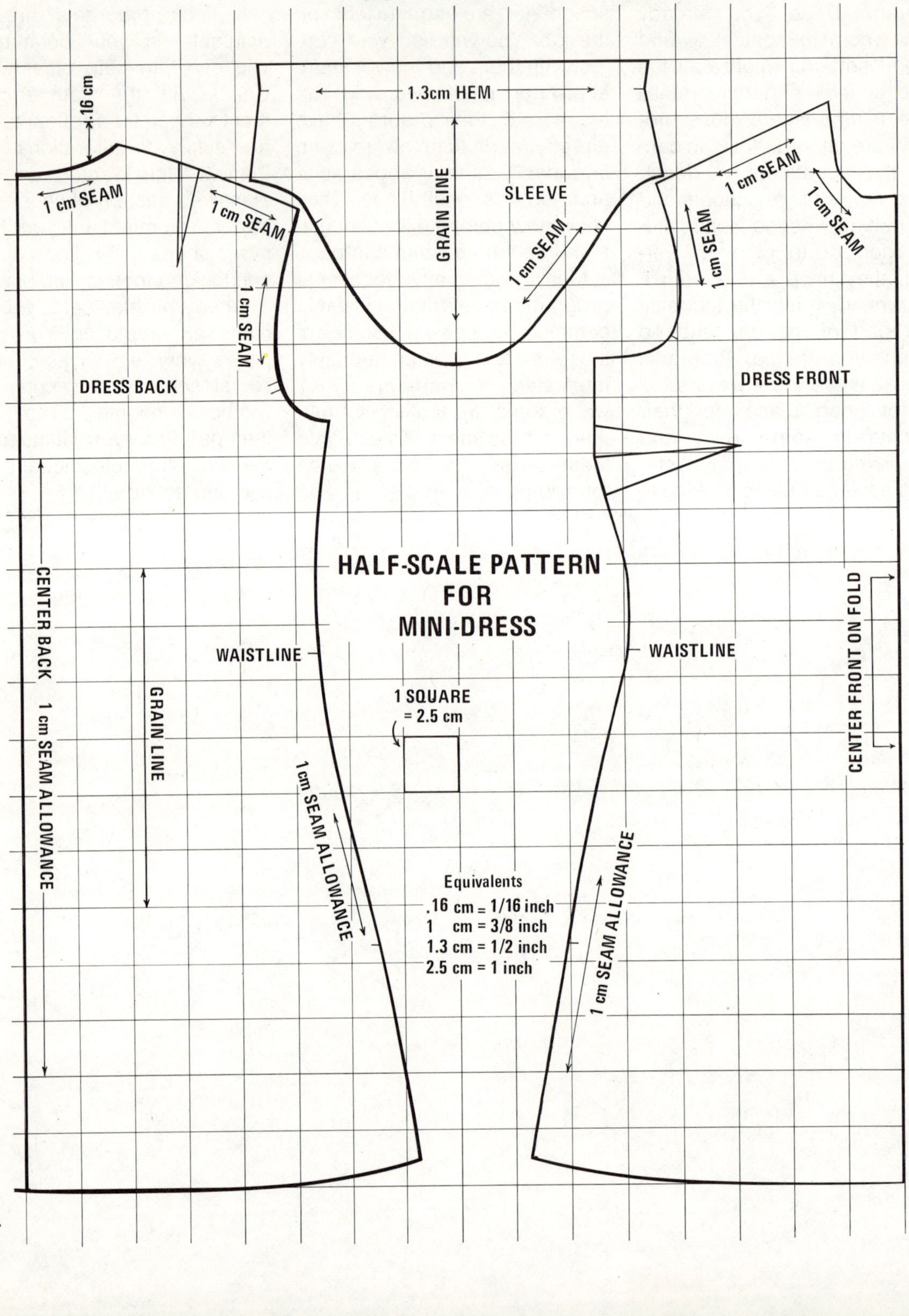

1.3cm HEM
.16 cm
1 cm SEAM
1 cm SEAM
GRAIN LINE
SLEEVE
1 cm SEAM
1 cm SEAM
1 cm SEAM
1 cm SEAM
1 cm SEAM
DRESS BACK
DRESS FRONT
HALF-SCALE PATTERN
FOR
MINI-DRESS
CENTER BACK 1 cm SEAM ALLOWANCE
GRAIN LINE
WAISTLINE
WAISTLINE
CENTER FRONT ON FOLD
1 SQUARE
= 2.5 cm
1cm SEAM ALLOWANCE
1 cm SEAM ALLOWANCE
Equivalents
.16 cm = 1/16 inch
1 cm = 3/8 inch
1.3 cm = 1/2 inch
2.5 cm = 1 inch

# Glossary

*abaissé* (a bess say)—lowered, as a hem or a waistline. (French)

*absorbent*—having the ability to absorb or take in moisture.

*agréments* (a grey monh)—ornaments or trimmings. (French)

*A-Line*—skirt fitted at waist and slightly flared at the hem.

*alongé* (a lonh zhay)—elongated, lengthened, stretched. (French)

*amincir* (a mahn seer)—to make thin, or look slender. (French)

*armhole*—a garment opening for the arm or sleeve.

*armscye*—another term for armhole.

*arêter* (ar re tay)—to fasten. (French)

*arrowhead*—an embroidered triangle used as decorative reinforcement for ends of seams, pleats, or pockets.

*asymmetric*—different on each side of the center; not symmetrical.

*atelier* (a tell yay)—workroom or studio, dressmaking establishment.

*au courant* (a coo ranh)—up to the minute, of the present, in vogue, fashionable. (French)

*awl*—a small, pointed instrument for piercing small holes.

*backing*—lightweight fabric used as reinforcement.

*basic*—fundamental; used to describe a dress with a plain skirt and bodice.

*Basque*—knitted shirt with stripes and crew neck; also, tight-fitted, low-waisted bodice.

*basting*—sewing temporarily by hand or with a large machine stitch.

*bell*—skirt gathered or pleated at waist to form a bell shape.

*bell-bottoms*—pants cut narrow through hips and thighs, flaring from knees to varying widths at the hems.

*belting*—a stiffening used as the backing for belt made of fabric, or a ribbon-like banding that is used as the waistline of a skirt or dress.

*bias*—diagonal grain line formed by folding the lengthwise grain parallel to the crosswise grain. True bias has the most stretch and elasticity.

*blazer*—single or double-breasted sport jacket with patch pockets; may be solid or patterned fabric with contrasting trim; worn by men and women.

*blouson*—loose, extra-length bodice gathered into waistline to give overblouse effect.

*bodice*—the waist or top part of a garment.

*bodkin*—a blunt needle used for threading elastic, tape, or ribbon through a casing or beading.

*body suit*—shirt or blouse with enough length to snap or button between the legs to hold it in place.

*bolero*—midriff length, buttonless jacket with curved bottom; usually collarless and sometimes sleeveless. (Spanish)

*bonded*—fibers or fabrics held together with an adhesive substance.

*bon goût* (bohn goo)—good taste. (French)

*boning*—flexible strips, usually plastic, used to stiffen seams or edges.

*bordé* (bor day)—bordered or edged. (French)

*bouffant* or *ballet*—very full, gathered skirt with narrow waist; effective with many layers of sheer fabric.

*boutique* (boo teek)—a small store in which accessories and special fashion items are sold. (French)

*bouttonnage* (boo ton azh)—closing. (French)

*box*—straight line, square-shouldered, beltless coat for men or women; single or double-breasted.

*buckboard*—a small, non-collapsible ironing board used on top of a separate base or support rather than having legs of its own.

*burnoose*—loose woolen cloak with hood; adapted from Middle East.

*canvas*—strong, plain-weave cotton, linen, or mixed fabric used for interfacings or as ironing board covers or press cloths.

*cape*—a flared, circular, or straight-lined, sleeveless outer garment that hangs from neckline closing; may be any length and hooded.

*cardigan*—collarless, button-front garment with rounded or V-neck; sleeveless, short, or long sleeves; style adapted to sweaters, coats, or dresses and worn by men, women, or children.

*carrier*—a thread or fabric loop used to keep a tie, belt, or strap in place.

*casing*—a facing, hem, or binding used to hold a drawstring, elastic, or boning so it will be covered on both sides.

*centure* (sanh toor)—belt or sash. (French)

*chain stitch*—used two ways; to stitch from one piece of fabric to another without cutting the threads between the two pieces; or, interlocking of a single thread into successive loops to form a long chain (as in single crochet).

*chain tacks*—varying lengths of chain stitch (see second definition above) used to hold two parts of a garment together loosely so some movement is allowed.

*chemise* (also sack)—straight line dress with no waistline or fitting darts.

*chesterfield*—slightly fitted, beltless coat with fly front, flap pockets, and velvet collar; originally a man's style but now adapted for women and children.

*chez* (shay)—in the home or shop of; such as chez Chanel. (French)

*chic* (sheek)—currently fashionable, smart style in dress. (French)

*clapper*—a smooth, flat piece of wood used by pressers to hold a crease in place while the steam dissipates and the fabric dries.

*clip*—a short snip or cut in the seam allowance, using just the point of the scissors; used as a marking.

*circular*—skirt cut in true circle pattern flaring out from hips.

*confectionné* (conh feck syonay)—ready-to-wear. (French)

*continental*—slim-cut man's trousers with fitted waistband, no belt loops, and slashed side pockets; straight or slightly tapered, cuffless legs.

*conservative*—man's trousers with belt loops, slashed side pockets; pleated, with cuffed full legs.

*corsage* (cor sahzh)—bodice or waist of a dress. (French)

*corselet*—garment with tightly fitted, laced midriff.

*coudre* (coo dr)—to stitch or sew. (French)

*couture* (coo toor)—needlework or sewing; products of a seamstress; seam. (French)

*couturier* (coo too ryay)—male dressmaker, designer, or head of a dressmaking establishment. (French)

*couturière* (coo too ryare)—woman dressmaker or designer. (French)

*crease*—a folded line which is pressed into the material.

*crosswise grain*—the filling or woof yarns running the width of the fabric from one selvage to the other.

*culottes*—skirt-like pants with concealing panel or pleats.

*cutaway*—single-breasted, formal daytime coat usually seen at weddings; curves from front waistline button to long tails in back.

*crotch*—the angle formed by the parting of two legs; in clothing refers to the center seam where the two legs of a pair of pants are sewn together.

*dart*—a tuck, tapered to a point at one or both ends; used to fit clothing over the curved areas of the body.

## Glossary

*décolleté* (day coll e tay)—low-cut neckline, one that exposes the neck and back or neck and shoulders. (French)

*démondé* (day mo day)—old-fashioned, out of style. (French)

*dénoué* (day noo ay)—untied, loose. (French)

*dernier cri* (dare nyay kree)—the last word in fashion; the latest thing. (French)

*dirndl*—gathered peasant skirt in colorful country prints; often worn with a corselet.

*dowel*—a round rod or stick.

*drape*—the cut or hang of clothing; also refers to controlled fullness held in place by gathers, pleats, or tucks.

*drill cloth*—a cotton fabric similar in weight and use to canvas but made with a twill weave.

*dropped shoulder*—a shoulder seam line, where the sleeve joins the shoulder, that is lower on the arm than the normal line.

*dungarees*—work pants worn by all ages; of dark heavy-duty fabric; reinforced stitching at all stress points.

*ease*—to fit seams of unequal lengths together so excess fabric does not pleat or pucker.

*ease allowance*—the extra room allowed in clothes so the wearer can move comfortably and the fabric does not appear to strain over the body.

*ease stitch*—a single line of regular machine stitches used to hold fabric in place and keep it from stretching.

*edge stitch*—a line of stitching close to a folded edge, usually on the outside of the garment; used for decoration or to hold bulky seams in place.

*edging*—a narrow lace, ruffle, zigzag stitching, or binding used as trimming.

*Edwardian*—single or double-breasted men's jacket with four-button closing, slight waist fitting, and center or side vents; of English origin.

*emery*—an abrasive powder used to clean and keep needles and pins free from rust.

*empire*—fitted garment with waistline seam directly under the bust.

*entre deux* (ontre du)—lace or embroidery insertion resembling hemstitching, narrow beading; used in seams, especially in lingerie. (French)

*étoffe* (ai toff)—material, fabric, cloth; or quality. (French)

*Eton jacket*—short, square jacket buttoned in front; usually worn with a round white collar; adapted from style worn by students at Eton school in England.

*étroit* (ai trwah)—close-fitting, narrow. (French)

*eyelet*—a small metal ring or hand- or machine-stitched hole; used for decoration, lacing, or for the prong of a buckle.

*face*—to finish an edge by applying a fitted piece of fabric to cover raw edges.

*facings*—fitted pieces of matching or other fabric applied to a garment edge as a finish.

*façon* (fa sonh)—fashion cut; make; shape. (French)

*fencer's jacket*—close fitting, waist-length jacket with side closing and high neckline.

*findings*—dressmaking supplies used to make a garment—matching thread, binding, tape, zipper, trims, buttons.

*flares*—any style pants that drape away from the hips into varying widths at the bottom.

*flap*—a shaped piece finished on three sides and attached to the garment by one edge; used as decoration such as a flap on a pocket.

*fleur de lis* (fler de lee)—iris flower, royal emblem of France; conventionalized motif used as a design. (French)

*flounce*—deep, slightly gathered ruffle.

*fold*—to turn under or double a piece of fabric along a given line.

*fourreau* (foo roe)—fitted, sheath-like gown. (French)

*fuse*—to blend by melting or adhering together.

*garni* (gar nee)—garnished or trimmed. (French)

*garniture* (gar nee toor)—ornamental trimming. (French)

### Altering Ready-To-Wear Fashions

*gather*—to control fullness by drawing up a thread.

*gaucho pants*—wide, calf-length pants fitted over hips and usually worn with boots; adapted from Argentine cowboy work pants.

*generic*—belonging to a class, kind, or group having common characteristics.

*gens du monde* (zhonh du mond)—refers to people of fashionable society. (French)

*glazing*—giving a smooth, shiny, or lustrous surface; may be an applied finish for some fabrics or caused by too much heat in pressing.

*godet*—a shaped piece of fabric set in a garment at the bottom for fullness and decoration; usually pointed at one end and wide at the other.

*gore*—a shaped, tapered section of fabric wider at the bottom than the top, as in a gored skirt.

*grading*—trimming seam allowances of facings, interfacings, and garment to different widths to eliminate bulk.

*grain*—the direction of the woven threads in a piece of fabric.

*greatcoat*—any full length, heavy, protective coat worn over suits, jackets, or dresses.

*gusset*—a shaped piece of fabric inserted in a garment to give ease and aid in fit; often diamond shaped.

*haute couture* (ote coo toor)—creative fashion design. (French)

*ham*—a firmly stuffed pressing cushion shaped like a ham.

*hand finishing*—the final touches done by hand sewing rather than by machine such as hems, sewing on buttons, hooks, eyes, and trims.

*hand picked*—a tailoring detail of hand-stitched finish used to outline a faced edge.

*heat-set*—pleats, creases, or shape permanently set in thermoplastic fabrics with the use of heat and pressure.

*hemline*—the line on which a hem is folded back or under.

*hip-huggers*—pants with waist that rests on the hips resulting in short crotch line; also used for shorts and skirts.

*Hong Kong finish*—a neat, decorative finish for inside seams and hem edges; covered with a binding.

*inseams*—the seams on trousers or pants which follow the inside of the pant leg from crotch to hem.

*inset*—a piece of fabric or trimming inserted within a larger piece for fit or decorative effect.

*insertion*—a narrow band of embroidery or lace with plain edges set between two sections of fabric as trim.

*interfacing*—an added piece of material between the garment and the facing to give added strength, shape, or body, and to prevent stretching and sagging.

*interlining*—a layer of fabric placed between the lining and the garment fabric for extra warmth.

*inverness*—an overcoat of plaid or houndstooth check with removable cape; can be applied to long cape of plaid or check.

*Ivy League*—conventional cut pants with belt loops, straight legs, and cuffs.

*Ivy League suit*—unshaped, three-button, single-breasted man's jacket with natural shoulders, center back vent, and narrow lapels; pants as in previous definition.

*jeans*—work pants of heavy-duty cloth cut with yoke front and back; finished with reinforced stitching and nailheads at stress points; now made in many fabrics and patterns.

*jodhpurs*—English-style riding pants flaring out over hips and narrowing back to the calves to be laced or zippered to fit to the ankles; worn with calf-length boots.

*jumper*—sleeveless, collarless, dress-like garment of medium- or heavy-weight fabric to be worn over shirts or sweaters.

*jumpsuit* (coverall)—any one-piece pants garment with full, straight, or pleated legs; front or back closing; made of any fabric and adapted to casual or semi-formal wear; worn by men or women.

*kilt*—traditional Scot's skirt that is pleated and wraps around with a side closing.

## Glossary

*kimono*—traditional garment worn by men and women of Japan; garment is unfitted with loose, wide sleeves; worn with obi or wide sash.

*knickers* (knickerbockers or plus-fours)—pants gathered and fitted to a band just below the knee; usually worn with knee-high socks or boots.

*lap*—the part of a garment that extends over another part; also to fold one section over another.

*lapel*—a part of a garment worn turned or folded back; as on a coat or jacket neckline.

*layout*—the arrangement of pattern pieces on fabric for cutting.

*lining*—a separate fabric covering used on the inside of a garment to cover the inside surface either partially or fully.

*lengthwise grain*—the yarns, threads, or wales of a fabric that run the length of the material parallel with the selvage edges.

*lingerie*—women's intimate apparel.

*lingerie keeper*—thread or fabric loop attached to a garment to keep lingerie straps out of sight.

*mackinaw*—boxy, lined shortcoat of heavy-weight wool plaid.

*manche* (monsh)—sleeve. (French)

*manchette* (monh shet)—wristband or cuff. (French)

*mandarin*—straight, unfitted coat with side slits, kimono sleeves, high collar, and side closing. (Chinese)

*man-tailored*—any garment that has a masculine or extremely tailored look; no curves or soft finishes.

*maxi*—term applied to ankle-length day-time wear.

*middy*—long-waisted, long-sleeved blouse with tight cuffs and large sailor collar.

*midi*—garment hem length that comes to the middle of the calf.

*midriff*—the section of the body below the bust and above the waist.

*mini*—any garment length that is four inches or more above the knee.

*mitt*—a small, padded pressing cushion made to fit over the hand.

*miter (mitre)*—the diagonal seam at the corner of a hem or straight band to form a square corner.

*mock*—something made as an imitation.

*modelliste* (moh del leest)—a dress designer whose designs are shown under the name of the house for whom he or she works. (French)

*monastic*—loose, kimono-like garment with hood; adapted from monk's robe.

*nap*—a fuzzy or downy surface of short fibers on a fabric that all lie in one direction; also refers to a one-direction design that must be used with all pattern pieces going the same way; some smooth surface fabrics reflect light differently depending on the direction used.

*Norfolk jacket*—belted, hip length jacket with patch pockets, yoke, box-pleated front and back; single-breasted.

*notch*—a small V-shaped nick cut in seam of garment to show where pieces go together.

*outseam*—the side seam on a pair of trousers that goes up the outside of the leg to the hip.

*ouvrage a l'aiguille* (oo vrahzh a lay gwee)—needlework. (French)

*overalls*—work pants worn by farmers and railroad workers; made of heavy drill cloth with bib front and shoulder straps that cross in back; plasterers, painters, and carpenters wear the same overall in white; now adapted in other fabrics for sportswear.

*overcast*—to cover the raw edges of a seam or cut edge with thread to prevent raveling.

*overcoat*—see greatcoat.

*pants suit*—women's coordinated outfit consisting of jacket and pants to match; skirt, top, and vest may be included.

*parka*—short, fleece-lined jacket with hood; copied from the Eskimo's fur parka.

*passementerie* (pahss monh tree)—trimmings, especially heavy edgings or embroideries. (French) *patte* (paht)—tab, flap, or strap. (French)

*pea jacket*—short, heavy, melton-cloth sailor's jacket worn by men and women; single- or double-breasted; sometimes with hood.

*peace jacket* (Eisenhower or battle jacket)—short, bloused, banded at waist and cuffs; with patch pockets and flaps.

*pegboard*—a piece of hard board pierced all over with small, evenly spaced, holes; comes with metal peg-like hooks to be placed in the holes as desired for hanging objects.

*peplum*—a flared, flounce-like detail attached to the top of a skirt or bottom of a bodice or jacket.

*piecing*—adding a small piece of fabric to a larger section to extend the size.

*pile*—weave of a fabric having upright surface threads such as corduroy or velvet.

*pinafore*—an over-garment that can be made of any fabric; usually sleeveless with bib front and gathered skirt; often ruffled.

*pin basting*—pinning seams or darts to hold them in place for stitching rather than basting with needle and thread.

*pinking*—a smoothly cut, finely notched edge used to prevent raveling of fabrics.

*placket*—an opening in a garment for ease in dressing.

*pleat*—a fold of fabric permanently stitched in place.

*plissé* (plee say)—fold; pleating; gathering. (French)

*polo coat*—top coat recognized by large buttons, welt seams, patch pockets, and box shape pulled in slightly with half or full belt; single- or double-breasted; usually in natural color camel's hair cloth.

*poncho*—a rectangular-cut, seamless garment with a hole in the center for the head; falls loosely from the shoulders; made of any fabric, some waterproofed.

*princess*—closely fitted garment with style line seams to fit the figure contours front and back; has no waistline seam or darts.

*raincoat*—full-length coat of any style that covers garments; made of waterproof fabric or material.

*ravel*—to pull or draw threads from the edge of a piece of fabric, forming a fringe; also refers to the pulling of threads due to wear or cleaning procedures.

*reefer*—princess-style coat with tailored sport look; single- or double-breasted with buttoned-on half belt.

*revers*—wide, shaped lapels on coats, suits, and dresses.

*riding coat*—special coat made for ease in riding horses; fitted to the waist with a flared skirt and back or side vents; single-breasted with slant pockets; may be fingertip length or slightly longer.

*rip*—to open a stitched area by removing the stitches.

*ruffle*—a strip of fabric pleated or gathered and used as a finish or trimming.

*rise*—the section of trousers from the waist to the bottom of the fly.

*safari jacket*—tropical hunting jacket of lightweight fabric; four button-down patch pockets with flap; lapels; epaulettes (straps over shoulder seams); and belt.

*sag*—degree to which a garment stretches after hanging.

*sari*—native Hindu style, contrived by draping five to eight yards of filmy fabric around the body and tucking it into an underskirt; one end is usually worn thrown over the shoulder or head.

*sarong*—patterned after the native garb of Tahiti; straight piece of fabric draped around the body to one side and tied in place.

*seam*—the line formed by sewing together parts of a garment or the edges of pieces of fabric.

*seam allowance*—the extra fabric allowed beyond the seam line.

*seam binding*—ribbon-like tape used to finish the edges of seams or the top of a hem.

## Glossary

*selvage (selvedge)*—the narrow, woven edge or border along the lengthwise edge of woven fabrics.

*set-in sleeves*—separate sleeves attached to the bodice with an armhole seam.

*sequin*—small, round, shiny, metal, or plastic spangle used to decorate fabric.

*shaper*—any form of elasticized foundation garment worn to firm the flesh of the body and give a smoother line under clothing.

*sheath*—straight-line garment slightly fitted at waist; no belt or waist seam.

*shift*—loose-fitting dress; can be straight or A-line; no waist seam.

*shirr*—to make three or more rows of gathers.

*shirtdress* or *shirtwaist*—bodice tailored like a man's shirt and fitted to a pleated, gathered, or straight skirt with belt; bodice may have long, short, or rolled sleeves or be sleeveless.

*shrink*—to contract fabrics by application of heat and moisture.

*shorts*—(Bermuda, Jamaica, short shorts, walking shorts)—pants of varying styles and lengths that stop above the knees; worn by both sexes of all ages.

*sizing*—a finishing process applied to fabrics and yarns to add strength and body to the fabric.

*ski jacket*—practical, lightweight, lined jacket with optional hood; made of waterproof and wind-resistant fabrics.

*ski pants*—fitted, tapered pants ending with a strap under the instep; made of warm, water-repellent, windproof stretch fabric.

*slash*—a cut in the fabric.

*slicker*—fisherman's raincoat of oil-treated fabric with metal buckle closings; style adapted to vinyl fabric.

*smocking*—a decorative embroidery stitching to hold fullness in a regular pattern.

*smoking jacket* (lounge)—man's fingertip-length house jacket; has shawl collar and tie belt.

*snip*—to cut with one short stroke.

*soigneé* (swahn yay)—highly finished, well-groomed, carefully done. (French)

*soutache* (soo tahsh)—narrow braid trim. (French)

*sport coat*—patterned or check, plaid coat worn casually over sport clothes.

*sport jacket*—can be any pattern, color, plaid, or check jacket worn with contrasting trousers.

*stay stitch*—a line of regular-length machine stitching through a single thickness of cloth; applied 1/8 inch (.3 cm) toward the raw edge from the seam line; used to keep fabric from stretching on curved or bias edges.

*steaming*—to expose fabric to controlled amount of moisture and heat.

*stiletto*—a small, pointed instrument used to punch neat holes in fabric.

*stitching-in-the-ditch*—a line of top stitching applied directly over the stitches of another seam in the space between the two edges of the seam; used to hold facings in place underneath without hand sewing.

*storm coat*—same as greatcoat or overcoat but with an additional, detachable warm lining.

*strié* (stree ay)—vertically striped in a variety of colors with the stripes very close together and narrow. (French)

*suit*—a man's suit is usually a jacket, one or two pairs of trousers, and optional vest, in same fabric and color; a woman's suit can be a jacket and skirt plus pants and vest.

*swing needle*—another term for a machine stitch in which the machine needle moves back and forth sideways as well as forward.

*tack*—to fasten two fabric surfaces together loosely.

*tail coat*—men's formal wear jacket with long tails.

*taille* (tie)—form or figure, size, waist. (French)

*tailor's tacks*—small, temporary thread loops applied to a fabric piece as a marking device.

*tension*—the tightness or looseness with which the upper and lower threads feed through the sewing machine.

*texturized*—a yarn manufacturing process in which fibers or filaments are permanently crimped or bulked to give greater flexibility to the use of the filaments.

*thermoplastic*—having the property of softening or fusing when heated and of hardening again when cooled.

*tiered*—layers of flounces, ruffles, or pleating, sometimes increasing in width from top layer to bottom layer.

*tissu* (tee syu)—texture; textile fabric. (French)

*toile* (twahl)—muslin copy of a design; may be sold to copiers or used as a pattern by the originator. (French)

*topcoat*—man's or woman's full length coat of lightweight fabric; sometimes called a "Spring" coat.

*topper*—(shortie or chubbie) short topcoat of any fabric or fur worn by women.

*top-stitching*—a line of stitching close to the seam line on the outside of the garment.

*trace*—to transfer pattern symbols or a fitting mark to fabric with a tracing wheel.

*train*—a part of a gown that trails behind the wearer.

*trapeze*—also referred to as "tent"; exaggerated A-line dress that starts flaring at the underarm; no waist seam.

*trim*—to cut away excess fabric.

*tuck*—a fold of fabric stitched in place.

*tunic*—straight, fingertip-length garment worn over skirt or pants.

*tuxedo* or dinner jacket—semiformal man's jacket with lapels or shawl collar, single- or double-breasted.

*undercollar*—the under section or facing of a collar.

*underlap*—the part of a garment which is covered by another part.

*underlay*—a piece of material placed under other pieces to effect joining, as in a slot seam.

*understitching*—a row of regular-length machine stitches through the facing and facing seam only; placed near the seam on the right side of the facing to hold the facing in place.

*vendeuse* (vohn deuz)—saleswoman in a dressmaking house who earns salary and commissions and has her own assistants. (French)

*vent*—a finished opening such as in the bottom of a jacket.

*vest* or *weskit*—waist-length garment of knitted or woven fabric; sleeveless with V-neck; can be pullover or with center-front closing; does not have to match other parts of outfit.

*volant* (vo lohn)—floating as a panel or flounce, flying loose. (French)

*weight*—a small, metal disc sewn into the hem of jackets or coats to help the garment stay in position when worn.

*welt*—a double-edge strip, insert, or seam for ornament or reinforcement.

*western shirt*—tailored, long-sleeved, fitted shirt with cuffs and yoke front and back; patch pockets with flaps and pointed collar.

*wrap-around*—any garment that is loosely lapped over front or back and kept in place with tie or concealed snaps or hooks.

*wrap-around coat*—styled same as wrap-around dress but made of heavier or waterproof fabric.

*zigzag*—see swing needle.

# References

## BOOKS

Better Homes and Gardens Editors. *Better Homes and Gardens Jiffy Cooking.* Better Homes and Gardens Books, Des Moines, Iowa. 1967.

Better Homes and Gardens Editors. *Better Homes and Gardens Junior Cook Book.* Better Homes and Gardens Books, Des Moines, Iowa. 1972.

Better Homes and Gardens Editors. *Better Homes and Gardens Make Ahead Cook Book.* Better Homes and Gardens Books, Des Moines, Iowa. 1971.

Better Homes and Gardens Editors. *Better Homes and Gardens Meals in Minutes.* Better Homes and Gardens Books, Des Moines, Iowa. 1973.

Better Homes and Gardens Editors. *Better Homes and Gardens Sewing Book.* Better Homes and Gardens Books, Des Moines, Iowa. 1970.

Brady, James. *Superchic.* Little, Brown and Co., Boston, Mass. 1974.

Cherry, Shirley, M. *Sew Your Own With Fashion Appeal*, 2227 Trescott Drive, Tallahassee, Fla. 32303. 1974.

Conners, Dorsey. *Save Time, Save Money, Save Yourself: Household Hints for a Happy Life-Style.* Hawthorne Books, Inc., New York, N.Y. 1972.

Crocker, Betty. *Betty Crocker's Family Dinners in a Hurry.* Western Publishing Co., Inc., New York, N. Y. 1970.

Cunningham, Gladys and Hutton, Jesse. *Singer Sewing Book: The Complete Guide to Sewing.* Random House, Inc., New York, N. Y. 1972.

Dariaux, Genevieve A. *Elegance.* Doubleday and Co., Inc., New York, N. Y. 1964.

Dyer, Ceil. *Plan-Ahead Cookbook.* Macmillan Inc., New York, N.Y. 1970.

Esquire Magazine Editors. *Esquire Fashions for Today.* Harper and Row, New York, N.Y. 1973.

Esquire Magazine Editors. *Esquire Book of Good Grooming for Men.* Grosset and Dunlap, Inc., New York, N.Y. 1969.

Ficarotta, Phyllis. *Sewing Without a Pattern.* Sterling Publishing Co., Inc., New York, N.Y. 1971.

Ford, Eileen (ed.) *A More Beautiful You in 21 Days.* Simon and Schuster, Inc., New York, N.Y.

Gawne, Eleanor J., and Oerke, Bess V. *Dress.* Chas. A. Bennett Co., Inc., Peoria, Ill. 1975.

Gawne, Eleanor J. *Fabrics for Clothing.* Chas. A. Bennett Co., Inc., Peoria, Ill. 1973.

Head, Edith, and Hyams, Joe. *How to Dress for Success.* Random House, Inc., New York, N.Y. 1967.

Heloise. *Heloise's Hints for the Working Woman.* Pocket Books, Inc., New York, N.Y. 1971.

Johnson, Mary. *Mary Johnson's Guide to Altering and Restyling Ready-Made Clothes.* E.P. Dutton and Co., Inc., New York, N.Y. 1964.

Johnson, Mary. *Sewing the Easy Way.* E.P. Dutton and Co., Inc., New York, N.Y. 1966.

Lane, Thelma. *Shortcuts to Sewing Skill.* Barnes and Noble, Inc., Scranton, Pa. 1971.

Lawson, Donna, and Conlon, Jean. *Beauty is No Big Deal: The Commonsense Beauty Book.* Bernard Geis Associates, Inc., New York, N.Y. 1971.

Marcus, Stanley. *Minding the Store.* Little, Brown and Co., Boston, Mass. 1974.

McCall's Editors. *McCall's Sewing Book.* Random House, Inc., New York, N.Y. 1968.

Simplicity Pattern Co., Inc. *Simplicity Sewing Book.* Doubleday and Co., Inc., New York, N.Y. 1971.

Skelsey, Alice. *The Working Mother's Guide to Her Home, Her Family and Herself.* Random House, Inc., New York, N.Y. 1970.

Spears, Charleszine W. *How to Wear Colors: With Emphasis on Dark Skins.* Burgess Publishing Co., Minneapolis, Minn. 1974.

## PERIODICALS

*Ebony*, Johnson Publishing Co., 1820 S. Michigan Avenue, Chicago, Ill. 60616.

### Altering Ready-To-Wear Fashions

*Esquire,* Esquire, Inc., 65 E. South Water Street, Chicago, Ill. 60601.

*Essence,* The Hollingsworth Group, Inc., 300 E. 42nd Street, New York, N.Y. 10017.

*Family Circle,* Family Circle, Inc., Mattoon, Ill. 61938.

*GQ (Gentlemen's Quarterly),* Esquire, Inc., 65 E. South Water Street, Chicago, Ill. 60601.

*Glamour,* Condé Nast Publications, Inc., Condé Nast Bldg., 350 Madison Avenue, New York, N.Y. 10017.

*Good Housekeeping,* The Hearst Corp., 717 Fifth Avenue, New York, N.Y. 10022.

*Harper's Bazaar,* The Hearst Corp., 717 Fifth Avenue, New York, N.Y. 10022.

*Ladies' Home Journal,* Ladies' Home Journal, 641 Lexington Avenue, New York, N.Y. 10022.

*Mademoiselle,* Condé Nast Publications Inc., Condé Nast Bldg., 350 Madison Avenue, New York, N.Y. 10017.

*McCall's,* The McCall Publishing Co., 230 Park Avenue, New York, N.Y. 10017.

*MsTIQUE,* Pullen-Walker Publishing Co., Inc., 8206 S. Cottage Grove Avenue, Chicago, Ill. 60619.

*Seventeen,* Triangle Communication, Inc., 320 Park Avenue, New York, N.Y. 10022.

*Woman's Day,* Fawcett Publications, Fawcett Bldg., Greenwich, Conn. 06830.

*Vogue,* Condé Nast Publications, Inc., Condé Nast Bldg. 350 Madison Avenue, New York, N.Y. 10017.

## NEWSPAPERS

*W,* Fairchild Publications, Inc. 7 E. 12th Street, New York, N.Y. 10003 (A bi-monthly women's fashion newspaper).

# Index

## A

Accessories for sewing machines, 35, 37
Acetate, 54
Acetate tricot underface, 61, 62
Adhesive interfacing, 49, 50
Adhesives for fabrics, 50, 51
Adjustable body forms, 42
Adrian, 29
Alterationist
   careers, 10–17
   establishing business, 360–383
   getting a job, 351–359
Alterations
   described and illustrated
      for men, 316–333
      for women, 197–244
   problems with permanent press, 63
   provided by stores, 10
   time schedule (chart), 337, 338
   work area for, 33, 37–41, 363–365, 375–377
   (Also see specific types of alterations)
Alteration ticket, 139, 197
Application forms for jobs, 356–359
Appointment book, 139, 374
Awl, steel, 47

## B

Backstitch, 282
Balance, as shown on statement, 371
Ball point needle, 37, 44
Ball (top) of snap, 294
Bargain department stores, 25, 26
Bar tack, Hong Kong, 288, 289
Basting stitches, 280, 281
Beaded fabrics, 268, 269
Beading-wire needles, 44
Beetling, 62
Belt
   alterations, 223
   backing, 50
   carriers, 285
Bias, 58
Bias facings, 255
Blending of fibers, 57
Blind stitch
   by hand, 257
   by machine, 259
Blind stitch industrial machines, 35, 36, 379
Blue "C" Polyester, 64
Bobbins, 37
Bodice alterations, 215–219
Bodice fittings, 156–164
   measuring length of, 143
   princess style, 180–183
Body proportions, 121, 122, 247
Bookkeeping for small business, 373, 382
Books on fashion, list of, 32
Bonded fabrics, 61
Boutique, 27
Bra carriers, 285
Bras, 132, 133
Bridal, formal wear, as specialty shop, 26, 27
Bridal gown with train, hemline fitting, 251, 252
Buckboard for pressing, 41, 73, 75, 83–85
Budget-priced garments, 18, 21
Bulletin board, 377
Burrows, Stephen, 31
Bushelman, 305
Business cards, 366, 367
Business, establishment of,
   conducting business, 368–379
   customer contact, 365–368
   enlarging, 379–383
   planning work area, 363–365
   procedures, 361–363
Bust darts
   altering, 219, 220
   fitting, 162–164
Bust, measurement for fitting, 142, 144
Buttonhole
   stitch, 289, 290
   twist thread, 48
Button loops, 286, 288
Buttons, 48, 292, 293

## C

Calendering, 62
Camouflage, 122
Cardin, 30, 31
Career opportunities, 10–17
Catalogues, pattern, 32
Catch stitch, 258, 259
Cellulose, cellulosic fibers, 54
Centered zipper, 298
Centimetre (cm), 17
Centi, metric prefix, 17
Chain sewing, 93
Chain stitch
   by hand, 284–287
   by machine, 33, 34
Chain weights, 302
Chair for sewing, 39
"Chanel chain" (See *Chain weights*)
Chanel, Coco, 28, 29
Charts
   alterations price list, 369
   bra sizes, 133
   clothing sizes, metric conversion, 136, 137, 138
   textile fibers—use, characteristics, care, 54, 55
   tricky textiles—machine and pre-sewing preparation, pressing, 68–71
Chemise (See *Shift*)
Circle of the armhole, 209
Clapper (See *Pounding block*)
Classified ads, 351, 352
Clips, 88, 89, 199
Closed lining on coat, to shorten, 273, 274
Clothes hooks, 41
Clothing labels, 23–25
Clothing maintenance specialist, 13
Cloth manufacturer's label, 25
Coat alterations
   hemline, 270–278
   neck and collar, 243
   seam, 243
   shoulder, 243
   sleeve, 243, 244
Coat fitting
   hemline, 252, 253
   shoulder, 195, 196
Coat, hook fastener for, 295
Collar
   altering necklines with, 206–208
   fitting necklines with, 149, 150
Color effects on clothing, 122–124
Combination manufacturer and designer label, 25
Commercial sewing methods, 88–120
Compatibility of fabrics and trim, 64
Construction methods, 91–114
Costume jewelry, 29
Cotton
   basting thread, 48
   fiber, 53, 54
   -polyester thread, 48
Coty (fashion) award, 31
Courreges, 30
Covered snaps, 294
Covers for ironing boards, 75
Crewel needle, 44
Crocheted fabrics, 60
Crosswise (filling) yarns, 58
Crotch piece, 312, 313
Crotch seam, 313
Cuffing tool, 319, 321
Cuffs, 319–321
Customer
   contacts, 365–368
   record file, 375
Cut edge finish for knit fabrics, 254

## D

Dacron, 64
Darning needles, 44
Darts
   bustline, 162–164
   how to make by commercial method, 92, 93
   how to press, 80, 81
   replacing old with new, 198
   waistline, 164–167
Decorative lines of garment, 126
Designer garment, 18
Designers, well-known, 28–31
Designer's label, 25
Designing to flatter figure, 121–133
Designs, fabric, 62, 131
Diagonal basting, 281
Dior, 29, 30
Domestic sewing machine, 33, 34
Double-edge stitched hem, by machine, 260

## Index

Double hem finish, 254
Double knit, 60
Dowel stick, 77, 82
Dress construction by manufacturers, 91–119
Dressmaker (See *Sample hand*)
Dressmaker's carbon paper, 46
Dress shirts for men, 331
Drop of hemline, 264
Dyeing fabrics, 62

### E

Ease-stitch
  for sleeves, 116
  on machine, 291
Easy care (See *Wrinkle-resistant*)
Elastic braid, 50
Elastic thread, 48
Elasticized waistline on pants, 236, 237
Electric scissors, 43
Embroidery needle, 44
Embroidery scissors, 42, 43
Emery bag, 47
Emery boards, 47
Employment agencies, 351
Establishing business, 360–383
Even basting, 281
Evening pants, wide-legged
  to shorten
    alteration, 269
    fitting, 252
Eyelets, 290
Eye (loop) of hook fasteners, 295

### F

Fabric bag for covering weights, 302, 303
Fabrics
  design, 62, 131
  general discussion, 52–71
  texture, 129, 130
Facing fabric in bonding, 61
Facings for hems, 255, 256
Fake fur coat, to shorten hem, 276
Fashion trends, 28
Fasteners, types of, 48, 49, 292–302
Federal Trade Commission, 65
Felling stitch, 283
Felt fabric, 60
"Felt" together, of wool fibers, 54
FHA home improvement loan, 381
Fiber
  generic name, 64
  synthetic and natural, 53–56
Fiber content and clothing care label, 25
Filaments, man-made fiber, 53
Filling knit, 59, 60
Finishes for hems, 48, 261
Finishing processes for fabrics, 62, 63
Finishing stitches, 282–290
Finish pressing, 80
Fitter, in stores, 10, 11
Fitter-alterationist, 11
Fitter-alterationist-salesperson, 11
Fitter's instructions (See *Alteration ticket*)
Fitting garments
  by pinning, 144, 145

measuring for, 142–144
procedures, 141, 142
second, after altering, 244
things to avoid, 145
tools for, 139
(Also see specific types of fittings)
Fitting platform, 42
Flat tack stitch, 290
Flat weights, 302, 303
Floor treadle, 34
Fluorescent light for work area, 39
Fly zipper, 301
Fogerty, Ann, 29
Folded edge finish for hems, 253, 254
Formal gown with train, hemline fitting, 251, 252
Formal shirts for men, 331
Forms, adjustable, for fitting, 42
Fortrel, 64
Fowler Taping Attachment, 36
French lining (See *Closed lining*)
Front dart or seam, men's jackets, 323
Full-length mirror, 42
Fur
  finisher, finisher-alterationist, 13
  hook fasteners for, 295
Fusible web material, 51

### G

Garment industry, 18–32
Garment(s)
  pressing of, 72–87
  sample mini, 88–91
  types by price, 18, 21
  well-fitted, 139, 140
Garment storage in work area, 39, 41
Gathering, on machine, 291, 292
Gauge, six-inch, 45, 46
Generic families of fibers, 64
Girdles, 133
Givenchy, 30
Glazing, 62
Glover needle, 45
Grain, 58, 59
Gram, 17
Grounding for sewing machine, 34, 35
Gusset, adding to sleeve, 175, 230, 231

### H

Half size classification, 135, 136, 138
Halston, 31
Ham, tailor's, 76, 77, 80
Hand hemming stitches, 256–259
Hand of fabric, 129
Hand stitches to finish garment, 279–290
Hanger bar or loops, 285
Head, Edith, 29
Health care, 339–341
Heavy-duty thread, 48
Helpers for alteration business, 382, 383
Hem
  facings, 255, 256
  finishes, 253–261
  marker, 46
Hemline alterations
  coat, cape, or coatdress, 270–278

  general discussion, 261, 262
  pants, lengthen or shorten, 269, 270
  to shorten, 266–269
  when even, 262–264
  when uneven, 264, 265
Hemline fitting
  coats and capes, 252, 253
  floor-length, 250–252
  general discussion, 245–247
  street-length, 247–250
  techniques of hemming, 253–261
Hemming on blindstitch machine, 35
Hepburn, Audrey, 30
Hip measurement for fitting, 143
Hong Kong finish for hems, 255
Hong Kong stitch, 288
Hook, hook fasteners, 295
Hook loops, 286, 288
Hooks and eyes, 48, 49
Horsehair braid for hems
  edge-stitch, 260
  facing, 256
  floor-length, 267

### I

Income tax payments when self-employed, 362, 363
Industrial sewing machine, 34–36
Inseam of men's trousers, 313
Insurance for business, 362
Interfacings, 49, 50
Interlocking fibers, 60
Interviews for job, 352–357
Invisible catch stitch, 259
Invisible zipper, 301
Iron
  short cuts with, 82
  steam, 72, 73
Ironing, 72
Ironing board and cover, 75

### J

Jackets for men, alterations, 323
  collar, 324, 325
  shortening sleeves, 328
  shortening length, 329
  shoulders, 326
  too full or too snug, 327, 328
Jackets for men, fitting
  collar, 314
  judging fit, 309, 310
  measuring, 313, 314
  shoulders, 314, 315
  too full or too snug, 315
Jackets for women
  alterations, 244
  fitting, 196
Jobs for alterationist
  accepting and keeping, 357
  application forms, 356–359
  interview, 352–357
  where to look, 351, 352
  (Also see *Career opportunities*)
Jewelry, "costume", 29
Johnson, Betsy, 31
Junior size classification, 135, 136, 138

# Index

## K
Kennedy, Jackie, 30
Kilo, metric prefix, 17
Knee press lever, 34, 35
Knits, 59, 60, 254
Knotting, 60, 61
Kodel, 64

## L
Labels
  applying when finishing, 304
  permanent care, 65, 66
  requiring fiber identification, 64
  types of, 23–25
Labor union label, 25
Lace
  for hem facing, 256
  for seam binding, 49
  (Also see *Openwork fabrics*)
Lap board, 37, 39
Lapped zipper, 297
Layered look, 31
Leather coat, to shorten hem, 278
Ledger, bookkeeping, 373
Legislation, federal, of fabrics, 64
Lengthwise yarn (See *Warp of yarn*)
"Lettuce" edge ruffle hems, 31, 260 (Also see *Ripple-edge stitch*)
Lever, knee press, 34, 35
Levi jeans, shirts, jackets, 31
Licensing of business in home, 361, 362
Lighting in working area, 39
Linen, 53, 54
Lines in clothing, 125–129
Lingerie keeper (strap holder), 287, 296
Lingerie, loungewear, as specialty of shop, 27
Lining
  altering sleeves with, 243, 244
  hemline alterations on coats with, 271–275
  materials, 49
Litre, 17
Lockstitch, 33, 34
"London Fog" finish for raincoat hemlines, 275
Loom, as weaving frame, 58
Loops, 285, 286, 290
Luster finish, 62

## M
Machine
  hem finishes, 259–261
  stitches, 291, 292
Magazines, 32
Maintenance supplies for sewing machine, 37
Management check list, 344
Manager of specialty shop, 11
Manufacturer's label, 25
Manufacturing garments, 18–21, 91–114
Marker for pattern, 21
Marking for alterations, 198, 199
Measuring tools, 45, 46
Mending and repair specialist, 12
Men only specialty shop, 26

Menswear
  altering, 316–333
  fitting, 312–316
  general discussion, 305–309
Mercerized cotton thread, 48, 257
Mercerizing, 62
Metre (m), 17
Metric system, 17
Metric tape measure, 45
Micro-mini skirt, 30
Midi-length skirt, 30
Milli, metric prefix, 17
Milliner's needle, 44
  for hand hemming, 257
  for hand stitches, 279
Mini patterns for samples, 91
Mirrors, 42
Misses size classification, 135, 136, 138, 139
"Mod" (fashion) look, 30
Moderate-priced garments, 18
Monogram machine operators, 12

## N
Natural fibers, 53, 54
Neckline alterations, 200–208
Neckline fittings, 145–150
  princess style, 178
Necklines, as related to face and figure, 126, 128, 129
Needle board, 78, 79
Needles
  ball point, 37, 44
  for hand sewing, 44, 45
  sewing machine, 37
Needle trades, 18
Net (See *Openwork fabrics*)
"New look", 29
Noncellulosic fibers (See *Synthetic fibers*)
Norell, Norman, 29
Nylon monofilament thread, 48

## O
Off-grain sleeves, 177
Off-grain stitching, 116
One-panel mirror, 42
Openwork fabrics, 60, 61
Optical illusion, 121, 122, 125, 131
Outseam of men's trousers, 313
Overhead, as business expense, 369
Over-the-door clothes bar, 39

## P
Padding materials, 50
Pamphlets on fashion, 32
Pants alterations
  crotch, 241, 242
  hips too tight, 238, 239
  legs, 242
  length, 242, 243, 269, 270
  too large, 239–242
  waistline, 236–238
Pants fitting, 188, 189
  crotch, 194
  hips too tight, 192, 193
  legs, 195

  length, 195, 252
  measurement for, 144
  too large, 193–195
  waistline, 190, 191
Patch label, 25
Pattern
  catalogues, list of, 32
  mini, for samples, 91
Peg board for sewing supplies, 39, 376
Pencil markings for alterations, 199
Permanent care labeling, 65, 66
Permanent press fabric finish, 63
Petite junior size classification, 135, 137
Petite misses size classification, 135, 137
Pick basting, 281
Pickstitch, 282
Piece dyeing, 62
Pill (small balls of fuzz), 56
Pin cushions, 47
Pin fitting of garments, 144, 145, 198, 199
Pinked edge, 254
Pinning garments, 94
Pins, dressmaker, 43
Plastic foot on sewing machine, 37
Platform for fitting floor-length garments, 250
Pliers, 47
Ply yarn, 56
Point pressers, 77, 82
Pounding block, 77, 78, 80
Preshrunk, 62
Press cloth, 78–80
Presser feet, 37
Pressing
  area, 41
  block, 85
  cushions, 85
  ham, 85, 86
  mitt, 75, 76; how to make, 86, 87
  of garments, general discussion, 72–87
Price, 26
Prices to charge for alterations, 369, 370
Princess-style garment alterations
  bodice, 233, 234
  shoulders, 231, 232
  skirt, 234
Princess-style garment fitting, 178
  bodice, 180–183
  shoulders, 179
  skirt, 184
Printing on fabrics, 62
Pucci, Emilio, 29, 30

## Q
Quality department stores, 25
Quant, Mary, 30

## R
Rack for hanging garments, 39
Raincoat, hemline alterations, 275, 276
Rayon, 54
Ready-to-wear sizes, 135–139
References for job, 354, 355
Regenerated fibers (See *Cellulosic fibers*)
Renting space for alteration work, 382
Residual shrinkage, 62
Resort shops, 27

397

## Index

Resumé for job, 354, 355
Retail stores
  as source of alteration work, 367, 368
  types of, 25–27
Right-, left-hand zipper feet, 37
Ripple-edge stitch
  by machine, 260, 261
  to shorten gown with, 267
Rolling foot on sewing machine, 37
Rough fabrics, hem facings for, 256
Rubber cement for altering leather, 51
Ruler, plastic see-through, 46
Running stitch, 282

S

Sack dress, 185
St. Laurent, 30
Salesperson, 12
Sample hand (dressmaker), 12, 13
Sample mini garments, 88–91
Samples, practice
  for finishing touches, 279
  for hemming techniques, 253
Sanforizing, 62
Scissors, 42, 43
Scoop neck, front neckline fullness
  alteration, 204
  fitting, 147
Seam binding, 48, 49
Seam ripper, 47
Seam roll for pressing, 76, 82, 86, 87
Seams
  alteration of, 197, 198
  how to press, 80, 81
  serged, 192
Second fitting, after altering, 244
Self-employment opportunities, 14, 361–383
Sequinned fabric, to shorten hemline of, 268, 269
Serged seams on pants, 192
Seventh Avenue, New York City, 18
Sewing, commercial methods, 88–120
Sewing machine
  accessories, 35, 37
  domestic, 33, 34
  industrial, 34–36
  maintenance, 37
Sewing scissors, small, 42
Sewing specialist, 11
Sewing supplies, general discussion, 48–51
Shades of color, 123
Shanks, button, 293
Sharp needle, 44
Shears, 42
Sheath (See *Shift*)
Shift, basic, alterations
  bodice too long, 234–236
  bodice too short, 236
Shift, basic, fitting, 185
  bodice too long, 186, 187
  bodice too short, 187
  waistline shaping, 188
Shirring, on machine, 291, 292
Shirts for men, altering, 331–333
Shoulder alterations
  line too high, 213, 214

too narrow, 212, 213
too wide, 208–211
when shoulders slope, 214, 215
Shoulder fittings
  line too high, 154
  measurement for, 144
  princess style, 180
  too narrow, 153
  too wide, 150–152
  when shoulders slope or droop, 155, 156
Shoulder pads, padding, 196
  applying when finishing, 303
  used in alteration for sloping shoulders, 214, 215
Shrinkage control of fabrics, 62, 63
Signature label, 25
Silhouette, 126
Silicone spray, 51
Silk, 54
Single-edge stitched hem, by machine, 260
Size, as specialty of shop, 27
Sizes, ready-to-wear classifications, 135–139
Skimmer (See *Shift*)
Skirt, 30
Skirt alterations, 224–226
Skirt fittings, 168–173
  measurement for length, 144
Sleeve alterations, 228–231
Sleeve board for pressing, 75
Sleeve, distributing fullness evenly, 116
Sleeve fittings, 174–177
  measurement for, 144
Slip basting, 280
Slip knot for hand hemming, 257
Slipstitch, 282
Slot zippers, 299–301
Smith, Willi, 31
Snaps, 48, 49, 294
Social security
  card, 353
  payments, when self-employed, 362
Socket (bottom) of snap, 294
Solution dyeing, 62
Specialists
  clothing maintenance, 13
  mending and repair, 12
  sewing, 11
Special-order garments, 142
Specialty shops, 26
Speed of sewing machines, 34
Sport shirts for men, 331
Sportswear, as specialty shop, 26
Staple, as fiber length, 53
Statement, as written bill to customers, 370–372
Static electricity in synthetic fibers, 56
Stay-stitching, 291
Steam iron, 72, 73
Stitch-in-the-ditch, 198, 291
Stock dyeing, 62
Storage, 39
Store(s)
  customer alterations by, 10
  label, 25
  retail, 25–27, 367, 368

Straight-grain facings, 255
Straight stitch (See *Lockstitch*)
Strap holders (See *Lingerie keepers*)
Structural lines of garment, 126
Suede, synthetic, coat, to shorten hem, 276–278
Suit jacket fitting, 196
Supervisor, alterations department, 11
Swing needle attachment, 34
Symbols for men's clothing alterations, 312
Synthetic fibers, 56

T

Tacks, chain stitch, 287
Tailored pants
  alterations, 269, 270
  fitting length, 252
Tailor's
  chalk, 47, 199
  ham for pressing, 76, 77, 80
  press board (See *Buckboard*)
  wax, 199
Tailor's findings (menswear supplies), 48
Tailor stitch, 258
Tall misses size classification, 135
Tape measure, 45, 312
Tape, seam and lace, for hem finish, 254
Tapestry needle, 44
Tax consultant, 362, 381
Textile Products Identification Act, 64
Textiles, tricky, 63, 64, 68–71
Texture of fabric, 129, 130
Texturized yarn, 53
Thermoplastic, 56
Thimble, 46
Thread chain (See *Chain stitch*)
Thread markings for alterations, 199, 279, 280
Thread, types of, 48
Three-way mirror, 42
Ticket, alteration or work, 139, 197, 372, 373
Time-study, time-saving methods, 334–338
Tints of color, 123
Tools for alterations, 42–48
Top pressing, 80
Top-stitched hem, by machine, 261
Tracing wheel, 46
Trade information, sources of, 31, 32
Train on bridal gown or formal
  hemline fitting, 251
  to shorten, 267, 268
Tray attachment for pressing long garments, 74, 75
Treadle, floor, 34
Triacetate, 54
Tricot fabric, 61
Trousers for men, alterations
  hemming when uncuffed, 318, 319
  making cuffs, 319–321
  replacing zippers, 322
  seat and crotch, 317, 318
  tapering legs, 318
  waistline, 316, 317
Trousers for men, fitting
  judging for fit, 310, 311
  legs too wide, 316

**398**

# Index

length, 316
measuring for, 313
seat and crotch, 315, 316
waistline, 315
True bias, 58
Tweezers for removing threads, 47

## U

Undergarments, 132, 133
Underlining
for garments, 119, 120
of bonded fabric, 61
Underpressing, 80
Uneven basting, 280
United States Extension Service bulletins, 32
Unlined coats, hemline alterations, 270, 271, 274

## V

Vests for men, alterations, 330, 331
Vinyl coat, alteration to shorten hem, 276
V-neck, front neckline fullness
alteration, 204
fitting, 147

Vocational training program students, as sewing helpers, 382, 383

## W

Waistbands on skirts and pants
alterations, 227, 228
fittings, 173
Waistline alterations, 221, 222
Waistline fittings, 164–167
measurement for, 142
Wales, in knitted fabrics, 59
Walking foot of sewing machine, 37
Warp knit, 60
Warp of yarn, 58
Wash and wear (See *Wrinkle-resistant*)
Wax markers, 47
Weaves, weaving, 58, 59, 62
Weights, lead, 50, 302, 303
Well-fitted garment, 139, 140
Whipstitch, 283
White glue, 51
Wick of fibers, 56
Women only specialty shop, 26
Women's size classification, 135, 136, 138

Wool, 54
Work area for alterations, 33, 37–41, 363–365, 375–377
Working with people, 345–350
Work organization for alterationist, 335–339
Work shirts for men, 331
Worktable, 37
Wrinkle-resistant, 63
Wrist pin cushion, 47

## Y

Yardstick, 45
Yarns, 56, 57; dyeing of, 62

## Z

Zigzag finish for hems
by hand, 255
by machine, 260
Zipper
applying, 296–301
replacement, men's trousers, 322
shorten at bottom, 301, 302
Zipper foot, 37